HUMAN ANTIQUITY

HUMAN ANTIQUITY

An Introduction to Physical Anthropology and Archaeology

FIFTH EDITION

Kenneth L. Feder
Michael Alan Park

Central Connecticut State University

Boston   Burr Ridge, IL   Dubuque, IA   Madison, WI   New York
San Francisco   St. Louis   Bangkok   Bogotá   Caracas   Kuala Lumpur
Lisbon   London   Madrid   Mexico City   Milan   Montreal   New Delhi
Santiago   Seoul   Singapore   Sydney   Taipei   Toronto

The McGraw-Hill Companies

Higher Education

Published by McGraw-Hill, an imprint of The McGraw-Hill Companies, Inc., 1221 Avenue of the Americas, New York, NY 10020.

1 2 3 4 5 6 7 8 9 0 DOC/DOC 0 9 8 7 6

ISBN-13: 978-0-07-304196-4
ISBN-10: 0-07-304196-3

Editor in Chief: *Emily Barrosse*
Publisher: *Phillip A. Butcher*
Developmental Editor: *Rosalind Sackoff*
Editorial Coordinator: *Teresa C. Treacy*
Marketing Manager: *Daniel Loch*
Media Producer: *Michele Borrelli*
Project Manager: *Carey Eisner*
Art Editor: *Robin Mouat*
Illustration: *John and Judy Waller, maps: Patti Isaacs*
Manager, Photo Research: *Brian J. Pecko*
Manuscript Editor: *Andrea McCarrick*
Senior Designer and Cover Designer: *Cassandra Chu*
Text Designer: *Linda Robertson*
Lead Production Supervisor: *Randy Hurst*
Composition: *10.5/12 Berkeley Book by Thompson Type*
Printing: *45# Pub Matte Plus, R. R. Donnelley*

Cover: *Machu Picchu, © Galen Rowell/Corbis*

Library of Congress Cataloging-in-Publication Data
Feder, Kenneth L.
    Human antiquity: an introduction to physical anthropology and archaeology /
    Kenneth L. Feder, Michael Alan Park.—5th ed.
        p. cm.
    Includes bibliographical references and index.
    ISBN-13: 978-0-07-304196-4
    ISBN-10: 0-07-304196-3
        1. Physical anthropology.   2. Archaeology.   3. Prehistoric peoples.
    I. Park, Michael Alan.   II. Title.
GN60 .F43 2007
599.9—dc22   2006045780

www.mhhe.com

TO THE INSTRUCTOR

Physical (biological) anthropology and archaeology, two subfields of anthropology, are really two starting points on the road to a common goal—the understanding of the human past. Both authors of this book research human antiquity: Feder is an archaeologist who conducts surveys, excavations, and analyses aimed at understanding the native inhabitants of southern New England. Park is a biological anthropologist interested in the application of evolutionary theory to the biological history of our species. But a full understanding of the human past is simply not possible without the kinds of research both of us do. Our approach in this book, then, is to truly combine the ideas, methods, and knowledge from our two subfields into the unified effort they really are.

Features

Accessibility. This book is written for students. It does not assume prior knowledge of archaeology or biological anthropology. We explain the material we present in clear, straightforward language, including, where appropriate, colloquialisms and personal comments; we want our readers to know this was written by real people.

We have attempted to at least touch on all relevant topics within this broad subject and to discuss all reasonable points of view around individual issues, giving the pros and cons of each and indicating our leaning—and the reasons for it—where we have one. Some items, naturally, will be left out or will not be covered as completely as some may wish. We can only say that our goal here is to help our readers understand what is known about the human past and how we have come to know it.

We have also included various study aids to help introductory students navigate their way through what must often seem like an overwhelming amount of new information. These study aids include definitions of key terms on the page where they first appear as well as in a comprehensive glossary at the back of the book; chapter summaries, study questions, lists of key terms, and suggested readings at the ends of chapters; a taxonomic glossary with pronunciations; and an extensive bibliography.

Science made interesting and relevant. Although we think all the topics in this book are inherently fascinating, they may not be to students, many of whom find the very idea of science rather daunting. So we include subjects that seem to naturally pique students' interest. Chapter 1, for example, consists of a unique discussion of three creation myths compared to scientific explanations for human origins. Throughout the text, we introduce the chapters with subjects or ideas that capture student interest—the Piltdown fraud (Chapter 8), for example, or the story of Archbishop James Ussher and his dating of the Creation (Chapter 2). And to demonstrate that the study of the past can apply to the present, "Contemporary Issues" sections show how the anthropological investigation of the human past can be applied to current concerns.

Use of narrative and analogy. Stories are often easier to remember than lists of facts, so we present our material as orderly and logical sequences of causality. In some places, this takes the form of a chronological narrative. In Chapter 3, for example, we provide a unique overview of the evolution of the universe, focusing, of course, on the latter stages of earth's history. This brief chapter accomplishes several things. It shows students that history—evolutionary as well as cultural—is made up of contingent series of events. It provides a perspective on the time scale involved in the history of our universe as well as a sense of the relative temporal placement of individual important events. Most importantly, it places the human story within a universal time frame. This chapter shows students that the evolution of humanity is not separate from the evolution of everything else but is, rather, just one story line within a much larger epic. And, for that portion of history that is the topic of this book, Chapter 3 previews and outlines what is to be detailed in the subsequent chapters about human evolution.

In other places, the "narrative" approach is accomplished simply by relying on the logic of the scientific method—developing inductive hypotheses and then deductively testing them. We show how scientific reasoning works (Chapter 1) and then apply it throughout the book. Chapter 8 describes and tests various explanations and scenarios about the evolution of hominid bipedalism. Chapter 10 applies an explicitly deductive approach to the question of the origins of anatomically modern human beings. Chapter 12 does the same with different hypotheses that have attempted to account for the origins of agriculture; and Chapter 13 presents our current understanding of the evolution of complex civilizations using this same deductive approach.

We also recognize the importance of analogy. For example, in Chapter 3, we help instill a sense of time by comparing the history of the universe to a calendar year (with thanks to Carl Sagan). In Chapter 6, we discuss the comparison of human behaviors to those of other primates, and of contemporary human foragers to ancient hunter-gatherers, stressing the limitations involved in all such comparisons. In Chapter 7, on methodology, the archaeological dating technique of seriation is explained using the analogy of changes in automobile styles. And in Chapter 9, we help students appreciate the rigors of the Pleistocene ice ages by describing a New England winter storm.

Organization

We begin in **Part One:** *Thinking about the Past* with some examples of mythological explanations of the past and a discussion of how these explanations differ from those offered by science. After discussing the nature of the science of anthropology, we give a brief account of some early scientific attempts to study and explain the human past. The part ends with a narrative overview of what is now understood about evolutionary history to help give the reader a sense of time and the sequence of events.

   Part Two: *The Study of the Past* focuses on the tools—material and intellectual—that we apply to our study of the human past. We include here, in separate chapters, a discussion of genetics and evolutionary theory, the evolution of the primates, the use of animal behavior in developing models of the behavior of our evolutionary ancestors, and the research methods used by archaeologists and paleoanthropologists.

   Part Three: *The Story of the Human Past* chronicles what we have learned so far about human antiquity. We begin with the origins of the human family and trace our evolutionary journey through the beginnings of civilization.

   We conclude with an *Epilogue* in which we pose some questions still unanswered in the field.

What's New in This Edition

Our understanding of the human past changes at a dizzying rate. New discoveries, new methods of analysis, and new interpretations of old data require a more or less constant reassessment of our models of human antiquity. Although intellectually exhilarating, the pace of change can be frustrating to authors of textbooks. We have made every effort to bring this book up-to-date by adding new material on many topics. In the four years since publication of the previous edition, a wealth of material has been discovered and published concerning, especially, the fossil evidence of the first hominids, DNA analysis of ancient bones, phytolith evidence of early agriculture, and newly excavated sites in Peru that provide insights into the development of state societies.

Previous Chapters 8 and 9 have been combined into a single chapter, Chapter 8, *The Emergence of the Human Lineage;* former Chapters 10 and 11 have also been combined into one chapter, Chapter 9, *The Human Lineage Evolves.* Merging these chapters eliminates redundancy that had crept into previous editions and contributes to the flow of the book. Succeeding chapters are renumbered accordingly.

In previous editions of the book, the authors felt forced to tiptoe around the controversial debate concerning the evolution of modern human beings because they, themselves disagreed. That was silly. Rather than gloss over the issue, in this edition the authors decided to incorporate their own disagreement in the chapter focusing on this topic—Chapter 10, *The Evolution and Nature of Modern Humanity.* As an object lesson in the scientific method, each author speaks in his own voice, providing a point–counterpoint presentation of the debate.

Following the lead set by the journal *Science,* the *Epilogue* has been entirely recast, presenting a discussion of the most important questions about human antiquity for which, as yet, we have no firm answers.

Supplementary Material

An Instructor's Manual and Testing Program (with more than 700 multiple-choice and short-answer/essay questions) is available for instructor download at the password-protected fifth edition Web site at www.mhhe.com/federha5.

Acknowledgments

We would like to thank all the folks at McGraw-Hill who have been our partners and colleagues in this work. Special thanks to Kevin Witt who was our sponsoring editor in the early stages of this edition; Rosalind Sackoff, developmental editor; Carey Eisner, production editor; Andrea McCarrick, copyeditor; Robin Mouat, art editor; Cassandra Chu, designer; Brian J. Pecko, manager, photo research; Randy Hurst, lead production supervisor; and Michele Borrelli, media producer.

Thanks are due to colleagues who generously supplied us with photographs of their own research for use in our book; we have credited each of them in the figure captions. We would also like to thank those colleagues in anthropology who reviewed the manuscript and provided specific advice and criticism for this edition:

Andrew Buckser, Purdue University; Linda J. Reed-Jerofke, Eastern Oregon University; Robert J. Mucci, Indiana University–Northwest; David R.

Schwimmer, Columbus State University; Daniel Sellen, Emory University; Linda M. Van Blerkom, Drew University; Renee B. Walker, Skidmore College; Terrance Weik, University of South Carolina. We, of course, remain responsible for the final content.

TO THE READER

Very simply, this book explains what we now know about the most basic questions regarding our species: Where do we come from? Why do we behave as we do? Why do we look like we do? What is our place in nature? What exactly has happened to us during our several million years on earth? And, just as important, this book tells how we have arrived at our answers.

Obviously, many academic disciplines focus on aspects of humanity's long tenure on this planet. Our perspective in this book is the perspective of anthropology—the field that broadly studies the entire human species and that looks for the connections between our past and our present, between one culture and another, and between human cultural behavior and biological endowments.

The two areas of anthropology most concerned with the human past are physical (or biological) anthropology, whose starting point is the biological nature of human beings, and archaeology, whose focus is the human cultural past. Commonly considered separate fields, these two anthropological subfields are clearly interrelated. One cannot fully understand the history of human culture without understanding how our ancestors lived before they had acquired culture and how the biological nature of our complex brains makes our cultural behavior possible. Similarly, one cannot understand how and why our biology changed over time without understanding how our behavior, especially our cultural behavior, helped us adapt to the various environments we have encountered during our 5- to 7-million-year evolution.

The study of the interrelationship of human biology and human culture is achieved by integrating the methods, the data, and the conclusions of both physical anthropology and archaeology, and it is this approach we use to answer the questions posed at the beginning of this section.

How to Use This Book

We have tried to make the text readable and easy to use. Each chapter begins with a photograph and a caption that asks the questions we will address within the chapter. Important terms are **boldfaced** in the text and are listed under "Key Terms" at the end of each chapter. These terms are defined in three places: in the text itself, in a running glossary found in the margins, and in the main "Glossary of Terms" at the back of the book. Although the wording of a definition may differ in these three places, they all carry the same meaning; we hope that defining a term in several slightly different ways will help you more fully grasp its meaning.

Scientific names of living and extinct primates are also boldfaced in the text where they first appear and defined (with pronunciations) in a separate glossary, the "Glossary of Human and Nonhuman Primates."

All references within the text are in parentheses, giving the author's last name, the date of publication, and page numbers where applicable. Details of these references may then be looked up at your convenience in the "Bibliography." For each chapter, a "Summary" is provided where the key concepts and ideas of the chapter are briefly discussed. Following this is a list of "Study Questions" that focuses on key issues of the chapter and will allow you to assess your understanding of the chapter contents. You can also go to the book's Web site and take advantage of the free online Study Guide. Each chapter ends with a section called "For More Information," where we list some additional works we think would be helpful should you wish to do further reading on a particular topic. Full references to these works are also in the "Bibliography."

Many of our chapters contain a "Contemporary Issue" section. Here we have applied the perspective gained in our study of the human past to a modern concern. The data of human antiquity are not merely interesting bits of information—fascinating, but esoteric and essentially useless. Rather, the perspective gained from understanding our roots is uniquely important to our full comprehension of ourselves, past and present.

CONTENTS

To the Instructor   v

To the Reader   xi

Part One
THINKING ABOUT THE PAST

1   Frameworks   1

Human Origins: The Framework of Myth   2
  The Yanomamö   3
  The Ancient Hebrews   4
  The Maya   6
Creation Myths   7
Human Origins: The Framework of Science   8
Anthropology: Studying Ourselves   11

Summary   14
Study Questions   15
Key Terms   15
For More Information   15

2   Eden Questioned: Historical Perspectives   17

Uniformitarianism: The Contribution from Geology   19
Natural Selection: The Contribution from Biology   23
  The Significance of Fossils   24
  Evolution   26

Cultural Evolution: The Contribution from Anthropology   32
  The Discovery of "New" People   32
  The Discovery of Mysterious Artifacts   35
  The Evolutionary Explanation   36
  A "Stone Age"   37

Summary   39
Study Questions   39

CONTEMPORARY ISSUE: *Scientific Creationism and Intelligent Design: Old Ideas in New Forms*   42

Key Terms   46
For More Information   46

3   Evolution: An Overview   49

Big Bang to Big Dinosaurs   50
Grasping Hands and Big Brains   58

Summary   66
Study Questions   68
Key Terms   68
For More Information   68

Part Two
THE STUDY OF THE PAST

4   Understanding Change: Modern Evolutionary Theory   71

Genetics   72
  The Genetic Code   72
  An Overview of the Human Genome   77
  The Inheritance of Characteristics   78
The Genetics of Populations   82
The Processes of Evolution   84
  Natural Selection   84
  Mutation   90
  Gene Flow   91
  Genetic Drift   92
The Origin of Species   94

Summary   99

CONTEMPORARY ISSUE: *What Is Genetic Cloning?*   100
Study Questions   101

Key Terms   102
For More Information   102

5   Learning about the Past: The Primates   105

Taxonomy   106
  Linnaean Taxonomy   106
  Cladistics   110
The Primates   113
  The Senses   113
  Locomotion   114
  Reproduction   115
  Intelligence   116
  Behavior Patterns   116
A Primate Portfolio   117
The Human Primate   127
Genetics and Primate Relationships   129
The Evolution of the Primates   132

Summary   138
Study Questions   139
Key Terms   139
For More Information   139

CONTEMPORARY ISSUE: *What Is the Status of Our Closest Relatives?*   140

6   Learning about the Past: Behavioral Models for Human Evolution   143

Behavior, Adaptation, and Evolution   144
Baboons   147
Chimpanzees   149
Bonobos   154
Ethnographic Analogy   158

Summary   161
Study Questions   162
Key Terms   162
For More Information   162

7   Learning about the Past: The Material Record   165

The Anthropology of the Past: Archaeology and Physical Anthropology   166

Where? The Process of Finding Sites   167

What? Recovering Archaeological Data   173

When? Dating the Past   176
   Stratigraphy   177
   Chronometric Techniques   179
   Cultural Techniques   186

How? Reconstructing Past Lifeways   187
   Technology   189
   Environment   191
   Diet   194
   Social Systems   199
   Trade: The Movement of Materials and People   200
   Ideology   202

Who? Identifying the Remains of Humans and Human Ancestors   203
   Species Identification and Definition   205
   Sex   208
   Age   210
   Health   211
   Appearance   215
   Behavior   217

Why? Explaining the Past   219

Summary   220

CONTEMPORARY ISSUE: *Preserving the Past*   221

Study Questions   222
Key Terms   222
For More Information   223

Part Three
THE STORY OF THE HUMAN PAST

8   The Emergence of the Human Lineage   225

The Early Hominids: Bipedal Primates   227

Searching for the First Hominids   236

Bipedalism   239
   The Benefits of Bipedalism   239
   Explaining the Emergence of Bipedalism   242

The Hominids Evolve   247
   More Australopithecines   247
   Still More Hominids   249
   Putting It All Together   252

CONTEMPORARY ISSUE: *Where Is the "Missing Link"?*   255

Summary   256
Study Questions   256
Key Terms   256
For More Information   257

9   The Human Lineage Evolves   259

The First Members of Genus *Homo*   260

To New Lands   265

The Evolution and Behavior of *Homo erectus*   277
  Stone Tools   280
  Quest for Fire   284
  Hunters or Scavengers?   286
  The Question of Language   288

Big Brains, Archaic Skulls   290

The Neandertals   296

Modern Humans   308

Summary   313

CONTEMPORARY ISSUE: *Who Are the "Hobbits" from Indonesia?*   314

Study Questions   316
Key Terms   316
For More Information   316

10   The Evolution and Nature of Modern Humanity   319

The Major Models in an Ongoing Debate   320
  The Recent African Origin (RAO) Model   320
  The Multiregional Evolution (MRE) Model   321
  The Key Requirements of Each Model   323

The Evidence   323
  The Fossil Record   325
  The Cultural Evidence   327
  Genetic Evidence   330
  Evolutionary Theory   335

Mostly-Out-of-Africa: An Alternative Model   337

Point–Counterpoint: The Authors Debate the Debate   339

Biological Diversity in Modern Humans   341
  Natural Selection and Human Variation   343
  The Question of Human Races   348

CONTEMPORARY ISSUE: *Is There a Connection between Modern Human Origins and Race?*   351

Summary   352
Study Questions   354

Key Terms   354
For More Information   354

11   New Ideas, New Worlds: Life in the Upper Paleolithic   357

Comparing the Middle and Upper Paleolithic   359

Art in the European Upper Paleolithic   368
  Cave Paintings   368
  Geometric Signs   373
  Human Depictions   373
  Carvings and Engravings   376
  Venus Figurines   377
  The Implications of Upper Paleolithic Artwork   379

Brave New Worlds   381
  Australia   381
  The Americas   385
  The Arctic   401

Summary   402
Study Questions   403
Key Terms   404
For More Information   404

12   The Origins of Agriculture   407

Life at the End of the Pleistocene   408
  Mesolithic and Archaic Cultures of the Early Holocene   408

The Food-Producing Revolution   410
  The Domestication of Plants and Animals   412
  From Wolf to Dog   413

Why Food Production?   415
  Hypotheses   415

Domestication: How Can You Tell?   424
  Recognizing Domesticated Plants   424
  Recognizing Domesticated Animals   426

Hearths of Domestication   428
  Southwest Asia   428
  Africa   436

East Asia   439
Europe   443
Mesoamerica   445
South America   451
North America   454
The Nutritional Impact of Agriculture   458
Can Agriculture Be Explained?   459
CONTEMPORARY ISSUE: *Our Worst Mistake?*   461

Summary   462
Study Questions   462
Key Terms   463
For More Information   463

13 The Evolution of Civilization   465

The Meaning of Civilization   466
Food and Labor Surplus   467
Social Stratification   467
Formal Government   468
Labor Specialization   470
Monumental Works   471
Dense Population   474
A System of Recordkeeping   474

Explaining the Evolution of Civilization   476
The Explanation of Race   476
Environmental Determinism   476
Unilinear Evolution   478
Marxism   479
The Hydraulic Hypothesis   480
The Circumscription Hypothesis   481
Hearths of Civilization   481
*Civilization's Roots: Chiefdoms in
  Southwest Asia*   482
Mesopotamia   485
Egypt   492
The Indus Valley   497
China   504
Mesoamerica   508
South America   518
Southern Europe   526
Africa, South of Egypt   528
North America   531
Southeast Asia   532
Why Did It Happen?   533

CONTEMPORARY ISSUE: *The Collapse of
  Civilization*   536

Summary   538
Study Questions   539
Key Terms   539
For More Information   539

Epilogue: What *Don't* We Know?   E–1

**Glossary of Human and Nonhuman
Primates   G–1**

Glossary of Terms   G–5

Bibliography   B–1

Index   I–1

To my parents, who ignited my sense of wonder
To Melissa, whose love makes life wonderful
To our children, first Josh and now Jacob, who are wonders
                                                    —KLF

To all my furry quadrupedal friends, past and present,
who kept me company and provided an
always humbling perspective
on the human species.
And to Jan
who knows why.
                                                    —MAP

This is the story of how we begin to remember.
                                                    —Paul Simon

How do these native South Americans explain the origin of humankind? In what ways is their explanation like that of Europeans prior to the eighteenth century? How do these explanations differ from those offered by science?

(R. A. Mittermeir/Bruce Coleman, Inc.)

FRAMEWORKS

CHAPTER CONTENTS

Human Origins: The Framework of Myth
Creation Myths
Human Origins: The Framework of Science
Anthropology: Studying Ourselves

Summary
Study Questions
Key Terms
For More Information

"Where do I come from?"

This is a question most of us, as children, ask our parents. Eventually, we come to understand that we haven't always been here; each of us has a beginning, we develop and change, and we will continue to do so. Finally—hardest to comprehend—we realize that we will not always exist: eventually we die.

People are also curious about their society's origins, development, and fate. "Where do *we* come from?" we ask as conscious, intelligent, curious beings. "How did our society come into existence? Where did our ancestors come from? How did our people come to live the life we do?" People attempt to answer these questions in a number of different ways.

FIGURE 1.1 The Ya̧nomamö live in villages that consist of a large circular building, surrounded by a log palisade and covered around the edges by a thatched roof, seen here in the background. The people in the picture are visitors to this village, waiting to be welcomed by their hosts for a ritual feast aimed at promoting political alliance and trade relations between villages. *(Napoleon Chagnon/Anthro-Photo)*

Human Origins: The Framework of Myth

For much of the history of our species, people have addressed the question of where we came from with **myths**—stories involving magic and gods. For a long time these supernatural accounts, taken on faith, provided at least partially satisfying answers to this most profound of questions. For many, they still do.

Virtually every culture has had its own myth explaining the creation of the earth, of plants and animals, and of human beings. For some, everything is the result of an act of creation by an all-powerful, supernatural being who cannot be seen but whose existence is inferred by the great power and beauty reflected in the world around us. For others, creation was merely an act of awakening, an arousing of elements inherent in an earth that had always existed. Still others developed complex tales of creation occurring as the sometimes accidental result of intrigue, alliances, and betrayal among spirits or gods. Such stories, though often quite different on the surface, are all myths, tales invented as the result of human curiosity concerning the origins of the universe, the world, and our societies.

Science, through a different process, attempts to explain the same things. To better understand the procedures employed in the scientific investigation of human origins and development and to comprehend how they differ from the processes of myth making, we will look at three origin tales, one of which you likely know. We will begin with the creation story of the Ya̧nomamö, Native Americans living in southern Venezuela and northern Brazil (Figure 1.1).

myth A story, usually invoking the supernatural, to account for some aspect of the world.

science The method of inquiry that attempts to explain phenomena through observation and the development and testing of hypotheses.

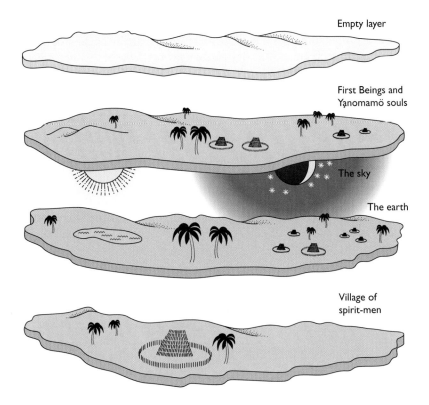

Empty layer

First Beings and
Yąnomamö souls

The sky

The earth

Village of
spirit-men

FIGURE 1.2 A schematic diagram of the Yąnomamö image of the cosmos. The layers resemble the layers of the rain forest canopy in which the Yąnomamö live. (*Redrawn from Verdun P. Chagnon in Napoleon A. Chagnon,* Yąnomamö: The Fierce People, *2d ed., New York: Holt, Rinehart and Winston, 1977, p. 27. Reproduced by permission of the publisher.*)

The Yąnomamö

The Yąnomamö hunt and farm in the jungles of the Orinoco River. They tell of their past this way (Chagnon 1997): In the beginning, they say, the cosmos was made of four layers (Figure 1.2). The first layer once had a function, but now it is empty. The undersurface of the second layer is the visible sky. The third layer is the earth, a huge jungle dotted with countless Yąnomamö villages. Even foreigners, who descended from the Yąnomamö, live in such villages. The fourth layer contains a single village inhabited by spirit people who sometimes travel up to earth to capture and eat the souls of children and so must be constantly guarded against.

The First Beings—the Yąnomamö gods—originated along with the layers of the cosmos. Each Being is credited with a specific function, usually the creation of something useful in Yąnomamö life—important plants, tools, fire, animals, knowledge of farming.

According to their creation story, the Yąnomamö themselves were created when one of the First Beings, Periboriwä, came to earth to eat the souls of children. Two other First Beings shot at him with arrows as he ascended to the second layer. One arrow found its mark, and Periboriwä was wounded. The wound bled, and each drop of blood that hit the earth became a Yąnomamö man. Because they were originally created of blood, all Yąnomamö men are, to this day, fierce warriors. One of the men created in this way became pregnant in his legs, and from his legs were born other men and a new type of being, woman. Unlike the men created from blood, these new Yąnomamö people were timid and docile. Later, all the First Beings became spirits and now dwell, along with the souls of departed Yąnomamö, on the second layer, a replica of the "real-world" third layer.

The Ancient Hebrews

The ancient Hebrews recorded two different versions of their creation story. One told of an all-powerful Being who brought order to a chaotic world of water. Over six days he created, in succession, light; Heaven; the

FIGURE 1.3 This stained-glass window, depicting Adam and Eve succumbing to temptation and accepting the serpent's offer of fruit from the tree of knowledge in the Garden of Eden—a key event in the Judeo-Christian creation myth—can be seen in the late-fifteenth-century Chateau Chaumont in the Loire Valley, France. *(K. L. Feder)*

FIGURE 1.4 Noah gazes out from the ark, and a few animals wander the deck as mermaids look on in this sixteenth-century artist's conception of the great flood. *(Historical Picture Archive/Corbis)*

earth with its dry land, oceans, and plants; the sun, moon, and stars; aquatic animals, flying creatures, and land animals; and finally, in his own image, man and woman. This Being—God—told the man and woman that all his other creations were for their use, instructing them to "be fruitful, and multiply." He placed humanity at the apex of his creation, telling the first man and first woman to "replenish the earth, and subdue it" and granting humans "dominion over the fish of the sea, and over the fowl of the air, and over every living thing that moveth upon the earth."

The second version of the Hebrew creation story provides additional details concerning the origin of humans and relates the early history of the Hebrew people. In this account, a fallible, humanlike god creates water on a dry world and produces a man out of "the dust of the ground." He plants a garden in a place called Eden for the man to care for and eat from. Feeling that the man needs a partner, God begins creating all sorts of beasts and fowl, which the man names, but none proves to be a suitable companion and helper. So God puts the man to sleep and makes a woman from one of his ribs.

All is well in the garden until one day, while walking there, God discovers that his two human creations have eaten from the forbidden tree of knowledge. Now they are too much like gods themselves because they know good and evil. Angry, God curses them, condemning women to the "sorrow" of bearing children and to the rule of men. God punishes the first man and all men thereafter by forcing on them the hard labor of farming

FIGURE 1.5 In the Maya creation story in the *Popol Vuh,* the creators, K'ucumatz and Tepew, first made the earth and its mountains, plains, and rivers.

the land to acquire food. God then expels the two humans he has created from the garden (Figure 1.3). Generations pass, during which their descendants become increasingly sinful. To punish them, God produces a catastrophic flood to destroy all his creations. But before doing so, he directs Noah (a descendant of the first two humans) to build an ark, on which he, his family, and a few representatives of other living creatures are saved (Figure 1.4). The story then describes in great detail how these survivors produced all the generations that became the Hebrews and related peoples.

The Maya

The Maya are indigenous to Central America. Beginning more than 2,000 years ago, they developed a complex civilization with magnificent pyramids, a sophisticated calendar, and far-reaching trade networks. The Maya also developed a writing system, and it is from one of their few remaining books, the *Popol Vuh,* that we can learn about their creation story (Savaria 1965).

Before creation, according to the *Popol Vuh,* there were no people, animals, birds, fish, crabs, trees, or stones. There was only the calm sea. The creators, K'ucumatz and Tepew (Figure 1.5), first made the earth, with its mountains, plains, and rivers, and then made animals, such as deer, jaguars, and snakes. The creators assigned each animal its own place to live in the newly created world.

The creators next ordered the animals to speak so that they might praise the creators for their work. The animals, however, could not speak, so the creators decided to make creatures that could; these would be people. The first people, made of mud, could speak, but they had no minds and dissolved in the water. Then the creators made people out of wood who multiplied and spread across the earth. They could speak but lacked blood and minds, and they did not remember the creators who made them. K'ucumatz and Tepew ordered that they be destroyed. Birds plucked out their eyes, and jaguars devoured their woody flesh. Some of these wooden men, nevertheless, managed to escape into the jungle, where all that remains of them today are the monkeys. According to the Maya, this is why monkeys are similar to human beings.

Finally, the fox, the coyote, the parrot, and the crow told the creators about the yellow and white corn that grew on the earth (Figure 1.6). The creators ground and mixed the yellow and white corn into a meal from which they made the flesh and blood of the first true people. These people had blood and minds, and they worshiped the gods who created them and the world in which they lived.

Creation Myths

The preceding stories are **creation myths.** A creation myth performs several functions. It provides an account of the origin of the world. It tells the story of a people's beginnings and their early history. It lays out the society's worldview and belief system. It explains the origin and meaning of a people's rules of social behavior. Ultimately, creation myths serve to codify, rationalize, justify, and stabilize a given social system—generally under the auspices of some supernatural power.

Consequently, a creation story reflects the environment, history, and cultural system of the society that tells it. The mythical layers of the Yąnomamö cosmos, for example, resemble the ecological layers of the rain forest canopy in which they live. Yąnomamö men see themselves as—and indeed they are—fierce warriors who regularly wage war on neighboring villages and generally lead lives centered on violent conflict. Such wars and conflicts have, of course, perfectly concrete explanations. But the Yąnomamö explanation—the abstract justification that maintains this behavior—is found in the creation story of men formed from drops of blood. The subservient position of women in Yąnomamö society and, presumably, the presence of a few men who are not fierce warriors are nicely accounted for in the story by the creation of the timid, docile Yąnomamö from the pregnant legs of one of the first men born from drops of blood.

Similarly, the *Popol Vuh,* the creation story of the Maya, represents the world in which they lived. It includes animals that were important inhabitants of their world and accounts for the vital role played by corn farming in their culture. The tremendous material investment in the construction of sacred Maya buildings, such as temples and pyramids, is also explained by their creation myth; according to the *Popul Vuh,* the entire purpose of humanity is to praise and glorify the gods.

The same sort of analysis, of course, can be applied to the creation myths of the ancient Hebrews. We have come to know these stories well,

FIGURE 1.6 Here, from the *Popol Vuh,* the parrot tells one of the Maya creators about the yellow and white corn. The creator then uses the corn meal to make the flesh and blood of the first true people.

creation myth A myth that explains the origin of the world and its inhabitants.

and they have exerted a great deal of influence on Western culture. They were written down in the book of Genesis—the first portion of the Jewish Torah and the first chapter of the Christian Bible. Parts of these stories have been traced to the creation myths of the Babylonians and other peoples living in Southwest Asia at about the same time as the Hebrews. But the specific details of the Genesis stories, and even the fact that they were written down, are direct results of the environment and history of the Hebrew people at specific times.

For example, Biblical scholars now think that the basic Hebrew creation story of the first man and woman was first put into writing about 3,000 years ago as a political protest against King David's having moved the seat of government to a new location (Asimov 1969; Buttrick 1952). This document's goal was to unify a people on the verge of fragmentation. It reinforced in the Jewish people the ideas of their common bond, heritage, and commitment to God. About 100 years later, in response to a subsequent political split between northern and southern Hebrew groups, the more detailed, second creation story—the one about the humanlike god, the garden, and the flood—was added to the mix. Again, the purpose was to demonstrate the common heritage of the Jewish people in order to reunite them.

This attempt failed to fully unite the Jews, and they were conquered by the Assyrians and the Babylonians. When the so-called Babylonian captivity ended in the sixth century B.C., the Jews needed to reestablish their uniqueness and identity and to formalize their history and cultural heritage. To help accomplish this goal, the old writings were edited, removing internal contradictions and adding some of the history that had taken place since. A "preface" was also added to the story of the garden and the flood: the account of the six-day creation by an all-powerful god, taken largely from a then-popular Babylonian myth called the *Enuma Elish*.

It is this Hebrew creation myth that is of direct concern to us here. As the very beginning of the basic document of the Judeo-Christian tradition, it has had an important impact on many aspects of the development of Western civilization—including the ways in which people have asked and answered questions about the history of their world and its inhabitants. This creation myth, in other words, has deeply affected how Western peoples have studied the past.

Human Origins: The Framework of Science

In this book, we focus on the scientific study of the origin and development of the human species—in essence, on the **evolution** of humankind. A scientific investigation of humanity differs fundamentally from mythic constructs of human origins of the sort just outlined.

Myths are highly variable and idiosyncratic, differing from culture to culture. The contents of myths may or may not be based on observations of the real world. Myths aren't testable explanations; they aren't tweaked

evolution The systematic change over time of organisms or social systems.

or refined as new evidence becomes available. Myth makers don't collect data, conduct research, or carry out experiments. They don't need to; myths are based on imagination and creativity. Myths are, in essence, like Rudyard Kipling's *Just So Stories* ("How the Camel Got His Hump," "How the Leopard Got His Spots," "How the Rhinoceros Got His Skin"). They are interesting attempts to explain things, but they are just that—interesting attempts without any process of assessment, verification, or proof. The point of myth making is the construction of satisfying stories aimed at explaining some aspect of reality and reinforcing or maintaining a social or political order. Creation myths, such as those of the Yąnomamö, the ancient Hebrews, and the Maya perform valuable functions, but they have no necessary grounding in fact.

In contrast, the **scientific method** is normally predicated on observations of the real world, generalizations from those observations, and tests of those generalizations. Creating general explanations of how things work based on specific observations is called **induction.** The general explanations, the "educated guesses" at the rules that govern the way things work, are called **hypotheses.** Scientists, however, do not stop with seemingly plausible explanations for how things such as volcanoes, the weather, or human behavior operate or for how things such as stars, planets, plants, animals, or people came into being. Science goes beyond its own reasonable, credible guesses to rigorously test those hypotheses. Science always asks the question: If a hypothesis induced from concrete observation is valid, if it accurately describes or explains how some part of reality functions, then what new, specific data can be predicted and what further study can test that prediction? This process of suggesting what specific data should be found if a general explanation is to be supported is called **deduction.**

Consider the story about two different species of ape—chimpanzees and gorillas—told in the nineteenth century by the Mpongwe people of Gabon in coastal Africa. Just as the Maya perceived similarities between monkeys and people and explained this in their creation myth, the Mpongwe recognized both the physical and behavioral similarities between apes and human beings and the differences between the two kinds of apes. They attempted to explain these through their myths. They viewed chimps as the physical incarnation of the departed souls of highly intelligent and peaceable people; they thought of chimps as reincarnated Mpongwe. They perceived gorillas as the embodiment of the souls of less intelligent but fiercer forest peoples, people other than the Mpongwe. Thus, a curious similarity between people and apes was explained within the context of a belief system that included the mobility of the soul and the Mpongwe's feeling of intellectual superiority to their neighbors.

In contrast to the Mpongwe explanation, scientists hypothesize that chimpanzees, gorillas, and human beings are similar because we share a relatively recent common ancestor; in other words, we are evolutionarily closely connected in time. That sounds reasonable, but, in contrast with myth, science doesn't stop there. If the hypothesis is correct that humans

scientific method The process by which phenomena are explained through observation and the development and testing of hypotheses.

induction Developing a general explanation from specific observations.

hypothesis A testable explanation of a phenomenon.

deduction The process of suggesting specific data that would be found if a hypothesis were true.

and these apes are biologically closely related, then our genetic codes should be quite similar (see Chapter 4), reflecting our recent divergence (see Chapter 8). In addition, the fossil record should show increasing similarity between human ancestors and the African apes as that record goes back in time (see Chapter 5), and behavioral studies of apes and humans should show detailed and specific similarities (see Chapter 6). These are the data science predicts must be found if the hypothesized biological relationship between apes and people is to be validated. As you will see in these subsequent chapters, this is precisely what has been found. Thus, scientists are not content merely to suggest what seems like a reasonable, pleasing, useful, or congenial explanation for the perceived similarity of humans and apes. They predict what must be true if the hypothesis is valid and then go about the task of seeing if those predictions pan out.

Scientists are well aware of one of the major pitfalls of our imperfect human thought processes—the subconscious desire to see only what we expect to see, to notice only those things that uphold our cherished beliefs (yes, even scientists have cherished beliefs), and to incorporate into our mind-set only those pieces of information that support what we already think is true. This is why in the formal workings of scientific thought, we do not attempt to "prove" our hypotheses; that would be dangerous, and we might never disprove our incorrect, or at least incomplete, explanations. Instead, we attempt to do just the opposite: we make every effort to overturn our hypotheses, to attempt aggressively to prove them wrong! Only when we are *unsuccessful* after applying our best efforts to show that our preliminary explanations are wrong, do we conclude that, at least so far, it looks like our hypothesis actually explains the phenomenon we are examining.

Science is all about taking intellectual risks, leaping into the unknown with imperfect and incomplete data and suggesting explanations for why things are the way they are. As a result, more often than we care to admit, we fall on our faces and are proved wrong. But that's precisely how science proceeds. Based on our observations, the experiments we conduct, and the observations we have made, scientists suggest explanations for puzzles such as how planets form, how our earliest human ancestors evolved, and how civilization developed. Next, we go about the process of testing those explanations with new data, new observations, new experimental results. If the new data contradict our proposed explanations, we refine, overhaul, or reject those explanations and try to come up with something better. If, on the other hand, the new data conform to and confirm our proposed explanations, our confidence in them grows and we continue to test and refine them with new information. Such constant critical testing and refining are the hallmarks of science, and these are what distinguish science from myth.

Eventually, a hypothesis that holds up under rigorous testing is elevated to the status of a **theory.** In common usage, the term *theory* refers to something that is uncertain or contingent on other events: "Are you going

theory A hypothesis that has been well supported by evidence and experimental testing.

to school tomorrow?" "In theory, if it doesn't snow." In this application of the word, you may hear some people say, "Evolution is *only* a theory," meaning it is only a plausible guess and that scientists must, therefore, be uncertain of its validity. This confusion stems from the fact that scientists use the term *theory* in a very particular and precise way that is quite different from its common usage. To a scientist, a theory is not something that is uncertain. Instead, in its scientific use, a theory is a hypothesis that has demonstrably held up to the most rigorous testing for so long that it is a virtual certainty. Every attempt to knock it down has itself failed to disprove the fundamental theme of the hypothesis. Hypotheses that have been elevated to the status of a theory show us in a fundamental way how some aspect of the world works.

Scientists have developed many theories; the theory of gravity and atomic theory are two developed by physics. As you will see, evolution, as an explanation of how life developed and changed on this planet, is a scientific theory from the field of biology. It is a hypothesis that has held up so well and for so long under scientific scrutiny that scientists are virtually certain of its validity in a general sense.

Although evolution is a general theory of the development of life, scientists are still testing many specific hypotheses that seek to explain particular aspects of how evolution operates. This book presents the data and arguments that have been generated by the extensive testing of the many specific hypotheses concerning human evolution.

The general theory of evolution, as well as some specific hypotheses concerning how evolution may have happened, developed within a cultural environment where the Judeo-Christian creation myth was important and influential. In the next chapter, we will outline how the theory of evolution itself evolved within that context.

Anthropology: Studying Ourselves

The specific science that focuses on humanity, including its biology, behavior, culture, and history, is **anthropology.** Anthropologists investigate humanity's origins and subsequent biological and cultural development. In simplest terms, anthropologists focus on the past and present nature of the human **species.**

To use an analogy, anthropology studies humans much the way a branch of biology, say zoology, studies its subjects (although anthropologists focus on a single species). Anthropologists try to make generalizations about the species on which they focus. They look for connections between the present condition and past history of that species. Anthropology assumes that all facets of human anatomy, physiology, behavior, environment, and evolution are interrelated and can only be fully understood in terms of those interrelationships. Thus described, anthropology is the

anthropology The holistic and integrative scientific study of the human species.

species A group of organisms that can produce fertile offspring among themselves but not with any other group.

holistic study of people. Anthropology studies the whole species and all its features in interaction with one another.

Such a broad subject is necessarily divided into a number of specialties or subfields. Perhaps the most characteristic feature of our species is cultural behavior, with all its various manifestations. The specialty of **cultural anthropology** focuses on this behavior, seeking to understand the nature of culture and its variety among different societies. In its most general definition, **culture** is the entirety of those things people have invented or developed and have passed down to later generations. Culture is our extrasomatic (nonphysical, literally "beyond the body") means of adaptation (the way in which we survive).

Our discussion of the origin myth of the Yąnomamö, for example, is based on the fieldwork of cultural anthropologists who have lived among the Yąnomamö for extended periods of time, observed their way of life, spoken to them at length about their lives, and, in fact, asked them how they think the world originated and where their people come from. Cultural anthropologists typically study living societies, yet they also study cultures of the past. Consider, for example, the Hebrew creation myth. Although cultural anthropologists cannot live among this ancient people of Southwest Asia, question them directly about their beliefs and ideologies, or observe their adaptations over time, they can study their surviving texts in order to illuminate their way of life and their beliefs concerning the origin and meaning of life and our universe.

Whereas most other animal species rely on very specific physical adaptations or adjustments to their environment, people, through culture, produce their own means of survival. In other words, culture constitutes all aspects of the human strategy for survival that people, as a result of their intelligence, have been able to think up. Cultural anthropology attempts to describe various cultural systems and to explain the variations these systems exhibit (Figure 1.7). It also searches for processes that account for change in culture over time.

Because language is unique to human beings and such an important part of what makes us different from other animals, some anthropologists focus on linguistics, the nature and structure of human language. **Anthropological linguistics** focuses on issues such as the evolution of speech, the historical connections between the many and various human language systems, and the ways in which language affects our perception of the world.

Cultural systems also have a past. **Archaeology** is the branch of anthropology that studies this past. Along with their written records, the ancient Hebrews and the Maya have also left behind physical traces of their existence. Those physical traces include the daily food remains they disposed of, the tools they lost or discarded, their temples, their burials, and even the remains of their ancient cities. These physical traces comprise the archaeological record, and these cultures—and myriad others—have been the focus of extensive archaeological research. These material remains are,

holistic A study that views its subject as a whole made up of integrated parts.

cultural anthropology The branch of anthropology that focuses on cultural behavior.

culture The nongenetic means of adaptation; those things people invent or develop and pass down.

anthropological linguistics The branch of anthropology that focuses on language.

archaeology The branch of anthropology that focuses on cultural evolution through the study of the material remains of past societies.

FIGURE 1.7 Raymond Hames, using a battery-powered computer and printer, gathers data from some Yąnomamö villagers about the history of their settlement patterns. *(Raymond Hames)*

in effect, the voice through which cultures of the past communicate their story to us in the present. Finding, recovering, and interpreting these remains is the job of the archaeologist, and much of this book focuses on the results of archaeological research.

Finally, we are, of course, living organisms, subject to the same biological processes that affect all other organisms. The study of how these processes apply to people is the focus of **physical,** or **biological, anthropology** (Figure 1.8).

You will be seeing lots of pictures of ancient bones in this book. Most of those bones were discovered and recovered through the work of physical anthropologists. Their analysis forms much of the database that enables us to hypothesize about the evolution of human beings—and to rigorously test those hypotheses.

physical (biological) anthropology The branch of anthropology that focuses on humans as a biological species.

FIGURE 1.8 *(Left)* Ken Feder conducting a field excavation along the Farmington River in Connecticut as part of the Farmington River Archaeological Project. *(Right)* Biological anthropology applied: the excavation of an early New England grave (at the family's request) and the study and eventual reburial of the bones. Nick Bellantoni, Connecticut State Archaeologist, hands Michael Park a bone for identification. *(Left: K. L. Feder; Right: photo by William F. Keegan; courtesy Nicholas Bellantoni)*

paleoanthropologist A biological anthropologist specializing in the study of human fossil remains.

primatologist An anthropologist who studies nonhuman primates.

Some specialists in this subfield gather biological data from living human populations. Others focus on groups of the past, represented by fossil remains; these are **paleoanthropologists.** Still others, **primatologists,** study the biology of our closest relatives, the other primates.

Our subject in this book is human antiquity. In terms of the field of anthropology, this book focuses on the data and methods of archaeology and paleoanthropology—the "anthropology of the past." Remember, though, that in a real sense the subfield designations in anthropology have limited meaning. They refer not to separate disciplines but to starting points or focuses in the general process of trying to understand the human species. Our subject—people—does not divide itself neatly into discrete categories such as present and past, cultural and biological. Neither does anthropology. All branches of anthropology work together toward a common goal: understanding the human species.

Summary

People use two basic frameworks for explaining the past. Myths are stories created to explain some aspect of the world as a group of people sees it at a given time. Myths satisfy the need to place events in chronological order and in a sequence of causality, and they address the basic questions of how, what, who, when, and why. Many myths, like the three described, specifically attempt to account for a people's origins, for their early history, and for their present lifestyle.

Science also seeks to answer these questions, but with a methodology that requires skepticism, testing, and continual reexamination. Science uses observations of real-world data to generate hypotheses. It then tests these hypotheses in an attempt to derive theories—generalizations based on factual data—about the hows, whats, whos, whens, and whys of the world in which we humans live, including our origin and our past.

What follows in this book is an account of what the scientific method has told us so far about the origin and early history of the human species.

Study Questions

1. What are creation myths? How do the three myths described account for the origins of the cultures that tell those myths?
2. What is the scientific method? How does it differ from the use of myth in accounting for human origins and evolution?
3. How does science generate its hypotheses, and how does it test them? What do we mean by *theory* in science?
4. What is anthropology, and why is it described as a holistic study? What are the subfields of anthropology?

Key Terms

myth	deduction	anthropological
science	theory	linguistics
creation myth	anthropology	archaeology
evolution	species	physical (biological)
scientific method	holistic	anthropology
induction	cultural anthropology	paleoanthropologist
hypothesis	culture	primatologist

For More Information

The best book on the Yạnomamö remains Napoleon A. Chagnon's *Yạnomamö*. A useful summary of the archaeology and history of the Maya is *A Forest of Kings: The Untold Story of the Ancient Maya*, by Linda Schele and David Freidel. There are many interpretations of the Bible story. A standard is G. A. Buttrick, ed., *Interpreter's Bible*. See also Isaac Asimov's *Asimov's Guide to the Bible* and John Romer's *Testament: The Bible and History*.

For more detailed discussions of scientific methodology, see *Science and Unreason*, by Daisie Radner and Michael Radner, and *Frauds, Myths, and Mysteries: Science and Pseudoscience in Archaeology*, fifth edition, by Kenneth L. Feder.

Features of the landscape, like the eroded spires of Bryce Canyon in Utah, were interpreted by some geologists as evidence of a young earth afflicted by natural cataclysms. Others saw such features as evidence of an ancient, uniformly changing planet. How did the modern scientific view of an ancient and changing earth arise? How did scientists in the centuries before our own view the place of humanity in their chronological schemes? *(K. L. Feder)*

EDEN QUESTIONED
Historical Perspectives

CHAPTER CONTENTS

Uniformitarianism: The Contribution from Geology

Natural Selection: The Contribution from Biology

Cultural Evolution: The Contribution from Anthropology

Summary

Study Questions

CONTEMPORARY ISSUE: Scientific Creationism and Intelligent Design: Old Ideas in New Forms

Key Terms

For More Information

So much of what is now known about the past was not known just a few hundred years ago. For most Europeans in prior centuries, the biblical framework of history—including the Judeo-Christian creation myth discussed in Chapter 1—was the only acceptable way of looking at the past. The Genesis stories of the six-day creation, the Garden of Eden, Adam and Eve, and Noah's flood were all regarded as genuine history. These myths clearly defined and constrained Western understanding of the actual past.

In the same way that the Maya and the Yąnomamö looked to their myths and legends for information about their worlds, Europeans invoked the Bible as the ultimate source of knowledge, even concerning specific questions of earth history. For example, many Europeans were curious about the actual age of the world. Based on an interpretation of the Bible, it was commonly believed, in past centuries, that the earth was less than 6,000 years old. When in the play *As You Like It* William Shakespeare had his heroine Rosalind state, "This poor world is almost six thousand years old," he was repeating what had become a generally held opinion by the 1590s, when the play was written.

Perhaps the best-known attempt to determine the precise age of the earth based on the Bible was that of Archbishop James Ussher (1581–1656), an Irish cleric. In 1650, through reference to biblical detail, astronomical cycles, and historical records—and after not just a few interpretive leaps—the archbishop determined that the world was created in the year 4004 B.C.; more precisely "upon the entrance of the night preceding the twenty-third day of October" (from Archbishop Ussher's Annales, as cited in Brice 1982:18). Ussher's calculation was widely accepted, and this date was printed in the margins of many English-language Bibles beginning in 1701.

Although Ussher was wrong, he was not as irrational as some modern writers suggest. After all, he arrived at his figure by careful calculation; there was no claim of divine revelation. His result derived from simple math and historical analysis, although it was based in part on a literal interpretation of the Bible (Gould 1993a).

While most Europeans saw the Bible as providing an accurate history of the world, some Europeans and Americans of the seventeenth, eighteenth, and nineteenth centuries, though still believing in God, began to seek enlightenment about the world around them from a source other than the Bible—that is, from nature itself (Greene 1959). Calling themselves natural scientists or natural philosophers, they began a vigorous exploration of various natural sources of information about the earth and the heavens. Make no mistake, these thinkers and writers were religious—the term usually used is *God-fearing*—folks. They were not, at least not initially in any fundamental way, questioning or challenging the story told in Genesis of the creation of the universe, the earth, and plant, animal and human life. Instead, many of these thinkers believed that they were merely practicing a different way of worshiping and venerating God by the study and glorification of his works. In 1691, the natural scientist and theologian Reverend John Ray (1627–1705) expressed the view of many scientists in the title of his book; the proper role of science, in fact, the primary rationale for the conduct of scientific inquiry, was to reveal *The Wisdom of God Manifested in the Works of the Creation.*

Uniformitarianism: The Contribution from Geology

Many of these early natural scientists accepted Ussher's claim of a recent divine creation, but when they looked directly at nature they saw evidence for extensive physical change in the earth itself. The new science of geology described natural features that clearly indicated the earth had undergone vast amounts of change in its appearance. How, then, to reconcile this evidence with the accepted biblical interpretation that the earth was created in its then-present form less than 6,000 years before?

The answer for some thinkers was to view the earth's appearance as the result of a series of natural catastrophes. Noah's flood was seen as one—and maybe the most catastrophic—of these occurrences, but not the only one. Many natural scientists believed that these catastrophes—floods, earthquakes, volcanic eruptions, operating not just locally but on a global scale as well—accounted for the diverse layers of rock and other evidence of substantial change that they had observed. Those who adhered to this general interpretation were called, appropriately enough, **catastrophists.**

Opponents to this view emerged. Geology was developing as an empirical science in which hypotheses proposed for explaining the condition of the earth were based on observation, and global catastrophes of the size and impact necessary to support the catastrophist view had never been observed or recorded. Instead, geologists observed mostly slow-acting, steady processes of change. Some interpreted this to mean that these slow-acting processes, not planetwide cataclysms, had produced the present appearance of the earth. For example, Reverend Thomas Burnet (1635–1715), writing in 1681, suggested that the condition of the earth could best be explained, and its age determined, by reference to ordinary, slow-acting, non-catastrophic natural processes of erosion by ice, wind, and water. Still, he concluded, the world was very young. He argued that if the earth had been ancient, erosion would already have worn away even the tallest mountains. Burnet was unaware that mountain building was still taking place, but he was on the right track by looking strictly at natural phenomena even if his conclusion of a young earth was incorrect.

Robert Hooke (1635–1703), another seventeenth-century English scientist, was fascinated by fossils (Figure 2.1). Whereas others contended that fossils were mere tricks of nature, Hooke correctly interpreted them as the remains of animals and plants that no longer existed. He contended that organisms became extinct because the earth was always changing. These changes were only partly a result, he said, of Noah's flood; they were also caused by long-term phenomena—ordinary occurrences such as erosion that went on all the time in nature.

Hooke was more correct than he knew. The geological and biological records are indeed the results of slow, ordinary, long-term phenomena *and* catastrophic events. For example, the extinction of the dinosaurs

catastrophist An adherent of the idea that the world was changed over time by a series of catastrophic events.

FIGURE 2.1 Early depiction of fossil hunters recovering ancient animal remains in a cave. The seventeenth-century natural scientist Robert Hooke was one of the first to recognize that fossils were the remains of extinct plants and animals. *(From Buckland 1823)*

65 million years ago appears to have been initiated by the impact of an asteroid with the earth, which radically altered the planet's climate. One difference between the modern understanding of such events and the catastrophism of the seventeenth and eighteenth centuries lies in the early thinkers' assumptions that these catastrophes had a divine origin and that all of the earth's features were the result of a regular series of catastrophic events.

Like Burnet, however, Hooke also believed that the earth was quite young. He was perplexed by the fact that ancient histories, such as those of Egypt and China, did not contain descriptions of fossilization actually taking place. He failed to realize that even the most ancient of human histories were far too recent to have borne witness to that process.

By the late eighteenth century, however, some scientists began doing what had heretofore been inconceivable—actually calling into question the historical accuracy of the Genesis account. In 1749, the first volume of *A Natural History* by the French scholar Georges Buffon (1707–1788) was published. In this work, Buffon articulated a perspective called **uniformitarianism.** In essence, he stated that in trying to explain the present appearance of the earth and to determine its age,

uniformitarianism The concept that biological and geological processes that affected the earth in the past still operate today.

We ought not to be affected by causes which seldom act and whose action is always sudden and violent. These have no place in the ordinary course of nature. But operations *uniformly* repeated, motions which succeed one another without interruption, are the causes which alone ought to be the foundation of our reasoning [emphasis ours]. (as cited in Greene 1959:55)

Buffon was saying something simple and straightforward: to learn about the earth, study the earth. The world looks the way it does because of known, natural, observable processes, not because of catastrophic events that no one has ever witnessed. Rivers cut channels, wind and rain wear away mountains, and waves bite into the shore today, as they always have done. These simple, everyday processes can be observed all around us. Given enough time—and here is the key—far more time than Ussher, Burnet, or Hooke had reckoned, rivers could eventually create deep canyons, tall mountains could be worn away leaving flat plains, and coasts could be entirely redrawn.

The implications of Buffon's work were not entirely lost on those who still maintained that the world, exactly as it presently appeared, was the very recent creation of God. In fact, by the fourth volume of *A Natural History,* as pressure mounted on Buffon, he felt obliged to retract just about everything he had said about the age of the earth in the first three volumes. In 1778, however, Buffon tried to accommodate the biblical story of Genesis with his uniformitarian perspective in his *Epochs of Nature.* He suggested that the world was indeed ancient and that earth's history could be divided into six distinct epochs. Although he estimated the duration of each epoch in thousands of years, the six epochs clearly echoed the six days of creation in the Bible.

Perhaps the most important eighteenth-century work on the uniformitarian approach was that of the Scottish geologist James Hutton (1726–1797). In *Theory of the Earth* (1788), Hutton explicitly advanced the notion that by studying natural, slowly working, repetitive processes— that is, uniform, natural processes such as erosion and weathering—we could explain the earth's geology and geography. Again, the key element was time. Given enough time—counted in at least hundreds of thousands of years, not merely thousands—the present appearance of the earth could be understood and explained.

According to Hutton, God had created the earth as what we today would call a self-regulating system. The slow erosion of mountains produced the soil in which plants could grow, which, in turn, could feed animals and humans, for whom it was all created (Figure 2.2). The pressure of this soil on the surface of the earth would, over a long period of time, push up more mountains, ultimately providing new sources of soil on which more plants could grow, and so on. Hutton presented uniformitarianism in a way that glorified even more greatly the creator who had produced such a clever, self-sustaining system for the benefit of his crown of creation, humanity. For such a system to work, a 6,000-year time span

FIGURE 2.2 Delicate Arch is one of several arches at Arches National Monument in southeastern Utah. These fantastic geological features exhibit some of the remarkable forms that have been sculpted by the natural processes of erosion and weathering that geologist James Hutton cited in his uniformitarian approach. *(© Digital Vision)*

was simply insufficient, which is why Hutton suggested that the earth was at least hundreds of thousands of years old. As we now know, however, even this radical suggestion greatly underestimated the actual age of the earth.

The English geologist Charles Lyell (1797–1875) was, perhaps, the most eloquent nineteenth-century advocate for the uniformitarian perspective. It was Lyell who uttered the memorable statement, "The present is the key to the past." In other words, the key to understanding the past rests in the study of those geological processes that can be observed in the present. By examining geological data, Lyell estimated the age of specific features of the earth. For example, because the present rate of deposition of silt at the mouth of the Mississippi River (Figure 2.3) can be measured and because the total size of the existing deposit in the Mississippi Delta can be estimated, the amount of time required for the delta to be formed can be approximated, assuming a uniform rate of deposition. Lyell's figure was about 100,000 years (1873:44–47). (The delta is actually not that old; deposition rates are not as constant as Lyell thought, nor were available measuring techniques precise enough.)

Many people were shocked at the time spans proposed by Hutton and Lyell. Their work was attacked, partly on scientific grounds but largely on the basis that it contradicted the accepted interpretation of Genesis. Then, early in the nineteenth century, a respected English cleric, Reverend Thomas Chalmers, accepted Hutton's work on the principle of uniformitarianism, proclaiming, "The writings of Moses do not fix the antiquity of

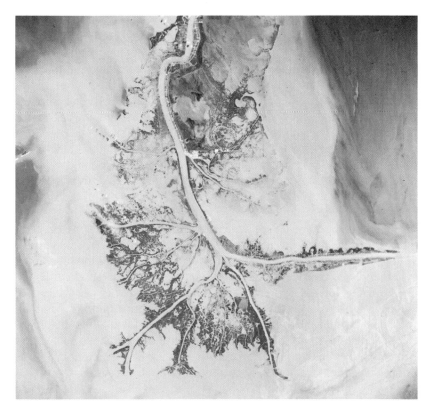

FIGURE 2.3 Aerial view of the Mississippi Delta. By estimating the amount of material deposited in the delta, nineteenth-century geologist Charles Lyell concluded (although mistakenly) that the delta was 100,000 years old. *(Courtesy NASA)*

the globe" (Howard 1975:69). Many other scientists followed suit, recognizing that though the Bible does state that the world was created in six days, there is no mention of when that six-day period took place. Eventually, almost all viewed the hypothesis of an ancient earth as contradicting only Archbishop Ussher, not the Bible itself. The work of Buffon and especially Hutton and Lyell had opened the door for the concept of an old earth—an earth that had existed long enough for the slow erosion of mountains, the cutting of great canyons, the changing of animal species, and even, perhaps, the evolution of humanity.

Natural Selection: The Contribution from Biology

It was shocking enough for people of the late eighteenth and early nineteenth centuries to realize that the earth on which they lived had undergone significant change. At the same time, they learned that the earth was far older than 6,000 years and that the vast changes recorded in the geological record were the result not of a series of relatively recent supernatural catastrophes but of entirely natural, mostly rather mundane, steady, everyday processes played out over an enormous stretch of time. What may have been most shocking, however, was another implication of these ideas: life on earth, including human life, may also have undergone change.

Despite the mounting geological evidence for a changing earth, some biologists denied the possibility of biological change. Like some geologists, however, many were anxious to investigate nature to seek support for divine creation. They sought to glorify creation by studying it. Perhaps the most famous was the Swedish botanist Carl von Linné (1707–1778), better known to us by his Latinized name, Carolus Linnaeus.

Linnaeus was a strict **creationist;** he believed the world and all its inhabitants had been divinely created all at once and had undergone no change (or perhaps only limited change) since that creation. But he also observed that living things resembled or differed from one another to varying degrees. A bear and a deer, for example, have far more features in common (they are warm-blooded, give birth to live offspring, suckle their young) than either has with an earthworm. There was, Linnaeus felt, a system to God's creative works, and he set out to describe it scientifically.

Linnaeus looked at the varying degrees of similarity and difference among organisms, a process today called **comparative biology.** Based on these comparisons, he devised a system of categories and names that identified living things and indicated their physical similarities as he felt God had planned them. Linnaeus's system of classification—a **taxonomy**—was published in final form in 1758. Scientists still use his system today, and we'll show you how it works in Chapter 5.

Although Linnaeus thought he was describing a static, unchanging world of living things, he was actually setting the stage for a more complex interpretation. The similarities and differences Linnaeus recorded might reflect not simultaneous creation but a series of biological relationships. That is, the reason bears and deer are similar in certain ways is that they are biologically related, having once had an ancestor in common—much as you and your cousin are related in that you share a set of grandparents. In other words, one could infer from Linnaeus's descriptions that life on earth had indeed undergone change—and many people were beginning to infer just that.

The Significance of Fossils

Folklorist Adrienne Mayor (2000, 2005) makes a persuasive argument that people in the past, including the Greeks and Romans of classical times (between about 700 B.C. and A.D. 500) and the native peoples of North America of past centuries, encountered the fossilized bones of extinct creatures and attempted to interpret them within their own understanding of the world. For example, Mayor suggests that Greek stories of the mythological creature called the griffin (a sort of half-eagle, half-lion beast) were based on travelers' observations of the fossilized bones of a small di-

creationist One who believes that a supernatural power was responsible for the origin of the universe, the earth, and living things.

comparative biology The study of the similarities and differences among plants and animals.

taxonomy A systematic classification based on similarities and differences.

nosaur—*Protoceratops*—while on trading expeditions into central Asia. *Protoceratops,* indeed, had a birdlike beak and a lionlike body. Closer to home, the Greeks also encountered the fossilized bones of extinct animals in naturally exposed layers on the Mediterranean island of Samos. A Greek myth about monsters called Neades that lived on Samos when the world was young is based, Mayor contends, on the presence there of readily visible, enormous fossil bones. Archaeologists have even found one of these bones in the ruins of a Greek temple on the island dedicated to Hera, the wife of Zeus.

In her latest work, Mayor (2005) explores Native American stories, searching for references to monsters or giants whose bases might have been actual fossil bones encountered by the tellers of the tales. For example, the Pawnee people of Oklahoma tell a story of giants who inhabited the earth at the beginning of time (Mayor 2005:192–195). These giants were quick and powerful but did not respect the creator, Tirawa. Angered, the creator flooded the land, producing a thick layer of mud in which the giants became mired. According to the source of the story as related by Mayor, one can still find the bones of these giants deep in the ground. Mayor suggests that this may be a reference to the Pawnee discovery of actual fossil bones. An even clearer example comes from the Kiowa people of the Southwest, with their legend of Tenocouny, an enormous snakelike monster. Mayor points to depictions of Tenocouny made in a ledger-book sometime between 1891 and 1894 and on a tipi in 1904. Both depictions are reminiscent of the fossilized skeletons of mosasaurs, large serpentine creatures that lived during the Late Cretaceous, between 85 and 65 million years ago. Mosasaur bones have been found in Kiowa territory in Texas, and Kiowa awareness of their existence may have inspired their story of Tenocouny.

All this means that as early as the eighth century B.C., some people were interpreting the fossilized bones of extinct animals as the remains of "strange beasts that no longer existed" (Mayor 2000:60). At least in a general sense, this is the modern interpretation as well.

Back in Europe in the seventeenth century A.D., more than 2,000 years after the Greek explanation of the bones of Samos, the hard evidence of the fossil record finally made the study of living things completely "natural." Like the Greeks before him, Robert Hooke had recognized that some fossils represented the remains of creatures that no longer existed (Figure 2.4). Unlike the Greeks, Pawnee, or Kiowa, Hooke viewed these creatures not as supernatural monsters but as ordinary animals that had simply become extinct. Clearly, this showed that life in general was anything but static. Other fossils showed that particular kinds of creatures had undergone change over time; for example, the skeletons of modern elephants did not look exactly like those of their ancient, extinct relatives.

Moreover, fossils were often found in identifiable layers of rock and soil. Scientists call these layers **strata** (singular, **stratum**) and their study

strata (singular, stratum) Layers of different rock and soil types.

stratigraphy. These strata indicate a chronological sequence of geological
events, the deeper strata generally representing older events and those
closer to the surface more recent ones (Figure 2.5). Thus, the fossils embedded within the strata reflected a history of life on earth.

Evolution

As with geological change, the rapidly mounting evidence for biological
change quickly became irrefutable, and by the late 1700s the idea had
been fairly well accepted within the scientific community and by much of
the educated public. The big question, as the 1800s began, was not if
change had occurred but how.

Even in their attempts to answer this question, some investigators still
tried to include an aspect of stability. If living things themselves could not
be stable and unchanging, they seemed to think, at least the process that
brought change about could be stable, dependable, and predictable. One
of the first popular proposals for a regular mechanism of biological change
was made by Jean-Baptiste de Lamarck (1744–1829).

Lamarck, who coined the term *biology*, was a French naturalist. In the
early years of the nineteenth century, he proposed an explanation for how
and why plants and animals had changed—in modern terms, how they had
evolved. One part of his idea was absolutely correct; the other two parts
were wrong. He correctly recognized that organisms and their environments

stratigraphy The arrangement of rocks and soil in
sequential layers.

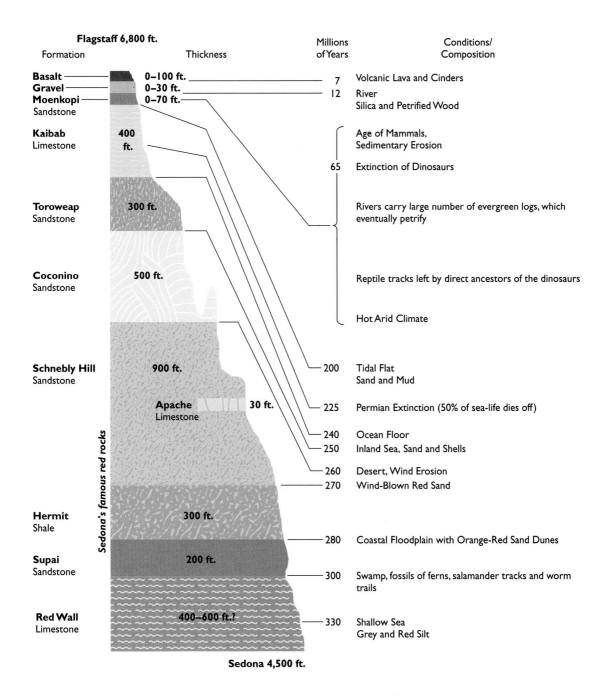

FIGURE 2.5 Geological cross section of the area around Sedona and Flagstaff, Arizona, showing the variation in composition and thickness of the strata and some of the events represented in those strata. *(From J. Best Publishing Co.)*

have an intimate and dynamic relationship: plants and animals are **adapted** to their environments; that is, they possess physical characteristics and patterns of behavior that help them survive under a given set of natural circumstances. When environments change (as the geological record shows they continually do), organisms must alter their adaptive characteristics if they are to survive.

Lamarck went astray, however, in his overall concept of the direction of evolution and in the specific mechanism he proposed for it. He believed that evolution was **progressive,** causing organisms to become increasingly complex and thus more perfect. It followed from this that no organisms would become extinct; creatures represented only by fossils were simply creatures that had undergone so much change that they existed today in unrecognizably different forms. Of course, if all organisms were evolving to become more complex, you might logically ask why very simple organisms still exist. Lamarck would have answered by saying—against a great deal of evidence to the contrary—that new, and therefore simple, living things were always being naturally created.

Progressive evolution is really the heart of Lamarck's idea, but it is not what he is remembered for. His name has come to represent the second erroneous part of his evolutionary concept, his mechanism for change. Lamarck supported an idea that had been around for some time called the **inheritance of acquired characteristics.** His own words in *Philosophie Zoologique,* published in 1809, describe this theory best:

> When the will guides an animal to any action, the organs which have to carry out that action are immediately stimulated to it by the influx of subtle fluids. . . . Hence it follows that numerous repetitions of these organized activities strengthen, stretch, develop and even create the organs necessary to them. . . . Now every change that is wrought in an organ through habit of frequently using it, is subsequently preserved by reproduction. . . . Such a change is thus handed on to all succeeding individuals in the same environment, without their having to acquire it in the same way that it was actually created. (as cited in Harris 1981:116–17)

When the environment changes, said Lamarck, organisms perceive the change and use, cease using, or even create the organs necessary to alter their adaptation. The effects of this use, disuse, or creation of a new organ are automatically passed on to succeeding generations (Figure 2.6).

Lamarck's scheme doesn't work, of course. Traits acquired during one's lifetime cannot be inherited by one's offspring. A bodybuilder's children will not be born with bulging muscles. The offspring of people with lots of tattoos or piercings won't be born with inked designs or holes all over their bodies. Furthermore, how can simple creatures or plants have some sort of will that allows them to know which organs to use and which not to use, or even to create new organs? How can a butterfly will itself to change color? How can a sightless creature sense the need for eyes and

adapted Adjusted to a particular set of environmental conditions.

progressive In a particular direction; in this case, toward increasing complexity.

inheritance of acquired characteristics The incorrect idea that traits acquired by actions taken during an organism's lifetime could be passed to its offspring.

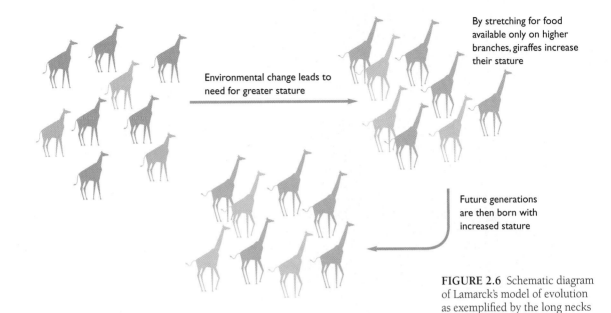

Environmental change leads to need for greater stature

By stretching for food available only on higher branches, giraffes increase their stature

Future generations are then born with increased stature

FIGURE 2.6 Schematic diagram of Lamarck's model of evolution as exemplified by the long necks of giraffes.

then develop them? These were the very sorts of objections many people voiced during Lamarck's time.

The hypothesis, though, maintained some popularity. First, nobody had come up with anything better. Second, it was a comfortable idea that if organisms were going to change, at least they were changing progressively and had some direct control over the process. Indeed, the supposed evolutionary impact of the use (or disuse) of particular muscles or organs and the inheritance of acquired characteristics seem to keep popping up in the history of evolutionary thought.

The scientific objections remained, however, and so the search was still on to explain why and how living things evolved. Enter Englishmen Charles Darwin and Alfred Russel Wallace. The story of these two scientists is fascinating in itself. (Consult the sources at the end of the chapter for fuller accounts.) For our purposes, suffice it to say that Darwin (1809–1882) and Wallace (1823–1913), as a result of separate worldwide travels, observations, and knowledge of the work and ideas of other thinkers, independently became aware of two important facts that had seemingly been overlooked by their predecessors.

First, both noticed that individual organisms within a species exhibit variation. Not every member of a species looks like every other member. Just look around your classroom. If Lamarck's idea were correct, you would expect very little variation because all members of a species would have used, not used, or created the same characteristics.

Second, both men expanded the inference from Linnaeus that similarities and differences among organisms represent biological relationships

FIGURE 2.7 Variation within a population represents the raw material for natural selection. The tiger swallowtail butterflies (*upper right* and *bottom*) are members of the same species. The dark one is a mimic of the pipe-vine butterfly (*left*) that is protected from predation by its foul taste. (*Robert F. Sisson,* © *National Geographic Society Image Collection*)

natural selection Evolution based on relative reproductive success of individuals within a species due to the individual's adaptive fitness.

resulting from their descent from previous organisms. Species, they concluded, descend from other species, just as members of your family descend from earlier members. Darwin and Wallace pictured life on earth as a gigantic and complex family tree.

Given these assumptions, how did Darwin and Wallace think evolution actually worked? Their theory, developed independently by each man, is known by the name Darwin gave it: **natural selection.** Like Lamarck's concept, natural selection is based on the premise that organisms are adapted to their environments and undergo adaptive change when the environments change. But the theory differs from Lamarck's in its explanation of the nature and source of variation.

Inheritance of acquired characteristics requires variation to arise when it is needed. The theory of natural selection, on the other hand, requires variation to already exist (Figure 2.7). Neither Darwin nor Wallace understood why variation existed within species—the nature of the genetic code (see Chapter 4) had yet to be discovered—but they realized that this variation was important. Nature "selects" from the existing variation within a species in the sense that those individuals who, by chance, are best adapted to environmental conditions are the most reproductively successful—that is, they produce the most offspring who survive—and so pass on their adaptive traits to more offspring. As a result, the most adaptive traits of a species tend to increase in frequency within the species; the less adaptive traits tend to decrease.

It follows that evolution has no particular direction. Organisms do not all evolve into more complex forms, as Lamarck had suggested, or into bigger or smarter ones. Rather, populations of organisms evolve to become better adapted, or at least to stay adapted, to the particular environment and time in which they live. There is no overriding principle of progression. Further, the variation from which nature selects is random, not willed by the organism.

It follows that if populations from one species are geographically separated, and thus reproductively isolated, the separate populations, in their different environments, will face different selective pressures. Because changes are selected for and accumulate over time, the populations may eventually become so different that they constitute separate species—that is, they will not be able to interbreed and produce fertile offspring. Thus, not only can a single species change over time as a result of environmental change, but it can also generate new species. This thinking is reflected in the title of Darwin's most famous book, published in 1859, *On the Origin of Species by Means of Natural Selection.*

Finally, it must be understood that such a process, using random variation as its raw material, can't always ensure that species successfully adapt. Sometimes there is simply no existing variation available that will allow for survival in the face of a particularly extensive or rapid environmental change. In such a case, a species becomes extinct. This, in fact, is the norm. Perhaps more than nine-tenths of all species that have ever existed are now extinct.

Wallace, younger and brasher than Darwin, was willing to go public with his new idea right away. But Darwin, who actually thought of natural selection some twenty years before Wallace, kept the idea a secret from all but his closest colleagues; even his wife didn't know about it. Darwin was finally talked into publishing by his friends only after Wallace had made his version known. Why had he kept quiet for so long?

Darwin's delay was not—as popular opinion had it for some time—because he feared public reaction to his support of the idea of evolution. Rather, Darwin was afraid that his mechanism for evolution, as confident as he was about it, was everything that Lamarck's was not and so would not be well received. Natural selection was not progressive, it did not involve the organism's conscious control, and it freely acknowledged extinction. And Darwin, a recluse who suffered poor physical and mental health and feared any sort of unpleasantness or controversy, may have been wise to delay. The world may not have accepted natural selection when he first came up with the theory, around 1836. As the second half of the century began, however—a period marked by rapid and extensive social, political, technological, and economic change—the Western world was ready. The first printing of Darwin's book sold out in a single day and was, for the most part, hailed as a major scientific breakthrough. One scientist of the time is said to have remarked, "How stupid of me not to have thought of that!"

In this way, the scientific revolution brought about by the work of geologists and biologists, put together so well by Charles Darwin, altered forever the scientific view of the past. The past was now seen as a series of events, often caused initially by random change, that were linked to each other over time and linked to the present by uniformitarian processes. This new concept even changed the view of human behavior.

Cultural Evolution: The Contribution from Anthropology

The Discovery of "New" People

Darwin and Wallace focused on variation in plants and animals, but what about a concept taken for granted today—variation in people and their cultures? We are aware that some people live in industrialized, technologically complex societies while others live in agricultural societies that use oxen for plowing their fields. Still others (at least until fairly recently) have relied on hunting animals and gathering wild plants for their subsistence. Most of us realize that different cultures representing different ways of life coexist in the modern world.

Before the Renaissance and the Age of Exploration, however, Europeans were unaware of the diversity of the world's cultures. They knew only a few cultures beyond their own—the Arabs to the south, for example, and the Mongols to the east, whom Marco Polo described in the thirteenth century. Most of the peoples living in Africa and Asia were unknown to Europeans. On maps before the sixteenth century, these areas were labeled *terra incognita*—literally, "unknown land" (Figure 2.8). The Americas remained largely unexplored by Europeans until the sixteenth, seventeenth, and eighteenth centuries.

Europeans looked to the Bible to explain the existence of those other cultures of which they were aware. Remember, the Judeo-Christian creation myth was accepted as a factual account of human history. Adam and Eve, the first people, were the ancestors of all human beings. After their eviction from the Garden of Eden, their direct descendants spread across the land. These people were simple, hard-working farmers, but eventually they strayed from the righteous life and were destroyed by God in a great flood. Only Noah, his family, and the animals on board the ark were saved from destruction. It was the view of most Europeans in these centuries that all living animals could be traced to those that were saved on the ark and all living people could be traced to one of Noah's three sons. Sometime after Noah's flood and the dispersal of Noah's sons and their families,

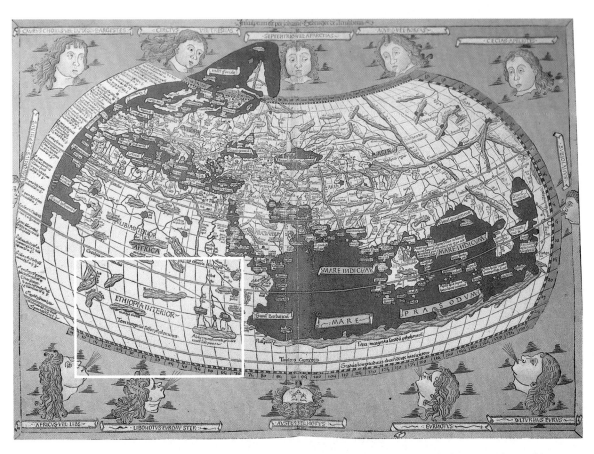

FIGURE 2.8 The world as perceived by Europeans in the fifteenth century. This popular map of the world is from a fifteenth-century edition of the second-century geographer Ptolemy's *Geography*. Much of Africa is labeled *terra incognita*—literally, "unknown land." (© *The Granger Collection, New York*)

the Bible maintains, God became angry at a group of people attempting to build a great tower, the Tower of Babel, up to Heaven. He caused them all to speak in different languages, ruining their plans by destroying their ability to communicate.

This is how the Bible accounts for the origin of language differences and, by inference, the origin of separate cultures. The European interpretation of subsequent history is derived from this biblical framework. The Egyptians, the Greeks, and others were each seen as having originated at Babel. Within this framework, human history was fairly neat and simple; it conformed to the Bible and could be accommodated within a 6,000-year-old universe.

Imagine the Europeans' surprise when early explorers brought home stories of previously unknown peoples—peoples not mentioned in the Bible. They didn't look like Europeans and followed ways of life quite different from what was familiar to Europeans. For example, Portuguese sailors who explored the coast of Africa encountered societies of dark-skinned people who knew nothing of the Bible. Looking for a route to the East Indies, Christopher Columbus sailed west and instead came upon an unknown world with unimagined cultures and peoples, none of which were described in the Bible (Figure 2.9). These new peoples and their cultures simply did not fit neatly into the accepted biblical account of human societies.

Many European thinkers were perplexed by these discoveries. Initially, they assumed that the newly encountered peoples of Asia and Africa were descendants of Noah's sons, Shem and Ham. (Europeans were supposed to be the descendants of the third son, Japheth.) The so-called simpler cultures of Africa and Asia were explained as the result of intellectual degeneration of the descendants of Noah's less-worthy offspring.

Unfortunately, this neat arrangement left no ancestor for the native peoples of the New World, a circumstance that gave rise to a tremendous amount of speculation about who, exactly, the Native Americans were and how they fit into the biblical chronology (Feder 2006; Williams 1991). Practically every European and Asian culture was proposed, at one time or another, as having given rise to Native Americans sometime after Noah's flood (Huddleston 1967). One idea was that a group of sailors or fishermen—perhaps Greeks, maybe "Hindoos," possibly even Norwegians—was lost at sea long ago, fortuitously washed up on the American shore, and established a population. Over the years they changed in appearance, forgot their religion, and became the Indians who Columbus encountered. For a while it was also popular to believe that American Indians were the Lost Tribes of Israel—groups of biblical Hebrews historically unaccounted for. Even the mythical lost continent of Atlantis was suggested as a source of American Indian culture. Europeans were indeed having a hard time trying to make an ever-expanding world fit within their creation myth.

FIGURE 2.9 A seventeenth-century Spanish version of a 1594 engraving (by de Bry) depicting Columbus's first contact with natives of the New World. (© *The Granger Collection, New York*)

The Discovery of Mysterious Artifacts

While some Europeans were exploring unknown lands and encountering unknown cultures, others were examining the soil beneath their own feet and discovering some rather strange-looking stone objects. Though the symmetry, sharp edges, and beauty of these flaked pieces implied that they had been manufactured by human beings, many writers denied the possibility that these objects represented human craftsmanship.

This denial was firmly rooted in biblical literalism. The Bible did not mention the existence of a primitive stage of human development, certainly not one in which people made tools of stone and knew nothing of metal. In Genesis, a seventh-generation descendant of Adam named Tubalcain (a brother or half brother of Noah) is identified as the "instructor of every artificer in brass and iron" (Genesis 4:22). With metallurgy traceable to this early a time in biblical history, there seemed no reason to believe that there had been a historical period when human beings relied on stone tools. Many thinkers in the seventeenth, eighteenth, and nineteenth centuries concluded that these tool-like objects of stone must have been tricks of nature. (Remember that fossils were also explained this way by those seeking to deny the earth's antiquity.) Some suggested that such objects were the handiwork of fairies and elves, calling the objects, in fact, "fairy stones." Others declared them to be the natural result of lightning striking the ground and labeled them "thunder stones." Still others did accept the objects as having been made by humans; they believed, however, that the makers of such simple stone tools must have been some degraded form of humanity that existed just before Noah's flood but after Tubalcain's invention of metallurgy.

The Evolutionary Explanation

At the same time, other thinkers challenged these Bible-based interpretations. Some researchers in the seventeenth century—for example, the French naturalist Isaac de la Peyrère—explicitly suggested that finely worked stone objects found deep in the earth must have been the result of ancient human manufacture. In the late eighteenth century, a young Englishman, John Frere, published a short note in the journal of the London Society of Antiquaries recounting his discovery of finely chipped stone axes at a great depth in a quarry in Hoxne, England (Figure 2.10). These tools were found *beneath* the bones of extinct animals, suggesting that they were even older than the bones, having been manufactured "by a people who had not the use of metals" (Frere 1800:204).

In his spare time, French customs official Jacques Boucher de Perthes collected hundreds of flint implements in excavations along the terraces overlooking the River Somme in northern France. Boucher de Perthes (1847) deduced that these chipped stone implements were ancient and, in the title of the first volume of his work on ancient history, called them *antediluvian,* meaning, literally, "from before the flood." Just as with the stone tools unearthed by John Frere in England, these French artifacts were discovered in deep excavations, recovered from soil layers that also produced the bones of extinct animals, including those of bison, woolly mammoth, woolly rhinoceros, and cave bear (Stiebing 1993). The stratigraphic context and association of the tools with fossil bones provided strong evidence for their great antiquity, dating them, in fact, to a time when people relied on stone, not metal, for their weapons and tools and when animals now long extinct roamed the European countryside.

FIGURE 2.10 Woodcut of one of the hand axes discovered in Hoxne and reported on by John Frere to the London Society of Antiquaries in 1797 (and first published in 1800). The hand axes from Hoxne were important because, perhaps for the first time, such artifacts had been found in stratigraphic position, deeply buried in the soil and in association with the bones of extinct animals. All this implied a great age for these specimens—and for the humans who had manufactured them. (© *Society of Antiquaries, London*)

In *The Geological Evidences of the Antiquity of Man,* first published in 1863, Charles Lyell, the ardent uniformitarianist we met earlier, presented detailed evidence for the association of some stone tools with the fossilized bones of extinct animals and even humans.

> For the last half-century, the occasional occurrence, in various parts of Europe, of the bones of Man or the work of his hands, in cave-breccias and stalagmites, associated with the remains of the extinct hyaena, bear, elephant, or rhinoceros, has given rise to a suspicion that the date of Man must be carried further back than we had heretofore imagined. (1873:1–2)

The discovery of stone tools at great depth and in direct association with the bones of extinct animals strongly supported the argument for the great antiquity of these artifacts (Grayson 1983; Van Riper 1993).

A "Stone Age"

De la Peyrère, Frere, Boucher de Perthes, Lyell, and others agreed that chipped-stone artifacts were the handiwork of people living in more primitive ways in the distant past. Some thinkers went on to propose that such tools were direct evidence of a previous and primitive stage of universal human **cultural evolution**—a stone age through which all people, including Europeans, had passed.

cultural evolution Changes in cultural patterns over time.

Evidence of previous stages of human cultural development mounted as more and more ancient artifacts were unearthed. The evidence became so compelling that in 1836, Christian Jurgensen Thomsen of the Danish National Museum in Copenhagen produced a guidebook describing the museum's collection of artifacts, which he organized into three prehistoric ages—stone, bronze, and iron. Inherent in Thomsen's three-age system was the notion that human culture had changed over time in a patterned and comprehensible way. Thomsen's ages were thought to reflect increasing technological sophistication over time, a progression of better tools made from increasingly difficult-to-work raw materials.

Others applied the notion of cultural evolution even more broadly. Anthropologist Edward Burnett Tylor, in his book *Primitive Culture* (1871), argued that the persistence of primitive—that is, less technologically complex—societies into the nineteenth century could be explained in one of two ways. Either culture was created more or less as is and primitive societies represent degeneration, or modern civilization developed over a very long period of time from an initial state of "barbarism" and modern primitives, for whatever reason, were still living in a stage of development that the rest of humanity had long ago left behind. For the former theory, Tylor concluded that there was absolutely no evidence. He championed the latter and became one of the first cultural evolutionists.

Lewis Henry Morgan, an American anthropologist and cultural evolutionist, followed Tylor's idea and suggested, in *Ancient Society* (1877), that all cultures change over time, evolving through stages of "savagery," "barbarism," and "civilization." Cultures could get stuck at a particular level if certain key inventions and advances were not made—the bow and arrow, the domestication of plants and animals, the smelting of iron. Modern primitives were such frozen societies.

Tylor and Morgan's schemes of cultural evolution were **unilinear.** Their view was that all cultures eventually pass through the same fixed stages of increasing technological complexity. Modern anthropologists no longer accept such simplistic schemes, viewing cultural evolution as **multilinear,** with different cultures passing through different possible sequences of change. Nevertheless, Tylor and Morgan are important early theorists because they recognized that human beings and their cultures have undergone great change, just as plants and animals have done. They showed that cultures have evolved and that processes of cultural change can be identified and understood.

Evidence for the great age of and change within humanity was mounting in the newly developing field of anthropology. As with geology and biology, the interpretation of the anthropological evidence virtually required that both the earth itself and the human race were ancient and always changing. Science was supplying enormous amounts of new data about human history and the world. And these data simply could no longer be contained within a 6,000-year-old, static universe (Figure 2.11).

unilinear The now-discredited notion that all cultures pass through the same sequence of change.

multilinear The accepted notion that different cultures pass through any one of a number of possible sequences of change.

Summary

Until a few hundred years ago, most European thinkers sought to inter-pret the nature of the world in the context of biblical history. The more they looked into nature itself, however, the more the biblical framework became supplanted by ideas derived from use of the scientific method—the inductive development of hypotheses to account for observed data and the deductive testing of these hypotheses to generate theories.

Science thus altered the European view of the world. Where they once saw earth as young and unchanging, Europeans came to see the earth as ancient and undergoing virtually continual change. The work of natural scientists such as James Hutton and Charles Lyell and their principle of uniformitarianism provided evidence for this ancient and changing earth. The discoveries of Frere, Boucher de Perthes, and de la Peyrère of flaked stone tools at great depth and in association with the bones of extinct ani-mals suggested a primitive period of great antiquity.

Where living things had been seen as the unaltered creations of a supreme being, species were now viewed as the ever-changing products of natural processes. The work of Alfred Wallace and Charles Darwin in the nineteenth century explained the mechanisms for these processes of change. Even humans themselves came to be seen as a topic for scientific investigation and as a species whose history stretched far into antiquity.

Study Questions

1. How did the study of the human past begin to move from the realm of belief systems to the realm of science?
2. What is uniformitarianism? How did it develop, and how did it contribute to our understanding of changes in the earth and its inhabitants?
3. What were the major ideas about how life on earth evolved? How does natural selection operate, and what does it imply about how life has changed?
4. What biblically based explanations were given for the finely shaped stone objects found at great depth in the late eighteenth and early nineteenth centuries? How were these objects seen within a scientific framework?
5. How were new peoples, encountered by Europeans during the Age of Exploration, first accounted for? How did the science of anthropology explain the observed variation in human cultural systems?
6. What are scientific creationism and intelligent design, and why are they considered a threat to both science education and religious freedom?

FIGURE 2.11 Timeline showing the chronology of key thinkers and events in the intellectual history of research into the age of the earth and the evolution of life on the planet.

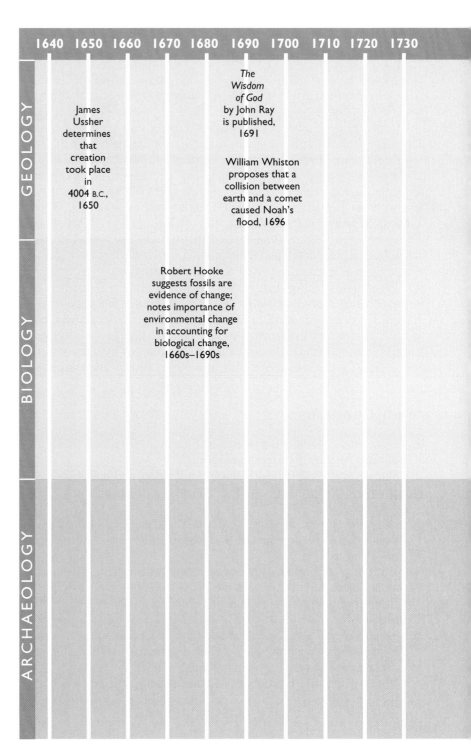

1740	1750	1760	1770	1780	1790	1800	1810	1820	1830	1840	1850	1860	1870	1880

Theory of the Earth by James Hutton published, 1788

Principles of Geology by Charles Lyell published, 1830

William Smith's stratigraphic tables first circulated, 1799

William Smith's stratigraphic tables published, 1815

Georges Buffon Uniformitarianism; longer timeframe for earth history, 1749

Linnaeus publishes his taxonomy of living things, 1758

Philosophie Zoologique by Jean-Baptiste de Lamarck published, 1809

Darwin begins his voyage on the *Beagle,* 1831

Darwin writes a synopsis of his theory of evolution, 1844

The Origin of Species by Charles Darwin published, 1859

The Descent of Man by Charles Darwin published, 1872

Alfred Russel Wallace proposed idea of natural selection, 1859

Gregor Mendel discovered basic laws of inheritance, 1860s

John Frere finds flint tools in soil layer deep in quarry in Hoxne, England, 1797

Flint tools and bones of extinct animals found in Kent's Cavern, England, 1824

C. J. Thomsen publishes museum guide and introduces three-age system, 1836

Primitive skull found in Neander Valley, Germany, 1856

Ancient Society by Lewis Henry Morgan published, 1877

Human bones found with bones of extinct animals in French cave, 1828

Geological Evidences of the Antiquity of Man by Charles Lyell published, 1863

Jacques Boucher de Perthes finds ancient flint axes, 1837

Researches in the Early History of Mankind by Edward Tylor published, 1865

CONTEMPORARY ISSUE

Scientific Creationism and Intelligent Design: Old Ideas in New Forms

The reliance on a literal interpretation of the Bible did not die out when the theories of uniformitarianism and natural selection were developed. These theories took many years to gain acceptance, and even today many people continue to have faith that their god or gods had some hand in designing the world.

For many Westerners, no conflict exists between such a belief and the actual processes of earth history and evolution so laboriously illuminated and described by science. Most Jews and Christians, for example, simply believe that God created these natural processes along with everything else. This is the official stance of the Roman Catholic Church. But a sizable minority still holds that the Judeo-Christian creation myth is factual. Like most Europeans in previous centuries, they take the stories in Genesis literally; in other words, they believe a literal interpretation of the story told in their creation myth is true.

Scientific knowledge involves a rational, logical attempt to understand the physical world. It is based on the scientific method described in the previous chapter. In honest science, this method of inquiry is continuous; no idea is ever accepted as proven for all time. Rather, it is tested, retested, refined, and changed as new evidence and new ideas accumulate. As the evolutionary scientist John Maynard Smith puts it, science tells us "what is possible" (1984:24). Or, in the words of Pope John Paul II (paraphrasing the Vatican librarian Baronio, a contemporary of Galileo), the function of science is to instruct us "how heaven is."

The other type of human knowledge consists of belief systems, which are not open to testing and experimentation. They are taken on faith, accepted as given. A belief in God, for instance, or a disbelief in God for that matter, simply cannot be subjected to the scientific method. What is the concrete evidence? How is it tested? What person, believing in a supreme deity, is going to change his or her mind in light of some scientifically derived theory about the physical world? What sort of rational thinking would convince someone that human life is not sacred? Rather than serving to describe the physical world,

belief systems function to tell people how to behave toward one another and toward that world. They also serve to define the meaning of life. They tell us, says John Maynard Smith, "what is desirable" (1984:24), and instruct us, say Galileo and Pope John Paul II, "how to get to heaven."

To the majority of people who hold them, religious beliefs usually fall into a category of knowledge that also includes ethical precepts, moral values, and philosophical tenets. There is no inherent conflict between this kind of knowledge and the kind labeled science. Indeed, the two usually live in harmony with each other.

In fact, these two spheres of knowledge—rather than being eternally in conflict with each other, as they are all too often seen—should interact harmoniously for any society to thrive and prosper. People require scientific knowledge, based on the scientific method, to tell them how to hunt animals, grow plants, make tools, and program computers. But people also require rules of behavior, taken on faith, to ensure unity, cooperation, and harmony within societies. It is perhaps part of the human condition to wonder why we are here, and belief systems also help answer this sort of question. Again, science tells us what is possible; belief systems tell us what is desirable.

Sometimes, however, the harmonious interaction of these spheres of knowledge is disrupted when they are forced into conflict with one another—when science attempts to challenge a belief system or when a belief system claims its tenets are scientifically valid. The latter occurred in Tennessee in 1925, when a bill was passed in the state legislature that declared it illegal to teach, in a state-supported school, any theory that denied the biblical creation story and claimed humans were descended from some "lower order of animals." Initially, the bill was not taken seriously (except by its sponsor, of course), but the governor signed it as a demonstration of Christian faith. No one thought it would be enforced.

The American Civil Liberties Union viewed the law as a serious threat and, with the cooperation of

William Jennings Bryan (*right*) and Clarence Darrow at the Scopes trial.
(© *AP/Wide World Photos*)

community leaders in Dayton, Tennessee, orchestrated a test case, hoping to shame the state into rescinding the law. The local high school's regular biology teacher wanted no part of the plot, but the school's football teacher, John T. Scopes, who also happened to be a substitute classroom teacher, agreed to the setup, deliberately and openly violating the law by assigning a text section that dealt with evolution. Scopes was arrested, charged with a crime,

and a trial followed. Then things got out of hand. People came from all over the country to watch the trial, not so much because of the issue but because the attorney for the prosecution was William Jennings Bryan, a fundamentalist speaker and failed presidential candidate, and the lawyer for the defense was Clarence Darrow, perhaps the best-known and most successful lawyer of his time.

(*continued*)

CONTEMPORARY ISSUE

Scientific Creationism and Intelligent Design: Old Ideas in New Forms   (*continued*)

The town of Dayton took on a circus atmosphere, though the trial itself turned out to be rather unspectacular and boring. Convicted and fined $100, Scopes later had his conviction overturned on a technicality. But the trial did feature a memorable and now-famous confrontation between Bryan and Darrow—which did not become part of the formal record. In an unprecedented move, Darrow put prosecutor Bryan on the stand and questioned him about his views on the literal truth of the Bible. During this exchange, which demonstrated the wit and oratorical skills of both men, the separate natures of science and religion became clear as Bryan was unable to support his interpretation of creation with anything other than faith. Here is a brief excerpt (Appleman 1970:543–44):

DARROW: [asking about the accepted date of 4004 B.C. for the creation of the world] Don't you know that the ancient civilizations of China are 6,000 or 7,000 years old, at the very least?

BRYAN: No; but they would not run back beyond the creation according to the Bible, 6,000 years.

DARROW: You don't know how old they are, is that right?

BRYAN: I don't know how old they are, but probably you do. I think you would give preference to anybody who opposed the Bible, and I give the preference to the Bible.

As this exchange became part of American folklore, the common interpretation was that science had "won." In fact, both science and religion suffered. One result of the trial was to draw attention to a conflict that didn't necessarily exist. Shortly after the trial, the topic of evolution began to disappear from textbooks, where previously it had occupied a prominent place. It only reappeared after 1957, when the Soviet launching of the Sputnik satellite prompted the United States to reexamine the quality of its science education.

The controversy in the schools, however, has not gone away; in fact, it has intensified in recent years.

Challenging the teaching of evolution has become a virtual cottage industry in the United States in recent years. In 1995, the Alabama state legislature mandated that an insert be pasted into high school biology texts stating that evolution has not been proven. A similar insert was also placed in biology textbooks in Georgia. In 1996, the Tennessee Senate debated (and eventually rejected by a vote of 20 to 13) a proposal that had been passed by the state House of Representatives to dismiss any public school teacher who presented evolution as a fact. Since 1999, the Kansas Board of Education has gone back and forth over the status of evolution as one of its knowledge "benchmarks," that is, fundamental elements of science that all students must understand. The Kansas board eliminated the evolution benchmark in 1999 and restored it in 2001. In 2004–2005, the Kansas board revisited the issue and proposed revising the evolution benchmark, proposing that teachers emphasize the controversial nature of evolution, maintaining that it is "a theory and not a fact," a statement that reflects the board's misunderstanding of the term *theory* (see Chapter 1). Controversies regarding the teaching of evolution have not been restricted to the South and Midwest. In 2005, bills were debated in the New York and Pennsylvania state legislatures that would have required general science and biology instructors to teach "intelligent design" (a scientifically baseless concept that we will discuss shortly) side by side with evolution.

Were it not for its larger implications and these present-day echoes, we might see the story of the Scope's trial (called the "monkey trial" because of the implications of Darwin's theory for our ancestry) as an amusing little bit of Americana. Clearly, however, the issue the trial brought to the public's attention has lingered, and recently a new version of creationism has emerged in a particularly complex and disturbing form.

Called **scientific creationism**, this latter-day notion has as its basic tenets (1) that real scientific evidence exists to support the biblical creation story, and (2) that no real evidence exists to support evolutionary theory. The Bible, according to this view, is a scientific and historical document as well as a religious one. Moreover, it posits that if evolution can be shown to be false, then scientific creationism must be true.

As we have outlined briefly and will discuss in detail later, an enormous quantity of evidence supports the idea of biological evolution. That is why these topics are part of mainstream science—and science curricula. Not one shred of scientific evidence supports scientific creationism.

One of the corollary ideas of the scientific creationists is that, as a science, creationism should be given equal time in schools alongside evolution as an equally viable scientific hypothesis. This argument has gained some support in the United States and in other countries. With a very basic national belief in religious freedom and tolerance, Americans are reluctant to deny people access to an idea with religious (especially Judeo-Christian) connections.

The fact is, though, that equal time is for equal things, and creationism is not the equivalent of evolution. Scientific creationism is based on one group's interpretation of the content and message of the Bible. It is a belief system and thus is not even open to scientific investigation. But some of the specific claims of scientific creationism *are* open to testing—and they have utterly failed these tests.

For example, believing that the world is a mere 6,000 to 10,000 years old, some scientific creationists have attempted to prove that dinosaurs and human beings lived during the same period of earth history and even that Noah saved dinosaurs on board the ark (Morris 1980). They deny the simple fact of **biostratigraphy,** wherein fossils often appear in a regular sequence of ancient soil and rock layers, or strata, from old (deeper) to recent (higher). Paleontologists and paleoanthropologists know that dinosaur and human bones are never found in the same layers (see Chapter 7) because dinosaurs and the immediate evolutionary ancestors of humans are separated by at least 60 million years. Scientific creationists rationalize the separation in this way: di-

nosaurs that drowned in Noah's flood didn't float as well as humans who died in the flood, so humans are found in higher geological layers.

In one of the few examples of actual fieldwork they have conducted, creationists excavated a series of fossilized footprints along the Paluxey River in Texas. They claimed that dinosaur footprints and giant human footprints were found side by side in the same layer, implying that dinosaurs and people lived at the same time. The so-called human footprints have been shown conclusively to be misidentified dinosaur footprints (Kuban 1989a, 1989b).

In its attempt to attribute scientific and historical accuracy to the Bible, scientific creationism is no less than a clever and insidious device for injecting a partisan religious view into public education. In fact, teaching the two models side by side in science classes would contradict the principle of religious freedom, for it would mean that one group's religious ideas were being taught as scientific theory to individuals who hold other religious views or no religious views at all. Furthermore, it would undermine the whole idea of free scientific inquiry and intellectual honesty.

Recently, a new twist on this problem has surfaced with a new degree of complexity and, thus, a potential for unquestioned acceptance. It is generally referred to as **intelligent design.** It comes in several forms, but one will capture the idea. This version of intelligent design says that the basic chemistry of life—the cell, with its DNA, RNA, resultant proteins, and myriad reactions—is far too complex to have evolved naturally and so *must* have been designed by some intelligent entity. The more involved arguments use statistics to convey the great odds against putting together just the right combination of molecules that we now know are needed for life. Intimidated by such large numbers, many people accept the proposed improbability, if not impossiblity, of life evolving by natural processes.

There are two problems with this idea. First, the initial improbability of something happening doesn't

(continued)

CONTEMPORARY ISSUE

Scientific Creationism and Intelligent Design: Old Ideas in New Forms   **(continued)**

preclude its happening. What was the probability at my birth that I would eventually become a biological anthropologist teaching at this university and, at this moment, writing a textbook? The answer is: infinitesimally small! And yet it happened, through all the contingent facts of my personal history—all the little things, many of them conscious decisions but many random, unpredictable, and accidental, which led to other things, and so on.

Similarly, for the evolution of life, a billion years or so passed from the formation of the earth to the first evidence of life (think of how long a billion years is). There are so many molecules, so many combinations of molecules to make compounds, so many individual chances for things to come together in different variations that we couldn't begin to even estimate the number. Among the things that did occur was the chemical combination, under just the right circumstances, that set in motion the chain of events that led to what we now call life. In other words, an intelligent designer is *not necessary*.

The second problem is that an intelligent designer is not a scientific (that is, testable) idea. The proposal of an intelligent designer based on supposed rational, scientific evidence (biochemistry and statistics) is just a thinly disguised version of scientific creationism. It ignores the majority of empirical evidence and substitutes an idea that cannot be tested, that *must* be taken on faith. It then becomes, by the definition I use here, a pseudoscience. There may well *be* some designer behind the universe we see, but a belief in such a designer is not a *substitute* for a scientific explanation of that universe.

We will describe a great many scientific hypotheses and theories throughout this book. We have no vested interest in whether any specific idea proves to be true or false. As scientists, we believe that our only vested interest is in seeking and understanding the nature of the world—whatever that may be. The strides made by science toward that goal and the resulting benefits to our species are only possible in an atmosphere of free inquiry and harmonious interaction between science and belief systems.

Key Terms

scientific creationism The belief that scientific evidence exists to support the religious claim that the universe is the product of divine creation.

biostratigraphy The patterned appearance of plant and animal fossils in strata. The fossils of more ancient organisms are found in older, deeper strata, while those of more recent organisms are found in younger, generally higher strata.

catastrophist
uniformitarianism
creationist
comparative biology
taxonomy
strata
stratigraphy

adapted
progressive
inheritance of
   acquired
   characteristics
natural selection
cultural evolution

unilinear
multilinear
scientific creationism
biostratigraphy
intelligent design

For More Information

Perhaps the most famous book on the history of evolution, which still holds up over thirty years after its publication, is John C. Greene's *The Death of Adam: Evolution and Its Impact on Western Thought*. Another treatment of the same subject, using excerpts from original writings, is *Evolution: Genesis and Revelations,* edited and with comments by C. Leon Harris. A collection of writings by Charles Darwin and many of his contemporaries, predecessors, and successors is *Darwin,* second edition, edited by Philip Appleman. A biography of Darwin that focuses on the man as well as the scientist is John Bowlby's *Charles Darwin: A New Life.*

Finally, paleontologist and science historian Stephen Jay Gould has written a number of essays on the history of evolutionary thought, many aimed at reexamining old ideas on the subject. They can be found in his books *Ever Since Darwin, The Panda's Thumb, Hen's Teeth and Horse's Toes, The Flamingo's Smile, Bully for Brontosaurus, Eight Little Piggies,* and *Dinosaur in a Haystack.*

For an idea as to the arguments of the scientific creationists, try *Evolution: The Fossils Say No!* by Duane T. Gish, and for a refutation of scientific creationism, go to Stephen Jay Gould and a series of articles on the subject in his *Hen's Teeth and Horse's Toes.* For more about the Scopes trial, the following Web site provides quite a bit of information including part of the trial transcript and contemporary newspaper accounts of the trial: www.law.umkc.edu/faculty/projects/ftrials/scopes/scopes.htm

intelligent design The idea that an intelligent designer played a role in some aspect of the evolution of life on earth, usually the origin of life itself.

This gaseous pillar in the M16 nebula is an incubator of new stars. Our own sun may have formed in just such a structure. What do scientists know about the history of the universe and the development of life on our miniscule part of it? (*J. Hestor, P. Srowen, and NASA, courtesy Space Telescope Institute, Baltimore*)

EVOLUTION
An Overview

CHAPTER CONTENTS

Big Bang to Big Dinosaurs   Study Questions
Grasping Hands and Big Brains   Key Terms
Summary   For More Information

In the remainder of this book, we'll be painting a picture of human antiquity. Our palette will be the methods of inquiry and investigation called science; some of these methods were described in Chapter 1. Our paints will be the hypotheses, theories, and facts that science has provided. The canvas we paint on will be the dimension of time.

Time can often be a problem for those who seek to learn about the past and so must deal with vast quantities of it. It is easy to conceive of a day, a week, a month, even a year. By stretching the imagination, it is possible to get a feel for the span of time that makes up an individual life. But it becomes increasingly difficult to imagine the time involved in the last few generations, or in the history of the United States, or in the period of time since the ancient Egyptians built the pyramids more than 4,000 years ago.

It gets even more difficult when thinking about the time since the invention of writing, since the beginnings of modern humans, and since the dawn of our evolutionary line. And it becomes a monumental task to conceive of the vistas of time back to the dinosaurs, to the first land animals, to the beginning of life on earth, and to the very origin of the universe.

But it's vital for someone interested in human antiquity to acquire a concept of the time involved in humans' tenure on earth and to appreciate just where that time fits into the broader scheme of events that makes up earth history. It's essential to understand that all the processes of evolution apply to all forms of life on earth and that the idea of evolution—change over time—applies to the whole history of the universe.

In the chapters that follow, we'll present many details about human evolution. It's difficult, we think, to develop a concept of time working from the specific to the general; so, in this chapter we'll provide a brief narrative outline of evolutionary history, focusing on human evolution. Then, as you read about the detailed evidence and ideas, you'll have a context—of time and basic events—in which to place those details.

Big Bang to Big Dinosaurs

A number of hypotheses attempt to account for the origin of the universe. According to the majority of scientists, in the beginning—the very beginning—all the energy, space, and matter of the known universe were compacted into a dense, hot, inconceivably tiny speck of pure energy. The laws of physics as currently understood can't account for the existence of this speck, so science has yet to answer the question of where it came from. Some people turn to mythology for an answer; some simply believe the universe has always been here, cycling through eternity; others wait, assuming science will one day be able to provide an explanation.

While science cannot yet determine where the universe came from or why it is here, science can account for most of the history of the universe by using the established fact that the universe is rapidly expanding. To this fact, scientists apply the current laws of physics and astronomy and work backward, rather like running a movie of an explosion in reverse. They hypothetically shrink the universe and determine what would happen to all its matter and energy under conditions of decreasing size and increasing density and heat. They also devise a time frame for the events involved.

Through this procedure, scientists trace the chronology of a long series of events and processes set in motion somewhere around 15 billion

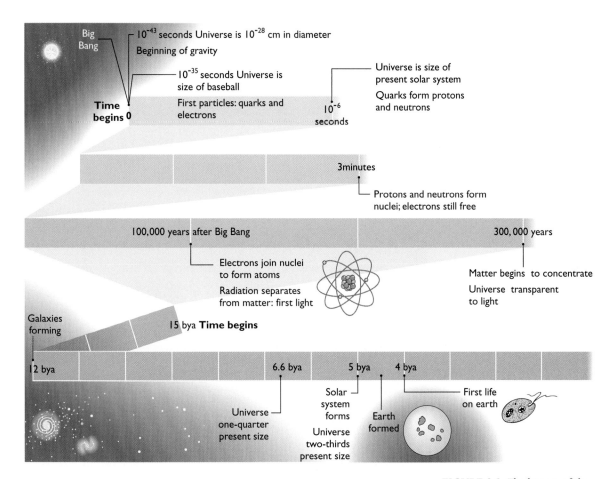

10^{-43} seconds Universe is 10^{-28} cm in diameter
Beginning of gravity

Big Bang

10^{-35} seconds Universe is size of baseball

Universe is size of present solar system

Quarks form protons and neutrons

Time begins 0

First particles: quarks and electrons

10^{-6} seconds

3minutes

Protons and neutrons form nuclei; electrons still free

100,000 years after Big Bang

300,000 years

Electrons join nuclei to form atoms

Radiation separates from matter: first light

Matter begins to concentrate

Universe transparent to light

Galaxies forming

15 bya **Time begins**

12 bya

6.6 bya

5 bya

4 bya

First life on earth

Universe one-quarter present size

Solar system forms

Universe two-thirds present size

Earth formed

FIGURE 3.1 The history of the universe, from the Big Bang to the origin of life on earth. The scale of the timeline changes because some events are condensed into incredibly small periods and others are stretched over unimaginable spans.

years ago (bya;* Figure 3.1). (We use *billion* here in the American sense, that is, as a thousand millions. In much of the world, *billion* means a million millions, what Americans call a trillion.) It was then that the tiny speck began to expand. This event is known as the Big Bang although it wasn't really an explosion. It was more like a balloon being rapidly inflated, a balloon that contained both energy and space. This inflation is hypothesized to have been caused by the accumulation of a material that created a repulsive force—the opposite of gravity's attractive force.

A fraction of a second after the expansion began, the space-energy speck, now the size of a baseball, began cooling off (relatively speaking; it still was enormously hot), and matter began to condense from energy. The first matter was in the form of the smallest subatomic particles, but as the infant universe continued to grow and cool, increasingly larger particles

*By convention, we will use the following abbreviations throughout the remainder of the book: *ya* for "years ago," *mya* for "million years ago," and *bya* for "billion years ago."

FIGURE 3.2 This color-enhanced photo, taken by the Hubble Space Telescope in 1995, shows huge pillars of gas in the M16 nebula in the constellation Serpens. Such pillars are the incubators for new stars, which form in the tips of the pillars by a process called *photoevaporation.* Each pillar in this picture is about one light-year (6 trillion miles) long. *(J. Hestor, P. Srowen, and NASA, courtesy Space Telescope Institute, Baltimore)*

FIGURE 3.3 The whole earth from space, showing Africa and the Arabian Peninsula. The island of Madagascar is just right of center. *(NASA)*

formed. By three minutes after the Big Bang, atomic nuclei appeared—but it took another 100,000 years to form the first atoms. They were atoms of hydrogen, the element with the simplest atomic structure.

To make a very long story short, expansion continued, and the cooling universe eventually saw simple elements condense to form galaxies and their stars. The first stars were made mainly of hydrogen, but in the nuclear furnaces of these stars, heavier elements with larger, more complex atoms were formed. When these early stars died in tremendous explosions called *supernovas*, these new elements were shot out into the universe, ultimately contributing to the formation of more galaxies, stars, and planets (Figure 3.2). On one planet at least, the atoms formed inside stars provided the raw material that eventually evolved into living creatures. When the late astronomer Carl Sagan (1980) says we are "star stuff," he is being literal.

By a little over 5 bya, the universe was about half its present size. At about this time, our star, the sun, was formed, and the earth took shape shortly thereafter (Figure 3.3). The early earth contained only inorganic molecules (that is, molecules not containing carbon), but about 4 bya

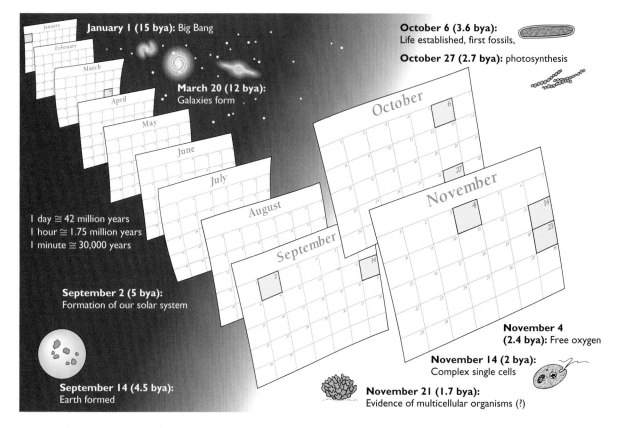

January 1 (15 bya): Big Bang

March 20 (12 bya):
Galaxies form

October 6 (3.6 bya):
Life established, first fossils,

October 27 (2.7 bya): photosynthesis

1 day ≅ 42 million years
1 hour ≅ 1.75 million years
1 minute ≅ 30,000 years

September 2 (5 bya):
Formation of our solar system

September 14 (4.5 bya):
Earth formed

November 4
(2.4 bya): Free oxygen

November 14 (2 bya):
Complex single cells

November 21 (1.7 bya):
Evidence of multicellular organisms (?)

FIGURE 3.4 Astronomer Carl Sagan likened the history of the universe to a single calendar year in his 1975 Pulitzer Prize–winning book *The Dragons of Eden.* This calendar has been recalculated to show the currently accepted dates for important events. One calendar day equals approximately 42 million years. *(Adapted from Sagan, 1975)*

some of these were rearranged and formed organic molecules, carbon-containing compounds that make up living organisms. Figure 3.4 summarizes what is known about the timing of important events in the evolution of life on earth.

Although creating organic molecules out of inorganic ones may sound like magic, it's not. Scientists have been producing a simple version of this reaction in laboratories for over forty years; all they do is add water to the chemicals that made up the early earth atmosphere and subject the mixture to a source of energy like electricity. Among the molecules that result are amino acids, the raw materials from which genes form proteins. These are the building blocks of all known life.

An amino acid, though, is still a long way from a living organism, and another 500 million years were required for these and other organic chemicals to react in just the right ways to form living, reproducing creatures. Scientists know that these reactions occurred because they have found fossils of bacteria-like cells—among the simplest of living things—in 3.6 billion-year-old strata exposed by various geological processes in Greenland, southern Africa, and Australia (Figure 3.5).

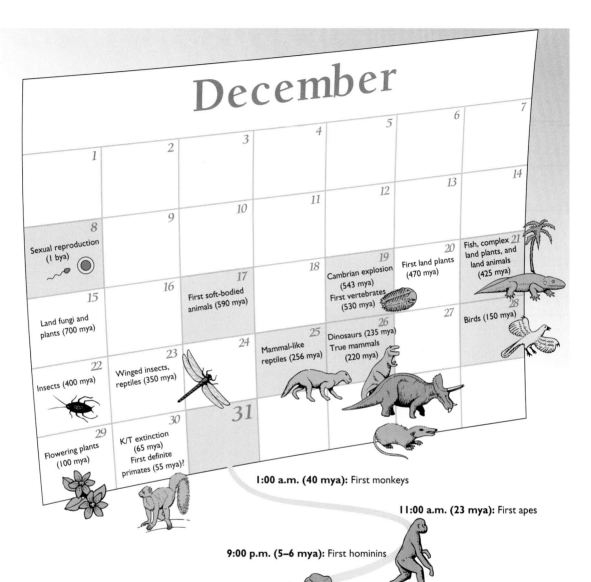

December

1	2	3	4	5	6	7
8 Sexual reproduction (1 bya)	9	10	11	12	13	14
15 Land fungi and plants (700 mya)	16	**17** First soft-bodied animals (590 mya)	**18** Cambrian explosion (543 mya) **First vertebrates (530 mya)**	**19**	**20** First land plants (470 mya)	**21** Fish, complex land plants, and land animals (425 mya)
22 Insects (400 mya)	**23** Winged insects, reptiles (350 mya)	**24**	**25** Mammal-like reptiles (256 mya)	**26** Dinosaurs (235 mya) True mammals (220 mya)	**27**	**28** Birds (150 mya)
29 Flowering plants (100 mya)	**30** K/T extinction (65 mya) First definite primates (55 mya)?	**31**				

1:00 a.m. (40 mya): First monkeys

11:00 a.m. (23 mya): First apes

9:00 p.m. (5–6 mya): First hominins

10:30 p.m. (2.5 mya): First stone tools

11:22 p.m. (0.5 mya): First use of fire

11:59 p.m. (30,000 ya): Cave paintings

11:59:35 p.m. (12,000 ya): Farming

11:59:55 p.m. (2,000 ya): Common Era begins

11:59:59 p.m. (500 ya): Renaissance

FIGURE 3.5 Stromatolites in Australia, formed when mats of blue-green algae (single-celled organisms) are covered with sand, silt, and mud, which the algae cement down and then grow over. Fossil stromatolites, and thus the organisms that made them, have been dated to 3.6 bya. (© *Fred Bavendam/ Peter Arnold, Inc.*)

The earth's first creatures were all asexual—that is, they reproduced by splitting or budding, making copies of themselves. Change was very slow because it relied solely on mutations, but it still took place. Evidence shows that 3.6 bya the first single-celled organisms appeared that could photosynthesize—or make nutrients from water, sunlight, and carbon dioxide—as modern green plants do. A waste product of photosynthesis is oxygen. Originally, no free oxygen was present in the earth's atmosphere, but as a result of photosynthesis it appeared by 1.8 bya. Shortly thereafter came the evolution of organisms that could use it. A new branch of the evolutionary tree had begun.

Evidence from the stratigraphic record shows that by 2 bya, cells that were more complex than bacteria had evolved. These cells had a nucleus and functionally differentiated internal parts. Multicellular organisms may have evolved as early as 1.7 bya. And around 1 bya, a sudden increase in diversity of living forms has been interpreted as indicating the beginning of sexual reproduction, which may have first evolved as a mechanism for counteracting the buildup of harmful mutations that can occur in species that reproduce asexually. With sexual reproduction came more possibilities for change because the genes of two parents were now recombined in the production of offspring. Natural selection had more variation from which to choose, and evolution accelerated as a result.

By the beginning of the Cambrian period, 570 mya, the world contained many new and different kinds of creatures—complex multicellular animals such as jellyfish and worms. About 543 mya came the sudden appearance of animals with hard outer coverings, forerunners of creatures like clams and lobsters. This has been called the Cambrian Explosion. And 530 mya saw the first vertebrates, creatures with internal skeletons. We, of course, are vertebrates.

The pace of change continued to accelerate. Around 425 mya, fish had evolved, and plants and simple animals began to colonize the land. Insects appeared 400 mya and evolved winged forms 350 mya. Reptiles first showed up 350 mya, and the form of reptile that would give rise to mammals appeared about 256 mya.

During all this time, the earth didn't look as it does now. The continents that seem so permanent today aren't. They move, or, in the term used by geology, *drift*. The process that explains continental drift, called **plate tectonics,** is complex, but basically the hard outer shell of the earth, the crust, is made up of about sixteen plates that fit together like a jigsaw puzzle. The continents are the portions of these plates that protrude above the oceans. The plates are in constant interaction with the inside of the earth, which is made up of liquid rock continually in motion. As this liquid moves, it adds solid rock to some parts of the crust and melts away solid rock from other parts, causing the plates with their continents to drift slowly but constantly around the surface of the planet (Figure 3.6). Where the plates meet, they grind against one another, producing the

More than 200 mya

180 mya

65 mya

Present

FIGURE 3.6 Movement of the earth's landmasses over the last 200 million years, caused by the process of plate tectonics.

plate tectonics The movement of the plates of the earth's crust caused by their interaction with the molten rock of the earth's interior. The cause of continental drift.

tremendous forces that are largely responsible for great geological events such as volcanoes, earthquakes, and mountain building.

About the time the dinosaurs were evolving, around 235 mya, landmasses that are part of all the present continents were drifting together to form a single supercontinent called **Pangea** (literally, "all lands"). This supercontinent was fully formed by 210 mya. Similar fossils of early dinosaurs and other organisms have been found in such diverse places as the Gobi Desert in China, the Badlands of South Dakota, and Antarctica because these were all part of one unbroken landmass.

Mammals first appeared around 220 mya, and about 150 mya a small upright dinosaur with feathers heralded the beginning of the birds (see Figure 4.16). Flowering plants appear only about 100 mya. By this time, however, Pangea had broken up, and it is here that the story of human evolution really starts.

Grasping Hands and Big Brains

Pangea broke up into six landmasses that are approximately the present-day continents, although they were not then in the same locations they are today. As these new lands drifted over the globe, a greater variety of separate environments was produced, offering a greater opportunity for the evolution of new types of living things.

One new evolutionary line began perhaps 65 mya or even earlier (Gibbons 1998a; Tavaré et al. 2002) on a large northern landmass called **Laurasia,** made up of parts of modern North America and Eurasia. It consisted of a group of mammals whose fossilized skeletons are reminiscent of rodents. But their multipurpose teeth, the beginning of grasping hands and feet, and other details of their anatomy were not rodentlike. They were more like the features of the **primates,** the group of mammals that today includes monkeys, apes, and humans (Figure 3.7).

Like the other mammals at the time, the early primates were mostly small, inconspicuous, nocturnal creatures (Figure 3.8). This was largely because the dinosaurs, one of evolution's most successful groups, dominated the world's major environments. Add the fact that many dinosaurs were carnivores that certainly included mammals on their menu, and it is understandable why mammalian evolution was slow at first.

But about 65 mya, something happened that we can probably thank for our very existence: dinosaurs became extinct. A major and rapid environmental change took place to which the dinosaurs were unable to adapt, and they disappeared (Figure 3.9). There is a growing consensus among scientists that the earth sustained a titanic impact from an asteroid about 65 mya, that had an enormous impact on our planet, including the extinction of the dinosaurs. We have witnessed such collisions on other planets,

Pangea The supercontinent that included parts of all present-day landmasses.

Laurasia The former landmass made up of parts of present-day North America and Eurasia.

primate A large-brained, arboreal mammal with stereoscopic color vision and grasping hands and (often) feet.

FIGURE 3.7 Humans are not typical primates. This rhesus monkey from Asia is perhaps as close as one could come to an "average" primate. The rhesus has been important in medical and behavioral experimentation. The Rh positive and negative blood types were named after it. (© Noel Rowe)

FIGURE 3.8 Of all living species, this Asian tree shrew, though not a primate, most closely resembles what we think the first primates looked like. (© Noel Rowe)

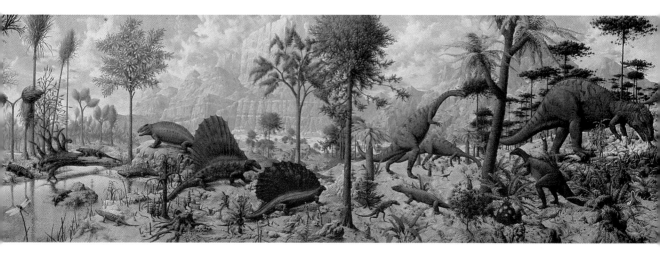

FIGURE 3.9 This painting, by the late Rudolph Zallinger, reflects some now outdated ideas about the appearance and behavior of the dinosaurs. It does show, however, some of the variety of these creatures as they existed over 170 million years of time (*from left to right in the mural*). The dinosaurs once dominated the earth's environments but became extinct about 65 mya. It is now thought that the cause of their extinction was an enormous asteroid that crashed into the earth where the Mexican Yucatán peninsula is now, leaving a crater perhaps 200 miles across. The resulting explosion caused a series of events that blocked sunlight, cooled the earth, started huge forest fires, and may have initiated volcanic eruptions. Perhaps 75 percent of the earth's marine species became extinct, along with many land animals. (*The Age of Reptiles, a mural by Rudolph F. Zallinger. Copyright © 1966, 1975, 1985, 1989, Peabody Museum of Natural History, New Haven, Connecticut, USA*)

most recently Jupiter, the size of which would have had a major impact on life on earth, and there is direct evidence that our planet has not been immune to such extraterrestrial impacts (Figure 3.10). Though the uniformitarianists (see Chapter 2) were correct that "existing causes" such as erosion and weathering characterize long stretches of earth history, the catastrophists (see Chapter 2) also were correct, at least in the sense that over the course of tens of millions of years, the earth is subject to catastrophic events—particularly impacts with astronomical objects—that profoundly affect life on our planet. Whatever caused their extinction, the only direct living descendants of the dinosaurs are the birds; snakes, lizards, and other living reptiles had a separate evolution.

The extinction of this major and widespread group opened the world up for the evolution of other organisms, especially the mammals. No longer forced to compete with the dinosaurs, the mammals flourished. Shortly after the extinction of the dinosaurs, the fossil record begins to show fossils of most major kinds of mammals—creatures as diverse as bats, whales, and primates. Mammals spread rapidly, filling in the ecological gaps left by the dinosaurs.

FIGURE 3.10 Meteor Crater in Arizona, nearly a mile across and originally 750 feet deep, is graphic proof of extraterrestrial impacts on earth, in this case of a 300,000-ton meteor around 50,000 ya. (© *National Geographic Society; photo by Jonathan Blair*)

FIGURE 3.11 A ring-tailed lemur, one of the living prosimians from Madagascar. (© *Noel Rowe*)

By 45 mya, North America and Eurasia drifted apart, and the Western and Eastern Hemispheres were formed. This split the populations of living things that had once inhabited Laurasia, setting the species in each hemisphere off on separate evolutionary courses.

As North America and Eurasia drifted northward toward their present locations, their climates began to get cooler and increasingly inhospitable to many of their inhabitants, adapted to tropical life. South America and Africa, then farther south than today, were also drifting northward and by 30 mya had joined their respective northern partners. Now warm-climate animals such as the early **arboreal** primates, the **prosimians,** had somewhere to go. In the Old World, some prosimians evolved into larger-brained, leaf-eating primates—the monkeys, which were successful and began to spread and diversify. They pushed the Old World prosimians into isolated areas. Most living prosimians now inhabit the island of Madagascar and the isolated islands of Southeast Asia (Figure 3.11). What happened in the

arboreal Adapted to life in the trees.

prosimian A member of the group of primates with the most primitive features, that is, that most resemble the earliest primates.

62

FIGURE 3.12 The savannas (open grasslands) of present-day Africa are sufficiently similar to those of 6 mya to give us a glimpse into what life was like at that time for its inhabitants, including our earliest ancestors. (© C. W. Perkins/Animals Animals)

New World is an involved topic, which we'll take up in Chapter 8. For now, suffice it to say there are at present only monkeys, no prosimians, in Central and South America.

Continental drift and climatic change continued, and more new niches resulted. The primates responded to these, and around 23 mya another new group evolved in the Old World. They were larger than the monkeys, had bigger brains, were tailless, and were adapted to a more varied diet that included some seasonal foods such as nuts and fruits and maybe even some meat. These were the first apes, smaller, more monkeylike forerunners of present-day chimpanzees, bonobos, gorillas, and orangutans.

Between 23 and 14 mya, various species of apes flourished across Europe, Africa, and Asia, which by this time occupied almost their present-day positions. Ape species ranged in size from that of a large monkey to a giant grain eater from India and China, larger than modern gorillas. But the heyday of the apes began to end about 10 mya. Many ape species became extinct. Populations of an ape that survived in the forests of Africa gave rise to modern-day chimps, bonobos, and gorillas. Another group, probably living where forest met **savanna**, changed in a different direction and became more adapted to terrestrial life, eventually occupying the vast and dangerous open plains (Figure 3.12). These were our ancestors.

Scientists can make an educated guess about when the human evolutionary line split from that of the apes. Based on existing fossil and

savanna Tropical grasslands with trees scattered throughout.

FIGURE 3.13 The importance of bipedal locomotion for our species can be seen in the drive of infants to master upright walking. *(K. L. Feder)*

geological evidence and on the genetic similarities between humans and chimpanzees (see Chapter 5), we think the human ancestor diverged from the ape line 6 to 5 mya. By the time the fossil record starts to provide more substantial evidence, a little over 4 mya, a new creature emerges, one with the face and brain size of an ape but with an added feature that sets it off from all other primates that had ever existed: it walked upright (Figure 3.13).

Bipedalism was the most important and earliest human characteristic—an adaptive response to early humans' life in mixed, often open terrestrial areas, as well as in the trees. This adaptation, seen in rudimentary form in modern apes, allowed our earliest ancestors to move efficiently over great distances and to carry things at the same time. Later, on the savannas, where food sources were more widely scattered and less varied than in the forests and where numerous creatures lurked that were ready to make meals out of small mammals, this ability was particularly important. It was a successful adaptation, for fossil evidence of these early humans is found all over eastern and southern Africa. In broad evolutionary perspective, then, bipedalism is our most distinguishing feature because it was first. In Chapter 8, we'll explore some ideas about just how and why this adaptation took place.

Our earliest ancestors, the topic of Chapter 8, have been collectively called australopithecines. The term means, literally, "southern apes," a holdover from the name given them, in 1925, by the South African pale-

bipedal Having the ability to walk on two feet.

ontologist Raymond Dart, who first identified one of their fossils; at the time, he recognized but wasn't quite ready to formally admit they were **hominids,** part of the human lineage. But they were. About 3 mya, the australopithecines diverged into two types. One, referred to as the robust early hominids, seems to have evolved toward an increasingly vegetarian diet. It appears to have become extinct about 1 mya.

The second type evolved a different adaptation. These hominids had bigger brains, smaller, more modern-looking teeth and chewing muscles, and a new and important behavior: they made stone tools. As a result, they began to be a major factor in the savanna environment. With their big brains and more complex intellect, and with the tools that they produced as a result, they could exploit savanna food sources more efficiently than other hominids.

Now the big brain became the adaptive focus of hominid evolution. By 1.75 mya, the brains of our African ancestors approached the lower limit of the range of modern human brain sizes. Their heads and faces were notably different from ours today, but from the neck down their skeletons were essentially of modern form. They are the topic of Chapter 9. Their bigger brains allowed them to improve on toolmaking and probably to devise schemes for social organization and cooperation. Their populations increased, and they began to spread rapidly; their adaptations, originally geared for life on the savannas of Africa, turned out to be useful all over the Old World. They devised different sorts of tools and other cultural adaptations specifically geared to their environments—from the savannas of Africa to the tropical forests of Southeast Asia to the temperate woodlands of Europe and China, some of these areas much colder than today. These cultural changes included the control of fire.

Perhaps as early as 750,000 ya and certainly by about 400,000 ya, we see another major change in human evolution: an increase in average brain size to that of modern people. What caused this development is unknown. Evolutionary processes, operating on the trend already begun and proven successful, may have promoted the reproductive success of those humans with still bigger, more complex brains. These people may have had a better ability to think up answers to the problems of survival. We discuss this period of our evolution in Chapter 9.

After this turning point, it becomes harder to generalize about our evolutionary history. The adaptation of culture, made possible by humans' big brain, allowed for great diversity in behaviors. Humans spread all over the Old World, fitting tools and social organizations to the specific problems the various environments posed. But these humans were to some extent still at the mercy of the environment, which still had some effect on biology. There are physical differences among populations of humans over the last three-quarters of a million years, and these have led to a controversy over just how many species of hominids have existed and how they

hominid The bipedal primate; modern humans and their ancestors.

are related to one another. At question too is when *Homo sapiens,* the species to which all modern people belong, first evolved. We will examine this controversy in Chapter 10.

Also in Chapter 10, we will discuss the continued success of the modern human species as it entered new habitats and populated new worlds. At least as early as 40,000 ya (and perhaps as many as 60,000 ya), humans entered Australia and at least 15,000 and more likely about 20,000 ya the Americas, crossing over a broad land connection between Siberia and Alaska. *Homo sapiens* now inhabited nearly the entire globe, and it was probably at this point that the species began to evolve the physical variation that characterizes people today (and that seems to present us with so many social problems). We will end Chapter 10 with a discussion of human biodiversity and race.

Culture change continued to accelerate; people increased their populations and adapted to new and increasingly specific ecological niches. Sometime after 12,000 ya, some populations found it necessary to use their vast knowledge of their environments to gain more control over their food resources. They invented farming and animal domestication (Chapter 12). With this came even more cultural diversity and a whole host of new cultural adaptations: cities, metallurgy, warfare, complex political and economic organization, and writing—the beginning of the historical record (Chapter 13).

Thus, the canvas of time on which we will paint the picture of human antiquity begins with the very first primates and continues to the recent past.

Summary

We hope this brief narrative will provide you with a basic context into which all the details of the next chapters can be easily fit. We also hope it has demonstrated three other general ideas. First, you should see that the story of human evolution, as complex as it is, takes up only the smallest fraction of time in the whole history of the universe; it is just the latest tick of the evolutionary clock. We find that a rather humbling thought (Figure 3.14).

Second, though we use terms like *beginning* and *origin,* notice that the whole story contains only one real origin: that tiny, dense speck of energy and space that started the whole thing. Since then, nothing brand new has entered the picture. There have only been rearrangements of what already existed: matter condensing from cooling energy, large particles forming from combinations of smaller ones, stars and planets coming together from cosmic dust, inorganic molecules shuffling their parts and producing the molecules of life, the genes of living things recombining in a nearly infinite variety of ways to evolve the wondrous array of creatures that have

FIGURE 3.14 All that our species has achieved—from observing the universe to its actual exploration, from the efficient transmission of knowledge to the drive of children to understand and participate in their world—all can be traced back to the Big Bang some 15 bya. *(Telescope: National Optical Astronomy Observatories; Astronaut: NASA; Computer kids: K. L. Feder; Boy: K. L. Feder)*

inhabited the earth. Indeed, uniformitarianism has a broader meaning than James Hutton and Charles Lyell could have imagined. We are all truly "star stuff."

Third, the specific history of the universe, the earth, and life on earth could have happened in countless other ways. Each event in the story is contingent on preceding events. Even the evolution of our species is dependent on a specific sequence of events. If those events had been different, we would probably be different—or we might not be here at all. What if that asteroid had not hit the earth 65 million years ago? The evolution of human beings—or any other species—was not inevitable. We're lucky we're here.

Study Questions

1. What are the major events in the history of the universe, the earth, and earth's living forms? When did these events occur?
2. What general ideas may we perceive from this history about the nature of evolutionary change?

Key Terms

plate tectonics	primate	savanna
Pangea	arboreal	bipedal
Laurasia	prosimian	hominid

For More Information

The evolution of the universe is one of the themes of Carl Sagan's *Cosmos*. For an update on the latest information about cosmology—the history of the universe—see the February 2000 issue of *Natural History*, especially "Genesis: The Sequel," by Alan Guth. For a good discussion of the science behind our understanding of the history of the universe, see Timothy Ferris's *Coming of Age in the Milky Way*.

The evolution of life is covered in more detail in Roger Lewin's *Thread of Life: The Smithsonian Looks at Evolution* and in the lavishly illustrated *The Book of Life,* edited by Stephen Jay Gould. For a more technical but still highly readable treatment, try Richard Cowen's *History of Life. National Geographic* has a series of articles called "The Rise of Life on Earth" in the March 1998, April 1998, May 1999, February 2000, and September 2000 issues.

On the relationship between dinosaurs and birds, see "Dinosaurs Take Wing" by Jennifer Ackerman in the July 1998 *National Geographic* and "Feathers for *T. Rex*?" by Christopher Sloan in the November 1999 *National Geographic*. And for a good discussion of the origin of feathers, see "Which Came First, the Feather or the Bird?" by Richard O. Prum and Alan H. Brush in the March 2003 *Scientific American*.

New data on the possible early age of the primates and other mammal groups is in "Genes Put Mammals in Age of Dinosaurs," by Ann Gibbons, in the May 1, 1998 issue of *Science,* page 675.

To see an animation of the breakup of Pangea and the movement of the continents into their present positions, go to www.scotese.com/pangeanim .htm. Drag your cursor across the map of the world from left to right to show the earth as it looked 200 mya. Then drag your cursor from right to left to show how the modern configuration of the continents came into existence.

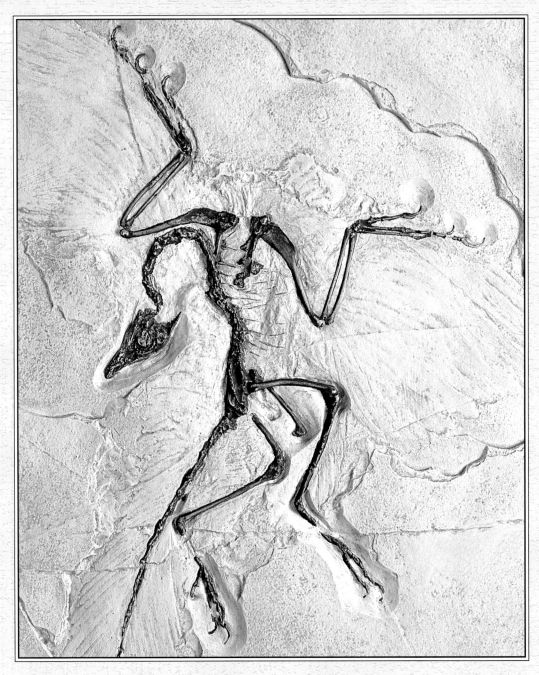

The 150-million-year-old fossil of *Archaeopteryx*, interpreted as a link between birds and dinosaurs, is evidence the earth's living creatures have evolved. How does evolution work?
(© Tom and Therisa Stack/Tom Stack & Associates)

UNDERSTANDING CHANGE
Modern Evolutionary Theory

CHAPTER CONTENTS

Genetics

The Genetics of Populations

The Processes of Evolution

The Origin of Species

Summary

CONTEMPORARY ISSUE: What Is Genetic Cloning?

Study Questions

Key Terms

For More Information

Chapter 2 ended with a discussion of scientific creationism and intelligent design. We said that the theory of evolution, unlike creationism and intelligent design, is supported by a massive amount of interrelated evidence gathered and interpreted according to the scientific method.

What is the evidence for evolution as we understand it today? How does evolution work? How do the processes of evolution apply to the human species?

Genetics

As we noted in Chapter 2, neither Charles Darwin nor Alfred Wallace understood the biological variation that was so crucial to their theory of natural selection. They knew that variation existed and was maintained even after a species had undergone years of natural selection, but as Darwin admitted, such variations "seem to us in our ignorance to arise spontaneously" (1898:239). Nor did Darwin understand how traits were passed on from parent to offspring—another important factor in natural selection.

Why did Darwin fail to understand these principles? The answer is that he was operating without knowledge of **genetics.** Adhering to the notion current in his day, he thought inheritance worked through some sort of "blending"—a mixing of parental substances in the offspring. There seemed to be ample evidence for this idea from plant and animal breeding, where offspring often exhibited traits that appeared to be 50:50 mixtures of their parents' traits—pink flowers from a cross of red-flowered and white-flowered parents, for instance.

Plenty of characteristics, of course, don't show this equal mixture of parental traits. Organisms inherit their sex from their parents, and, with few exceptions, they are not 50:50 blends but either male or female. Traits that seem to blend, though, like flower color, appear to have been more influential in early thinking about the mechanism of inheritance.

Ironically, at about the same time Darwin was writing *The Origin of Species,* an Augustinian monk named Gregor Mendel (1822–1884), working in a monastery in what is now the Czech Republic, established that inheritance did not operate by blending but rather was **particulate.** By conducting breeding experiments with the pea plants in the monastery garden (the culmination of many years of experimentation with plants and mice), Mendel showed that an organism's traits are passed from generation to generation by individual particles, which Mendel called *factors*—what we now call **genes.**

As a further irony, Mendel's work was neither widely read nor fully appreciated by those who did know about it. They failed to see any implications beyond some interesting facts about pea plants. After Mendel's death, his work fell into obscurity, and it was not until 1900 that it was rediscovered. By then the implications of his experiments were clear, and so the stage was set for the series of discoveries that led to our modern understanding of genetics.

The Genetic Code

We now understand that a gene is actually a set of chemical instructions for the production of a **protein.** Proteins serve many functions in a living thing. Some are structural, shaping the cells (Figure 4.1); supporting the

genetics The study of the mechanism of inheritance.

particulate The idea that biological traits are controlled by individual factors rather than by a single hereditary agent.

gene The portion of the DNA molecule that codes for a specific protein.

protein The family of molecules that makes cells and carries out cellular functions.

enzyme A protein that controls chemical processes.

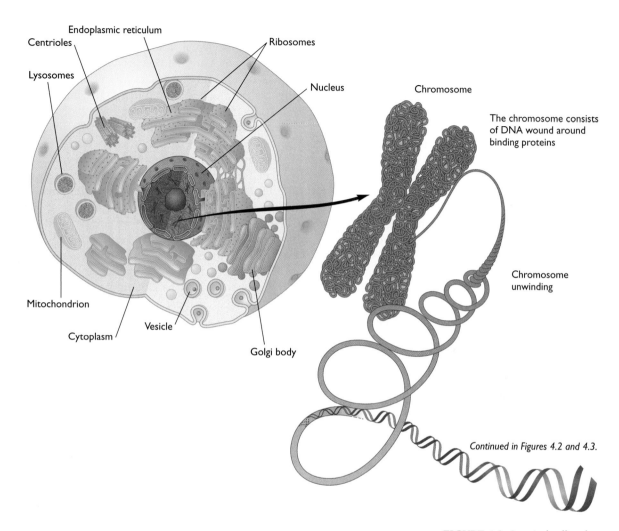

Centrioles

Endoplasmic reticulum

Ribosomes

Lysosomes

Nucleus

Chromosome

The chromosome consists of DNA wound around binding proteins

Mitochondrion

Chromosome unwinding

Cytoplasm

Vesicle

Golgi body

Continued in Figures 4.2 and 4.3.

FIGURE 4.1 A typical cell and its important parts. This cell represents all types of cells, from the more complex single-celled organisms such as amoebas to the cells in the human body. The ribosomes are the sites of protein synthesis (see Figure 4.3). The mitochondria are the cells' energy factories, converting energy stored in nutrients into a form the cells can use to perform their various functions.

cells' internal structure; linking the cells together; and building membranes, muscles, and connective tissue. Collagen, a key constituent of skin, tendons, ligaments, and cartilage, is an example of the latter. Some proteins are **enzymes,** catalysts that speed up the body's chemical reactions. Still others transport chemicals through the body; hemoglobin, which we will discuss further below, is a protein that carries oxygen to the cells. A few proteins are hormones, chemicals that send messages among cells. Thus, it could be said that, in a sense, living things *are* proteins. About half an animal's dry body weight is protein. Humans can produce at least 100,000 different proteins.

The genetic code is made up of a variable sequence of bases (a family of chemicals) that are part of a long chemical strand called **deoxyribonucleic acid (DNA).** The strands of DNA are themselves wrapped around series of protein cores to make up **chromosomes,** found in the nuclei of all cells. Four bases are involved in the code: adenine (A), thymine (T), cytosine (C), and guanine (G). Chemical bonds between these bases hold the DNA molecule together, but the bases are bonded only in A-T or T-A and C-G or G-C pairs.

The first function of this pairing is to enable the DNA molecule to make copies of itself during cell division. The DNA molecule is shaped like a ladder with the ends twisted in opposite directions, a configuration called a double helix. During cell division the helix unwinds, and each strand, with its now unpaired bases, picks up the proper complementary bases, which are in solution in the cell. This is called **replication.** Thus, when the whole cell divides, each new daughter cell has a complete set of DNA base pairs (Figure 4.2).

A gene can be thought of as a portion of the DNA molecule that carries a code that instructs the cell to manufacture a particular protein. Our current understanding of how proteins are manufactured according to the genetic code is a process known as **protein synthesis** (Figure 4.3). Follow along in the diagram as you read the description.

During protein synthesis only a portion of the DNA molecule is unwound (in contrast to the complete unwinding seen in replication). **Messenger ribonucleic acid (mRNA)** is assembled against one strand of this unwound DNA. (Only one strand carries the code; the other is structural.) The mRNA transcribes the gene by matching complementary bases to those exposed in the coding strand of DNA, except that uracil (U) replaces thymine (T). We refer to each consecutive sequence of three DNA bases as a **codon.** Think of them as three-letter words. A gene, then, is a sequence of codons, a sentence made up of many words.

After mRNa has transcribed the code, it leaves the nucleus of the cell and moves to specialized structures in the cell called ribosomes where the message is decoded and translated into an actual protein. Another type of RNA called **transfer RNA (tRNA)** reads the three-letter codes as instructions for assembling a chain of **amino acids.** Each set of three exposed RNA bases codes for one amino acid. Thus, for example, a sequence of 300 bases codes for a sequence of 100 amino acids. A sequence of amino acids is a protein. Although there are only about 20 or so types of amino acids, it is possible to arrange them in a nearly infinite variety of sequences and lengths. In this way, the sequence of DNA bases represents a sequence of amino acids, and it is this sequence that determines the shape and function of the protein.

The measurable, observable chemical or physical traits of an organism are the results of the actions of proteins that have been manufactured by the cells according to genetic instructions. Some traits are coded for by

deoxyribonucleic acid (DNA) The molecule that carries the genetic code.

chromosome A strand of DNA in the nucleus of cells.

replication The copying of the genetic code during the process of cell division.

protein synthesis The process by which the genetic code puts together proteins in the cell.

messenger ribonucleic acid (mRNA) The molecule that carries the genetic code out of the nucleus for translation into proteins.

codon A section of DNA that codes for a particular amino acid.

transfer RNA (tRNA) RNA that lines up amino acids along mRNA to make proteins.

amino acid The chief component of proteins.

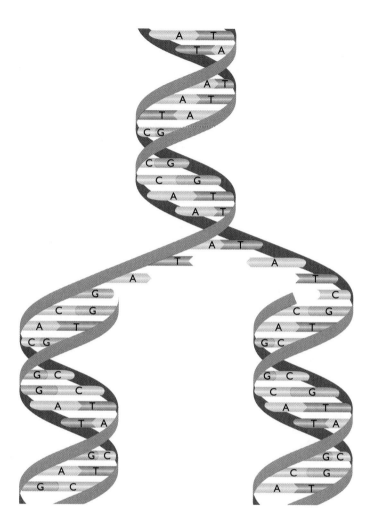

FIGURE 4.2 The DNA molecule. This molecule is shown in the process of unwinding and copying itself prior to cell division.

one or just a few genes. The blood component hemoglobin is a protein made up of two paired amino acid chains and thus is determined by two genes. Skin color is made up of many proteins and is thus coded for by many genes.

Each species has a characteristic number of chromosomes. Bacteria have a single chromosome. Humans have forty-six; chimpanzees, forty-eight; wheat, forty-two; and dogs, seventy-eight. In sexually reproducing species, chromosomes come in pairs. An organism inherits one chromosome of each pair from each parent and thus gets half its genetic material from each parent. It follows that the genes also come in pairs.

The catch is that a gene can have variants, called **alleles**, each with a slightly different set of codons. The alleles of a gene influence the same trait but may produce different expressions of that trait. For example, for

allele A variant of a gene.

1. Section of DNA molecule with base pairs

2. DNA molecule temporarily separates at bases. mRNA lines up its bases (with U replacing T) with their complements on the coding side of the DNA. (The other strand is structural and is not copied.)

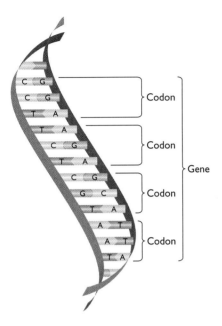

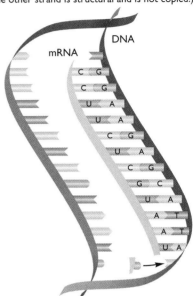

3. mRNA moves out of cell nucleus to ribosomes. As ribosomes move along mRNA, tRNA picks up amino acids and lines up along mRNA according to base complements. Each tRNA transfers its amino acid to the next active tRNA as it leaves, resulting in a chain of amino acids.

4. This chain of amino acids forms a protein.

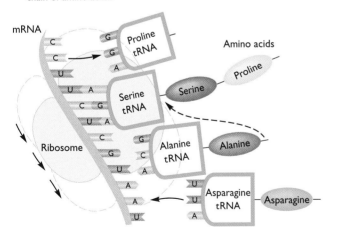

FIGURE 4.3 Protein synthesis as described in the text. In reality, no protein is only four amino acids long, but the process works exactly as shown.

blood type in the ABO system, there are three possible alleles, A, B, and O. Whether you have blood type A, B, AB, or O depends on which pair of alleles codes for the amino acid chain determining blood type. Each allele codes for a version of the chain with a different specific sequence of amino acids. Your allele pair is your **genotype.**

An Overview of the Human Genome

As of spring 2003, nearly the entire human **genome** had been sequenced. What this means is that we know the sequence of the 3.1 million base pairs (the As, Ts, Gs, and Cs) of two representative humans' DNA. (There were two organizations working on the genome sequence, each primarily focusing on a different participant's DNA.) We now have a baseline from which scientists will be able to further research the genome and compare other people and populations.

There is still much to learn. We need to figure out just where in that 3.1-billion-base-pair sequence the genes are, what proteins they code for, what those proteins do, and what functions the other nongene DNA serves. In other words, we still need to discover how the DNA "builds" an organism. But in the last few years, some remarkable new information has come to light.

It turns out that most of the genome is not composed of genes. That is, most of the genome—possibly 98 percent—doesn't code for proteins. We refer to this nongene material as *noncoding DNA.* Although this DNA used to be referred to as "junk DNA," we now know that much of it is not *without* function. Some of it acts as punctuation, marking the beginnings and ends of coding sequences. Some serves to regulate gene function and activity level. Some jumps around carrying other DNA with it, allowing the genetic code to reshuffle its elements; this provides a partial explanation for why a surprisingly small number of genes (20,000 to 40,000 by current estimates) can produce such a huge variety of proteins (around 50,000) in an organism as complex as a human being. Some noncoding DNA is made up of repetitive sequences, some hundreds of thousands of base pairs long, that may do nothing. Some of our DNA may be very ancient, from a remote common ancestor, and some may have been transferred from microbes.

Moreover, we have learned that the coding sequences are not lined up neatly together but are scattered and interrupted by noncoding sequences. A single coding sequence might code for more than one protein, depending on just which part is transcribed.

And recently it was discovered that RNA is more than just the means of converting the DNA code into proteins. Some classes of RNAs have other functions, such as turning on or off some genes, blocking the action of mRNA in producing a protein (which may be important in disease research), shutting down genes and thus operating as a defense against

genotype The alleles possessed by an organism.

genome The total genetic endowment of an organism.

harmful DNA or viruses, and even shaping the genome itself by keeping and discarding certain genes. Realizing that at least some of these noncoding RNAs are produced by the DNA genome has expanded the definition of a gene. Some genes (that is, coding DNA sequences) produce proteins as their end products, but others have noncoding RNAs as end products. By this definition, then, the estimated number of genes in the genome would increase.

Thus, the nice neat view we've had of the genetic code and how it works, even until recently, has radically changed. In the words of Lewis Carroll, the nature and operation of the human genome keeps getting "curiouser and curiouser" and will be an important area of study for years to come.

The Inheritance of Characteristics

An organism has two of the same allele—i.e., is **homozygous**—when both parents have contributed the same allele of that gene. An organism has two different alleles—is **heterozygous**—when the genes contributed by the parents carry different codes. Alleles are products of **mutations,** genetic mistakes that alter the code in a cell of reproduction and thus may transform an existing allele, say, one coding for brown eyes, into a new and different allele, say, one coding for blue eyes.

The expression of a genotype—the trait that results from the genetic code—is called the **phenotype.** In homozygotes both alleles are the same, so the way the trait is expressed is simply in accordance with these alleles. There is no alternative. In heterozygotes, the situation is more complex. In many, the influence of both alleles is expressed in the phenotype. This is what gives rise to the appearance of blending. But on occasion, the expression of one allele in heterozygotes may be hidden. Such alleles are said to be **recessive.** The other member of the pair, the one expressed, is **dominant.** The words dominant and recessive carry no implications of value, no significance for adaptation. Dominant alleles are not necessarily better or more common than recessive alleles.

When an organism reproduces, it obviously cannot pass on both alleles of each pair to its offspring. If this were the case, the offspring would end up with twice the normal number of genes. Instead, organisms produce reproductive cells that are different from the cells that make up the rest of the organism. These are the sex cells, or **gametes** (sperm and egg, for instance). Gametes are produced through the process of meiosis, which splits the chromosome pairs—and thus the allele pairs—so that each gamete only has one of each gene (Figure 4.4). Mendel called this effect **segregation.**

When a sperm from the male parent fertilizes an egg from the female, the resultant **zygote** once again has pairs of chromosomes and thus pairs of each gene. But because the members of each pair have two different sources, the combination of genes in each pair will necessarily be different from that of either parent. This produces genetic variation among individuals of the same species and, in fact, among offspring of the same parent.

homozygous Having two of the same allele.

heterozygous Having two different alleles in a pair.

mutation A change in an organism's genetic material.

phenotype The chemical or physical results of the genetic code.

recessive An allele of a pair that is not expressed.

dominant An allele of a pair that is expressed.

gamete The cell of reproduction.

segregation The breaking up of allele pairs during gamete production.

zygote A fertilized egg before cell division begins.

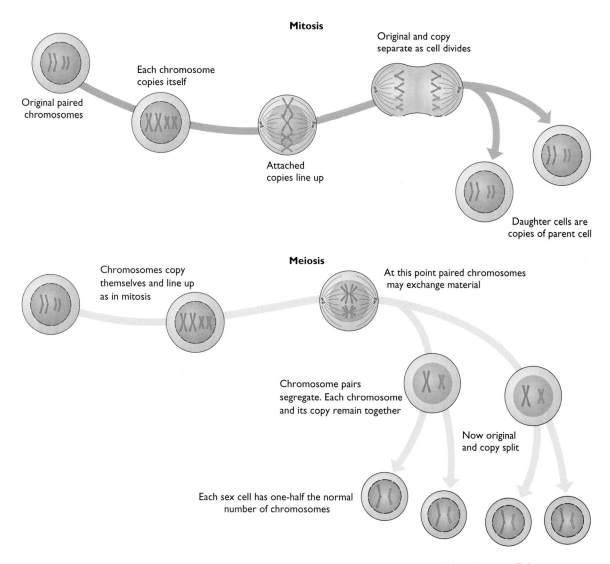

Mitosis

Original paired chromosomes

Each chromosome copies itself

Attached copies line up

Original and copy separate as cell divides

Daughter cells are copies of parent cell

Meiosis

Chromosomes copy themselves and line up as in mitosis

At this point paired chromosomes may exchange material

Chromosome pairs segregate. Each chromosome and its copy remain together

Now original and copy split

Each sex cell has one-half the normal number of chromosomes

FIGURE 4.4 Cell division occurs in two ways. Mitosis produces exact copies of the parent cell and is the most common form of cell division. Meiosis results in four daughter cells, each with one-half the genetic content of the parent cell. Meiosis is the process by which gametes, or sex cells (sperm and egg), are manufactured. It ensures that when fertilization occurs, the new individual has a complete set of genes, one-half from each parent.

These principles can be demonstrated in a concrete example. Sickle cell anemia is a genetic disease of the blood often associated, erroneously, only with African Americans. The association results from the high frequencies of the disease found in a band across central Africa, a region from which most American blacks trace their ancestry. But sickle cell anemia is also found in southern Europe, the Middle East, India, and Southeast Asia.

Sickle cell anemia, the result of a mutation of a gene on chromosome 11, affects hemoglobin, the protein on the red blood cells that carries oxygen from the lungs to the body's tissues. Hemoglobin is made up of two paired amino acid chains, an alpha chain of 141 amino acids and a beta chain 146 amino acids long. If, through a mutation, the amino acid

FIGURE 4.5 Normal red blood cells and one showing the abnormal shape characteristic of sickle cell anemia, which result from the presence of hemoglobin with one incorrect amino acid. Such cells fail to transport oxygen properly to the body's tissues. (© *Meckes/Ottawa/Photo Researchers, Inc.*)

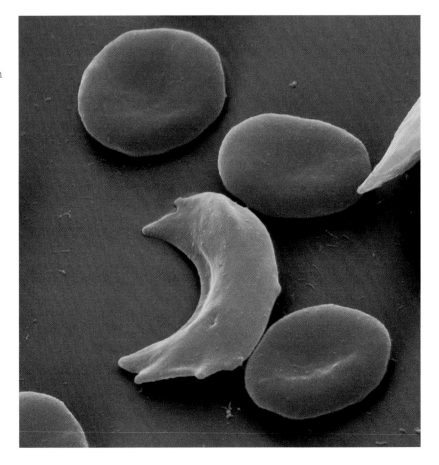

valine is substituted for glutamic acid at position 6 on the beta chain, the disease results. In terms of the genetic code, this means that the mutation is one wrong "word"—a mistake in one codon, often a single incorrect base—in a sentence of 287 words. This is a **point mutation.**

When the abnormal hemoglobin is present and stress, high altitude, or illness lowers an individual's oxygen supply, the red blood cells take on peculiar shapes. Some resemble sickles (Figure 4.5). In this condition, they cannot carry sufficient oxygen to nourish the body's cells. Results can include fatigue, retarded physical development in children, miscarriage in pregnant women, fever, severe pain, and increased susceptibility to infection. People with sickle cell anemia frequently die before their twenties; even if they live longer, they have a very low reproductive rate. In terms of evolutionary success, sickle cell anemia has been considered nearly 100 percent lethal. (It should be noted that there have been recent breakthroughs in the treatment of the disease, including a new means of repairing the RNA message with the result that normal hemoglobin is produced.)

point mutation A mutation of a single letter in a codon.

The abnormal allele for sickle cell acts like a recessive in the sense that a person must have the homozygous abnormal genotype to be afflicted with the disease. Heterozygotes, however, still carry the sickle cell allele. When two individuals carrying one allele each for sickle cell mate, they have a one-quarter chance of producing an offspring homozygous for sickle cell anemia. A device called a Punnett square shows how this process works (Figure 4.6).

Sickle cell anemia also demonstrates some of the complexity of genetics and its intricate relationship to the environment and to evolution. The sickle cell allele is not completely recessive. Heterozygotes possess about 40 percent abnormal hemoglobin, and, under extreme conditions of low oxygen, they experience sickle cell symptoms, although not as severely as homozygotes. Indeed, complete dominance and complete recessiveness are the exception; the different alleles of most genes are both expressed to some degree. A heterozygote may be somehow intermediate between either homozygote or may show the phenotypes of both alleles. Alleles that exhibit these characteristics are said to be **codominant.**

The general rule is that the phenotype is usually not a clear-cut indication of the genotype. Besides various relationships among alleles, most phenotypic traits are simply not coded for by a single gene (**monogenic**) but by many genes (**polygenic**). This effect becomes clear in complex traits like stature or skin color, where numerous individual cellular and chemical actions operate together to make up those phenotypes.

Moreover, not all genes are always in operation. Some are switched on by others in response to environmental changes or some internal timing. In other words, not all genes are equally influential in producing phenotypic traits. In addition, many genes can influence several seemingly unrelated traits. Think of the many symptoms of sickle cell anemia—highly variable specific expressions all resulting from a point mutation.

Finally, the relationship between genotype and phenotype can be influenced by environmental factors, that is, any factor outside the codon-to-trait process just outlined. Your skin color, for example, though coded for in your DNA, can change noticeably depending on your health, how much sun you get, and even your emotional state. All these factors can be considered environmental in the broadest sense of the word. Heterozygotes for sickle cell anemia, who all have the same genotype, nonetheless vary greatly in the degree to which they exhibit the symptoms of the disease and in how easily those symptoms are triggered. This variation occurs because of a complex interaction of numerous factors that affects the relationship between genotype and phenotype.

With the rediscovery of Mendel's work in 1900, an understanding of the mechanism of inheritance and of the basic source of variation was added to Darwin's framework for a theory of evolution by natural selection. From this synthesis, over the next century, our current knowledge both of genetics and of the processes of evolution has developed.

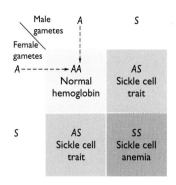

FIGURE 4.6 Punnett square showing sickle cell inheritance. (*A* is the normal allele; *S* is the sickle cell allele.) Two individuals, each heterozygous at the hemoglobin locus, produce gametes with normal and abnormal alleles in about equal numbers. When they mate, they have a one-quarter chance of producing a child with normal hemoglobin, a one-half chance of producing a heterozygote like themselves, and a one-quarter chance of producing a child who will exhibit the symptoms of sickle cell anemia.

codominant The expression of both alleles of a gene pair.

monogenic A trait coded for by a single gene.

polygenic A trait coded for by more than one gene.

The Genetics of Populations

The physical evidence for evolution is change in the phenotypic features of organisms over time. If evolution manifests itself as phenotypic change and if the genetic code is responsible for generating phenotypic traits, then evolution may be accurately regarded as genetic change over time. Because the overall genetic makeup of an individual does not change (except for isolated mutations), individuals don't evolve. The unit of evolution is the **population,** defined generally as a group within which mates are normally found.

Technically, a whole species could be treated as a genetic population because members of an animal species, by definition, can only reproduce within that species. (Some plants *can* reproduce across species.) But most species are unevenly distributed within their range and so contain subunits of interbreeding individuals, often further defined by a particular locality and perhaps even by particular adaptations and physical characteristics. These groups are called **breeding populations,** or **demes.** The evolution of a species can be seen as the collective evolution of the demes within that species as those populations change independently and as they interact by exchanging genetic material.

A breeding population is characterized genetically by identifying how often a certain allele appears in the population relative to the other alleles of the same gene. This is called **allele frequency.** Thus, the genetic definition of evolution is change in allele frequency over time. The processes of evolution, then, are all those factors that bring about changes in allele frequency.

To understand how this concept can help us study and explain the nature and operation of evolutionary processes, let's use sickle cell anemia in a hypothetical breeding population (Park 1999 from Relethford 1997). In a population of 145 individuals under study, the following numbers were found:

Phenotype	Genotype	Number
Normal	*AA*	35
Heterozygote	*AS*	100
Sickle cell	*SS*	10
Total		145

To study the population, it is necessary first to find the allele frequency. Because individuals with normal hemoglobin have genotype *AA,* there are twice as many *A* alleles as there are "normal" individuals. In addition, all heterozygotes possess one *A* allele, so this must be added to the total *A* allele count. Thus,

$$\text{Number of } A \text{ alleles} = (35 \times 2) + 100 = 170$$

population A reproductive unit.

breeding population A population with some degree of genetic isolation from other populations of the species.

deme Generally, the same as a breeding population.

allele frequency The number of times (in percentage) that a particular allele appears in a population.

Similarly, for the S allele,

$$\text{Number of } S \text{ alleles} = (10 \times 2) + 100 = 120$$
$$\text{Total number of alleles} = 290$$

Now, in order to calculate the frequency (the percentage) of occurrence of each allele, divide the number of each allele by the total number of alleles in the population. Thus, for the A allele,

$$170/290 = 0.59$$

Similarly, for the S allele,

$$120/290 = 0.41$$

In a population of 145 individuals, the allele for normal hemoglobin occurs 59 percent of the time, and the allele for sickle cell occurs 41 percent of the time. These are the allele frequencies for that population.

Given those allele frequencies, we can now calculate the expected genotype and phenotype frequencies under conditions where no evolution is in operation. This procedure is known as *testing the null hypothesis*. If you can state the condition under which nothing occurs, you can then compare it to situations where something *does* occur, observe the nature and direction of the difference, and possibly discern factors that are responsible. With reference to the genetics of populations, the null hypothesis is specifically known as the **Hardy-Weinberg equilibrium** (named after the mathematician and physician who independently derived it in 1908).

Using our two alleles, A and S, we designate the frequency of A as p and the frequency of S as q. (These letters are used because of a mathematical convention.) The probability of creating each of the possible genotypes is the product (the result of multiplication) of the frequencies of the alleles of that genotype. Thus,

Genotype	Product of Frequencies
AA	$p \times p = p^2$
AS	$p \times q = pq$
SA	$q \times p = qp$
SS	$q \times q = q^2$

$$\left. \begin{array}{l} p \times q = pq \\ q \times p = qp \end{array} \right\} 2pq$$

Because all genotypes are now accounted for,

$$p^2 + 2pq + q^2 = 1$$

(that is, 100 percent of the genotypes).

We can now return to our hypothetical population to see what its genotype frequencies would be if they were based solely on the frequencies of the alleles, if, in the terminology of population genetics, the population were in Hardy-Weinberg equilibrium.

Hardy-Weinberg equilibrium The formula that shows genotype percentages under hypothetical conditions of no evolutionary change.

Genotype	Expected Frequency	Expected Number	Observed Number
AA	$p^2 = 0.59^2 = 0.3481$	$0.3481 \times 145 = 50$	35
AS	$2pq = 0.59 \times 0.41 \times 2$ $= 0.4838$	$0.4838 \times 145 = 70$	100
SS	$q^2 = 0.41^2 = 0.1681$	$0.1681 \times 145 = 24$	10

The observed numbers are not in equilibrium. The allele frequencies have changed relative to the null hypothesis situation. Evolution, by definition, is taking place; there are fewer "normal" individuals than expected, more heterozygotes, and fewer sickle cell homozygotes. An evolutionary trend seems to favor heterozygotes. Given what we know about sickle cell anemia, this makes perfect sense. (We'll see why in the next section.) Indeed, data similar to this hinted at the nature of the disease and led to our understanding of it.

In real life, we would still have to run certain statistical tests on the above results because even if the expected and observed numbers do not match, they could still result from simple chance. One such test, called *chi-square,* showed that the results are probably not a matter of chance. They are, in mathematical terms, statistically significant.

What processes, then, can bring about changes in allele frequency in populations and thus alter the phenotypic nature of the group?

The Processes of Evolution

Natural Selection

As Darwin explained, from the physical and behavioral variation within a species, nature selects the characteristics best adapted to a particular environment. The measure of nature's selection is the relative reproductive success of the individual organisms that possess those characteristics. This is called **differential reproduction.** Individuals with the most adaptive traits tend to produce more offspring on the average, thus relatively more often passing on the alleles that code for their advantageous traits. In this manner, the better adapted traits accumulate over time and the poorly adapted ones become less frequent—even disappearing if their possessors fail to reproduce at all. The result is that the species as a whole stays adapted to its environmental **niche**—the particular set of environmental circumstances with which it comes in contact and to which it must adjust.

The traits that make an individual better adapted will, of course, vary with the species in question and with that species' particular niche. Bigger size, smaller size, bright colors, dull colors, speed, stealth, intelligence, reliance on built-in instincts—each can be adaptive depending on the species and niche.

differential reproduction The differing reproductive success of individuals within a population.

niche The environment of an organism and its adaptive response to that environment.

In addition, selection of mating partners takes place in many species. Males may directly compete with one another for access to females. The famous head-clashing duels of bighorn sheep are an example. In other cases, females choose mates based on things such as the establishment of a nesting site or colorful feather displays, as with the peacock (although the adaptive benefit of these displays is still not fully understood). This form of selection is called **sexual selection,** and as we'll see it may have played a part in early human evolution.

Thus, by ensuring that the more advantageous traits are passed to more offspring, natural selection maintains a species' adaptation to its environment. As we have seen, however, environments change. When this happens, traits that were once adaptively neutral or even poorly adapted may actually become better adapted. These traits will begin to occur in higher frequencies because their possessors become increasingly successful reproductively. At the same time, traits that once were adaptive may become increasingly rare and perhaps even nonexistent. Even under new environmental conditions, then, the species can remain viable and adapted, though its adaptive features may be different.

A striking example of natural selection in changing environments comes from pioneering work by Rosemary and Peter Grant and their colleagues (Grant and Grant 2000, 2002; Weiner 1994) among the famous birds of the Galápagos Islands collectively known as Darwin's finches (Figure 4.7). Among the important adaptive features of this group of birds are their beaks, which have evolved to help each species of finch exploit particular food sources. In 1977 there was a severe and nearly yearlong drought on one of the small islands that the Grants' team was using as a study area. Insects virtually disappeared, and the only plant seeds available were larger than average and had tougher than average exteriors to preserve their moisture. The finches on the island suffered a serious food shortage.

The next year, when the rains returned, the researchers found that just one finch in seven (a mere 14 percent) had made it through the drought. Moreover, the surviving birds of one species common to the island (the medium ground finch) were 5 to 6 percent larger than those that had perished and had beaks that were slightly (in fact, less than a millimeter) longer and deeper than the average before the drought. It's not a big difference on a human scale, but the size difference allowed some of the finches to more easily crack open the larger, tougher seeds during the drought, enabling them to survive; males survived much better than females because they are about 5 percent larger.

Now, however, because evolution takes place across generations, it had to be seen if this change would be passed on to the offspring of the surviving finches. This was, indeed, the case. It is the female finches that select males with which to mate. The males that the few surviving females selected were the largest and had the deepest beaks. As a result, the finches

sexual selection The active, rather than random, selection of mating partners by individuals within a population.

FIGURE 4.7 Some of the species of Darwin's finches found on the Galápagos Islands with indications of their basic adaptations for acquiring food.

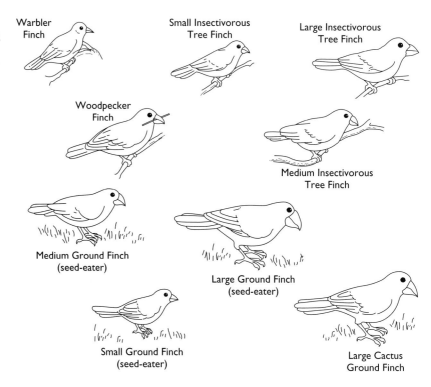

of the next generation were both larger and had beaks that were 4 to 5 percent deeper than the average before the drought. Moreover, when conditions, and thus food sources, returned to normal for a time, the average beak size decreased over several generations toward its previous dimensions. Larger beaks were no longer a distinct advantage and so were no longer selected for. These changes showed natural selection in action. Because of the severity of the situation, it took place rapidly enough for human observers to measure and record it.

It is important to note that in this case, as in any example of natural selection, the variation that proved useful under changed circumstances was already present. It did not appear when it was needed or because it was needed. The finches that survived *already* had larger body and beak size; they did not develop these after the drought altered their food source. It was, in other words, already an aspect of their variation, although only a small number of finches would possess large beaks and bodies since, under usual conditions, they conferred no distinct advantage and may even have been disadvantageous. This is the essential difference between Lamarck's inheritance of acquired characteristics and Darwin's natural selection (Figure 4.8).

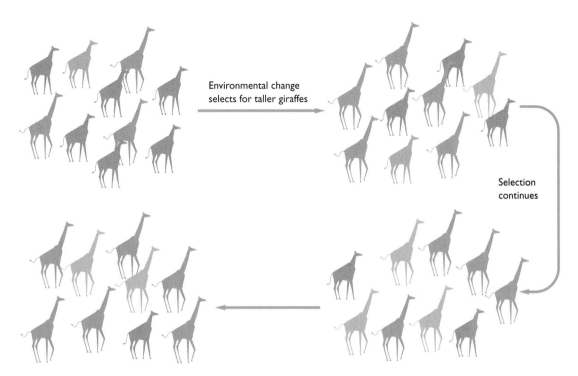

Environmental change selects for taller giraffes

Selection continues

FIGURE 4.8 Schematic diagram of Darwinian natural selection. As in the case of the finches, an environmental change makes the larger individuals more reproductively successful, and they become the most common representatives of their species. Compare with Figure 2.6, Lamarck's concept of evolutionary change.

A more complex example comes once again from sickle cell anemia. Despite the fact that it is so disadvantageous, sickle cell anemia is found in high frequencies in certain areas of the world (Figure 4.9). One would expect a lethal allele to disappear quickly or, in evolutionary terms, to be *selected out.* But in some parts of Africa, the sickle cell disease is found in at least one in every sixty-four people. There's clearly more to the persistence of this disease than first meets the eye.

The reason for the high frequency of sickle cell disease is that the heterozygous condition conveys an adaptive benefit. Besides not usually having severe symptoms of sickle cell anemia, heterozygote individuals also have a resistance to malaria, a potentially fatal disease caused by a parasitic single-celled organism and transmitted by mosquitoes. This resistance comes about because red blood cells with abnormal hemoglobin (remember, heterozygotes have 40 percent abnormal hemoglobin) take on abnormal shapes when infected by the malaria parasite and die, failing to transport the parasite through the system. Sickle cell is found in highest frequencies where malaria is found in highest frequencies (Figure 4.10). In no environment is there any advantage in being homozygous for the abnormal allele. In malarial environments, however, heterozygotes do have an advantage. As you saw in the Punnett square, when two heterozygotes

FIGURE 4.9 The distribution of high frequencies of sickle cell anemia. Compare this with the map of high frequencies of malaria (Figure 4.10).

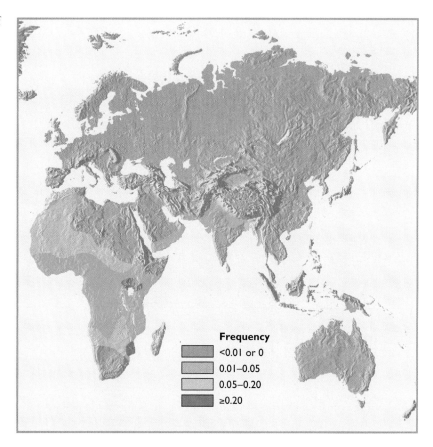

Frequency
<0.01 or 0
0.01–0.05
0.05–0.20
≥0.20

mate, they have only a one-quarter chance of producing a homozygous child who will probably die at an early age from sickle cell whereas they have a one-half chance (twice as good) of producing more heterozygotes who carry the defense against malaria.

Adaptive fitness, then, is relative to particular environmental conditions. What is adaptive in one environment may not be adaptive in another. What is adaptive at one time may not be at another. A lethal allele (such as sickle cell) may actually be adaptive in certain genotypic combinations within certain environments. As we will see later, a genetically determined ability to, say, walk on two legs more frequently and with greater ability might provide an advantage to those members of a species that possess those characteristics and abilities, but only under certain environmental conditions. The gene-environment relationship is a complex one.

This is something to keep in mind as we discuss the various phenotypic evolutionary changes our species has undergone. Few evolutionary events are as simple as they first seem. When we discuss the evolution of

FIGURE 4.10 The distribution of high frequencies of malaria shows a correspondence with high frequencies of sickle cell anemia (Figure 4.9).

our upright posture or our large brains, you should appreciate the complex genetic changes that must have occurred, as well as the complex interactions between genotype and phenotype and between phenotype and environment.

It is also important to remember that because it operates on variation already present in existing traits, natural selection is not always successful in maintaining the viability of a species. When some environmental change is too severe or too rapid, there may simply not be any variation within a species that enables some of its members to reproduce in quantities sufficient to perpetuate the species. Extinction is the result—indeed, it has been the fate of over 90 percent of all species that have ever existed.

For example, dinosaur species occupied a great diversity of niches and were around in some form for over 100 million years. Yet a rapid and substantial environmental change occurred to which none of the dinosaurs (or too few to matter) had sufficiently adapted traits. As a result, the dinosaurs died out in a fairly short period of time. Human activity also constitutes a

FIGURE 4.11 Processes of evolution. A species is in an adaptive relationship with its environment. This relationship is maintained by natural selection. Environments, however, are constantly changing, so the adaptive characteristics of species change over time. In addition, the gene pool of a species is always changing, altering the phenotypes on which selection acts. Processes that alter a species' gene pool are also, by definition, processes of evolution because they change allele frequency. Mutation provides new genetic variation by producing new alleles or otherwise altering the genetic code. Gene flow and genetic drift mix the genetic variation within a species, continually supplying new combinations of genetic variables.

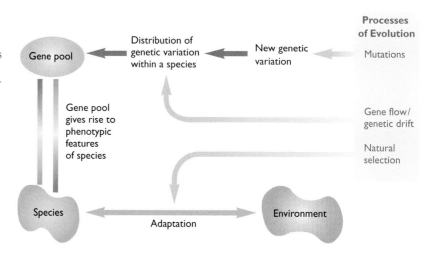

form of environmental change and can bring about the same kinds of results. Overhunting of passenger pigeons in North America, coupled with the felling of forests that provided their habitat, resulted in the extinction, by 1914, of a species that once numbered in the billions.

Natural selection is not magic, nor is it the only process that changes allele frequency and thus contributes to evolution. Whereas natural selection produces change in the direction of better adaptation, other processes have no adaptive direction. But since they cause the frequency of alleles to change over time, they are considered evolutionary processes (Figure 4.11), and they also provide variation on which natural selection acts. These processes are mutation, gene flow, and genetic drift, which we will examine next.

Mutation

Mutations are random—that is, unpredictable—changes in the material of inheritance. Mutations may affect individual genes, as in the case of sickle cell anemia, the result of one wrong codon in a sequence of 287. Or they may affect a whole chromosome, or a portion of a chromosome, and therefore many genes. Mutations may occur spontaneously as a result of mechanical errors during the processes by which the genetic code either copies itself during cell division or is translated into working proteins. Mutations may also result from certain outside stimuli such as cosmic or nuclear radiation, various chemical pollutants, and some insecticides.

Mutations are frequent. Some have taken place in cells somewhere in your body since you started reading this page. The only ones that matter to the evolution of sexually reproducing species, though, are those that occur in the sex cells or the cells that produce the sex cells. These are the mutations that can be passed on and can thus change the allele frequencies of a population over time.

Because mutations are sudden, random changes, they may logically be considered mistakes. As mistakes, many have deleterious effects. Such mutations tend to disappear because individuals having them are less reproductively successful. In other words, these mutations are selected against. Other mutations may produce alleles that are neutral in terms of adaptation—that is, at the time they occur they are neither more nor less adaptive than the original allele. And some mutations may even be more adaptive than other variations. In this case, natural selection is provided with new raw material that may be selected for.

Mutation, then, is a source of variation on which natural selection can act. It is also itself a process of evolutionary change because it alters the hereditary material of a species. The effect of a mutation on the species depends, of course, on just what traits are affected and on how important those traits are to the relative reproductive success of individuals possessing them. A small, inconsequential mutation has little or no effect on the individual. As a result, it may or may not be passed to a proportionately large number of offspring; that depends on the success of the individual based on other traits it possesses. A large mutation, or a small one with extensive effects (such as the sickle cell allele), will be passed on to decreasing numbers of individuals if it is deleterious. A trait that kills carriers before they become old enough to mate is unlikely to become common in a population because those with the trait are not able to pass it on. On the other hand, a genetic trait may spread rapidly through the species in subsequent generations if it confers a distinct advantage on those who carry it.

Mutations are changes that affect the hereditary material itself. Natural selection operates on the physical manifestations of the hereditary material based on the adaptiveness of those manifestations. Two other processes of evolution, **gene flow** and **genetic drift**, work at a level between selection and mutation. These processes change allele frequency by altering the frequencies of genotypes, that is, allele combinations. They work, however, without regard to their specific adaptive characteristics.

Gene Flow

Members of a species interbreed with one another. But species tend to be divided into breeding populations, or demes, that are delimited by geographic distance, a specific environmental range and niche, and social organization. These breeding populations within a species may undergo natural selection for their particular environmental situations and may therefore exhibit minor differences among one another. So when members of different populations do interbreed with other populations as a result of migration or the exchange of genes with neighboring populations—when

gene flow The exchange of genes among populations through interbreeding.

genetic drift The change in allele frequency by random fluctuations.

the genes of one "flow" into the **gene pool** of another—the offspring have new genetic combinations. New physical manifestations appear in the mixed population and provide even more raw material for natural selection on the species level.

When flow is extensive among populations within a species, it has the effect of reducing the genetic variation among those populations. A perfect example is our own species; our mobility and tendency to interbreed have blurred physical distinctions among individual populations—the reason why our species cannot be divided into biologically meaningful racial groups (see Chapter 10).

Genetic Drift

Several distinct processes fall under the heading of genetic drift. **Fission** is the opposite of gene flow. When a population within a species splits, the new subpopulations will differ from one another and from the original population in the average phenotypes and genotypes. This may not seem obvious at first, but an example can demonstrate the point. Suppose you calculate the average stature of members of your anthropology class to be 5′ 9″ with a range from 5′ 1″ to 6′ 7″. If you divide the class population into two samples without considering height, do you think the average stature and range for each new group will be the same as the original? The two samples might have a similar mean height and range, but, by chance, they may not; in fact, they may end up being very different. The same applies to genes in natural populations. Any population split—a common enough occurrence—will provide evolutionary change as well as new gene pools for selection to operate on (Figure 4.12).

This effect is enhanced when the split is uneven—when, for example, 10 percent of a population splits from the original and founds a new population. It is virtually impossible for that 10 percent to possess the same average physical traits, gene combinations, and allele frequencies as the original. This is known as the **founder effect.** The founder effect and fission together form one type of genetic drift.

The other form of genetic drift is **gamete sampling**. When fertilization takes place in sexually reproducing species, the genetic material from two parents is mixed. The potential number of new genetic combinations in the offspring is enormous. You may resemble your parents, but you are not a carbon copy of either, and your specific genetic makeup is absolutely unique to you (unless you have an identical twin). With sexual reproduction, then, change occurs every generation, based solely on the laws of probability applied to the recombination of parental genes in their offspring. This change is not related to the adaptive fitness of the traits involved because it is produced at the time of fertilization, before the environment has a chance to act on the physical traits.

gene pool All the genes of a population.

fission The splitting up of a population to form new populations.

founder effect Differences in populations caused by genetic differences in the individuals who establish the populations.

gamete sampling The genetic change caused when genes are passed to new generations in frequencies unlike those in the parental population.

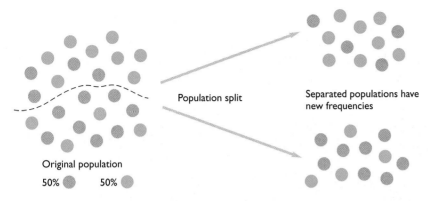

Population split

Separated populations have
new frequencies

Original population

50% ⬤   50% ⬤

FIGURE 4.12 Diagram of fission, where a population split produces new populations with distinct gene pools. Gene flow, which produces one new genetic population from two or more, can be pictured by reversing the direction of the arrows.

As described in the preceding paragraph, the process of gamete sampling affects only the offspring of one set of parents, but the combined effects of this process at the population level, in many sets of parents and offspring, can bring about a great deal of change from one generation to the next. Especially if the phenotypes coded for by the new genetic combinations are adaptively unimportant, the specific expressions may change at random across generations, "drifting" in whatever direction chance takes them—hence the name genetic drift.

Suppose, for instance, two parents are both heterozygous for a certain locus, say, *Aa*. A Punnett square would reveal that they stand a one-quarter chance of producing an *AA* offspring, a one-half chance of producing an *Aa* offspring, and a one-quarter chance of producing an *aa* offspring. These figures, however, are probabilities, not certainties. Each fertilization is an event independent of all previous fertilizations. They may, for example, produce nothing but *AA* offspring. In that case, all their *a* alleles are lost. In a large population, there is a good chance that two other parents of genotype *Aa* will produce only *aa* offspring, and it will all balance out. But in a small population—of, say, under 100 individuals—the chance of such a balance is very small. In fact, all forms of genetic drift have greater effects in small populations. In this way, some alleles may ultimately be lost and others may reach a frequency of 100 percent all with no necessary relation to adaptation.

As with the other processes, drift produces evolutionary change as well as new population variation on which natural selection may then operate. It may not, however, always be a positive process. A further threat to species already on the brink of extinction because of low population size is the fact that what little genetic variation they have left may be further depleted by the drifting of some alleles to high frequencies and others to low frequencies. The less genetic variation, the less chance a species has of containing enough individuals well enough adapted to reproduce in sufficient numbers. This is part of the current plight of cheetahs, African lions, gorillas, condors, and other endangered species.

The Origin of Species

Although natural selection was the cornerstone of Darwin's theory of evolution, it was not the phenomenon he ultimately sought to explain. What interested Darwin, and Wallace, was the question of where all the species of plants and animals had come from in the first place. Natural selection was the mechanism they proposed as the answer. Darwin, in fact, felt it was *the* answer. Natural selection, he said, brought about "the accumulation of innumerable slight variations, each good for the individual possessor" (1898:267). He added,

> What limit can be put to this power, acting during long ages and rigidly scrutinizing the whole constitution, structure, and habits of each creature,— favoring the good and rejecting the bad? I can see no limit to this power, in slowly and beautifully adapting each form to the most complex relations of life. (1898:267)

So, according to Darwin's view, one way new species arise is as a direct result of constant adaptive change within existing species. Eventually, a species will change so much it evolves into a new species.

In addition, such constant selection, Darwin said, will also produce variation among populations within a species in response to slight differences in their environments. He referred to these populations as "varieties." Eventually, selection brings about such marked distinctions in varieties that two or more new species branch from the old one. These species, said Darwin, "are only well-marked varieties, of which the characters have become in a high degree permanent" (1898:285).

Darwin, then, saw natural selection as more than a mechanism for the origin of species. To him, it was the driving force behind the origin of

FIGURE 4.13 Darwinian gradualism.

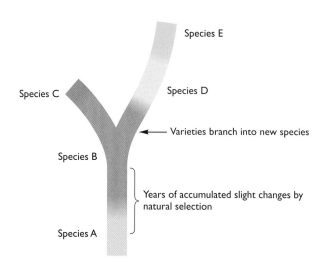

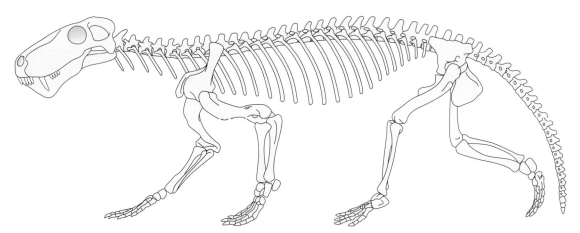

FIGURE 4.14 *Lycaenops,* a mammal-like reptile from 240 mya. Its legs were long and under its body, allowing it to keep its body continually off the ground, like mammals in general but unlike earlier reptiles. *Lycaenops* also had long canine teeth like mammals, though its other teeth were reptilian. *(Neg. #2A3387. Courtesy Department of Library Services, American Museum of Natural History)*

species, constantly choosing from among innumerable small variations those best suited to an environment. The result is the turning of one species into another, whether it occurs gradually but inexorably or produces first new varieties within the species and finally a new species, forming in the process "an interminable number of intermediate forms . . . linking together all the species in each group by [fine] gradations" (1898:271–72). Evolution, according to Darwin, is a long string of small adaptive changes over time. This model of evolution is called **gradualism,** or sometimes **Darwinian gradualism** (Figure 4.13).

Darwin was challenged, however, on one aspect of his model of speciation. If evolution were slow and gradual, where, some of his contemporaries asked, were all those "intermediate forms" in the fossil record? Darwin's answer was that the fossil record was "imperfect," that more time and study would reveal all the transitions. He was overly optimistic.

Although the last 140 years have brought to light fossils representing the transitions between major forms of life (dinosaurs to birds and reptiles to mammals, for example; Figure 4.14), transitional forms between individual species have, for the most part, failed to appear. Moreover, species, for the most part, seem to remain fairly stable throughout their tenure on earth. The concrete evidence does not fully support Darwin's model.

Moreover, Darwinian gradualism presents a theoretical problem. If each small variation selected for is "good for the individual possessor," then we must account for the adaptive benefit of each small step toward the development of some completed characteristic. Could one-tenth of a wing, or one-hundredth of an eye—like a millimeter in those finches' beaks—*always* convey to its possessor a reproductive advantage over the members of its species that lack this trait?

It would seem, then, that evolutionary change over great spans of time is not the result of gradual change *within* species (individual species changing

gradualism The view that speciation is slow and steady with cumulative change.

Darwinian gradualism The same as gradualism.

so much they become a new species) but, rather, the result of new species branching from existing species. Indeed, natural selection is not the creative "scrutinizing" force that Darwin envisioned, but a more conservative force, simply eliminating what doesn't work adaptively and allowing to reproduce what does. Change *within* a species is limited.

This does not mean that natural selection has *no* effect on a species over time. Traits that are important may change back and forth as environmental conditions change. Recall the changes in beak size among the Darwin's finches studied by the Grants and their team. The data indicate that a slight difference in beak size among members of one species—as little as a millimeter or two—can be of adaptive importance during sudden, prolonged, or radical environmental changes such as droughts. In fact, small variations made the difference between life and death, and so, after such an environmental episode, the average beak size of an affected finch species could be significantly altered. When conditions—and, thus, food sources—returned to normal, the average beak size often returned to its previous measurement. The average expression of important traits of a species, then, may change back and forth as environmental conditions change. This is called **oscillating selection.** But it is adaptive variation—a sort of fine-tuning—around a norm, rather than continual change in a particular direction.

Speciation, however, is a frequent process in the sense that new species of some sort evolve all the time (although most events of speciation involve smaller species with short generations). It is also a relatively rapid process in a geological time frame where thousands of years constitute a few seconds on our cosmic calendar. Speciation occurs when a portion or portions of a species are isolated from the species as a whole. If sufficient variation exists to allow this new population to survive and reproduce in its new environment, it may accumulate enough differences from its parent species to become a separate species, reproductively isolated from the parent species. This isolation may be physical. For example, the thirteen species of Darwin's finches that inhabit the Galápagos were descended from a single South American species. Over a long span of time, individuals from the original population were blown or floated out to sea from the mainland, and a few managed to end up on the dozen or so major Galápagos Islands, where they adapted to the various niches on the islands. Natural selection to those niches, along with the relative isolation of the islands and long periods of time, allowed the finch populations to diverge to such a degree that they are now considered separate species, characterized by such features as differences in size and other features such as their beaks. Subsequent movement has resulted in a dispersal of the various species among the islands. Some of the larger and more ecologically varied islands of the group support as many as ten finch species (Figure 4.15).

The isolation may also be genetic. Mutations were once thought to involve only slight alterations. Now, however, we recognize that not all genes

oscillating selection Adaptive variation around a norm, rater than in one direction, in response to environmental variation in a species' habitat.

speciation The evolution of new species.

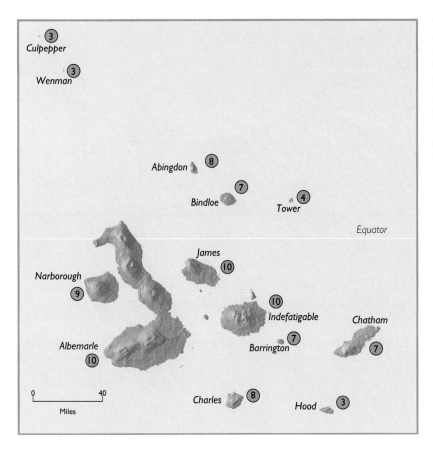

FIGURE 4.15 The various species of Darwin's finches evolved when small groups from an original species underwent adaptation to the varying environmental conditions found throughout the Galápagos Islands. The numbers on the map represent the number of finch species found on each major island.

are of equal importance and that a mutation of large numbers of genes or of genes that code for important phenotypic traits can produce a major change in the offspring of the organism that passes that mutation on.

There are, for example, genes influencing developmental changes that act on the individual at an early age but may have important consequences for the structure and function of the adult organism. There appears to have been one such change, more than 140 mya; that altered the development of dinosaur skin to produce featherlike structures, thus beginning the evolution of the birds (Figure 4.16). Thus, if multiple members of an existing species (say, all the members of a litter or all the hatchlings in a nest) share such a mutation, with the result that they cannot interbreed with the rest of the species, or their differences severely limit interbreeding, speciation may take place very rapidly.

This model of evolutionary change, first proposed in its modern form in 1972 by paleontologists Niles Eldredge and Stephen Jay Gould (1972), is called **punctuated equilibrium**. It says that the evolutionary histories of species are marked by equilibrium—long periods of little change—with

punctuated equilibrium
The view that species tend to remain stable, with evolutionary change arising fairly suddenly through the breaking off of a new species.

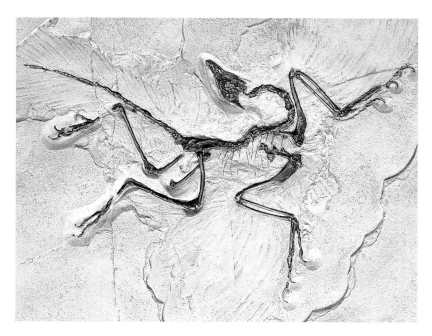

FIGURE 4.16 The fossil remains of *Archaeopteryx* ("ancient bird"), about 150 million years old. It is actually a small, bipedal dinosaur with feathers. These feathers, modifications of dinosaurian scales, are an example of a sudden but sizable alteration in a species' genetic makeup that eventually gave rise to a whole new group of organisms. (© *Tom and Therisa Stack/Tom Stack & Associates*)

natural selection acting largely in a conservative way to maintain the species' adaptation to its environment, mostly by selecting against maladaptive variations but also by bringing about, if possible, small changes back and forth as adjustments to environmental alterations (oscillating selection). This equilibrium, however, is punctuated by bursts of change in the form of speciation events. These events occur when a portion of a species is isolated, either physically or genetically. In time, a new species may evolve. This is not an instant process; it may take thousands of years. Indeed, although we recognize thirteen species names for the Galápagos finches, some of these species can interbreed when altered environmental circumstances cause their niches to overlap. In other words, they might be considered as still somewhere in the process of becoming true species. But speciation is not the gradual evolution Darwin had proposed, marked by a long series of small transitional steps. It begins with a big step—the isolation of a portion of a species or a macromutation—providing natural selection with something brand new and very different to work with (Figure 4.17).

So the evolution of life on earth cannot be depicted as a ladder or chain representing a steady march of progress toward complexity, as

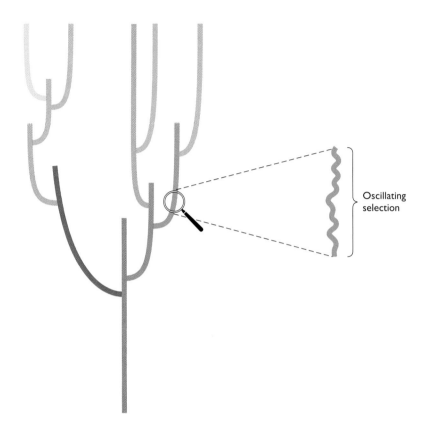

FIGURE 4.17 The shape of evolution according to the punctuated equilibrium model. Major evolutionary change is the result of speciation, the branching of new species from existing ones. Individual species change relatively little over time, although natural selection still acts constantly to maintain a species' adaptation to its environment.

Oscillating selection

Lamarck and other early scientists believed. Nor is it a gracefully branching tree, as Darwin pictured it. Instead, evolution is, in the words of Stephen Jay Gould (1994:91), a "luxuriant bush," more complex than we will probably ever know—or, as Gould puts it in another work (1985:355), a "blooming and buzzing confusion."

Summary

To fully account for the evolution of species, an understanding of the workings of genetics is vital. Genes code for the traits that make up the physical organism by giving instructions for the synthesis of proteins. Proteins make cells and control their functions, and cells, in turn, make up the tissues that make up the organism.

The gene pool of a species changes over time because of four processes that alter the frequencies with which the alleles of genes appear. Mutations produce new alleles or, on the chromosomal level, new sequences or combinations of alleles. Gene flow shuffles the alleles of populations within a

CONTEMPORARY ISSUE
What Is Genetic Cloning?

Since advances in genetic technology enabled the cloning of Dolly the sheep in 1997, that ability and its potential applications have been areas of both great scientific interest and heated controversy, much of the latter due to a poor general understanding of what the term *cloning* means. What immediately comes to mind are the plots from popular science fiction novels and movies. For example, in Ira Levin's *The Boys from Brazil,* a Nazi scientist produces clones of Hitler, each, of course, with Hitler's personality.

Not only is something like that impossible, but it doesn't even come close to exemplifying the scientific meaning of cloning. The term *clone* simply refers to an exact or nearly exact copy of a biological entity, whether an individual or a cell. Identical twins, by that definition, are natural clones because they began life as a single fertilized egg cell and are, essentially, genetically the same.

In terms of artificial cloning, there are two main types. And the distinction is important. Dolly and members of at least seven other species are examples of *reproductive cloning.* Here, the goal is the production of a genetic duplicate of an organism.

Motivations range from increasing productivity of food animals to producing organs for transplantation to replicating pets. Not only are the functions of reproductive cloning open to ethical considerations, but at present there are severe limitations on its success, including the fact (probably mercifully) that it doesn't seem to work with primates (Simerly et al. 2003).

Specific techniques differ, but in the most widely used method, the chromosomes are removed from an unfertilized egg shortly after ovulation, when it would be ready to develop if stimulated by the sperm. The donor cell, the one to be copied, is a somatic (body) cell, often a skin cell or a mammary cell. It is fused with the egg cell with the help of electric pulses, which also mimic the stimulation of fertilization. After about four or five days in a chemical solution, if all goes well, the fused cells will have developed into an embryo of several hundred cells. At this point, the embryo is transferred to the uterus of a surrogate mother of the species in question with the hope that it will develop normally. If it does, as was the case with Dolly, the new organism will be an

species to produce new genotypic frequencies. Due to genetic drift, new genotypic frequencies occur each time a population splits and each time a new generation is produced. And natural selection affects allele frequencies via the differential reproduction of the carriers of adaptive phenotypes.

Given sufficient change and the right circumstances, new species can evolve from existing ones. Charles Darwin thought this occurred as a result of the gradual yet inexorable force of selection slightly changing each species every generation. We now understand that natural selection is more a conservative force than a creative one, largely acting to maintain the adaptation of a species to its environment. Speciation occurs when a portion of a species is isolated, physically or genetically, and, if it gains an adaptive foothold, starts off on its own evolutionary path, becoming different enough to be reproductively isolated from its parent species.

exact genetic copy of the individual from whom the donor cell was taken.

One misconception about this technique is that the clone will be a phenotypic duplicate of the donor. To be sure, clone and donor will be very much alike. But genes do not act alone in producing phenotypic traits, and many variables are involved in the path from single egg to multicellular organism. The more complex the trait, the more variable the potential results. So a clone of me would look like me but would not have all my personality traits. Even if we could clone humans, we would not be making exact copies.

The second type of genetic cloning is *therapeutic cloning,* in which cells and eventually tissues are grown *in vitro* (in a chemical culture) for medical purposes. No reproduction of individuals is involved. The idea is to make copies of stem cells. These are cells, such as a fertilized egg and cells from early in embryonic development, that have the potential to become all the different cell types in the body. In a few days, cells begin to specialize. At this stage (which is the same stage an embryo is implanted into a surrogate in reproductive cloning),

certain cells are removed from the embryo in the hope of differentiating them into specific types of tissues to replace or repair a patient's tissue damaged by certain diseases, including Parkinson's disease, muscular dystrophy, and diabetes.

An objection to stem cell cloning is that an embryo—a potential life—is intentionally created only to be destroyed when the wanted cells are removed. But a new technique can "trick" an egg cell into "thinking" it has been fertilized so that it clones itself into an embryo. Such embryos are nonviable and could not lead to a pregnancy. In addition, there are stem cells still present in adult animals, and these could potentially be cloned and artificially differentiated. Ethical objections to therapeutic cloning seem easier to overcome than those to reproductive cloning, and the benefits to human health are of potentially inestimable value.

Both research and debate will continue on cloning, as well they should. But the former should be done with clear and beneficial goals in mind and the latter with sound, accurate knowledge of the science involved.

Study Questions

1. What are genes, and through what steps do they produce the traits that make up a living organism?
2. What are the basic laws of inheritance; that is, how are traits passed on from parent to offspring?
3. How may we study the genetic makeup of populations as well as genetic change in populations through the use of mathematics?
4. What are the processes of evolution? How do they interact to bring about evolutionary change?
5. How do existing species give rise to new species?
6. How is sickle cell anemia an example of all aspects of modern evolutionary theory?

Key Terms

genetics	homozygous	Hardy-Weinberg
particulate	heterozygous	equilibrium
gene	mutation	differential
protein	phenotype	reproduction
enzyme	recessive	niche
deoxyribonucleic acid	dominant	sexual selection
(DNA)	gamete	gene flow
chromosome	segregation	genetic drift
replication	zygote	gene pool
protein synthesis	point mutation	fission
messenger ribonucleic	codominant	founder effect
acid (mRNA)	monogenic	gamete sampling
codon	polygenic	gradualism
transfer RNA (tRNA)	population	Darwinian gradualism
amino acid	breeding population	oscillating selection
allele	deme	speciation
genotype	allele frequency	punctuated
genome		equilibrium

For More Information

Many excellent books on evolution and evolutionary processes are available. We recommend Mark Ridley's *Evolution,* second edition. The history of evolutionary thought, with excerpts from original sources, is covered in C. Leon Harris's *Evolution: Genesis and Revelations.*

A must for anyone interested in genetics—or, for that matter, the nature of scientific inquiry in general—is *The Double Helix* by James D. Watson, about the race to discover the nature of the genetic code and thereby win the Nobel Prize. The author was one of the winners. For an up-to-date piece on new discoveries in genetics, and their applications, see "Secrets of the Gene" by James Shreeve in the October 1999 *National Geographic.*

For the original announcement of the completion of the human genome, see the "Science Times" section of the February 3, 2001 *New York Times,* the February 15, 2001 issue of *Nature,* and the February 16, 2001 issue of *Science* (in the last publication, see page 1163 for a list of Web sites on the genome project and data).

The reseach on Darwin's finches and the people who conducted it are the subjects of Jonathan Weiner's Pulitzer Prize–winning *The Beak of the Finch: A Story of Evolution in Our Time.* For an update, see Peter and Rosemary Grant's article "Non-Random Fitness Variation in Two Populations of

Darwin's Finches," in the January 22, 2000 issue of the *Proceedings of the Royal Society of London: Biological Sciences* and their "Unpredictable Evolution in a 30-Year Study of Darwin's Finches" in the April 26, 2002 issue of *Science*.

Cloning technology is summarized in "Cloning for Medicine," by Ian Wilmut (who cloned Dolly), in the December 1998 *Scientific American*.

The Southeast Asian orangutan is, like us, a primate. What do we have in common with this tree-dwelling ape—and with nearly 200 other living primate species? How is our species unique? (© *Noel Rowe*)

LEARNING ABOUT THE PAST

The Primates

CHAPTER CONTENTS

Taxonomy

The Primates

A Primate Portfolio

The Human Primate

Genetics and Primate Relationships

The Evolution of the Primates

Summary

Study Questions

Key Terms

For More Information

CONTEMPORARY ISSUE: What Is the Status of Our Closest Relatives?

"What is man, that thou art mindful of him?" asks David in the biblical psalm. It is a question we must ask as well, but in a broader form: "What is a human being?" Before we embark on our journey through human evolution, we must understand modern humans, the species with which our journey ultimately ends.

Two problems are encountered in defining humanness. First, all modern human beings belong to a single species, and we lose perspective if we refer only to ourselves. Try describing any animal without referring to other organisms: "Well, a spider has body segments and jointed legs like an insect, only it has eight legs instead of six. . . ." Second, we are members of the very species we're describing. It's difficult to step back and see ourselves from an objective perspective. We have a tendency to focus on things that are important to us in a certain cultural setting at a certain time. For example, Carolus Linnaeus, the great eighteenth-century Swedish naturalist (see Chapter 2) listed as the distinguishing characteristics of *Homo sapiens* "diurnal [active during the day]; varying by education and situation." He then described five subspecies of humans using a combination of physical features and subjective European attitudes. Of the Native American, for instance, he said: "Hair black, straight, thick; nostrils wide, face harsh; beard scanty; obstinate, content free. Paints himself with fine red lines. Regulated by customs" (Kennedy 1976:25). (We will look at Linnaeus's classification of humans more fully in Chapter 10.)

Clearly, we need to look at ourselves not from cultural (and subjective) perspectives like Linnaeus's but in terms of how we compare objectively with other living organisms. Demosthenes, a fourth-century B.C. Greek orator, described us as "featherless bipeds"; twentieth-century biologist Desmond Morris dubbed us the "naked ape." These are better definitions because they are free from cultural values and recognize both our similarities to other organisms and our distinctive differences.

Taxonomy

We have already discussed the concept of the species, the natural unit of classification. Each organism belongs to a *specific species* (the words come from the same root), a group of potentially interbreeding individuals that are reproductively isolated from other groups.

The most cursory examination, however, shows clearly that there are larger units of classification of living things. Some species are more similar to one another than they are to other species. The book of Genesis, for example, does not name each species that God created, but it lists general categories: "the fish of the sea," "the fowl of the air," "every herb of the field," "every beast of the earth."

Linnaean Taxonomy

taxonomy A classification based on similarities and differences.

The idea that species share similarities so struck Linnaeus that he devised a taxonomic system to name and thus categorize all living creatures. A **taxonomy** is a system of classification, based on similarities and differences, that is organized into categories and increasingly specific subcategories.

TABLE 5.1 Linnaean Taxonomy of Five Familiar Species

	Human	Chimpanzee	Bonobo	Gorilla	Orangutan
Kingdom	Animalia	Animalia	Animalia	Animalia	Animalia
Phylum	Chordata	Chordata	Chordata	Chordata	Chordata
Class	Mammalia	Mammalia	Mammalia	Mammalia	Mammalia
Order	Primates	Primates	Primates	Primates	Primates
Family	Hominidae	Pongidae	Pongidae	Pongidae	Pongidae
Genus	Homo	Pan	Pan	Gorilla	Pongo
Species	sapiens	troglodytes	paniscus	gorilla	pygmaeus

Linnaeus (who used Latin names and, as mentioned earlier, even latinized his original name, Carl von Linné) devised a system, published in final form in 1758, that used four nested categories—*class, order, genus,* and *species.* Other scientists soon added *kingdom, phylum,* and *family,* giving us the seven Linnaean categories recognized by modern taxonomy (which uses additional categories when needed). Table 5.1 shows a traditional Linnaean taxonomy for five familiar species. We'll detail the taxonomy of our species to show what Linnaeus's system accomplishes.

It should be noted that a species is never referred to by just the species name, listed in the bottom row of the table. The species name is usually descriptive, and so there may be many species that share the same name. Many African animals have the species name *africanus,* for example. The chimpanzee shares its species name, *troglodytes,* with the winter wren, a small North American bird (the name conveying the erroneous assumption that these species are cave dwellers). It takes *both* the genus and species names to denote a particular species. We are, for instance, *Homo sapiens.*

Humans are members of the kingdom Animalia (Table 5.2). We share this grouping with the other four species in Table 5.1 by virtue of the fact that we all ingest our food, have sense organs and nervous systems, and are capable of intentional movement. We are not members of any of the other three kingdoms of eukaryotes (organisms whose cells have nuclei): complex single-celled organisms (amoebas and the like), fungi (mushrooms, mildews, molds), and plants (roses, ferns, broccoli, pine trees). There are, in addition, two main groups of prokaryotes, single-celled organisms that lack nuclei: bacteria and archaea. These are the microbes that make up the bulk of the earth's biomass.

TABLE 5.2 A Linnaean Taxonomy of Humans (with defining criteria)

Kingdom	Phylum	Class	Order	Family	Genus	Species
Animalia	Chordata	Mammalia	Primates	Hominidae	Homo	sapiens
Ingestion	Notochord	Hair	Arboreal	Habitual bipeds	Toolmaking	Brain size 1,000–2,000 ml*
Movement		Warm-blooded	Developed vision		Omnivore	
Sense organs		Live birth	Grasping hands			
		Mammary glands	Large brains			
		Active and intelligent				

*Note: This definition is a matter of controversy and will be taken up in Chapter 10.

Within kingdom Animalia are about thirty *phyla* (singular, *phylum*), groups such as sponges, jellyfish, starfish, three types of worms, mollusks, arthropods (insects, spiders, crustaceans), and chordates. We are members of phylum Chordata because we have a bony spine, the evolutionary descendant of a **notochord,** a long cartilaginous rod running down the back to support the body and protect the spinal chord, the extension of the central nervous system (Figure 5.1). Chordates with a bony spine are grouped into a subphylum, Vertebrata. All five species in Table 5.1 are chordates and, more specifically, vertebrates.

There are seven classes within the vertebrates: the jawless fishes (an ancient group represented by only a few existing species), cartilaginous fishes (sharks and rays), bony fishes (guppies, tunas, and so on), amphibians (frogs and salamanders), reptiles (snakes, lizards, and alligators), birds, and mammals. All our sample species are members of class Mammalia because they maintain a constant body temperature (commonly called *warm-blooded*), have hair, give birth to live young, nourish the young with milk from mammary glands, and have relatively large, complex brains.

We need to stop here for an important point. You may have noticed that some of the traits listed for mammals are also possessed by other classes. Birds, for example, are also warm-blooded; so, according to many, were some of the dinosaurs, and so are a number of other creatures, including great white sharks. Some sharks, some bony fishes (such as guppies), and some snakes give birth to live young. By the same token, you might know two mammals that do not possess all the mammalian traits. The spiny anteater (or echidna) and the duckbill platypus, both from Australia, lay eggs. Obviously, though, birds, dinosaurs, and great white sharks are *not* mammals, while the spiny anteater and platypus *are*. What's the resolution to this seeming contradiction?

notochord The evolutionary precursor of the vertebral column.

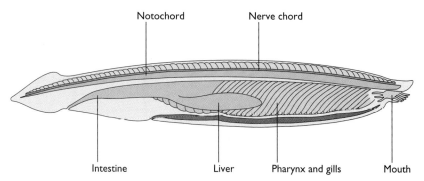

Notochord   Nerve chord

Intestine   Liver   Pharynx and gills   Mouth

FIGURE 5.1 Shown here is an amphioxus, a chordate with a notochord but no bony spine (shown about four times life size).

The answer is that inclusion into a taxonomic category is more than simply a matter of possessing a list of traits. The traits of an organism make possible that organism's *adaptation,* and it is adaptation, measured by reproductive success, that is the criterion of natural selection. Thus, taxonomic categories become statements about adaptation, as well as biological relationships, with each taxonomic level becoming more specifically focused. Mammals, whether they lay eggs or not, are animals that are adapted through active lifestyles and a reliance on learned behavior facilitated by a set of shared traits. Mammalian young, therefore, require a great deal of direct care and nurturing. Mammals also require a constant body temperature to sustain their level of activity, and they require hair (or in the case of whales, a thick layer of fat) to maintain that temperature. That's not a very concise definition of a mammal, but the real world doesn't always make things easy for those of us who try to describe it.

Within class Mammalia are about nineteen existing orders—nineteen rather specific adaptive strategies and resulting sets of characteristics. There are, for example, the flying bats; the fully aquatic whales and dolphins; the partially aquatic seals, sea lions, and walruses; two orders of hoofed plant eaters (the difference being a skeletal feature of the feet); the rabbits and hares; the rodents; the meat eaters; the insect eaters; the pouched marsupials (kangaroos and opposums); and a group of large-brained tree-dwellers with three-dimensional vision and dexterous hands. These last mammals are the members of order Primates.

All the species in Table 5.1 are primates, but they differ at the level of family. Humans traditionally have been classified in family Hominidae, while the other four are members of family Pongidae, the great apes. Within the pongids we recognize three *genera* (singular, *genus*). The only Asian species, the orangutan is placed in genus *Pongo.* The African gorilla, although similar to the other African apes, is different enough to be placed in a separate genus, *Gorilla.* The chimp and bonobo are recognized as two species within the same genus, *Pan.* A Linnaean taxonomy thus indicates the relative relationships among named organisms.

FIGURE 5.2 Evolutionary tree based on phenetic analysis. We infer the evolutionary relationships from the taxonomic classifications.

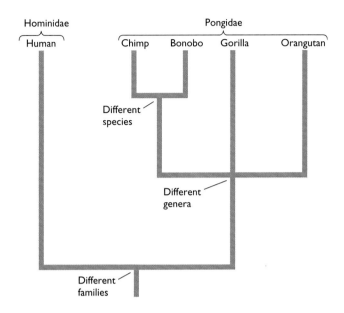

Linnaeus's goal was to describe the system that, as he believed, God had in mind when he created all the earth's living things. Linnaeus was a creationist, as were just about all scientists of his time. But as you can probably see, to modern scientists his taxonomy indicates not only present-day similarities and differences but evolutionary relationships as well. For example, the reason the chimp is more similar to the bonobo than to a human is that the chimp and bonobo diverged from each other more recently than they did from humans. The chimp and bonobo are thought to have had a common ancestor from which they split less than 1 mya. Humans and the chimp/bonobo line branched about 5 mya. Humans and chimps have had a longer time to evolve in different ways than have the bonobo and chimp, which is why they are more different and why they are placed in different taxonomic families.

So, a Linnaean taxonomy, or **phenetic taxonomy** (one based on existing phenotypic features and adaptations), can be translated into an evolutionary tree, showing the relative order of branching of the classified species and other **taxa** (categories; singular, *taxon*). Figure 5.2 shows an evolutionary tree derived from the classification of the five species in Table 5.1.

Cladistics

The tree in Figure 5.2 demonstrates the basis of a current debate within taxonomy. The tree was *inferred* from phenetic categories—physical comparisons of living species. Many such evolutionary trees prove quite accurate with regard to relative branching times and, thus, the overall pattern

phenetic taxonomy A classification system based on existing phenotypic features and adaptations.

taxon A category within a taxonomic classification.

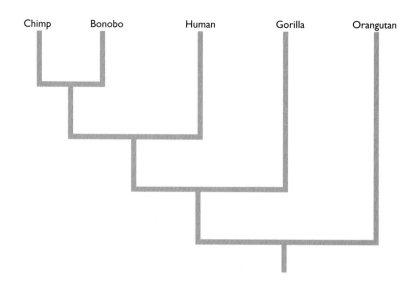

FIGURE 5.3 Accurate evolutionary tree based on cladistic analysis.

of branching. But as we learn more about the fossil ancestors of living species and as we improve our techniques of genetic comparison, we also learn more about the details of the evolutionary relationships among those species—particularly about the exact times and patterns of their evolutionary divergences.

Current knowledge from the fossil record and from genetic comparisons indicates that the orangutan line diverged earliest, the gorilla line next, and the human and chimp/bonobo lines most recently. In other words, the tree inferred from the phenetic taxonomy (see Figure 5.2) is inaccurate. The actual evolutionary tree should look like Figure 5.3. Thus, there is a contradiction between the traditional taxonomic names and categories for these species and their evolutionary relationships.

Cladistics (from *clade,* meaning "branch") works the opposite way from phenetics by starting with the evolutionary tree and placing organisms in taxonomic categories based on their order of branching, regardless of how their present-day appearances and adaptations might assort them into groups.

Branching order is determined in two ways. First, we use **shared derived characteristics.** If two groups share phenotypic features not found in other groups and if it can be supported that those features were derived from a common ancestor, the groups must be lumped into the same category at whatever taxonomic level is appropriate. For example, we could justify lumping birds with dinosaurs in the same taxon and placing reptiles in a different taxon because birds and dinosaurs share a feature of the pelvis not found in any other group, including reptiles. Second, branching order is determined by genetic comparison, now done at the level of the base sequence of the genetic code itself.

cladistics A classification system based on order of evolutionary branching rather than on present similarities and differences.

shared derived characteristics Phenotypic features shared by two or more taxonomic groups that are derived from a common ancestor and that are not found in other groups.

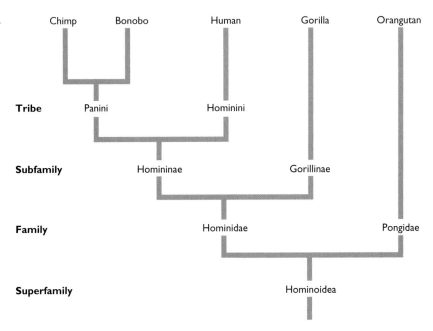

FIGURE 5.4 One possible taxonomic classification based on cladistic analysis. Note that new categories have had to be added.

What are the implications for the primates? Under a phenetic scheme (see Figure 5.2), there is a family division between hominids and pongids—in other words, between humans and apes. This is intuitively obvious since the four ape species resemble one another in some basic phenotypic features and adaptations more than they do us humans.

But in cladistics (Figure 5.4), there is no such thing as an "ape." There is no clade that *includes* the four great apes and *excludes* humans. Cladists have proposed a number of different taxonomies to reflect this. In one taxonomy, family Pongidae includes only the orangutan, and humans and the African apes are lumped into family Hominidae. Subfamily and tribe categories are then added to make further distinctions.

Is a phenetic or a cladistic system better? Phenetics captures obvious phenotypic and adaptive relationships but may fail to accurately reflect actual patterns of branching. Cladistics is evolutionarily accurate but requires redefinition of taxonomic categories that make sense in terms of obvious adaptive focuses. For instance, if we accept the preceding cladistic taxonomy, *hominid* is no longer restricted to "the **bipedal** primate" but now includes the **quadrupedal** chimps, bonobos, and gorillas. Its definition then becomes much more complex.

The debate continues, with no consensus in sight. Our own preference is to classify taxa by branching order (that is, cladistically) and then, although it can get wordy, describe the phenotypic and adaptive differences that may have arisen within a taxon and figure out why they arose. Having said that, however, we will stick with the traditional phenetic classification for the primates in this text. Our focus is to show how primate

bipedal Walking on two legs.

quadrupedal Walking on all four limbs.

species, especially the so-called higher primates, look and behave and how those looks and behaviors have evolved. It is simpler to start with phenetic categories because they are based on looks and adaptive behaviors and *then* see how categories change under cladistic analysis. We will discuss some examples as we continue.

Now, let's focus on the adaptive strategy and the phenotypic traits that characterize the members of order Primates.

The Primates

The essential primate environment is the trees; primates are arboreal, or tree-dwelling. The fact that the human species is obviously built for locomotion on the ground—and clearly not for moving around in the trees—should not be misinterpreted. Although among the primates we humans are exceptional for our mode of locomotion, our bodies and behaviors still reflect that arboreal theme.

There are, of course, many other arboreal creatures. Squirrels, birds, many insects, and even a few snakes all have adaptations for a tree-dwelling way of life. Primates don't have a monopoly on that environment, but they do adapt to it in a way none of these others do. It has obviously been a successful adaptation. For even now, with all the changes and disruptions to the natural environment brought about by the human primate, there are still about 200 species of primates spread pretty much worldwide—in Central and South America, Africa, Asia (including northern Japan), and Europe (on Gibraltar).

To examine the characteristics that make possible this arboreal adaptation, we'll use categories that reflect an organism's relationship to its environment: the senses, locomotion, reproduction, intelligence, and behavior patterns. Keep in mind that these are generalizations. Because of the large number of primate species and their wide geographical range, this order displays a good deal of variation, which we'll detail later.

The Senses

The world in which an organism lives is to a great extent determined by its senses. All the information a creature takes in about its environment comes through the sense organs, which send signals to the brain for interpretation and (if possible) storage. The predominance of one sense over the others can make an enormous difference. Sound rules the sensory world of a dolphin or a bat; smell predominates for dogs. The primate's world is a visual one.

Most primates see in color. Although many mammals are not entirely colorblind (dogs and cats can see some pastel tints), full color vision is rare. Primate eyes face forward instead of out to the sides, so that each eye sees just about the same scene as the other eye but from a slightly different

FIGURE 5.5 Stereoscopic vision. The fields of vision overlap, and the optic nerve from each eye travels to both hemispheres of the brain. The result is true depth perception.

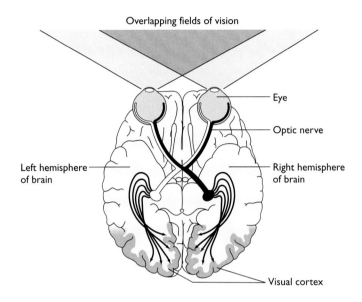

Overlapping fields of vision

Eye

Optic nerve

Left hemisphere of brain

Right hemisphere of brain

Visual cortex

angle. When the signals from such eyes are interpreted by the brain, the result is a world of three dimensions. Primates are said to have true depth perception, or **stereoscopic vision** (Figure 5.5). To protect their delicate muscles and nerves, primate eyes are enclosed in a bony socket.

This emphasis on the visual sense in primates seems connected to a reduction in the sensitivity of the other senses, at least as compared with many other mammals. Primates have neither the olfactory (smell) nor auditory (hearing) acuity of such familiar animals as dogs, cats, cattle, and horses. The areas of the primate brain that interpret these data are reduced in comparison with those of other mammals, and primates tend to have flat faces, reducing the olfactory receptor area within the nose. But no living creature, except possibly birds of prey, sees as well as we primates do.

Locomotion

Most mammals are quadrupedal; they walk on all fours. With the notable exception of humans, so do primates, but how they use their four limbs differs from other mammals. Whereas the limbs and feet of mammals in general are built for firm, solid contact with the ground (via hooves or paws with pads), primate limbs are highly flexible; the hands and, in many primates, the feet have the ability to grasp objects. Such hands and feet are said to be **prehensile** (Figure 5.6). Primates use this trait for several forms of locomotion. Some, called *vertical clingers and leapers,* jump from branch to branch or trunk to trunk, using the grasping ability of all four limbs. The apes are suspensory climbers with the ability to hang and climb by the arms. An extreme form of this mode of movement is **brachiation,**

stereoscopic vision Three-dimensional vision; depth perception.

prehensile The ability to grasp.

brachiate To swing through the trees using arms and hands.

swinging arm over arm through the trees (see Figure 5.15). When on the ground, most primates use all fours. Asia's orangutans walk on their fists. The African apes have a unique quadrupedalism, supporting themselves on the knuckles of their hands instead of the palms. Primate species may use one or more of these locomotor methods, depending on their anatomy and the situation.

Most primates also have some degree of **opposability**—the ability to touch the thumb to the tips of the other fingers on the same hand, enabling them to pick up small objects. And most primates have flat nails instead of claws on the ends of their fingers and toes. Nails lend support to the sensitive tactile receptors of the fingertips, and they don't get in the way as claws would when the hand is closed.

Reproduction

In contrast to many other mammals that bear litters or to fish and reptiles that may produce dozens of offspring at a time, nearly all primates have only a single offspring at a time. A small number of primate species normally

opposability The ability to touch the thumb to the tips of other digits on the same hand.

give birth to twins or triplets. As mammals, the primates take direct care of their young, protecting, nursing, showing affection, and (even if indirectly) teaching. Particularly because of their large, complex brains, primates take a long time to mature. This time is related to size, so a mouse lemur (which you could hold in the palm of your hand) grows up faster than a gorilla or a human. Relative to size, however, the primates have the longest period of **postnatal dependency** of all mammals.

Intelligence

Intelligence means the relative ability of an organism's brain to acquire, store, retrieve, and process information. To a great extent, these abilities are related to brain size. A bigger brain simply has more room for the neural connections that make it all work. (Brain-size variation *within* a species is another matter, which we'll mention later.) But intelligence is also related to the complexity of the brain—how many parts it has and the relative size of the parts—and to the brain's overall size relative to the organism's body. No primate has a brain the size of a whale's or an elephant's; when adjusted for body size, however, primates have the largest and most complex brains of all mammals.

The relatively large and absolutely more complex brains of primates allow them to take in, store, retrieve, and process more information in more complicated ways than other mammals. Primates are smart.

Behavior Patterns

Primates are social creatures. Most live in social groups, but even solitary primates interact with other species members in ways far more complex than would be found among, say, a herd of antelope. The difference is that primates (like some other mammals, especially social carnivores such as wolves and African lions) recognize individuals, and individuals each hold a certain status within a primate group. Some primates—baboons, for example—exhibit a form of **dominance hierarchy** in which individuals have differential social power and influence and, perhaps, access to mates. Nearly all primates recognize a special status for females with infants. Chimpanzees have varying attitudes about members of their group that can only be described by our human term *friendship*.

Much of the reason for this social structure stems from the long dependency period of the young. Born helpless and with much to learn about their world using large brains that take a long time to grow, primate babies need protection. With a close maternal bond to her infant—a bond common among all primates—the mother provides most of this protection. But especially in dangerous areas such as the open plains of Africa, the presence of a group adds greatly to the chance of successfully rearing offspring to become functioning members of the species' next generation.

postnatal dependency The period, after birth, of dependency on adults.

intelligence The relative ability to take in, store, access, and use information.

dominance hierarchy Individual differences in power, influence, and access to resources and mating.

FIGURE 5.7 Francois's langurs, monkeys from Southeast Asia, grooming. Grooming serves not only to rid the primates of parasites and dirt but also helps maintain group unity and harmony. (© *Noel Rowe*)

Care of offspring thus becomes another distinguishing feature of the primate behavior pattern.

Primate social systems are maintained through communication. Although only humans have a complex symbolic language, most primates have a large repertoire of signs and signals with specific meanings. These take the form of facial expressions, body movements, and vocalizations. Touch, usually through mutual **grooming** to remove dirt and parasites, is another form of communication common to most primates and seems to serve as a source of reassurance to maintain group harmony and unity (Figure 5.7).

Given this set of mutually reinforcing traits, the primates may be generally defined as arboreal mammals with a well-developed visual sense who, by virtue of a large, complex brain, complex social organization, and a long period of infant dependency with extensive and direct care of the young, adapt to life in the trees. They learn about, move with agility through, and manipulate this environment, with the last two abilities made possible by grasping and dexterous hands and feet.

A Primate Portfolio

For groups with numerous species and a variety of geographical locations and environmental niches, it is necessary to add to the basic seven Linnaean taxonomic categories (see Table 5.1).

Order **Primates** (Figure 5.8) is divided into two major groups, suborders **Prosimii** and **Anthropoidea**. Prosimians represent the most primitive

> **grooming** Cleaning the fur of another animal, a behavior that promotes social cohesion.

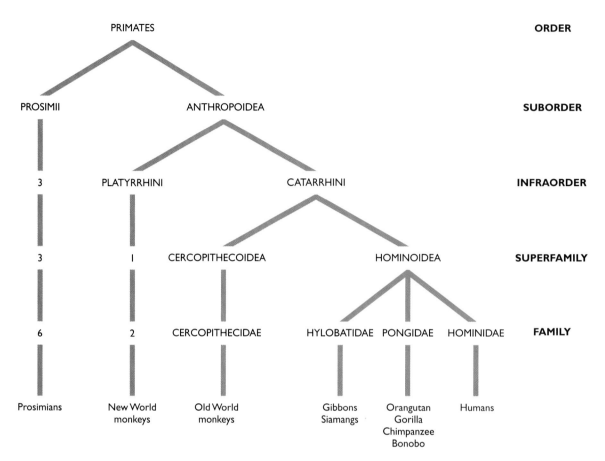

FIGURE 5.8 A traditional primate taxonomy. Numbers refer to living groups in that category. Alternative taxonomies exist.

primate. Biologically, the term *primitive* implies no value judgment but merely refers to age. Prosimians are said to be primitive because they most closely resemble the earliest primates as revealed by the fossil record discussed later in this chapter. As newer, more adaptively flexible primates evolved, the early prosimians were pushed into isolated, protected areas. Most prosimians now inhabit the island of Madagascar, which newer primates never reached, with other species on mainland Africa and India and on the isolated islands of Southeast Asia (Figure 5.9).

As a group, prosimians show some differences from the general primate pattern outlined in the last section (Figure 5.10, and see Figure 3.11). About half of the prosimians are **nocturnal.** These tend to live on mainland Africa and in Southeast Asia, where this adaptation helps them avoid competition with the **diurnal** anthropoid primates. As nocturnal creatures, prosimians have a better sense of smell than most primates. To aid this sense, they have a protruding snout with a large olfactory receptor area and a moist, naked nose (like a dog or cat) to help pick up molecules that provide olfactory signals.

nocturnal Active at night.

diurnal Active during the day.

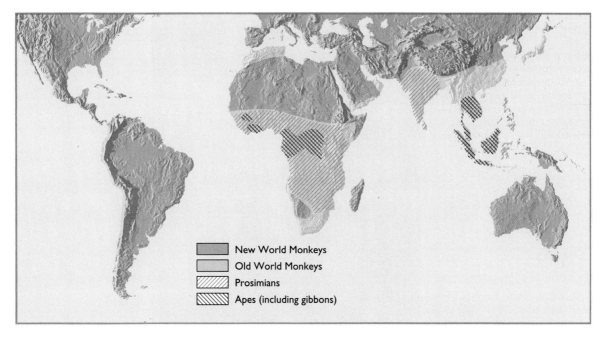

New World Monkeys
Old World Monkeys
Prosimians
Apes (including gibbons)

FIGURE 5.9 Distribution of the living primates.

Like nocturnal creatures everywhere, prosimians have large eyes to gather more light, but they have virtually no color vision because it's not useful at night. They do, however, have stereoscopic vision because, like all primates, they need to judge distances in bushes and trees. Many use this ability to catch insect prey.

Prosimians have prehensile hands and feet, but their opposability is different from the other primates. Rather than being able to touch the thumb to the other fingers on the same hand individually, the four other digits of prosimians (or three, as some prosimians lack an index finger) move together. In addition, some prosimians have claws on a couple of fingers or toes. These grooming claws are used for cleaning fur.

Prosimians spend most of their time in trees or, if they are small, in bushes. Their form of locomotion depends, of course, on their ability to grasp with their hands and feet the trunks and branches on which they are moving. The characteristic way many move about is vertical clinging and leaping—jumping from branch to branch in an upright position, pushing off with their legs and landing with both arms and legs. This trait differs from the behavior of other primates that "walk" one limb at a time through the trees, or brachiate, swinging arm over arm (see Figure 5.15).

A few of the Madagascar primates, the lemurs (see Figure 3.11), give birth to twins or even triplets on a regular basis. Transporting them seems to pose no problem because a male or older sibling often helps the mother take care of the babies. Some species also build nests in which offspring may be kept.

FIGURE 5.10 The slender loris, a prosimian from India and Sri Lanka. Note the large eyes and moist naked nose—adaptations to a nocturnal way of life. Note also the grooming claw, just visible on one toe in the foot at the top of the picture. Those typical primate prehensile hands and feet are easily seen. *(© Noel Rowe)*

A particularly interesting primate is the tarsier (Figure 5.11) of Southeast Asia, a small (4 or 5 ounces) primate noted for its powerful hindlimbs for leaping, enlarged fingertips and toetips for friction, ability to turn its head 180 degrees like an owl, and almost exclusively insect diet. Although traditionally classed as a prosimian, some authorities think it may be evolutionarily more closely related to members of the suborder Anthropoidea because, like all anthropoids, it lacks a moist, naked nose and has color vision.

The suborder Anthropoidea (meaning "humanlike") includes the monkeys, the apes, and the hominids (humans and human ancestors). It is divided into two infraorders, **Platyrrhini** and **Catarrhini.** This division is geographical, the platyrrhines (all monkeys) inhabiting the Western Hemisphere, or New World, and the catarrhines (monkeys, apes, and hominids) inhabiting the Eastern Hemisphere, or Old World.

The platyrrhines have several physical characteristics that distinguish them from the catarrhines (Figure 5.12). One distinguishing feature is the nose. *Platyrrhine* means "flat nose," and the noses of the New World mon-

FIGURE 5.11 The tarsier of Southeast Asia. Note the huge eyes (each eye is as big as the entire brain) for nocturnal vision, the powerfully built legs for jumping, and the enlarged finger and toe tips for friction. Grooming claws are also visible on some of the toes. (© *Noel Rowe*)

keys have widely spaced nostrils separated by a broad septum. Compare this with your own catarrhine nose, with its closely spaced nostrils that face downward. (We are considered Old World primates because that is where humans first evolved.) In addition, platyrrhine primates have more teeth than the catarrhines—twelve premolars or bicuspids compared to eight for the Old World primates (including humans). Because most New World monkeys are almost completely arboreal, they have evolved long limbs and long, curved clawlike nails; a few even have prehensile tails capable of grasping things and supporting their weight. No Old World primate has this kind of tail. Finally, one group of platyrrhines, the marmosets, normally gives birth to twins.

Referring to Figure 5.8, we see that the Old World primates are divided into two superfamilies. The monkeys of Europe, Africa, and Asia make up superfamily **Cercopithecoidea** and family **Cercopithecidae**. The apes and humans comprise superfamily **Hominoidea**.

Within the cercopithecids are two subfamilies and about a dozen genera with numerous individual species. These monkeys have the nasal

FIGURE 5.12 The northern woolly spider monkey, a platyrrhine primate from Brazil. Note the prehensile tail with the bare strip of skin on the inner surface to enhance grasping ability. (© *Noel Rowe*)

shape and tooth number of Old World primates, and most have tails, though none are prehensile. Males tend to be larger than females, unlike the New World species, which show little sexual dimorphism. The cercopithecids have fully opposable thumbs (also unlike the platyrrhines). In general, the monkeys of the Eastern Hemisphere seem more adaptively flexible. One large genus, **Macaca,** has representative species all the way from North Africa to India to the mountains of northern Japan, where they are called "snow monkeys" (Figure 5.13).

Another genus, **Papio,** is of particular interest to us because it contains most of the baboons, the large, long-snouted monkeys of the African savannas (Figure 5.14; see also Figures 6.2 and 6.3). This is an important environment for the early evolution of our lineage. The savannas are nearly the same today as when early hominids lived on them. By observing the adaptations of another primate to the same environment, we may get some idea of how our ancestors survived. We'll discuss this topic in detail in Chapter 6.

Superfamily Hominoidea, the large, tailless primates, is made up of three families. Family **Hylobatidae** includes the gibbons and siamangs of Southeast Asia and Malaysia, sometimes referred to as the "lesser apes" because they are smaller than the African apes. These species are especially

FIGURE 5.13 Japanese macaques, or "snow monkeys," are well adapted to life in cold, mountainous areas, even to the point of warming themselves in volcanic hot springs. (© *Steven Kaufman/Peter Arnold, Inc.*)

noted for their brachiating form of locomotion (Figure 5.15). To aid in this movement, the arms of gibbons and siamangs are much longer and more powerful than their legs and end in hands with short thumbs and long, hooklike fingers. The hylobatids have, for the primates, an unusual social group: male and female are monogamous, establish and defend a territory, and may even help their offspring set up a territory.

Family **Pongidae** comprises the "great apes," of which there are four living species: the orangutan of Southeast Asia (genus **Pongo**) and three African species—the chimpanzee and the bonobo (genus **Pan**), and the gorilla (genus **Gorilla**) (Figure 5.16). These are the most robust primates, heavy-boned with large, powerful jaws and chewing muscles used for eating a wide range of fruits and vegetables and, in the case of the genus *Pan*,

FIGURE 5.14 A group of gelada baboons on the grasslands of Ethiopia. *(© Brand X Pictures/ PunchStock)*

FIGURE 5.15 White-handed gibbon from Southeast Asia suspended by one arm. Notice the long, hooklike fingers and that it is also grasping with its feet. *(© Noel Rowe)*

FIGURE 5.16 The great apes (*clockwise from top left*): the orangutan of Southeast Asia and the gorilla, bonobo, and chimpanzee of Africa. (*Orangutan: © Noel Rowe; Bonobo: © Ron Garrison/The Zoological Society of San Diego; Gorilla: M. A. Park; Chimpanzee: © Steve Turner/Animals Animals/Earth Scenes*)

meat. The apes are essentially quadrupeds. Chimps and gorillas spend a large portion of their time on the ground, whereas the orangutan spends almost all of its time in the trees. In fact, the orangutan is so well adapted to arboreal locomotion that its feet look and function like two additional hands. All the great apes are built like brachiators, with large and powerful shoulders and arms, but they are too large to do much traveling in this fashion. Though predominantly quadrupedal, the apes can and do walk upright on occasion, usually when they want to look around or carry something. These two specific benefits made possible by the ability to stand upright may have been crucial in the evolution of a primate that could stand—and move about—habitually, as we will discuss in Chapter 8.

Orangutans are solitary, but chimps, bonobos, and gorillas live in social units marked by a changing group membership, loose organization, and some degree of dominance recognition. Because the apes don't live in areas that present the dangers faced by savanna primates, dominance and its recognition may be even looser and more flexible than among baboons.

Apes have large brains, some measuring about half the size of the smallest modern human brains. Many features of the anatomy of pongid brains are also similar to those of humans. Apes are intelligent. They have, for example, a vast knowledge of a great number of food sources. Because many of these foods are fruits, they need to be aware of seasonal changes so they can be at the right place when the fruits ripen, a cognitive behavior found also in some monkeys.

Chimpanzees can even make simple tools. Their most well-known tools are the "termite fishing sticks" they make from twigs and blades of grass. They stick these down termite holes, wiggle them around, and draw out a meal of termites that have attacked the "invader" by clinging to it with their powerful pinchers (Figure 5.17). This is a cultural behavior: it is learned. It also involves abstract concepts; the chimps must visualize the tool within the bush or grass as well as the behavior of the unseen termites. It involves an **artifact**—a natural object consciously modified for a specific purpose. This tool-using behavior also differs from individual to individual and from group to group, with each chimp having a raw material that is her favorite (usually only females perform this activity). Most chimp troops don't do it at all, a sure sign that the behavior is learned rather than genetic. And among chimps that do make tools, different groups have different styles. Humans are clearly not the sole possessors of cultural behaviors.

Chimps are also known to hunt small mammals, including young baboons, which they capture with their hands, kill by biting through the back of the skull or neck, and then tear apart with their hands and teeth. In some groups, just one chimp—nearly always a male—does the hunting and killing, but in other groups it is a cooperative venture that appears to have some sort of group strategy. The meat acquired is the one food that chimps share with one another. Bonobos also hunt and eat meat, although less often.

artifact A natural object consciously modified for a specific purpose.

FIGURE 5.17 Chimps using tools they have made to extract termites from a mound. (*Jane Goodall/ National Geographic Society*)

Like all primates, apes use vocalizations, facial expressions, and body language to communicate. They have nothing like a human language, but, because of their complex ecological niches and rich social lives—not to mention the large, complex brains they have correspondingly evolved—they are capable of learning the rudiments of human language. Chimps, gorillas, and orangutans have been taught to use various symbolic representations of language, most notably American Sign Language for the hearing impaired (Ameslan), because these species lack the vocal apparatus to make the full range of human sounds. Some researchers claim that these apes can communicate at about the level of a 4- or 5-year-old human, linking words in grammatically correct ways. Others refute this, saying the apes are only mimicking their trainers. This research remains controversial, although most evidence seems to point to some elementary linguistic ability on the part of our closest relatives.

The other family within the hominoids, **Hominidae,** includes living humans, all of whom belong to the same genus and species, *Homo sapiens.* Humans of the past, when at times several genera and species existed, also belong to family Hominidae, the hominids.

The Human Primate

It should now be clear that humans are primates. We share with some 200 other living species a common set of basic physical and behavioral traits. Each primate species, though, has its own unique expression of the primate adaptation. Humans are no exception; our expression of the primate adaptation involves not being arboreal at all. Let's review the five categories discussed earlier and see how we compare.

1. The senses.   Our sensory organs are basically the same as those of the anthropoid monkeys and apes. Sense of smell seems exactly the same. Monkeys can hear higher sound frequencies than we can, but we are more sensitive to changes in pitch and intensity. Color vision is the same in humans, apes, and monkeys, except that humans may be more sensitive to slight differences in colors than monkeys. It is possible, though, that this may be because we have assigned cultural names to slightly different shades of color and so recognize them because we have learned them. It has also been suggested that we can distinguish many colors because we can concentrate harder on such tasks (Passingham 1982). In general, in terms of the five senses, humans, apes, and monkeys perceive the same world.

2. Locomotion.   The most striking physical difference between us and the other primates is the way we move about. We are the only primate that is habitually bipedal, walking on two feet. The bones of our back, pelvis, legs, and feet are all structured to balance us and hold us erect (see Figure 8.12). Our musculature has evolved to serve the same purpose. Even the rather spherical shape of our head, as opposed to the more elongated heads of other primates, may have evolved in part to be more balanced atop a vertical spine. Because our legs are the limbs of locomotion, they are longer and more muscular than our arms—just the opposite of apes. Completely freed from locomotor functions, our hands have become organs of manipulation. We have the most precise opposability of the primates, facilitated by the longest and relatively strongest primate thumb.

3. Reproduction.   Like nearly all primates, we normally have one offspring at a time. Though we are not the largest primate (gorillas are), we have the longest period of dependency and maturation. Chimps, for example, reach sexual maturity in about nine years and physical maturity in about twelve years. For us, the averages are thirteen years and twenty-one years. Not only do we grow up more slowly, we are born relatively more immature and helpless than other primates, so we get off to a late start.

4. Intelligence.   We are clearly the most intelligent primate because we can store and process more information in more complex ways than the others. Our cultural behavior—our languages, societies, abstract belief systems, scientific knowledge—attests to these abilities. Our intellect is made possible by our big brain, the result of and reason for the extended period of growth after our immature births. Although some primates, such as squirrel monkeys from South America, have larger brains relative to body size than ours, our brains are still three times the size expected for a primate of our body mass. In absolute terms, our brains are larger and more complex than any primate's. Especially large is our **neocortex**, the outer layer of the brain where abstract thought, problem solving, and attentiveness take place (Figure 5.18).

neocortex The part of the brain responsible for memory and thought.

5. Behavior patterns.   Like most primates, humans live in social groups that are made up of individuals with differential identities and statuses.

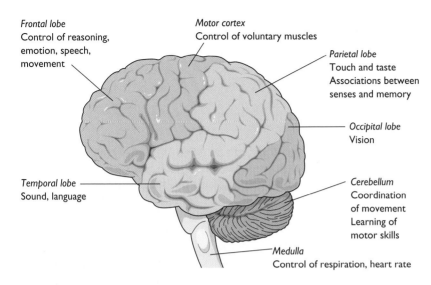

Frontal lobe
Control of reasoning, emotion, speech, movement

Motor cortex
Control of voluntary muscles

Parietal lobe
Touch and taste
Associations between senses and memory

Occipital lobe
Vision

Temporal lobe
Sound, language

Cerebellum
Coordination of movement
Learning of motor skills

Medulla
Control of respiration, heart rate

FIGURE 5.18 The human brain, with major parts and their functions. The lobes and motor cortex are all part of the neocortex.

The difference is that human groups are structured and maintained by cultural values—ideas, rules, and behavioral norms we have created and share through complex communication systems.

Our big brains have allowed us to move well beyond purely biological evolutionary processes. Certainly, natural selection brought about the evolution of our big brains in the first place, but the way in which this organ functioned permitted us to think up answers to the problems of our survival. As human societies moved around and encountered varying environmental situations and other human groups, these answers became so complex that strikingly different social systems evolved. In a sense, culture became our environment, to which we responded with still newer cultural ideas, systems, and artifacts.

Chimps may exhibit some cultural behaviors, may be able to learn to use the basic features of human language, and may differ from us genetically by approximately 2 percent of their genes, but our behavior—the extent to which we use and indeed rely on culture—is very different from that of the other primates.

Genetics and Primate Relationships

Physical features are controlled by a complex interaction of genetic loci, evolutionary processes, and environmental factors. Therefore, trying to examine evolutionary relationships based solely on physical traits can be misleading. A trait may look the same in two organisms, but the expressions of the trait may be based on very different genetic and developmental processes, and the traits themselves may differ in their adaptive significance.

A famous example (Gould 1980) is the "thumb" of the panda, a bear. It looks very much like the thumb of many primates, but its use is specialized: it enables the panda to handle and strip the leaves off bamboo stalks. And it's not a finger at all but an elongated wrist bone.

Some investigators asked, then, would it not be more informative to look at the genes themselves—or at least at the immediate products of the genes? Two organisms with similar genes must certainly be closely related evolutionarily.

In the 1960s, Vincent Sarich and Allan Wilson of the University of California at Berkeley pioneered research along just such lines (Sarich 1971). They compared the blood proteins of a number of organisms, with the goal of quantifying similarities and differences. Blood proteins such as albumin are large, easy to work with, and made up of amino acids—the immediate products of the genes. Sarich and Wilson's research indicated that the blood proteins of humans and chimpanzees are almost identical.

But there was an even more startling inference from this research. Sarich and Wilson wondered if their figures might provide a relative idea not only of evolutionary distance but also of the timing of the evolutionary split. Because evolution involves the accumulation of mutations, the differences between two species in a genetic product such as albumin might act as a "clock" if the mutations causing those differences take place at a fairly constant rate and if we can then figure out how many of those mutations take place over a certain period of time.

Comparing species whose time of divergence was well established from the fossil record, Sarich and Wilson concluded that the small difference in blood proteins between chimps and humans corresponded to an evolutionary separation of only 5 million years. At the time, the accepted date for the divergence of our two lineages stood at between 12 and 15 million years. Based on the "protein clock," Sarich said that no primate that old could be a hominid no matter what it looked like. He was right.

Other types of genetic comparisons yielded the same basic results. Comparisons of the amino acid sequence of certain blood proteins such as hemoglobin among primates showed a difference of 2.8 percent between humans and orangutans, and the amazingly low figures of 0.6 percent for humans compared with gorillas and 0.3 percent for humans compared with chimpanzees. Another method that compares the bonding reaction between DNA of different species showed humans and chimpanzees to have nearly the same DNA.

Yet another method, one that gives visible results, involves comparing patterns of bands appearing on chromosomes treated with certain dyes that show areas of active genes (Figure 5.19). Eighteen of the twenty-three pairs of human chromosomes are virtually identical to chromosomes of chimpanzees. Moreover, although chimps have twenty-four pairs of chromosomes, it appears as if one of our chromosomes may have been derived from two of theirs (the far left comparison in Figure 5.19).

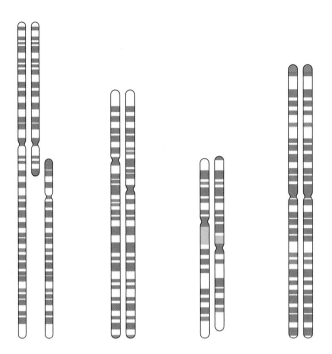

FIGURE 5.19 Human chromosomes, on the left in each pair, compared to those of chimpanzees. The similarities in banding pattern are clear. In the far lefthand pair, the pattern of human chromosome 2 is similar to that of two chimp chromosomes. The far righthand pair are virtually identical. This is one piece of evidence for the 98 percent genetic similarity between our two species.

Now, recent technology has allowed us to look at and compare the most basic genetic components—the sequence of base pairs that make up the codons, which in turn make up the genes. This is the same technology that is applied to the investigation of criminal and missing-person cases. For example, blood samples from crime scenes can be genetically compared with samples from suspects, virtually assuring accurate identifications. DNA sequencing also helps in locating genes involved in various diseases. And, relative to our topic here, we can now precisely compare the genetic makeup of primate species, establishing just how genetically similar or different they are and, using the logic described above, estimate how long ago their evolutionary lines diverged. There has even been an attempt to reconstruct the ancestral genome of all living primates (O'Brien and Stanyon 1999).

To be sure, until we can compare *all* the base pairs of the species in which we're interested, there will be some differences in the estimated relationships. Comparisons of different sections of the genomes may yield slightly different results. But this new technology is accurate enough that we are, for example, confident in the 2 percent genetic difference identified between humans and chimpanzees and of the evolutionary branching pattern that has been genetically determined for the hominoids.

An interesting new question that has resulted from these studies is the matter of just *which* genes differ between humans and chimpanzees and *what* those genes do. In other words, what genetic differences make chimps chimps and humans humans? Recent studies suggest that the difference may be as few as 50 coding genes (out of an estimated 100,000) (Wade 1998) and that one of those differences—a 92-base pair section of a single gene—leads to humans' lack of a certain chemical on the surface of all body cells that all other mammals, including the apes, possess (Gibbons 1998b; Muchmore et al. 1998; Normile 2001). The results of this difference are still being investigated, but it is known that the chemical acts as a receptor for messages from other cells, is used by pathogens to attach to a cell, and, importantly, may be involved in cellular communication during brain development and function, something that could influence the timing and extent of brain growth. This last function has obvious implications for the story of human evolution.

Another specific difference is in some genes for enzymes called *proteases,* which are important to the immune system. This could explain why chimps are less severely affected by some diseases such as AIDS and Alzheimer's. And most recently, a difference between nonhuman primates and humans has been located on a gene for a protein important in the building of some jaw muscles. Because of a mutation, the human version of the gene is inactivated, resulting in reduced muscle fibers and even a reduced size of some jaw muscles (Stedman et al. 2004). Moreover, the origin of this mutation has been placed at about 2.4 mya, a date, as we shall see, that is about the time of the first fossils identified as belonging to our genus, *Homo.*

In addition to these specific differences, it has also been established that five chromosomes in our two species show significant differences in the arrangement of the same genes. Some sequences, for example, have been flipped (or inverted) in one species as compared to the other. These changes could lead to different roles for those genes. Identifying their functions is a current goal, as is the establishment of a primate genome project to provide a complete sequence of the genomes of our closest relatives (Gibbons 1998b).

The Evolution of the Primates

To say that the fossil record of the early primates is confusing is to understate the case. There are a large number of fossil specimens of primates, but, as one authority notes, 65 percent of extinct primate species are based on fossils that are "extremely fragmentary," mostly pieces of jaw or sometimes just teeth (Martin 1990:39). Although one extinct species may be represented by many specimens, fossils of its contemporaries are lacking, giving us little basis for comparison. For certain periods of primate evolution, all fossils are found in one or two locations. Still, we have been able to piece together the basic picture of the primate evolutionary story (Figure 5.20).

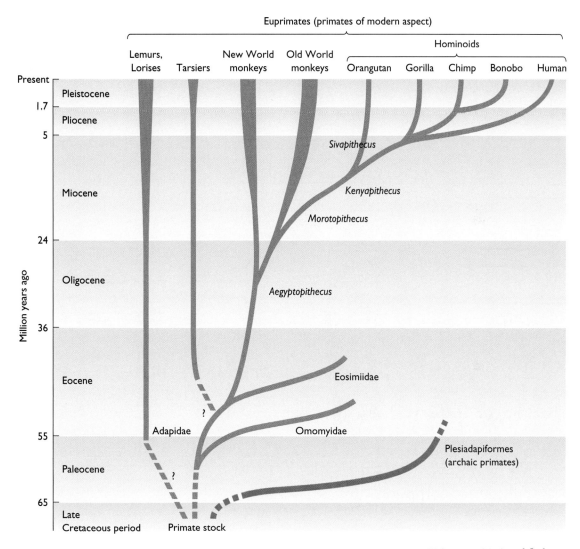

FIGURE 5.20 Simplified evolutionary tree for the primates, with major geological epochs and dates. Question marks and dashed lines indicate insufficient data to establish evolutionary relationships. This tree represents one of several possible interpretations.

Very little exists to tell us about the beginnings of the primates. Some genetic comparisons, such as those described in the last section, point to the origin of the primates at 90 to 80 mya, well back into the time of the dinosaurs (Gibbons 1998a; Tavaré et al. 2002). In terms of hard evidence, a few primatelike teeth from Montana dated at 65 mya and some bones from Wyoming from 60 mya show primatelike anatomical features related to climbing. Remember that at that time, North America and Europe were still very close together and possibly still connected in some locations (see Figure 3.6), so the primates probably originated on the large northern

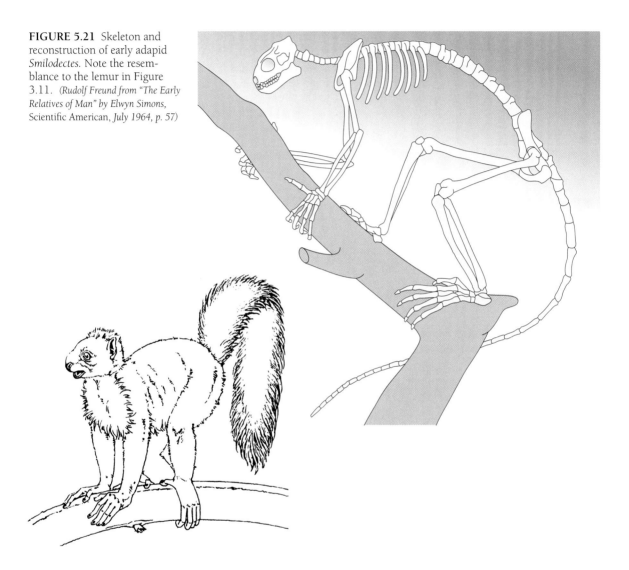

FIGURE 5.21 Skeleton and reconstruction of early adapid *Smilodectes*. Note the resemblance to the lemur in Figure 3.11. *(Rudolf Freund from "The Early Relatives of Man" by Elwyn Simons, Scientific American, July 1964, p. 57)*

landmass called Laurasia. It is not until about 55 mya that fossils of undisputed primates are found.

The traits of modern primates that we associate with an arboreal adaptation may not have first evolved specifically to facilitate that adaptation. Anthropologist Matt Cartmill (1992) suggests that prehensile extremities and stereoscopic vision may have evolved to aid leaping as a means of locomotion in the forest canopy or the shrub-layer undergrowth and to promote fruit eating and "visually directed predation" on insects. Some modern primates such as the tarsier (see Figure 5.11) track insects by sight and seize them by hand. As the early primates evolved, then, these basic traits also proved a useful adaptive theme for life in the trees in general.

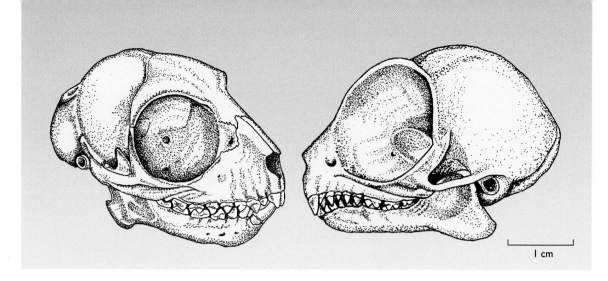

FIGURE 5.22 Comparison of fossil omomyid *Necrolemur* (left) with modern tarsier. *(From R. D. Martin,* Primate Origins, *p. 61 © 1989. Reproduced with permission of Kluwer Academic Publishers)*

Some new fossil finds from Wyoming (Bloch and Boyer 2002; Sargis 2002)—representing several families of **Plesiadapiformes,** an extinct branch of archaic primates (as opposed to the euprimates, or primates of modern aspect)—clearly show features related to grasping, indicating that that adaptation evolved early in primate evolution.

The early primate fossils come in two groups, and both have been found in North America, Europe, Asia, and Africa. One group, the lemur-like **Adapidae** (Figure 5.21), is thought to be ancestral to modern lemurs and lorises. The other group, the tarsierlike **Omomyidae** (Figure 5.22), which may date back to 60 mya, may be ancestral to both tarsiers and anthropoids. A recently discovered group, the **Eosimiidae** from Asia, appears to represent the more direct ancestors of monkeys, apes, and hominids (Gebo et al. 2000; Jaeger et al. 1999; Kay et al. 1997). Important evolutionary shifts that mark the origin of the anthropoids were changes from a nocturnal lifestyle to a diurnal one, from less leaping to more climbing through the trees with all fours, and from an insect-based diet to a more herbivorous diet. (How we can discern such changes among often fragmentary fossils is a topic we'll discuss in Chapter 7.)

By the time the omomyids were moving into Asia, the Eastern and Western Hemispheres were separate. The New World has so far offered virtually no fossil evidence to tell us what happened next. It may be that the prosimian forms that ended up in the New World moved into South America once it joined North America and evolved into the present-day platyrrhine monkeys. A second view is that prosimian evolution got no farther in the Western Hemisphere and that early monkeys from the Old World "rafted" over to South America, floating on logs and branches, or crossed over on a chain of volcanic islands when South America and Africa were still fairly close together. The degree of physical similarity among all modern anthropoids suggests a single origin and so argues for the second scenario, as does a recent find of a 25- to 27-million-year-old monkey from Bolivia (Takai et al. 2000) whose teeth are very similar to an older

FIGURE 5.23 Skull of *Aegyptopithecus* from the Fayum in Egypt, considered an early monkeylike form that may be ancestral to later Old World monkeys and apes. (© *David L. Brill 1985/Brill Atlanta*)

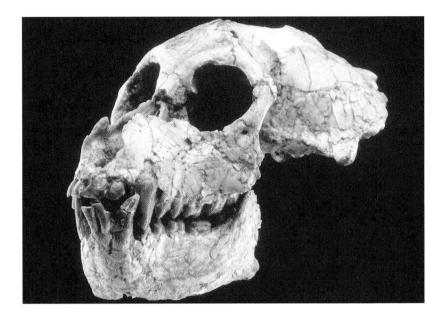

fossil form from Egypt, suggesting that the New World monkeys originated and diversified first in Africa. That this scenario is plausible is demonstrated by a report (Yoon 1998) of fifteen iguanas (large lizards) floating on a huge raft of trees 200 miles from the Caribbean island of Guadeloupe, where this particular species was native, to the island of Anguilla, where they had not previously been found. They are established and reproducing in their new habitat.

Much of the early evolutionary history of the Old World monkeys themselves is known from a single site, though it has yielded a large number of fossils. This is a desert depression, the remains of an ancient lake southwest of Cairo, Egypt, called the Fayum. New evidence has recently come from other sites in Africa and Southwest Asia. For more detail on this complex period of primate evolution, see Benefit 1999 and Simons and Rasmussen 1994.

From the Fayum come a number of monkeylike forms dated 40 to 25 mya, perhaps the best known of which is **Aegyptopithecus** (Figure 5.23) dated at 34 mya. From its postcranial skeletal remains, this anthropoid of about 10 pounds seems to have been an arboreal quadruped. It shows a number of features of the teeth, brain, and skull that resemble those of the later hominoids, the apes and humans. *Aegyptopithecus* may be an early ancestor of the hominoids, although it is still primitive enough to be ancestral to the modern Old World monkeys as well.

Definite apes appeared beginning about 23 mya and became more numerous over the next 10 to 15 million years. We refer to these as "dental apes" because their teeth have the characteristics of modern apes. Their bodies, though, are distinctly different. Do not get the impression that modern-looking chimpanzees were running around in these very ancient times. The classification of these primates as apes is based on a number of physical features, the most important of which is a trait of the molar teeth found only in modern hominoids and no other primate—the Y-5 cusp pattern (Figure 5.24).

Between 23 and 5 mya, there were an estimated thirty or more different types of apes—larger-bodied, tailless, larger-brained primates. Only one lineage, however, gave rise to modern apes and hominids. Evidence is scanty, but new fossil finds point to two African forms as candidates for the earliest hominoid. **Kenyapithecus,** from around 15 mya, has some modern ape features of the jaw, face, and teeth. Newer fossils, placed by some into a new genus, **Equatorius** (Ward et al. 1999), indicate similarities in the arm and ankle bones that are related to the modern chimpanzee's abilities to hang in trees and to rotate the foot, which permits walking flat-footed on the ground and grasping (McCrossin 1997).

A more ancient and more arboreal form, **Morotopithecus** from Uganda, dated at 20 mya, also shows similarities. It has a mobile shoulder joint that would have aided in hanging from trees by the arms, as chimps and orangs do, and vertebrae that suggest a short, stiff spine, a feature of modern apes that allows them occasional upright posture (Gebo et al. 1997).

Starting about 12 mya, we find fossils of more ground-dwelling, open-country apes, whose larger back teeth with thicker enamel point to a more mixed vegetable diet that included harder foods such as nuts. Fossils of these apes have been found in Africa, India, Pakistan, China, Turkey, Hungary, and Greece. One group from India and Pakistan, **Sivapithecus,** shares features with the modern orangutan and so is most likely an ancestor of that species or closely related to it (Figure 5.25). A new form from Turkey, **Ankarapithecus,** dated at 9.8 mya, also shows similarities to this group.

Another form, however, **Ouranopithecus,** so far only found in Greece and dated at 10 to 9 mya, shares some features with hominids. Though clearly an ape, about the size of a female gorilla, it is thought by some to be a member of the ape line that eventually led to the hominids (DeBonis and Koufos 1994).

Yet another interesting fossil form in this general group is a giant ape from China, Vietnam, and northern India called **Gigantopithecus.** So far, only its massive jaws and teeth have been found, but estimates from these indicate that it may have been 10 to 12 feet tall when standing upright and weighed from 700 to 1,200 pounds. It lived from 7 mya to perhaps as recently as 300,000 ya. Evidence from its teeth indicates that, like the gorilla, it was a vegetarian. Certain features of the teeth link it to the sivapithecid group.

Current evidence indicates, then, that the apes evolved in Africa and diverged into a number of evolutionary lines all over the Old World. Gradually, these lines decreased, leaving relatively few forms to evolve into the

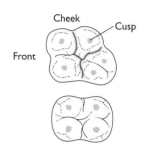

FIGURE 5.24 Y-5 cusp pattern found only in hominoids (*top*), and the four-cusp pattern found in all anthropoids. The chewing surface is shown. A look in the mirror will probably give you a firsthand glimpse of a Y-5 tooth, but not all molars of all hominoids show this feature.

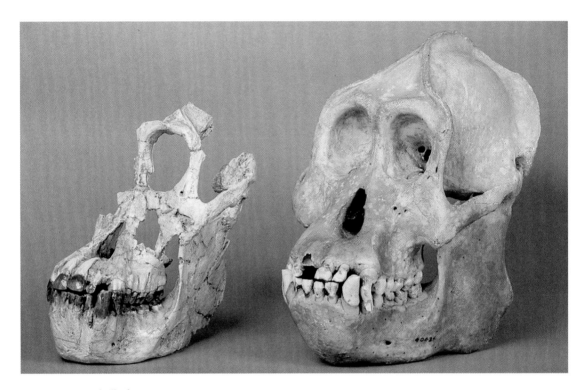

FIGURE 5.25 Skull of
Sivapithecus (left) compared
to modern orangutan. They
are essentially identical.
*(From Dr. Ian Tattersall, American Museum of Natural History,
The Human Odyssey, 1993)*

modern hominoids. One line that we are fairly certain of is that from *Sivapithecus* to modern orangutans. Some African form—or an African population of that form—gave rise to the line leading to modern African apes and the hominids. This is the subject of Chapter 8.

Summary

One important tool for learning about the past is an understanding of the results of the events that made up the past. By determining our place in nature and our relationships with other primates, we can see what the present-day products are of the 65 million years (or more) of primate evolution. This gives us a road map for journeying into the past and looking at our other tool, the fossil record.

Humans are among some 200 species of living primates. In many ways, we are typical of this group—with three-dimensional color vision; prehensile, opposable hands; emphasis on social groups; a long period of dependency shown by single-birth offspring; and the intelligence and flexibility of our brains for dealing with our world.

In other ways, however, we are atypical primates. We are not arboreal. Our feet are not prehensile but are built to support the entire weight of our upright locomotion. We have especially dexterous hands with long, strong opposable thumbs. We take the longest time of any primate to mature, and we have the largest, most complex brains. Finally, we rely for our very survival on one of the products of those brains: our culture.

The primate fossil record is a complex one that may stretch back to the time of the dinosaurs. Much remains to be explained, especially about the early stages of primate evolution. Clearly, though, our group, the hominids, is a late arrival on the primate scene, splitting off from the African apes a mere 6 to 5 mya.

Study Questions

1. What is our place in nature; that is, where do we humans fit—from a scientific point of view—in the world of living things? How does taxonomy help us describe our place in nature?
2. What are the characteristics of the members of the primate order?
3. What are the different groups of primates? What are their characteristics, basic behaviors, and geographical distribution?
4. In what ways are humans like the other primates? In what ways are we unique?
5. What is the genetic evidence for our relationship with the other primates?
6. What is the basic story of primate evolution?

Key Terms

taxonomy	bipedal	intelligence
notochord	quadrupedal	dominance hierarchy
phenetic taxonomy	stereoscopic vision	grooming
taxon	prehensile	nocturnal
cladistics	brachiate	diurnal
shared derived	opposability	artifact
characteristics	postnatal dependency	neocortex

For More Information

An excellent book that examines humans as an animal species is Richard Passingham's *The Human Primate*. Perhaps the major reference work on the nonhuman primates is *The Natural History of the Primates* by J. R. and P. H. Napier. The National Geographic Society's *The Great Apes: Between Two Worlds,* by M. J. Nichols and colleagues, discusses not only the four species of apes but also talks about the scientific studies conducted on

CONTEMPORARY ISSUE
What Is the Status of Our Closest Relatives?

In a nutshell, the answer is, not good. The International Union for Conservation of Nature and Natural Resources (www.redlist.org) recognizes 296 species of primates.* Of these, 20 are listed as "critically endangered," 48 as "endangered," 46 as "vulnerable," and 47 as "near threatened." The rest are "lower risk/ conservation dependent," "least concern," or "data deficient" (none of which are necessarily good signs).

And it's getting progressively worse, especially in Africa and especially among the great apes. An estimated 80 percent of the world's gorillas and most chimpanzees live in the West African countries of Gabon and the Republic of Congo. In Gabon, the populations of those species have decreased by more than half over the last twenty years. Two-thirds of the gorillas in a sanctuary in Congo died in 2003. At its present rate of decline, the bonobo will be extinct in the wild in a decade. In the mountains east of those countries, the population of the rare mountain gorilla (made famous by the book and film *Gorillas*

*There are not that many acknowledged species, so some of these are certainly named subspecies.

in the Mist) is thought to be down to fewer than 650 individuals.

What is causing this disastrous decline? Worldwide, we humans threaten the primates, as well as other endangered species, through our overpopulation, depletion of resources, warfare, habitat destruction, pollution, hunting, and other direct exploitation of innumerable species, both plant and animal. In the case of the African apes, the effects of hunting have been recently exacerbated by the "bushmeat" trade, targeting any number of large native animals, including chimpanzees, bonobos, and gorillas. The encroachment of logging and mining into these animals' habitats (particularly in Congo, which is rich in coltan, an ore used in the production of cell phones and laptops) has brought an influx of workers who subsist on the meat of whatever animals are available to hunt, whether endangered or not. Elsewhere, local peoples in need of food in their poverty-stricken countries are also turning to hunting. And most egregiously, and the main motivation for hunting, there is a lucrative commercial market for bushmeat in African cities and towns as well as abroad. Some believe that hunting caused the first recorded primate

them in the wild and the dangers they now face from their closest primate relative. For an informative and beautifully illustrated book on the primate order, see Noel Rowe's *The Pictorial Guide to the Living Primates*. Most of the primate photos in this chapter were taken from that book.

More on the linguistic abilities of the apes can be found in "Chimpanzee Sign Language Research" in *The Nonhuman Primates,* by Phyllis Dolhinow and Agustín Fuentes.

On the importance of brain size, see the interesting article in the December 1999–January 2000 issue of *Natural History* by Göran E. Nilsson, "The Cost of a Brain."

For the evolution of the primates up to the hominids, see John G. Fleagle's *Primate Adaptation and Evolution*. The story of *Gigantopithecus* is extinction—of the wonderfully named Miss Waldron's red colobus, an African monkey.

Related to the bushmeat trade is a serious threat to humans—the virus that causes Ebola, the hemorrhagic fever whose origin is still unknown (Walsh et al. 2003). Ebola decimated the gorillas at the sanctuary in Congo and is now spreading toward a national park that has one of the largest, densest ape populations in the world. Outbreaks of the disease in apes coincide with outbreaks in human populations, so it is likely that humans are contracting Ebola from apes, largely as a result of hunting and eating them. It's unclear whether the apes are transmitting the disease to one another or are, because there are more and more humans in the forests, being forced into closer contact with the source of the virus (hypothesized to be bats, mice, or birds). But we do know that outbreaks have occurred among apes in regions remote from human habitation as well.

The debate now centers on what action to take. Walsh and his colleagues (2003) recommend that the apes' status be changed from "endangered" to "critically endangered." They also suggest that only a "massive investment" in law enforcement to prevent hunting will stem the bushmeat trade. As for Ebola, some have suggested transporting apes to a safe area or otherwise dividing infected groups from noninfected groups. If, however, the apes are continually contracting the disease from its still-unknown source, these measures won't do much. There is an experimental vaccine that works on monkeys, but it still requires testing, and administering it to wild animals would be a difficult task.

The prospects, in other words, don't look good—either for the apes of West Africa or, in the long run, for the world's other primates and all the other endangered species of life. At times, the situation seems hopeless, but various organizations are working tirelessly to prevent the local zoo from ultimately being the *only* place to see the apes and other species. For more information on the crisis, what is being done, and how we can help, see http://pin.primate.wisc.edu and click on "Conservation" under the heading "About the Primates." Also see www.unep.org/grasp for information on the United Nations Great Apes Survival Project. To paraphrase Gandhi, whatever we do might be insignificant, but it is very important that we do it.

told in *Other Origins: The Search for the Giant Ape in Human Prehistory,* by Russell Ciochon et al. For a more technical piece on early primate evolution, see R. D. Martin's "Primate Origins: Plugging the Gaps" in the May 20, 1993, issue of *Nature.*

The status of the mountain gorilla is discussed in "Gorilla Warfare" by Craig B. Stanford in the July–August 1999 issue of *The Sciences,* and for a consideration of the endangered status of many of the primates from the perspective of a primatologist, see "A View on the Science: Physical Anthropology at the Millennium," by Richard Wrangham, in the April 2000 issue of the *American Journal of Physical Anthropology.*

For conservation information, try the Web sites listed in this chapter's "Contemporary Issue" box, as well as http://primatecenter.duke.edu.

It is no accident that this bonobo, or pygmy chimpanzee, strikes us as so humanlike; our behaviors, including upright walking, have the same evolutionary origin. What can we learn about the evolution of human behavior by examing our close relatives?

(© Frans Lanting, Minden Pictures)

LEARNING ABOUT THE PAST

Behavioral Models for Human Evolution

CHAPTER CONTENTS

Behavior, Adaptation, and Evolution

Baboons

Chimpanzees

Bonobos

Ethnographic Analogy

Summary

Study Questions

Key Terms

For More Information

In reconstructing the human past, our primary focus is the concrete evidence from the fossil and archaeological records. Neither fossil bones nor artifacts alone, however, tell us what our ancestors were like in the most profound biological sense—in terms of how they were adapted to their environments; how they lived; in short, how they behaved.

Were the early hominids social? If so, how were their societies organized? Were group members social equals, or were there leaders and followers? How did they communicate? What did they eat, and how did they acquire their food? Were there family units within the group? Did they care for the sick and aged? Did they share food? Were they individually self-sufficient, or did they divide their labors? Did groups recognize a territory, and did they defend it?

Fossils and artifacts alone cannot normally be used to answer these questions directly, although inferences can be made. Another source of information is living animals that may serve as models for prehistoric hominid behavior. The rationale for such studies is that, although living animals do not represent "fossils" of ancient human behavior, they can provide insight into behavior patterns that may resemble those of ancient humans, who are known only from their bones and their material remains.

Behavior, Adaptation, and Evolution

Studying nonhuman primate behavior to shed light on human behavior is based on the same premise as studying the physical traits of nonhuman primates and comparing them with our own: we share a common heritage with the other primates and so have inherited our shared features from the same source, a common ancestor. It is not a coincidence, for example, that all primates have prehensile hands. Our common prehensile ability comes from the same ancient ancestor and serves the same basic function. Such traits, shared by multiple species through inheritance from a common ancestor, are called **homologies.** Thus, we can gain some perspective on our prehensile hands by fully examining the prehensile appendages of species with whom we share an ancestor from whom we all derived the trait.

Homologous traits need not share a common function, however. Your arms and the wings of a bat, although they are used for different things, are homologues. They are similar by virtue of having evolved from the same source, the forelimb structure of an early mammal.

On the other hand, the wings of a bat and the wings of an insect, although they share the same function, have evolved independently and are not at all similar in structure. These functional but evolutionarily unrelated similarities are known as **analogies.** We can certainly learn something about the physics of flight by comparing these wings; however, we can get only a limited amount of information about the wings of bats by studying the wings of insects because they evolved quite separately from one another to facilitate very different adaptive systems (Figure 6.1).

Just as organisms pass on anatomical and physiological features in their genes, they also pass on behavioral characteristics. In some groups— ants, for example—complex behavioral repertoires are inherited. Ants completely rely on built-in instinct; they don't really think or, in fact, have much of anything to think *with*. So, even though ants live in highly complex societies and act in elaborate ways, all their behaviors are coded for in their genes, to be triggered by outside stimuli but with little or no flexibility or variation in their response.

Other organisms, with larger and more complex brains, can vary their behavior as needed to cope with specific situations. They have behavioral potentials or themes carried in their genetic codes. They respond to their

homology A trait shared by two or more species through inheritance from a common ancestor.

analogy A trait shared by two or more species that is similar in function but unrelated evolutionarily.

(a)

(b)

(c)

FIGURE 6.1 Homology and analogy. The arm of a human (a) and the wing of a bat (b) are homologous—they have different funtions but share the same evolutionary source. The wing of a bat (b) and the wing of an insect (c) are analogous—they share a function but are evolutionarily different.

environments by building onto these potentials—taking in information from the outside, remembering it, and using stored information in appropriate circumstances. In other words, they think.

The nature of the inborn behavioral potentials in complex organisms is still a matter of debate, especially when humans are the topic. Some argue that we are born as blank slates or, in a more modern image, as computers with internal hardware but no programming. Others hold the extreme opposite view: our brains come equipped with *specific* behaviors that are only modified to a degree by outside stimuli—like a computer with basic programs already in the system.

The reality is no doubt somewhere in the middle—to extend the computer metaphor, at birth we are like computers with a common operating system loaded onto our hard drives but no application software. Certainly, we come into this world with some basic, built-in behavioral responses. Facial expressions such as smiling, nursing behavior among infants, the bond between a mother and her offspring, and the drives to walk upright and learn language are all recognized as universal in our species and as being preprogrammed in our biology. But just as certainly we are not programmed for *particular* ways of expressing behaviors. Consider the highly complex structures of our brains and the great variability in our psychologies, intellects, personal behaviors, and cultural systems. Language ability, for example, may be instinctive, but there are thousands of languages, and the one you speak is learned within your specific cultural and individual context.

At any rate, if it is the case that at least behavioral themes can be inherited, then we can shed light on our behaviors by looking into the behaviors of other creatures. In doing so, however, we need to take into account the concepts of homology and analogy. In comparing the behaviors of humans with those of chimpanzees or bonobos, it is highly likely that a behavior is shared because it is the *same* basic behavior, derived by all three species from our common ancestor of 6 to 5 mya with subsequent modification during those millions of years. Understanding the nature and function of that behavior in chimps or bonobos is likely to provide insight into the origin of the behavior in humans because the behavior in question is *homologous*. A behavior similar in humans and baboons is more likely to be *analogous*. Our two species have evolved independently for about 36 million years, so there is a greater chance that the behaviors evolved separately, under separate environmental circumstances, for different adaptive reasons. Still, they may be variations on some general behavior pattern common to the primates and inherited from an early common ancestor. Analogy and homology are not separate categories but differences in degree.

The likelihood that two similar behaviors are analogous increases as the species being compared become less closely related. Some investigators have compared the behavior of humans with that of social carnivores such as lions, wolves, and African wild dogs. There are strikingly "human" behaviors in these species. All three hunt cooperatively. Members of a lion pride will eat from the same carcass. Mothers, of course, will bring food—sometimes still alive—back to their young. But lions do not share food in the sense of one actively giving a portion of a kill to another. Wolves and wild dogs have complex social relationships, use vocal and gestural signs to maintain them, and actively feed their young. Wolves are territorial.

These collections of similarities, however, are probably not derived from a common ancestor but have, at most, evolved independently from some general mammalian traits of social interaction, care for young, and relatively large complex brains allowing for flexibility of behavior. What we do learn from the behavior of such species is that complex social behavior is one possible route to the adaptive success of mammals that include meat in their diet, especially meat from large animals. But it is only one route; other carnivores—the fox and the leopard, for example—are solitary hunters.

Comparing analogous behaviors, then, can be informative and can point out possible clusters of adaptive traits. But analogies must be used with the understanding that the more evolutionarily distant the species, the less useful the comparison. Ants live in highly complex societies to which investigators often apply human names (*slave, caste, queen, nurse, soldier*), but studying the social behavior of ants probably tells us nothing directly about our own societies.

With this understanding of the benefits and pitfalls of species comparison, we can now look at the behavior of some other species that have, to varying degrees, been used as models for the origin and evolution of human behavior. For years, nearly all our information about other species came from studies of their behavior in the artificial environments of zoos and laboratories. Only when the science of **ethology** started to study creatures in the wild, under natural conditions, could we see how they were *really* adapted. And only then did we begin to learn some of the truly remarkable adaptations that our fellow species possess.

Baboons

The five named species of genus *Papio* have long been of interest to anthropologists because of the obvious complexity of the baboon's social organization and because baboon habitats include the savannas of East and South Africa—the very habitat of some of our early hominid ancestors.

In the past, baboon society was thought to have a rigid social order with large males dominating the group, and some suggested that ancient hominids may have behaved in a similar way. Recent detailed field observations of wild baboon troops (Fedigan and Fedigan 1988; Smuts 1985, 1995; Strum 1987) show instead that although male baboons have individual identities and differential social power and influence and that they protect and defend the troop from members of other troops and from predators (Figure 6.2), a formal, tightly structured dominance hierarchy among males does not exist. Rather, the structure of the troop is based on "a network of social alliances" (Fedigan and Fedigan 1988:14), including friendships between females and between females and males. These friendships may be so strong that a male will aid his female friend's infants even though he is not their father. Such friendships, rather than the social position of the males, may be what determines who mates with whom.

ethology The study of the behavior of organisms under natural conditions.

FIGURE 6.2 A male baboon shows his long canine teeth and flashes his white eyelids in a "threat gesture," probably directed toward a less dominant male. (© *Irven DeVore/Anthro-Photo*)

Differential social positions exist, based on an individual's (male or female) "experience, skill, and . . . ability to manipulate others [and] mobilize allies" (Fedigan and Fedigan 1988:15). If any subgroup is central to a troop and ties generations together, it is that of related females, the males being a more mobile and less stable part of the troop than was previously supposed. In fact, the competition that may be most important to the troop is not that among males but among females competing with one another "over access to the resources necessary to sustain them and their offspring" (Fedigan and Fedigan 1988:5). Finally, it appears that mate choice is often more a female than a male prerogative. Males make overtures toward **estrus** females (Figure 6.3), but the females decide with whom they mate.

Again, we must remember that we can share with baboons only the most general primate homologous traits. Similarities between us and baboons exist because behaviors derive from the same behavioral themes. The specific expressions of those themes in the two species, however, are the results of long separate and independent evolutionary histories.

Those separate histories, however, have produced general results that are similar in baboons, humans, and, as we will see, chimpanzees and bonobos: the adaptive focus of a social structure built around a family unit, friendships, mutual aid within the group, defense of the group, and recognition of individuals. This at least tells us that such a focus is one possible adaptive path among primates. It is thus conceivable to propose that something like it was the key to the survival of the early hominids. Given that our closest relatives, the chimpanzees and bonobos, exhibit this cluster of traits, it seems an even more reasonable proposition.

estrus In many nonhuman mammals, the period during which a female is fertile; the signals indicating this condition.

FIGURE 6.3 A baboon in estrus. The skin around her genital area is swollen, a clear visual sign that she is fertile and sexually receptive. *(M. A. Park)*

Chimpanzees

Some of the most remarkable results of ethological observations have come from three landmark studies of the great apes, all initiated by paleoanthropologist Louis Leakey: Jane Goodall's study of the chimpanzee (***Pan troglodytes***), Dian Fossey's study of the gorilla (***Gorilla gorilla***), and Biruté Galdikas's study of the orangutan (***Pongo pygmaeus***). Each of these studies is interesting in its own right and tells us something of the variations possible on the basic primate pattern of social organization. The species most relevant to our present subject, however, are the chimpanzee and its close relative, the bonobo (***Pan paniscus***).

The orangutan is an Asian ape and, as we have seen (in Chapter 5), is separated from us by 12 million years or more. The gorilla, although according to some as close to us genetically as the chimp and although exhibiting many of the same basic social behaviors, is a rather specialized ape. Unlike the chimpanzee, the gorilla spends most of its time on the ground, and its almost exclusively vegetarian diet consists largely of ground plants. It will, however, take to the trees in search of fruit, an important part of the diet for many gorilla groups, all of which are exclusively vegetarians. It makes its sleeping nests on the ground. It is not known to make or use tools in the wild. The gorilla's huge size (males in the wild average 400 pounds) means that it has no enemies (except humans), and this, along with its easily obtained plant diet, makes its life fairly laid-back. Gorilla groups are headed by a dominant male, and there is evidence for male fighting and infanticide, but on the whole the groups

FIGURE 6.4 A group of mountain gorillas peacefully resting on a sunny slope. Note the silver fur on the back of the large male in the center. These "silverbacks" are usually the group leaders. *(© Michael A. Nichols/Magnum Photos Inc.)*

are unified and peaceful (Figure 6.4), without the almost constant tension over social position that is more characteristic of baboon and chimp societies. As zoologist and writer David Attenborough puts it, the gorilla has "no need [to] be particularly nimble in either body or mind" (1979:291). Although perhaps overstated—gorillas, like chimps, can be taught to communicate through sign language, for example—this statement seems an accurate impression of the nature of gorilla adaptation.

In contrast, the chimpanzee is "both agile and inquisitive" (Attenborough 1979:291). Much of what we know of the ethology of the chimp comes from the more than thirty years of research at Gombe Stream National Park in Tanzania led by Jane Goodall (1971, 1986, 1990). Goodall's studies have shown that in addition to physical and physiological traits, we share with chimps a number of behavioral characteristics centered on aspects of social interaction. This commonality is instructive for our understanding of our own behavior.

The bond between mother and infant is strong in chimps, as it is in most mammals (Figure 6.5). These apes, though, have large, complex brains and have much to learn about their world before they can become

FIGURE 6.5 A chimpanzee mother and infant. The bond between them is strong and will last a lifetime. (*© Nancy Nicolson/Anthro-Photo*)

functioning adults. Thus, the mother-infant bond is particularly long-lived and important, and the nature of that interaction can have a lasting effect on the rest of a chimp's life. Poor treatment by its mother, for example, often makes a chimp a poor mother herself when she bears young. Chimps have been seen to help their mothers with younger siblings, and siblings often remain close to each other into adulthood. Chimps, in other words, don't just give birth to an offspring and then cast it out on its own. Chimps *raise* their young, and the family bonds that result may last a lifetime.

The chimps in a group are arranged in a dominance hierarchy. Males are generally dominant over females, but a loose hierarchy exists among females. Males compete with one another, often by fighting aggressively, in an attempt to achieve the highest position possible. The rewards are access to feeding places and females. Social position, although attained in males through violent but seldom injurious actions, is maintained via a series of expressions, gestures, and vocalizations (Figure 6.6). One of the most important behaviors is grooming (see Figure 5.7), which preserves social cohesion and, on occasion, is a sign of dominance when a subordinate male grooms his superior. Other expressions of social interaction include kissing, hugging, bowing, extending the hand, making sexual gestures, and grinning; we can freely use these terms because the meanings of these actions in chimp society seem to be precisely what they are in human society.

Though a dominance hierarchy exists, chimp society is in no way some sort of dictatorship. Instead, it is marked by cooperation and mutual concern. This is seen mostly within the family unit of mother and offspring (because chimps are sexually promiscuous, the father is unknown). Throughout their lives, members of this family unit protect and care for one another, especially during illness and injury. Males have even been known to help brothers in their competition for dominance.

But care also extends outside the family unit. When chimps hunt, for example, portions of the kill are often shared, sometimes proportionately depending on the degree of friendship between the hunter and the chimp begging for food. Offspring are important to the group as a whole, and unrelated adults come to the aid or protection of a youngster threatened with some harm, even risking their own welfare. In one case observed by a researcher, an adolescent male adopted an unrelated youngster who had been orphaned (Goodall 1990:202).

Group membership is somewhat fluid. Chimps, for various reasons, leave a group, and outsiders occasionally enter it. Despite this, there is a sense of group identity and territory. Small bands of males sometimes patrol the boundaries of the group's range; and when they encounter members of other groups, they treat them as outsiders. In one rare but chilling series of events, males from Goodall's main study group attacked and killed a female and all the males of a group that had broken away to establish its own territory. Goodall thinks the motivation may have been to reclaim the area. Although other examples of similar behavior have been reported, there is still debate over whether it is typical of the species. It has been suggested (Power 1991, for example) that because the researchers at Gombe interfered with the chimps' normal activities by providing food, they may have influenced the apes' behaviors, including this event. Others (Sussman 1997) question how convincing the evidence is for similar occurrences.

Among the chimpanzee's wide range of food sources is meat. Chimps from some groups, including those studied by Goodall and associates, are hunters (Stanford 1995, 1999). Males, and occasionally females, will hunt and kill small pigs, antelopes, and monkeys, including young baboons (Figure 6.7). The Gombe chimps, sometimes hunting in cooperative groups, kill over 100 red colobus monkeys a year, nearly a fifth of that species within the chimps' range. Meat is the one food that chimps share, and male chimps are more likely to share with friends. They even withhold meat from rivals. There is evidence, too, that males hunt in order to get meat as an offering to an estrus female.

The vast majority of our information about this species comes from Goodall's research, but work on other chimp groups amply bears out her observations and conclusions and lends support to the idea that chimp behavior is flexible, adaptable, and the result of a great degree of intelligence and reasoning. We have known that there is variation among chimp groups in such behaviors as hunting and body language. W. C. McGrew (1998) has suggested that this is evidence of cultural differences. And a

FIGURE 6.7 A chimp in Tanzania eats the carcass of a baboon he has recently hunted and killed. He may share some of his prize with close friends in his group. (© *Kennan Ward/DRK Photo*)

recent synthesis of data from seven well-established chimpanzee field sites across Africa, comprising an accumulated 151 years of observation, has shown variation in thirty-nine different behavior patterns, not including those with obvious ecological explanations (such as not nesting on the ground where leopards and lions are common). The behaviors include tool use, grooming, and courtship behavior, and the nature of the variation points to the chimp's ability to invent new behaviors and pass them on socially—in which case the behaviors might be thought of as "customs" (Whiten et al. 1999; Whiten and Boesch 2001).

Bonobos

Even more intriguing information has come to light about the other species of chimpanzee: the pygmy chimpanzee, or bonobo (de Waal and Lanting 1997; Ingmanson and Kano 1993; Kano 1990; White 1996). The bonobo lives in the lowland forests of the Democratic Republic of the Congo (for-

FIGURE 6.8 A bonobo walking bipedally. Note that she is doing so because she is carrying something in her hands. (© *Frans Lanting/Minden Pictures*)

merly Zaire) and has been estimated by molecular studies to have been separate from the common chimp for about 930,000 years (Kaessmann et al. 1999).

Not really pygmies, the bonobos are as large as chimps, although more slender and with smaller heads and shoulders. They walk upright more often than do chimps (Figure 6.8). Like chimps, they do some hunting, but there are differences in the two species' hunting behavior. Bonobos hunt rarely, there is no evidence of cooperative hunting, females are some-times the hunters, and the game is small (flying squirrels or a tiny forest antelope; Ingmanson and Ihobe 1992). Also like the chimps, bonobos use tools, but never in acquiring food. Rather, bonobos use leaves as rain hats and drag branches to serve the social purposes of initiating group move-ment and indicating the direction of movement (Ingmanson 1996).

The bonobos are more peaceful and gregarious than the chimps. There is a dominance hierarchy among males, but, unlike the case with chim-panzees, the hierarchy is easily established with brief aggressive chases. Female hierarchies appear to be based on seniority. And, also unlike the chimps, females may dominate males (de Waal and Lanting 1997). Bono-bos more readily share food with one another than do chimps, and the food shared is not limited to luxury items such as meat. They have never been observed to kill another of their kind, and they appear to bind their group together with sex.

Bonobos, especially when feeding, constantly posture toward one an-other, rubbing rumps or "presenting" themselves as if initiating sexual ac-tivity. When sex does follow, it is usually face-to-face, a position common in humans but notably uncommon in nonhuman primates. Sexual activity is not limited to opposite-sex partners. Females commonly rub genitalia with other females, and males mount each other.

Moreover, the signs of fertility, the estrus signals, seem nearly always present in bonobo females. There is some swelling almost all the time, and, indeed, bonobos seem almost constantly sexually receptive. Sexual activity in this species has become separate from purely reproductive ac-tivity. The motivation for sex may be as much psychological and social as it is reproductive.

The function of food sharing and sexual receptiveness in the bonobos seems to be the same as with grooming and as with some of the expres-sions and gestures among chimps: to prevent violence; to ease tension, es-pecially while feeding; to offer a greeting, a sign of reconciliation, or a sign for reassurance (Figure 6.9). Sex or some form of sexual activity, hetero-sexual or homosexual, has even been seen to precede food sharing.

While on the subject of bonobos, we should mention Kanzi, a teenage male bonobo at the Language Research Center at Georgia State University (Savage-Rumbaugh and Lewin 1994). Kanzi is one of the most successful apes at communicating through a language with the characteristics of human communication. He uses symbols on a computer keyboard, and he can even recognize and, using his computer, respond to a large number of spoken English words. In addition to his linguistic skills, he has been taught to make and use simple stone tools. Although not resembling even the earliest known hominid stone tools (see Chapter 9), Kanzi's tools are, nonetheless, true artifacts, and so may show us what the *very* earliest stone tools of our lineage might have looked like. Neither of these behaviors—using a humanlike language and stone toolmaking—are seen among wild

FIGURE 6.9 Bonobo society is characterized by peaceful relationships, with sexual activity and—as seen here on the left—food sharing as mechanisms to maintain harmony, ease tensions, reassure other members, and show reconciliation.

(© Noel Rowe)

bonobos, but they do give us an idea as to the cognitive potentials of the brains of these apes.

Now, if the behaviors of the chimp and bonobo sound more than vaguely human, the reason may be simple. We share certain behavioral patterns because we inherited them from a common ancestor. To be sure, our line and that of the chimps have been going their separate and independent ways for 5 or 6 million years, and even shared features have had the chance to become modified by all the processes of evolution—to be changed, eliminated, enhanced, and differently adapted to our species' different niches. Chimps and bonobos are not "living fossils," stuck in some 5-million-year-old rut while our ancestors continued to evolve. But because our common ancestor is relatively recent and there is a striking similarity between their bodies and behaviors and ours, we can argue that our shared behaviors are homologous.

This does *not* mean that we humans have specific genes for friendship, food sharing, territoriality, or continual sexuality. These are complex behaviors, and chimps, bonobos, and humans are complex species. The suggestion is that, as with the chimps and bonobos, the focus of the human adaptation—the thing that adapted our earliest hominid ancestors and has been the adaptive theme of our line—is social interaction based on individual recognition, a strong bond centered around family relationships (generally, mothers and their offspring), long-term friendships, sexual consciousness, mutual care within the group, and recognition and defense of the group. It seems reasonable to propose that our hominid ancestors—represented by the fossils to be discussed in Chapters 8 through 10—behaved in similar ways. As Goodall says,

> The concept of early humans poking for insects with twigs and wiping themselves with leaves seems entirely sensible. The thought of those ancestors greeting and reassuring one another with kisses or embraces, cooperating in protecting their territory or in hunting, and sharing food with each other, is appealing. The idea of close affectionate ties within the Stone Age family, of brothers helping one another, of teenage sons hastening to the protection of their old mothers, and of teenage daughters minding the babies, for me brings the fossilized relics of their physical selves dramatically to life. (1990:207)

Ethnographic Analogy

One more method has been used to try to open a window into our behavioral past. Modern human societies vary greatly in their cultural systems, including their degree of technological complexity and the extent to which they manipulate their environments to extract needed resources. Perhaps by examining the least technologically complex societies, those that live close to the land, we can see ways of life that may parallel in some aspects the lives of our ancestors. Such groups are collectively called **hunter-gatherers**, or **foragers**.

Such studies, however, must be made with caution. It is important to remember that modern foraging peoples are just that—modern. Though "primitive" perhaps by the **ethnocentric** standards of the industrial world, they are decidedly *not* humans arrested at some previous stage of evolution. They possess fully modern human intellectual capabilities, and these have given them cultural assets unknown to any humans until recently. Many, for example, use the bow and arrow, which is only about 20,000 years old.

In addition, evidence indicates that modern foraging groups, however isolated, are not as untouched by outside influences as we had thought or hoped. The most infamous example is the Tasaday, discovered in the jun-

hunter-gatherer A human society that relies on naturally occurring sources of food.

forager A synonym for hunter-gatherer.

ethnocentric Judging another society's values in terms of one's own social values.

gles of the Philippines in 1971. This group of twenty-five people were thought to be hunter-gatherers (if catching frogs can be considered hunting) who used very simple stone tools and had been completely isolated for 2,000 years. This was a glimpse into the past if ever there was one! But it turns out that at the very least, the Tasaday were part of or had traded with a larger agricultural group. There is even some evidence that they were a publicity hoax, a small group of farming people paid to act like "a stone age tribe" (Berreman 1991). Indeed, it can fairly be said that all societies today have been influenced and changed by contact with other groups, and so probably none accurately represents our species' previous way of life.

Moreover, like all humans, foraging peoples are culture-bearing. They consciously create and modify cultural systems to fit their environments and the basic ways they cope with those environments. So, rather than reflecting some lifestyle directly inherited from our ancient past, the social systems of foragers must be seen as the collective cultural responses of groups of people to the world they know and have to deal with. Now, however, with these cautions in mind, we may look at the lifestyles of foraging people to see if they shed some light on the human past.

Foragers are peoples who rely on naturally occurring resources for their subsistence. Rather than produce food, they collect it, by hunting wild animals and gathering wild plants. They don't farm, and they don't have domesticated animals (except for dogs). This is how all our ancestors lived until only about 12,000 ya (see Chapter 12). Thus, by observing modern foragers, we are observing something similar to the lifestyle of most humans throughout most of human history.

It is probably safe to say that no true foragers are left in the world. But until recently, there have been groups whose adaptive focus was on this pattern of subsistence, and they have been observed and studied. Examples include a number of Native American cultures, most notably the Inuit (Eskimo), the native populations of Australia, some societies from the Philippines, and, perhaps the most studied, the Ju/'hoansi (pronounced "zhut'-wah-see") from the Kalahari Desert of southern Africa, formally called the !Kung San and sometimes derogatorily referred to as Bushmen (Figure 6.10). (The ! and / represent click sounds in this language.) The Ju/'hoansi have always seemed the best model because they inhabit dry, open areas of Africa, environments with much the same potential sources of plant and animal food available to some early hominids.

The specific cultural systems of foraging peoples show a great deal of variation, but we can make some generalizations. Foraging bands are usually small collections of related family units, each known as a **nuclear family**—a mother, father, and their offspring. Band sizes vary according to particular environmental circumstances, but the average number supported by this form of subsistence seems to be around twenty-five people.

nuclear family The family unit made up of parents and their offspring.

FIGURE 6.10 The Ju/'hoansi from the Kalahari Desert in Namibia, Botswana, and South Africa are, of course, fully modern humans. Yet their way of life, until recently that of hunters and gatherers, can give us a window into the lives of our ancestors before the invention of farming and animal domestication. Here, members of a Ju/'hoansi family are on the move, carrying with them their children, tools, weapons, and other possessions. The lives of the Ju/'hoansi have been changed forever by political and military events in southern Africa since this photo was taken nearly 40 years ago. (© *Irven DeVore/Anthro-Photo*)

Foragers often have a home range within which they are mobile as they follow the travels of the animals they hunt and the seasonal cycles of the plants they gather.

Foraging societies tend to be **egalitarian**—that is, they don't have formalized social or economic hierarchies. Not everyone, of course, can do an equal amount of labor or fend completely for themselves. Thus, sharing is a vital feature of such groups, to ensure that everyone benefits equally from the labors of the group as a whole. There is no labor specialization—no full-time occupations—but tasks do tend to be associated with one sex or the other. Generally, men hunt and women gather. This, of course, makes practical sense in that hunting is more strenuous, more dangerous, more time-consuming, and often takes hunters far from home. Participating in hunting is probably seen as normally too much of a burden for pregnant females or women nursing small children.

When women gather, they may do so in groups, but each woman normally works by and for herself and her immediate family. Plants are usually a more reliable food source than meat and, as in the case of the Ju/'hoansi, may comprise up to 75 percent of a foraging group's diet. Hunting, on the other hand, especially if large game is the target, requires cooperation among the men; the meat acquired, usually much more scarce and less dependable than plant foods, is shared, sometimes via elaborate, ritualized exchanges to symbolize group unity.

egalitarian A type of society that does not recognize differences in social position or wealth.

Although foraging societies are egalitarian with regard to politics and economics, the people themselves still have differential relationships with one another. As in any group, there are friends of varying degrees and individuals who are not so friendly. Indeed, irreconcilable conflicts are one of the things that contribute to the flexibility of foraging-band membership. People come and go in these groups for various reasons—from personal choice to economic necessity, as when a scarcity of resources causes a band to split apart to seek food in different areas.

Despite the cautions we noted before, the behavioral themes running through this discussion can hardly be ignored. Striking similarities exist between many of the general traits of foraging societies and the societies of chimpanzees and bonobos—particularly the importance of the mother-infant bond, the presence of a home range, differential relationships within the group, the flexibility of group membership, and, most notably, the focus on the group itself and the vital role of cooperation. Because we humans have been foragers for most of our time on earth, it seems a reasonable proposition that a similar set of behavioral features characterized the earliest humans.

What foraging cultures may show us is that our cultural ability to vary our specific behaviors over an incredible range may, in fact, be based on certain general patterns of behavior established in our prehominid past. And so, when we look at baboons and, especially, at chimpanzees and bonobos, we are not necessarily seeing ourselves in the past, but we are seeing the patterns of behavior that adapted the early members of the hominid family and from which modern human behavior has evolved.

Summary

As noted in Chapter 5, one way to guide us as we look into our past is to understand the results of the events that made up that past. This approach works for behavior as well as for physical adaptations. We can compare the behavior of various modern human groups to that of species with whom we share general traits or environmental conditions. We search for trends or tendencies that may indicate how our ancestors might have adapted to similar circumstances. The importance of a well-defined organization among social African carnivores such as the lion and wild dog and in another savanna primate, the baboon, is a good hint that an analogous behavior was a key to the survival of early savanna hominids.

More useful is the behavior of close evolutionary relatives, especially the chimpanzee and bonobo. Chimp and bonobo behavior differs in specifics from ours and has been evolving separately from ours for 5 or 6 million years, helping those species adapt to their particular niches. The basic patterns for the behavior of our three species, however, are homologous. They are homologous because we inherited them from a common ancestor. It is highly likely, then, that our remote hominid ancestors also manifested these patterns.

Such studies indicate that early hominids of the plains of Africa may very well have been highly social creatures and that their social organization was built around differing interpersonal relationships, a family unit, conscious sexuality, recognition of group membership and territory, and mutual care at both the individual and the group level.

Study Questions

1. What ideas must we consider in trying to explain the behavior of a living creature, especially one as complex as our species?
2. What are some of the basic behaviors of our close relatives? What light do they shed on the evolution of our own behaviors?
3. How may the study of living humans contribute to our understanding of human behavioral evolution? What limits must we recognize in conducting such studies?

Key Terms

homology	estrus	ethnocentric
analogy	hunter-gatherer	nuclear family
ethology	forager	egalitarian

For More Information

More on baboon behavior can be found in Shirley Strum's *Almost Human* and in Barbara Smuts's *Sex and Friendship in Baboons*. Dian Fossey recounts her study of gorillas in *Gorillas in the Mist;* her own story in turn, including her murder, is told by Farley Mowat in *Woman in the Mists* and in the 1988 movie *Gorillas in the Mist*. Biruté Galdikas tells about orangutans in *Reflections of Eden: My Years with the Orangutans of Borneo*. Jane Goodall's latest popular work on the chimps and her experiences studying them is *Through a Window: My Thirty Years with the Chimpanzees of Gombe*. See also the article about her work in the December 1995 *National Geographic*.

Chimpanzee hunting behavior and the possible influence of meat eating on human evolution are the topic of Craig B. Stanford's *The Hunting Apes: Meat Eating and the Origins of Human Behavior*. His position—that the quest for meat was what helped select for our big brains and gave rise to many human social behaviors—is a controversial one. For a critique, see the review of Stanford's book by Christophe Boesch in the June 17, 1999, issue of *Nature,* page 653.

Bonobos are described in *Bonobo: The Forgotten Ape,* by Frans de Waal with photographs by Frans Lanting. For more on the amazing Kanzi and other bonobos, see *Kanzi: The Ape at the Brink of the Human Mind,* by Sue Savage-Rumbaugh and Roger Lewin, and *Apes, Language, and the Human Mind,* by Savage-Rumbaugh et al.

Some basic information about foragers can be found in *Man the Hunter,* by Richard Lee and Irven DeVore, and *Woman the Gatherer,* edited by F. Dahlberg.

Built nearly 800 years ago in a protected niche in a cliff, Square Tower House in Mesa Verde, Colorado, is symbolic of the often hidden nature of the data of human antiquity. Physical anthropologists and archaeologists have developed many methods for finding and analyzing evidence of the human past. How can scientists know what happened in the ancient past? How can we reveal the human story? *(K. L. Feder)*

LEARNING ABOUT
THE PAST
The Material Record

CHAPTER CONTENTS

The Anthropology of the Past: Archaeology and Physical Anthropology

Where? The Process of Finding Sites

What? Recovering Archaeological Data

When? Dating the Past

How? Reconstructing Past Lifeways

Who? Identifying the Remains of Humans and Human Ancestors

Why? Explaining the Past

Summary

CONTEMPORARY ISSUE: Preserving the Past

Study Questions

Key Terms

For More Information

This book focuses on the data of human antiquity, but how do we collect, analyze, and interpret these data in order to learn about the ancient past of our species? Our approach to understanding the human past will be through the field of anthropology, defined previously as the study of humanity. If you think about it, though, nearly all the courses you're now taking deal in some fashion with people or their works. What makes anthropology different?

The Anthropology of the Past: Archaeology and Physical Anthropology

Many people have some very strange ideas about what archaeology and physical (or biological) anthropology are and what scientists in these fields do. Some people think archaeologists study dinosaurs. (They've seen too many episodes of *The Flintstones*.) In reality, dinosaurs became extinct nearly 60 million years before even our earliest human ancestors appeared on the scene. Thanks, at least in part, to such movies as the Indiana Jones series, many think that archaeologists are tough, globe-trotting vagabonds who loot sites for treasure. Physical anthropologists are often stereotyped as those who identify the skeletal remains of dead people. These days on the Discovery Channel and, especially, on Court TV, most physical anthropologists are shown conducting CSI-style forensic work, helping solve crimes through the examination and identification of a murder victim's remains. The most common question both of us get, even from university colleagues, is "Dig up any interesting bones lately?"

Actually, archaeology is simply that branch of anthropology focusing on the human cultural past. Whereas other anthropologists may study a people by actually living among them, archaeologists must study a people through analysis of what they left behind—yes, including bones. Archaeology is necessary because the only way we can learn directly about people in the past, especially those who lived before the invention of writing, is by studying their remains and the things they made and used—and that, luckily, have been preserved. So archaeologists have, as their primary data, the material consequences of human behavior—the tools, edifices, art, and even garbage a society leaves behind. From potsherds to pyramids, from arrowheads to Stonehenge, these are the archaeologist's raw data. Because the materials archaeologists deal with—pyramids, cave paintings, pots, and the like—can be so interesting in and of themselves, it is easy to lose track of why we are studying them. Just remember that archaeologists are anthropologists; they are interested in the same sorts of things. They aim to understand how ancient people lived, not simply to collect interesting antiques.

Similarly, whereas some physical anthropologists collect data from living individuals, paleoanthropologists deal with the skeletal remains of people, and even then usually not with the complete skeleton. Nevertheless, they also seek to learn about the biology of the people who made the tools and pots and paintings. What did they look like? What diseases did they suffer from, and what sorts of injuries caused their deaths? What were the sex ratios and average ages of their populations? Moreover, paleoanthropologists are interested in how and why human biology changed over the more than 6 million years we and our upright-walking ancestors have been around. In other words, how do the processes of evolution apply to our species? Biological anthropologists also address these matters. The answers to such questions round out the understanding of ancient people.

The goals of the study of the past can be broken down into a series of general questions anthropologists wish to ask of the data:

1. *Where* did people live?
2. *What* materials did they leave behind?
3. *When* was an area occupied, and when did certain human activities occur?
4. *How* did people in a given region or time period live?
5. *Who* were the people, biologically?
6. *Why* did they live the life they did, and what rules or processes did they use to adjust their ways of life to respond to changes in their surroundings?

Through asking and attempting to answer these questions, anthropologists illuminate the story of human biological and cultural evolution. In the rest of this chapter, we will briefly describe how the anthropologists who study the past go about this task.

Where? The Process of Finding Sites

To know where prehistoric people settled, where they lived, and where they died, it is necessary to find the material remnants of their existence. These are archaeological **sites**—locations where humans once lived or worked and where their traces were left behind and have been preserved. These traces are in the form of **artifacts**—objects made by people, such as spear points or clay pots—and **features**—nonportable remains reflecting human activity, such as hearths, trash piles, or burials. For nonarchaeologists, the ability to find sites may seem almost magical. It would probably not be giving away any trade secrets to tell you that, in reality, the discovery of archaeological sites does not depend on intuition, psychic power, or magic. Instead, sites are discovered through a scientific process demanding hard work and, admittedly, a bit of luck (Feder 1997).

Archaeological site survey, the actual process of finding sites, often begins with a set of basic, commonsense techniques, among them: (1) reference to previous research conducted in an area, (2) examination of local history for stories of discoveries made by inhabitants, and (3) contacting local collectors of artifacts. Unfortunately, there are many people who, legally or otherwise, collect artifacts—sometimes doing little better than looting sites—for their own personal collections or to sell to the highest bidder; you can actually find some of this stuff on eBay. Though these people might be extremely knowledgeable about local archaeological sites, it would be ethically dubious for archaeologists to use such people as an information source—and it is unlikely that these individuals would share their information anyway. On the other hand, there are plenty of people with an abiding interest in the past who are happy to share their knowledge with

site A place that contains evidence of a past human presence.

artifact Any object made by humans.

feature A nonportable element of a site, composed of artifacts; for example, a grave or fireplace.

professional archaeologists about local artifacts that they uncover by walking over plowed fields or construction sites, doing little damage to these intact sites. There are professional archaeologists today whose interest in the past was ignited initially by finding an arrowhead or pottery fragment in the furrow of a plowed field. Even people who do not go out consciously looking for artifacts or sites sometimes have valuable information for archaeologists. Farmers plowing their fields, homeowners building an addition to their house, workers constructing a highway, and gardeners planting their tomatoes all disturb the soil and as a result may encounter the remains of buried artifacts. Many of the important archaeological sites mentioned in this book were found accidentally by people engaged in nonarchaeological pursuits.

Once these initial sources of site data have been explored, site survey may proceed with a consideration of environmental variables. Whether they are prehistoric hunters, primitive farmers, or twenty-first-century Americans, all people depend, ultimately, on nature's bounty. Archaeologists use that fact to help find archaeological sites. For example, all people need a source of fresh water, and no one is likely to live too far from one. Locations with readily available wood—for construction and for use as fuel—are attractive places to settle. Hunters tend to concentrate their settlements in areas where animals are likely to be found. Farmers may prefer extensive areas of fertile flatland to make a living. People with hostile neighbors may choose to settle in protected areas. Pottery-making people may want to live close to a source of clay. The archaeologist must consider a constellation of environmental variables to isolate the kinds of areas where sites are most likely to be found.

All of this background research paves the way for the **field survey,** which includes both a surface and a subsurface investigation of an area. Before using procedures in which the soil is actually turned over in search of archaeological evidence, in some cases archaeologists can apply techniques of **remote sensing.** You've likely seen someone scanning a beach or park with a metal detector, looking for buried metal objects, often coins or jewelry. Though this kind of treasure hunting certainly doesn't qualify as archaeology, it is an example of remote sensing, and archaeologists sometimes use metal detectors at sites where metal artifacts are expected. Beyond using metal detectors, there are other ways of scanning the subsurface before digging. For example, **electrical resistivity survey** involves passing an electrical current through the ground in order to search for variations in the electrical signal that might suggest the presence of buried cultural material; a wall or a trash pit, for example, might create a level of electrical resistance measurably different from the surrounding soil. Another remote-sensing technique, **proton magnetometry,** gauges minor variations in the earth's magnetic field that might indicate, again, the presence of archaeological materials below ground. A proton-magnetometry survey conducted at the Knife River Indian Villages National Historic Site

field survey The process of discovering archaeological sites.

remote sensing Noninvasive examination of sites where no soil is removed.

electrical resistivity survey A noninvasive procedure used in archaeological prospecting in which an electrical current is passed through the ground. Variations in resistance to the current may signal the location of archaeological artifacts or features.

proton magnetometry A noninvasive technique used in archaeological prospecting in which a proton magnetometer measures the strength of the earth's magnetic field at the surface. Variations in that magnetic field may signal the location of buried remains, including walls and foundations.

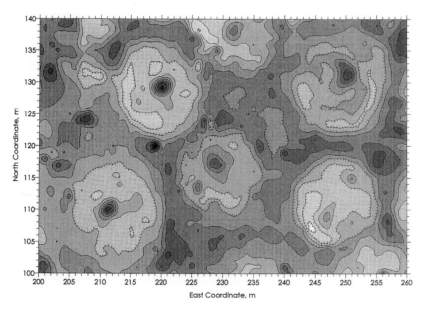

FIGURE 7.1 An example of remote sensing—proton magnetometer map produced for the Knife River Indian Villages National Historic Site. This map depicts a small portion of magnetometer survey at the Big Hidatsa Village. The larger circular features represent the magnetic anomalies produced by earth lodges. The small circular anomalies within each of the larger features are fire hearths.

showed a distinct pattern of these variations, or anomalies, in the earth's magnetic field, reflecting the presence of the remains of houses, called "earth lodges," not visible on the surface (Figure 7.1). **Ground penetrating radar,** or **GPR** (Conyers 2004), is another remote-sensing procedure used in archaeology. In the above-ground use of radar, an electromagnetic pulse is propagated through the air, and a receiver scans for the signal once it has reflected off an object—an airplane, for example. In GPR, the electromagnetic signal is propagated through the soil, and a receiver looks for return signals bouncing off cultural material, for instance, the loose soil of a burial or the buried wall of a house foundation. Lawrence Conyers has used GPR extensively (www.du.edu/~lconyer) and with great success for locating and identifying buried architectural features and graves. Figure 7.2 shows a GPR image of a previously unknown *kiva*—a religious structure of the Hopi people—in southeastern Utah.

Remote-sensing methods are noninvasive, like a medical CAT scan. Photographs taken from an airplane or satellite, radar images, analysis of magnetic anomalies in the ground, and variations in subsurface resistance to an electrical current or an electromagnetic pulse can provide the archaeologist with data concerning the potential presence of archaeological materials unavailable by simple inspection and without having to dig holes in the ground. The results of these remote-sensing procedures cannot ordinarily replace those obtained from excavation, but they certainly are valuable in helping the archaeologist decide where to use surface inspection and subsurface investigation to investigate further.

ground penetrating radar (GPR) A noninvasive technique used in archaeological prospecting in which an electromagnetic pulse is passed through the soil. Variations in the pulse as it reflects off buried objects may signal the location of archaeological remains, for example, walls or foundations.

FIGURE 7.2 Ground-penetrating radar imaging at Bluff, Utah. The circular feature just a little below and to the left of the center of the image is the GPR signal of the buried walls of a *kiva,* a circular, ceremonial structure of the native people of the American Southwest. *(Courtesy of Lawrence Conyers, University of Denver)*

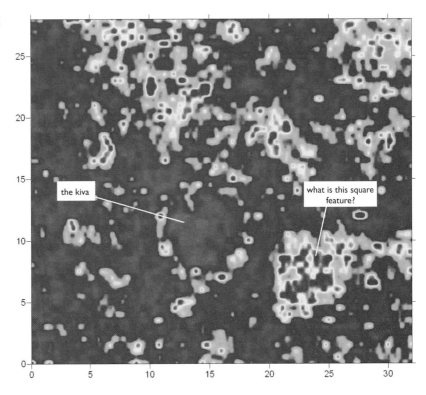

FIGURE 7.3 Where preservation is high and where people built structures in durable materials, archaeologists can find sites simply by walking across an area. Hovenweep National Monument, in the American Southwest, is one such area. Remnants of ancient stone towers built by the ancestors of the modern Hopi Indians still stand at the site. *(K. L. Feder)*

FIGURE 7.4 Olduvai Gorge, Tanzania, one of the world's most productive sites for paleoanthropologists. The strata represent more than 2 million years of the evolution of humans and our ancestors. (© E. E. Kingsley 1984/ Science Source/Photo Researchers, Inc.)

Where prehistoric people have left above-ground structures of relatively resilient material (as in the case of the ancient Egyptians or native people of the American Southwest), sites can be discovered simply by a visual inspection of the surface (Figure 7.3). In densely settled parts of the world, most sites visible on the surface have probably been inventoried, but the discovery of unknown surface sites in less-populated areas is still common.

An above-ground inspection is also valuable when nature itself has conducted its own kind of excavation through erosion. A river eroding its bank or a gulley being cut by a flash flood may expose previously unknown archaeological material. In many instances, the fossil remains of human ancestors have been found in places where ancient soil levels have been exposed by natural processes. Olduvai Gorge, in Africa, is a famous example of this effect. Searching for and surveying areas where such ancient deposits have been exposed by natural erosion is an important part of the search for the vestiges of prehistoric humanity (Figure 7.4).

Most prehistoric archaeological sites, however, have been buried by natural processes of deposition. Rivers deposit soil when they flood, sand gets blown about by winds, volcanoes erupt and spew out lava and ash,

test boring A small excavation to establish the presence of an archaeological site, often a narrow column of soil extracted by the use of a hollow metal tube.

sounding A test excavation. Usually a small pit or column dug to expose stratigraphic layers and to search for archaeological material. A test pit.

test pit A synonym for sounding.

compliance archaeology Archaeological research mandated by government regulations aimed at historic and environmental preservation.

random sample Randomly selected points within a research area tested for the presence of archaeological material with the goal of obtaining a representative sample of sites in a region.

representative sample A small sample of a large population in which the characteristics of the sample (ages, sizes, activities, functions, etc.) proportionally match those found in the overall population.

transect A line of systematically located test borings.

mountains erode, and cave roofs collapse. All these processes can bury the remains of a town, camp, or cemetery; in fact, such natural burial may be the most common reason that archaeological remains are preserved. To find sites subjected to thousands and even millions of years of these natural processes of deposition, we must dig.

A research area may be enormous, and generally the archaeologist cannot turn over every square meter of soil to determine the presence or absence of sites. Instead, the archaeologist may sample an area by excavating **test borings, soundings,** or **test pits**—soil corings, shovel-dug holes, and even test trenches excavated by mechanized equipment such as backhoes.

Researchers may appraise the archaeological potential of a region and select specific areas to test based on local history, the reports of amateur archaeologists, and an assessment of the local environment. In some cases, archaeologists select a place to dig based simply on the desire to cover a given area—for example, if the area is to be destroyed as a result of development. Many countries have passed and vigorously enforce laws regarding the preservation of historical resources within their borders and require archaeological surveys before major construction projects are undertaken. In this kind of **compliance archaeology,** a project area may be thoroughly tested by archaeologists before construction begins in an effort to assess the impact of a proposed project on the archaeological record. The sampling may need to be quite intensive to prevent an unknown site from being destroyed or to avoid costly delays or even having to shut down construction should a site be discovered midway through the project.

Especially in those instances where there is no immediate threat of site destruction, areas may be tested archaeologically by the investigation of a **random** and **representative sample** of an area. Here, there are no preconceptions or biases about the best places to test or where sites will most likely be found—and, therefore, no self-fulfilling prophecies about where sites will be located. For example, if only areas adjacent to rivers are tested, then all sites found will be adjacent to rivers. By random sampling, the sites detected should be representative of all the sites in a region, not just those located in places where archaeologists expect them to be.

Within an area to be analyzed, test pits are placed according to a number of different sampling strategies. They may be placed at regular intervals—for example, every 10 meters—along a straight line, or **transect** (Figure 7.5). They may be placed in a square grid or checkerboard pattern. Thousands of these shovel-dug holes may be excavated without finding much of anything. It may seem like looking for the proverbial needle in a haystack—and it is. There are no shortcuts to finding archaeological remains. If the archaeologist has done his or her homework, however, the most likely areas are isolated before test pits are excavated, and there is a good chance of finding something.

What? Recovering Archaeological Data

All scientists are faced with the problem of data collection. Astronomers may need optical or radio telescopes and microbiologists may need high-powered optical or scanning electron microscopes to bring the data they analyze into view. Archaeological data, the stuff people made and used, is neither enormously far away nor, usually, extremely tiny, but most of it ends up being deposited in the ground and, through the processes mentioned, buried. Once sites have been discovered through site survey, the main tools of archaeological data collection are decidedly low-tech and involve removing the soil from around the artifacts.

Not everybody recognizes the difficulty in retrieving the artifacts while still preserving the *information* that a site contains. For example, a local developer uncovered some 10,000-year-old woolly mammoth bones and invited one of the authors to take a look and dig them up; perhaps the mammoth had been killed by prehistoric people. We arrived with our dental picks and trowels, ready to spend days or even weeks removing the handful of bones and tusk fragments from the ground. The developer, however, assured us that he could accomplish the same task with his backhoe in a few minutes, swearing he would be "real careful"!

The materials that archaeologists ordinarily study have been lying in the ground for hundreds, thousands, or even millions of years. It would be a terrible irony if, in attempting to recover these objects, we were to destroy them instead. Consequently, archaeologists need to be meticulous and exacting in excavation. Using small hand tools, including masons' trowels for careful scraping of the soil, dental picks, artists' brushes, and

FIGURE 7.5 In areas of the world where natural processes have not exposed ancient sites, archaeologists must dig to reveal buried cultural deposits. Test pits are often excavated to explore an area for buried archaeological material. Here, fieldworkers excavate a test pit transect—a line of pits placed at 10-meter intervals (*left*). One of the workers (*right*) can be seen extracting soil from a test pit. The soil will be placed in the sifter shown just in front of her and passed through ⅛-inch mesh hardware cloth in the search for small bits of archaeological evidence. (*K. L. Feder*)

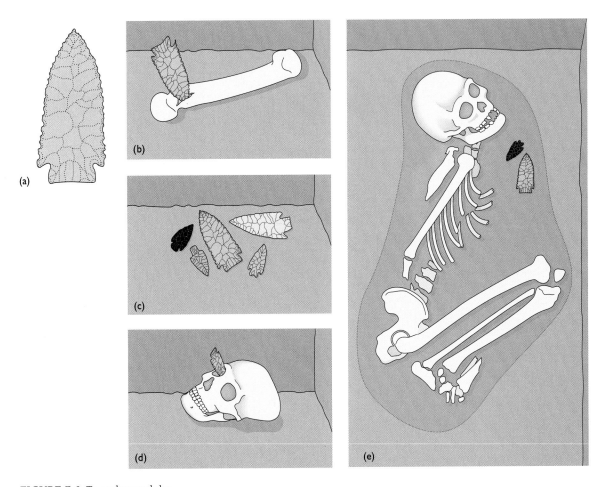

FIGURE 7.6 To understand the significance of archaeological material, context is crucial. Archaeologists must identify where each object was found and what it was found with—in other words, its associations. Here, a spear point (a), is shown in four different hypothetical contexts: (b) piercing the bone of an animal, (c) in a "cache," or hidden reserve, of stone tools, (d) in the skull of a person, and (e) as a grave offering to a deceased hunter. In each case, the artifact is exactly the same, but its context—and, therefore, its inferred use—is different.

whisk brooms, archaeologists remove the soil from around the remains exactly where they were discovered.

Not only do we want to preserve the items themselves, but we also want to preserve their **spatial contexts.** Knowing where an arrow was left or placed thousands of years ago can reveal as much about what it was used for as the arrow itself. An arrow found in an isolated spot with no other objects nearby might be a weapon lost during a hunt. One found with a cluster of arrows inside the remains of a hut could be part of a hunter's storage area. An arrow found in a fireplace may have fallen out of the animal it killed. One discovered in a human grave could be a tool to accompany the deceased to the afterlife. In each case, the tool itself would look exactly the same. But where it was found (its **provenience**) and what was found with it (its **associations**) tell us quite a bit about what the people who used it were doing (Figure 7.6). A backhoe would make short work of this wealth

FIGURE 7.7 Excavation grid at the 1,000-year-old Tulmeadow North site in West Simsbury, Connecticut (*top*). Wooden stakes mark the corners of each excavation unit, and string demarcates their boundaries. (*bottom*) Detail of one of the 1-meter-square excavation units as the crew member scrapes down the soil level with a mason's trowel, a standard tool in the archaeologist's toolkit. (*K. L. Feder*)

spatial context Where and with what an artifact is found in a site.

provenience The precise location of an artifact.

association The spatial relationships of artifacts, one to another.

excavation units Individually dug sections at an archaeological site.

of valuable evidence. Spatial contexts provide crucial information about the behavior of ancient people. Without spatial context—which is absent with spear points, pottery, or carvings for sale by tomb looters—we can learn little about the behavior of the people who used these objects.

Archaeological sites are excavated in an extremely orderly and logical fashion (Figure 7.7). Ordinarily, a site is segmented into grids or squares, often 1 or 2 meters on a side, although this practice varies. These **excavation units** are dug individually or in clusters. Individual soil layers, distinguishable by color and texture may, in turn, be scraped back very carefully.

FIGURE 7.8 By leaving each of the blades at the Glazier Blade Cache site in place as they were encountered in excavation, archaeologists were able to expose the entire archaeological feature exactly as it was left by the ancient inhabitants of north-central Connecticut. (K. L. Feder)

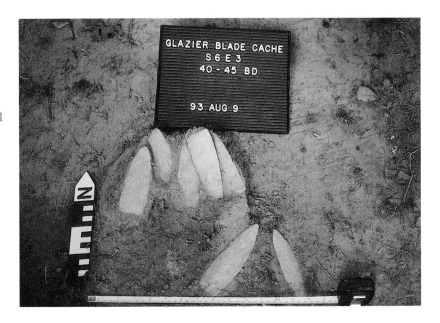

In instances where distinct layers are not apparent or else quite thick, the soil may be scraped down instead in regular increments, only a few centimeters at a time. The soil is then sifted through screens with 1/4-inch, 1/8-inch, or even smaller mesh to catch anything that may have escaped the watchful eye of the archaeologist.

When possible, artifacts encountered in excavation are left in place (**in situ**) so they can be viewed in their spatial contexts, as they were placed and last seen by the inhabitants of the site (Figure 7.8). Maps are made and photographs taken in an attempt to create a permanent record of the spatial contexts. In digging a site and taking to the laboratory or museum the materials found, of course, archaeologists do destroy the site. They do so systematically, however, to be able to study it. The careful recording of all information is crucial for reconstructing what took place at the site from the often meager remains left behind.

When? Dating the Past

in situ In place. An artifact or feature that remains in its exact place of discovery is said to be *in situ*.

How old is a site? When did specific cultural developments occur in human prehistory? When did people begin walking on two feet? When was agriculture invented? How old is a given artifact or the pieces of a skeleton? When did certain environmental changes occur? There are a number of techniques for answering these questions related to time. We will describe the most important ones here.

FIGURE 7.9 Stratigraphic profile of the east wall of a 1-meter-square excavation unit at the Tulmeadow North site in West Simsbury, Connecticut. The upper, darker layer represents the *plow zone,* the soil commonly turned over by a plow in cultivation. Most of the artifacts recovered at this site were found just beneath that plow zone. (*K. L. Feder*)

Stratigraphy

The study of the origin, composition, and sequence of the layering of the earth's soil is **stratigraphy.** You saw in Chapter 2 how recognizing this layering was an important step in the development of uniformitarianism and the modern concept of biological evolution.

Geologists recognize that the history of the earth is written in its rock. Rock and soil (rock and mineral particles mixed with organic material) are deposited by the wind, flooding rivers, eroding mountains, and erupting volcanoes—the same processes that bury archaeological sites. Soil is often deposited in distinguishable layers or may develop such layers later. The layering may result from different sources, or **parent materials.** For example, in the same spot one layer of soil may be from a river flood, another from a dust storm, and another still from a rock slide. Layering may also result from different conditions of deposition. For example, some layers may have been deposited underwater and others under dry conditions. Different climatic conditions after deposition may cause layering because soil texture is altered by temperature. Plants growing on the soil may also have an impact; layering develops as a result of the specific chemical and biological action of various plants extracting nutrients from the soil (Figure 7.9).

Whatever the cause of the layering, soil layers are superimposed, one on top of another, over time. Thus, barring disturbance, successively older layers are encountered as you dig deeper. Archaeologists, paleoanthropologists, and geologists use this **law of superposition** to help place sites in what is known as a **relative chronological sequence.**

stratigraphy The arrangement of soil and rock in layers.

parent material The source material for a particular soil.

law of superposition The principle of stratigraphy that, barring disturbances, more recent layers are superimposed over older ones.

relative chronological sequence A sequence arranged in an older-to-younger relationship without the assignment of specific dates.

FIGURE 7.10 This stratigraphic section from the Old Farms Brook Site in Avon, Connecticut, shows a sequence of three prehistoric occupations and one historic occupation of the same location.

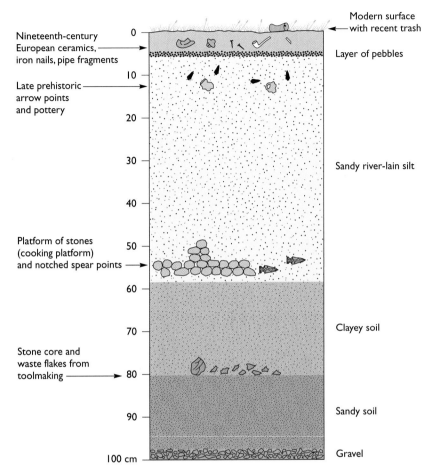

Modern surface with recent trash

Nineteenth-century European ceramics, iron nails, pipe fragments

Layer of pebbles

Late prehistoric arrow points and pottery

Sandy river-lain silt

Platform of stones (cooking platform) and notched spear points

Clayey soil

Stone core and waste flakes from toolmaking

Sandy soil

Gravel

0
10
20
30
40
50
60
70
80
90
100 cm

Many of the objects people make and use eventually become incorporated into the soil beneath their feet through a number of cultural processes—loss, discard, storage, and abandonment (Schiffer 1978). After the people are gone, soil may be deposited over the artifacts. Sometime later, another group may move in, and their objects become a part of the stratigraphic record—at a level *above* that of the previous group—and soil-formation processes act to cover their materials as well (Figure 7.10).

Imagine that many years later you have a picnic on the very spot where these prehistoric people lived. Some change falls out of your pocket, and you leave, unaware of your loss. Next spring a nearby river floods, depositing a fine layer of silt over your artifacts. Now your personal detritus has been incorporated into the stratigraphic record of this site. Not only is the history of the earth written in the soil, so too is the history of humanity.

Chronometric Techniques

Stratigraphy can provide only a relative chronology. It reveals the order in which a series of different cultures inhabited a spot but not *when* those cultures existed—archaeologists cannot determine an age in years simply from the layering of soil. They do, however, have techniques that enable them to derive actual dates from material: **chronometric** and **absolute dating** techniques. Chronometric dating techniques are not necessarily precise, but most enable us to date an object or a site to within a range of years. There also are a few chronometric techniques that allow us to determine a date or age to within a very narrow range or even precisely to an individual year.

Chronometric dates can be expressed in a number of ways: B.C.E. (before the common era) or B.C. (before the birth of Christ); A.D. (not "after death," as many assume, but *anno Domini*, literally, "in the year of our Lord," in other words, after the *birth* of Christ); or B.P. (before present). (For B.P., the "present" is fixed at 1950. Virtually all sites we will be discussing are far too old and the dating techniques too imprecise for it to make a difference; but technically, if the "present" were not set at some fixed point, all dates expressed in this way would need to be changed each year.)

One set of chronometric methods is called **radiometric dating.** This means that the dating procedure is based on the decay of a **radioactive isotope.** The term *radioactive* shouldn't concern you in this context; it only means "unstable," not dangerous or deadly. A radioactive isotope is merely a variety of an element that is not in balance and—given sufficient time—will decay or morph into another, usually far more stable isotope of the same element or even transform into the stable form of another element altogether.

Radioactive decay transpires at a fixed pace, providing what is sometimes referred to as a "natural clock" (a more accurate term would be "natural calendar") by which we can gauge the age of an archaeological artifact or **ecofact**—something that may be stratigraphically associated with an archaeological remain. Radioactive isotopes decay by a variety of natural processes. Scientists can measure the rate of decay of most radioactive isotopes—that is, how fast they change from an unstable to a stable form. They can also measure how much of the radioactive isotope is left in a given archaeological, biological, or geological specimen. By first estimating how much of the isotope must have been present initially, archaeologists can determine how old the object is—how long it must have taken for the initial quantity of the radioactive isotope to decrease to whatever the level is today.

There are many radioactive isotopes in nature, all with measurable decay rates. Most are useless to archaeologists and paleoanthropologists, though, because the elements are so rare that it would be unlikely to find any of them in cultural or biological specimens. Many are also useless because their decay rates are so fast that even fairly recent specimens are

chronometric dating A dating technique in which an actual age or range of years can be applied to archaeological objects or sites.

absolute dating See chronometric dating.

radiometric dating A chronometric dating technique using the decay rate of a radioactive substance.

radioactive isotope An unstable form of an element that decays to a stable form by giving off radiation.

ecofact An element found in an archaeological context that exhibits human activity but was not made by people and so is not, strictly speaking, an artifact.

unlikely to have any of the radioactive isotope left to be measured. Other radioactive elements have such slow rates of decay that even the oldest of anthropological specimens have not been around long enough for any measurable decay to have taken place; thus, no age can be derived.

A few elements, however, are present in many varieties of archaeological specimens and have decay rates that make them useful for the dating of sites. Radioactive carbon is one of those. It provides the raw material for the **radiocarbon dating** technique.

Carbon is found in the atmosphere, linked to oxygen, in the form of carbon dioxide (CO_2). Plants respire carbon dioxide and, through photosynthesis, break the bonds between the carbon and oxygen atoms, releasing the oxygen into the atmosphere and incorporating the carbon into their roots, leaves, fruits, stems, and bark.

Most carbon atoms have an atomic weight of 12 (and thus are labeled ^{12}C) for the twelve particles in their nuclei (six positively charged particles called *protons* and six neutral particles called *neutrons*). Some carbon atoms, however, have two additional neutrons in their nuclei—these atoms are called ^{14}C (pronounced C-14 or carbon 14) and are produced when swiftly moving neutrons collide with nitrogen atoms in the atmosphere. These ^{14}C atoms combine with oxygen to produce carbon dioxide, just like ^{12}C does, and the carbon dioxide with ^{14}C is respired by plants just like carbon dioxide with ^{12}C. The different varieties of carbon are used identically by plants; there is no biological process that filters out or prefers ^{12}C or ^{14}C. As a result, the ratio of ^{12}C to ^{14}C in plants is the same as it is in the atmosphere. Animals then eat the leaves, seeds, fruits, and roots of these plants, incorporating the plants' carbon into their own bodies, again at the same ratio as is found in the plants. Carnivores eat these animals, incorporating ^{12}C and ^{14}C, again in the same proportion as that present in their prey, in plants, and in the atmosphere.

Though chemically nearly identical to ordinary ^{12}C, ^{14}C is a radioactive (meaning "unstable") variety, or isotope, of carbon; in other words, it decays or changes into a nonradioactive, or stable, element over time at a fixed rate. The rate at which a radioactive isotope decays is called its **half-life**. The half-life of ^{14}C is measured at about 5,730 years (more precisely, $5,730 \pm 40$ years).

The unstable ^{14}C in a plant or an animal is constantly decaying or changing back into nitrogen at this fixed rate, but as long as an organism is alive, it is constantly respiring or ingesting new ^{14}C, so its ratio of ^{12}C to ^{14}C remains constant. Once an organism dies, however, there is no further replenishing of the decaying ^{14}C. It slowly dissipates until there is essentially none left.

So, in 5,730 years about half of the ^{14}C in a dead organism is gone, having decayed to nitrogen. Looked at another way, if only about half of the ^{14}C that would be in an organism if it were alive right now is actually present in a bone, seed, or piece of wood recovered at an archaeological

radiocarbon dating A radiometric technique using the decay rate of a radioactive isotope of carbon found in organic remains.

half-life The amount of time needed for half of a radioactive isotope to decay to a stable one.

site, what remains must be about 5,730 years old. Thus, the radioactive isotope of carbon acts as a sort of atomic clock, slowly ticking away through time by decaying back to nitrogen at a known rate.

After another 5,730 years, half of what was left after the first half-life has then decayed, leaving one-quarter of what was there initially, and this same statistical process continues until there is no ^{14}C remaining. Since we know the rate of decay as measured in the half-life, and because we can extrapolate how much ^{14}C was present initially and can measure how much is left now, we can figure out how old the item is—how long it has been since ^{14}C replenishment by respiration in a plant or ingestion in an animal has ceased. It's like knowing how much sand there is in an hourglass, how fast it flows to the bottom, and how much has flowed out of the top. From that, you know how much time has elapsed since the hourglass was overturned. From the measure of ^{14}C, we can know how many years have elapsed since the death of a living thing.

This method has a few constraints. Radiocarbon dating is a destructive technique; the material dated is consumed in the analysis. The size of the sample needed for dating and the amount of an artifact or ecofact that is destroyed in the process varies by raw material. Using the standard radiocarbon method, a leading radiocarbon dating lab recommends 30 grams of charcoal (a little more than an ounce), but as little as 1.7 (.06 oz) may suffice. On the other hand, as much as 500 grams (17.64 oz) of bone is recommended by this same lab, and 200 (7.05 oz) is considered sufficient.

Obviously, archaeologists are loathe to sacrifice a rare or precious object just to obtain a date. Until recently, some objects and some sites went undated as a result. This problem has been ameliorated with the development of the **accelerator mass spectrometry (AMS)** method of carbon dating. A much smaller sample is needed here; as little as 5 milligrams (barely a whisper) of charcoal and 2 grams (.07 oz) of bone. When the Shroud of Turin, posited by some to be the actual burial shroud of Jesus Christ, was analyzed using the AMS method, the destruction of only a very small swatch of the fabric was required. Three labs obtained virtually the same date for the linen from which the shroud was woven; not 2,000 years old, as it would have been were it genuine, but more like 700 years old, indicating that it is an artifact of the medieval period in Europe (Gove 1996).

Another restriction of radiocarbon dating concerns its chronological range of applicability. If something is only a few hundred years old, not enough decay has taken place to allow for its age to be determined reliably. Further, although AMS dating has extended the upper range of carbon dating to a theoretical limit of about 70,000 years, if something is much more than 40,000 years old, not enough ^{14}C is ordinarily left for the technique to work.

Further complicating the interpretation of a radiocarbon date derived from an archaeological specimen is the fact that we now know that the

accelerator mass spectrometry (AMS) A technique in radiocarbon dating in which the actual number of ^{14}C atoms (or a proportion of them) is counted.

ratio of ^{12}C to ^{14}C in the atmosphere has changed significantly, over at least the last 10,000 to 20,000 years, creating a built-in error factor. A tree or bush or animal that was alive during a period when the ^{14}C concentration in the atmosphere was lower than it is today would have incorporated that same lower concentration into its branches, seeds, fruits, or bones when it was alive. Starting with a lower concentration means that the organism will appear to us to be *older* than it actually is in terms of its ^{14}C concentration. If we could go back in time and sample one of these specimens while it was alive and measure its ^{14}C, we might conclude that the organism was already hundreds or even thousands of "radiocarbon years" old because it wouldn't have as much ^{14}C as we would expect it to have if it were alive today. We would be wrong, of course; it wouldn't have lost any ^{14}C due to decay over time, it would simply have less ^{14}C in the first place because the atmospheric concentration was lower when it was alive. Of course, in the reverse case, anything that was alive during a period when the atmospheric ^{14}C concentration was high compared to modern levels would have incorporated that higher concentration of ^{14}C. Beginning with a higher concentration means that it will appear to be *younger* than it actually is.

This complication has led archaeologists to make a distinction between "radiocarbon years" and "calendar years," the former referring to the radiocarbon age of an object and the latter to its actual calendar age. Of course, we are most interested in the actual age (in calendar years) of artifacts, ecofacts, and sites. Fortunately there is a bit of a work-around for this problem, at least for the last 10,000 to 12,000 years, which we'll examine shortly, in our discussion of dendrochronology (tree-ring dating).

If an organic remain was part of an archaeological site that is more than a few hundred and less than about 50,000 years old, archaeologists often can obtain a fairly good idea of how old the site is using the radiocarbon technique. This range is more than enough to cover the entire period of human settlement in the Americas and Australia (see Chapter 11), for example, but cannot be applied to the far older early hominid sites in Africa, Asia, and Europe (see Chapters 8–10). Compared to other dating techniques, radiocarbon dating also is relatively inexpensive: a standard date usually runs around $300, and an AMS date will cost around $600.

Another important, commonly used radiometric technique is **potassium/ argon,** or **K/Ar, dating,** which uses as its atomic clock the rate of decay of a radioactive isotope of potassium (^{40}K) into argon gas. The most recent refinement of this technique is called **argon/argon (Ar/Ar) dating,** which measures the decay of one isotope of the gas argon (^{40}Ar) into another (^{39}Ar). Argon/argon dating is more accurate and is now used more often than the older procedure, but it is still based on measuring the amount of argon that has accumulated in volcanic rock (Deino et al. 1998).

The K/Ar and Ar/Ar methods measure the age of volcanic rocks. In both procedures, the amount of argon gas that has built up in the rock is

potassium/argon (K/Ar) dating A radiometric technique using the decay rate of radioactive potassium, found in volcanic rock, into stable argon.

argon/argon (Ar/Ar) dating A recent refinement of potassium/argon dating. Measures the decay of one isotope of the gas argon (^{40}Ar) into another (^{39}Ar).

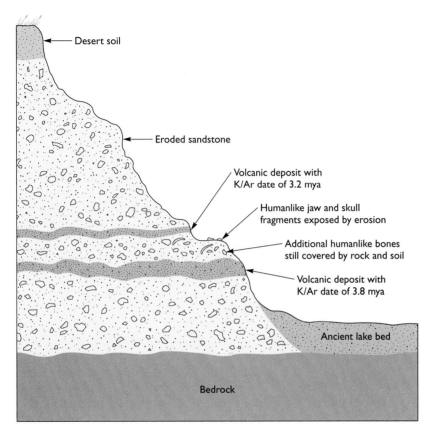

- Desert soil
- Eroded sandstone
- Volcanic deposit with K/Ar date of 3.2 mya
- Humanlike jaw and skull fragments exposed by erosion
- Additional humanlike bones still covered by rock and soil
- Volcanic deposit with K/Ar date of 3.8 mya
- Ancient lake bed
- Bedrock

FIGURE 7.11 Hypothetical geological profile showing human remains between two layers of volcanic rock. The archaeological material must be younger than the volcanic deposit below it (3.8 mya) and older than the volcanic deposit above it (3.2 mya).

measured. Because the half-life of ^{40}K is known (1.31 billion years), how old the rock is—when it last solidified—can be determined by measuring how much argon has accumulated. Because of the very long half-life, there is virtually no upper limit to the technique—nothing is too old to be dated. On the other hand, although it is technically feasible to date rock that is only 10,000 years old, the long half-life generally renders the technique inaccurate for anything less than 100,000 years old.

Potassium/argon and argon/argon dating reveal the age of the rock, that is, how long ago it came out of a volcano. It is not, therefore, a direct measure of the date of a site but, instead, the age of a layer of volcanic rock. Archaeologists can, however, combine K/Ar and Ar/Ar dating with stratigraphic analysis. For example, if artifacts or bones are found in a stratigraphic layer *above* a volcanic flow that is dated by either technique to 3.8 mya and *below* a subsequent flow dated to 3.2 mya, then they are reasonably certain that the occupation of the site is not more than 3.8 million and not less than 3.2 million years old (Figure 7.11). Many fossil human sites were dated with the original potassium/argon technique; many are now being dated using the argon/argon method.

Still another series of radiometric techniques is based on calibrations of the decay rate of uranium isotopes to their various "daughter" isotopes and elements. For example, ^{234}U decays to thorium, and ^{235}U decays to protactinium. Rather than disappearing entirely, these isotopes decay at a known rate to an equilibrium level with their daughter isotopes. When a carbonate or phosphate has been deposited at the time of site occupation, typically as in a cave deposit called *travertine,* the site can be dated. En-crustations found on bones have also been dated using this technique. The decay to thorium is extremely useful because the half-life of ^{234}U is about 247,000 years and that of thorium, 75,400 years. As a result, sites too old to date with radiocarbon but too young to use K/Ar or Ar/Ar dat-ing can sometimes be dated by means of **uranium series.**

Electron spin resonance, or **ESR, dating** is based on measurement of the cumulative "damage" produced on a paleoanthropological specimen (typically a tooth) by radioactive decay in the specimen itself as well as in the soil in which it was deposited (Grün 1993; Grün and Stringer 1991). Once the background radiation rate and susceptibility of the specimen to radiation damage are accounted for, the amount of damage present can be used to determine the age of the specimen. ESR dating is applicable to teeth that are several thousand years or older. The upper limit for ESR is estimated at somewhere between 10 million and 100 million years (Grün and Stringer 1991:165).

Dendrochronology, or tree-ring dating, is an extremely accurate bio-logical dating technique. It is very limited in its application, however, and depends on four principles:

1. Trees add one growth ring for each year they are alive.
2. The size of a ring in a given year varies according to some environ-mental condition or set of conditions such as rainfall or temperature.
3. Any sequence of varying tree-ring widths over a long period of time will be unique.
4. All trees in a given area reflect the same changes in tree-ring width.

By overlapping ring sequences of living trees with those of old dead trees, a **master sequence** of tree-ring width variation over many years can be developed. Such master sequences have been developed for several world areas, extending back to nearly 12,000 years. When an archaeologi-cal site is located that contains wood or even entire logs, the unique se-quence of thick and thin rings in the ancient specimens can be compared to the master sequence (Figure 7.12). In this way, the exact year a tree was cut down can be determined. This may or may not coincide with the date of house construction, however, because an old log may have been reused in the building or a new beam may have replaced an original long after initial construction.

uranium series A dating technique based on the cali-bration of the decay of ura-nium isotopes to their various "daughter" isotopes and ele-ments including thorium and protactinium.

electron spin resonance (ESR) dating A dating tech-nique based on measuring the buildup of electrons in crystalline materials.

dendrochronology A dating technique using tree-ring sequences.

master sequence The gen-eral and relatively consistent pattern of tree-ring width variation over time within a given region.

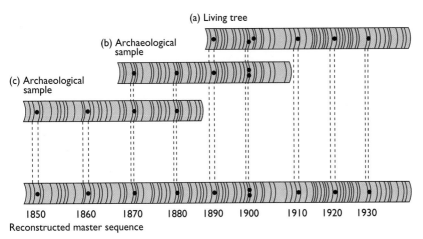

FIGURE 7.12 Cross section of tree rings from a living tree (a) overlaps the ring sequence from an archaeological sample (b) which, in turn, overlaps part of the sequence of another archaeological sample (c). The overlapping of many samples allows for the construction of a "master sequence" of tree-ring patterns shown at the bottom. (*Archaeology: Discovering Our Past, 2d ed., Sharer and Ashmore, 1993:320, Mayfield Publishing*)

This brings us back to the primary problem mentioned earlier in interpreting radiocarbon dates: How do we interpret radiocarbon dates? In other words, how do we convert radiocarbon dates to actual calendar-year dates? Dendrochronology provides an answer. Tree-ring dates are extremely precise and accurate; under most circumstances, a tree-ring year date corresponds exactly to the actual calendar year in which the ring was formed. Therefore, tree-ring dates provide us with our fixed, absolutely accurate chronometer, presenting us with actual calendar years. Next, we can obtain radiocarbon dates for wood samples taken from each of a long sequence of individual tree rings. Each of these radiocarbon dates reflects the year in which the ring was laid down by the living tree. This works because old tree rings are no longer growing and are, therefore, removed from the carbon cycle; decaying ^{14}C is not being replenished in them. A ring laid down 1,000 years ago in a *living* redwood tree, for example, will produce a carbon date of about 1,000 years before the present. A very large sample of carbon dates derived from old tree rings has been carefully compared to the actual calendar age of each ring. A graph in which tree-ring dates represent the independent variable and radiocarbon dates represent the dependent variable provides us with a **calibration curve** covering the last 11,000 years. This graph allows a radiocarbon date within this period to be converted to a calendar-year date (Figure 7.13). Moving up the curve from the bottom right to the top left, you can see that from the present to about 3,000 ya, radiocarbon dates derived from individual tree rings (the black, squiggly line) are a very close match for the actual (calendar-year) tree-ring dates (the straight, red line). Further back in time, however, the radiocarbon dates begin to diverge somewhat from the tree-ring dates, consistently falling below the tree-ring calendar line, indicating that the radiocarbon dates are too young. This implies, following our previous discussion, that the atmosphere before 3,000 ya had a higher concentration

calibration curve The curve derived for the correlation of tree-ring and radiocarbon dates.

FIGURE 7.13 Calibration curve for radiocarbon dates. The vertical axis represents the radiocarbon dates derived for a large number of tree-ring samples, and the horizontal axis represents the actual dendrochronologically derived dates for those same tree rings. As you can see, for tree rings that are more than about 3,000 years old, radiocarbon dates generally understate the true age of a sample.

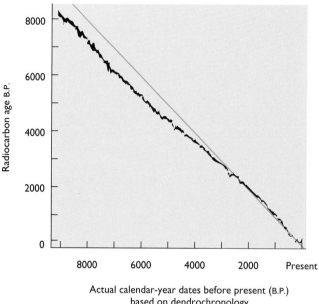

of ^{14}C than at the present. This means that radiocarbon dates that are more than 3,000 years old consistently underestimate the actual, calendar age of the dated material. When receiving dates from a radiocarbon lab, archaeologists receive both the radiocarbon date itself as well as the calendar date as interpolated from the calibration graph.

Cultural Techniques

The final dating methods to discuss are based on our knowledge of material culture and common patterns of cultural change. As a group, these methods are called **cultural techniques.**

For example, imagine that you are walking down the street and a car drives by. It is large with sharp tail-fins and built low to the ground. You can tell almost immediately that this car is a 1950s model. Suppose I hand you a photograph of a young woman with a ponytail who is wearing saddle shoes, knee socks, a frilly blouse, and a swing skirt featuring an embroidered poodle. Again, the time period is the 1950s. But how do you know this? You know because you are aware of certain style changes that have taken place in our own culture (Figure 7.14).

Archaeologists perform a similar kind of identification when they determine the age of a site based on the style of the architecture or artifacts found there. Archaeologists can pick up a piece of pottery or a stone tool

cultural technique A dating technique using cultural comparisons.

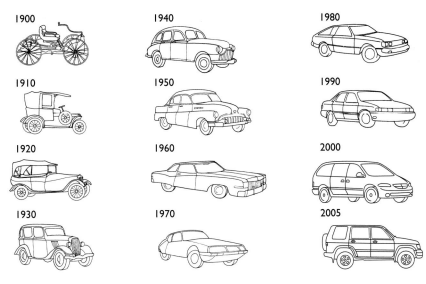

1900 1910 1920 1930 1940 1950 1960 1970 1980 1990 2000 2005

FIGURE 7.14 Styles of artifacts change over time as technology and tastes change. Automobiles are one example. (*Archaeology: Discovering Our Past*, 2d ed., *Sharer and Ashmore, 1993:307, Mayfield Publishing*)

and estimate its age because they are familiar with style changes in the ancient past. They can apply actual dates to these items if identical styles have been found at other sites where absolute dates have been obtained.

Archaeologists also measure the rates of change and gauge how quickly styles replace each other by a process called **seriation.** This technique assumes that styles of certain artifacts, such as pottery, arrowheads, gravestones, and even soda cans, change in fairly regular patterns. When a new way of doing something—decorating ceramics, making arrowheads, designing gravestones, opening soft drink cans—is introduced in a culture, it starts off slowly, gains in acceptance until it reaches a peak, and then is slowly replaced by another, newer way of doing the same thing. An interesting example of this process can be seen in gravestones in seventeenth-, eighteenth-, and nineteenth-century New England (Dethlefsen and Deetz, 1966; Figure 7.15). The predictable pattern of this process is used as a relative dating technique by placing sites in the most logical chronological order based on these changes in style.

Many other dating techniques are available to the archaeologist. Table 7.1 presents a list and some details of their applicability.

How? Reconstructing Past Lifeways

How did the people at a given archaeological site get by? What did they eat, how did they make their tools, how did they obtain resources necessary for their survival, how did they organize their societies, how did they

seriation Establishing a relative chronological sequence using the pattern of replacement of artifact styles.

FIGURE 7.15 Seriation graph of tombstone design in central Connecticut cemeteries from 1700 to 1860. Here, as elsewhere in New England, the so-called death's head, or skull design, was replaced by the cherub, or smiling angel face, which was, in turn, replaced by the urn and willow tree design. The statistical pattern of design replacement is typical for many artifact types analyzed by archaeologists. *(K. L. Feder)*

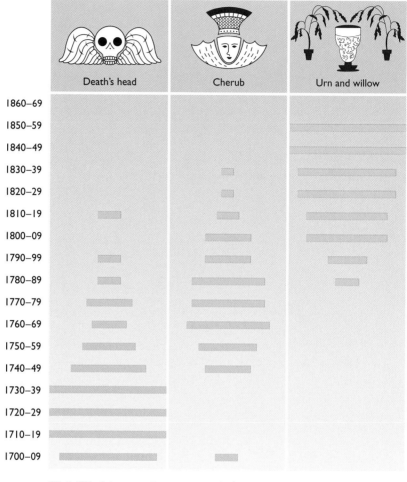

= 10% of the stones in a ten-year period

bury their dead? How did people respond to changes in the environment? How did agriculture develop? How did the first cities evolve? A major problem in answering these questions is, of course, that the people being studied are dead. We can't ask them about their relations with their neighbors. We can't examine their social networks or political practices. We can't observe their religious ceremonies. We can't interview them about their reasons for adopting agriculture.

One way around this is through **ethnoarchaeology.** With this approach, archaeologists examine living groups in the same manner as ethnographers, but they focus on how human behavior becomes translated into the archaeological record. This is an important approach when analyzing

ethnoarchaeology Observing living peoples to understand how archaeological records are produced.

TABLE 7.1 Other Dating Methods

Dating Method	Age Range	Material Dated	Basis
Thermoluminescence	No effective limits	Fired clay, pottery, bricks, burned rock	Measure of amount of energy captured in material from decay of radioactive elements in surrounding soil; amount of energy captured is proportional to age
Paleomagnetism	2,000 B.P.– present	Material with magnetic minerals	Movement of earth's magnetic poles and known dates of the position of the poles
Amino (aspartic) acid racemization	1,000,000– 2,000 B.P.	Bone	Shift in polarity of amino acids
Obsidian hydration	800,000 B.P.– present	Obsidian (volcanic glass)	Regular buildup of "hydration layer" caused by chemical reaction of obsidian with water over time
Fission track dating	1,000,000– 100,000 B.P	Volcanic rock	Radioactive decay leaves microscopic damage "tracks" in rock at regular rate

the general processes by which sites are produced. But when it comes to attempting to reconstruct a particular culture, all that archaeologists generally have are physical remains, the hardware left behind, the stuff made and used and then lost, discarded, or abandoned. Much methodology, then, concerns itself with this task: How can the static archaeological record consisting of such things as a bunch of broken pots, pieces of bone, arrowheads, and ruins be transformed into a dynamic picture of a once-vibrant, now past culture? Anthropologists who live with a people to understand their way of life are performing **ethnography** (literally, "cultural description"). Archaeologists trying to understand an ancient way of life are performing **paleoethnography.**

Paleoethnography includes a series of general categories of cultural inquiry: technology, environment, diet, social systems, trade, and ideology. Certainly, society's activities could be categorized other ways, but these should encompass many of the major questions an anthropologist might ask.

Technology

The study of prehistoric technology involves figuring out how past people made the things they used and how they used them. This can include everything from a simple stone spear point to an enormous pyramid. Technology is one of the areas of ancient life an archaeologist can study most directly. After all, most of what we find are physical objects, the direct products of a given technology. Archaeologists can use information from a

ethnography The intensive study and description of a particular culture.

paleoethnography Reconstructing a past cultural system through archaeological remains.

FIGURE 7.16 Experimental archaeologist Terry del Bene produces replicas of stone tools with stone and antler hammers. By replicating stone tools, the archaeologist can gain some insight into how prehistoric specimens were made and used. *(Courtesy Terry del Bene)*

direct historical approach
One method of ethnographic analogy. The historically recorded behavior of descendants of a group whose archaeological remains are being studied is used as the source for models or analogies in an attempt to understand the ancient culture.

ethnographic analogy A technique in archaeological analysis in which a written description of the lifeway of a contemporary or historically recorded group is used as a model for interpreting the archaeological record.

number of sources to give them clues about how the things dug up were actually made by prehistoric people.

The historical record is one source of data. For example, the early Spanish settlers in Mexico described in writing how the Aztecs manufactured artifacts of silver and gold. We know how the longhouses of the Iroquois Indians of New York State were made because the early Jesuit missionaries wrote extensively about Iroquois lifestyles. We know about the trading networks and patterns of the aboriginal people of Australia because European settlers, missionaries, and early anthropologists wrote much about how various native groups obtained from their neighbors, both nearby and distant, raw materials such as stone for axes and stingray barb spines for hunting weapons. The archaeologist simply attempts to extend the historical record back into the prehistoric past. Using these ethnohistorical sources, studying ethnographic accounts describing the cultures of the actual descendants of the ancient people whose artifacts are being studied (the **direct historical approach**), or relying on the written descriptions of people who lived ways of life generally similar to those of the ancient people being investigated are all part of an analytical technique called **ethnographic analogy.** Archaeologists use the detailed descriptions of historically examined and recorded cultures as analogies to provide models for the way of life of a particular prehistoric group.

Another way to study prehistoric technology is by experimentation. The archaeologist attempts, through a process of trial and error, to replicate objects that have been recovered (Figure 7.16). If you wish to know how a certain variety of prehistoric stone tool was made, you try to make one exactly like it—using the same raw material, same size, and same proportions. Following a research model developed by archaeologist Lawrence Keeley (1980), students in my (Feder's) experimental archaeology course spend a few weeks making stone tools and then using them in a wide variety of ways (cutting, piercing, scraping, engraving, drilling, etc.) on an equally wide range of raw materials (wood, bone, leather, antler, etc.). The students then examine each utilized replica tool under the microscope, looking for the distinct types of wear or damage Keeley (1980) enumerated, such as polishing, abrasion, striations, and scalar and half-moon scarring (Figure 7.17). After a while, students are able to identify the specific uses that result in the types of wear and damage produced on utilized stone tool edges. They figure out pretty quickly, for example, that the working edge of a stone drill used to make holes in wood often exhibits some polishing. Similarly, they learn that a stone knife used to cut meat off of bone will (like a drill) display polishing, but it will also exhibit striations parallel to the working edge, as well as scalar scars along that edge.

The true measure of their **wear pattern** knowledge comes next, in a blind test. Students randomly switch tools with their classmates. Without knowing how the tools they are about to examine were used and with only the patterned evidence of wear and damage to figure that out, they do very well, more often than not correctly deducing both how the tools were used and the raw materials on which they were used.

Archaeological experiments can try to replicate anything from a single artifact type—say, prehistoric axes from France—to an entire way of life (Figure 7.18). A series of ambitious experiments were aired on the British science program *Horizon* (and shown in the United States on PBS's *Nova* series). Combining their skills and expertise, archaeologists, sculptors, engineers, and stonemasons made experimental replicas of Stonehenge, Inca walls, the roof over the Coliseum in Rome, an Egyptian obelisk, and an Egyptian pyramid (see Chapter 13 for some of the original works). In the case of the pyramid—through historical research, archaeological analysis, and more than a little trial and error—they were able to quarry the stone, move it to the construction site, and build a small replica of a pyramid using techniques available to ancient Egyptians (Figure 7.19). Other experiments related to monumentally scaled, ancient architectural projects have been conducted including those by scientists wishing to determine how the enormous Easter Island statues were carved and transported (van Tilburg 1995). These exercises have been extremely successful in testing ways that such tasks could have been performed by ancient people without benefit of modern technology.

Yet another experiment was carried out in Denmark by a group of people who lived for about four months in a dwelling patterned on the remains of Danish **Bronze Age** structures. They worked and slept in the house in an isolated part of Denmark. They grew their own food, kept animals, and made tools. They immersed themselves in what life was thought to be like in the Bronze Age based on archaeological findings. By actually attempting to live according to reconstructions of the past, archaeologists can get a pretty good idea of what was possible. Experiments show how people *may* have accomplished a task such as building a pyramid or making a tool, but they cannot be used to *prove* that people worked in this way—there are always other possibilities.

Environment

A number of techniques are available for ancient environmental reconstruction. For example, the dating technique of dendrochronology can be used to reconstruct general rainfall patterns in some areas; the width of tree rings are proportional to the amount of rain that falls in a given year—the more rain, the thicker the ring.

More broadly, changes in worldwide climate can be recognized through an analysis of the ratio of two isotopes of oxygen, ^{16}O and ^{18}O, in seawater. This ratio varies over time as a function of changes in the earth's climate. Simply stated, water bearing ^{16}O, the lighter isotope, evaporates more readily than does water containing ^{18}O. In generally warm periods, this has little impact on the $^{16}O{:}^{18}O$ ratio in the ocean because most of the

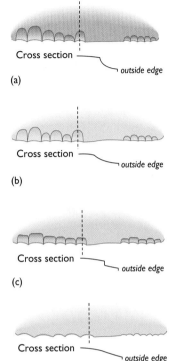

Cross section — outside edge
(a)

Cross section — outside edge
(b)

Cross section — outside edge
(c)

Cross section — outside edge
(d)

FIGURE 7.17 A compendium of edge damage types, all of which result from tool use recognized and defined by archaeologist Lawrence Keeley: (a) deep scalar scars (large, *left*; small, *right*), (b) shallow scalar scars (large, *left*; small, *right*), (c) step scars (large, *left*; small, *right*), and (d) half-moons. (*After Lawrence Keeley, 1980*)

wear pattern A mark indicative of certain uses, left on a tool.

Bronze Age The period of European history when bronze toolmaking began.

(a)

(b)

(c)

(d)

FIGURE 7.18 Assortment of archaeological replicative experiments designed and conducted by students in my (Feder's) experimental archaeology course: (a) fire starting; (b) bow and arrow; (c) ballista (ancient Greek siege weapon); (d) trebuchet (mid-thirteenth-century weapon). (K. L. Feder)

seawater that evaporates falls as rain and returns to the sea. When the planet as a whole is colder, however, large quantities of seawater evaporate, fall as snow in northern latitudes and high elevations, and do not melt off. This effectively depletes the ocean of some of its ^{16}O, changing the ratio of the two isotopes.

How can the $^{16}O{:}^{18}O$ ratio in ancient seawater be measured? It can't be—directly. Fortunately, however, the ratio can be measured in the an-

FIGURE 7.19 In this archaeological experiment, an archaeologist, an experienced stonemason, and a small group of Egyptian stoneworkers tested various hypotheses regarding the construction of the ancient Egyptian pyramids by actually attempting to put suggested techniques into practice. Notice the ancient pyramid in the background. *(Courtesy Mark Lehner)*

cient skeletons of small marine organisms called **foraminifera.** These organisms incorporate oxygen into their skeletons, reflecting the $^{16}O:^{18}O$ ratio in the surrounding seawater.

Stratigraphic columns of suboceanic deposits have been dated by assuming a constant rate of deposition and by reference to a 180-degree shift in the earth's magnetic field dated by K/Ar to 780,000 ya (Monastersky 1992). A chronological sequence of changes in the $^{16}O:^{18}O$ ratio has been constructed by Nicholas Shackleton and Neil Opdyke (1973; see Figure 9.13). Currently, the $^{16}O:^{18}O$ ratio is also being analyzed a bit more directly in ancient ice brought up in cores taken from deep in the Greenland ice sheet. It is hoped that the cores will cover 200,000 years of weather history (Monastersky 1991).

A widely applicable procedure for environmental reconstruction is **palynology**—the study of pollen. The pollen from each species of plant is unique in its appearance (Figure 7.20). Every year, great quantities of pollen are produced, and much of it ends up in the soil, where it preserves quite well under the right conditions. Palynologists can recover prehistoric pollen, identify the species represented, and date the pollen by reference to stratigraphy or by carbon-dating organic remains associated with

foraminifera Microscopic marine organisms whose exoskeletons are used in oxygen isotope analysis.

palynology The identification of plants through their preserved pollen remains.

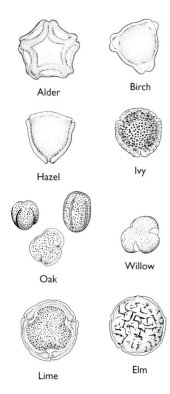

Alder   Birch

Hazel   Ivy

Oak   Willow

Lime   Elm

FIGURE 7.20 Pollen from a number of plant species, drawn to scale. (The grains are magnified about 5,000 times actual size.) Palynology, the study of pollen, can provide information about the plant communities growing in an area. This, in turn, can be used to reconstruct the environment.

midden A pile of trash produced by the inhabitants of a settlement.

flotation A technique in which soil matrix and archaeological material are separated by the use of water.

it. (Usually, pollen itself is not dated because there is too little of it by weight.) Because individual plant communities thrive under varying environmental conditions, knowing which plants grew in an area in given periods provides insight into what the climate was like. Knowing what grew there, and when, gives an idea of what the people who lived there may have eaten.

Diet

One of the most important pieces of information about a prehistoric people is the nature of their diet. This is especially true when trying to answer questions related to the origins of agriculture (see Chapter 12). Archaeologists can approach diet in a number of ways.

They can study diet indirectly by figuring out what people might have eaten based on what was available in their natural environment. For example, deer, moose, raccoon, duck, turkey, and fish are known to have been available in New England for about 7,000 years. A hunting and gathering people in this area are likely to have used such resources at one time or another. This method of reasoning, however, has a weakness simply because the modern environment may be quite different from the prehistoric one.

On the other hand, archaeologists can approach the question of diet more directly if there has been good preservation. In many instances, the food remains themselves are still present in archaeological sites. Archaeologists can study the fireplaces, hearths, and garbage heaps, or **middens,** of the people who lived at a site (Figure 7.21). From these, we may recover food material if it has been preserved.

Such remains as bone, seeds, and nuts are often fragile and fragmentary, however, making it difficult to get them out of the ground and back to the lab for identification and analysis. In many cases, an archaeologist takes the entire feature, including all soil, back to the laboratory, instead of attempting to separate the dry soil matrix from the fragile archaeological remains in the field. In the lab, through a number of different procedures collectively called **flotation,** the archaeologist takes advantage of the fact that soil and rock will not float in some liquids, whereas organic remains will (Pearsall 1989). Liquid, then, does the delicate job of separation.

The next task in the reconstruction of a prehistoric diet is the identification of the species of plant or animal represented by the remains. This task can be difficult because of the fragmentary nature of such remains. In some cases, no precise identification can be made—the piece of bone is too small or the seed too broken up to tell with any degree of confidence. But by using a **comparative collection**—a sort of "library" of bones, nuts, and seeds—archaeologists can often identify many of the dietary remains found at a site (Figure 7.22).

Examining the animal remains found at a site is called **faunal analysis.** Here, the species represented, their sex, ages at death, health, and

FIGURE 7.21 The excavation of features allows archaeologists to recover the remnants of a discrete behavior at a particular time. A hearth, like this one, can tell us about prehistoric diet. Features also include burials, stoneworking areas, pottery kilns, and structural remains. *(K. L. Feder)*

physical characteristics are identified. Knowing the species of the remains as well as their age, sex, and health status can provide insight into the hunting practices of prehistoric people. Were the people hunting large numbers of herd animals in group hunts, or were their prey solitary creatures that could be hunted by individual hunters? Were the ancient people able to kill large animals in their prime, or only the very young, very old, or sick? Also, because many animals give birth to their young seasonally, during restricted periods, knowing the age of death of a juvenile helps determine the season of the hunt. For example, the North American white-

comparative collection A "library" of animal bones or seeds and nuts used for comparison with archaeological specimens.

faunal analysis An examination of animal remains from archaeological sites.

FIGURE 7.22 Even quite small bones recovered at a 2,000-year-old archaeological site can be identified by matching them to known, modern bones from an osteological comparative collection or "bone library." The archaeological specimens *(the two bones on the bottom)* match the form of the two foot bones of a white-tailed deer from our comparative collection *(top)*. *(K. L. Feder)*

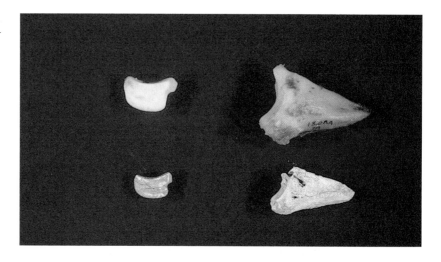

tailed deer usually bears its young in May or June. If the bones of a deer found at an archaeological site indicate an age of 9 months, the animal must have been killed, and the site was most probably occupied, in February or March.

An important factor that must be taken into account in using faunal analysis to reconstruct prehistoric diet is taphonomy. **Taphonomy** involves the analysis of how bones (animal or human) become part of the archaeological or paleontological record. How did the animal die? Was it killed by animals or by people? What happened to the bones of the animal after its death? Was it scavenged or immediately buried, say, in a flood? How were the bones deposited? Were they moved from the kill site by scavengers or some other process?

Taphonomy is a crucial consideration when trying to generate and test hypotheses concerning the behavior of an ancient people. Were they the hunters—or the hunted? Did they engage in organized communal hunts, or did they merely scavenge the remains of creatures killed by carnivorous animals? Were they ritualistic cannibals, or were their bones simply picked over by scavengers? Before concluding that an animal was hunted, killed, and eaten by humans, archaeologists must distinguish between the marks left on animal bones by stone tools and the traces left by animal teeth. Before making inferences about hunting practices from a pile of bones in a cave, they must distinguish between an assemblage of bones left by people and one left by carnivorous animals. Detailed analyses of how carnivores and scavengers kill, dismember, and deposit bones (Binford 1978, 1981; Read-Martin and Read 1975) and microscopic analysis of cut marks and tooth marks on bones (Shipman and Rose 1983) are contributing to the understanding of taphonomy and, ultimately, to the nature of the diet of our prehistoric ancestors.

taphonomy The study of how organisms become part of the archaeological or paleontological records.

General information about diet can sometimes be gathered from an animal's skeletal remains. For example, in mammals the nature of the dentition is a clue to overall food sources. Carnivores such as dogs and cats, for example, have slicing teeth adapted to meat eating. Humans have a more generalized dentition, built for chewing a varied diet. Certain wear patterns on the teeth, examined microscopically, can reveal whether the diet was made up of soft foods such as fruits or more abrasive, gritty foods such as roots and tubers (see Figure 8.16). The chemical content of ancient bones can be examined for their proportion of strontium and calcium to determine whether plants or meat made up the bulk of the diet of certain populations. An inadequate diet leaves its mark on the human skeleton too. For example, nutritional deficiencies may show up in porous bones or abnormal bone growth. Two specific deficiencies, those of vitamin D (rickets) and vitamin C (scurvy), leave characteristic signs on the skeleton.

Plants produce a mineral residue consisting of microscopic particles called **phytoliths.** Because they are made up of mineral particles—technically opal silica bodies—phytoliths can be quite durable, surviving for centuries and even millennia in the soil and, in certain circumstances, on the surfaces of tools used to process the plants that produced them. Each plant species produces a morphologically unique set of phytoliths (Figure 7.23). Therefore, when phytoliths are recovered from archaeological artifacts or soils, specialists can identify the kinds of plants that grew in the area when the site was occupied and can deduce the plant's species on which the tools were used. For example, at the Aguadulce Shelter site in Panama, Dolores Piperno, Anthony Ranere, Irene Holst, and Patricia Hansell (2000) recovered phytoliths embedded in imperfections on the surfaces of a number of milling stones. The plants represented in the phytolith assemblage included manioc, arrowroot, and yams, all food sources utilized by the residents of this 7,000-year-old site.

Carbon isotope analysis can also be used to identify diet patterns in some cases. Along with ^{12}C, the most abundant and stable isotope of carbon, and ^{14}C, the isotope used in radiocarbon dating, there is another stable variety of carbon, ^{13}C. Carbon 13 has the same number of protons as ^{12}C and ^{14}C, but it differs in its number of neutrons; ^{13}C has seven neutrons (7 neutrons + 6 protons = 13; thus the 13 in ^{13}C). About 1 in 100 carbon atoms are ^{13}C. It turns out that different varieties of plants use the ^{12}C and ^{13}C isotopes differentially in photosynthesis. The differences in ^{12}C and ^{13}C absorption is detectable not only in the plants themselves but also in the tissues of the animals that eat them. Thus, under certain circumstances, human bones can be analyzed for their $^{12}C{:}^{13}C$ ratio, and the kinds of plants that were abundant in the diet can be determined. This approach has been applied in the examination of the domestication of maize (corn), which uses a photosynthesis process different from most of the wild plants that grow in the same area in Central America (Farnsworth et al. 1985; and see Chapter 12).

phytoliths Microscopic fragments of opal silica produced in plant cells. Phytolith form is species-specific, enabling researchers to identify plants that grew in an area and those that may have been used by ancient humans or human ancestors.

carbon isotope analysis Analysis of the ratio of ^{12}C to ^{13}C in a sample.

FIGURE 7.23 Phytoliths, like pollen, are durable and species-specific. When phytoliths are recovered from the soils at an archaeological site or on the surfaces of tools, the species of the plants growing in the area or even on which the tools were used can be identified. Phytoliths produced by maize are shown here. *(Courtesy Deborah Pearsall/University of Missouri Paleoethnobotany Lab)*

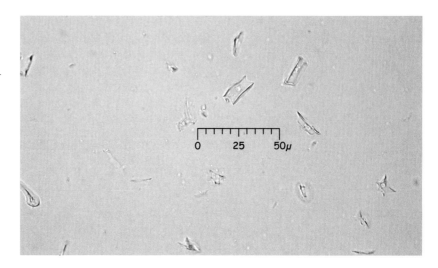

Another important method used in dietary reconstruction is usually applicable only in very dry areas of the world, where the level of organic preservation is high. This technique is based on the simple fact that most animals, including human beings, do not completely digest everything they eat. In other words, some of what goes in very often comes out—and in recognizable form. The data in question are the preserved remains of prehistoric feces, or **paleofeces.** Paleofeces (often called **coprolites**) contain undigested particles of food that survived an organism's digestive system. Though not one of the more romantic activities in archaeology and paleoanthropology, there are few better ways of reconstructing an ancient person's last meal than by examining what passed through his or her system. Because many caves were used repeatedly, a large sample of paleofeces may be present and provide a broad view of the diet of an ancient group—at least during the time they used the cave.

A new line of research indicates that blood traces might be preserved on the edges of stone tools used to kill animals or process animal products. When this occurs, the blood can be analyzed and the animal species identified. For example, using standard forensic procedures to identify blood at crime scenes, Australian archaeologist Tom Loy has identified blood residues on a stone artifact recovered at a 9,000-year-old archaeological site in Turkey as belonging to sheep, humans, and an extinct form of cattle (Bower 1989a). Archaeologists Noreen Tuross and Tom Dillehay (1995) report the identification of mastodon blood on a 13,000-year-old stone tool found in Chile. There are a series of ongoing debates about the accuracy of such identifications (Kaiser 1995), but all agree that blood-residue analysis is a procedure that deserves consideration.

paleofeces Preserved fecal remains.

coprolites Fossilized feces, useful in reconstructing a paleo-diet. Paleofeces.

Social Systems

Studying prehistoric technology and diet may be difficult tasks, but at least tools and food remains are often preserved, allowing archaeologists to study these aspects of culture directly. Social systems, or the interrelationships of people, leave little in the way of direct material remains, however. Who do people marry, and with whom do they live? Who do they consider to be family, and who not? To whom do they owe their allegiance, and on whom do they depend in time of trouble? All these ties are crucial to human survival, but direct remains are few.

Nevertheless, reconstruction of social systems is possible because the objects that people make and use—the material remains found at archaeological sites—were made, used, and discarded within a *social context.* The very careful analysis of sometimes minute details of artifact manufacture and design can provide information about the social system of the people being studied because social information is *encoded* into the things that people make.

A good example of this phenomenon is found in archaeologist James Deetz's classic study of Arikara ceramics (Deetz 1965). According to the historical record, the Arikara, Native Americans who lived in what is now Nebraska, were a **matrilocal** society. That is, upon marriage a young woman remained in her home village and her husband, usually someone from another village, moved in with her. At any given time, therefore, a village is composed of grandmothers, daughters, and granddaughters, who all grew up in the same village, and their husbands, who have moved in from different villages. Deetz was able to show that in these matrilocal Arikara villages, the pottery, which was made by the women, was homogeneous. In other words, because all the women were related and learned their craft from women who were related, their styles were highly similar. Different villages, then, each had their unique style.

When the matrilocal pattern broke down after European contact, however, women no longer stayed in one place, and the **postmarital residence pattern** became **patrilocal.** The pottery in any one village was now heterogeneous, having been made by women who moved in from different villages with their different styles. Deetz could trace these changes in pottery styles as the social system changed over time. The material objects—the pots—reflected changes in the social context in which they were made.

In an example of a similar kind of analysis, but one where there is no historical data to indicate the kind of postmarital residence pattern practiced by the people, at the 11,000-year-old Lindenmeier site in Colorado there were two major concentrations of a particular kind of spear point used in killing big-game animals (Wilmsen 1974). Careful analysis of the points in the two concentrations showed subtle differences in the style of the points, which led researcher Edwin Wilmsen to conclude that two separate bands of hunters had inhabited Lindenmeier at the same time. The

matrilocal A type of society in which a married couple lives with the wife's family.

postmarital residence pattern Where a new couple lives after they marry.

patrilocal A type of society in which a married couple lives with the husband's family.

points were probably made by men living in two different patrilocal bands. In Wilmsen's view, like the Arikara women making pottery in their matrilocal groups, men learned spear making from their fathers and brothers, all of whom stayed in the band when they got married. Thus, each patrilocal band developed a unique style of point making.

Trade: The Movement of Materials and People

Archaeologists are also interested in the relationships among the inhabitants of different ancient societies. Many prehistoric people, even those living at great distances from one another, engaged in trade. Obsidian (natural volcanic glass) from Turkey is found at sites in Syria, hundreds of miles from its source. Copper from Michigan is found in New York State. Turquoise from the American Southwest is found in Mexico. Shells from the Pacific Ocean are found in highland New Guinea. Once the source of raw materials can be ascertained, maps showing the movement of such materials can be drawn.

We can sometimes determine the precise sources of raw materials by macroscopic (naked-eye) inspection. Often, however, it is not so easy, and much more sophisticated techniques are needed. In **petrographic analysis,** a thin slice can be cut from a stone artifact and examined microscopically. The "fabric" of the rock from which an artifact was made can then be compared to the fabric of various possible natural outcrops in order to associate the artifact's raw material with its particular source. Another procedure is called **trace element analysis.** This technique measures the quantities of so-called trace elements in materials. For example, whereas obsidian, wherever it comes from, is made up largely of silica, there are also tiny amounts (traces) of other elements—impurities such as arsenic and copper. The precise proportions of these trace elements are generally unique to the area where the raw material originated and thus can serve as a sort of "fingerprint" for a raw-material source. Archaeologists can determine the trace elements in the raw material of an artifact and then match up that fingerprint to a source with the same trace element chemistry.

In the Lindenmeier example just discussed, Wilmsen performed trace element analysis on the obsidian tools from the two different concentrations. The tools from one of the concentrations exhibited a profile of trace elements very similar to that displayed by an obsidian source located in northeastern Wyoming; the tools in the second Lindenmeier concentration matched the trace element composition of obsidian found at a source in central New Mexico. The hypothesis of two separate hunting bands, therefore, was supported. Two distinct bands, making tools in their own styles and traveling in different territories (one moving through, and collecting raw materials in, Wyoming, the other gathering their material in New Mexico), came together at Lindenmeier. That we can know this 11,000 years after the fact is a testament to anthropology of the past.

petrographic analysis Examination of the morphology of a lithic source by the analysis of thin slices of rock.

trace element analysis Determining the source of a material by identifying small (trace) amounts of impurities.

FIGURE 7.24 An example of turquoise inlay done by the indigenous people of Mesoamerica. Interestingly, since there aren't extensive deposits of turquoise in Mesoamerica, the question is where they got the raw material! Using neutron activation analysis, researchers have been able to trace the source to deposits located in the southwestern United States.
(Werner/Forman Art Resource)

Archaeologists, cultural anthropologists, and historians have long recognized that the indigenous people of Mesoamerica placed a high value in the semiprecious stone turquoise and used it to produce beautiful works of sculpture and jewelry (Figure 7.24). Those same scientists have also long recognized that there simply aren't any extensive natural deposits of this lustrous blue-green stone in Mesoamerica. Naturally enough, this leads to the question: Where did people including the Aztecs, Toltecs, and Maya (discussed in Chapter 13) obtain their raw turquoise?

In a project that has spanned more than thirty years, archaeologist Phil Weigand has attempted to answer this question. Weigand has collected samples of raw turquoise from forty-four significant known sources in the American Southwest and California (Powell 2005). As an undergraduate student at what was then called the State University of New York at Stonybrook (now, Stonybrook University), I (Feder) worked on an early phase of the project, preparing samples from these turquoise sources for **neutron activation analysis,** a very powerful trace element procedure. Through this technique, Weigand has been able to establish the chemical "signatures" of each of these sources.

Along with Brookhaven National Laboratories physicist Garman Harbottle, Weigand has also applied neutron activation analysis to finished turquoise artifacts excavated from archaeological sites in Mexico, and he

neutron activation analysis A procedure that reveals the chemical signature of a raw material, such as turquoise, obsidian, or clay; used to associate an artifact with the source from which its raw material originated.

has compared their trace element compositions to the sources he has investigated in the Southwest. The result: many of the turquoise artifacts found in Mexico revealed trace element signatures quite similar to those of sources located north of the border. The conclusion: ancient Mexicans likely obtained turquoise—whether by trade through intermediaries or by long-distance travel—from sources located in what is now the southwestern United States.

Ideology

It might not seem that ideology, philosophy, or religion are topics an archaeologist could readily deal with. After all, archaeologists study physical or material remains. Ideology, by its very nature, is a nonmaterial, abstract aspect of human existence. The same argument applies here that did regarding the archaeologist's ability to reconstruct social systems. Because everything we do takes place within the context of a specific social system, what we make bears some imprint of that system. Similarly, what we do also takes place within the context of an ideological system. In a general sense, all our artifacts are made within the context of an ideology and should reflect certain aspects of that ideology.

It is also necessary to point out that, although culture can be divided into categories such as social systems and ideology, human beings do not compartmentalize their lives. Culture is not simply a bundle of vaguely connected parts; it is an integrated approach to survival. Very often artifacts or features simultaneously reflect several of the separate aspects that make up a culture. One example of this expression of multiple cultural features is burials. The manner in which a human being is buried, for example, reflects a number of abstract concepts. Think in terms of our own culture. Our tombstones—and tombstones are certainly very important "artifacts"—often record the accomplishments of individuals and their family lives as well as reflect their religious beliefs (Figure 7.25). If some future archaeologist were to walk into a twenty-first-century graveyard, he or she would almost certainly gain some insight into our perspective on life, society, religion, and, of course, death.

Prehistoric archaeology and paleoanthropology, however, do not yield tombstones and the legible information they provide. Yet in burying their dead, prehistoric people made as much of a statement about their ideological beliefs as we do. Instead of using a written language, these people wrote their epitaphs in the language of artifacts. Tools and food were often placed in graves to accompany the deceased to the afterlife. Sometimes animals, or even other people, were killed and buried, apparently to serve the needs of the departed. Precious objects manufactured from valuable raw materials were placed in some graves; other burials contain no artifacts. In some instances, huge pyramids were raised over the remains of the dead; other bodies were thrown away in trash heaps. Information

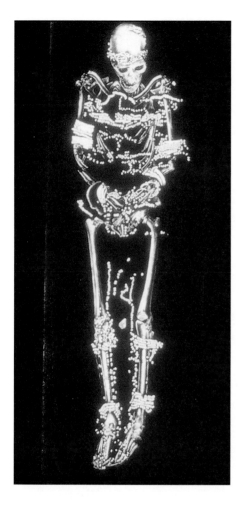

FIGURE 7.25 Artifacts associated with death and burial—such as the more than 300-year-old tombstone from colonial America (above) and the ivory beads in the 25,000-year-old Sungir' burial site (left) near Moscow, Russia—reflect the religious, social, economic, and political systems of the people who produced them. (Tombstone: K. L. Feder; burial site: © O. Bader/Musée de l'Homme)

about social status, trade, religion, and even economics is contained in burials. (An economic system with many "extra" people is needed to build a pyramid every time a ruler dies.) This is why archaeologists are often so anxious to excavate grave sites: they provide valuable data not otherwise available. In addition, of course, the physical remains of the people themselves provide a great deal of information about just who they were.

Who? Identifying the Remains of Humans and Human Ancestors

We are all aware, from newspaper accounts, television, and movies, just how much information can be derived from examining the remains, through autopsies, of recently deceased humans. On rare occasions,

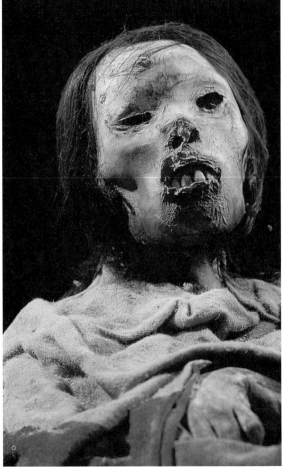

FIGURE 7.26 The famous "Ice Man" *(above),* preserved for over 5,000 years in the Italian Alps, was naturally mummified by cold and wind. He was discovered by hikers in 1991. His excellent state of preservation has allowed anthropologists to discover his age, health status, diet, time of death, genetic affiliations, and even, through artistic reconstruction, his facial features. The "Tollund Man" *(top right),* preserved for 2,000 years in a Danish peat bog, was probably a sacrificial victim—the rope noose was still around his neck. He was well enough preserved that the remains of his last meal (barley and linseed gruel) were still in his stomach. A young Inca girl *(bottom right)* was discovered in 1995 near the summit of the 20,760-foot mountain Nevando Ampato in Peru. Five hundred years ago the girl, nicknamed "Juanita," was sacrificed to the gods of the mountains. She was preserved by the cold and dry conditions of the high altitude. *(Ice Man: © Gerha Hinterleitner/ Gamma; Tollund Man: © Ira Block 1986; Inca girl: © Stephen Alvarez/National Geographic Society Image Collection)*

anthropologists can examine well-preserved ancient remains such as the "Ice Man" from the Alps and the bodies preserved in peat bogs in northern Europe (Figure 7.26).

But such finds are exceptional. Even though anthropologists studying the past cannot usually gather these kinds of data about an individual, they are nevertheless interested in the study of the deceased to learn, in a general sense, who the people were whose lifestyle is being studied. Moreover, anthropologists are interested in humans as a biological species, and the study of human remains addresses certain biological and evolutionary questions.

Finally, they are also concerned with issues, such as cause of death, that reveal something important about the lives of the subjects. The problem paleoanthropologists face is that the remains they study are almost always in the form of bones. The further back in time one goes, the more fragmentary those skeletal remains become. So just what can one hope to discover from this biological data?

Species Identification and Definition

When skeletal remains are unearthed, often in connection with an archaeological excavation, perhaps the most basic task is identifying the species to which the bones belong. How do anthropologists know if the bones are human? A survey of **comparative osteology** (the study of bones of different species) is far beyond the scope of this book. Suffice it to say, though, that the anthropologist interested in this area of study is intimately familiar with the 206 bones of the adult human and is generally able to identify a recovered bone (Figure 7.27). To help in this endeavor, many universities maintain comparative bone collections so that a bone or bone fragment that cannot be readily identified can be compared with similar ones from many species until a match is found.

The identification process gets more complicated when the bones belong to species that no longer exist. Throughout this book, however, we will be designating the species of ancient fossil remains. How is this done? Using the system formalized by Linnaeus (see Chapter 5), scientists classify living animals on the basis of morphology and behavior. Animals that look very similar and share a common behavioral pattern are thought to belong to the same species when—and this is the key—they are *interfertile*. A species is defined as a group of animals in which fertile males and females can mate and produce fertile offspring.

For example, brown bears (genus *Ursus*, species *arctos*) from Eurasia, Alaska, Canada, and the western United States (called grizzly bears in the Western Hemisphere) are all placed in the same species because they look very similar, share the same general environmental niches, and can interbreed to produce offspring who can, in turn, produce offspring of their own. But brown bears are quite different in size, color, and behavior from

comparative osteology The study of bones of different species.

FIGURE 7.27 The human skeleton, with the major bones identified. Adults have a total of 206 bones, many of which are the results of fusing of the nearly 270 bones present at birth. Each bone has features that characterize it as belonging to a member of our species.

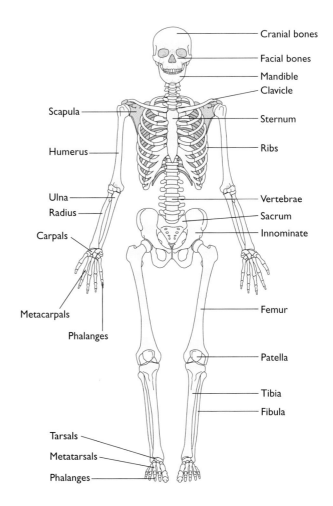

black bears (*Ursus americanus*), the common bear from eastern North America. Both varieties are still recognizable as bears, but they are different in form and behavior and they cannot mate with one another and produce fertile offspring; similar enough to be placed in the same genus (*Ursus*), they are different enough to be placed in separate species (*arctos* and *americanus*).

You can readily see the problem species definition poses for paleoanthropology. Fossil bones are not found stamped with a species designation; paleoanthropologists name and define species. Further, fossil species are all extinct and are represented only by their bones—which often are quite fragmentary. As a result, two fundamental sources of data concerning species are not directly available: behavior and the ability to mate and produce fertile offspring. In assessing species designations, paleoanthropologists ordinarily can directly analyze and compare only the skeletal morphology of different specimens.

How, then, do paleoanthropologists know if two skulls or two thigh bones—or one skull and one thigh bone—from different locations, or even the same site, belonged to members of the same species? They base their conclusions on the degree of similarity or difference between the individual specimens: if they are very similar and, especially, if they share specific anatomical traits not seen in other specimens, they place them in the same species and distinguish them from other species.

How similar or different do two specimens have to be before paleoanthropologists conclude that they belong in the same or two separate species? To answer this question, consider the degree of morphological variability present within living species. Some living creatures—for example, dogs—exhibit a great deal of physical and behavioral variation yet are able to interbreed—and therefore belong to the same species (see Figure 12.3). Even within our own species, we see a striking amount of variation (see Chapter 10). If humanity were extinct and extraterrestrial physical anthropologists had only the incomplete and fragmentary skeletal remains of an Inuit (Eskimo), a native Australian, a Scandinavian, and a Masai (people native to East Africa), they might not place them all within a single species, though we know that they all are demonstrably *Homo sapiens*.

Naming fossil species and assigning specimens to a species, then, are difficult and imperfect tasks. Labeling specimens can often be controversial. Some researchers accept more variation within a single group and lump many different specimens together. Others, the "splitters," allow for less variation and, therefore, create more fossil species with fewer specimens assigned to each. We will see this quite clearly when we discuss the fossils belonging to family Hominidae (see Chapters 8–10), which are lumped or split differently by different researchers.

Fortunately, we are entering a remarkable new age of fossil species identification and analysis. Actual DNA has been recovered from ancient remains—including those of human beings. Human bones from Illinois dated to more than 600 ya (Stone and Stoneking 1993), 500–800 year-old Chilean mummies (Rogan and Salvo 1990), a 2,400-year-old Egyptian mummy (Pääbo 1985), and some well-preserved, 7,000-year-old human brains found in waterlogged conditions at archaeological sites in Florida (Pääbo et al. 1988), have all produced ancient human DNA. Even if the remains had been too fragmentary in these cases to identify them as human, the preserved DNA extracted from those remains would have provided definitive evidence of their source.

In two separate studies, small segments of mitochondrial DNA (see Chapter 10) were extracted from Neandertal bone fragments, allowing scientists for the first time to compare some of the genetic instructions for an earlier form of humanity with the DNA of modern humans (Krings et al. 1997; Ovchinnikov et al. 2000; and see Chapter 9). Under most conditions,

DNA deterioration makes species identification impossible in ancient specimens, but in these rare instances where it has been preserved, we are afforded a new and exciting window into the past.

When applying this technique across species, however, we have more variables to take into account, particularly the matter of analogy and homology (as we discussed for physical and behavior traits in Chapter 6). We have to decide, to put it simply, which genetic similarities and differences are relevant to the assignment of species identity. At one level, for example, there are important genetic similarities between humans and fruit flies—hardly a criterion for species classification. In this regard, these new genetic techniques are in their infancy but promise to be vital tools in the future. (We will show how these techniques have been used to look at possible species of genus *Homo* in Chapter 10.)

Sex

Once a skeleton or, more usually, a portion of one is identified as a human or a human ancestor, the next detail to be discerned is usually its sex. Generally, this is fairly easy to determine because human beings, like many other species, exhibit **sexual dimorphism.** The two sexes look different, even when only bones remain. For example, a complete human skull alone can be "sexed" with over 90 percent accuracy; a skull and pelvis together provide about 98 percent accuracy.

The general rule is that males on the average are larger and more heavily muscled than females. In fact, this generalization applies to many of the primates, especially our closest relatives, the great apes. Thus, researchers look at a skull for overall size and for the size and presence of certain features on the bones related to muscle attachment: the bigger the muscles, the more prominent the attachment area.

Similarly, the pelvis of a male tends to be larger and more rugged than that of a female. The human female pelvis must be adapted to the process of giving birth to very large-headed babies. So the pelvises of females are generally wider in their openings and angles than those of males. Where the sex of a skull may be ambiguous, the pelvis is usually a dead giveaway (Figure 7.28).

These rules, of course, represent *averages.* Averages can vary from group to group; similarly, an individual may not conform to the average and can be misidentified. For this reason, it is preferable, as in any kind of skeletal analysis, to deal with a large sample of skeletons, which allows comparisons to be made. In the case of sex identification, many females are larger than the average male, and many males are smaller than the average female. No absolute criteria can be applied to sexing a skeleton or, for that matter, most other forms of skeletal analysis. It is a skill that takes practice and a great deal of observation of bones of known sex. With all

sexual dimorphism The anatomical features that distinguish the sexes of a species.

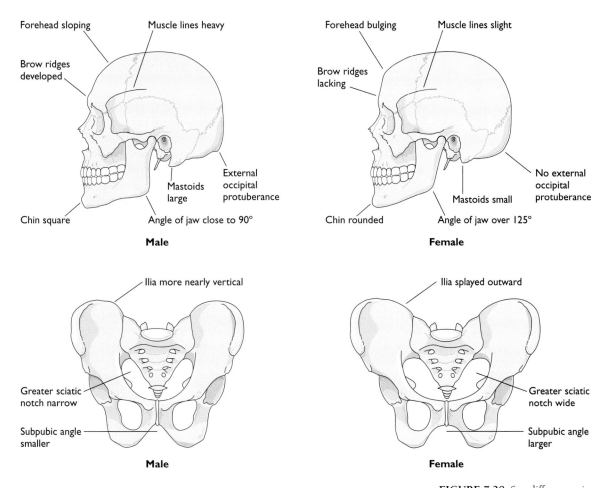

FIGURE 7.28 Sex differences in the skull and pelvis.

this, though, experienced anthropologists can sex most human skeletal remains with acceptable accuracy.

But what about the remains of premodern humans? What happens with a skeleton from 30,000, or 300,000, or 3 million years ago? Anthropologists really have little choice but to begin with the assumption that the same criteria apply. After all, these are members of the same basic evolutionary line, and they are primates. One of the earliest sets of human remains, from 3.18 mya, was determined to be that of a female, using just such reasoning. (She is called "Lucy," and we'll tell you about her in Chapter 8.)

This approach, though, has its limitations because anthropologists don't know for sure if the degree of sexual dimorphism was always the same in the past. In Lucy's case, more representatives of her stage of evolution

AGES OF TOOTH ERUPTION

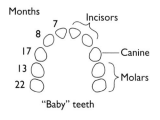

"Baby" teeth

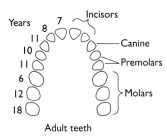

Adult teeth

FIGURE 7.29 Average ages of eruption of the deciduous (baby) teeth (*top*) in months and of permanent teeth (*bottom*) in years. Individuals may deviate from these dates for some teeth, but most people display this basic pattern.

suture A line of contact between the bones of the skull.

diaphysis The shaft of a long bone.

epiphysis The end, or cap, of a long bone.

epiphyseal union The fusion of the ends of long bones with the shafts.

pubic symphysis Articulation between the two halves of the pelvis at the pubis.

were found, and the assessments of sex were substantiated. In other words, researchers had not just an individual but a sample of a population.

Age

What about a person's age at death? The body goes through many physical changes as it develops, matures, and grows old. Many of these changes are reflected in the skeleton and take place at certain times in a human's life. By determining which changes have already occurred and which have yet to occur in a given set of remains, researchers can approximate a person's age at death. Perhaps the best-known method for "aging" a skeleton is the use of dental eruption dates (Figure 7.29). Like many mammals, humans have two sets of teeth: deciduous, or "baby," teeth, and adult teeth. Each tooth in both sets erupts through the gum line at a certain average age. Dental remains (among the most common because the outer layer of the teeth, the enamel, is the hardest substance the body produces) can reveal which tooth was the last to erupt and which unerupted tooth would have erupted next. The dates of eruption of those two teeth determine the minimum and maximum probable age at which that person died. Once all the adult teeth have erupted, of course, this method is no longer applicable.

Another aging technique makes use of the skull. A baby's head has *fontanelles,* or "soft spots," which are actually spaces between the bones of the skull. The bones develop separately, in part to allow some flexibility of our large heads during the birth process. Shortly after birth, the bones grow and fit together like a jigsaw puzzle. Later still, additional bone is added to the lines of attachment, called **sutures,** eventually forming a single cranial bone late in life. Because the sutures close at a fairly regular rate, a range may be derived for age at death from the last closure that has occurred and the next closure that would have occurred (Figure 7.30). This method, which can be used from about ages 18 to 50 and even beyond, has been judged as fairly unreliable, although there have been recent attempts to revive its use with more sophisticated analytical techniques. It may, however, be the only method available if just a cranium is recovered.

A third important aging technique makes use of the bones of the arms, legs, hands, and feet. These bones all grow in three sections: a shaft, or **diaphysis,** and two caps, or **epiphyses.** When growth is complete, the cartilagenous disks between caps and shaft become ossified (turn to bone), and a single arm, leg, finger, or toe bone is produced. Since ages for **epiphyseal union** are known, the same logic outlined before is used to determine age at death (Figure 7.31).

Another established aging method uses the inner surface of the area where the two halves of the pelvis meet in front. This is called the **pubic symphysis.** Between the ages of 18 and 50+, the appearance of this surface undergoes characteristic changes. By assessing the phase to which a

AVERAGE DATES FOR CRANIAL SUTURE CLOSURE (YEARS)

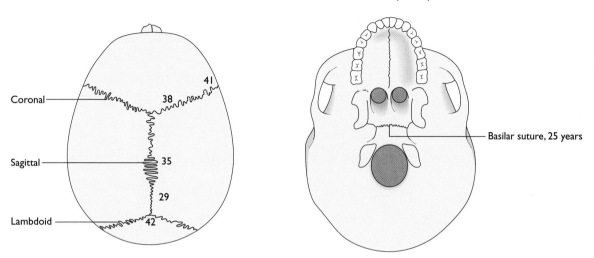

FIGURE 7.30 Patterns of cranial suture closure. A great deal of individual variation is seen in the shapes of the sutures and in their closure dates, making the method of questionable reliability.

specimen belongs, approximate age at death may be determined. Other aging methods include the appearance of the ends of the ribs and the auricular surface of the pelvic bones (where they articulate with the sacrum).

As with sexing, methods for aging rely on averages. No two humans are identical, and not everyone's growth pattern and rate follow the rules. Thus, the more data one can gather from a skeleton, the more accurate the determination will be. As with sexing, anthropologists must assume similar growth patterns and rates for our early ancestors, at least until they have a large enough number of fossils to establish separate criteria for different stages of human evolution.

Health

The anthropologist of the past, like a medical examiner, plays detective and tries, where possible, to determine the presence of illness and injury as well as cause of death. This area of study is called **paleopathology.** What people suffer and die from can tell a great deal about the nature of their environments, their diets, and their relations with other humans. Many diseases leave characteristic marks on the human skeleton. These include such ailments as certain forms of arthritis, tumors and other cancers, tuberculosis, leprosy, some anemias, syphilis, osteoporosis, and various infections such as dental abscesses (Figure 7.32). Any developmental anomalies, such as curvature of the spine or other deformations, will, of course, be clearly evident on the bones.

People also die from wounds and accidents. Bones have revealed that people of the past suffered from fractures, dislocations, and accidental

paleopathology The study of ancient disease.

FIGURE 7.31 Pattern of epiphyseal union, one of the most
reliable indications of skeletal
age.

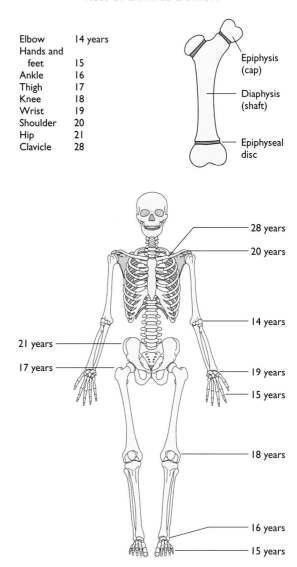

AGES OF EPIPHYSEAL UNION

Elbow	14 years
Hands and feet	15
Ankle	16
Thigh	17
Knee	18
Wrist	19
Shoulder	20
Hip	21
Clavicle	28

Age at which the epiphyses in the indicated area fuse to the shafts.

amputations. Deaths from arrow, spear, knife, and gunshot wounds have
also been seen. Scalping (usually done after death) shows up as a characteristic set of cut marks on top of the skull. Large holes cut into the skull
show that **trephining,** a form of prehistoric skull surgery, was not always
successful, although healing around some holes indicates that many obviously survived the operation (Figure 7.33).

trephining Cutting a hole in
the skull to treat an illness.

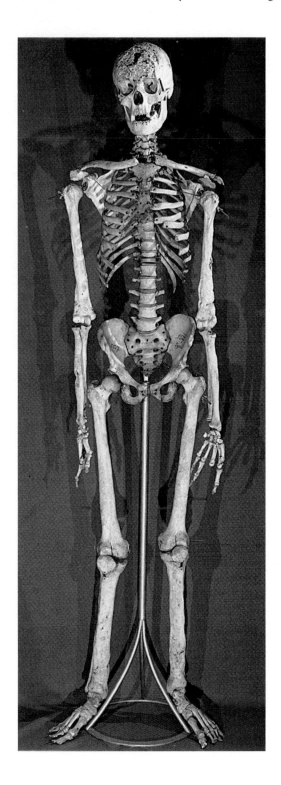

FIGURE 7.32 The effects of syphilis on the human skeleton. Note the extensive lesions on the skull and at the ends of the humeri and tibias. (Identification of Pathological Conditions in Human Skeletal Remains, *Ortner and Putschar, 1985:195, Smithsonian Institution Press*)

FIGURE 7.33 A trephined skull from Peru. The arrow shows the outer margin of the wound. The edge of the hole indicates that healing has taken place. (Identification of Pathological Conditions in Human Skeletal Remains, *Ortner and Putschar, 1985:98, Smithsonian Institution Press*)

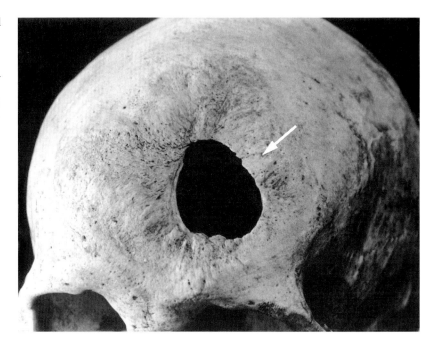

growth arrest lines Horizontal cracks at the ends of the long bone shafts resulting from malnutrition during childhood.

Harris lines Another term for growth arrest lines, named after the researcher who first recognized their cause.

enamel hypoplasia Damage in the form of pits and cracks in the enamel of the adult teeth resulting from disease and malnutrition during early childhood, long before the adult teeth appear in the mouth.

As we are all aware, a nutritious diet is especially important for growing children. When for any reason, nutrition is insufficient, a child's growth can be affected, even interrupted, leaving permanent scars on the skeleton. An example of this kind of permanent scarring is called **growth arrest lines,** or **Harris lines** (named after the researcher who initially diagnosed them). During periods of severe malnutrition, the lengthwise growth of a child's long bones (for example, the bones of the arms and legs) can actually be halted. When adequate nutrition is restored, the bones recommence growing, but the interruption can be marked by horizontal lines at the ends of the long bones, literally marking a period during which growth was arrested. These lines may be visible to the naked eye as well as show up on an X-ray (Figure 7.34).

Childhood malnutrition may also manifest itself in the enamel surfaces of the adult teeth. The buds, or "germs," of the adult teeth are present in a child's mouth, obviously beneath the baby teeth. These buds are extremely susceptible to health and nutrition problems experienced during early childhood and can be permanently scarred by a pitting called **enamel hypoplasia.** The presence of growth lines and/or enamel hypoplasia provides the biological anthropologist with direct evidence of dietary problems or disease experienced by individual children or populations of children in antiquity.

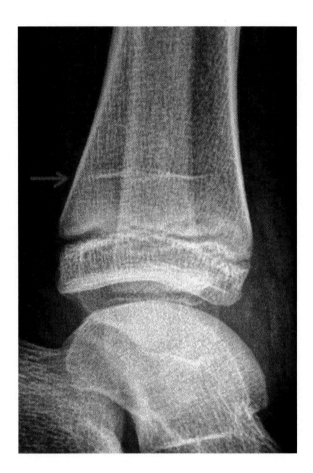

FIGURE 7.34 The red arrow points to a growth arrest, or Harris, line, a defect in this lower leg bone (specifically the tibia) marking a point during maturation when nutrition was insufficient to sustain growth. *(Courtesy of Brian Tidey, www .radiographersreporting.com)*

Appearance

The skeleton acts as a framework for the body as a whole; thus the size and shape of the bones can reveal something of the appearance of the entire living person. For example, the sheer size and ruggedness of their bones shows that the Neandertals, humans from ancient Europe (see Chapter 9), were big, brawny, and extremely strong. Anthropologists can obtain a more exact idea of size, especially stature, by using a series of mathematical formulas. By measuring, say, a femur, they can calculate the height of the individual who once owned it.

There is a direct relationship between bone and muscle because muscles attach to bones. This relationship has led a number of investigators to attempt to reconstruct the faces of our ancestors from the shapes of their skulls and facial skeletons. Using their knowledge of human anatomy, they artistically add missing bones, eyes, fatty tissue, cartilage, muscle, and

FIGURE 7.35 Using a cast of a fossil skull, modeling clay is added to "flesh out" the face of an ancient human ancestor. (© *Karen Huntt Mason/Corbis*)

skin to ancient skulls, literally "fleshing out" the picture of early humans (Figure 7.35). As before, of course, these reconstructions assume that present anatomical relationships also held true in the past. Researchers have yet to find an entire ancient face preserved as a fossil. (The same procedure is used also in law enforcement to try to identify skeletal remains and match them with missing persons.)

The relationship between bone and soft tissue also provides a basis for determining geographical location or origin. In living humans, a number of physical and chemical characteristics show variation on a geographical scale. Such traits as skin color, eye shape, nose shape, hair color and texture, blood type, and other genetic features are all variable in our species, and all show some geographical regularity.

Similarly, some skulls look as if they come from a certain place or belong to a certain general population (we will discuss this phenomenon in more detail in Chapter 10). Such analysis, to be sure, can be rather subjective, but with enough examples and enough practice, anthropologists can often make a reasonably accurate identification of the general population from which a skull came. Some numerical generalizations can also accomplish the same task. Average head length, relative length of arms and legs, and other measurements tend to differ geographically. Last, some very specific traits can be found most often in certain populations. Shovel-shaped incisors—upper front teeth with an appearance rather like a shovel—are not exclusive to, but are very common among, Asian groups. This trait can help distinguish Native American skeletal remains from those of Europeans since Native Americans are of Asian origin.

Behavior

Finally, the skeleton can be a source of information about behavior. In evolutionary perspective, the first distinguishing feature of human anatomy was upright posture and locomotion. Anthropologists know when this feature first evolved because the skeleton directly reflects it; the nature of the bones of the pelvis and the femur, along with the position of the hole in the base of the skull, are clear indications of locomotor posture. It is obvious from such evidence that humans have walked upright for over 4 million years.

Sometimes skulls are found deformed in uniform ways, although the individuals themselves seem otherwise normal. Such artificial deformation was sometimes performed to reflect standards of beauty. Historic records—from ancient Egypt, for example—can substantiate the practice. The famous Queen Nefertiti had a cranial deformation of this sort. Sometimes, however, the deformation was accidental, caused by pressure from a cradleboard, a device used in many parts of the world to hold an infant's head (and thus the infant itself) steady and secure while the parents were otherwise occupied (Figure 7.36).

Methods from engineering have been applied to the assessment of strength from cross sections of human bones (Bridges 1995). Some interesting relationships between arm and leg strength and subsistence pattern have been proposed. For example, one study indicates that arm and leg strength declined among males when Native American populations along the Georgia coast moved from hunting and gathering to maize agriculture.

FIGURE 7.36 An example of the effects of cradleboarding from ancient Illinois. The board flattened the forehead and, especially, the back of the skull, but probably caused no ill effects. *(Illinois State Museum, reproduction by written permission only)*

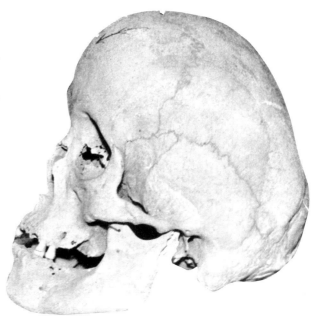

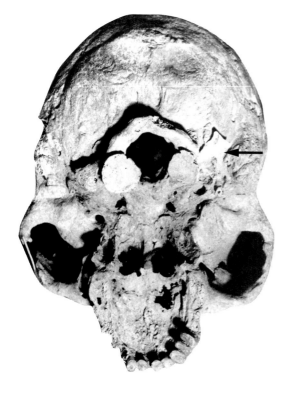

FIGURE 7.37 The small arrow point embedded in the base of the skull of this ancient Illinois Native American no doubt caused this individual's death. *(Illinois State Museum, reproduction by written permission only)*

Another study shows a decrease in right-arm strength among males in the American Midwest during the Late Woodland period when the *atlatl* (spear thrower) was replaced by the bow and arrow around A.D. 900.

Finally, evidence of wounds from arrows, spears, and guns indicates another kind of human behavior (Figure 7.37). Such evidence tells something about the relations of a group of people with its neighbors.

It should be noted here that researchers are now beginning to go beyond appearance to study certain chemical characteristics of ancient bone. Presently, for some bones preserved under the right conditions, blood type in the ABO system can be determined. This not only reveals something about an individual but also—if a large enough sample of skeletal material is found at one site—may provide some genetic information about an entire population. Moreover, we are learning, as noted before, to extract DNA from ancient bone, a technique that will give us even more detailed and intimate information about populations of the past.

While studying these remains, however, anthropologists must keep in mind an ethical consideration. In the case of recent remains, these data are the bodies of people whose living descendants belong to an identified group. This is true for many Native American populations, whose ancestral burial areas have long been sources of human skeletal remains for the anthropologist. The scientific value of such studies cannot be denied and can provide important information. But the rights and values of the people involved should also be respected. Remains ought not to be treated as mere specimens or curiosities.

Why? Explaining the Past

Over 6 mya, the first humans stood upright. Why? At least 80,000 ya, our human ancestors began the practice of burying their dead. Why? About 30,000 ya, the Neandertals apparently disappeared. Why? Soon after 11,000 ya, in Southeast Asia and the Middle East, we find evidence that human beings were raising their own crops and domesticating animals, instead of simply hunting and gathering what nature provided. Why? About 5,000 ya, in the Middle East, and soon after in Egypt, India, China, Mesoamerica, and South America, people began to live in cities and build enormous monumental works such as pyramids and temples. Why?

Why, indeed! The final question that anthropologists studying the past confront is perhaps the most difficult of all. They can locate sites, figure out how old they are, describe the people themselves, and to a large extent reconstruct what went on. But answering the many whys poses the greatest challenge.

It is indeed difficult to suggest why a given people 3 million, 10,000, or even 500 years ago made a certain decision or changed their culture in a certain way. As difficult as it is, however, the answers to certain crucial "why" questions about humanity in general can only be pursued by the application of anthropological data. Many of the important questions that people want to answer have roots extending far back into the mists of antiquity. Anthropologists can only penetrate these puzzles if they apply the types of biological and cultural analysis described here.

Imagine a book 400 pages long. Imagine that each page represents a period of time in the development of humanity. The very first sentence on the first page represents the first time a human ancestor stood upright on the African savanna. The very last sentence on page 400 is today. The amount of space in the book devoted to certain time periods is proportional to their actual length. There's just one hitch; we can only read that part of the book corresponding to the period after human beings invented writing some 6,000 ya. The pages before the invention of writing are blank.

Can you guess where the writing would begin? On the last half of the final page! Imagine reading a 400-page book with writing only on the last half of the last page and then being asked to explain what happened. If the book were a detective novel, you might know that "the butler did it," but it is unlikely you would know what he did, when, to whom, or, most importantly, why.

So the first 399.5 pages of the book about our human story are blank, at least as far as writing is concerned—for they are filled not with words but with spears and pots, burials and monuments, bones and seeds. In the story of our species, the first 99.99 percent of our existence on this planet is prehistoric and therefore the purview of archaeologists and paleoanthropologists. To ask who we are and why we are is to be, almost by definition, an anthropologist studying the past.

Summary

The study of human antiquity includes the methodologies of the archaeologist and the biological anthropologist. Their research attempts to answer the general questions where, what, when, how, who, and why. Investigating the human past begins by determining *where* the physical evidence of ancient people can be found. Various techniques are used to locate and recover the physical remains of these people—*what* they left behind, the artifacts and features clustered in the sites where they once lived. Techniques from various disciplines are applied to determine the age of these remains, establishing *when* the people lived. Acting as ethnographers, anthropologists analyze the remains of the human past to establish *how* these people survived—how they made their tools, what their physical environment was like, and what diet, social systems, trading networks, and ideology comprised their culture. Studying the physical remains of the people

CONTEMPORARY ISSUE

Preserving the Past

We have tried to impart here the importance of anthropological research in our quest to understand human physical and cultural evolution. Unfortunately, however, the raw data of archaeology and paleoanthropology are in great danger. Many agricultural practices, mining techniques, and construction projects, along with general greed and indifference, contribute to the destruction of important sites all over the world each year. Farmers in some countries practice land-leveling techniques that destroy buried sites. Strip mining in some places causes terrific destruction of archaeological resources. In developed and developing nations alike, the construction of roads and water projects contributes to the destruction of the fragile prehistoric record. In some countries, including our own, sites are looted for their more aesthetically pleasing artifacts, which are then sold to the highest bidder.

No more ancient sites are being made. They are, in a sense, nonrenewable resources like coal and oil. Some nations have recognized the importance of protecting these fragile remnants of the past. A series of federal, state, and even town laws in this country afford at least some protection to archaeological sites. Other countries have patrimony laws that make it illegal to export the artifacts of their ancestors—which are usually sold to the wealthy of other nations for their amusement. Many countries and some states have laws against the disturbance of ancient human burials.

Laws are very important, but people's attitudes are perhaps most important of all. If people would only recognize the importance of understanding the past, site destruction would become unthinkable. Ancient sites would be preserved for future study, money would be made available for archaeological research, and the market for antiquities would dry up. It would be a terrible tragedy and irony indeed if, just as our study of the past is becoming a sophisticated scientific enterprise, the raw data of the past were to become as extinct as the cultures we are attempting to understand.

Looters dug more than 450 holes in this Kentucky field in search of Native American artifacts. *(Courtesy Cheryl Ann Munson, Indiana University, and David Pollack, Kentucky Heritage Council)*

Construction-related development often poses the greatest threat to archaeological resources. Here an archaeological excavation is conducted in the shadow of highway expansion in Southbury, Connecticut. *(K. L. Feder)*

themselves—their bones—helps us understand *who* they were as individuals and as populations. Finally, anthropologists attempt to discern and reveal *why* they lived the lives they did. Through the application of the procedures outlined in this chapter, anthropologists studying the human past attempt through science to illuminate the story of our species.

Study Questions

1. List and describe the general questions archaeologists and paleoanthropologists ask about the human past.
2. How are archaeological and paleoanthropological sites discovered? How is evidence of a past people's way of life recovered from such sites?
3. How can the behavior of ancient people be analyzed? How can we reconstruct the ancient environment and a people's diet, social system, trading patterns, technology, and belief system?
4. How can archaeologists and paleoanthropologists determine the age of specimens?
5. What information can be gathered from the skeletal remains of humans and human ancestors?

Key Terms

site
artifact
feature
field survey
remote sensing
electrical resistivity
   survey
proton magnetometry
ground penetrating
   radar (GPR)
test boring
sounding
test pit
compliance
   archaeology
random sample
representative sample
transect
spatial context
provenience

association
excavation units
in situ
stratigraphy
parent material
law of superposition
relative chronological
   sequence
chronometric dating
absolute dating
radiometric dating
radioactive isotope
ecofact
radiocarbon dating
half-life
accelerator mass
   spectrometry
   (AMS)
potassium/argon
   (K/Ar) dating

argon-argon (Ar/Ar)
   dating
uranium series
electron spin
   resonance (ESR)
   dating
dendrochronology
master sequence
calibration curve
cultural technique
seriation
ethnoarchaeology
ethnography
paleoethnography
direct historical
   approach
ethnographic analogy
wear pattern
Bronze Age
foraminifera

palynology
midden
flotation
comparative collection
faunal analysis
taphonomy
phytoliths
carbon isotope
   analysis
paleofeces
coprolites

matrilocal
postmarital residence
   pattern
patrilocal
petrographic analysis
trace element analysis
neutron activation
   analysis
comparative osteology
sexual dimorphism
suture

diaphysis
epiphysis
epiphyseal union
pubic symphysis
paleopathology
trephining
growth arrest lines
Harris lines
enamel hypoplasia

For More Information

Although we have been able to devote only a chapter to the techniques of learning about the human past, many fine texts deal with the methodology of archaeology and physical anthropology. A few of the best are *Archaeology: Discovering Our Past,* second edition, by Robert Sharer and Wendy Ashmore; *In the Beginning: An Introduction to Archaeology,* by Brian Fagan; and *Archaeology,* second edition, by David Hurst Thomas. For archaeological field and laboratory methods, see *Field Methods in Archaeology,* by Tom Hester, Harry Shafer, and Ken Feder.

For more detailed discussions of analysis of the human skeleton, see the excellent books *Human Osteology: A Laboratory and Field Manual of the Human Skeleton,* by William Bass, and *Handbook of Forensic Archaeology and Anthropology,* by Dan Morse, Jack Duncan, and James Stoutamire. Especially noteworthy for its beautiful photographs is *Human Osteology,* second edition, by Tim White and Pieter Folkens. See also *Skeleton Keys,* by Jeffrey Schwartz, and for a broader treatment of human anatomy, *The Human Strategy: An Evolutionary Perspective on Human Anatomy,* by John Langdon.

A nice collection of articles showing how skeletal analysis is put to specific use is *Bodies of Evidence: Reconstructing History Through Skeletal Analysis,* edited by Anne L. Grauer.

Ancient Disease in the Midwest, by Dan Morse, is a good source for information on paleopathology.

The 3,500-mile-long Rift Valley in East Africa is thought to be intimately connected to the beginnings of hominid evolution. What happened in Africa 6 to 5 mya that began the human story? (© Emory Kristof/National Geographic Society Image Collection)

THE EMERGENCE OF THE HUMAN LINEAGE

CHAPTER CONTENTS

The Early Hominids: Bipedal Primates

Searching for the First Hominids

Bipedalism

The Hominids Evolve

CONTEMPORARY ISSUE: Where Is the "Missing Link"?

Summary

Study Questions

Key Terms

For More Information

In 1912, amateur scientist Charles Dawson announced the recovery, from a gravel pit in Pilt-down, England, of perhaps the best-known and most controversial bones in the history of anthropology. The find consisted of a mandible and several cranial bones in association with some primitive stone tools. The cranial bones were clearly those of a large-brained human, but the mandible was indistinguishable from that of an ape. This combination of traits was precisely what many scientists of the time expected of the evolutionary "missing link" be-tween ape and human.

FIGURE 8.1 Reconstruction of the skull of the Piltdown fraud. This modern human braincase was planted in the same site with an orangutan jaw and claimed by the discoverers to belong together. The result was exactly what science at the time expected of the earliest human. (© *The Natural History Museum, London*)

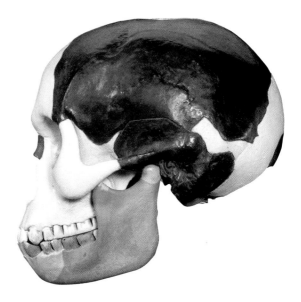

The remains were named **Eoanthropus,** meaning "dawn man" (Figure 8.1). For nearly forty years, many scientists, especially in Britain, accepted "Piltdown Man" as the earliest human. In other countries, however, opinion ranged from withheld judgment to downright skepticism. Many felt the combination of the apelike jaw and human braincase was too good to be true. Furthermore, during those forty years no similar fossils were found that could provide supporting evidence for *Eoanthropus.*

The skeptics were proved correct. In the early 1950s, in a classic example of the self-correcting nature of science, Piltdown was unmasked as a fake—it was *literally* the cranium of a modern human and the jaw of a modern orangutan. Both had been filed, stained, and otherwise modified to appear ancient. With that revelation, other early remains suddenly took their rightful place in our understanding of human evolution. Though there are plenty of suspects, to this day no one knows for certain who perpetrated the fraud. Piltdown remains one of the great mysteries of science. (For accounts of the story—with different solutions as to "whodunit"—see Blinderman 1986; Feder 2006; Gould 1983; Millar 1972; Spencer 1990; Walsh 1996; and Weiner 1955.)

Despite a great deal of skepticism, the Piltdown find appeared in many books on human evolution during the forty years before its fraudulence was established. What accounts, then, for the popularity and acceptance of so obvious a fake as Piltdown for so long a time? The answer, in part, is nationalism. No important fossil human had yet been found on British soil, so the possibility that the "dawn man" might be British had obvious appeal. More important, Piltdown fulfilled expectations of what the earliest human *should* look like. At that time, the most important difference between human and ape was believed to be humans' big brain. Therefore, it was reasoned, the large brain differentiating us from the apes must have been evolving the longest because it was the most changed part of our anatomy. If the brain had been evolving longest, it must have evolved first, before the other features that distinguish us from apes. The "missing link" should therefore be essentially an ape with a big head.

In this expectation, scientists committed a classic error in the study of evolution, thinking that a modern situation represents the original situation—in this case, that the most characteristic feature of modern humans would also have been the first feature of our lineage. This mistaken idea is part of the reason why the evolutionary position of the australopithecines, (see Chapter 3), whose remains had first come to light in 1925, was unclear for so long. Their bipedal posture but ape-sized brains did not fit expectations of what the earliest humans should look like.

It is now clear, as it has been for nearly fifty years, that the large brains of humans appeared relatively late in hominid evolution. Our brains achieved their modern size 780,000 ya at the earliest, whereas the feature that first distinguished us from the apes—our bipedalism—is over 4 million years old. So the first question in our discussion of the emergence of the human lineage is not how and why humans evolved big brains—but how and why humans stood up and walked around on two legs.

The Early Hominids: Bipedal Primates

The first evidence from the dawn of hominid evolution came in 1925. South African paleoanthropologist Raymond Dart was given a fossil found in a limestone quarry at a site called Taung (Figure 8.2). It took Dart seventy-three days to separate the fossil from the limestone around it. When freed, it revealed the face, braincase, and brain cast of a young primate, apelike but for two important differences. First, the canine teeth—which are long and large in apes, with gaps to accommodate them when the jaws are shut—were no bigger than those of a human child. Second was the position of the **foramen magnum.** This is the hole in the base of the skull through which the spinal cord extends from the brain and around the outside of which the top vertebra articulates. In the Taung specimen, this hole was well underneath the skull rather than toward the back, as in apes, indicating an upright, bipedal posture rather than a quadrupedal one (Figure 8.3). Dart hypothesized that the "Taung Baby," as it came to be known, was an intermediate between apes and hominids. Nevertheless, he named it ***Australopithecus africanus,*** the "southern ape of Africa"; because of its many apelike traits, he wasn't ready to formally classify it in the human family.

Further finds in Africa substantiated Dart's assessment of the anatomy of his fossil and his opinion that it represented a new type of primate. Those finds also made it clear that *Australopithecus,* rather than being an intermediary, was in fact a hominid, a bipedal primate. (The rules of scientific nomenclature, or taxonomic names, however, require that first-used

foramen magnum The hole in the base of the skull through which the spinal cord emerges and around the outside of which the top vertebra articulates.

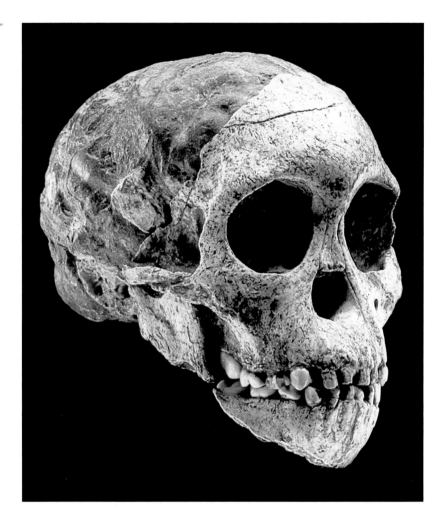

FIGURE 8.2 The "Taung Baby," the first specimen of *Australopithecus*. Note the naturally formed cast of the brain (see page 288, Figure 9.20).
(*© David L. Brill 1985/Brill Atlanta*)

names stick even if they later prove to be descriptively inaccurate. Thus, these hominids are still named "southern apes.")

The story that the early hominid fossils tell is by no means clear or agreed on by everyone. But we can begin with some reasonably well-established fossil forms and dates, which will provide a basic understanding of this period of human evolution. With these as a basis, in the following section we can examine some of the newer and more controversial fossils and consider some of the ways to put all these data together.

First, a general orientation. All the fossils discussed here belong to family Hominidae. Within that family, anthropologists now generally acknowledge four well-established genera: *Ardipithecus*, *Australopithecus*, *Paranthropus*, and *Homo*. Only the last genus still exists; the other three are extinct. These groups may be distinguished by the following definitions, on which we'll elaborate:

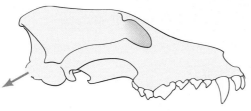

Wolf

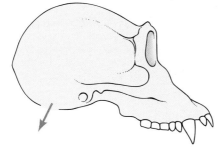

Chimpanzee

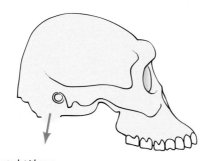

Australopithecus

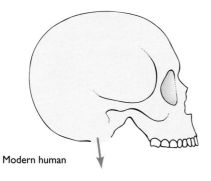

Modern human

FIGURE 8.3 Comparison of the placement of the foramen magnum and orientation of the spinal column relative to the skull in a nonprimate quadruped and three primates. The wolf, with equally long fore and hind limbs, has a foramen magnum toward the back of the skull and oriented almost horizontally. The chimp, still a quadruped but with longer arms than legs, has a more forward placement, with the spine extending at an angle. In the bipedal hominids, we see a trend toward even more forward placement and vertical orientation of the spine. *(Wolf by M. A. Park; primates from Biegert 1963)*

TABLE 8.1   Summary of Well-Established Early Fossil Hominid Species

	Ard. ramidus*	A. anamensis	A. afarensis	A. africanus	P. robustus	P. boisei
Dates	4.4 mya	4.2–3.8 mya	3.9–3 mya	3–2.3 mya	2.2–1.5 mya (?)	2.2–1 mya
Sites	Middle Awash/ Aramis	Lake Turkana	Hadar Omo Laetoli Maka Lake Turkana	Taung Sterkfontein Makapansgat Lake Turkana (?) Omo (?)	Kromdraai Swartkrans Drimolen	Olduvai Lake Turkana Omo
Cranial capacity (in ml)	(no data)	(no data)	380–500 mean = 440	370–515 mean = 440	520 (based on one specimen)	500–530 mean = 515
Estimated size (average, in lb)	(no data)	114	110	100	105	101
Skull	Canines human-shaped but large Small molars as in apes Foramen magnum forward (?)	Canines large, but hominid-like canine roots More apelike chin than A. afarensis Tooth rows parallel as in apes	Very prognathous Receding chin Large teeth Pointed canine with gap Shape of tooth row between ape and human Hint of sagittal crest	Less prognathous than A. afarensis Jaw more rounded Large back teeth Canines smaller than P. robustus, larger than A. afarensis No sagittal crest	Heavy jaws Small canines and front teeth Large back teeth Definite sagittal crest	Very large jaws Very large back teeth Large sagittal crest
Postcranial skeleton	(no published data)	Bipedal knee and ankle joints Fibula intermediate between ape and hominid	Long arms Short thumb Curved fingers and toes Bipedal	Similar to A. afarensis but possibly with longer arms and shorter legs	Hands and feet more like modern humans Retention of long arms	Similar to P. robustus

*There is another, older proposed species of *Ardipithecus,* which we will discuss in the next section under new, more controversial forms.

Family Hominidae: the bipedal primates (by the traditional definition we'll use here)

Genus *Ardipithecus:* the most apelike hominids

Genus *Australopithecus:* small-brained, gracile (slender) hominids with a mixed vegetable/fruit diet

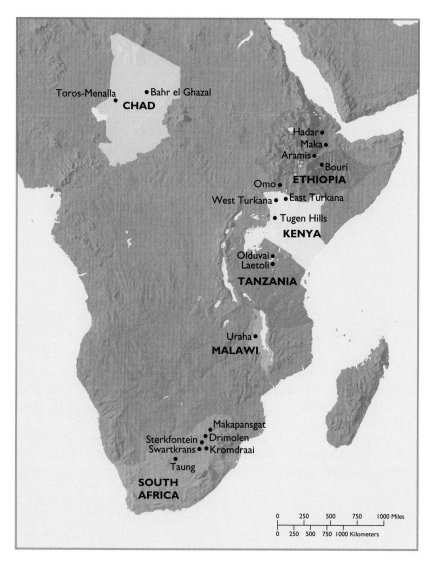

FIGURE 8.4 Map of major early fossil hominid sites.

Genus *Paranthropus:* small-brained, robust hominids with a grassland vegetable diet

Genus *Homo:* large-brained, omnivorous hominids

Table 8.1 summarizes information on the well-established species of these genera, and Figure 8.4 shows the important fossil sites discussed in this chapter.

It should be noted that authorities are about evenly divided on the issue of whether *Paranthropus* is a separate genus or is part of *Australopithecus.*

FIGURE 8.5 Fossil tooth and portion of jaw from *Ardipithecus ramidus ramidus.* (© 1994 Tim D. White/Brill Atlanta)

We will use the first option here, in part because we think the evidence warrants it but mostly because using a different name makes understanding the evolutionary trends of this complex period a little easier.

The earliest-known hominid fossils were first discovered in Ethiopia in 1992 and 1993. The finds consisted of seventeen fossil fragments, including some arm bones, two skull bases, a child's mandible, and some teeth (Figure 8.5). These fossils were different enough from any found previously to warrant creating a fourth hominid genus, **Ardipithecus ramidus** (the genus name means "ground ape," and the species name means "root" in the Afar language; a second species has been added because of some new finds—which we will discuss in the next section). The fossils are dated at 4.4 mya.

In 1994, more fossil bones were recovered in Ethiopia, close to the first site. These consisted of ninety fragments representing about 45 percent of a skeleton, including the telltale pelvis, leg, ankle, and foot. These new finds, however, still await published analysis.

Ardipithecus ramidus is considered a hominid because the foramen magnum is more forward than in apes and because of some detailed features of the elbow joint and the teeth. At the same time, it is "the most apelike hominid ancestor known" (White et al. 1994). Among other things, the canine teeth are larger, compared to the other teeth, than in later hominids. It seems, then, that *Ard. ramidus* existed very close to the

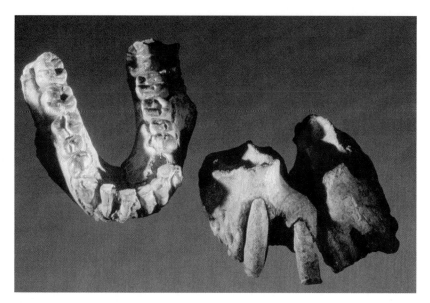

FIGURE 8.6 Mandible (*left*) and maxilla of *Australopithecus anamensis*. The chinless jaw is apelike, but the vertical root of the canine is clearly a hominid trait (the canine roots of apes are angled). (*© Kenneth Garrett/ National Geographic Society Image Collection*)

time when the hominids and the apes split and so may be, as the name implies, the "root" hominid species. These fossils, however, remain somewhat enigmatic for the moment. Although the evidence from the foramen magnum indicates that this species was bipedal, conclusive evidence from the legs, pelvis, and feet must wait until the newest finds can be fully examined and the results published.

In August 1995, another hominid species was announced (Leakey and Lewin 1995; C. Ward et al. 1999). Called **Australopithecus anamensis,** it consists, so far, of twenty-one specimens from the Lake Turkana region of Kenya (*anam* means "lake"), including jaws, teeth, a skull fragment, a tibia, and a humerus (Figure 8.6). The specimens are dated at 4.2 to 3.8 mya. Although they exhibit apelike features such as large canine teeth and parallel tooth rows (Figure 8.7), the root of the canine is vertical as in later hominids rather than angled as in apes, and the tooth enamel is thicker than in apes or in *Ardipithecus ramidus* and more like that in later hominids. Most notably, the leg bones are clearly those of a biped. There appears to be some consensus that *A. anamensis* may represent the ancestor of all later hominids, with *Ard. ramidus* representing a side branch of the hominid family.

The next species is also well established, and its nature is generally agreed on. The species is **Australopithecus afarensis,** and its first and most famous specimen is the 3.2-million-year-old skeleton, also from Ethiopia, known as "Lucy" (Figure 8.8), found in 1974 by Donald Johanson and his team. Lucy is remarkable because, as old as she is, nearly 40 percent of her skeleton was preserved, and all parts of her body were well represented

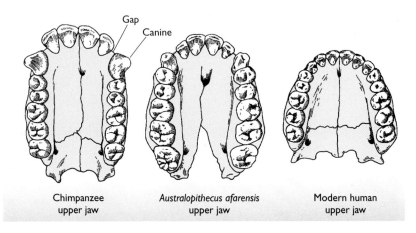

Gap
Canine

Chimpanzee
upper jaw

Australopithecus afarensis
upper jaw

Modern human
upper jaw

FIGURE 8.7 Comparison of upper jaws and tooth rows of chimpanzee, *Australopithecus afarensis,* and modern human. Note the parallel postcanine teeth in the chimp, the slightly divergent tooth row in the early hominid, and the divergent row in modern humans. Note also the large canines and the large gap (diastema) in the chimp, the lack of these in modern humans, and the intermediate state in the early hominid. *Australopithecus anamensis* has slightly larger canines than the later *A. afarensis* and tooth rows more like the ape. *(From Lucy: The Beginnings of Human Kind. © 1981 Donald C. Johanson & Maitland A. Edey, drawings by Luba Dmytryk Gudz)*

FIGURE 8.8 Skeleton of "Lucy," the first specimen of *A. afarensis.* *(© John Reader/Science Photo Library/ Photo Researchers, Inc.)*

except the cranium, the remains of which are fragmentary. We know—based on the kind of osteological analysis described in Chapter 7—that she was a female and that she stood about 3 feet 8 inches and weighed about 65 pounds. Although there is some disagreement about details, there is no doubt that Lucy and her kind were bipeds.

Other fragmentary specimens, including a portion of a skull dated at 3.9 mya, were unearthed in Ethiopia and Tanzania and assigned to this species. Based on this evidence, a reconstruction of the head of *A. afarensis* was attempted, but a single complete fossil skull was not found until 1992. In February of that year, Donald Johanson and his team discovered 200 skull fragments, again in Ethiopia. Once reconstructed, the skull closely resembled the previously discovered fragments, except that it was large and rugged, probably the skull of a male. It was dated at about 3 mya (Figure 8.9).

The evidence so far—over 300 specimens—indicates that there was a well-established hominid species, *A. afarensis,* that lived from 3.9 to 3 mya. The variation in size of the specimens fits the pattern of sexual dimorphism of apes and other early hominids. We are probably looking at the remains of both males (for example, the skull found in 1992) and females (for example, Lucy) of one species.

However, in 1995 a French team found the remains of a partial hominid jaw in Chad, in north-central Africa, dated at 3.5 to 3 mya. The team

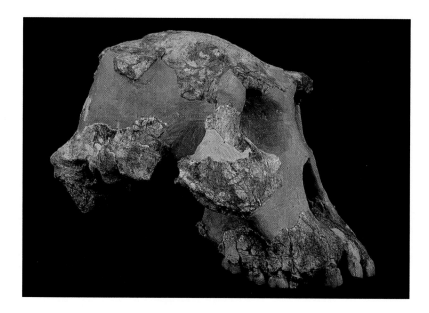

FIGURE 8.9 Side view of a cranium of *Australopithecus afarensis*. Spaces between missing bones have been filled in using information from other specimens and knowledge of related species. (© *Institute of Human Origins, photography by W. H. Kimbel. Used with permission*)

announced that this find represents a second species of hominid living during that time (Simons 1996). The species has been named ***Australopithecus bahrelghazalia*** (after an Arabic name for a nearby riverbed), and it suggests that early hominids were more widely spread on the continent than previously thought. Full acceptance of this classification and the implications of the fossil await further study.

What did Lucy and her kin look like? They might be described as "bipedal apes." Their average brain size was about 440 ml (a can of soda holds 355 ml), close to the average for chimpanzees and with the same maximum size of about 500 ml. *A. afarensis* had the **prognathism** (projection of the lower face and jaws), the pointy canine teeth, and the gaps in the tooth rows characteristic of apes, though the canine teeth and gaps were not as pronounced as in apes. There was a hint of a **sagittal crest**, a ridge of bone along the top of the skull for the attachment of major chewing muscles. Gorillas have pronounced crests (Figure 8.10). In modern humans, these muscles are attached on the side of the head. (Put your hand on your head, about 2 inches above one ear, and then clench and unclench your teeth. You'll feel the muscle called the *temporalis*.)

At first there was some disagreement as to just how bipedal *A. afarensis* was, especially considering the apelike nature of much of the rest of its anatomy. (Disagreements continue; see Stern 2000 for a summary.) All the interpretations, after all, were based on fossilized bones; no one, obviously, had ever actually seen one walk. But in 1976 at a site in Tanzania called Laetoli, Mary Leakey recovered the next best thing—a set of footprints made in a fresh layer of volcanic ash that quickly hardened and preserved

prognathism The jutting forward of the lower face and jaw area.

sagittal crest A ridge of bone, running from front to back along the top of the skull, for the attachment of chewing muscles.

FIGURE 8.10 Skull of a male gorilla. Compare the sagittal crest with those of *Paranthropus* (see Figures 8.17, 8.18, and 8.19).

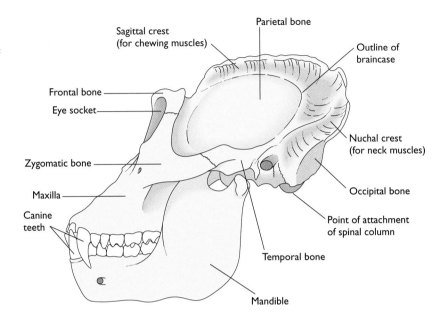

for us a striking picture of an event that took place 3.7 mya. Two hominids—one large, one small—had walked side-by-side through the ash shortly after an eruption. The hominids' footprints show an anatomy and stride no different from ours today (Figure 8.11).

Thus, fossils assigned to the various species of genus *Australopithecus* are generally agreed to represent an important early stage in the establishment of the hominid family, with *Ardipithecus ramidus* being a reasonable representative for an even earlier, more apelike stage. For many years, this was all the concrete evidence we had to study our beginnings. But in the last few years, mostly older fossils have been discovered, and while they will eventually shed light on hominid origins, at the moment the waters are even muddier.

Searching for the First Hominids

There are four new fossil forms that have been described and named recently. Some authorities think that each form represents an important step in the evolution of the hominids in general or of genus *Homo* in particular. As always, of course, there are disagreements and controversy.

In March 2001 Meave Leakey, daughter of Louis and Mary Leakey, announced a new hominid genus (Leakey et al. 2001). It is based on a fairly complete, although distorted cranium and a mandible, found in 1998 and 1999 in Kenya and reliably dated at 3.5 mya. The fossils show a

FIGURE 8.11 The Laetoli footprints from Tanzania, and the reconstruction of the hominids that probably produced them, from the American Museum of Natural History in New York City. *(Laetoli footprints: © John Reader/Science Photo Library/Photo Researchers, Inc.; reconstruction: Negative #4744(5). Photo by D. Finnin/C. Chesek. Courtesy Department of Library Services, American Museum of Natural History)*

combination of features unlike that of any other forms. The brain size, some dental features, and details of the nasal region are like those of genus *Australopithecus*. But its face appears flat, it has a tall, vertically oriented cheek area, and shows no depression behind the brow ridges. In these ways, it bears a resemblance to a later hominid form from East Africa. This set of traits in a fossil contemporaneous with *A. afarensis* led its discoverers to give it not only a new species name but a new genus name as well—**Kenyanthropus platyops** ("flat-faced hominid from Kenya"). Some authorities have suggested that this new form may be a better common ancestor for *Homo* than any species of *Australopithecus*. More evidence, however, is needed to even establish that these fossils do represent a whole new taxon; more examples with the same set of features will have to be found (White 2003).

In March 2004, a new subspecies of *Ardipithecus* was announced (Haile-Selassie et al. 2004), **Ardipithecus kadabba** (*kadabba* means "base family ancestor" in the Afar language). Found in the same Ethiopian location as *Ard. ramidus,* these fossils are older, 5.8 to 5.2 mya, and comprise a mandible, teeth, partial clavicle, hand bones, and, most important, a toe bone. The last item is said to show an angle at the joint that indicates a "toe-off" stride, as in modern human walking—in other words, evidence of habitual bipedalism at an early date. The interpretation, of course, is not without controversy; some authorities even claim these fossils represent chimpanzee ancestors (see discussion by Gee 2001; the fossils were found earlier and originally assigned to a subspecies of *Ard. ramidus*).

In October 2000, an even older possible hominid ancestor was proposed by French paleoanthropologists (Balter 2001a), based on thirteen fossil fragments from the Tugen Hills in northwestern Kenya. The dating of these fossils—femurs, teeth, portions of a mandible—is agreed on; they are about 5.6 to 6.2 million years old. Their identity, however, is a matter of debate. The discoverers claim the fossils represent the real ancestor of modern humans and that the other early hominids, the species of *Australopithecus,* are side branches. *Ardipithecus kadabba,* they say, is a chimp ancestor. They base their claim on their assessment that this hominid—placed by them into a new genus and species, **Orrorin tugenensis** (*orrorin* means "original man" in the local dialect)—was bipedal and exhibited expressions of certain traits that were more modern than those of other early hominids. Features of the head of the femur and grooves for muscle and ligament attachments are said to point to bipedalism. If true, that would place the origin of bipedalism nearly 2 million years earlier than the earliest existing bipedal fossil forms. Other authorities disagree with this analysis, and some question whether this form even *is* a hominid (Haile-Selassie 2001).

The most recent candidate for "first hominid" is a find from the Toros-Menalla site in northern Chad consisting of a cranium, jaw fragment, and several teeth and dated from 7 to 6 mya (Brunet et al. 2002). It has been placed in a new genus and species, ***Sahelanthropus tchadensis*** (after the Sahel region of Africa that borders the southern Sahara), and is known popularly as "Toumaï" ("hope of life" in the local Goran language). This form is described as having a "mosaic" of features. It is very apelike in its brain size (estimated at 320 to 380 ml), widely spaced eye orbits, and other details of its morphology, but according to its discoverers it has a number of striking features characteristic of later hominids. These include small canines of a hominid size, shape, and wear pattern; a face with reduced prognathism; and a continuous brow ridge. The forward position of the foramen magnum, while not enough evidence to reliably infer habitual bipedalism, still makes such an inference "not . . . unreasonable" (Brunet et al. 2002:150). The primary investigators thus claim that this form represents "the oldest and most primitive known member of the hominid clade, close to the divergence of hominids and chimpanzees" (151).

This view, of course, has its detractors. One group (Wolpoff et al. 2002) claims that the supposed hominid features of *Sahelanthropus* have other explanations and, in fact, that this form was not bipedal and, indeed, "was an ape" (582). (See Brunet 2002 for a counterargument.)

Clearly, however—no matter what these fossils turn out to be—bipedalism was the first hominid trait to evolve. Those changes in posture and locomotion are essentially the only changes we see in the early hominids for a few million years, indicating that the original branching that led to the hominids occurred relatively quickly. If the branching had been a slow process, it would have involved a collection of traits in concert with bipedalism. Instead, bipedalism was strongly and quickly selected for, and all the other traits that came to be characteristic of our family of primates came later. Bipedalism is thus the first adaptation that began our family of primates.

Bipedalism

The Benefits of Bipedalism

What's the benefit of standing upright, an adaptation that involved major realignments of much of the body of a quadrupedal animal? Under what circumstances was it selected for in the earliest members of our lineage?

Not many creatures use this form of locomotion. Kangaroos do and birds do—and many dinosaurs did—but they also use their tails for balance and support and walk with the knees bent and the trunk sloping forward. Birds' feet are essentially prehensile; they can even sleep perched on a branch. Human bipedalism, although it obviously works quite well, involves a large number of individual physical features and evolutionary changes (Figure 8.12) and remarkable acts of coordination. When we stand and walk, with our trunk erect and knees straight, we have to balance our

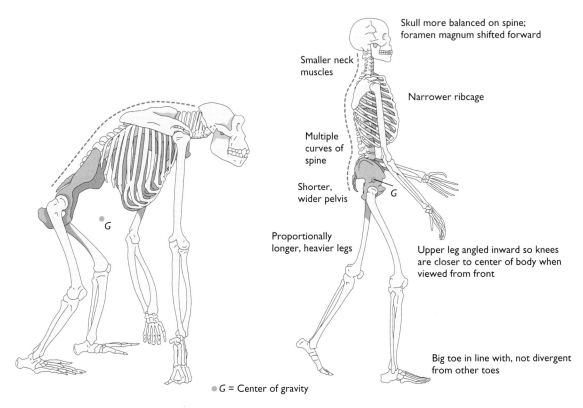

Skull more balanced on spine; foramen magnum shifted forward

Smaller neck muscles

Narrower ribcage

Multiple curves of spine

Shorter, wider pelvis

G

Proportionally longer, heavier legs

Upper leg angled inward so knees are closer to center of body when viewed from front

Big toe in line with, not divergent from other toes

G

● G = Center of gravity

FIGURE 8.12 The anatomical changes and, thus, the physical evidence associated with bipedalism in the human primate. Compare each human feature with the corresponding one in the gorilla. *G* represents the center of gravity when standing bipedally. The ape expends much more energy to keep from falling forward. *(Modified from John Napier,* The Antiquity of Human Walking, © *1967 Scientific American. Drawing by Enid Kotschnigo)*

knuckle walking Walking on the backs of the knuckles of the hand, typical of the African apes.

bodies vertically on two relatively small points of contact with the ground. We can't run particularly fast, and we aren't very stable on rough or slippery surfaces.

What makes this adaptive change even more puzzling is some strong evidence suggesting that rather than evolving from completely arboreal ancestors who came directly "out of the trees," we evolved from apes with a specialized terrestrial adaptation. This adaptation, called **knuckle walking** (exhibited by modern apes), is a form of locomotion that involves placing the backs of the middle joints of the fingers on the ground (see the gorilla in Figure 8.12). This adaptation allows the individual to hold a small object in its prehensile hand and walk at the same time. The wrist joints (specifically the distal portion, or hand end, of the radius) of the earliest established hominids, *Australopithecus anamensis* and *A. afarensis*, share a trait with chimps and gorillas that helps keep the arm rigid while walking in this fashion (Begun 2000; Collard and Aiello 2000; Richmond and Strait 2000). It seems reasonable, then, that the common ancestor of the African apes and hominids also had this feature. So if our common ancestor *already* had a specialized adaptation to walking on the ground (on

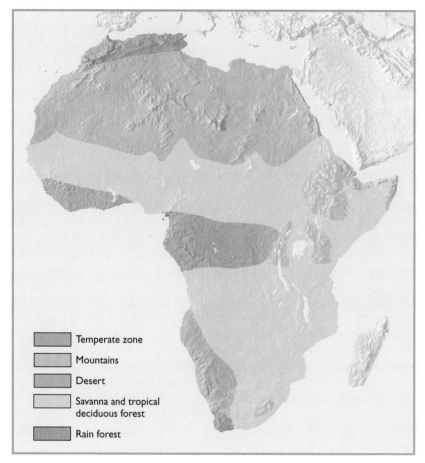

FIGURE 8.13 The general climatic and vegetation zones of Africa today. Except for the large deserts in the north and south, the zones are much the same as when our evolutionary story began some 5 mya, although specific local conditions may have differed. Moreover, where zones meet, the conditions grade into one another, producing an area of mixed vegetation and other conditions. *(Redrawn with permission from: Bernard Campbell, Human Ecology [New York: Aldine de Gruyter] © 1983 by Bernard Campbell)*

Legend:
- Temperate zone
- Mountains
- Desert
- Savanna and tropical deciduous forest
- Rain forest

all fours), why did our lineage evolve an even more specialized and complex one (bipedalism)?

Compare the map of early hominid sites (see Figure 8.4) with the map of Africa's climatic and vegetation zones (Figure 8.13). Note that the sites are located in savannas or tropical deciduous forests (open grasslands or woodlands more open than the rain forest and with trees that undergo seasonal cycles of growth). Where these zones meet, there is a mix of forest and open areas, as one zone grades into another.

Open areas, particularly the savannas, present a very different set of problems to a primate than do dense forests. Primates are basically vegetarian. Although there are plenty of plants on the savannas, there are not as many that can be utilized by the digestive systems of most primates. Most primates cannot digest cellulose as can the *ungulates* (grazing animals such as the African antelopes). Edible plants or plants with edible parts—at least for a hominoid primate—are not as concentrated on the open plains or even open forests. As a result, primates living in such areas have to travel over a wider area to find food. These areas are more affected by seasonal change than are the rain forests, and so there may be greater variation between the wet and dry seasons. This, too, creates the need for more traveling in search of food. Finally, there is more danger involved in acquiring these widely dispersed foods. Lions, leopards, cheetahs, wild dogs, hyenas, and other predators of the plains and open forests are more than happy to make a meal out of a small primate.

There are, of course, sources of meat, both in the forests and especially on the open savannas with their great herds of herbivores. Chimpanzees are known to hunt, kill, and eat small mammals such as monkeys. They are even known to scavenge kills that leopards have left hanging in trees—although rarely (Byrne and Byrne 1988; Cavallo 1990). While our earliest ancestors may have hunted small animals, it is unlikely they preyed on big game or even animals as large as those hunted by chimps. They were not as mobile in the trees as the chimps (having legs adapted to bipedalism), and they lacked the powerful musculature and large interlocking canine teeth of the apes (see Figures 6.6 and 8.10). And, so far at least, there is no physical evidence of big-game hunting on the plains. There is, however, evidence that they scavenged kills, which we will cover in the next chapter. Still, although scavenging provided access to meat, it was dangerous. The carcasses had to be taken away and kept away from other predators or scavenged after the predators had finished.

So, we may ask not only how bipedalism could be a benefit for terrestrial walking, but we can structure our inquiry more precisely by asking how it would be adaptive in such a mix of environments.

Explaining the Emergence of Bipedalism

Six different models have been proposed to account for the evolution of bipedalism under the environmental conditions just described.

1. Carrying model. Bipedalism could have allowed our early ancestors to search for and collect food in greater safety and with greater efficiency. Freeing the arms and hands from a role in locomotion would have meant that our ancestors could transport food from open areas to safer locations, such as a grove of trees or perhaps the foot of a steep hill. This would have been especially important if the food were part of an animal carcass, since other meat eaters would also have found it attractive. Moreover, bipedalism would have allowed mothers to carry children in their arms while walking in search of food. Perhaps our ancestors carried sticks and rocks to throw at predators and scavengers to scare them away from a kill. (Chimps will occasionally hurl rocks and sticks, though not particularly accurately.) Under experimental conditions (Videan and McGrew 2000), it has been shown that having something to carry is a major stimulus for bipedal locomotion in chimpanzees and bonobos (see Figure 6.8). However, Jablonski and Chaplin (2000) claim that if bipedal carrying of anything other than small, light objects had been a major selective focus, there would have been other changes as well, such as an enlargement of the lower (lumbar) vertebrae, as seen in modern humans. But this feature did not appear early on in our evolution, not even in the earliest members of genus *Homo* (about 2.4 mya).

2. *Vigilance model.* It has been proposed that bipedalism, by elevating the head, helped our ancestors locate potential sources of food and danger. Observe, for example, how squirrels sit upright to better look around. Videan and McGrew's (2000) experiment, just noted, showed this to be an important factor in the use of bipedalism, at least in their controlled studies among captive apes. In fact, it was the most frequent context of upright posture. It should be noted here, however, that this model only addresses upright posture, not necessarily upright locomotion.

3. *Heat dissipation model.* According to another view, the vertical orientation of bipedalism helps cool the body by presenting a smaller target to the intense equatorial rays of the sun and by placing more of the body above the ground to catch any cooling air currents. The savanna can be hot, and the heat built up by hours of walking in search of food needs to be dissipated. (This factor may also explain the adaptive significance of the relatively hairless bodies of modern hominids. Having no hair allows sweat to evaporate more quickly and cool the body more efficiently.) This model, of course, would not apply to the forests, where primates would be sheltered by the shade of trees.

4. *Energy efficiency model.* Data indicate that although bipedalism is an energy-inefficient way of running compared to quadrupedalism, it is *more* efficient for walking. For example, a 154-pound man uses 140 more joules of energy per meter walking than standing still and 260 more joules running than standing still. A 154-pound quadrupedal mammal uses 200 more joules of energy per meter both walking and running (Alexander 1995). Long periods of steady bipedal walking in search of food, then, would seem to require less energy. Remember, however, that the first hominids may not have walked bipedally quite like later members of our family, and they may not have been any more efficient at walking upright than are chimpanzees. Moreover, it is not certain that what makes our walking more efficient is simply our upright stance. Body mass and other anatomical features may be related as well. So, as Steudel (1996) maintains, efficiency may not have been the initial key factor in selection for bipedal locomotion. It may be that bipedalism had, at first, other advantages and that once it was established, further anatomical changes made it more energy efficient.

5. *Foraging/bipedal harvesting model.* This idea refers to the benefits of standing upright to reach sources of food on bushes and trees, particularly those difficult or impossible to climb. The introduction of raised feeding structures in Videan and McGrew's (2000) experiment stimulated bipedal posture in chimps.

6. *Display model.* Jablonski and Chaplin (2000) propose that the important factor of bipedalism was an upright display posture like that seen in chimps during dominance confrontations and, to a lesser extent, in male bonobos (who sometimes also stand erect, in both senses, as a sexual display). Among these primates, an upright display posture conveys meaning because it makes the individual seem larger; it is also directly related to mating success. Although chimps and bonobos devote relatively little time to this behavior, its adaptive and evolutionary impact among our ancestors, the authors suggest, could still have been great. In their experiment, Videan and McGrew (2000) noted that the introduction of display objects (things the animals could wave around or make noise with) increased rates of bipedalism among chimps, though not among bonobos.

Each of these models has logic and evidence in its support, and each could be argued against as being an important adaptive focus. It seems reasonable, at the moment, to provisionally suppose that *all* these factors, acting together, could have played an adaptive role in the emergence of the hominid lineage and its characteristic mode of locomotion. But do these models—other than the display model—explain why bipedalism would have made some individuals, and eventually some groups, more reproductively successful? Remember that reproductive success is the measure of natural selection. Simple survival and longevity are only part of it.

Once again, we may get a clue from our close relatives, the chimps and bonobos, the former an open-forest species and the latter an inhabitant of dense forests. Although chimps normally have no need to share resources, they do share meat from a hunt, possibly because it is—in some chimp way—considered a luxury item. Bonobos, on the other hand, share even foods that are plentiful. This serves to avoid conflict and to establish and maintain peaceful coexistence within the group. Food sharing is, in a sense, a symbol of group peace and unity. In times of need, of course, food sharing might have practical consequences. Moreover, as you recall from Chapter 6, the bonobos use sex—in various combinations and with a variety of techniques—to strengthen and maintain group unity and to defuse tension. Sex for them is separate from purely reproductive activity. It has social and psychological meaning as well.

Perhaps, then, our earliest ancestors survived by the enhancement of adaptations that promoted peaceful cooperation and group unity, including the sharing of resources. The acquisition of these resources was made easier, safer, and more energy efficient by the ability to walk habitually upright.

Such a set of adaptations would certainly have been one way of aiding survival on the floor of open forests and out on the savannas. But remember that our earliest ancestors also exhibited traits associated with an arboreal adaptation: relatively long arms; heavy shoulder girdles, arm bones, and arm muscles; and curved finger and toe bones. Perhaps in the earliest stages of our lineage, our ancestors were adapted to both a tree-climbing *and* a terrestrial, open-area way of life. And environmental data bear this out.

Reassessment of the specific local environments of some important early hominid sites has shown them to be more forested than previously thought (see Shreeve 1996b for a summary and C. Ward et al. 1999 for recent descriptions). *Ardipithecus ramidus* lived in a high-altitude, dense woodland and *Ard. kadabba* in a wet, wooded environment. *Orrorin* lived in a wooded habitat. *Sahelanthropus* inhabited a "swampy, vegetated" area near some open grasslands and gallery forest (Vignaud et al. 2002:155). The Lake Turkana site where *Australopithecus anamensis* was found may have been an arid area, but the lake itself was surrounded by forest, and there were woodlands associated with rivers. Lucy, the first specimen of *A. afarensis,* probably lived in a mixed forest and bushland area, and Laetoli was open grassland with scattered trees and forests nearby. *A. bahrelghazalia* from Chad is thought to have inhabited forests with grassy patches. There is, in fact, evidence that East Africa at the time was a "heterogeneous mosaic" of environments, from forests to open plains (Kingston et al. 1994:958). The same appears to be true of southern Africa, home to other early hominids to be discussed in the next section.

Indeed, Richard Potts (1996, 1998) gives evidence that the past 6 million years marks a period of increasing environmental fluctuations that produced great oscillations in moisture and vegetation in Africa. Our early ancestors, he says, encountered a variety of environments and underwent selection for the ability to live in both densely wooded and open habitats. Potts calls this "variability selection"—adaptations that result in "flexible, novel responses to surroundings and diversity" that can "buffer" a species against "episodic change" in its environment (1998:86). The retention of arboreal features accompanied by the enhancement of bipedal locomotion would seem to be a perfect example of this sort of adaptation, along with, perhaps, other changes that enhanced social cooperation and resource sharing.

Finally, the isolation of our ancestors from the ancestors of the modern African apes may have been reinforced by a geological change—the formation of the Great Rift Valley in East Africa starting about 8 mya (Figure 8.14). Tectonic movements caused some land to sink, forming the valley, with mountains on its western rim. This in turn caused a localized climatic change: the area west of the valley remained moist and heavily forested, and that east of the valley turned drier to become savanna and more open forest. Today, chimpanzees are found only in the valley or to

FIGURE 8.14 A portion of the Great Rift Valley in southern Kenya. The rift, formed some 8 mya, stretches 3,500 miles from Mozambique to the Red Sea and is, in places, over 2,000 feet deep. Many lakes such as the Little Magadi, shown in the photograph, lie in the valley. (© *Emory Kristof/National Geographic Society Image Collection*)

the west. Early hominid fossils, with the exception of the Chad find, have been found only in the valley or to the east.

The details about the early evolution of our hominid family and its characteristic traits are still being debated. Clearly, however, the hominid line had emerged by perhaps 6 to 5 mya in a mixed and fluctuating woodland and savanna environment. Clearly, too, the trait that distinguishes the hominids from the other primates is bipedalism, although it first evolved in organisms that retained arboreal features as well—an adaptation to a variable and changing environment. Accompanying upright locomotion was, perhaps, an emphasis on group unity and survival facilitated by food sharing and perhaps by sexual activity separated from purely reproductive functions and linked to emotional, social, and personal relationships.

Whatever happened, it was successful. At least one hominid species was well ensconced in East Africa by 3 mya. From there our family began to branch out.

FIGURE 8.15 Skull of *Australopithecus africanus* (female?) from Sterkfontein, South Africa. Note the general similarity to *A. afarensis* (see Figure 8.9). *(Transvaal Museum, D. C. Panagos)*

The Hominids Evolve

More Australopithecines

The basic set of early hominid features represented by Lucy and her kin continued for another three-quarters of a million years. Although little changed from *Australopithecus afarensis,* the fossils representing the next period are still called by their original name, *A. africanus* (Dart's "southern ape of Africa"). The remains of this species have been found mostly in South Africa, but there are some fossils from Kenya and Ethiopia as well. They have the same body size and shape and the same brain size as *A. afarensis.* There are a few differences, however (Figure 8.15). Their faces are a bit less prognathous, and they lack a sagittal crest. Their canine teeth are smaller, there are no gaps in the tooth row, and the tooth row is more rounded, as in a human rather than an ape (see Figure 8.7).

The relative size and shape of the teeth of both *A. afarensis* and *A. africanus,* on the whole larger than those of modern humans, indicate a mostly mixed vegetable diet of fruits and leaves. This is confirmed by analysis of microscopic scratches and wear patterns on the teeth (Figure 8.16). There is no direct evidence of meat eating, but a recent study (Sponheimer and Lee-Thorp 1999) of a carbon isotope (^{13}C) in the tooth enamel of a sample of *A. africanus* indicated that members of this species ate either tropical grasses or the flesh of animals that ate tropical grasses or both. (Grasses

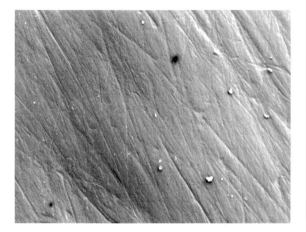

FIGURE 8.16 Scanning electron microscope pictures of the surfaces of early hominid teeth. The enamel of the teeth of *Australopithecus africanus (left)* is polished and scratched, while that of *Paranthropus (right)* is pitted and very rough. This is evidence of the hard, tough, gritty foods eaten by the latter. *(Micrographs courtesy of Dr. Frederick E. Grine, SUNY, Stony Brook. Photographed by Chester Tarka)*

have more ^{13}C in their tissues than do other types of plants.) Because the dentition examined by these researchers lacked the tooth wear patterns indicative of grass eating, the carbon may have come from grass-eating animals. While these grass-eating animals may have been plant-eating insects, there is the possibility that the australopithecines either hunted small animals or scavenged the carcasses of larger ones. There is also evidence that early hominids dug up rootstocks (tubers, rhizomes, and bulbs), although prior to the use of fire for cooking, this would have required some other means of deactivating toxins found in some of these food sources, such as crushing, soaking, or drying (Ragir 2000). It is noteworthy in this regard that some early bone tools from South Africa, formerly interpreted as showing signs of tuber digging, are now seen as having wear patterns associated with opening termite mounds (Holden 2001).

The essential similarity of *A. afarensis* and *A. africanus* suggests a plausible, and simple, interpretation: that *A. africanus* is a continuation of *A. afarensis,* more widely distributed in southern and possibly eastern Africa and showing some evolutionary changes. It should be noted that this interpretation is not agreed on by all investigators and remains hypothetical. Moreover, this simple linear relationship is confounded by the suggestion of some older dates (4 mya) for the South African site of Sterkfontein (Patridge et al. 2003). So if *A. africanus* and *A. afarensis* are contemporaries, their relationship is more complex; perhaps they are either members of the same species or of different species living at the same time.

Some recent evidence lends support to the meat-eating interpretation and to the definition of another new hominid species. The site of Bouri, in Ethiopia, dated at 2.5 mya, has revealed (in separate locations) hominid cranial and postcranial bones, as well as the bones of antelopes, horses, and other animals that exhibit cut marks made by stone tools (Asfaw et al. 1999; Culotta 1999b; de Heinzelin et al. 1999). The cranial bones indicate a brain size of 450 ml, and the prognathous jaw is similar to that of

A. afarensis. Several features of the teeth resemble those of early *Homo,* but the molars are unusually large, even larger than those of the southern African robust hominids called *Paranthropus* (to be discussed next). This set of traits led investigators to designate these bones as a new species, **Australopithecus garhi** (*garhi* means "surprise" in a local language). The postcranial remains from Bouri, not clearly from the same species as the cranial specimens, show the relative lengths of the upper arm and upper leg to be humanlike, while the lower arm remains long, as in apes. This may indicate that in the evolution of human limb proportions, the leg elongated first and the arm shortened later. Finally, the stone-tool cut marks on the animal bones show that whatever hominid (not necessarily *A. garhi*) made them was butchering animals for meat and smashing bones to get at the fat-rich marrow.

The evolutionary relationship of *A. garhi* to other hominids is still a matter of debate. Its discoverers (Asfaw et al. 1999) feel it is descended from *A. afarensis* and is a direct ancestor of *Homo.* Others disagree (Strait and Grine 1999; and see Culotta 1999a). Clearly, more evidence is needed to interpret these specimens more precisely, but they do show the extent of the variation among hominids during this period.

Still More Hominids

Between 3 and 2 mya, two new types of hominids appear in the fossil record, two new genera by the approach used here: *Paranthropus* and our genus *Homo.* One type retains the chimpanzee-sized brains and small bodies of *Australopithecus* but has evolved a notable robusticity in the areas of the skull involved with chewing. This is genus *Paranthropus.* As noted before, some authorities place these fossils in genus *Australopithecus,* but we will use *Paranthropus* both for clarity and because we lean toward that interpretation of current evidence (McCollum 1999).

The fossils representing the beginning of this genus are a single skull from Lake Turkana, Kenya—dubbed the "Black Skull" because of its dark color resulting from minerals in the ground (Figure 8.17)—and some fragmentary fossils from Ethiopia. These fossils are grouped into a separate species, **Paranthropus aethiopicus,** and are dated at between 2.8 and 2.2 mya.

The Black Skull is striking for several reasons. First, it has the smallest adult brain—at only 410 ml—ever found in any well-established hominid. Also, it has the largest sagittal crest of any hominid, the most prognathous face, and an extremely large area in the back of the mouth for the molar teeth. Although no teeth were found, its molars appear to have been four or five times the size of a modern human's.

The Black Skull represents the beginning of a second major type of hominid, sometimes referred to as "robust" hominids. Although they were pretty much the same as *Australopithecus* in brain and body size, the members of genus *Paranthropus* were considerably more robust in all those features

involved with chewing. The sagittal crest; broad, dished-out face; large
cheekbones; huge mandible; and back teeth that are much larger relative
to the front teeth—all point to a diet of large amounts of vegetable matter
with an emphasis on hard, tough, gritty items such as seeds, nuts, hard
fruits, and tubers. This is confirmed by microscopic wear pattern analysis
(see Figure 8.16).

A little over 2 mya, two more types of robust hominids appear. One
species, **Paranthropus robustus,** was found in South Africa and dates between 2.2 and 1.5 mya or even later (Figure 8.18). It retains the body size
of *Australopithecus,* but there is a slight increase in average brain capacity
to about 520 ml. The jaws are heavy, the back teeth are large, and there is
a sagittal crest—all indications of a mixed, tough vegetable diet. The crania, though, are obviously not as robust as in *P. aethiopicus.*

The second robust species continues the extreme ruggedness of
P. aethiopicus, though it is not quite as pronounced. Found in Tanzania,
Kenya, and Ethiopia and existing from 2.2 to 1 mya, **Paranthropus boisei**
shows features that, along with those of *P. aethiopicus,* are sometimes referred to as "hyperrobust" (Figure 8.19). The specimen that defined the

FIGURE 8.18 Skull of *Paranthropus robustus* from Swartkrans, South Africa. Note the remnant of a sagittal crest. *(Transvaal Museum, D. C. Panagos)*

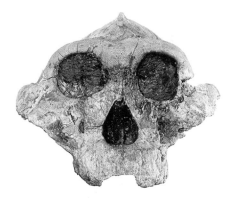

FIGURE 8.19 Three views of *Paranthropus boisei* from Lake Turkana, Kenya. Note the large sagittal crest, heavy brow ridge, prognathism, large cheekbones, and the huge space between the zygomatic arch and the skull. The zygomatic arch is the bony arch that runs from the cheekbones to just in front of the ear, clearly seen in the top view of the skull (*bottom*). All these indicate very large chewing muscles and thus an adaptation to a diet of tough, hard, gritty foods. *(© The National Museums of Kenya)*

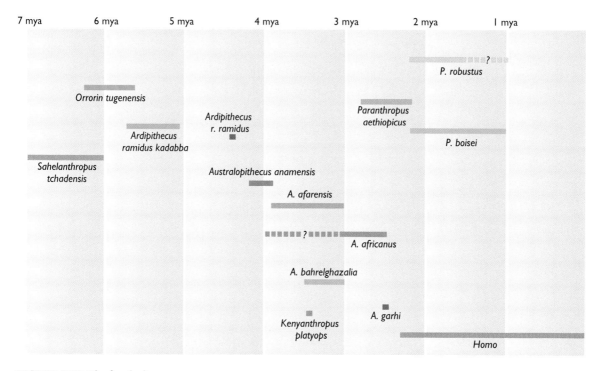

7 mya   6 mya   5 mya   4 mya   3 mya   2 mya   1 mya

P. robustus

Orrorin tugenensis

Ardipithecus
r. ramidus

Paranthropus
aethiopicus

Ardipithecus
ramidus kadabba

P. boisei

Sahelanthropus
tchadensis

Australopithecus anamensis

A. afarensis

A. africanus

A. bahrelghazalia

Kenyanthropus
platyops

A. garhi

Homo

FIGURE 8.20 The fossils discussed in this chapter, with their currently accepted time ranges. The dotted lines indicate possible extensions of those ranges.

species is the famous "Zinjanthropus," found by Mary and Louis Leakey in 1959. Dubbed "Nutcracker Man," this specimen has extremely large jaws and back teeth and a large sagittal crest. Otherwise *P. boisei* has the body and brain size of the South African robust hominids.

A more recent *P. boisei* fossil from Ethiopia (Suwa et al. 1997) consists of the first cranium of this species with an associated mandible. The largest-known skull of the species, it comes from a new site that extends the species' known range in Africa and is clearly associated with a dry grassland environment. It also shows some physical differences from existing *boisei* fossils that indicate a considerable range of phenotypic variation within the species.

The second new hominid genus that appeared about 2.5 mya is the one to which modern humans belong, *Homo*. We will discuss the early species of our genus in the next chapter. For now, however, we need to discuss the overall shape of the early hominid family tree.

Putting It All Together

Figure 8.20 shows the dates of all the established and proposed early hominid fossils discussed in this chapter (with *Homo* added for perspective and a preview of what's to come). A number of different specific models have been proposed for connecting all these fossils into an evolutionary tree. Most authorities generally agree that the hominids from about 4 mya on can be grouped into two natural categories, the gracile and the robust (here, *Australopithecus* and *Paranthropus,* although some lump them all into the first genus). We've grouped them in the timeline to reflect this. There is also general agreement that it was some member of the gracile hominids that gave rise to *Homo.* A simple tree, then, would look like this:

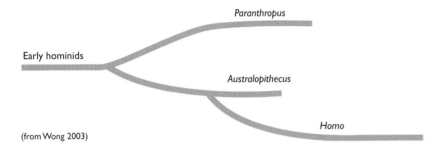

(from Wong 2003)

There is a difference of opinion as to *which* australopithecine is the direct ancestor of *Homo,* and authorities have different favorite candidates. Some have suggested that our direct ancestor was not an australopithecine at all but *Kenyanthropus platyops,* although more specimens are required to verify the validity of this taxon and its traits.

There is even more debate over the newest fossil finds: *Ardipithecus kadabba, Orrorin tugenensis,* and *Sahelanthropus tchadensis.* With relatively scanty evidence so far, and with different body parts represented by the existing fossils, comparison and analysis are necessarily very tentative. At one extreme (see Wong 2003) is the idea that those three are lineal descendants, all on the line to *Homo:*

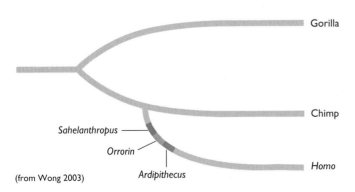

(from Wong 2003)

The opposite extreme has the three representing ancestors of three different genera:

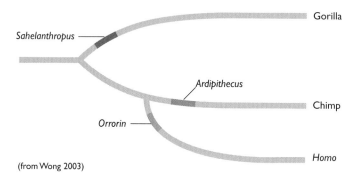

(from Wong 2003)

What *is* clear, however, is that with these three fossils (if further evidence shows they represent valid groups and are not anomalous individuals), we are close to the common ancestor of the chimps and us. Perhaps, as Bernard Wood has suggested (2002:134), none of these is *the* earliest hominid; instead, these fossils are "the tip of an iceberg of taxonomic diversity" during early hominid evolution, and there were many different combinations of traits in "an adaptive radiation of fossil ape-like creatures that included the common ancestor of humans and chimpanzees." Time and more fossils will presumably clarify the whole story.

We may address some other general questions about this period. What might have caused the branching that founded the new genera of *Paranthropus* and *Homo*? What caused the extinction, around the same time, of genus *Australopithecus*? Finally, what might have caused the extinction of the *Paranthropus* species about 1 mya?

We can't answer these questions with certainty, but recall Richard Potts's evidence for a sharp increase in environmental variability in Africa starting about 6 mya and continuing—and further increasing—over time (1996, 1998). There is also evidence for a major and abrupt change about 2.8 mya—an intensification of cycles that produced a shift toward grasslands (Kerr 2001). Increased environmental variability resulting in a series of newly emerging, complex, and diverse habitats may have initially promoted different adaptations among hominid populations, as seen in the branching that gave rise to the robust hominids and to *Homo*. But if the degree of the fluctuations continued to increase, this may have put such pressure on the hominid adaptive responses that those groups less able to cope eventually became extinct. Unable to survive well enough to perpetuate themselves in the face of decreasing resources (this may have been the case for *Paranthropus*, who were specialized vegetarians), these now-extinct hominids were possibly outcompeted for space and resources by

CONTEMPORARY ISSUE

Where Is the "Missing Link"?

A headline in the December 19, 1912 issue of the *New York Times* proclaimed, "Paleolithic Skull Is a Missing Link." The skull referred to was the now-infamous "Piltdown Man," discovered in England, named *Eoanthropus* (the "dawn man")—and forty years later shown to be a fraud (see Feder 2006 for details). At the time, however, it was touted as the "missing link" because it possessed traits that were a perfect mix between those of human and ape. Its cranium was the shape and size of a modern human's, and its mandible was decidedly apelike. (In fact, the cranium *was* of a modern human and the jaw *was* of a modern orangutan—modified by the still-unidentified perpetrator to appear ancient.)

For much of the history of evolutionary thought, evolution was conceived of as a ladder or a chain, progressing from primitive to modern, with living forms representing points on that chain. Even when it was generally acknowledged that humans had descended from apes, this evolution was thought of as unilinear—a single line of progress from ape to man. Thus, as we go back into the fossil record, we should eventually find something that is intermediate—half ape and half human. Since modern apes were thought of as the remnants of primitive forms that had never evolved further, the missing link (notice the chain metaphor) was conceived of as a mix of the traits of *modern* humans and *modern* apes. In our hubris, we were sure it was our big brains that separated us from the apes and that had evolved first, so the combination fabricated to concoct the Piltdown skull fit the bill perfectly. It had that big-brain hallmark of humanity, perched on top of an otherwise apelike jaw.

Indeed, even when evolution was recognized as being a branching tree rather than a ladder or chain,

the idea of fossil forms that were intermediates between modern species still held. Famed anatomist Sir Arthur Keith wrote that "to unravel man's pedigree, we have to thread our way, not along the links of a chain, but through the meshes of a complicated network" (1927:8). Then, on the next page, he accepted the Piltdown find as authentic.

We recognize today that living species are not leftover primitive links on an evolutionary chain but are, themselves, the products of evolution. A missing link in the traditional sense—between modern humans and modern apes—simply does not exist. What *does* exist is a common ancestor of humans and our closest relatives, the chimpanzees and bonobos—and it did not look exactly like any of those modern species. Granted, we have reason to think that the common ancestor resembled a bonobo or chimp more than a modern human, but this is just because evolution happened to take place at a more rapid pace in hominids than in the apes. The apes are still modern species.

So what we *can* look for is that common ancestor. It is a "link" not in the sense of a chain but in the sense of being that point where our two evolutionary lines converge. At the moment, that form is still missing. But as we find older and older fossils, we are closing in on our common ancestor.

What will it look like? It should have characteristics shared by both modern hominids and pongids, but it will look, on the whole, like neither. Genetic evidence suggests that our common ancestor is 5 to 7 million years old. So for the moment, the closest we've come to that elusive "missing link" are the fossils of *Ardipithecus* (see Figure 8.5), *Orrorin*, and *Sahelanthropus*.

---

the better adapted, a phenomenon known as **competitive exclusion.** In this case, only the adaptive response that included an increase in brain size, with its concomitant increase in ability to understand and manipulate the environment, proved successful in the long run.

competitive exclusion
When one species outcompetes others for the resources of a particular area.

Summary

The primates are one of the earliest of the existing mammal groups to evolve after the mass extinction of 65 mya. They appear to have evolved first in what are now North America and Europe, but the success of their adaptations allowed them to radiate over the Old World and into the New World.

About 23 mya, the hominoids appear in the form of primitive apes. This successful group has left fossils all over Africa, Europe, and Asia. It is from one of the African apes that our family, Hominidae, branched off 6 to 5 mya.

The evolution of habitual bipedalism marks the beginnings of our family and was the major distinguishing characteristic of this family for the first half of its time on earth. Bipedalism may have begun as part of one group's adaptation to the forests. We still see this trait—along with food sharing and sexual consciousness—in today's bonobos. However, these adaptations would also prove useful in Africa's increasingly variable environment, and the hominids soon were well established and radiated into three distinct groups, often classified as separate genera: *Australopithecus, Paranthropus,* and *Homo.*

The first two genera, *Australopithecus* and *Paranthropus,* with their chimp-sized brains, remained largely vegetarian and persisted until nearly 1 mya. They eventually lost out to a combination of environmental change and competition from the third hominid genus, *Homo,* with its bigger brain and ability to manipulate its environment. Our genus is the subject of the next chapter.

Study Questions

1. What is the fossil evidence for the beginnings of hominid evolution? How do these fossils support the idea that bipedalism was the first defining hominid trait?
2. Why was bipedalism adaptively important to the early hominids? When, and under what circumstances, did it evolve?
3. What do we know about the evolution of the now-extinct hominid lineages? How might they be related to one another and to the branch of the hominids that survived?

Key Terms

foramen magnum	sagittal crest	competitive exclusion
prognathism	knuckle walking	

For More Information

The primates and their evolution are covered in John G. Fleagle's *Primate Adaptation and Evolution.* The intriguing story of *Gigantopithecus* is told in *Other Origins: The Search for the Giant Ape in Human Prehistory,* by Russell Ciochon, John Olsen, and Jamie James. For a more technical account of early primate evolution, see R. D. Martin's article in the May 20, 1993 issue of *Nature,* "Primate Origins: Plugging the Gaps."

The story of the study of the human fossil record and of some of the major recent discoveries is told in *Lucy: The Beginnings of Humankind,* by Donald Johanson and Maitland Edey, and in a sequel, *Lucy's Child: The Discovery of a Human Ancestor,* by Donald Johanson and James Shreeve. Both of these books are somewhat outdated but still convey the excitement of paleoanthropology. A slightly different perspective on much of the same material is found in Richard Leakey and Roger Lewin's *Origins Reconsidered: In Search of What Makes Us Human.* A beautifully illustrated treatment of the subject, based on an exhibit at the American Museum of Natural History in New York, is Ian Tattersall's *The Human Odyssey: Four Million Years of Human Evolution.*

A *National Geographic* series, "The Dawn of Humans," covering the 6 million years of our evolution, appears in the following issues: September 1995; January and March 1996; February, May, July, and September 1997; August 1998; and May, July, and December 2000. The photographs and graphics are, as usual, superb. And see the October 2001 issue for photos of *Kenyanthropus.*

For more on the early apes and possible hominid ancestors, see David R. Begun's "Planet of the Apes" in the August 2003 *Scientific American.*

You might be interested in seeing what a primary report on an important fossil looks like. A good example is the first report on the discovery of *Sahelanthropus* by Brunet et al. in the July 11, 2002 issue of *Nature,* "A New Hominid from the Upper Miocene of Chad, Central Africa." And for a piece on all the new finds, see "An Ancestor to Call Our Own," by Kate Wong, in the January 2003 *Scientific American.*

For a nice summary of the different views on the possible climate-change influences on human evolution, see "Sunset on the Savanna," by James Shreeve, in the July 1996 issue of *Discover.* A nicely illustrated explanation of the Great Rift Valley, by Yves Coppens, appears in the May 1994 *Scientific American,* "East Side Story: The Origin of Humankind."

A review of two books on the bipedalism question and a nice discussion of the topic itself is Ian Tattersall's "Stand and Deliver" in the November 2003 *Natural History.*

A veritable river of ice, the Moreno Glacier is located in Patagonia, a region of Argentina.

(© Geoffery Clifford/Woodfin Camp and Associates)

9

THE HUMAN LINEAGE
EVOLVES

CHAPTER CONTENTS

The First Members of Genus *Homo*

To New Lands

The Evolution and Behavior of *Homo erectus*

Big Brains, Archaic Skulls

The Neandertals

Modern Humans

Summary

CONTEMPORARY ISSUE: Who Are the "Hobbits" from Indonesia?

Study Questions

Key Terms

For More Information

A swirling white powder cascaded past the streetlights as a heavy snowfall began to blanket the campus. School and business closings scrolled across television screens, airlines cancelled flights, and those huddled at home braced for the two to three feet of snow predicted by local meteorologists. Even with our technological sophistication in the late twentieth century, the "blizzard of 1996" paralyzed communities and frightened even long-time residents of the Northeast.

As cold as it got and as high as the snow piled, however, we could all rest easy in the knowledge that it would end. Spring would come and with it a thaw and a halt to the snow and cold—at least until next winter. The promise of spring has not always been a reality for much of the Northern Hemisphere, however. For long periods of time—sometimes lasting thousands of years—spring simply didn't come. We call this "deep freeze" the Pleistocene, and it is perhaps the most striking, but not only, example of the challenges that confronted our evolving lineage.

FIGURE 9.1 A sample of Oldowan tools. The two at lower right are flake tools. The others are core tools. *(© Eric Delson)*

The First Members of Genus *Homo*

When the Leakeys found Zinjanthropus in 1959, they uncovered some simple stone tools at the same level of the Olduvai Gorge (Figure 9.1). At first, they thought Zinjanthropus had made the tools, but they began to feel that "Zinj" was too primitive to have made something so sophisticated.

Marking the beginning of what paleoanthropologists call the **Lower Paleolithic** (or Early Stone Age), these tools, called **Oldowan** after Olduvai Gorge, seem very simple to us. Also called **pebble tools,** they are nothing more than water-smoothed cobbles 3 to 4 inches across, modified by knocking off a few chips from one or two faces to make a sharp edge. But unlike the termite sticks of the chimpanzees, there is nothing in the raw material—the unmodified stone—that immediately suggests the tools that can be made from it or the method of manufacture. A stone tool requires that the maker be able to imagine within the stone the tool he wants to make and to picture the process needed to make it. Making even a simple Oldowan tool is also a far more complex technological feat than stripping the leaves off a branch to make it narrow enough to fit down the hole of a termite mound (Figure 9.2). This leap of the imagination and increase in technological skill are what make the first evidence of stone toolmaking so important.

Authorities originally thought that the Oldowan tools were all **core tools** and that the flakes were the waste products of their manufacture. Recently, however, it has been shown that though some flaked cores may have been used as tools, the majority were the raw materials for the manufacture of **flake tools,** which were used for a variety of tasks, such as cutting meat and plant material, scraping meat off a bone, and sawing wood or bone (Schick and Toth 1993; Toth 1985). Under microscopic analysis, the edges of these flakes show a polish that is characteristic of these activities.

Lower Paleolithic Term used to label the earliest period of hominid toolmaking in Africa, Europe, and Asia; dates to as much as 2.5 mya (in Africa) to about 250,000 ya throughout the Old World.

Oldowan A toolmaking tradition from Africa associated with early *Homo*.

pebble tool The earliest type of hominid stone tool, made from water-smoothed stones with a few flakes taken off one or both sides.

core tool A tool made by taking a flake off a stone nucleus.

flake tool A tool made from a flake removed from a stone core.

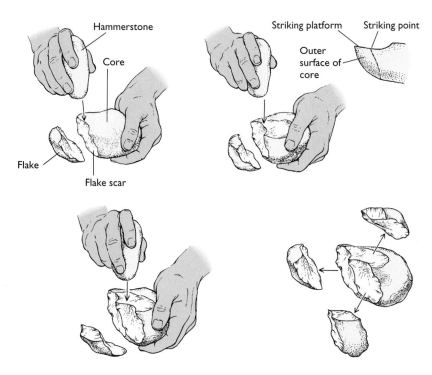

FIGURE 9.2 The process by which flakes were removed from a stone core in the Oldowan tradition: A hard stone was struck with another stone in just the right locations to allow for the removal of sharp, thin flakes. *(From "The First Technology" by Nicholas Toth. Copyright © 1987 by Scientific American, Inc. All rights reserved)*

It also appears that the makers of the Oldowan tools may have traveled some distance to find a source of stone known to be superior for the production of sharp, durable tools. The cores themselves were probably carried around to wherever flakes were needed; it is common to find flakes at a site but not the cores from which they were struck. All this shows a high level of planning (Schick and Toth 1993).

Although there is some evidence for bone tool manufacture among the earlier hominids (Holden 2001b), no evidence of stone tool manufacture has been found. One study (Susman 1994) concluded that the thumbs of *Australopithecus* and *Paranthropus* had features that allowed the dexterity required to make stone tools—although this conclusion has been challenged (Gibbons 1997a). Furthermore, some simple stone tools have recently been found in Ethiopia that date to 2.6 mya, 300,000 years earlier than the earliest accepted fossils of *Homo* (Semaw et al. 1997). Still, no hard evidence links any hominid other than *Homo* with the manufacture of stone implements.

It appeared in 1959, and still does, that Zinjanthropus was not a good candidate for having been the maker of the pebble tools. Then, in 1961, the Leakeys found a second hominid from the same time period. Actually, they had found fragmentary fossils of this form in the same year that they

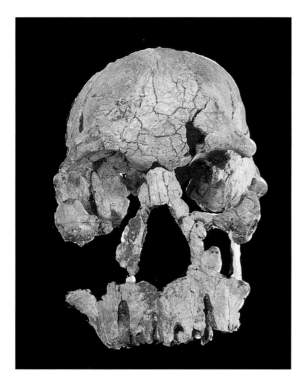 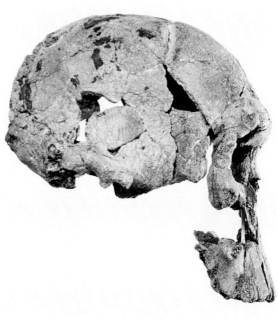

FIGURE 9.3 The well-known skull ER 1470 from Lake Turkana, Kenya, front and side views. Note the flatter face, smoother contours, lack of a sagittal crest, and more rounded braincase as compared to other early hominids. This find is usually considered an early member of genus *Homo,* but there still remains controversy over its exact classification. *(© National Museums of Kenya)*

found Zinjanthropus, but they had not fully recognized them as something different. They named the new form **Homo habilis** ("handy man"; Figure 9.3).

The reasons for including these fossils in genus *Homo* are twofold. First, *H. habilis* shows a notable increase in brain size, from the average of about 480 ml for *Australopithecus* and *Paranthropus* to an average of 680 ml, with a possible maximum of 800 ml. Second, the presence of the stone tools indicates that those larger brains were capable of a complexity of thought not seen in the record of the other two hominid genera. Thus *H. habilis* seems to mark the beginning of a new trend in hominid evolution—toward bigger brains and greater intelligence. Fossils of *H. habilis* have now been found in Tanzania, Kenya, Ethiopia, and perhaps southern Africa and have been dated at 2.3 to 1.6 mya.

The exact taxonomic affiliations of this group of fossils, however, are far from agreed on. The specimens from East Turkana, Kenya, are considered different enough by some to be placed in a new species, **Homo rudolfensis.** The specimen pictured in Figure 9.4 is an example. Differences include a larger body and brain size than in *H. habilis* and the lack

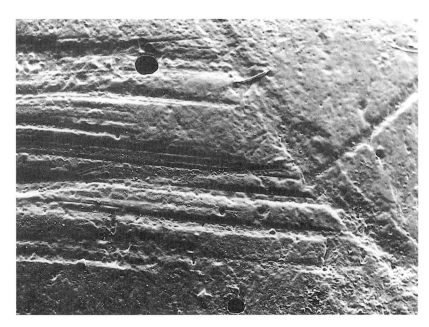

FIGURE 9.4 This micrograph of a fossil bone from Olduvai Gorge shows tool marks (the horizontal lines and the diagonal line beginning at the top of the photo) and a carnivore tooth mark (beginning on the right side and angled toward the center). The tooth mark overlies the tool mark, indicating that the hominids sliced meat off this part of the bone before a scavenger began eating. *(Photo by Pat Shipman)*

of a continuous brow ridge over the eyes. (See Tattersall 1992 for a review of this argument.) Others (Blumenschine et al. 2003) believe that all these specimens belong in *H. habilis.* Still others (Wood and Collard 1999) feel that the fossils labeled *H. habilis* and *H. rudolfensis* are in important ways closer to *Australopithecus* than to *Homo* and should thus be lumped into the former genus. This assessment is based on similar body proportions, evidence of continued arboreal ability, and similarity of brain size *relative to body size* (rather than absolute differences in brain size). Still others (Sherwood 2000) agree that while *H. habilis* might be lumped into *Australopithecus, H. rudolfensis* should remain in *Homo.* For the remainder of this discussion, we will use the term "early *Homo,*" in keeping with what is, at the moment, the majority view, and we will also consider all the fossils together. As more fossils that cover a broader span of time are found, the picture of hominid evolution during this period may become clearer. But the debate will probably never be fully resolved.

Finally, on the matter of evolutionary relationships, the arm-to-leg proportions of early *Homo* more closely resemble those of *Australopithecus africanus* (long arms, short legs) than they do *A. afarensis.* This argues for the former species being the direct ancestor of our genus (Berger 1998), even though later in our evolution the relative limb lengths became reversed (short arms, long legs).

What is it about the stone tools that may have given early *Homo* an edge? Paleoanthropologist Richard Leakey, the son of Louis and Mary, suggests that sharp stone tools allowed these hominids to more quickly cut meat and bones off a carcass, making the addition of meat to the diet through scavenging safer and more efficient. There is evidence for this suggestion.

Ten Olduvai sites from the early *Homo* period contain Oldowan tools, flakes, and animal bones. Once thought to be some sort of "home bases," these areas are now considered "stone cache" sites (Potts 1984) where hominids left supplies of stones and to which they took scavenged animal remains for quick, safe processing and eating. Analysis indicates that these sites were used for short periods, but repeatedly, as one would expect of such places.

Archaeologist Lewis Binford (1985) has analyzed the animal bones from these sites and found that they are mostly the lower leg bones of antelopes. These bones carry little meat and, along with the skull, are about the only parts left after a large carnivore has finished eating. However, such bones are rich in marrow, so a major activity at the sites in question may have been to cut off what little meat remained on these bones and then to break them open for the nutritious marrow inside.

Finally, Pat Shipman has studied the taphonomy of these and other bones with a scanning electron microscope (1984, 1986). She found that cut marks left by stone tools were usually on the shafts of the bones as if pieces of meat were cut off, not near the joints as if an entire carcass had been butchered (Figure 9.4). Also, the hominid tool marks sometimes overlapped carnivore tooth marks, showing that the carnivores had gotten there first.

We may envision early *Homo* in small cooperative groups, maybe family groups, foraging in a mixed grassland/woodland area (Blumenschine et al. 2003) for plant foods and always on the lookout for the telltale signs of a carnivore kill—a group of scavengers gathered on the ground or a flock of vultures circling overhead. Their big brains allowed them to better understand their environment and to manipulate it, making imaginative and technologically advanced tools from stone. With these tools they may have cut apart the carcasses they found and taken the pieces back to a safe place, maybe where they had stored more tools. There they cut the remaining meat off the bones and, using large hammerstones, smashed open the bones for marrow. It was no doubt a harsh life, but it was successful. The adaptive themes of bipedalism, large brains, social organization, and tool technology set the stage for the rest of hominid evolution.

Fossils indicate that forms with the characteristics of early *Homo* were around for only about half a million years. Before they disappeared from the fossil record, a new hominid species came on the scene—one that continued and enhanced the trends of big brains and tool technology, adaptations that soon carried this hominid all over the Old World.

To New Lands

Most of the fossils at the beginning of genus *Homo* (subsequent to the still-debated fossils of early *Homo*) are included in species **Homo erectus.** Some authorities split the fossils of this group from Kenya into a second species, **Homo ergaster** (Table 9.1 and Figure 9.5).

The Dutch physician Eugene Dubois made the first finds ever of *H. erectus* in Java in 1891. Dubois chose Java to look for hominid fossils largely because he was already stationed there with the military. But the choice was also a logical one for the time because most people thought that humans had first evolved in Asia, despite Darwin's clear suggestion that Africa was the hominid homeland. The idea that our evolutionary line was originally African apparently did not sit well with many Europeans.

When Dubois found a skullcap and a diseased femur at the site of Trinil (Figure 9.6), he thought they represented the "missing link" between apes and humans, and he dubbed the specimens "Pithecanthropus erectus" (the "upright ape-man"), popularly known as "Java Man." Since Dubois's work, numerous other fossils have been located in Java (see Table 9.1) and are now recognized as fully hominid and assigned to our genus, *Homo.* The fossils found in Java are similar in phenotype to the African and other Asian specimens, although their average brain size is larger than in some of the earlier fossils, and many are over 1,000 ml.

Perhaps the most famous *H. erectus* fossils are those from Zhoukoudian, a cave outside of Beijing, China. Starting in the 1920s, six nearly complete skulls, a couple dozen cranial and mandible fragments, over a hundred teeth, and a few postcranial pieces were recovered from the cave. Stone tools and animal bones, including those of horses and hyenas, were also recovered. The hominid remains are clearly similar to those of other specimens of *H. erectus.* Dating indicates that the cave was first occupied about 460,000 ya and was used until about 230,000 ya, although new evidence (Boaz and Ciochon 2001) suggests that most of the *H. erectus* bones in the cave were the remains of hyenas' meals.

The fame of the Zhoukoudian fossils, called "Peking Man" (from the old spelling of Beijing), lies mostly in the fact that they are missing. When Japan invaded China in 1937, U.S. Marines attempting to get the fossils out of the country were captured by Japanese troops. The fossils were never seen again. Their whereabouts remain one of the great mysteries in anthropology. Fortunately, extensive measurements had already been taken of the bones, and accurate casts had been made (Figure 9.7).

Since then, numerous fossils classified as *H. erectus* have been recovered, and we are filling in—although not without controversy—our knowledge of this important period in hominid evolution. Among the oldest fossils of this group are those that some authorities (see, for example, Tattersall 1997) place in a separate species, *H. ergaster* ("work man," a

TABLE 9.1   Major Fossils of *Homo ergaster* and *Homo erectus*

Country	Locality	Fossils	Crania	Age (million years)	Est. Brain Size (ml)
Homo ergaster					
Kenya	East Turkana	Cranial and postcranial fragments including mandibles and pelvis and long bone fragments	KNM-ER 3733	1.78	850
			KNM-ER 3883	1.57	800
		Cranial fragments	KNM-ER 42700	1.55	—
	West Turkana	Nearly complete juvenile individual	KNM-WT 15000	1.6	880
Homo erectus					
Algeria	Ternifine	3 mandibles and a skull	—	0.5–0.7	—
China	Hexian (Lontandong)	Partial skull	"Hexian Man"	0.25–0.5	1,000
	Lantian (Gongwangling)	Cranial fragments and mandible	"Lantian Man"	>1	800
	Longgupo(?)*	Mandible fragments	—	1.8	—
	Yunxian	2 crania	—	>0.35	—
	Zhoukoudian	Cranial and postcranial remains of 40 individuals	II	<0.46	1,030
			III	<0.46	915
			VI	<0.46	850
			X	<0.46	1,225
			XI	<0.46	1,015
			XII	<0.46	1,030
			Locality 13	0.7	—
	Tangshan Cave	Fragments	—	0.58–0.62	—
Ethiopia	Bouri	Cranial and post-cranial fragments	BOU-VP-2/66	1.0	995
Georgia	Dmanisi	3 mandibles, 16 teeth, 3 crania	D2280	1.75	780
			D2282	1.75	650
			D2700(?)	1.75	600

sagittal keel A sloping of the sides of the skull toward the top, as viewed from the front.

occipital The rear portion of the skull.

torus A bony ridge at the back of the skull, where the neck muscles attach.

reference to stone tools found in association with the fossils). The oldest well-established find, from East Turkana in Kenya, is dated at 1.78 mya (Figure 9.8). In some ways, it is typical of *H. erectus* crania. It has heavy brow ridges, a prognathous face, a sloping forehead, an elongated profile, a **sagittal keel**, a sharply angled **occipital** bone with a pronounced **torus,** and a cranial capacity of 850 ml (Figure 9.9). (The sagittal keel should not be confused with the sagittal crest. The crest is a ridge of bone for the attachment of chewing muscles. The keel is an aspect of the skull's shape). The average cranial capacity for this hominid group is about 980 ml, just slightly under the modern human minimum of 1,000 ml, but a consider-

TABLE 9.1   Major Fossils of *Homo ergaster* and *Homo erectus* (continued)

Country	Locality	Fossils	Crania	Age (million years)	Est. Brain Size (ml)
Homo erectus (continued)					
Israel	'Ubeidiya	Fragments	—	<1	—
Italy	Ceprano(?)	Cranium	—	0.8–0.9	—
Java	Modjokerto	Child's cranium	—	1.8(?)	—
	Ngandong	Cranial and postcranial fragments from >12 invidiuals	N-1	<0.1	1,170
			N-6	<0.1	1,250
			N-11	<0.1	1,230
			N-12	<0.1	1,090
	Sambungmachan	Large cranial fragment	Sambungmachan	<0.1	1,000
	Sangiran	Cranial and postcranial fragments from ~40 individuals	S-2	0.7–1.6	800
			S-4	0.7–1.6	900
			S-10	0.7–1.6	850
			S-12	0.7–1.6	1,050
			S-17	0.7–1.6	1,000
			1993 cranium	1.1–1.4	856
	Trinil	Skullcap and femur	"Java Man"	<1	940
Morocco	Salé	Cranium	Salé	0.4(?)	880
	Sidi Abder-rahman	2 mandible fragments	—	—	—
	Thomas Quarry	Mandible and skull fragments	—	0.5	—
Tanzania	Olduvai(?)	Cranial and postcranial fragments, including mandibles and pelvis and long bone fragments	OH9	1.4	1,060
			OH12	0.6–0.8	700–800
				Mean	**984.79**

*The (?) indicates that the species identification or age of that fossil is in question.

able jump from the 680 ml average for early *Homo*. Some *H. erectus* fossils have cranial capacities within the modern human range (see Table 9.1).

In other ways, however, the Turkana skull differs from others labeled as *H. erectus*. It is thinner and higher in profile, with smaller facial bones. These modern-looking features are what have led to its placement in the species *H. ergaster*. The cranium is thought to have belonged to a female. A similar skull from East Turkana dated at 1.57 mya is more ruggedly constructed. It is thought to have belonged to a male.

From the neck up, then, *H. erectus/ergaster* is quite distinct from early *Homo* in overall size, ruggedness, and especially brain size. The skull still

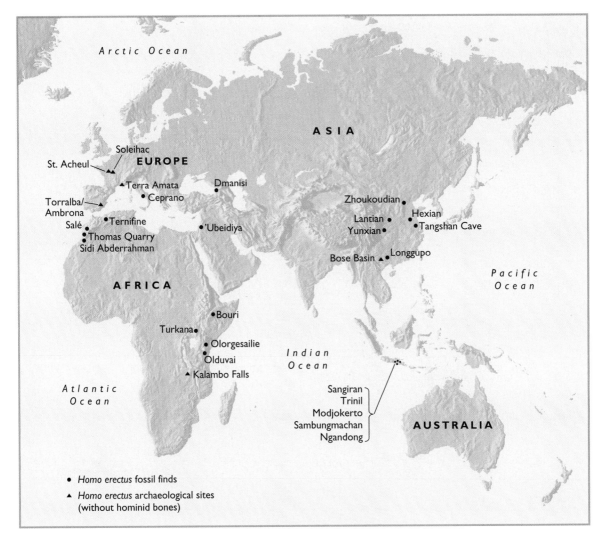

FIGURE 9.5 Map of major
Homo erectus/ergaster sites.

retains primitive features that distinguish it from modern *H. sapiens*. From the neck down, however, *H. erectus/ergaster* is essentially modern and apparently was so from its beginnings.

We know this because one of the oldest fossils of the group—also included in *H. ergaster*—is also the most complete. It is a nearly whole skeleton found at West Turkana in Kenya and is dated at 1.6 mya (Figure 9.10). The shape of the pelvis indicates that it was a male. Based on dental eruption and lack of any epiphyseal union, it is estimated that he was 12 years old when he died. "Turkana Boy," as he is commonly known, was about

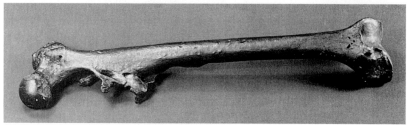

FIGURE 9.6 Skullcap and femur of "Java Man" *Homo erectus.* The growth toward the top of the femur is the result of a pathological condition. *(Top, © Rijksmuseum, Leiden. Bottom, Neg. #319781. Courtesy Department of Library Services, American Museum of Natural History)*

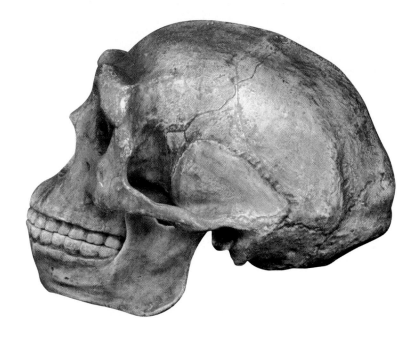

FIGURE 9.7 A replica of one of the famous "Peking Man" skulls lost during World War II. *(The Human Origins Program, Smithsonian Institution)*

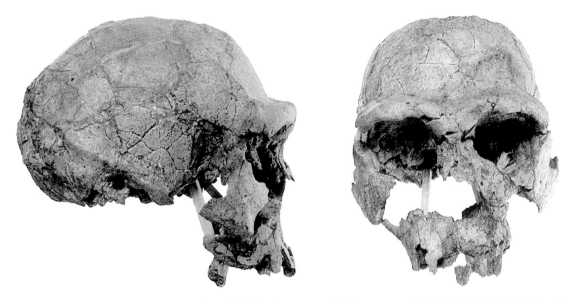

FIGURE 9.8 The *Homo erectus* (or *Homo ergaster*) skull of KNM-ER 3733 from the east shore of Lake Turkana, Kenya, is fairly typical of this group. (© *The National Museums of Kenya*)

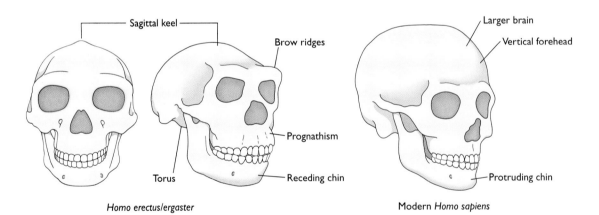

FIGURE 9.9 Cranial features of *Homo erectus/ergaster* (side and front views) compared with those of modern *Homo sapiens*.

5½ feet tall; he might have been 150 pounds and 6 feet tall had he lived to adulthood.

All other fossils from this group—including those from Africa outside Kenya—are assigned to *Homo erectus* (although a few are awaiting confirmation of their species affiliation). For the moment, we will treat them all as potentially *H. erectus*.

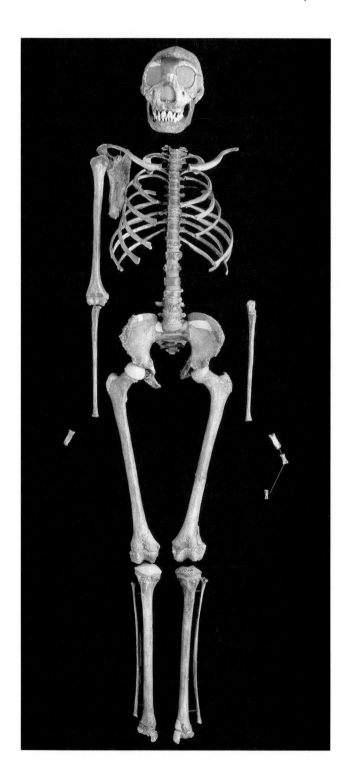

FIGURE 9.10 The skeleton of the 12-year-old boy from the west shore of Lake Turkana in Kenya (fossil KNM-WT 15000) is the most complete specimen of *Homo erectus* yet discovered. (© *The National Museums of Kenya*)

The *H. erectus* fossils from Africa—except for OH9 from Olduvai Gorge, dated at 1.4 mya, and a recent find from Ethiopia, dated at 1 mya (Asfaw et al. 2002)—are younger, from 400,000 to 800,000 years old. This means that *H. erectus* spread throughout the African continent and that populations of the species remained there for about a million years.

However, *H. erectus* did not remain only in Africa. According to recent data, members of the species had reached China and Southeast Asia by at least 1 mya and perhaps as much as 1.8 mya. What prompted the people of this species to leave the savannas to which they were apparently so well adapted?

We can't know the answer for sure, but a good guess is that the spread of *H. erectus* was simply an outcome of their reproductive success. Their big brains enabled them to exploit the savannas to a greater extent than had the other hominids to date. They had better and more varied tools (which we'll discuss later), the ability to learn more about their environment and to reason out the problems that their habitat presented, and, no doubt, a more complex social organization. With these adaptations, *H. erectus* would have rapidly increased in population size.

Population increase, however, puts pressure on resources and, perhaps, on social harmony as well. So groups of *H. erectus* probably fissioned and moved outside of familiar areas in search of less competition over food, space, and two other resources that may have been even more important—water and shelter. Water can be scarce on the savannas. There are lakes, rivers, and waterholes, but many of these are seasonal and are dry for months on end. And *H. erectus* may have needed shelter as well. With bodies virtually the same as ours, they were no longer good tree climbers and so had to seek shelter on the ground, in groves of trees, or, if they could locate one, in a cave or rock shelter. But, of course, a leopard or other animal may have already taken up residence in the cave and had to be dealt with. They may also have been following migrations of animal herds.

In search of food, water, shelter, and perhaps space and social harmony, *H. erectus* wandered the Old World. Those wanderings eventually carried them as far from their African homeland as what is now Beijing, China, and the Indonesian island of Java, and perhaps to Europe as well. Not only did these journeys take them to new climates, but the travels also brought them into contact with the changeable environments of the ice ages, known technically as the **Pleistocene.**

For reasons that are still debated, worldwide temperature began a long period of decline about 3.2 mya (Shackleton and Opdyke 1976). An additional, steeper temperature drop occurred about 2.4 mya (Shackleton et al. 1984; Stipp et al. 1967).

This cooling of the earth may have resulted from a decrease in the heat generated by the sun. It may have been precipitated by interplanetary dust blocking out a portion of the sun's radiation. It may have been caused

Pleistocene The geological time period, from 1.6 mya to 10,000 ya, characterized by a series of glacial advances and retreats.

by a substantial increase in volcanic activity here on earth, with material spewed out by volcanoes blocking the warming rays of the sun. It may have been initiated by a deviation in the geometry of the earth's orbit, resulting not in a change in the total amount of solar heat reaching our planet but merely in its distribution. The reasons have yet to be determined.

The initial drop in worldwide temperature occurred during the **Pliocene** (see Figure 5.20). The temperature decline was at its most severe and the spread of ice most extensive after about 1.6 mya in the Pleistocene.

Though initially regarded and still commonly referred to as an "Ice Age," the Pleistocene was actually a climatologically complex period with a series of lengthy, extremely cold episodes separated by a number of phases with mean temperatures as warm as—and occasionally even warmer than—today's. Geologists and **paleoclimatologists** have established that eight or nine lengthy and distinct cold periods separated by warmer spells occurred during the last 780,000 years of the Pleistocene (Shackleton et al. 1984; Shackleton and Opdyke 1973, 1976). Another ten cold phases separated by warmer periods may have characterized world climate between 1.6 mya and 780,000 ya (Bowen 1979).

During these cold phases, some of which lasted tens of thousands of years, worldwide temperatures dropped, and ice and snow accumulated in higher elevations and northern latitudes. As these ice fields grew in size—hundreds of meters to a few kilometers in thickness—internal pressures forced the ice to move in frozen rivers and great ice sheets called **glaciers** (Figure 9.11). These glaciers covered many higher elevations in the world, much of Canada and the northern United States, part of South America, much of Europe, and part of Asia (Bradley 1985; Flint 1971; Figure 9.12). Nonglaciated parts of the world, the tropics and subtropics, also underwent climate changes, experiencing generally cooler summers along with wetter winters in some regions and drier conditions elsewhere. The coasts of the continents were redrawn as sea level dropped as much as 125 meters (about 400 feet), a result of so much of the planet's water being locked in land-based glaciers.

The periods during which world ice cover expanded are called **glacials** or **glacial periods.** The times between the glacials, when the glaciers temporarily receded and temperature warmed up, are called **interglacials.** The glacials themselves were punctuated by shorter, colder bursts called **stadials** and relatively warmer periods called **interstadials.** The end of the Pleistocene and the beginning of the **Holocene,** the modern epoch in which we live, is marked by the inception of warmer temperatures worldwide and the regression of much of the glacial ice of the Pleistocene about 10,000 ya. Few paleoclimatologists, however, believe that the cycle of glacials and interglacials, stadials and interstadials ended with the beginning of the Holocene. Most scientists believe that our modern epoch is merely an interglacial remission, with another glacial period

Pliocene Geological epoch that dates from 5 million to 1.6 million years ago. This is the epoch during which the first hominids appeared in Africa.

paleoclimatologist A specialist in ancient climate conditions.

glacier A massive body of ice that can move and expand.

glacial A synonym for glacial period.

glacial period A phase of Pleistocene glacial expansion.

interglacial A period between glacial advances.

stadial A short period of rapid glacial advance and extreme cold.

interstadial A short period of glacial retreat during a longer phase of glacial advance.

Holocene The modern epoch that began 10,000 ya with the retreat of glacial ice and a worldwide warming.

FIGURE 9.11 A veritable river of ice, the Moreno Glacier is located in Patagonia, a region of Argentina. (*© Geoffery Clifford/ Woodfin Camp and Associates*)

certain to follow some time in the future. Most previous interglacials lasted about 10,000 to 20,000 years. Remember that the warmer temperatures of the Holocene began about 10,000 years ago, presenting some interesting scenarios for life in the twenty-first century and beyond (Shackleton and Opdyke 1976).

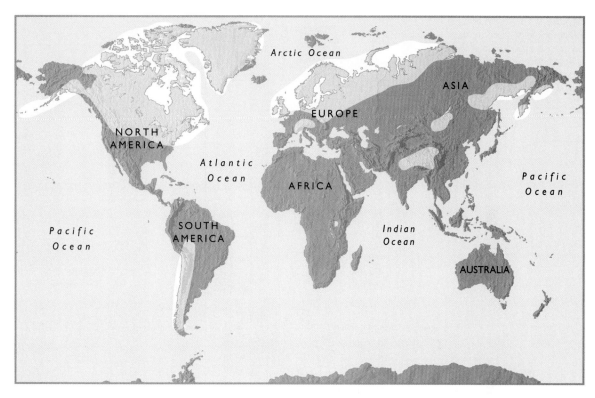

FIGURE 9.12 Maximum worldwide glacial expansion during the Pleistocene. The Antarctic ice cover, not shown here, also expanded during this epoch. *(Data compiled from Bowen 1978; Bradley 1985; and Flint 1971)*

Worldwide temperature trends might seem impossible to reconstruct thousands, hundreds of thousands, and even millions of years after the fact. The nature of glaciers makes the problem even more difficult. Though glaciers leave traces of their presence in the form of geological deposits and diagnostic patterns of erosion, the precise sequence of glacials and interglacials is difficult to study on land because ice advances are discontinuous and destructive events. Each subsequent movement of ice erases much, if not all, of the evidence of previous glacial expansions.

The stratigraphy of the ocean floor, however, provides a more or less continuous column of sediment for the entire Pleistocene and even for some time before. The sea floor was not scoured by glacial advances; as a result, subsequent glacial periods do not obscure evidence of previous ones. We may not be able to study ancient temperatures directly from seawater, but we can examine an indirect effect of temperature variations and the attendant expansion and melt-off of ice in the ratio of two isotopes of oxygen, ^{16}O and ^{18}O, in seawater. The oxygen isotope curve derived by Nicholas Shackleton and Neil Opdyke (1973, 1976) and discussed in Chapter 7 gives a fairly detailed picture of general worldwide climate change during at least the last 780,000 years of the Pleistocene (Figure 9.13).

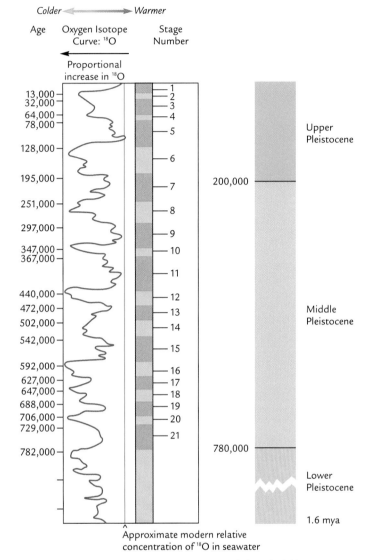

FIGURE 9.13 Pleistocene glacial chronology based on the oxygen isotope ratio in seawater as derived from foraminifera. *(Data compiled from Shackleton and Opdyke 1973)*

Colder ◄——————► Warmer

| Age | Oxygen Isotope Curve: ^{18}O | Stage Number |

Proportional increase in ^{18}O

13,000
32,000
64,000
78,000

128,000

195,000

251,000

297,000

347,000
367,000

440,000
472,000
502,000

542,000

592,000
627,000
647,000
688,000
706,000
729,000

782,000

1
2
3
4
5
6
7
8
9
10
11
12
13
14
15
16
17
18
19
20
21

200,000

780,000

Upper Pleistocene

Middle Pleistocene

Lower Pleistocene

1.6 mya

^
Approximate modern relative concentration of ^{18}O in seawater

Odd-numbered stages (in orange) = warmer periods, less glacial ice cover
Even-numbered stages (in blue) = colder periods, more glacial ice cover

Lower Pleistocene Part of the Pleistocene from 1.6 mya to 780,000 ya.

Middle Pleistocene Part of the Pleistocene from 780,000 to 200,000 ya.

Upper Pleistocene Part of the Pleistocene from 200,000 to 10,000 ya.

The Pleistocene is commonly divided into three sections. The beginning of the Pleistocene, about 1.6 mya to 780,000 ya, when the earth's magnetic field shifted, is called the **Lower Pleistocene** (Monastersky 1992); 780,000 to 200,000 ya is the **Middle Pleistocene;** and 200,000 to 10,000 ya is the **Upper Pleistocene.** The world of the Pleistocene was the world through which *H. erectus* was able to migrate and establish themselves, and we find their remains in some of the far corners of the Old World. They undoubtedly also inhabited the areas in between, but we have yet to uncover fossils in these areas.

The Evolution and Behavior of *Homo erectus*

Redating of early finds from Java has posed interesting questions regarding the spread of *H. erectus* around the Old World. Using new versions of the potassium/argon dating technique, researchers have redated the Sangiran *erectus* fossils to 1.6 mya and the Modjokerto remains to 1.8 mya (see Table 9.1)—twice as old as previously thought and at least as old as the oldest African *erectus/ergaster* fossil. This could mean that *H. erectus* evolved somewhere other than Africa. But all previous hominid fossils come only from Africa, so it's unlikely that *erectus* evolved anywhere but there.

That leaves two plausible explanations. Perhaps *H. erectus* (or *ergaster*) actually first evolved in Africa earlier than any of the fossils we have—remember how rare fossilization is—and then spread. The other possibility is simply that their expansion began very shortly after they first evolved. Science writer James Shreeve (1994:86) notes that Java is 10,000 to 15,000 miles from Africa, depending on the route, and that parts of Indonesia were connected to Asia at the time due to lower sea levels during the Pleistocene. If *erectus* walked just a mile a year, it would only have taken about 15,000 years to reach Java. That's still pretty fast, considering that they did not necessarily move 1 mile every year *in the right direction*. If the Java dates are correct, they probably mean that *H. erectus/ergaster* is older than we now assume based on existing fossils *and* that the species' expansion began early on.

New evidence for this interpretation comes from the Republic of Georgia and from Kenya. In 2002, a third cranium (D2700) from the Dmanisi site was discovered (Vekua et al. 2002). Dated at 1.75 mya, as were the previous Dmanisi fossils, this one was distinct in that it was smaller (an estimated 600 ml cranial capacity) and more "primitive" than the others, so much so that although it is provisionally assigned to *Homo erectus,* it has some features that resemble early *Homo* (Figure 9.14). In other words, hominids may have ventured out of Africa sooner and at an earlier evolutionary stage than we had previously assumed (Balter and Gibbons 2002). (In late 2003, anthropologists announced the discovery of some leg and ankles bones at the Dmanisi site, but details and technical reports are still forthcoming.)

Then in 2003, Meave Leakey (Leakey et al. 2003) announced the discovery of a skull in Kenya, dated at 1.55 mya, that bears a resemblance to the new Dmanisi skull in its size and some detailed features. The skull is assigned to *H. erectus,* but like the Dmanisi skull, it shows that early *H. erectus* had a transitional or intermediary stage—as compared with early *Homo*—and it was at this stage that the species first left Africa.

Moreover, new dating on a site in northern China shows the stone tools there to be 1.36 million years old, by far the oldest evidence of human presence in that region (Zhu et al. 2001). This is further evidence for an earlier initial migration of some populations from Africa than previously thought.

FIGURE 9.14 One of the previously discovered crania from Dmanisi, Georgia, dated at 1.75 mya and provisionally assigned to *Homo erectus*. The skulls from this site show a remarkable degree of variation, and some have traits that resemble early *Homo* from Africa. (© *AP/Wide World Photos*)

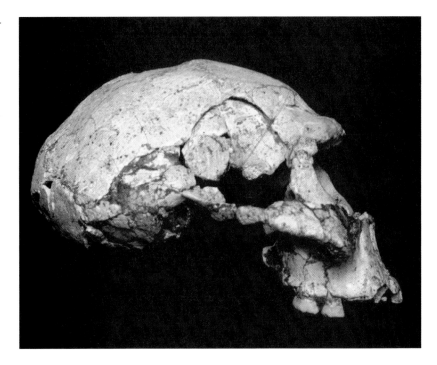

Another important date concerns the Java site of Ngandong. There is evidence that some *erectus* fossils there may be younger than 100,000 years—perhaps as young as 27,000 to 53,000 years old. If so, there were populations of *erectus* still around well after modern *Homo sapiens* had evolved.

It should be noted that with the exception of the Ceprano find, the European evidence of *H. erectus* comes in the form of cultural artifacts dated at times that have been associated with that species from other locations. At the site of Soleilhac in France are tools and animal remains dated at 800,000 ya. Another French site, Terra Amata on the Riviera, has been proposed as a site where *H. erectus* built shelters and established a village around 400,000 ya. This interpretation has recently been called into question, however. Some individuals lived there, but probably not in a village of huts. In Spain, at two adjacent sites called Torralba and Ambrona, dated at 400,000 ya, are the remains of some large mammals, including elephants, along with some stone tools that suggest a hunting or, more probably, a scavenging site. Until, however, we locate definite fossils of *H. erectus* from Europe—other than the cranium from Ceprano, Italy—we can only conclude that the species was there but was not widespread or, perhaps, that these sites are associated with another hominid species.

Though the *Homo erectus* skull certainly was larger than that of *Homo habilis*, it was not disproportionately larger than should be expected given

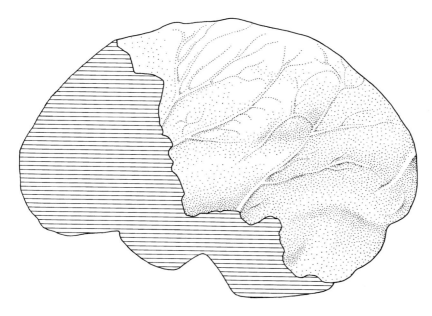

FIGURE 9.15 Drawing of an artificial cranial endocast made on the Sangiran 17 cranium by anthropologist Ralph Holloway. *(Redrawn from R. C. Holloway 1981)*

the larger body size of *erectus* (Walker and Shipman 1996:215–216). In other words, the *Homo erectus* brain was larger to control a larger body, but it falls right in line with what would have been expected based on the brain-size-to-body-size ratio of early *Homo.*

But how about the actual appearance of the brains of various hominids? Although their brains have not been preserved, the containers that held them sometimes have. The skull is not a dead, inert vessel but a living part of an organism. It is made of living bone that reacts with the material it is in contact with, whether muscle, arteries, or brain tissue. As a result, the inside surfaces of skulls often bear evidence of the external appearance of the brains they housed.

Endocasts of some fossil crania have been created naturally when fine sediments filled in the skull as the brain decayed. These sediments then fossilized, leaving a model in stone of the prehistoric brain (see Figure 9.20). Where natural endocasts did not form, they can be made artificially by pouring or painting liquid latex into the interior of the skull to make an impression of the inside surface and therefore produce a model of at least the major features of the exterior surface of the ancient brain.

Ralph Holloway (1980, 1981) has produced a series of endocasts for the Ngandong and Sangiran *Homo erectus* fossil skulls from Java and compared them with endocasts made from the skulls of gorillas, chimpanzees, orangutans, and forty ancient hominid fossil crania, including australopithecines, *Homo habilis,* other *erectus* samples, and *Homo sapiens* (Figure 9.15). Holloway notes some interesting similarities between the *H. erectus* and modern *H. sapiens* endocasts. The *erectus* endocasts show that the brains of this

endocast A natural or human-made cast of the inside of a skull.

species were asymmetrical. In *Homo sapiens,* this asymmetry is caused by the hemispheric specialization of our brains; because the two halves perform different functions, they look a bit different. For example, in general the left hemisphere houses abilities for language and symbol use, whereas the right hemisphere controls spatial-visual manipulation, as in hand-eye coordination.

The endocasts made from the Sangiran and Ngandong crania and the African *erectus* skulls KNM-ER 3733, KNM-ER 3883, and OH9 show a similar kind and degree of brain asymmetry as that seen in modern humans. From this evidence, we can infer that *H. erectus* possessed a level of hemispheric specialization similar to that of modern humans. The fascinating inference that Holloway draws is that more than 1.7 mya, *Homo erectus* possessed linguistic skills and the ability to manipulate symbols, along with a level of hand-eye coordination similar to, or at least approaching, that of modern humans. Although the scientific jury is still out on this suggestion, Holloway's is an extremely interesting approach that will probably contribute greatly to our understanding of the intellectual abilities of extinct hominids. At the least, we can be certain that the brain of *erectus* resembled ours in some very specific ways.

As Alan Walker (1993) points out, cerebral asymmetry is also present to a certain degree in some Old World monkeys and in chimpanzees. Interestingly, their larger left hemispheres house the areas of their brains employed in recognizing vocalizations used in communication, further supporting the hypothesis that enlargement of the left brain of the hominids is related to communication (which we will discuss shortly).

The greater intellect of *Homo erectus* certainly allowed for the elaboration of culture and innovations in behavior. There is a good deal of debate, however, on how this is reflected in the archaeological record. We will look at four important areas of such possible innovation: tool manufacture, the controlled use of fire, cooperative hunting, and language.

Stone Tools

The essentials of the stone tool tradition practiced by the precursors of *Homo erectus* were continued by them. Stone tool technology did not immediately or drastically change upon the appearance of a new, larger-brained hominid in Africa. Simple chopping tools created by the removal of a relatively small number of flakes from a stone cobble are present at many *H. erectus* sites. A new, more sophisticated toolmaking tradition, however, was developed by Middle Pleistocene hominids. Called **Acheulian** after the site of St. Acheul in France where it was first identified (though the tradition is actually older in Africa), it involved an elaboration on the removal of a few flakes. The end result is called a **hand axe**: a symmetrical, edged, pointed **bifacial** (flaked on both sides, or faces) tool (Figure 9.16). Hand axes were probably all-purpose tools for piercing animal flesh, butchering, scraping hides, cutting wood, digging roots—a sort of

Acheulian The toolmaking tradition of *Homo erectus,* including hand axes, cleavers, and flake tools.

hand axe A bifacial, symmetrical, all-purpose tool first produced by *H. erectus.*

bifacial A stone tool that has been worked on both sides.

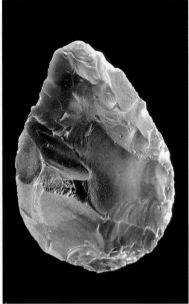

FIGURE 9.16 Hand axes symmetrically flaked on both sides, produced by *Homo erectus* beginning 1.4 mya, represent an advance in stone tool technology over the Oldowan tradition. This popular tool has been found in a variety of sizes and varying degrees of quality. (© *Boltin Picture Library/Bridgeman Art Library*)

Middle Pleistocene Swiss Army rock. It has even been suggested that they may have served as projectiles when thrown like a discus (O'Brien 1984).

Experimental archaeologist Mark Newcomer (1971) has produced replicas of Acheulian hand axes in order to understand how they were made. In one attempt, he produced a hand axe weighing 230 grams (about half a pound) from a stone nodule of around 3 kilograms (6.6 pounds). In producing this one hand axe, he also generated 51 large and potentially usable flakes with sharp edges and more than 4,500 smaller pieces.

From this and other experiments, Newcomer concluded that the manufacture of a hand axe probably progressed in three stages: First, a rough form, or "blank," was produced from a nodule of stone by striking the nodule directly with a stone hammer. Next, that rough blank was thinned and shaped by percussion with a softer tool, perhaps an antler. Finally, the tool would have been finished, again with a soft hammer, straightening the edge of the axe and producing the final, symmetrical shape.

That the Acheulian tradition of toolmaking evolved from the Oldowan, however, seems clear. Oldowan choppers from Sterkfontein in Africa were well enough made to resemble crude hand axes. The hand axe, however, shows more forethought, greater skill, and more utility in its design and manufacture than Oldowan tools. The hand axe tradition began in Africa about 1.4 mya and continued through the Middle Pleistocene, lasting even into the Upper Pleistocene. It spread into Europe after its invention in Africa.

Acheulian represents a more sophisticated technology in the sense that it produced more standardized tools that were more regular in form

FIGURE 9.17 Flake tools and a chopper associated with *Homo erectus* from the cave at Zhoukoudian. *(Drawings by Patricia J. Wynne)*

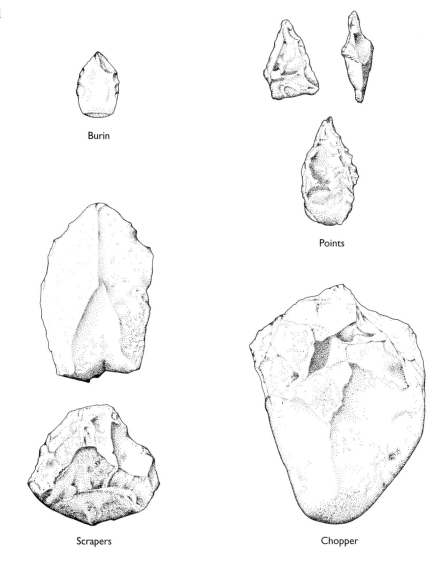

Burin

Points

Scrapers

Chopper

and, therefore, more consistently useful. This, combined with the technology's more efficient use of raw material (a greater proportion of usable edge for the same amount of rock—"more bang for the buck") represents a great technological advance over the ability of previous hominids.

Homo erectus also made cleavers with a straight, sharp edge. (The hand axe, in contrast, had a point.) Along with these core tools—both hand axes and cleavers were shaped from cores of stone—*erectus* also used flake tools (Figure 9.17). Stone flakes removed from a core in the process of making hand axes or cleavers were often used, without further modifica-

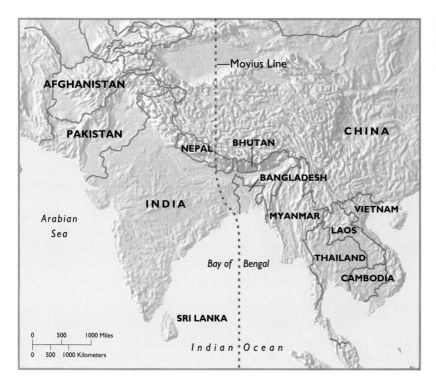

FIGURE 9.18 Location of the Movius Line. Hand axes are common to the west of this line and generally quite rare to the east.

tion, for cutting, scraping, or piercing animal flesh as well as for cutting or scraping plant material, including wood. Some flakes were themselves worked to produce a desired shape or cutting edge.

Though hand axes are commonly found in Africa and Europe, they are absent from most *H. erectus* sites in Asia east of India. There is such a clear geographic dividing line between the makers of hand axes in the west and those who made simple chopping tools from stone nodules in the east that a name has been applied to this division: the **Movius Line,** named for the researcher (Hallam Movius) who first articulated it (Figure 9.18). Movius viewed the line as geographically distinguishing technologically more advanced hominids to the west from those in East Asia, which he characterized as a "marginal region" (cited in Davis and Ranov 1999).

This rather extreme view is not supported by recent data. The Movius Line, though revealing a general and genuine technological difference between most contemporaneous stone tool technologies on either side of the line, should not be viewed as an impenetrable barrier to the movement of hominids or stone tool technologies east and west. At the same time, the general—but by no means absolute—absence of symmetrical, bifacially flaked hand axes east of the line in the Lower and Middle Paleolithic does not prove that the stone tool makers to the east were less intelligent than

Movius Line A geographic break between the manufacture of hand axes and that of simple stone chopping tools. Hand axes appear to the west of this line—located in eastern India—but not often east of it.

those to the west or in any way incapable of making tools that required greater precision in percussion flaking. A lack of suitable stone or a reliance on material other than stone may be at the root of this geographical difference. For example, paleoanthropologist Geoffrey Pope (1989) has suggested that bamboo replaced stone as a major raw material for making tools east of the Movius line. In this scenario, East Asians didn't make stone hand axes but rather tools out of bamboo that served the same functions. Bamboo does not preserve nearly as well as stone, however, and tools made of this material have not been found.

There are some hand axe–like implements found at a few sites located far to the east of the line where stone that could be chipped into large bifaces was abundant. For example, research in the Bose Basin of southern China, just north of the border with Vietnam, has revealed a technology quite similar to that of Acheulian, dated to 800,000 ya (Yamei et al. 2000). More than thirty large (180 mm, or about 7 inches, in length), bifacially flaked cobbles and flakes were recovered in the Bose Basin. In general form, these artifacts resemble Acheulian hand axes found in Africa and Europe dated to the period just after 1 mya.

Though the Bose Basin finds are interesting, it is still the case that they are exceptional. The Bose Basin material is geographically isolated in eastern Asia; there is nothing like an archaeological trail tracing the Bose technology back to an older source on the west side of the Movius Line.

The Movius Line demarcating Acheulian from other technologies might be explained by the fact that hominids left Africa and arrived in East Asia before the hand axe first was developed back in Africa around 1.4 mya. In other words, hominids arrived in east Asia without hand-axe technology because it hadn't developed when they left Africa in the first place. The fact that hand-axe manufacturing did not expand into and become widespread in East Asia after its invention in Africa is interpreted by some paleoanthropologists as supporting the view that the east Asian hominids that date to this period were a different species (*Homo erectus*) than those who invented and perfected the technology (*Homo ergaster*) in Africa. If so, the Bose tools show that both of these mid-Pleistocene hominid species were capable of independently developing the technology for making large, bifacially flaked, symmetrical tools.

Quest for Fire

The ability to control fire is extremely significant. Fire provides heat, which may have helped our tropically adapted ancestors survive in the inhospitably cold climate of Pleistocene Europe and Asia. Fire may have also provided protection from predatory animals, and its use for cooking would have made the meat they ate more digestible and thus more nutritious.

Perhaps just as significantly, says science writer John Pfeiffer (1969), fire would have extended the day. Our ancestors were—just as we are—a visually oriented species. *Homo erectus* depended on vision for most sensory input and could not see well in the dark. The light produced by fires would have increased the number of hours during which *H. erectus* could interact and create.

There is some limited but tantalizing evidence that as much as 1.6 mya—quite soon after the species' evolution—*Homo erectus* was able to produce and control campfires. Four roughly circular red patches of earth were excavated at the Koobi Fora site in Kenya by Ralph Rowlett, Michael Davis, and Robert Graber (1999). Though no charcoal remains were found in the deposits, phytoliths—microscopic fragments of silica produced in plant cells (see Chapter 7)—were recovered in abundance in the soil stains. The stains also exhibited archaeomagnetic indicators of having resulted from burning. Like pollen grains, the form of phytoliths is species-specific, allowing researchers to identify the type of plants that had contributed to the burning in the red-stained earth. Had the Koobi Fora red stains been the product of a burn of a single tree trunk or stump, as might happen in a natural fire caused by a lighting strike, the phytoliths of only a single species, that of the burned tree, would have been found in the stain. Instead, the Koobi Fora researchers found a mixture of phytoliths in three of the four stains they examined. These phytoliths came from woody plants, including plant types that could have served as tinder. Also, many of the phytoliths were of a variety produced by palm wood. Palm wood catches fire without much effort and burns quickly—facts not lost on modern campfire producers as well as, possibly, *Homo erectus.*

There is some additional evidence for the possible controlled use of fire by *H. erectus* by 1.5 mya in Africa (James 1989; Sillen and Brain 1990), 750,000 ya at the French cave of L'Escale, and soon after 500,000 ya at Zhoukoudian in China (Binford and Chuan 1985; Binford and Stone 1986).

Residues of million- or half-million-year-old fireplaces, however, are not so easy to distinguish from other, natural phenomena. Even the evidence for fire at Zhoukoudian, long thought to be definitive, has been questioned at least in part by Lewis Binford and Kun Ho Chuan (1985) and by Binford and Nancy Stone (1986), who remind researchers that indisputable hearths have not been found in the cave. Instead, large deposits of supposed ash have been interpreted as the result of hominid-controlled fires. Binford and Chuan point out, however, that these so-called ash deposits are not generally found in the same strata as the tools and hominid remains. Some of the animal bones found in the ash deposits appear to have been mineralized, not burned. Finally, they have reidentified much of the so-called ash as owl (or other bird) droppings. Though Binford and Stone agree that fire belonged in the cultural repertoire of *H. erectus,* they maintain that the evidence, at least in Zhoukoudian, occurs late in the sequence. A more recent analysis confirms Binford and Stone's skepticism regarding the control of fire by the hominids whose bones have been found in the cave (Weiner et al. 1998). Though some of the animal bones found at the same level in the cave as the oldest *Homo erectus* remains showed some evidence of burning, there is no direct proof of a fire in the cave itself; there were no hearths nor are any ash or even charcoal remains found in the cave.

We can only conclude that *H. erectus* may have used fire in Africa and elsewhere, but more research needs to be conducted to determine with any certainty how long ago and where this occurred.

Hunters or Scavengers?

The sites of Torralba and Ambrona in Spain, Olorgesailie in Kenya, and Olduvai BK II in Tanzania—all dating back to at least 400,000 ya and associated with the artifacts of *Homo erectus*—have been interpreted by some as seasonal camps where groups of related individuals came together perhaps on a yearly basis to hunt, socialize, and exchange information. At these sites, according to some, we see the earliest evidence of cooperative hunting by our hominid ancestors.

Torralba and Ambrona are two hills flanking a major pass in the Guadarrama Mountains of Spain, a natural migration route for people and animals. The remains of at least fifty prehistoric elephants, twenty-six horses, twenty-five deer, ten wild cattle, and six rhinoceroses have been excavated. It has been suggested that they represent perhaps as many as ten separate cooperative *H. erectus* hunts (Butzer 1971, 1982; Howell 1966). The animals may have been stampeded into swampy, boggy traps where they would become mired and then be killed and butchered by *H. erectus* hunters. Some researchers suggested that the animals were stampeded and directed to the wetlands by the use of fire.

At the BK II locality at Olduvai Gorge, groups of wild cattle were also thought to have been driven into a swamp, where they were then killed and butchered by *H. erectus.* Olorgesailie, in Kenya, is a site where a *H. erectus* population living west of a large lake is said to have cooperatively hunted baboons (Isaac 1977). Recent K/Ar dating indicates that the site may be from 700,000 to 900,000 years old (Bower 1987a). More than sixty individuals of a now-extinct baboon species have been discovered. All around the bones were large, unmodified, round cobbles that Isaac believes were thrown by the hominids as weapons. Other stone tools, used in butchering the animals, were also found. In Isaac's reconstruction, the hominids surrounded the baboons in their tree roosts, forced them to flee by throwing rocks at them, and clubbed them to death as they attempted to escape. Next, the animals would have been butchered and their bones cracked open to extract the nutrient-rich marrow inside. A more recent excavation at the same site has revealed possible evidence of an elephant kill. The bones of a now-extinct elephant species were discovered surrounded by hand axes, and there appear to be tool marks on some of the bones (Bower 1987b).

If this interpretation of hunting is correct, we can infer a high level of knowledge, cooperation, and coordination among hominids living several hundred thousand years ago. The *H. erectus* hunters of the Middle Pleistocene would have had to possess a sophisticated understanding of animal behavior, including migration schedules and patterns, herding behavior, and reactions to a threat. The level of cooperation and coordination necessary for such hunts implies an ability to communicate, divide labor, delegate responsibilities, and possibly even distribute the results of a successful hunt.

Based on our discussion of the possible similarity of the brain of *H. erectus* to ours, such a reconstruction, though remarkable, is certainly not out of the question. Recent careful investigation of the taphonomy of these alleged *H. erectus* kill sites, however, has called the cooperative hunting scenario into serious question (Binford 1981; Shipman and Rose 1983). In the case of Torralba and Ambrona, for example, the animal bones were found in an area where carnivorous animals were likely to have been active. Very few indisputable tools were found in association with the bones.

One way of determining human activity at these sites involves the search for cut marks on animal bones. Are there marks made by stone tools present on animal bones found at these sites? In an analysis of approximately 3,000 bones from Torralba and Ambrona, Pat Shipman and Jennie Rose (1983) determined that over 95 percent of the specimens were so heavily damaged that they could not be used in the search for cut marks. In fact, they maintain that the great majority of marks on the Torralba and Ambrona bones previously identified as cut marks are merely the scratches left by soil abrasion and root growth. Of the fifty-five specimens intact enough for analysis, a scanning electron microscope revealed only sixteen stone-tool cut marks on fourteen bones (1983:467), and these show no pattern that could be interpreted as systematic butchering (Figure 9.19). Shipman and Rose also found very little evidence of animal tooth marks, indicating that carnivores, including scavengers, may not have played a major role in producing the assemblage either.

Given that it is impossible to determine whether the rest of the bones had been cut with stone tools, the most that can be said is that *H. erectus* was present at Torralba and Ambrona and cut some meat off some animal carcasses there. The site, however, cannot be used to support a hypothesis of big-game hunting for *H. erectus*.

Our understanding of the cultural capabilities and achievements of *H. erectus* is in flux. As with early *Homo*, projecting modern hunter-gatherer analogues into the past to explain *H. erectus* settlement and subsistence, though once popular, now seems to be unwarranted. The evidence can no longer be interpreted as supporting the idea that *H. erectus* hunted cooperatively—though it should also be said that the evidence does not necessarily disprove that this group of hominids was capable of a coordinated hunt, either. They almost certainly scavenged animal meat where

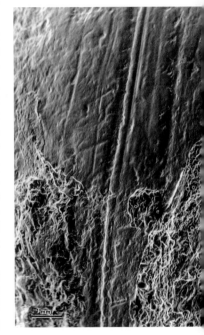

FIGURE 9.19 Scanning electron microscope photograph of cut marks on an elephant bone recovered at Ambrona, Spain. These longitudinal marks made by stone tools 400,000 ya are some of the bits of evidence that indicate the butchering of animals by *Homo erectus* at this site. *(Courtesy Pat Shipman)*

FIGURE 9.20 Natural endocasts from South African australopithecines showing the degree of detail possible. Notice the blood vessels that show, especially in the upper right cast. Such casts can be made artificially as well, allowing comparison of the brains of our ancestors with those of modern humans. (© *John Reader/Science Photo Library/Photo Researchers, Inc.*)

they could. They may have hunted, although probably not big game and not habitually. As seen at the Kalambo Falls site, they probably gathered wild plant foods where they could. They used fire, and they may have built shelters.

The Question of Language

As mentioned earlier, by making endocasts of the inside surfaces of fossil crania, anthropologist Ralph Holloway (1980, 1981) was able to produce images of the very brains of our ancestors (Figure 9.20). What these endo-

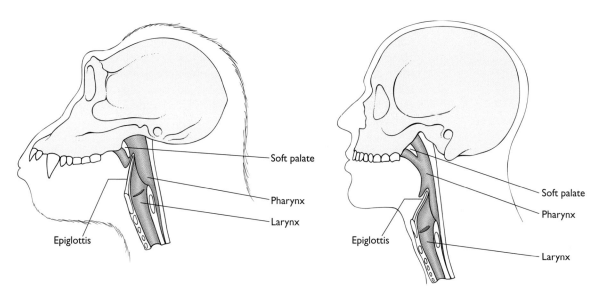

FIGURE 9.21 The vocal apparatus of a chimp (left) compared to a modern human's. The chimp's pharynx is straight, and it and the larynx are positioned high in the throat, limiting the ability to produce a wide range of sounds. The human pharynx is bent and is lower in the throat. This allows a broader range of sounds. *(Redrawn and reprinted by permission of the Smithsonian Institution Press from Roger Lewin,* In the Age of Mankind: A Smithsonian Book of Human Evolution, *1989:181, Smithsonian Institution Press)*

casts demonstrate is that the brains of *H. erectus* were asymmetrical—the right and left halves weren't the same shape. This asymmetry is found to some extent in apes but to a greater extent in modern humans, because the halves of our brains perform different functions. Language and the ability to use symbols, for example, are functions of our left hemisphere, while spatial reasoning (such as the hand-eye coordination needed to make complex tools) is performed in the right hemisphere. That *H. erectus* is also shown to have had hemisphere asymmetry suggests that our ancestors had the ability to communicate through a symbolic language.

Further evidence of language use by *H. erectus* is suggested by the reconstruction of the vocal apparatus based on the anatomy of the cranial base. Even though the vocal apparatus is made up of soft parts, those parts are connected to bone, and so the shape of the bone is correlated with the shape of the larynx, pharynx, and other features (Figure 9.21).

Reconstruction work on australopithecines indicates that their vocal tract was basically like that of apes, with the larynx and pharynx high up in the throat. While this would have allowed them to drink and breathe at the same time (as human infants can do up to 18 months), it would not have allowed for the precise manipulation of air that is required for modern human languages. The early hominids could make sounds, but they would have been more like those of chimpanzees.

Homo erectus, on the other hand, had vocal tracts more like those of modern humans, positioned lower in the throat and allowing for a greater range and speed of sound production. Thus, *H. erectus* could have produced vocal communication that involved many sounds with precise differences. Whether or not they did so is another question. But given their ability to manufacture fairly complex tools, to control fire, and to survive in different and changing environmental circumstances, *H. erectus* certainly had complex things to talk *about*. It is not out of the question that *H. erectus* had a communication system that was itself complex, although there are authorities who feel that a communication system with the attributes of modern human language is associated only with the sophisticated behavior of modern *Homo sapiens* (see Holden 1998 for a detailed discussion).

If we can consider it a separate species, *H. erectus*—although now extinct—was a smashing success by any standards. The species evolved nearly 2 mya in Africa, possibly from an earlier species, *H. ergaster,* and by perhaps 1.8 mya had spread as far as Java. By 500,000 ya, they had reached northern China and Europe. They lasted as an identifiable group in Africa and China until 250,000 ya and may have persisted in Java until less than 100,000 ya. (See the "Contemporary Issue" box at the end of this chapter.) Their adaptations—now focused on learning, technology, and the cultural transmission of information—allowed them to exploit a number of different environments.

There is some debate over just how much *H. erectus* changed during their tenure on earth. There is a small increase in average cranial capacity over this time (about 180 ml), as well as some refinement in their hand axe–making technique and variation in their flake tool production. These changes, however, are small and slow, so the overall impression is one of stability—not a bad thing in evolutionary terms.

Perhaps as early as 800,000 ya, there was another sudden surge in brain size, to an average matching our own. This marks the beginning of perhaps the most complex part of our story.

Big Brains, Archaic Skulls

The next three hominid species are marked by brain sizes within the modern human range that, indeed, match or approximate the modern human average; nonetheless, they have other features, especially of the cranium, that retain primitive characteristics. These hominid groups are sometimes collectively referred to as "archaic." The most recent of these, *Homo neanderthalensis,* will be considered separately in the next section. Here we will discuss the earlier *H. heidelbergensis* and the even earlier *H. antecessor* (Table 9.2 and Figure 9.22).

The newest suggested hominid species, named in mid-1997, is **Homo antecessor** ("advance guard" or "explorer"). Many authorities do not recognize the fossils involved as a separate species, but the discoverers see sufficient distinctions to warrant the new name (Bermúdez de Castro et al. 1997). Fossils have been discovered at the site of Gran Dolina cave in the Atapuerca hills in northern Spain. They consist of more than eighty fragments, including skulls, jaws, teeth, and other portions of the skeleton.

TABLE 9.2 Major Fossils of *Homo antecessor* and *Homo heidelbergensis*

Country	Locality	Fossils	Age (years)	Est. Brain Size (ml)
Homo antecessor				
Spain	Gran Dolina	More than 80 fragments	>780,000	>1,000
Homo heidelbergensis				
China	Dali	Cranium	200,000	1,120
	Jinniushan(?)*	Nearly complete skeleton	200,000	1,350
	Maba(?)	Cranium	130,000–170,000	—
	Xujiayao(?)	Fragments of 11 individuals	100,000–125,000	—
England	Swanscombe	Occipital and parietals	276,000–426,000	1,325
	Boxgrove	Tibia, teeth	362,000–423,000	—
Ethiopia	Bodo	Cranium	600,000(?)	1,250
France	Arago	Cranium and fragmentary remains of 7 individuals	250,000	1,200
Germany	Bilzingsleben(?)	Cranial fragments and tooth	320,000–412,000	—
	Mauer	Mandible	500,000	—
	Steinheim(?)	Cranium	200,000–240,000	1,200
Greece	Petralona	Cranium	160,000–240,000	1,200
Hungary	Vértesszöllös	Occipital fragment	250,000–475,000	1,250
India	Narmada	Cranium	200,000	1,300
Spain	Sima de los Huesos	2,500 fragments from at least 33 individuals	300,000	— 1,390
Tanzania	Ndutu (Olduvai)(?)	Cranium	400,000–700,000	1,100
Zambia	Kabwe (Broken Hill)	Cranium and additional cranial and postcranial remains of several individuals	400,000–700,000	1,280
			Mean	**1,247.00**

*The (?) indicates that the species identification or age of that fossil is in question.

There are also associated tools. Using paleomagnetism (see Table 7.1), the site has been dated at more than 780,000 ya. If that date is correct, these would be the oldest well-accepted fossil humans found in Europe.

The most striking fossil is the partial face of an 11-year-old boy (Figure 9.23). His features, described by the researchers as "fully modern," include a projecting nose region with a sharp lower margin, hollowed

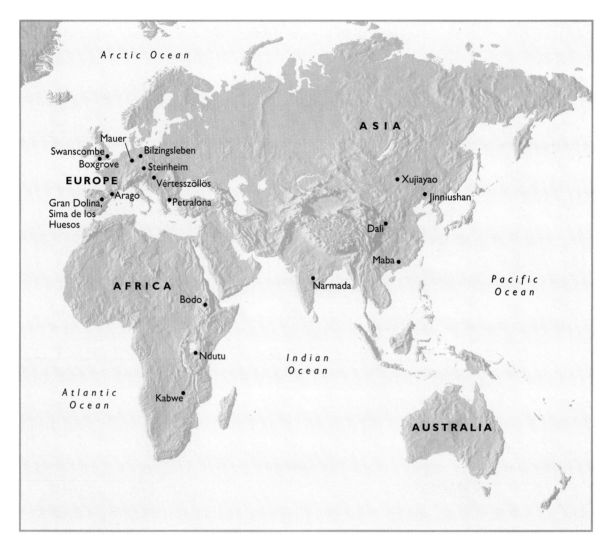

FIGURE 9.22 Map of major *Homo antecessor* and *Homo heidelbergensis* sites.

cheekbones (technically, the *canine fossae*), and several details of the dentition. Analysis of the specimens indicates a cranial capacity of greater than 1,000 ml.

On the other hand, other fossils from this site show primitive features such as prominent brow ridges and premolars with multiple roots (modern human premolars have a single root). This unique mix of traits, especially the very modern appearance of the face, is what led the investigators to assign the new species name—and to further suggest that this species is the direct ancestor both of modern humans and of *H. heidelbergensis* and *H. neanderthalensis*.

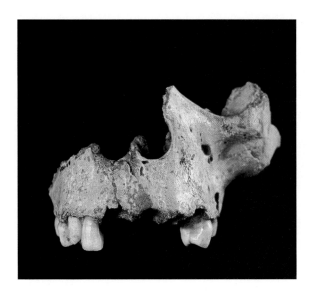

FIGURE 9.23 Fossil ATD6-69 from Gran Dolina cave, Atapuerca, Spain. This partial face of an 11-year-old boy who died perhaps more than 780,000 ya is fully modern in many features, including the hollowed cheekbone easily seen here. (© *Javier Trueba/Madrid Scientific Films*)

A logical objection to the analysis of the Gran Dolina boy is that the modern-looking traits seen so clearly in the boy's face might be juvenile features, not present in adults of his group and, therefore, not of diagnostic value for species assignment. The investigators, however, report that some of the other fragmentary facial bones from the site also show these modern traits and that *later* fossils from a nearby site, Sima de los Huesos, do not (Gibbons 1997b).

The fossil bones from Gran Dolina are striking for their antiquity, but some of the 200 tools found at the site are even older, dating back to 1 mya. These early tools resemble pre-hand-axe tools from Africa, such as cores and simple cutting flakes. Later tools found in the same strata as the human remains are more sophisticated. One long flake has a sharp edge on one side and a dulled flat edge on the other. It was presumably formed to be used as a knife. None of the tools at the site, however, are as complex as some of the Acheulian tools being made by *H. erectus* and *H. ergaster* at the same time period or earlier.

Finally, there is some intriguing evidence of the diet of the Gran Dolina people. Bison and deer bones, as well as some from other species, have been found that show stone tool cut marks, implying that the people hunted. According to the investigators, there are also cut marks on some of the human bones that were mixed in with animal bones, suggesting cannibalism (Kunzig 1997).

It should also be noted that there is a site in southeastern Spain, called Orce, that some contend is even older than Gran Dolina—900,000 years old or even older. It contains simple stone tools and alleged hominid bones. Other authorities, however, have identified the fragmentary bones

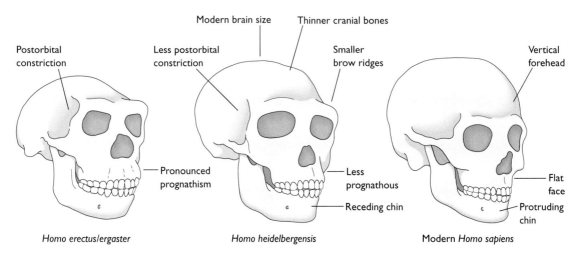

FIGURE 9.24 Cranial features of *Homo erectus/ergaster, Homo heidelbergensis,* and modern *Homo sapiens.*

as those of wild horses, and the dating is still contested (Bower 1997a). More study is clearly needed at this location.

Table 9.2 and Figure 9.22 show that the fossils assigned to **Homo heidelbergensis** are geographically widespread and range over about 275,000 years in time (longer if one includes *H. antecessor*). The species was first named for a mandible found in 1907 at Mauer, near Heidelberg, Germany. Note that the inclusion of several of the fossils is questioned by those who recognize this group as a species.

Members of this group show an average brain size of nearly 1,300 ml, a more than 30 percent increase over the average for *H. erectus.* The brains are also differently proportioned than those of *H. erectus,* with greater emphasis on the forebrain, reflected by steeper foreheads. This may be important because the frontal lobes of the human brain are the areas thought to be most involved in the control of voluntary movements, speech, attention, social behavior, planning, and reasoning (see Figure 5.18).

The bones of the cranium, compared with those of *H. erectus,* are thinner; the overall size of the face is reduced; the profile is less prognathous; the brow ridges, though still present, are less pronounced; and the **postorbital constriction,** characteristic of *erectus,* is lessened (Figure 9.24). The postcranial skeletons, essentially modern in overall shape, are more rugged and muscular than in modern humans. The 500,000-year-old tibia from Boxgrove in southeast England, for example, is strikingly thicker in cross section than the tibia of a modern person. Figures 9.25 and 9.26 show two of the more complete examples of *H. heidelbergensis* crania.

Given the fragmentary remains of many of these fossils, the fact that some were found early in the history of anthropology or by nonscientists, and the widespread range of the species, fairly little can be specifically said about the lifestyle of these early humans. We do know, however, some

postorbital constriction A narrowing of the skull behind the eyes, as viewed from above.

FIGURE 9.25 The nearly intact cranium of a *Homo heidelbergensis* from Steinheim, Germany. Note the more rounded appearance of the skull and the higher forehead than in *Homo erectus*. However, also note the large brow ridges. *(State Museum for Nature, Stuttgart, Germany)*

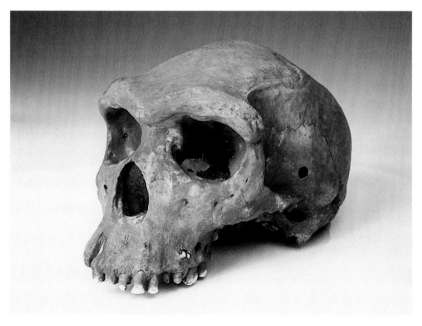

FIGURE 9.26 The Kabwe (formerly called Broken Hill) specimen is one of the best-known examples of *Homo heidelbergensis* from Africa. Note the extremely large brow ridges on this skull, which has a cranial capacity of 1,280 ml, quite close to the modern mean. *(© The Natural History Museum, London)*

things about their tools. For example, we have evidence from Boxgrove that the hand axe was in use by 500,000 ya. And by about 200,000 ya, people included in *H. heidelbergensis* invented a new and imaginative way to make stone tools. The method appears first in Africa and later in Europe. Called the *prepared core,* or **Levallois** technique (after the suburb of Paris where it was first recognized), it involved the careful preparation of the rough stone core so that a number of flakes of a desired shape (up to four or five) could be taken off. The flakes could then be used for cutting, scraping, or piercing. Figure 9.27 shows the steps involved and a replica of such a tool. There is also evidence of other materials used for manufacturing tools, such as some wooden spears from the 400,000-year-old site of Schöningen in Germany. The size and characteristics of these approximately 6-foot-long weapons suggest that they were meant to be thrown at fairly large animals (Thieme 1997).

Finally, an intriguing but still dim glimpse into the lives of the people of this era comes from another site in Atapuerca, near Gran Dolina (Kunzig 1997). Known as Sima de los Huesos ("pit of bones"), it is a shaft inside a cave, dated by electron spin resonance (see Chapter 7) at about 300,000 ya. It contains the bones of animals and the remains of at least thirty-three humans—many so well preserved that they include even fingertips and small inner ear bones. Most of the bones are from teenagers and young adults, both male and female. Although the bones show signs of chewing by a carnivore, it is unlikely that some predator would have selected just that age group, and the nonhuman remains in the pit are not those of prey animals but those of foxes and bears, which may have fallen in and chewed on the human bones before dying. Investigators think the bodies were thrown into the pit after death (one seems to have died from a massive infection), probably not as part of a formal funeral ritual (no artifacts were found) but more likely for simple disposal purposes. Perhaps they all died together in some catastrophe or at least over a short period of time. Many of the bones show signs of childhood malnourishment.

No doubt the peoples labeled *H. antecessor* and *H. heidelbergensis* had other mental, cultural, and perhaps physical adaptations to help them deal with the various and changeable environments they encountered as the Pleistocene continued. We certainly know this was true for one famous group of humans from Europe and the Near East. Some crania from Sima de los Huesos are said to show traits that might be ancestral to this next group, the Neandertals.

The Neandertals

Levallois A tool technology involving striking uniform flakes from a prepared core.

The Neandertals—***Homo neanderthalensis*** (see Chapter 10)—were named after one of the first human fossils found and recognized as a human fossil, a skullcap from the Neander Valley in Germany recovered in

Side Views

Top Views

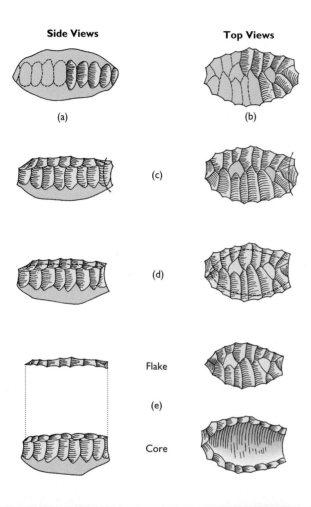

(a)

(b)

(c)

(d)

Flake

(e)

Core

FIGURE 9.27 The Levallois technique step-by-step: (a) produce a margin along the edge of the core, (b) shape the surface of the core, (c, d) prepare the surface to be struck (the "striking platform"), (e) remove the flake, and return to step (b) for additional flake removal. Shown below is a replica of a Levallois core and tool. (*Courtesy Dr. Ian Tattersall, from* The Human Odyssey)

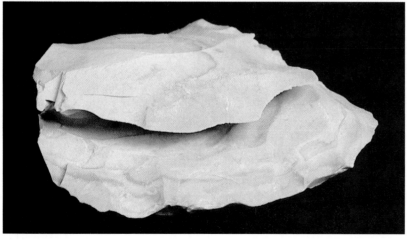

FIGURE 9.28 The skullcap found in the Neander Valley in Germany in 1856. This find gave the name *Neandertal* to all similar specimens in Europe. The cranial vault held a very large brain, but the brow ridges betray obvious differences with modern humans. *(Reinisches Landesmuseum, Bonn, Germany)*

1856 (Figure 9.28). This was before Darwin wrote *Origin of Species*. (In German, *thal* means "valley" and is always pronounced *tal*. Recent spelling drops the silent *h*, but some still use it. The formal species name retains its original spelling.) Table 9.3 and Figure 9.29 show the basic data for fossils of this species and the locations of these finds.

The Neandertals have had an interesting history in anthropology. At one time, they were considered brutish, hunched-over, dim-witted members of a dead-end side branch of human evolution. At other times they have been thought of as just an ancient, slightly different-looking form of modern *Homo sapiens* (Figure 9.30). These are both exaggerations. We now recognize the sophistication of the Neandertals' intellectual and cultural achievements. They were certainly similar to modern humans physically but still different in significant ways. So debate at present centers on whether the similarities place them within our species or whether the differences make them a separate species (see Chapter 10). Figures 9.31 and 9.32 compare the skulls and skeletons of a Neandertal and a modern *Homo sapiens*.

The crania of the Neandertals are striking in appearance. They had, essentially, more pronounced versions of the cranial features of *Homo heidelbergensis*. Their cranial capacities ranged from about 1,300 ml to 1,740 ml, well within the modern range, but their foreheads were still sloped, the backs of their skulls broad, and the sides bulging. The brow ridges were still large, but smaller at the sides than in *H. erectus*, and they were filled with air spaces (called the *frontal sinuses*), unlike the solid ridges of *H. erectus*. The brow ridges of the Neandertals were also rounded over each eye, rather than forming a straight line, as in earlier archaics. The face was

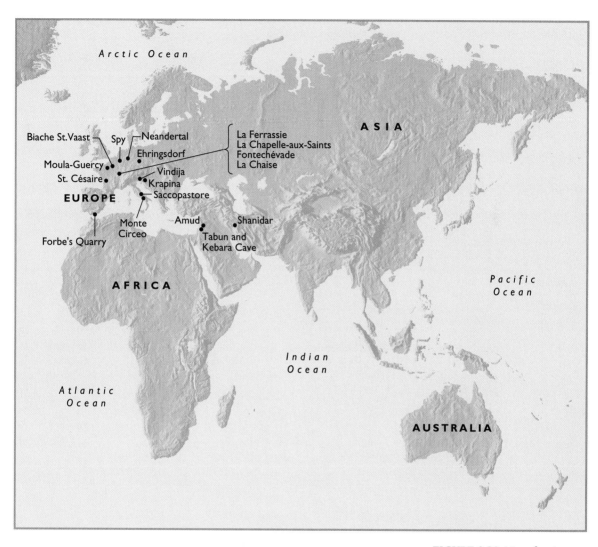

FIGURE 9.29 Map of major Neandertal sites.

large and prognathous, with a broad nasal opening and wide-set eyes. The chin was receding.

From the neck down, there were striking features. The bones of the Neandertals, even the finger bones, were more robust and had heavier muscle markings than their modern counterparts. The Neandertals were stocky, muscular, powerful people. This is seen even in the bones of Neandertal children, so it is assumed to be a result of inheritance, not simply of a hard-working lifestyle.

TABLE 9.3   Major Fossils of *Homo neanderthalensis*

Country	Locality	Fossils	Age (years)	Est. Brain Size (ml)
Belgium	Spy	2 skeletons	—	—
Croatia	Krapina	Cranial and postcranial fragments of >45 individuals	130,000	1,200–1,450
	Vindija	52 fossil fragments	28,000–42,000	—
France	Biache St. Vaast	2 crania	150,000–175,000	—
	Fontechévade	Cranial fragments of several individuals	100,000	1,500
	La Chaise	Cranium	126,000	—
	La Chapelle-aux-Saints	Skeleton	—	1,620
	La Ferrassie	8 skeletons	>38,000	1,680
	St. Césaire	Skeleton	36,000	—
Germany	Neandertal	Skullcap	—	>1,250
	Ehringsdorf	Cranial fragment	225,000	—
Gibraltar	Forbe's Quarry	Cranium	50,000	—
Iraq	Shanidar	9 partial skeletons	70,000	1,600
Israel	Amud	Skeleton	70,000	1,740
	Kebara Cave	Postcranial skeleton	60,000	—
	Tabun	Skeleton, mandible, postcranial fragments	100,000	1,270
Italy	Monte Circeo	Cranium	—	—
	Saccopastore	Cranium	—	—
			Mean	**1,478.89**

Although very strong and stocky, the Neandertals were relatively short. Estimates put the average for males at 5 feet 6 inches and for females at 5 feet 3 inches. Their short stature was partially a result of relatively short lower legs. The lower arms were short as well. All these physical features hint at adaptations to a strenuous lifestyle and to cold climates. Shorter, heavier bodies with short limbs conserve heat better than narrow, long-limbed bodies (Holliday 1997, and see Chapter 10). As evidence, the limbs of the Neandertals from warmer Southwest Asia are relatively longer than the limbs of those living in ice-age Europe, who faced some of the extreme climates of the glacial advances.

Another possible adaptation to cold has been suggested by several investigators (see Menon 1997). In eight Neandertal skulls, they found triangular bony projections in the nasal cavity unlike anything seen in

FIGURE 9.30 An old reconstruction from the Field Museum in Chicago (*left*) reinforces stereotypes of Neandertals as brutish, hairy, stooped-over distant cousins. In contrast, anthropologist Milford Wolpoff poses with a reconstructed Neandertal in modern dress to show that the differences between us and them were not that extreme. (*left, © The Field Museum, Neg. #A66700. Right, © Paul Jaronski/ University of Michigan Photo Services*)

modern humans or in any other human ancestors. These projections are thought to have provided increased surface area for the nasal mucous membranes, which would have helped warm and moisten the cold, dry air of Europe during the Pleistocene glaciations. It has also been suggested that the large sinus cavities served a similar function. Moreover, it is thought that the larynx of the Neandertals was higher in the throat than in modern humans (see Figure 9.21), which would have prevented them from gulping in cold, dry air through the mouth.

Neandertal fossils date from 225,000 to as recently as 28,000 ya (see Table 9.3). During this time, it has been proposed, Neandertals were responsible for a number of important cultural achievements. What do we know about their behavior?

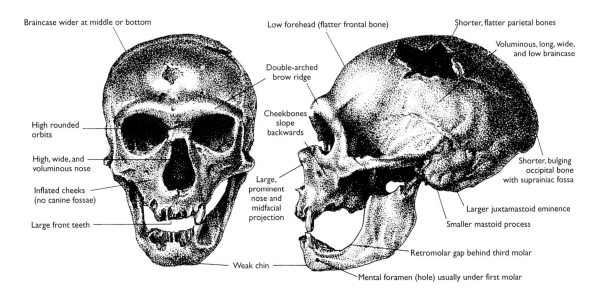

Braincase wider at middle or bottom

High rounded orbits

High, wide, and voluminous nose

Inflated cheeks (no canine fossa)

Large front teeth

Low forehead (flatter frontal bone)

Double-arched brow ridge

Cheekbones slope backwards

Large, prominent nose and midfacial projection

Weak chin

Shorter, flatter parietal bones

Voluminous, long, wide, and low braincase

Shorter, bulging occipital bone with suprainiac fossa

Larger juxtamastoid eminence

Smaller mastoid process

Retromolar gap behind third molar

Mental foramen (hole) usually under first molar

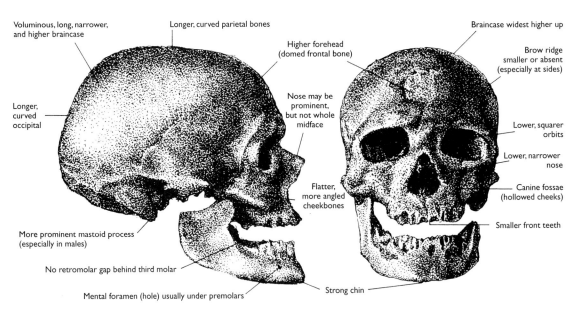

Voluminous, long, narrower, and higher braincase

Longer, curved occipital

More prominent mastoid process (especially in males)

No retromolar gap behind third molar

Mental foramen (hole) usually under premolars

Longer, curved parietal bones

Higher forehead (domed frontal bone)

Nose may be prominent, but not whole midface

Flatter, more angled cheekbones

Strong chin

Braincase widest higher up

Brow ridge smaller or absent (especially at sides)

Lower, squarer orbits

Lower, narrower nose

Canine fossae (hollowed cheeks)

Smaller front teeth

FIGURE 9.31 Cranial features of the La Chapelle specimen of Neandertal (*above*) compared with modern *Homo sapiens*. (*From* In Search of the Neanderthals *by Clive Gamble and Christopher Stringer. Reprinted by permission of Thames & Hudson, Ltd.*)

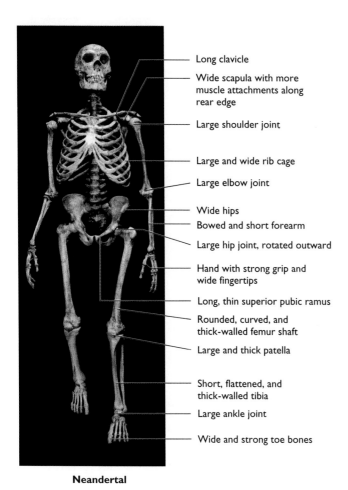

Long clavicle

Wide scapula with more muscle attachments along rear edge

Large shoulder joint

Large and wide rib cage

Large elbow joint

Wide hips

Bowed and short forearm

Large hip joint, rotated outward

Hand with strong grip and wide fingertips

Long, thin superior pubic ramus

Rounded, curved, and thick-walled femur shaft

Large and thick patella

Short, flattened, and thick-walled tibia

Large ankle joint

Wide and strong toe bones

Neandertal

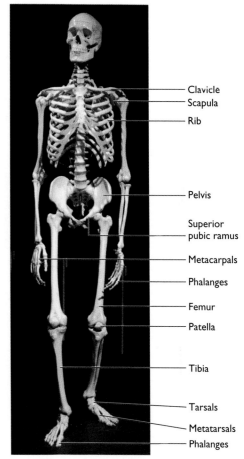

Clavicle
Scapula
Rib

Pelvis

Superior pubic ramus

Metacarpals

Phalanges

Femur

Patella

Tibia

Tarsals

Metatarsals

Phalanges

Modern *Homo sapiens*

FIGURE 9.32 Skeletal features of Neandertal compared with modern *Homo sapiens*. (*Courtesy American Museum of Natural History Library*)

Among the well-established accomplishments of the Neandertals is an elaboration on the Levallois stone toolmaking technique. Called the **Mousterian** technique, after the site of Le Moustier in France, it involved the careful retouching of flakes taken off cores. These flakes were sharpened and shaped by precise additional flaking, on one side or both, to make specialized tools (Figure 9.33). One authority has identified no less than sixty-three tool types (Bordes 1972).

Several specific uses of Mousterian tools have been inferred from microscopic wear-pattern analysis on specimens from the Kebara Cave site in Israel. Archaeologist John Shea (1989) notes wear patterns that indicate animal butchering, woodworking, bone and antler carving, and working of animal hides. There are also wear patterns like those produced by the

Mousterian A toolmaking tradition associated with the European Neandertals.

FIGURE 9.33 Unifacially re-touched Mousterian flakes from the original site, Le Moustier, France. *(K. L. Feder)*

friction of a wooden shaft against a stone spear point. The Neandertals may have been the first to **haft** a stone point.

Although there is still debate about whether the Neandertals were big-game hunters or mostly scavengers, there is no doubt that they were de-pendent on the animals that abounded during the Pleistocene—animals such as reindeer, deer, ibex (wild goats), aurochs (wild oxen), horses, woolly rhinoceroses, bison, bear, and elk. Bones of these creatures have been found in association with Neandertal remains.

While we now have earlier evidence of intentional human burials (dis-cussed in the next section), the first and most famous evidence comes from the Neandertals. Although many of these "burials" have now been attributed to natural causes, at least thirty-six Neandertal sites show evidence of in-tentional interment of the dead, and in some graves there were remains of offerings—stone tools, animal bones, and, possibly, flowers (Figure 9.34).

There is some debate, however, regarding the ritual significance of these Neandertal burials. Did they represent belief in an afterlife or rever-

haft To attach a wooden handle or shaft to a stone or bone point.

FIGURE 9.34 An undisputed Neandertal burial from La Ferrassie, France. Here, the individual was interred in the flexed position, with knees drawn up to the chest. (The basket belongs to the excavators.) (© *Musée de l'Homme. Photo by M. Lucas*)

ence for the physical remains of the deceased, or were the people simply disposing of a corpse, as seems to have been the case much earlier at Sima de los Huesos? Were animal bones present in the graves as offerings, or did scavengers and predators drag them there, along with Neandertal bones, where they were subsequently buried by natural processes? The pollen found in a Neandertal grave at Shanidar, Iraq, may not have been

FIGURE 9.35 In the last few decades, reconstructions of Neandertal physical features and cultural practices have emphasized similarities to modern humans. Here, a painting by Rudolph Zallinger depicts Neandertals making a shrine into which they are placing the heads of bears they have killed, the equivalent of modern hunting trophies. Recent analysis indicates, however, that there is little evidence for this behavior among the Neandertals. *(Courtesy of R. F. Zallinger and* Life *magazine/Photo © Herb Orth/Getty Images)*

from flowers placed in the grave but may have been brought in by burrowing rodents, carried in by water, or blown in by wind at the time of burial. The jury is still out on this issue. But we know the Neandertals did sometimes bury their dead, for whatever reason.

Along the same lines, evidence has traditionally been cited for a Neandertal cave bear "cult" in Europe (Figure 9.35). The cave bear, now extinct, was a huge, impressive species, about 12 feet tall when standing upright. Caves in Switzerland and France are supposed to contain a number of cave bear skulls placed in special stone chests or in niches in the cave walls. But these interpretations were apparently wishful thinking on the part of early investigators. Reanalysis of the site descriptions indicates

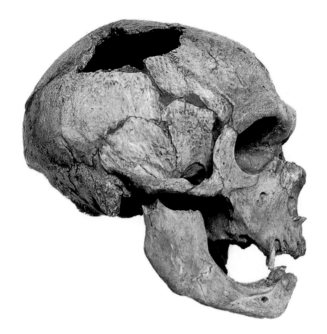

FIGURE 9.36 The famous "Old Man" of La Chapelle-aux-Saints, France. (See front view and labels in Figure 9.31.) (© *John Reader/Science Photo Library/Photo Researchers, Inc.*)

that the placement of the skulls was the result of natural processes such as cave-ins. Moreover, none of the bear bones show any signs of cut marks. This intriguing story has fallen to scientific investigation.

It has also been suggested that Neandertals were among the first to care for their elderly, ill, and injured. According to an early interpretation, the famous "Old Man" of La Chapelle-aux-Saints in France (Figure 9.36) was aged, lacked most of his teeth, and had a debilitating case of arthritis. That he survived for a time with these infirmities, according to the interpretation, indicates that he was cared for by his group.

Recent reexamination, though, shows that much of his tooth loss was after death and that his arthritis may not have been quite as debilitating as previously thought. Nor was he really old. He died when he was less than 40, probably rather quickly, as did the vast majority of Neandertals. Care of the elderly was probably not something they had to contend with very often.

On the other hand, there is a skeleton of a man from Shanidar, Iraq, that shows signs of injuries that may have resulted in blindness and the loss of one arm. He lived with this condition for some time and, therefore, was obviously cared for by his comrades.

But things may not have been completely peaceful among Neandertal populations. There is evidence of cannibalism from the Neandertal sites of Moula-Guercy in France (Defleur et al. 1999) and Krapina and Vindija in Croatia (White 2001). Fragmentary bones from at least six individuals show stone tool cut marks in the same anatomical locations as those found on bones of wild goats and deer at the site. Some of the human long bones also show signs of having been smashed, in the way that would have allowed access to the rich bone marrow. Whether the inferred cannibalism was ritual (ingesting part of, or ashes of, a group member at a funeral ceremony) or gustatory (eating the flesh as food) cannot be determined.

Finally, we have the question of the linguistic abilities of the Neandertals. Some investigators have reconstructed the vocal tract of Neandertals based on the structure of the underside of the cranium. They have concluded that because of the higher larynx noted before, Neandertals were not capable of making all the vowel sounds of modern humans. However, a recently found hyoid bone—a horseshoe-shaped bone in the throat—from the Neandertal site of Kebara in Israel appears fully modern. This would mean that the vocal tract of the Neandertals *was* like ours and that they *could* make all the sounds of which we are capable. The point, of course, is—as we said for *Homo erectus*—that the Neandertals had sufficiently complex things to talk *about,* and just how they did so is less important than the fact that they did talk.

Archaic members of genus *Homo* were successful in adapting to different environments and, in the case of the Neandertals, harsh and demanding climates. They were clearly intelligent. We will no doubt find more fossils of archaics in new areas in the future. But the archaics differed in their complex of physical features from humans alive today. To begin the story of anatomically modern *Homo sapiens,* we once again return to Africa.

Modern Humans

Beginning perhaps as early as 300,000 ya, fossils with what are considered to be near-modern or modern features appear, earliest in Africa and later in Southwest Asia, Europe, and East Asia. Later still, modern humans migrated to Australia, the islands of the Pacific, and North and South America. There is no general agreement about the exact species affiliation of some transitional forms—fossils with a mix of archaic and modern traits. Table 9.4 and Figure 9.37 give the basic information and locations of some of the more important fossils of early **Homo sapiens,** as well as transitional forms.

We call these fossils "anatomically modern" because they lack some features characteristic of earlier hominids and possess features common in humans today. Gone is the prognathous profile. The modern human face is essentially flat. There are no heavy brow ridges. The skull is globular rather than elongated, and the forehead is more nearly vertical. The face is smaller and narrower, and there is a protruding chin. The postcranial skeleton is less robust. Refer back to Figures 9.31 and 9.32, and then look in the mirror.

TABLE 9.4 Some Important Fossils of Early *Homo sapiens*

Country	Location	Age (years)
Kenya	Ileret	270,000–300,000 (trans.)*
South Africa	Florisbad	100,000–200,000 (trans.)
Ethiopia	Omo (Omo II cranium)	195,000 (trans.)
	(Omo I cranium)	195,000
Tanzania	Ngaloba	120,000 (trans.)
Morocco	Jebel Irhoud	100,000 (trans.)
Ethiopia	Herto	154,000–160,000
South Africa	Klasies River Mouth	84,000–120,000
	Langebaan Lagoon (footprints)	117,000
	Border Cave	62,000–115,000
Israel	Qafzeh	92,000–120,000
	Skhul	81,000–101,000
Germany	Stetten	36,000
France	Cro-Magnon	<30,000
	Abri Pataud	>27,000
China	Zhoukoudian	10,000–18,000
Australia	Lake Mungo	40,000
United States	Midland, Texas	11,600

*The abbreviation *trans.* indicates those fossils that are considered transitional between archaic and modern *Homo*.

Note in Table 9.4 that the earliest fossils are all from eastern and southern Africa and that they are considered, at least by some authorities, as transitional between archaic and modern *Homo*. There is also a transitional form from Morocco (Figure 9.38). The implication is that modern humans—whether a new species or just the modern form of an existing species—arose in Africa. Until recently, the earliest dates for the appearance of transitional forms was about 200,000 ya from South Africa, but recent finds from Kenya (Bräuer et al. 1997), dated by several methods that appear to correspond well, have pushed this date back to perhaps 300,000 ya.

By around 195,000 ya, we begin to find fossils that represent humans of fully modern appearance relative to their geographic area. The earliest

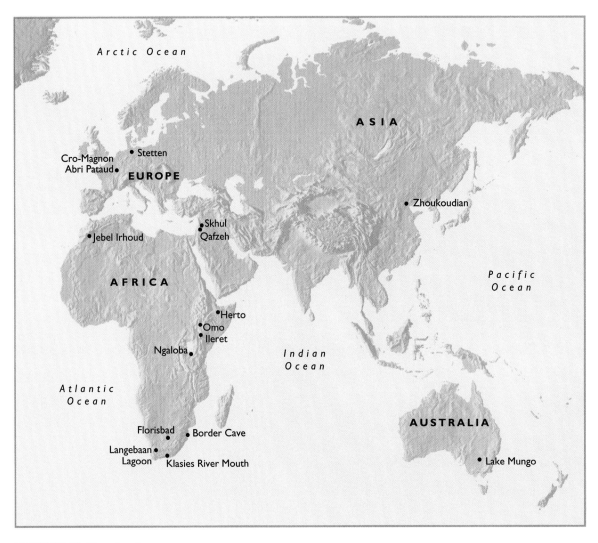

FIGURE 9.37 Map of major early *Homo sapiens* sites in Africa, Asia, Australia, and Europe.

of these at present are recent finds from Ethiopia (Clark et al. 2003; White et al. 2003; McDoughall et al. 2005). Three partial skulls, one fairly complete (Figure 9.39), show very modern features, including a large cranial capacity of up to 1,450 ml. They are thought to constitute the "oldest definite record of what we currently think of as modern *Homo sapiens*" (Stringer 2003). These remains are associated with a mix of primitive and more sophisticated stone tools, and the skulls show some signs of postmortem manipulation, possibly for ritual purposes.

Slightly more recent fossils are from South Africa and Israel (Figure 9.40). At the South African site of Langebaan Lagoon, a small human,

FIGURE 9.38 Cranium from Jebel Irhoud, Morocco. This skull, dated at about 100,000 ya, is considered by some to be transitional between archaic and modern *Homo*. The braincase is low, the face is relatively large, and it has distinct brow ridges. Otherwise, its features are modern. (© *Musée de l'Homme*)

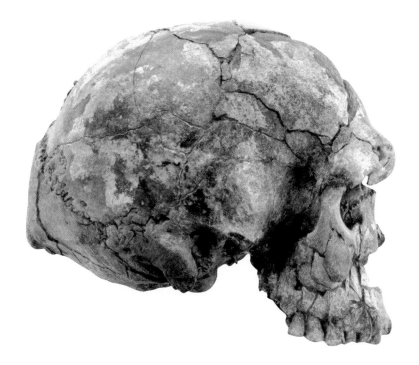

FIGURE 9.39 The most complete early *Homo sapiens* skull from Herto, Ethiopia, dated at 160,000 ya. The wide upper face, rounded forehead, divided brow ridge, flat midface, and large cranial capacity are all modern traits. (© *David L. Brill*)

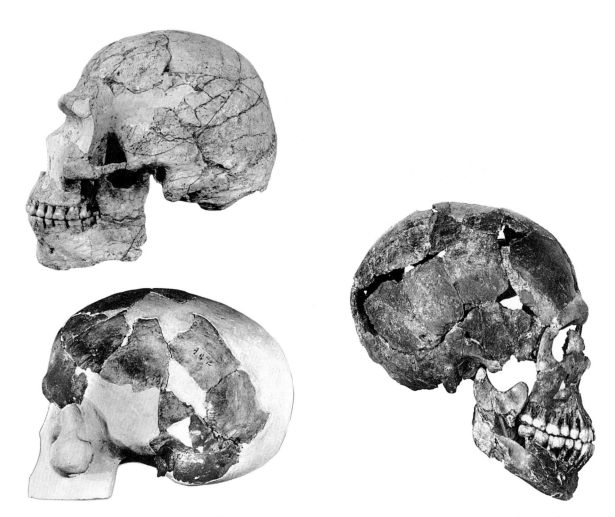

FIGURE 9.40 Examples of early modern *Homo sapiens* from (*counterlockwise from top*) Skhul, Israel; Border Cave, South Africa; and Qafzeh, Israel. Note the higher foreheads, protruding chins, and flatter faces compared with archaic *Homo*. Despite the rather prominent brow ridges in the Skhul specimen, it is still considered fully modern due to its other features. (*Top, © Peabody Museum, Harvard University. Photograph by Hillel Burger. Photo No. N26470; Bottom left, Photo by A. R. Hughes. Courtesy Professor P. V. Tobias, University of the Witwatersrand, Johannesburg, South Africa; Bottom right, Courtesy B. Vandermeersch, Laboratoire d'Anthropologie, Universite de Bordeaux*)

possibly a female, left her footprints in rock claimed to be dated at 117,000 ya —a moment frozen in time reminiscent of the Laetoli footprints from Tanzania (see Figure 8.11). As we move farther away from Africa and Southwest Asia, the dates for the early appearance of modern *H. sapiens* get more recent, a further indication that Africa is the birthplace of modern humans.

The behavior of modern humans and the artifacts that provide some of the evidence for that behavior are the focus of Chapters 11, 12, and 13. But first we need to confront a continuing debate within anthropology: the identity of our species, *Homo sapiens.* Just how many species of genus *Homo* have existed, and how are they related? This the topic of the next chapter.

Summary

The record of the latest 2.5 million years of hominid evolution is complex. The fossils from the first 99 percent of this period are scarce, often fragmentary, scattered geographically, physically variable, and, in some cases, questionably dated. Not surprisingly, the interpretations of these fossils vary as greatly as do the fossils themselves. Our survey uses as a starting point the model that recognizes six species within genus *Homo* after the early *Homo* stage. We will discuss this model, and alternatives, in the next chapter.

The earliest species, *H. ergaster,* is found only in Kenya, but a possible branch of this group, *H. erectus,* spread through the rest of Africa and into Asia and possibly southern Europe. These two species are characterized by virtually modern postcranial skeletons, brain sizes close to and even overlapping the modern human range, and the invention of more sophisticated stone tools and other cultural innovations, including the use of fire. In Java, *H. erectus* may have persisted until as recently as 27,000 ya.

A geographically and chronologically scattered species, *Homo heidelbergensis,* appears next. The earliest examples of this group, from Spain, are placed by some authorities into a new species, *H. antecessor.* Located from England to South Africa to China, *H. heidelbergensis* displays brain sizes within the modern human range and at the modern human average, though their crania retain primitive features, giving them the label "archaic." They are known, starting about 200,000 ya, for the invention of the Levallois stone toolmaking technique—a sophisticated way of "mass producing" flake tools. They may have done some hunting as well.

The most famous of the "archaic" humans are the Neandertals, a separate species, *Homo neanderthalensis,* according to many. Living in Europe and Southwest Asia from 225,000 to 28,000 ya, this group exhibits traits that distinguish it from both *H. heidelbergensis* and later *H. sapiens.* These traits include large, prognathous faces, ruggedly built skulls, and robust, muscular bodies—possibly adaptations to the cold glacial conditions many of their populations encountered. Neandertals are known for their retouched flake tools, which may have been used to carve bone and work wood, and for abstract cultural achievements such as burial of the dead and care of the elderly and infirm. They may also have been the first to haft stone points on wooden shafts.

CONTEMPORARY ISSUE

Who Are the "Hobbits" from Indonesia?

In October 2004 came a potentially astonishing announcement (Brown et al. 2004)—the discovery, on the Indonesian island of Flores, of a human skeleton dated to as recently as 13,000 ya. Such a find would not have been remarkable except that the skeleton is of an adult female who stood a mere 106 cm tall (about 3 feet 5 inches) and had an estimated brain size of 380 ml, about the stature and cranial capacity of *Australopithecus afarensis.* And yet the specimen's physical features seem fairly clearly to assign it to genus *Homo,* with particular similarities to *Homo erectus.* The discoverers have given the specimen the status of a new species, **Homo floresiensis.**

Even for those who propose multiple species of our genus over the last 2 million years (see Chapter 10), this is an amazing find, because as far as we know there have been no humans other than us— fully modern *Homo sapiens*—on earth for at least

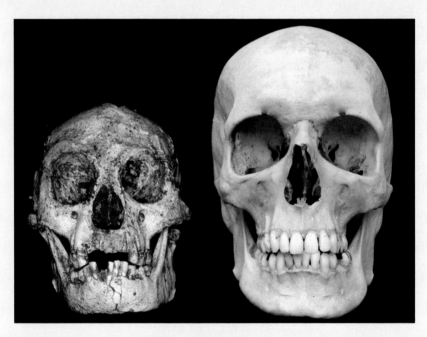

The skull of *Homo floresiensis (left)* compared to a modern human skull. (© *Dr. Peter Brown, University of New England, Armdale, Australia)*

Fossils transitional between archaic and modern *Homo* appear in Africa perhaps as early as 300,000 ya, and the first fully modern *Homo sapiens* are found in Africa and Southwest Asia beginning around 160,000 ya. From there, modern-appearing humans spread throughout the Old

27,000 years. And for those of us who feel that only one species of *Homo* has existed, the implication of this find and its interpretation is obvious.

What are we to make of this specimen, referred to in the popular press as a "Hobbit" (a reference to the small characters in J. R. R. Tolkien's *Lord of the Rings*)? Given its body and brain size, could it *be* an australopithecine, indicating that there were populations of this genus outside of Africa? Probably not, since it has phenotypic characteristics that place it clearly in genus *Homo* and it was found in association with stone tools and evidence of hunting and possibly fire and cooking. None of these cultural features are associated with *Australopithecus,* although some authorities say the pelvis and body proportions are australopithecine (Balter 2004). And the game *H. floresiensis* hunted was not small; it included pygmy elephants and Komodo dragons (the world's largest existing lizard). Certainly a high level of cooperation and communication would have been necessary to accomplish such hunting. Moreover, no fossils of australopithecines have been found outside of Africa, much less as far away as Southwest Asia.

Perhaps this is one individual within a group of pygmy humans or simply a modern human who had an anomalous condition, some form of dwarfism. Small humans, however, and humans with anomalous conditions tend to have smaller than average bodies but retain brains within the modern human range (1,000 to 2,000 ml). *H. floresiensis* had a brain approximately one-third the modern human average *minimum.*

On the other hand, perhaps once evolution achieved a modern human brain complexity, size became less important and a complex brain could develop in a small package (Falk et al. 2005). Consider, in a loose analogy, how we can now put hard drives of increasing capacity in smaller and smaller computers, MP3 players, and other devices.

At the moment, the best accepted guess is that this specimen comes from a population of descendants of *Homo erectus* that responded to a phenomenon of dwarfing common to island species, especially mammals. Free from predators and/or restricted in room and resources, mammalian species isolated on islands can evolve to be much smaller than their ancestors.

But several questions remain. First, is this specimen characteristic of a whole population? As of this writing, the discoverers of the original specimen have reported the recovery of the remains of perhaps seven more individuals with the same features. But until more of these remains are fully described and verified, we can only surmise that the original find is representative of an entire group.

Second, even if the original and subsequent finds do represent a population, is this population a separate species? We can't, of course, experiment to see if *H. floresiensis* could interbreed with other populations, so there is no definitive way to answer that question. Thus, as we will discuss, opinions on the number of species of *Homo* continue to differ, and there will probably never be a way to resolve the debate for sure.

One thing is certain, however. Unless this individual proves to be just that—one individual with a unique set of physical features—our genus *Homo* is a lot more variable than we once imagined.

World and eventually to the islands of the Pacific and to the Americas. Archaic peoples—or archaic traits—disappear. During this time, big-game hunting develops, tool technology advances, sophisticated shelters are built, and humans create art.

Study Questions

1. How and when did genus *Homo* first evolve? Why are the first fossils of our genus placed in that taxonomic category?
2. How does the cranial anatomy of *Homo erectus* differ from that of early *Homo habilis*?
3. What are the behavioral innovations associated with *Homo erectus*? How might these help explain the rapid expansion of this species within and beyond its African homeland?
4. What are the features of the Pleistocene? What do we know about its cause and ramifications for human evolution?
5. What do we know about the evolution of language? What techniques have been used to determine when human language first evolved?
6. Who were the Neandertals? Describe their anatomy, biological adaptations, behavior, and cultural innovations.
7. When and where did anatomically modern *Homo sapiens* evolve? What characteristics define our species?

Key Terms

Lower Paleolithic	glacier	endocast
Oldowan	glacial	Acheulian
pebble tool	glacial period	hand axe
core tool	interglacial	bifacial
flake tool	stadial	Movius Line
sagittal keel	interstadial	postorbital
occipital	Holocene	constriction
torus	Lower Pleistocene	Levallois
Pleistocene	Middle Pleistocene	Mousterian
Pliocene	Upper Pleistocene	haft
paleoclimatologist		

For More Information

For more on the new Dmanisi find, see a typically well-illustrated article in the August 2002 *National Geographic,* "New Find." For more on the Atapuerca finds from Spain, see the also well-illustrated book *The First Europeans: Treasures from the Hills of Atapuerca,* published by Junta de Castilla y León.

An interesting article linking an increase in human brain size with dietary change is "Food for Thought," by William R. Leonard, in the December 2002 *Scientific American.* And for more on ancient cannibalism, see Tim D. White's "Once We Were Cannibals" in the August 2001 *Scientific American.*

For summaries of human evolution, see *The Last Neanderthal,* by Ian Tattersall, and *Extinct Humans,* by Ian Tattersall and Jeffrey Schwarz. Be aware that these authors advocate a maximum number of separate species for *Homo* and the other hominid genera. The books, however, are accurate, up-to-date, and beautifully illustrated.

For the fascinating story of Eugene Dubois and the discovery of "Java Man," see Pat Shipman's *The Man Who Found the Missing Link: Eugene Dubois and His Lifelong Quest to Prove Darwin Right.* The story of the missing "Peking Man" fossils is the topic of *The Search for Peking Man,* by C. Janus.

For still more on Atapuerca, try www.ucm.es/info/paleo/ata/english. And for some Paleolithic art from Chauvet Cave, see www.culture.fr/culture/arcnat/chauvet/en.

For more on the Indonesian "Hobbits," see "The Littlest Human," by Kate Wong, in the February 2005 issue of *Scientific American.*

Humans come in a wide variety of shapes, sizes, colors, and other physical and chemical features. How and when did anatomically modern humans evolve? How are we related to premodern groups? How do we account for our current biodiversity, and what does it mean in terms of the concept of "race"? (© *George Steinmetz*)

THE EVOLUTION AND NATURE OF MODERN HUMANITY

CHAPTER CONTENTS

The Major Models in an Ongoing Debate

The Evidence

Mostly-Out-of-Africa: An Alternative Model

Point–Counterpoint: The Authors Debate the Debate

Biological Diversity in Modern Humans

CONTEMPORARY ISSUE: Is There a Connection between Modern Human Origins and Race?

Summary

Study Questions

Key Terms

For More Information

In Chapter 1, we discussed the nature of science and the scientific method. The power of science to help us understand our world lies in two of its characteristics. First, it requires the empirical testing of *testable* hypotheses. This is what separates science from myth.

And this leads to science's second strength: science is self-correcting. Scientific ideas, even some very well-accepted ones, often fall by the wayside in light of new data, new analytical techniques, new interpretations.

Thus, debates within science exemplify the scientific method in action, and the debate covered in this chapter—the evolutionary origin of modern humans—is no exception. And making it an even better example is the fact that the authors of this book don't agree on it!

We'll first discuss the two major schools of thought in the debate and then describe an alternative model. Then we'll tell you what each of us thinks about the issue and why. We'll end with a discussion of human biodiversity and the concept of race.

The Major Models in an Ongoing Debate

It would appear based on current available evidence (see Table 9.4) that fully modern-*looking* people first appeared 195,000 to 165,000 ya, with transitional forms showing the beginnings of modern traits as far back as 300,000 ya. It also appears that these traits first evolved in Africa. But at issue is the question, Do these traits accurately define and distinguish a new species of hominid, *Homo sapiens,* or is the collection of traits we think of as modern just the latest set of variable features in the evolution of a much older species?

We can define two major models for the origin of our species. The single-species model is known formally as the **Multiregional Evolution (MRE) model.** Models that recognize *H. sapiens* as only the most recent of multiple species of *Homo* are called by a number of names, most commonly the **Out-of-Africa model.** However, the MRE model also acknowledges that our species arose in and expanded out of Africa—just a lot earlier—so I prefer to call the latter model the **Recent African Origin (RAO) model.** Figure 10.1 has generalized diagrams that depict these two models. Once you have grasped the arguments for and against these well-known and quite opposite models as a basis, we'll examine an alternative, the **Mostly-Out-of-Africa model.**

The Recent African Origin (RAO) Model

Major proponents of the Recent African Origin model are Christopher Stringer of the Natural History Museum in London (Stringer and McKie 1996) and Ian Tattersall of the American Museum of Natural History in New York (Tattersall 2001; Tattersall and Schwarz 2000). Although various supporters of this model recognize different numbers of species within genus *Homo,* they all share the view that modern *Homo sapiens* is a separate species that branched from a preexisting archaic *Homo* species in Africa around 200,000 to 150,000 ya. This new species then spread over the Old World, replacing archaic populations when they came in contact, presumably because *H. sapiens* was a better-adapted species. (This model is sometimes called the *replacement model.*)

If this model is correct, we must be able to find distinctions between our modern species and premodern (or archaic) humans that clearly distinguish us *as separate species.* There must be an anatomical definition of modernity; in other words, there must be traits that all *Homo sapiens* share that are not found in premoderns, and traits found in premoderns that are lacking in modern humans. We would also expect to find genetic distinctions of a degree that would indicate separate species.

If we can anatomically define and distinguish premodern from modern humans, then we can deduce that fossils transitional between premodern and modern humans should occur only in the single region in which mod-

Multiregional Evolution (MRE) model The hypothesis that *Homo sapiens* is about 2 million years old and that modern human traits evolved in geographically diverse locations and then spread through the species.

Out-of-Africa model Another name for the Recent African Origin model.

Recent African Origin (RAO) model The hypothesis that *Homo sapiens* evolved recently as a separate species in Africa and then spread to replace more archaic populations.

Mostly-Out-of-Africa model The hypothesis that *Homo sapiens* is about 2 million years old as a species but that most of the genetic variation and phenotypic features of modern humans have an African origin.

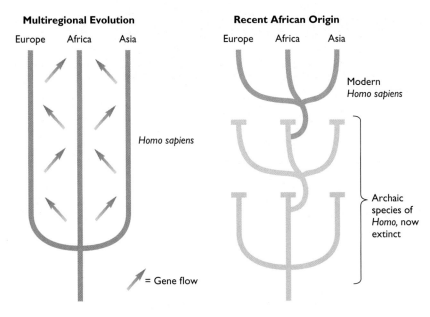

Multiregional Evolution

Europe   Africa   Asia

Homo sapiens

= Gene flow

Recent African Origin

Europe   Africa   Asia

Modern
Homo sapiens

Archaic
species of
Homo, now
extinct

FIGURE 10.1 Generalized models for the origin of *Homo sapiens*.

erns evolved. Elsewhere, there should be evidence of anatomical premoderns and anatomical moderns coexisting in the same regions, once the latter spread out from their initial source area. Eventually, the premodern human forms would have become extinct, unable to compete with their anatomically modern cousins. Figure 10.2 shows one way this model interprets the relationships among the six species of *Homo* we used in Chapter 9.

The Multiregional Evolution (MRE) Model

The names most often associated with the Multiregional Evolution model are Milford Wolpoff and Rachel Caspari of the University of Michigan (Wolpoff and Caspari 1997). This model—a bit more complicated than the RAO model—also claims that *Homo sapiens* arose in Africa, but it pushes back the date of *H. sapiens*'s appearance to as much as 2 mya. Members of this new species (traditionally called *Homo erectus*) spread throughout the Old World, evolving genetic and phenotypic regional differences in response to the wide variety of environmental circumstances they encountered and the complex population movements, isolations, mergings, and fissionings that must have taken place. The degree of species mobility resulted in sufficient gene flow to maintain a single species, as no population was isolated long enough or to a great enough degree for speciation to occur. As successful advantageous adaptive features arose, they were dispersed across the species through gene flow. Ideas and technologies spread and were exchanged as well (Wolpoff et al. 2001). Physical features

FIGURE 10.2 One possible set of relationships for the six proposed species of *Homo*, according to the RAO model.

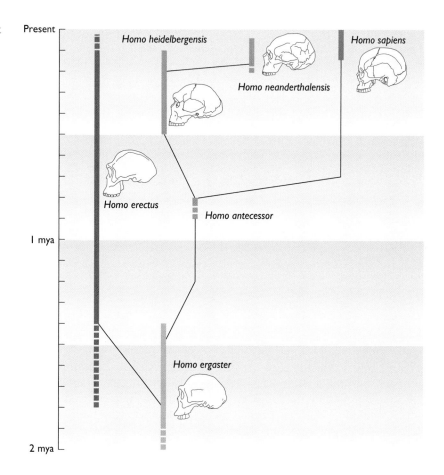

we associate with modern humans appeared everywhere but may have been manifested in different ways in different populations and in different environments. Thus, we are today and have always been a variable species—but a single species.

It is important to understand that this does *not* mean that *every* population within this long-lived and widespread species survived to contribute genes to modern humans. Certainly, individual isolated populations could have become extinct with few or none of their genes passed down. Nor does this deny the distinctive sets of traits that characterize some of the premodern (archaic) populations such as the Neandertals. The MRE model simply says that these populations were not separate species, that *Homo sapiens* did not arise in the recent past, and, thus, that it did not spread and become dominant by replacing other species of *Homo*.

If the MRE model is correct, we should find no clear evidence that modern *H. sapiens* is a separate species from any of the so-called premodern groups. In other words, there should be no biologically meaningful definition of modernity—no set of traits that is found among all populations classified as modern that is lacking among all premodern populations. However, populations with transitional sets of traits should be found in many locations. Ideally, there should be some evidence of interbreeding in the form of a mix of traits in fossils from those areas where groups co-existed. Finally, there should be regional continuity of traits—features characteristic of geographic areas that appear not only in modern populations but premodern ones as well.

One conclusion of this model is that if premodern groups are in fact members of our species, then the rules of taxonomy dictate that the earliest name used for any of them must be applied to them all. Thus, if all six species of *Homo* are indeed the same species, they would all be *Homo sapiens,* the name first used by Linnaeus in 1758. Figure 10.3 shows how the MRE model views the interrelationships among the various regional fossil populations discussed in Chapter 9.

The Key Requirements of Each Model

As we evaluate the evidence in this debate, here are the main points to keep in mind about each model:

RAO

- Requires an anatomical definition of modernity that clearly distinguishes modern humans from premodern species
- Requires genetic distinctions of a degree that indicates modern humans are a separate species
- Requires that transitional forms appear only in the single region in which modern humans evolved

MRE

- Requires that there be no biologically meaningful definition of modernity; that is, no set of "modern" traits that is lacking among all premodern populations
- Requires that populations with transitional sets of traits be found in many locations
- Requires a regional continuity of traits; that is, features characteristic of a given geographic area should appear in premodern and modern populations within that region

The Evidence

Clearly, the evidence for the past 2 million years of our evolution is limited. Fossils exist, but they are often fragmentary, and they are scattered across space and time. The same can be said for archaeological evidence of

FIGURE 10.3 Diagram of the MRE model. The red arrow represents the initial expansion out of Africa nearly 2 mya. Vertical lines represent direct regional descent. Diagonal lines represent gene flow among regional populations. (See Figure 10.9 for a more complete diagram representing a somewhat different model.) *(Adapted from Templeton 2002:48)*

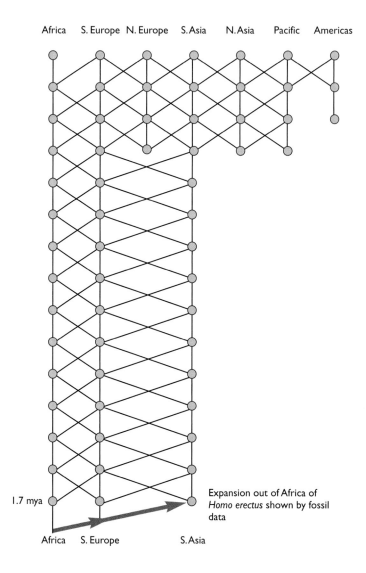

our ancestors' cultural activities. Genetic data are available, but only from fully modern populations alive today—or at least recently. And evolutionary theory is still being debated, both in general terms and more specifically when applied to the history of a specific group.

Thus, in reviewing the extensive literature on modern human origins, we find that different authorities have very different interpretations of the same data. Indeed, the same general data have been convincingly used to support both the MRE and RAO models, but proponents differ in which specific pieces of data they emphasize. Following, then, is a general summary of the available evidence and interpretations by both the MRE and RAO "camps."

The Fossil Record

In using the multiple-species model for our discussion of genus *Homo* in Chapter 9, we have already presented the fossil evidence as interpreted by the Recent African Origin proponents. Look again at the tables and maps in that chapter.

As suggested by the RAO model, forms transitional between archaic species (*H. heidelbergensis* and *H. neanderthalensis*) and *H. sapiens* are found only in Africa. Modern forms appear first in Africa and then show up at increasingly recent dates as one moves away from that continent. And archaics and moderns overlap in time in some areas. Note, for example, that the modern fossils from Skhul and Qafzeh in Israel actually predate the Neandertals in the same country and that the two groups shared the area for a time (see Tables 9.3 and 9.4).

In stark contrast, Wolpoff and Caspari assert that the variation seen within the fossil record of *Homo* does not warrant division into separate species. They claim, for example, that in broad perspective "just about every way *H. erectus* differs from its australopithecine ancestors also characterizes *H. sapiens:* virtually no features are unique to *H. erectus*" (1997:256). In other words, *H. sapiens* and *H. erectus* are the same species. They also contend that modern traits did not all arise in one location but in many and that they spread throughout the species through gene flow, to be expressed differently in different geographic locations. As required by the MRE model, transitional forms are found in many locations.

Moreover, Wolpoff and Caspari feel that "it has proved impossible to provide an acceptable [physical] definition of modernity" in the first place (1997:313). Some features proposed to define modern humans *do not* include all recent or living peoples. For example, it has been suggested that Neandertals' large, continuous brow ridges are a major diagnostic feature helping to distinguish them from modern humans. But some living indigenous people of Australia—fully modern biological humans in every sense of the word—also have large, continuous brow ridges (Figure 10.4). There is sufficient variation among modern humans, says Wolpoff, that modernity must be defined regionally, as no general definition includes all clearly modern humans and excludes all other proposed species.

The Neandertals are frequently used to establish a definition of modern. But to use the Neandertals in a comparison with modern populations is sort of stacking the deck, since they are *more* different from moderns in some ways than are other archaics. Moreover, the Neandertals were a small population, isolated by distance and ecology in an Old World backwater. Even if most of their populations, and thus their phenotypes, became

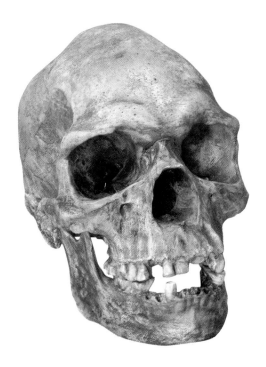

FIGURE 10.4 Cast of a Native Australian skull. Note the heavy brow ridges, as well as other so-called primitive traits—prognathism, a receding chin, and a sagittal keel. Obviously, a lack of such traits cannot be used to define modern humans because it would exclude some modern groups. *(Photo © Bone Clones®)*

extinct, that does not preclude their being members of our species, nor does it negate the MRE model. A physical definition of modernity thus seems to be in the eye of the beholder, based on one's interpretation and choice of populations and characteristics.

Wolpoff and colleagues (2001) also see continuity of individual traits in certain areas, especially Asia and Australia and also between Neandertal and modern populations in Europe. In another study, they compared anatomical features of skulls from both moderns and archaics from different parts of Europe, Africa, and Asia and found a series of similarities and differences that pointed to a mixed ancestry of the modern populations.

As further potential evidence of the MRE model, we have a 1998 find from Portugal of a 3½- to 5-year-old child who lived 24,500 ya (Duarte et al. 1999). The child's mandible displays a protruding chin and proportionately small front teeth, diagnostic of moderns. The postcranial bones, however, are robust, with proportionately short lower arms and legs, diagnostic of Neandertals. The investigators' interpretation is that the boy represents a hybrid, making those two groups, by definition, members of the same species. Not unexpectedly, of course, RAO proponents reject this claim, suggesting that the child was simply a "chunky" anatomically modern human (Holden 1999).

In regard to this debate, the fossil record is ambiguous. It can clearly be interpreted to support either point of view, and there is wide disagreement between those points of view. Note that even RAO proponents cannot agree on the exact number of premodern species of *Homo*. They only agree that *Homo sapiens* is a recent, separate species. The fossils that do exist are usually incomplete, not necessarily representative of the populations from which they came, and often of questionable age. Moreover, many of the morphological features being used for these analyses are of unknown heritability; that is, we don't know how much they tell us about actual genetic distinctions (Minugh-Purvis 1995). Finally, it is hard to translate physical features into species classification (see Chapter 7).

The Cultural Evidence

There is, of course, another source of data that we may use to assess the two models of modern human origins. If some premodern populations of *Homo* evolved as a separate species into modern *Homo sapiens* only in Africa, then there should be an attendant jump in the sophistication of material culture—more elaborate tools—first in Africa, marking the greater intelligence of anatomically modern human beings.

Africa   The artifacts recovered at some, though certainly not all, early modern human sites in Africa do show a more sophisticated technology than contemporary tool assemblages in Europe and Asia associated with premodern humans. Anthropologist Sally McBrearty has discovered the world's oldest blade tools in Kenya (Gutin 1995). The tools were recovered at a site near Lake Baringo and dated to about 240,000 ya. The form of the blades indicates that their makers carefully prepared the stone cores from which they were struck to ensure the tools' precision and consistency (Figure 10.5). As McBrearty indicates, this kind of core preparation implies a high level of abstraction and planning on the part of the toolmakers. These stone blades offer a tantalizing first glimpse of the intellectual advance of hominids in Africa during a period of transition from premodern to modern *Homo sapiens*.

At Klasies River Mouth in southern Africa, there are long, bifacially worked spear points made on stone blades detached from cores by means of a punch technique (Singer and Wymer 1982; Figure 10.6). In this technique, long blades are removed from stone cores by striking a punch, usually made of antler, with a hammerstone, instead of striking the core directly with the stone hammer. The punch directs the force of the blow precisely, resulting in longer, narrower, thinner flakes of predictable shape and form (see Figure 10.6). Such a technique, although more highly developed, occurs much later in Europe.

Three sites located in Katanda, Democratic Republic of Congo, provide further evidence that more sophisticated toolmaking appeared earlier in Africa than in either Europe or Asia (Yellen et al. 1995). The sites, dated to about 90,000 ya, have produced rather remarkable bone tools including

FIGURE 10.5 The stone blades found near Lake Baringo in Kenya date to about 240,000 ya. These tools were produced after carefully preparing the stone core from which they were struck, implying a high level of planning on the part of the tool-makers. *(Sally McBrearty)*

FIGURE 10.6 These precisely worked blade tools were recovered from Klasies River Mouth in association with the skeletal remains of early anatomically modern human beings dating to about 100,000 ya. *(From* The Middle Stone Age at Klasies River Mouth, South Africa, *by Ronald Singer and John Wymer, University of Chicago Press)*

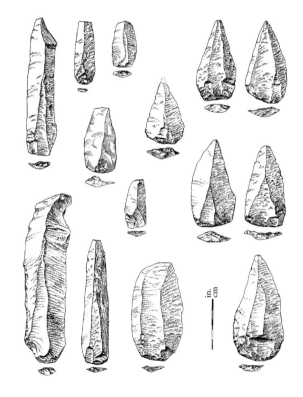

FIGURE 10.7 Barbed bone artifacts found in Katanda, Democratic Republic of Congo. These sophisticated implements date to more than 90,000 ya and may reflect the greater intelligence and technological sophistication of the first anatomically modern *Homo sapiens* when compared to premodern members of our species. *(Allison Brooks, George Washington University)*

barbed, harpoonlike piercing tools (Figure 10.7). These well-made tools required quite a bit of skill to produce. Premodern *Homo sapiens* are not known to have produced anything at this level of skill.

Outside of Africa   If the replacement model is correct, the more intelligent moderns should have brought their more sophisticated tools with them as they expanded out of their African homeland. These new, advanced tools should show up in the archaeological record along with the skeletons of the first anatomically modern human beings.

The artifactual evidence is interesting, although not entirely supportive of this model. The stone tool assemblage of the earlier Neandertals of Europe and Southwest Asia simply does not look very different from the **toolkits** of the early moderns of Africa and Southwest Asia (Wolpoff 1989). Whatever advantage anatomically modern human beings may have had, outside of Africa it does not seem to have been in a more sophisticated material culture. As Alan Thorne and Milford Wolpoff (1992) point out, for example, the artifacts associated with the anatomically modern crania from Skhul and Qafzeh are virtually identical to those recovered from nearby, contemporaneous sites associated with typically Neandertal crania. There are striking similarities at 100,000 ya and even later, and it is not until fairly recently that the Upper Paleolithic modern human inhabitants of Europe produced the far more sophisticated tools of the **Aurignacian** tradition, to be discussed in Chapter 11.

toolkit A group of tools often found in spatial association at an archaeological site, that were used together to perform a particular task.

Aurignacian The toolmaking tradition of anatomically modern *Homo sapiens* of the European Upper Paleolithic.

On the other hand, some scientists do see elements of replacement in the archaeological sequence. Archaeologist Frank Harrold (1989), for example, studied the older Mousterian industry associated with the European Neandertals (see Chapter 9) and a later industry, the **Châtelperronian**, also associated with the later Neandertals; it is the tool industry seen at the Neandertal sites of Saint Césaire (36,000 ya) and Arcy-sur-Cure (34,000 ya). Châtelperronian is considered more "advanced" than Mousterian because it represents a more efficient use of stone (more edge is produced from the same size core) and because it includes tools more finely made with long, precisely sharpened blades (Lévêque 1993).

Harrold compared Mousterian and Châtelperronian with the Aurignacian tool industry of Europe's first anatomically modern humans (see Chapter 11). Aurignacian tools found at Istallöskö in Hungary and Bacho Kiro Cave in Bulgaria (Straus 1989) have been dated to 43,000 ya. Those from the El Castillo and L'Arbreda sites in Spain have been dated to 38,000 ya (Bischoff et al. 1989; Valdes and Bischoff 1989). Harrold found that the Châtelperronian possesses more sophisticated tools than the Mousterian, and the Aurignacian, in turn, is more sophisticated than the Châtelperronian. But there is no sign of an evolution of the simpler Mousterian tradition of the Neandertals to the more sophisticated Aurignacian tradition of the first anatomically modern humans in Europe. Harrold suggests, instead, that Mousterian-wielding Neandertals in Europe developed the more advanced Châtelperronian after coming into contact with and borrowing some ideas from Aurignacian-wielding modern humans who had entered Europe probably from Southwest Asia. In other words, it may be that Neandertals and anatomically modern humans, living at the same time in Europe, came into contact on a regular basis, sharing technology and perhaps even interbreeding. It is a fascinating scenario.

Although the Aurignacian and Châtelperronian share many elements, Harrold suggests that the modern toolkit was slightly better and provided an advantage to the modern humans who used it. So, although the artifactual evidence seems to support the replacement hypothesis, it must be admitted that there is no good evidence in most areas for the wholesale replacement of a primitive tool technology practiced by premodern humans by an advanced technology practiced by modern humans.

Genetic Evidence

We mentioned genetic evidence in Chapter 5 regarding the relationship between humans and the nonhuman primates. Genetic data can also be used to compare living human populations and examine the question of modern human origins. Genetic lines of inquiry have usually been interpreted to support the Recent African Origin model, that is, a recent African source for modern humanity. As we will see, there are other possible interpretations.

Châtelperronian The stone tool industry associated with late Neandertals in Europe.

In general, living human beings exhibit very little genetic variation—in fact, less than that seen within ape species (Stringer and Andrews 1988:1264). Indeed, some chimpanzee DNA exhibits ten times the amount of variation as does human DNA (Wilson and Cann 1992:71; see also the section on biological diversity in this chapter). This suggests a relatively recent, common source for all living humans, which is consistent with the RAO hypothesis. In other words, if there is little genetic diversity, not much time has elapsed since the species first evolved.

On the other hand, the Multiregional Evolution model can also account for this genetic homogeneity. As a mobile species with a network of constant genetic exchange among populations, regional genetic differences would become increasingly lessened as the species increased its population and improved its ability to move around. In such a species, even a very old one, we would also expect relatively little *modern* genetic variation. Thus, our species' genetic homogeneity does not help us distinguish between the two models.

Although overall genetic variation is low in modern human beings, when some details of our DNA are compared across geographic populations, some potentially interesting patterns emerge. There are three basic types of DNA that are used in this regard. We may look at the DNA in the nucleus of our cells, the **nuclear DNA.** Most nuclear DNA is noncoding, and this noncoding DNA is especially useful because it appears to be selectively neutral. Thus, mutations that accumulate in it are neither selected against, resulting in their disappearance, nor selected for, resulting in an increase in their frequency. Therefore, nuclear DNA may provide a more accurate record of the genetic history of two or more divergent lineages.

Of special interest to us is **mitochondrial DNA (mtDNA).** Mitochondria are the energy factories within the cells of plants and animals. They possess their own distinct DNA, which, in complex interaction with the nuclear DNA, codes for the mitochondria's function of producing the biological fuel that energizes the cell. Most human cells contain hundreds or thousands of mitochondria. Mitochondria are particularly useful for some genetic studies because mtDNA accumulates mutations at a rate five to ten times faster than nuclear DNA, and there is evidence that the mutation rate is fairly constant. In addition, the entire mtDNA genome is known; that is, all the **base pairs** have been identified, and there are large noncoding sequences. Finally, mtDNA is inherited only through the female line; although both human eggs and sperm contain mitochondria, the 50 to 100 mitochondria from the sperm disappear from the egg shortly after fertilization. Thus, one's mtDNA is not a combination of the mtDNA from two parents, as is nuclear DNA.

The third type of DNA used is that on the Y chromosome. Analogously to mtDNA, Y-chromosome DNA is inherited only from one's father and is passed on only by males. Thus Y-chromosome analysis allows us to trace inheritance through one parental line with little or no influence from the other.

nuclear DNA The genetic material in the nucleus of a cell.

mitochondrial DNA (mtDNA) The genetic material found in the cell's mitochondria rather than in the cell's nucleus.

base pair Any pair of the four bases (A with T or G with C) in the DNA molecule. These pairings are the basis of the genetic code for the synthesis of proteins.

How are data from these types of DNA used to study the question at hand? The basic idea is that with our ability to sequence DNA, we can specifically compare species and populations within a species at the most basic genetic level. Since at that level evolution is the accumulation of genetic variation through mutation, the genetic differences among populations tell us how many mutations have taken place since they were a single population. We get a measure of relative evolutionary relationships, which allows us to construct "family trees."

Moreover, if we can estimate the mutation rate for a given type of DNA, we can turn these data into a "molecular clock." We ask how long it would take for a certain degree of difference to accumulate between two groups. This, we assume, is how long they have been evolving separately (if two species) or relatively separately (if populations within a species). Then, we may add dates to the family tree.

So what have the studies based on this reasoning told us about the question of modern human origins? Two conclusions from many of these studies are that (1) the world's peoples tend to cluster into two genetic groups, those from sub-Saharan Africa and those from everywhere else, and (2) Africa is more genetically diverse than the rest of the world put together (Figure 10.8). This evidence seems to support the RAO model and a recent African origin of modern humanity. If people have been evolving in Africa longer than elsewhere and only recently spread to the rest of the world, then the African population should be distinct from those of Europe and Asia and should show greater genetic diversity.

The data from these studies could, however, also result if the species were an old, single evolving lineage. Since most of hominid evolution occurred strictly in Africa, that continent has had the largest population for most of human history. A large population on a large and environmentally diverse continent would be expected to have a great deal of genetic diversity and thus be genetically different from all the rest of humanity, which (whether 2 million or 200,000 years old) is more recent (Relethford and Harpending 1995). Moreover, it might be the case that given the geography of the continents, there was more gene flow within Africa and within populations in the rest of the world than *between* Africa and the rest of the world. This would also contribute to a genetic distinction.

All these studies have used DNA from living populations. What about DNA from ancient remains? DNA is not a very stable molecule, and scientists at one time doubted that it could be recovered from old bones. But this has proved possible. Perhaps the most famous ancient DNA samples have come from four Neandertal specimens. The first, from the Neandertal shown in Figure 9.28, consisted of a short sequence of 379 base pairs of mtDNA (out of a total of about 16,500 for human mtDNA). When compared with the same sequence in modern humans, there were more than three times the number of differences between the Neandertal and the moderns than between any two groups of moderns (Krings et al. 1997).

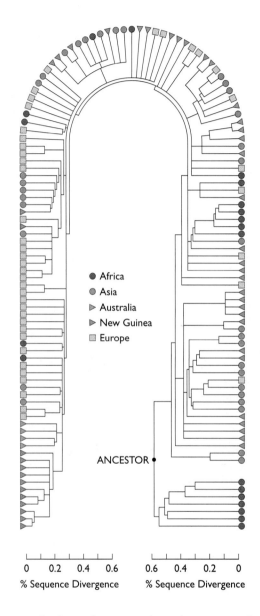

● Africa
◉ Asia
▷ Australia
▷ New Guinea
◻ Europe

ANCESTOR ●

0   0.2   0.4   0.6   0.6   0.4   0.2   0
% Sequence Divergence   % Sequence Divergence

FIGURE 10.8 This computer-generated tree is from an early, limited study (Cann et al. 1987) but demonstrates how such studies work. It shows the lines of descent of 147 women. The diagram is drawn as a horseshoe simply to fit on the page; mentally straighten it out, and you have a more familiar-looking family tree. The higher the percentage figure at the point of divergence (measured against the scale at the bottom of each end), the more different were the women's mtDNA and so the longer ago the divergence took place. Note the cluster of African women at the lower right. They are distinct from other African women and all others (0.6 percent on the scale). They also show greater diversity in their mtDNA, as seen by the fact that their lines of descent converge closer to the center of the diagram, that is, in the more distant past. *(Courtesy Mark Stoneking, Pennslyvania State University)*

Moreover, the sample showed no special similarity to modern Europeans, being equally distinct from all modern populations. The investigators concluded from this that the Neandertals made no contribution to modern human mtDNA and that our two lines diverged 690,000 to 550,000 ya. A follow-up study from the same sample on another section of mtDNA, this time with about 600 base pairs, came to a similar conclusion (Krings et al. 1999). Three more Neandertal samples (Ovchinnikov et al. 2000; Scholz et al. 2000) showed similar results.

In another case (Scholz et al. 2000), DNA was extracted from the bone of an ancient, anatomically modern human found at the Stetten site in Germany. The DNA recovered from this ancient, anatomically modern human bone was much more similar to the DNA of living people than it was the Neandertal DNA of the same period.

MRE proponents have questioned these conclusions. The DNA sequences are short, they note. And, says geneticist Simon Easteal, the fact that chimpanzees have much more mtDNA diversity than do humans shows that "the amount of diversity between Neanderthals and living humans is not exceptional" (Wong 1998). Moreover, one would expect there to be more genetic diversity in the human species in the past, before the larger populations, less isolation, and extensive gene flow of more recent times increased our genetic homogeneity. Clearly, more and larger ancient DNA samples will have to be obtained and studied.

Moreover, in 2000 mtDNA was extracted from ten skeletons in Australia dated at 60,000 to 2,000 ya (Holden 2001a). The oldest skeleton had an mtDNA sequence that differed both from that of similarly dated fossils from other regions and from modern peoples as well. This sequence is, in fact, now extinct in modern mtDNA. This means that an anatomically modern individual with very old, very different DNA lived thousands of miles away from where modern humans are supposed to have originated, supporting the idea that moderns are the result of a multiregional ancestry.

Yet another conclusion from the early mtDNA studies is that the origin of all modern mtDNA can be traced—based on the degree of diversity and the estimated mutation rate—back to somewhere around 150,000 ya. This has been supported by a study (Ingman et al. 2000) that used, for the first time, the entire mtDNA sequence of approximately 16,500 base pairs in a comparison of fifty-three individuals of diverse geographic origins. The study shows a tree rooted in Africa with the most recent common ancestor of all modern humans dated at 171,500 ya, plus or minus 50,000 years. This general age has also been supported by some studies on Y-chromosome DNA (Gibbons 1997b; Ke et al. 2001). One of these studies also found two important variants on the Y chromosome that are shared by other primates and in humans are found today only among Africans—mostly among Khoisan peoples from the Kalahari Desert area. This seems strong support for the RAO model.

Other studies on repeating segments of nuclear DNA (Bower 1995b) and segments of chromosome 12 (Tishkoff et al. 1996) provide similar dates. But all these dates have been called into question. Additional studies, particularly those of Y-chromosome genes, have given widely divergent dates, some as old as 500,000 ya and some as recent as 135,000 ya (Donnelly et al. 1996; Fu and Li 1996; Rogers et al. 1996; Weiss and von Haesler 1996), showing there is less than complete consistency and agreement.

A more general problem is the fact that the history of mtDNA or any other gene "does *not* reflect population history" (Wolpoff and Caspari 1997:302). Rather, it reflects the history of a specific genetic system, in the same way the history of "a single Scottish name might be different from the history of the Scottish people" (304). The evolutionary history of a population involves the histories of many genes. If there was a recent origin of a separate modern human species, then all genetic systems should have similar histories, which does not seem to be the case.

As with fossils and artifacts, the genetic evidence is ambiguous. While most of the analyses appear to support an RAO model, there are serious questions due to the fact that we have so far been able to look at only portions of specific genetic systems. Now, however, with our ever-increasing knowledge of the entirety of the human genome, we should see more extensive research and, eventually, better results. Still, with such a huge amount of data, analytical techniques will have to be refined. For example, even for the data shown in the tree in Figure 10.8, there are millions of different versions, with significantly different results, depending on just how those data are analyzed (Barinaga 1992; Hedges et al. 1992). Genetics may hold the key to resolving this debate, but not yet.

Evolutionary Theory

From the preceding discussion, it is clear that much of the haggling over these two major hypotheses focuses on details of the data. What about some of the broader considerations of evolutionary theory? What happens when we step back and look at the bigger picture? A major issue from this perspective is the plausibility of the gene flow required by the Multiregional Evolution model. Could such gene flow have taken place, and if so, how?

Christopher Stringer (Stringer and McKie 1996:142), representing the Recent African Origin view, thinks that such gene flow is unlikely at best. First, he says, until recent times hominid populations were too thinly spread across the three continents of the Old World to be so connected by gene flow. The gaps between groups were too large for genes to move around as much as MRE requires.

Second, there were too many geographic barriers. There were mountain, desert, and water barriers, and over the past million years or so, large portions of the world were in the grip of the Pleistocene ice ages, which caused extreme climatic disruptions and fluctuations. The flow of genes would have been severely limited by these geographic obstacles.

There are—as you must suspect by now—responses to these issues from the MRE point of view. The apparently thin spread of early human populations across the Old World may be in part attributable to the nature of the fossil record. Remember that most individual hominids who ever lived did not leave fossilized remains, nor have we found but a fraction of all the fossil hominid remains that *were* left. The actual distribution of early populations may have been quite different from the distribution of the fossils recovered.

Moreover, there are two processes involved in gene flow. One is the kind of genetic exchange Stringer cites, where "populations essentially sat still while genes passed through them" (Stringer and McKie 1996:144), that is, exchanged between neighboring groups. But genes also flow as a result of migration. For the past 2 million years, we humans have been a migratory genus. In a short period of time, members of *Homo erectus* got all the way from Africa to Java. There is no reason why humans, having once arrived in these far-flung areas, would necessarily all stay put. They moved because they were following needed resources or looking for better conditions—and the Pleistocene climatic changes may have required a great deal of moving.

In response to the second issue, geographic barriers to human habitation and movement certainly existed and still do. They did not, however, prevent the spread of human populations. Even if there were six different species of *Homo,* the fossil record shows that most managed to move around a bit (see the tables and maps in Chapter 9). And the climatic disruptions of the Pleistocene fluctuated. Barriers changed in severity and location. Sea levels rose and isolated some land areas but then dropped again. Dry periods followed wet periods. Glaciers covered huge masses of land but then retreated. Spread over a 2-million-year period, such temporary and changeable barriers might not have presented severe limitations to gene flow.

Furthermore, we must consider the evidence of possible hybridization between archaics and moderns. We've already discussed the young child from Portugal with both modern and Neandertal features. While some supporters of the RAO model insist the child must be one species or the other, Christopher Stringer, a major RAO proponent, has said that even if this child was a hybrid, hybridization between moderns and Neandertals was rare and had little impact on evolution (Bower 1999a). Elsewhere, Stringer (1994) has claimed that interbreeding may have taken place between archaics and moderns in Eurasia but that it was limited and left no genetic or physical results in modern populations. In a later article, G. Bräuer and Stringer (1997) indicate they think interbreeding did occur, and O. M. Pearson (2000), writing on postcranial remains, admits the possibility of some admixture between moderns and Neandertals.

The problem here is that if there was *any* interbreeding between Neandertals and moderns that led to hybrid and *fertile* individuals, then, by definition, they were members of the same species. This is true even if few or no Neandertal genes or morphological features are still present in modern humans (a debatable point itself). Gene flow between archaics and moderns, no matter how limited, refutes the RAO model and is, rather, basic to the MRE model (Wolpoff et al. 2001:296, n. 3).

Another relevant aspect of evolutionary theory involves the process of speciation (see Chapter 4). New species evolve when a portion of an existing species is completely isolated from the parent species long enough that subsequent genetic and phenotypic change eventually creates an absolute barrier to reproduction. Humans are and have been a mobile species, and our big brains have allowed our genus to experience increasing control over our environments and adaptations to those environments. It would seem to be a rare event for any individual group of such a genus to be isolated long enough to evolve sufficient differences in reproductive behavior or biology to become a technically separate species. The most extreme RAO model (see Lahr and Foley 2004) recognizes as many as *ten* species of *Homo*. In terms of how new species evolve, and the nature of genus *Homo,* this appears highly unlikely indeed.

Perhaps we have been misled because we have examined every available minute genetic and phenotypic variation in living humans and our fossil ancestors through a microscope—literally and figuratively. A single species, as it responds to the processes of evolution over time, may change, of course, and it certainly may show regional variation. But over the long haul, the temporal changes and regional variation within a species occur around some central adaptive theme that defines that species. Our central adaptive theme is our big brains and the resultant behaviors, especially culture, that those brains make possible. Evidence of this theme is found in all accepted members of genus *Homo*—and is absent in all other hominids.

Mostly-Out-of-Africa: An Alternative Model

The data from the fossil and archaeological records, genetics, and evolutionary theory are incapable of unambiguously supporting either the Multiregional Evolution model or the Recent African Origin model. The debate over these models, then, seems to be without solution. But there is now another model that appears to reconcile the existing data. Forms of this model have been expressed by, among others, biologist Alan Templeton, who titles his article "Out of Africa Again and Again" (Templeton 2002), and bioanthropologist John Relethford (2001, 2003). Relethford calls it the "Mostly-Out-of-Africa" model.

The basic idea is straightforward enough: that while *most* of the ancestors of modern humans are from Africa, not *all* are. The Mostly-Out-of-Africa model agrees that our species is an old one, perhaps as old as almost 2 million years, and that a network of gene flow maintained that species' identity across all geographic regions. Thus, it is a multiregional model.

But it also acknowledges the evidence from the fossil record that modern human anatomy, for the most part, seems to have originated in Africa. And it acknowledges the evidence from genetics that tends to point to greater genetic diversity in Africa and a degree of differentiation between

FIGURE 10.9 The multiple expansion, or Mostly-Out-of-Africa, model. Vertical lines represent direct regional descent, that is, regional continuity. Diagonal lines represent a network of recurrent gene flow among regional populations. (Actual gene flow, of course, would not have been this regular or even.) The red arrows represent major population expansions. In the original diagram, Templeton indicates that there is genetic evidence for the timing and direction of each of these expansions, as well as for certain sections of the network of gene flow. Note that, at least early on, Africa made major contributions to the gene pool and, thus, to the traits of the rest of the world. Also note that none of the expansions is a replacement or a speciation event, just the spread of a sample of genes among an existing, widespread species. *(Adapted from Templeton 2002:48)*

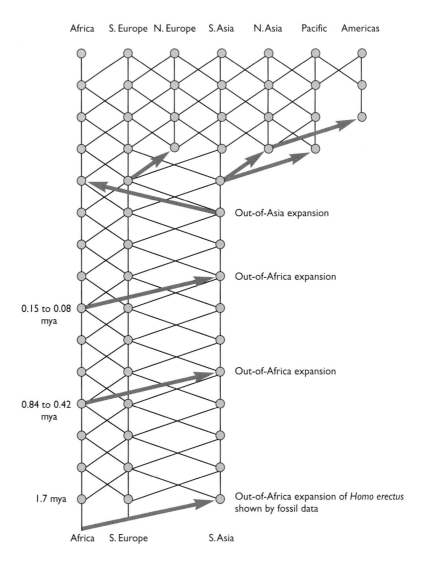

African DNA and that of every other regional population, in the sense that all other populations are really subsets of the genome of Africans. How can these ideas work together?

Perhaps there were at least two major expansions out of Africa, the first being in *Homo erectus* times and the latest around the time suggested as the origin of modern *Homo sapiens* (Figure 10.9). There may well have been other expansions, not all necessarily "out of Africa." These expansions would have spread collections of genes and traits across geographic space. Thus, the evolution of at least some features of modern human anatomy, and the genes that coded for them, could have occurred first in Africa, but their spread around the world would not necessarily have resulted in the replacement of one species by a new one. Rather, the features spread via gene flow among existing populations that descended from the first and subsequent expansions. Indeed, Templeton's study (2002), using seven types of genetic data and a sophisticated statistical analytic procedure, has suggested times and directions of some of the expansions, both out of Africa and elsewhere.

Moreover, the genetic data can be explained, because Africa—being the homeland of the hominids and the only place hominid evolution took place for millions of years—would have had for a long time a larger human population than the rest of the world. Thus, the contribution of African genes and traits would have been disproportionately large. As a result, African DNA is the most diverse (being the oldest), with the DNA of other populations being a subset of the African genome.

Point–Counterpoint: The Authors Debate the Debate

Science can be exciting, exasperating, and infuriating. Our knowledge is never perfect or even complete; there are always more data to collect and new interpretations of the data we have in hand. Nevertheless, in order to truly explain some aspect of the universe—how our planet formed, how life evolved, or how humanity developed—scientists attempt to connect the dots, even though we don't know where most of the dots are located and even while we continue looking for those missing dots. Science is characterized by uncertainty. Rather than being intellectually paralyzed by this uncertainty, however, science is typified by its courage to go out on a limb and suggest—some might call it "guess"—an explanation for some element of the universe, despite the fact that we don't have all the data and maybe never will. To use another analogy, approaching this uncertainty is like trying to predict the appearance of an entire jigsaw puzzle when only a small fraction of the pieces have been found and fewer still have been joined together. To extend the analogy, the prediction of the "big picture"—made up of the paleoanthropological record, or the puzzle pieces—provides a template that actually helps in putting that picture together.

As you have seen in this chapter's discussion, this is certainly the case for the big picture of the evolution of modern humanity. Our data are complex and incomplete and have been interpreted and explained in many ways, producing multiple big pictures. Randomly select any two anthropologists—maybe even two long-time colleagues, even coauthors of a textbook—and ask for their opinion concerning the evolution of modern human beings. You are likely to get two very different interpretations. You need to understand that this is not a weakness of science; in fact, it is a significant strength. The utility and validity of proposed explanations can only benefit from skeptical questioning. This leads us to our version of point–counterpoint concerning the evolution of modern *Homo sapiens*.

Feder: It appears that those who support the Multiregional Evolution ("out-of-everywhere") model now agree that some of the evidence confirms at least an attenuated version of the Out-of-Africa (or Recent African Origin) model. How has this shift in thinking occurred?

MRE supporters are absolutely correct in asserting that we cannot know for sure whether any of the premodern versions of humanity discussed in this text—or, for that matter, other named groups, such as *Homo erectus*—and modern human beings actually belong to the same or to separate species. We are uncertain because we can't answer the fundamental question: Could they mate and produce fertile offspring? I imagine, however, that even the most steadfast proponent of MRE is comfortable with the assertion, for example, that modern human beings and *Tyrannosaurus rex* don't belong to the same species, though we are faced with the same challenge in testing that assertion. I am being facetious, but at any given time in the course of scientific research, we need to base our reasoning on the kind of data we actually have access to. We have bones and artifacts, and our hypothesis testing must be based on our analysis of bones and artifacts.

In testing any scientific hypothesis, we need to make predictions concerning what new data must necessarily be found to support the hypothesis. The hypothesis that anatomically modern humans appeared first in one location fairly recently (within the last 200,000 years) and spread out from there, encountering older, archaic or "premodern" varieties of human beings who they then replaced, has held up pretty well, though by no means definitively, in such testing. For example, before any mtDNA was recovered from fossil hominid bones, it was understood that if such recovery were possible, the DNA of premoderns and modern human beings would have to show significant differences in order to support the Recent African Origin, or replacement, model. As discussed here, this is precisely what has been found. Before the discovery of sophisticated tools in Africa at sites occupied by ancient, anatomically modern human beings, it was understood by RAO supporters that the existence of such tools—implying more sophisticated toolmaking abilities and, therefore, greater intelligence when compared to other ancient hominids—should be found. Such tools have been found in Africa, dating to a time significantly before they are found outside of that continent.

Neither of these predictions flowed readily from the MRE model. Many MRE proponents have recognized that the fulfillment of these predictions lends a degree of support to the RAO model, though certainly not the most extreme versions. This has resulted, most recently, in the proposal of the Mostly-Out-of-Africa hypothesis, which in my view is essentially the RAO model, though with some significant caveats. We all agree that hominids originated in Africa, perhaps as much as 6 mya. There is a growing consensus that anatomically modern humans originated there as much as 200,000 ya. We also all agree that we have only touched on the complexity of modern human origins and, cliché though it may be, it is the case that only additional research will enable paleoanthropologists and archaeologists to more completely illuminate that complexity.

Park: The fossil and archaeological data are, at this point at least, irrelevant, since they cannot support one model over the other. No cultural evidence can possibly determine a species distinction between two populations, and there is no way to go back in time and conduct the only biological test that would determine species identity—a test for the ability to interbreed.

Thus, we are left to sort through this scientific dialogue with genetic evidence and evolutionary theory. While genetic data have been variously interpreted, most of it does lean toward a recent African origin of many of the genetic systems examined and a pattern suggesting that many African populations and all non-African populations are a genetic subset of the gene pool of sub-Saharan Africa. This appears to offer "hi-tech" support for the RAO model.

However, a strict RAO model calls for at least a species distinction between anatomically modern humans and archaics, and most versions of this model recognize multiple—as many as ten—species of genus *Homo* among archaics. This strikes me as absurd.

Speciation requires isolation that is long enough and complete enough to allow the accumulation of genetic distinctions that (by chance) include some biological barrier to reproduction. For this to happen as many as ten times in the 2-million-year history of *Homo* staggers the imagination. Our genus has always been highly mobile, exchanges genes regularly, and is increasingly culturally adapted (as opposed to completely relying on natural selection). These factors argue against populations of our genus becoming isolated and differentiated enough to be technically separate species warranting different taxonomic names.

Thus, I favor the Mostly-Out-of-Africa model or something like it, which acknowledges our single-species status back as far as 2 million years (when we first see anatomical and behavioral characteristics that define our type of primate) but also explains, in demographic terms, the distribution of our genetic diversity as pointing to a major influence of some fairly recent African genes in the total human gene pool.

Biological Diversity in Modern Humans

Anatomically modern *Homo sapiens* inhabits a wide geographic range. Indigenous populations of our species are found on all the continents but Antarctica. We live in environments ranging from frigid Arctic tundra to

FIGURE 10.10 A European American photographer with a group of Yali people from the highlands of Irian Jaya (the western half of New Guinea). There is little doubt as to who is who or that members of our species can display a striking degree of phenotypic variation. The major question then becomes: Does this degree of variation mean that there are distinguishable human races? *(© George Steinmetz)*

endogamy Marriage restricted to those within the same social group.

polymorphism A trait showing variation within a species as a result of genetic variation.

hot, dry deserts; from low-lying, humid tropical rainforests to the cold, thin air of mountains thousands of feet high. One would certainly expect evolution to have acted on us over these many years and in these many environments to bring about a great deal of biological variation.

In addition, such widespread populations must have a degree of isolation from one another (isolation by distance). Indigenous populations of Central Africa do not exchange genes directly with peoples in the North American Arctic. Moreover, human populations add to their reproductive isolation through cultural rules of **endogamy,** which, for purposes of maintaining cultural, religious, or ethnic identity, require people to find mates only within their group. As a result, even human populations living side by side may not exchange genes on a regular basis.

Our wide geographic spread coupled with this cultural isolation makes it no surprise that modern humans display a large number of **polymorphisms** or that certain clusters of these polymorphisms are characteristic of particular geographic areas (Figure 10.10). Nor can there be any doubt that the explanation for human polymorphisms lies in the processes of evolution acting on populations as they spread out into their incredible variety of environments.

At issue are two concerns: first, the nature and extent of the role of natural selection and the other evolutionary processes in producing our variation, and second, whether our variation is such that we are divisible into identifiable biological races.

Natural Selection and Human Variation

To determine the role of natural selection in bringing about the variable expressions of a trait, one must first try to link those expressions to particular environmental circumstances. This is a difficult task with humans. For one thing, we have always been a mobile species, and with modern modes of transportation and motives for travel, we are becoming more so. As a result, urban centers contain a wide cross section of human biological variation; nearly every corner of the world must be represented by the inhabitants of New York City, for example. We must try, then, to make generalizations about the distributions of our polymorphisms, usually by using only indigenous groups, those that we can assume represent populations that have been in certain geographic areas for long periods of time.

In addition, as we have shown in previous chapters, culture allows us to adapt to new environmental conditions much more quickly than natural selection can evolve adaptations. Thus, one of our most notable biological traits, our big brain, has actually allowed us, via culture, to buffer ourselves increasingly against some of the action of natural selection. Traits that may have been selectively disadvantageous may now, in the context of our cultural adaptations, be neutral. Biological fitness is relative to the environment in which a trait is found. Where a society can correct physical impairments, these are no longer a barrier to reproductive success. If they have a genetic basis, they may then be passed on to future generations. Similarly, if some infectious disease is cured, then any genes it selected for or against may now vary at random through genetic drift. As a result, it can be difficult to tell just how important natural selection is in determining the existence and distribution of a human polymorphism.

For instance, the variation in blood type for the ABO system, a trait controlled by a single gene with three alleles, remained a mystery for some time—and is still not entirely understood. All people have one of four phenotypes: A, B, AB, or O (as do chimps and gorillas, by the way). These types appear in markedly different frequencies around the world (Figure 10.11). Type A, for example, is totally absent among some native South American groups but is found in frequencies of over 50 percent in parts of Europe, native Australia, and among a few native North American groups (although in North America it is still generally found among less than a quarter of the population). Type O, the most common worldwide, still ranges from 40 percent in parts of Asia to 100 percent among some native South Americans.

Studies have indicated that persons with particular blood types have greater susceptibility to such disorders as duodenal ulcers, stomach cancer, forms of anemia, bronchial pneumonia, smallpox, bubonic plague,

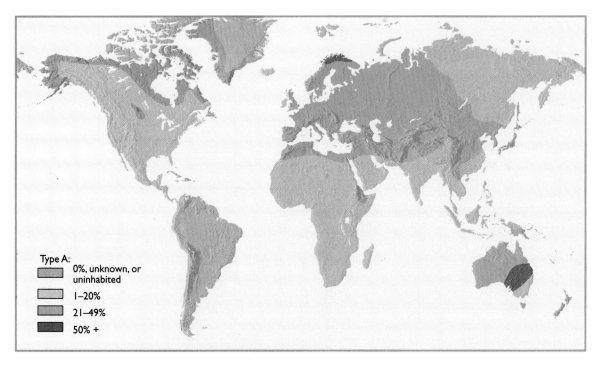

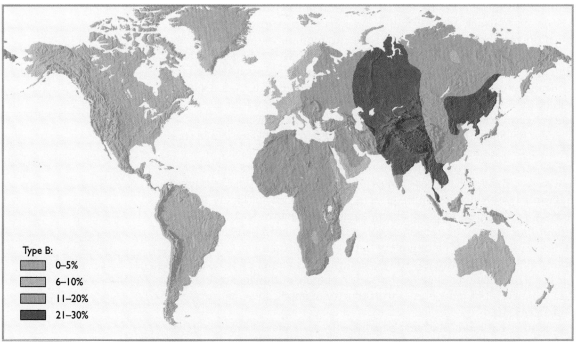

FIGURE 10.11 Approximate frequency distributions of type A and type B blood, demonstrating the lack of a pattern in the distribution of this polymorphism.

and typhoid. Type O persons seem more attractive to mosquitoes, which, as we saw in the discussion of sickle cell anemia, can be disease carriers (see Chapter 4). But the completion of such blood-type studies is hindered by two obstacles. First, because humans have gained a good deal of control over many of these diseases, it is difficult to gather data about their links to blood type on a worldwide scale. We are forced to look into the past, before such control was gained, and thus make inferences based on historical records—data that are less than ideal. Second, we have yet to establish a cause-and-effect connection: What is it about certain blood types that makes the people who have them more or less susceptible to a disease or to the bite of an insect?

Perhaps phenotypic traits more directly and obviously affected by outside environmental conditions would be easier to explain adaptively. The human polymorphism of skin color is the classic example. Skin color is determined largely by the amount of the pigment melanin produced in the lowest layer of skin and distributed in the upper layers. This is a genetically controlled trait, though the exact genetic mechanism is still unknown.

Looking at indigenous populations, we see that darker skin is generally found closer to the equator, and skin color gets lighter north and south of that line (Figure 10.12). Sunlight is more intense and less affected by seasonal fluctuations at the equator, and too much ultraviolet (UV) radiation from the sun can cause sunburn, with accompanying cell destruction, infection, and heat exhaustion. Excessive exposure to the sun has also been shown to cause skin cancer. More directly related to reproductive success, UV radiation can break down folic acid, a chemical required for normal embryo development and sperm production. On the other hand, ultraviolet light is necessary for the synthesis of vitamin D, important for proper bone growth. Because human evolution began in the tropics (some early hominid fossils are found right on the equator), our distant ancestors probably had dark skin. Populations that stayed in tropical regions retained this dark skin; those that moved away from the tropics underwent selection for lighter skin pigmentation.

It was thought that in such populations, those with darker skin could not manufacture sufficient vitamin D for normal bone growth and maintenance. Those with lighter skin, therefore, had an adaptive advantage. Over time, lighter skin became the normal, inherited condition in such groups. Skin color was thus seen as a balancing act—dark enough to protect from the damaging effects of UV radiation but light enough to allow the beneficial effects.

There are, however, some human polymorphisms for which selective explanations, of varying strengths, exist. We discussed sickle cell anemia in Chapter 4. Another example is body build, which tends to be linear in hot climates to promote heat loss and, as with the Neandertals, stockier in cold climates to preserve heat (Figure 10.13). Noses are long and narrow in cold or dry areas to help warm and moisten the air taken into the lungs.

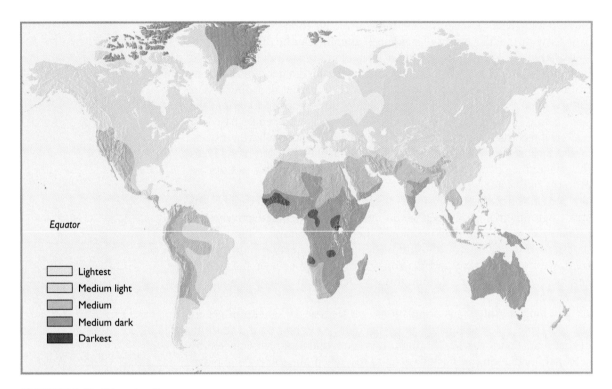

FIGURE 10.12 Skin color distribution. Darker skin is concentrated in equatorial regions. Compare the distribution of this polymorphism with the blood groups from Figure 10.11.

Short and broad noses are more common in places where air is already warm and moist.

Of course, some phenotypic variation may result not from natural selection to particular environmental circumstances but from one of the random processes of evolution—gene flow and genetic drift (see Chapter 4). This especially may be the case because human groups tend to be temporarily genetically isolated through geography or culture but are generally mobile and prone to genetic exchange. Groups have also, for most of human history, been relatively small. These are, as you recall, the conditions under which gene flow and genetic drift work best. For example, the high incidence of blood type A among the Blackfeet Indians might be attributed to the founder effect—the population being originally founded by a small group that, by chance, was uncharacteristically high in type A. Or, in a small ancestral Blackfeet population, allele frequencies may have drifted toward a high percentage of type A.

If natural selection is not actively selecting for or against the frequencies of a set of alleles, these random processes are free to operate. Because not all variation is adaptively important all the time—and some variation may not be important at all—gene flow and genetic drift can have major effects on the distribution of alleles. For example, one of us (Park 1979,

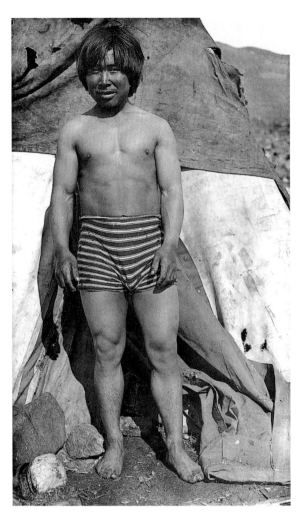 

FIGURE 10.13 Body build is in part selected for conservation of heat, as in the Inuit (*left*) or promotion of heat loss, as in the Masai cattle herder from Kenya (*right*). (*Inuit: Courtesy Department of Library Services. American Museum of Natural History. Photo by D. B. MacMillan, July 1916, Neg. #231604; Masai: Bruce Dale/NGS Image Collection*)

2005) found a significant degree of variation in inherited features of fingerprints among populations and between generations of the Hutterites, a religious group that lives in isolated communities in the western United States and Canada. Because these variables in fingerprints are of no known adaptive significance, this variation could only be the result of gene flow, founder effect, and gamete sampling.

In addition, variation results from environmental effects operating on the genotype-phenotype relationship. Although not entirely understood, there is clearly some nongenetic influence on certain aspects of human fingerprints. One's skin color at any point in time is certainly affected by nongenetic factors such as a person's health status and the amount of ultraviolet radiation he or she is exposed to. So some of the variation in certain phenotypic traits may be caused by complex direct environmental action. One's blood type, however, is only under genetic control. No influence from the environment can change it.

Modern humans display numerous variable traits. Some can be explained as the result of natural selection to certain environmental contexts. Others are accounted for by flow and drift. Many show regularity in terms of their geographic distribution. Does this mean that our species consists of identifiable subspecies, semispecies, or races?

The Question of Human Races

Look again at Figure 10.10. Although all the people in that photograph are members of the same species, *Homo sapiens,* the man in the middle and the other men are about as different as humans can look. Not only that, but with some background knowledge one could easily place them geographically. Surely, then, they belong to two definable, nameable biological subgroups within the species—that is, two subspecies or races. And surely, then, if we accept these two, there must be others.

The fact is, however, that *on a biological level,* human subspecies or races do not exist. There is no scientifically valid way to divide us up into any number of meaningful biological groups below the species level. And this is more than just wishful thinking. There are four areas of clear evidence that support this conclusion.

First, biologists in general are abandoning the concept of defined, named groups below the species level, that is, subspecies or races. Although most species show regional variation, there are no clear-cut boundaries between groups of variants. Remember, a species is held together by gene flow. As a result, variable traits (polymorphisms) within a species are distributed as **clines,** that is, variable expressions that grade into one another over geographical space (Figure 10.14).

Second, the situation with human polymorphic traits is no different. Although some human traits or trait clusters tend to be geographically localized (see again Figure 10.10), nearly all our features are spread across many populations and geographic areas. Dark skin, as just one example, is an equatorial trait, not only an African one, as many are inclined to consider it. In fact, no real boundaries exist between trait expressions. Although we divided skin-color expression into five categories for the sake of diagramming its distribution (see Figure 10.12), skin color doesn't change abruptly as the map might imply. It changes gradually in populations close to or farther from the equator. Such a clinical distribution simply cannot be divided into discrete units because its expressions don't come in neat packages with clear geographic boundaries. The same can be said with the distribution of blood groups (see Figure 10.11). Again, the categories on these maps are arbitrary. We could have divided the range of

cline A geographic continuum in the variation of a specific phenotype.

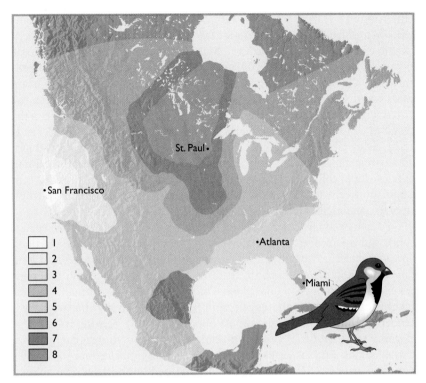

FIGURE 10.14 Distribution of size variation in male house sparrows, determined by sixteen skeletal measurements. The larger the number, the larger the sparrow. The classes, however, are arbitrary. If a line is drawn from Atlanta to St. Paul or from St. Paul to San Francisco, the size variation in the sparrows is distributed as a cline, a continuum of change from one area to another.

frequencies into more groups or fewer, and the maps would have looked very different. But, no matter how many categories, the distribution of this polymorphism is also a cline.

In addition, when we compare the distributions of human polymorphisms, we see incongruities. The distribution of one trait seldom matches the distribution of any other. A racial division based on one trait will invariably differ from that based on another. Compare the maps for blood type and skin color (Figures 10.11 and 10.12), for instance. The variations of these traits are very different in their distributions. It would be hard to force either of these traits—or nearly any human trait—into biologically meaningful units. At the phenotypic level, human variation *does* exist, but human races *don't*.

Third, as recent studies have shown, we are a very homogeneous species genetically. New technologies now allow us access to the most basic genetic level. We are quickly gathering data about the extent of diversity at that level—the variations of base pairs, or single nucleotide polymorphisms (SNPs), that account for most human genetic variation and, of course, phenotypic variation. There are about 10 million SNPs in the human population, but any two people differ, on average, by only 3 million SNPs

(International HapMap Consortium 2003; Stoneking 2001). This means that, on average, any two humans are more than 99 percent genetically identical at the most basic genetic level. Moreover, because most of the genome is noncoding, most of those SNPs are in noncoding regions. Only an estimated 60,000 are in actual genes (International SNP Map Working Group 2001), and many of those may be involved in the differences between the two sexes. All the phenotypic variation that we try to assort into race is the result of a virtual handful of alleles. The genetic variation that does exist is relatively evenly distributed. Richard Lewontin (1982:123) calculates that if some great cataclysm left only Africans alive, that remnant of the human species would still retain 93 percent of the variable genes of the former world population. As with phenotypic features, we cannot divide genetic variation up into meaningful biological units at the level of subspecies or races.

Fourth, we may look at evolutionary theory as it applies to our species. Since our species arose (whenever that was) and while we have been spreading and moving about, no human population has been isolated long enough or completely enough to allow absolutely separate and independent genetic changes to take place. During all that time, humans have in fact become increasingly mobile, and it seems fair to say that we have a tendency to exchange genes at most opportunities. To be sure, rules of endogamy exist, and they tend to isolate certain populations genetically at certain times. But such rules are not always fully upheld, and sometimes they are changed. Also, the populations defined by the rules change over time. Endogamy is a temporary condition. Geographic isolation is temporary. Gene flow is the real rule.

Then there is the matter of culture—our major adaptive mechanism. Even where natural selection had an effect on certain characteristics, such as skin color, these adaptive differences were minor compared to the major adaptation of culture. The cultural adaptation was well developed and part of our hominid line long before modern humans appeared. Our big brains—the basis of our cultural potential—are shared by all modern humans and are so important and basic that they are unlikely to show much major variation. Further, the products of the cultural ability—social systems, beliefs, technology—act as a buffer against much of the effect of natural selection.

Our variation, then, is part of ongoing dynamic processes: the editing by natural selection of traits within a widespread, highly mobile, generalized species combined with the operation of the other processes of evolution on our temporarily isolated but generally highly mobile individual populations. Such a situation doesn't allow for the kinds of conditions necessary to produce distinguishable subspecies or races.

If the above sounds familiar, that's because it is much the same argument supporters of the Multiregional Evolution model use to explain why genus *Homo* did not branch into multiple species. If an organism with our

CONTEMPORARY ISSUE

Is There a Connection between Modern Human Origins and Race?

"The Out-of-Africa model makes mincemeat of racial difference" reads a quote on the back of Christopher Stringer and Robin McKie's *African Exodus: The Origins of Modern Humanity* (1996). The title of Milford Wolpoff and Rachel Caspari's (1997) book is *Race and Human Evolution: A Fatal Attraction.* What is the connection between race and the models we examined?

The biological unity of our species is now a well-documented fact, and it leads to certain socially relevant ideas and ideals—namely, that although individual humans vary in many ways, there exist no profound inherent differences *among human groups* that would warrant differential treatment in social and cultural environments. Skin color, for example, is no predictor of intellectual capabilities.

A majority of anthropologists have leaned toward the Recent African Origin model not only because many believe the data support it but also because it neatly explains our species' current homogeneity. If our species is very young—only a few hundred thousand years at most—and if it arose from one localized population, then it could not possibly display deep and profound variations among its populations. There simply hasn't been enough time. If the RAO model is correct, human races could not exist. This makes the RAO model attractive indeed.

Moreover, it has been stated by some RAO supporters that one fatal problem with the Multiregional Evolution model is that it does "suggest, at face value, that modern humanity's constituent races are divided by fundamental and deep-rooted differences" (Stringer and McKie 1996:60). If, such arguments go, local populations show continuity of features into the distant past, that implies that modern racial groups are themselves very ancient and profoundly different. Such a suggestion goes against current social ideals, not to mention the scientific facts regarding our relative homogeneity.

There were, to be sure, earlier models of a multiregional perspective that did make such suggestions. In his 1962 book *The Origin of Races,* anthropologist Carleton Coon proposed that five subspecies, or races, of *Homo erectus* independently evolved into five major races of *Homo sapiens,* crossing "a critical threshold from a more brutal to a more *sapient* state" (658). To make matters worse, he claimed that the different races crossed the "sapiens threshold" at different times and that this accounted for some of the differences we see today in levels of cultural complexity. "If all races had a recent common origin," he asked, "why were the Tasmanians and many of the Australian aborigines still living during the nineteenth century in a manner comparable to that of Europeans of over 100,000 years ago?" (4). It is clear who Coon thought crossed the threshold first and last. Such ideas may well have sensitized anthropologists against any model of our evolution that included great time depth for the species and regional continuity of traits.

The modern MRE model, however, is quite different from Coon's and other early ideas. The MRE model does not claim that *populations* show continuity but that some regional *traits* do, especially traits that are found in fairly isolated areas, such as Australia and other places on the margins of the human geographic range. So-called racial groups are not now, nor were they ever, completely isolated. Rather, the species has displayed continual gene flow, enough to maintain species identity and spread physical features and their genes all over the world.

But this is all really a nonissue. Even if the extreme single-species MRE model proves correct, today's human species is *still* genetically and physically homogeneous. We know this because of well-established scientific studies of genetics and morphology. How we got to be this way doesn't change how we are, and either major model under debate could account for our current nature. As anthropologist Matt Cartmill puts it, "We are what we are, not what our ancestors were. . . . The truth of racial egalitarianism hinges on the facts about living people. Their genealogies are irrelevant" (1997:62).

characteristic network of genetic (and cultural) exchange has not divided into definable *subspecific* groups, how likely is it to have split into different related *species*?

This does not mean, however, that the modern human species is one gigantic stew of people, with no discernible groups and thus no way to trace the history of populations. Whereas phenotypic traits only serve to confuse the matter, increasing knowledge of genetics does permit precise comparisons of living indigenous populations to one another and, thus, the creation of "family trees" showing where populations originated and how they spread.

Some of the genetic studies noted earlier with regard to the origin of modern *Homo sapiens* have allowed researchers to produce trees indicating the relationships among populations from which the DNA samples were drawn. One early study by L. L. Cavalli-Sforza (Cavalli-Sforza 1991) found that the distribution of genes coincided to a great degree with the distribution of languages. Languages and genetic populations can be correlated because as human populations split and separate, "each fragment evolves linguistic and genetic patterns that bear marks of shared branching points" (Cavalli-Sforza 1991:109). In addition, "linguistic differences [and the cultural differences they reflect] may generate or reinforce genetic barriers between populations. Hence, some correlation is inevitable" (1991:109). Figure 10.15 is a simplified diagram of this correlation.

Our species doesn't sort itself into the clear-cut, ancient, and profoundly different racial groups assumed by earlier generations. We are too mobile, too genetically homogeneous, and too culturally adapted for that. But the richness of our genetic, ethnic, and cultural variety is not lost within some worldwide melting pot. And to say that there are human populations, identified by several correlated factors, is not to say that such groups are in any way so different as to warrant differential social treatment. We have far more similarities than we do differences. Still, racism—often based on a misreading of the biological facts—remains one of our most vexing problems.

Summary

Although the evidence is far more substantial for the most recent 500,000 years of hominid evolution than for the first 3.5 million, the origin, nature, and development of anatomically modern human beings are still points of contention and controversy for paleoanthropologists. Neither of the two competing models—Multiregional Evolution or Recent African Origin—has been definitively supported at this time. The evidence currently available from paleontology, genetics, archaeology, and evolutionary theory is ambiguous, incomplete, and can be interpreted differently by

Genetic Groups	Living Populations	Linguistic Groups
African	San	Khoisan
	Masai	Nilo-Saharan
	Mbuti	Niger-Congo
	Ethiopian	Afro-Asiatic
Caucasoid	Southwestern Asian	
	Mediterranean	Indo-European
	Northern European	
	Indian	
American	North American	Amerind
	Central American	
	South American	
Arctic	Eskimo	Eskimo-Aleut
	Siberian	Altaic
Northeast Asian	Japanese	
	Korean	
	Tibetan	Sino-Tibetan
Mainland Island Southeast Asian	Southern Chinese	
	Indonesian	
	Philippine	Austronesian
	Polynesian	
Pacific Islands	Melanesian	Indo-Pacific
	New Guinean	Australian
	Australian	

FIGURE 10.15 The correlation between genetic and language groups within modern humans. The living populations listed are a representative sample. Note that where populations live close to one another under similar conditions, as is the case for Ethiopians and Southwest Asians, they may speak languages of the same group even though they are genetically different. (*Data from Cavalli-Sforza 1991*)

each camp in support of its position. Some alternative model, such as the Mostly-Out-of-Africa model, may provide the solution.

The current state of our species includes a striking degree of phenotypic variation. Our polymorphic traits, some showing geographical regularity in distribution, may be explained as the result of the processes of evolution acting on a widespread, populous, mobile, and culture-bearing species. These traits, however, do not sort themselves into clear-cut, discrete categories that would constitute subspecies, semispecies, or races.

Study Questions

1. Contrast the MRE and RAO models of the evolution of anatomically modern *Homo sapiens.*
2. How, and in what ways, does the hominid fossil record support or refute each of the models to explain the evolution of anatomically modern *Homo sapiens?*
3. How, and in what ways, does modern human genetics support or refute each of the models to explain the evolution of anatomically modern *Homo sapiens?*
4. How, and in what ways, does material culture—the artifacts recovered by archaeologists—support or refute each of the models to explain the evolution of anatomically modern *Homo sapiens?*
5. How, and in what ways, does evolutionary theory support or refute each of the models to explain the evolution of anatomically modern *Homo sapiens?*
6. Explain one alternative model for the origin of modern humans.
7. What is the nature of the biological diversity within the human species? What processes account for variable phenotypes?
8. Based on this knowledge, what can we say—on a biological level—about the existence of human races?

Key Terms

Multiregional Evolution (MRE) model	Mostly-Out-of-Africa model	mitochondrial DNA (mtDNA)
Out-of-Africa model	toolkit	base pair
Recent African Origin (RAO) model	Aurignacian	endogamy
	Châtelperronian	polymorphism
	nuclear DNA	cline

For More Information

There is extensive literature about the RAO/MRE debate. We especially recommend the two books by the major proponents of each point of view: *Race and Human Evolution: A Fatal Attraction,* by Milford Wolpoff and Rachel Caspari, in support of the MRE model, and *African Exodus: The Origins of Modern Humanity,* by Christopher Stringer and Robin McKie, in support of the RAO model. The Wolpoff and Caspari book includes a good historical review of the issue. For the newer Mostly-Out-of-Africa model, see Alan Templeton's "Out of Africa Again and Again" in the March 7, 2002 *Nature* and John Relethford's two highly readable books, the more technical *Genetics and the Search for Modern Human Origins* and the more popular and broader *Reflections of Our Past: How Human History Is Revealed in Our Genes.*

On race, we highly recommend Stephen Molnar's *Human Variation: Races, Types, and Ethnic Groups.* This text covers the entire issue of race from an anthropological viewpoint. It includes detailed sections on our variable traits. Another treatment of the same subject, but from a biologist, is Richard Lewontin's *Human Diversity.* A book on the subject, and one that includes an extended discussion of race and athletic ability, is Jonathan Marks's *Human Biodiversity: Genes, Race, and History.*

For a collection of articles on the nonexistence of human biological races, see *The Concept of Race,* edited by Ashley Montagu, and for a nice treatment of the history of race studies, try Kenneth A. R. Kennedy's *Human Variation in Space and Time.* Also, see the chapters on race in Jonathan Marks's *What It Means to Be 98% Chimpanzee.*

The analysis of human genetic differences and what they tell us about the history of human groups is nicely covered by Luigi Luca Cavalli-Sforza and Francesco Cavalli-Sforza in *The Great Human Diasporas: The History of Diversity and Evolution.*

The best books on racism are Stephen Jay Gould's *The Mismeasure of Man* and *Race Is a Four-Letter Word,* by C. Loring Brace.

For some of the latest information on the study of human genetic diversity, see "The Greatest Journey" by James Shreeve in the March 2006 *National Geographic.*

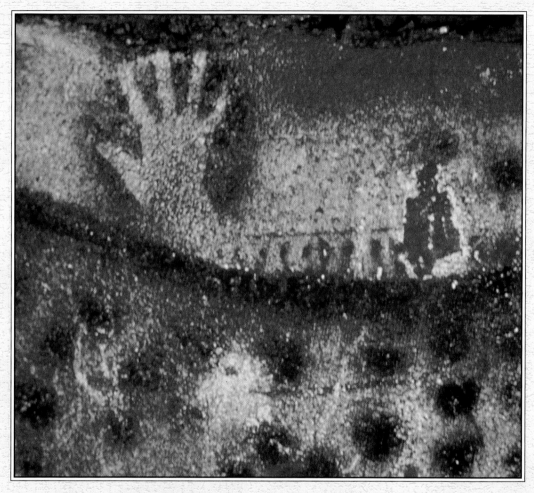

The cave paintings of the Upper Paleolithic are recognizable as modern human behavior; they are, in fact, art. What is the significance of the apparent intellectual leap forward that characterizes this period? How and when did the Upper Paleolithic inhabitants of the Old World expand into Australia and North and South America? *(© Musée de l'Homme. Photo by B. et G. Delluc)*

11

NEW IDEAS, NEW WORLDS
Life in the Upper Paleolithic

CHAPTER CONTENTS

Comparing the Middle and Upper Paleolithic

Art in the European Upper Paleolithic

Brave New Worlds

Summary

Study Questions

Key Terms

For More Information

Regardless of when our species first evolved, soon after 200,000 ya, people who looked just like us appear in the fossil record of Africa. With modern-sized brains, these anatomically modern humans are assumed to have been intellectually modern as well, in the sense that they possessed the same level of intelligence as us. Certainly, their cultures differed from ours, but the consensus is that their intellectual capabilities were identical; if an anatomically modern human being from 200,000 ya could be transported to the present and given your education, he or she could read this book and understand it as well as you.

As shown in Chapters 9 and 10, the fossil record indicates that human beings attained what appears to be anatomical modernity soon after 200,000 ya. In particular, the cranial capacities and overall skull shapes of fossils such as Omo I (195,000 years old) and Herto (165,000 years old) are fundamentally modern; they looked just like us. This leads to the implication that their brains were like ours as well, with the same innate capacity for intelligence. Herein lies an apparent mystery: though their skeletons look modern, by and large their cultures, as reflected in the archaeological record, do not appear to differ greatly from those of their anatomically premodern predecessors and contemporaries.

There are, however, glimmers of intellectual leaps forward among the earliest anatomically modern *Homo sapiens:* for example, the 240,000-year-old blade tools found near Lake Baringo in Kenya, the 100,000-year-old blade tools found at Klasies River Mouth in South Africa, and the finely made bone tools found at the Katanda sites in the Democratic Republic of the Congo, dating to over 90,000 ya (see Chapter 10). The efficient use of stone reflected in the stone blade tools and the precision required to produce the Katanda bone tools imply great intelligence, exceeding, perhaps, the capabilities of premodern humans.

Hints at the existence of modern intelligence are found not only in utilitarian tools, but also in the earliest evidence for artistic and symbolic expression reflected in nonutilitarian objects. For example, consider the 71 lumps of red ochre found in Qafzeh Cave, Israel, dating to 90,000 ya (Hovers et al. 2003). There are no naturally occurring deposits of this mineral in Qafzeh Cave, so the specimens recovered there must have been intentionally brought in from sources located in the general area surrounding the cave. Red ochre is a form of hematite, a mineral consisting of iron oxide that ranges in shade from red and orange to darker varieties. There is no utilitarian function for red ochre in its raw form; however, ground up into a powder and mixed with a binder (animal grease, egg white, or even saliva), it has been used by people all over the world to produce red-hued paint. Interestingly, the Qafzeh ochre was found near the human skeletons excavated in the cave and, in fact, appears to have been used intentionally to impart a red stain to some of the stone tools found there. It is impossible to know what meaning this had to the people who lived in the cave, but certainly it could have been a symbolic representation, perhaps of blood. Whatever its purpose, the presence of ochre in the cave implies a thought process ascribable to human intelligence.

Items of personal adornment are typical among members of our species. We identify, define, and even magnify our individuality and uniqueness by altering our appearance, sometimes permanently. Look around your classroom, and consider the necklaces, bracelets, earrings, nose rings, etc. worn by your classmates. In essence, we decorate ourselves. One of the oldest sites where such items of adornment have been found is Blombos Cave in South Africa (Figure 11.1). There, researchers have found

FIGURE 11.1 These perforated shell beads, found in Blombos Cave, South Africa, date to 75,000 ya. They are among the earliest nonutilitarian artifacts found that reflect a modern human capacity to produce decorative art. (*Courtesy Chris Henshilwood and Centre for Development Studies, University of Bergen*)

Upper Paleolithic Term used for the final phase of the Paleolithic in Europe, dating to between 40,000 and 10,000 ya, associated with the first appearance of anatomically modern humans in Europe.

Late Stone Age Final phase of the Stone Age in Africa, dating to between 40,000 and 10,000 ya.

Middle Paleolithic Term used for the time period in Europe after the Lower Paleolithic and before the Upper Paleolithic, dating to between 250,000 and 40,000 ya, encompassing the cultures of premodern varieties of human beings, including the Neandertals.

Middle Stone Age Term used for the time period in Africa after the Early Stone Age and before the Late Stone Age, dating to between 250,000 and 40,000 ya, encompassing the cultures of premodern varieties of human beings, including those transitional between premodern and anatomically modern *Homo sapiens*.

more than 40 perforated mollusk shell beads dating to 75,000 ya (Henshilwood et al. 2004). The location of the holes in the Blombos shells is rarely seen in nature and clearly seems to have been intentional, perhaps to hang the beads from a necklace.

Highly efficient blade tools, red ochre lumps, and shell beads are the rare exceptions; largely, the material culture of the earliest anatomically modern human beings does not reflect an intellectual leap forward but rather a baby step. This remains the case from the first appearance of anatomically modern *Homo sapiens* until about 50,000 ya. Most scientists agree with paleoanthropologist Anthony Marks (1990:56), who characterizes what happens after 50,000 ya as "a profound and fundamental change in both behavior and human potential." The period of this fundamental change—the Upper Paleolithic, or Late Stone Age—is the focus of this chapter.

Comparing the Middle and Upper Paleolithic

Cultures of the **Upper Paleolithic** (Europe) and the equivalent **Late Stone Age** (Africa), dating to between 40,000 and 10,000 ya, exhibit significant increases in technological sophistication when compared to their antecedents in the **Middle Paleolithic** (Europe) or the **Middle Stone Age** (Africa), generally dated to 250,000 to 40,000 ya. Randall White, both alone (1982) and together with Heidi Knecht and Anne Pike-Tay (Knecht et al. 1993), has examined some of the major differences between cultures

FIGURE 11.2 Illustration showing blade removal from a core. The hammerstone strikes the core at an angle (shown by the red arrows), contacting the edge of the striking platform and removing a long, sharp-edged stone blade. Each blade peeled off the core in this fashion leaves a remnant concave scar on the surface of the core.

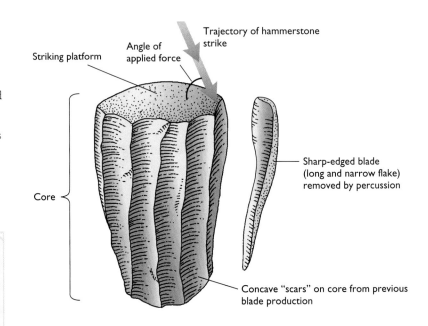

Gravettian An Upper Paleolithic toolmaking tradition, characterized by the production of small and denticulate knives. Dated from 27,000 to 21,000 B.P.

Solutrean Stone toolmaking tradition of the European Upper Paleolithic, dating from 21,000 to 16,000 ya.

projectile point A pointed tool or weapon—generally a stone, bone, or antler tip hafted onto a shaft, often of wood—which is thrown or shot at a target, usually a hunted animal. Includes spear points and arrowheads.

Magdelanian A late Upper Paleolithic culture in Europe dating from 16,000 to 11,000 B.P. Includes finely made barbed harpoons, carved decorative objects, and cave paintings.

microblades Small, usually extremely sharp, stone blades. Microblades were set into handles of bone, wood, antler, and so forth.

of the European Middle and Upper Paleolithic, identifying several significant cultural innovations. His list applies equally well to Africa and Asia:

1. Stone tool technologies based on the production of elongated blades rather than flakes.
2. Broadening of the subsistence base to include big-game hunting, small-mammal trapping, fishing, and catching birds.
3. Increased use of bone, ivory, and antler for making tools.
4. Manufacture of nonutilitarian objects, particularly items of personal adornment.
5. Larger, perhaps more sedentary, settlements.
6. Movement of raw materials across long distances, implying greater social integration of distant and diverse groups.
7. Elaborate burials including personal items to accompany the deceased.
8. Production of the first recognizable works of art in the form of paintings and sculpture.

1. Stone tool technologies based on the production of elongated blades rather than flakes.   Blades are commonly defined as a special variety of flakes at least twice as long as they are wide (Figure 11.2). Blade production involves significant planning and careful preparation of the stone core in order to maximize both the consistency and number of the elongated, sharp-edged tool blanks that are produced from it. This preparation and planning pays off; often, more than five times the amount of usable edge

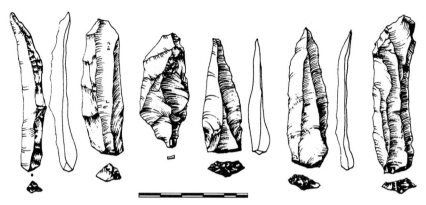

FIGURE 11.3 Upper Paleolithic stone tool technologies marked by elongated blades can be seen at Ksar Akil in Lebanon (examples shown here), dated to 52,000 ya. *(Reprinted from Paul Mellars, ed.:* The Emergence of Modern Humans: An Archaeological Perspective. *Copyright © Edinburgh University Press. Used by permission of the publisher, Cornell University Press)*

results from the same core in the production of blades as compared to regular flakes.

As already mentioned, stone tool traditions based on the production of blades did develop substantially before 50,000 ya; however, those technologies were exceptional and did not mark a general shift toward blade production by early humans. In fact, it isn't until about 52,000 ya that we see the beginning of a systematic movement toward this method of stone tool production. In southwest Asia, stone blade technologies have been found dating to as early as 52,000 ya at Ksar Akil in Lebanon (Figure 11.3), 45,000 B.P. at Boker Tachtit in Israel (A. Marks 1993), a bit before 40,000 B.P. in central and southeastern Europe (Svoboda 1993), and 40,000 B.P. at Haua Fteah Cave in Africa (Van Peer and Vermeersch 1990).

A blade-based stone tool technology developed in western Europe by about 35,000 B.P. (Allsworth-Jones 1990). The earliest such tools, belonging to the so-called Aurignacian culture mentioned in Chapter 10, date to between 34,000 and 27,000 ya (Figure 11.4). The Aurignacian includes long, sharp cutting tools; engraving tools called *burins;* and stone scrapers. The Aurignacian is followed by the **Gravettian** tradition (27,000 to 21,000 B.P.), with its emphasis on smaller blades and denticulate knives— cutting tools with numerous small, pointed projections along their cutting edges. The **Solutrean** tradition, dated from 21,000 to 16,000 ya, includes the production of exquisite, bifacially flaked, symmetrical, leaf-shaped **projectile points** (Figure 11.5). The Solutrean was followed by the **Magdelanian** from 16,000 to 11,000 B.P., which produced very small **microblades.** The Magdelanian is best known for the manufacture of bone and antler tools.

Blade tools were also becoming an important element in the stone tool repertoire of Late Stone Age Africans. For example, among the many regional cultures of the later Pleistocene in Africa, the Iberomaurusians inhabited the coastal plain and interior of what is today Tunisia and Morocco (Klein 1993). By about 16,000 B.P. they were making small stone blade

FIGURE 11.4 Aurignacian flint blades from France. This Upper Paleolithic industry made use of a core and blade technology in which long, thin, extremely sharp stone blades were struck from stone nodules. *(K. L. Feder)*

FIGURE 11.5 Bifacially flaked Solutrean spear points of the European Upper Paleolithic are examples of some of the finest stonework the world has ever seen. *(K. L. Feder)*

artifacts used as scraping and piercing tools—the former for scraping animal hides in clothing manufacture and the latter as arrow or spear points for hunting.

2. *Broadening of the subsistence base to include big-game hunting, small-mammal trapping, fishing, and catching birds.* Leslie Freeman (1973) has compared faunal assemblages from seventy-seven levels at twenty Middle and Upper Paleolithic cave sites in northern Spain. He found that the older assemblages showed that a small number of animal species were exploited and few members of each species were represented. He concludes that the Middle Paleolithic inhabitants of this area were opportunistic hunters, killing what they could when they could.

In the Upper Paleolithic levels, however, Freeman identified a consistent increase over time in the number of prey species represented, indicating, perhaps, more efficient hunting strategies. The evidence seems to indicate that the anatomically modern inhabitants of these caves were habitual hunters.

At Dolni Vestonice I in the Czech Republic, the remains of more than 100 mammoths slaughtered and butchered by the inhabitants have been identified (Soffer 1993). Butchering marks have been located on the remains of horse and reindeer as well. Subsistence at Mal'ta, in south-central Russia near modern Irkutsk (Chard 1974), clearly was based on the hunting of the big-game animals that migrated across the tundra in a yearly pattern, especially woolly rhinoceros, woolly mammoth, and reindeer.

These hunters almost certainly used the animals' hides for clothing. They also trapped foxes and other small mammals for their pelts. Interestingly, they buried the remains of the skinned foxes.

Recent evidence indicates that hunting and trapping smaller mammals also supplied food in the Upper Paleolithic. Back at Dolni Vestonice I and at the nearby Czech site of Pavlov, there is indirect evidence of the use of nets, likely used in hunting small game (Adovasio et al. 1996; Pringle 1997). The bones of small mammals, especially hare and fox, were abundant in the archaeological deposits of these sites; nets would have facilitated hunting these small, quick animals for their meat and for the warm pelts that they could provide. Though net fibers themselves have not been preserved, sections of nets were accidentally pressed into the clay floors of the inhabitants' houses. In a few cases those houses burned, leaving the impressions of the netting in the baked clay. The layers at both sites that produced these impressions date to around 26,000 ya. According to James Adovasio, an archaeologist and expert in ancient textiles, the net impressions found in these Czech sites reflect a sophisticated weaving technology, probably indicating a long tradition of net weaving (Adovasio et al. 1996).

Bones tend to preserve better than other food remains, and, as a result, archaeologists might overemphasize the importance of meat in an ancient diet. Archaeologists applying new, intensive methods of recovery, however, are beginning to find the remains of seeds, fruits, and even roots used by people in the Upper Paleolithic. For example, a team of researchers led by archaeologist Sarah Mason has found the burned residue of edible taproots of plants from the daisy or dandelion families in hearths at Dolni Vestonice I (Mason et al. 1994).

Archaeological evidence in southern Africa shows a similar expansion in the human diet at the same time. At sites that date to the African Late Stone Age, the bones of large, dangerous game animals such as buffalo are found along with those of tortoises, shellfish, and birds. Along with the bones of terrestrial mammals, the bones of fish and shellfish have been recovered at Blombos Cave (Henshilwood et al. 2002) in levels dating back to as much as 100,000 ya. Archaeologist Richard G. Klein ascribes the expansion in subsistence to the invention of new technologies—including snares and fishing and fowling gear—by the Late Stone Age people of Africa (Klein 1989).

Though it is likely that only adults in their prime would have been capable of hunting large and dangerous game animals, children, older adults, and women far along in pregnancy could have collected small animals and plant foods. In other words, a broad approach to subsistence allowed most members of a society to contribute to the food quest.

It is unlikely that Upper Paleolithic people overlooked important sources of nutrition. Evidence is now beginning to show that they subsisted on a broad spectrum of foods including the meat from animals both large and small, birds, fish, seeds, nuts, berries, and starchy roots.

FIGURE 11.6 Reconstruction of a hut at the 18,000-year-old site of Mal'ta in south-central Russia. Because wood was not plentiful on the tundra, the bones of woolly mammoth and the antlers of reindeer were used as construction materials.

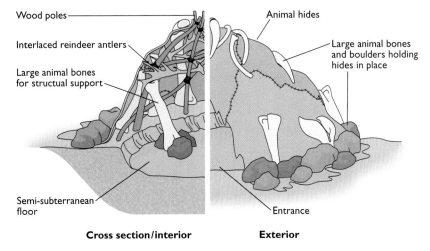

Wood poles

Interlaced reindeer antlers

Large animal bones for structural support

Animal hides

Large animal bones and boulders holding hides in place

Semi-subterranean floor

Entrance

Cross section/interior   **Exterior**

3. Increased use of bone, ivory, and antler for making tools. In the Upper Paleolithic, our ancestors perfected technologies that they had previously only experimented with, employing raw materials other than stone, including bone, ivory, and antler. The tools they made include sewing equipment such as awls, punches, and eyed-needles, as well as hunting equipment such as projectile points. Barbed bone harpoons; antler hammers; and wrenchlike, bone "shaft-straighteners" all have been found in Upper Paleolithic sites from western Europe to East Asia. The bone, antler, and ivory technology hinted at by the Katanda sites (see Chapter 10) flowered during the Late Stone Age and Upper Paleolithic. In South Africa, Late Stone Age sites such as Nelson Bay Cave exhibit a complex toolkit of finely made bone tools that exhibit polishing. These tools include spear points and "fish gorges"—bipointed bones that may have served as fishhooks (Klein 1989).

People living in the harsh glacial climate at the site of Mal'ta would have needed shelter from the Pleistocene cold. During its occupation, however, the site was located in tundra, so trees would have been largely unavailable for construction purposes. The people at Mal'ta developed an ingenious solution to this problem. They used the leg and rib bones of large animals such as the woolly mammoth for the framework of their dwellings. For the roof, where the weight of such bones would have been too great, they used lighter material such as reindeer antlers. On this bone-antler frame, they attached animal hides, held in place on the ground with large bones and boulders (Figure 11.6).

4. Manufacture of nonutilitarian objects, particularly items of personal adornment. At the 13,000-year-old site of Rocher de la Peine in France, researchers have found a beautiful necklace made of dentalium shell beads,

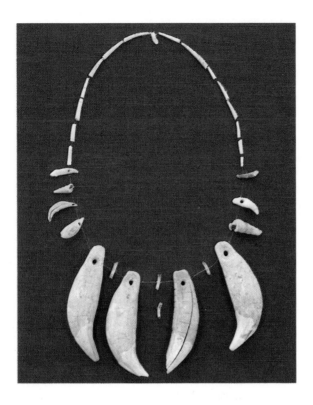

FIGURE 11.7 This 13,000-year-old necklace from Rocher de la Peine in France is made of dentalium shell beads, three large, perforated bear teeth, and a European lion's tooth. The shell came from the coast, which is 160 kilometers (100 miles) from the cave. Decorative art, including painting, engraving, sculpture, and jewelry, are found in abundance in the Upper Paleolithic and Late Stone Age. *(Beloit College, Logan Museum of Anthropology, LMA 4.7.253)*

three large bear teeth, and one tooth of a European lion (Figure 11.7; Dennell 1986). The shell came from the coast, located about 160 kilometers (100 miles) away from the site. At Mal'ta, we see a tradition of carved artwork, perhaps as part of a religious pattern. The three-dimensional bone and ivory carvings found there included jewelry, as well as carvings of waterfowl and human female figures (Figure 11.8). The people of Mal'ta also incised on antler and bone intricate, two-dimensional, abstract designs of curved lines and occasional realistic pictures of animals such as the woolly mammoth. At Nelson Bay Cave in South Africa, the bone tools mentioned previously were accompanied by nonutilitarian bone objects, including beads, pendants, and other items of adornment (Klein 1989).

As Randall White (1982) points out, the appearance of well-made items of personal adornment—often manufactured from exotic material that must have been difficult to obtain—is diagnostic of the Upper Paleolithic. In White's view, items of personal adornment imply a growing awareness and significance of the individual in Upper Paleolithic society.

5. Larger, perhaps more sedentary, settlements. The size of an ancient community can be assessed by calculating the area over which the material objects made, used, and discarded by that community's inhabitants

FIGURE 11.8 This carving of a human female, found in central Asia at the Mal'ta site, was produced from the ivory of a woolly mammoth. The carving dates to approximately 21,000 ya and marks a widespread Upper Paleolithic tradition of sculpted images of human females. *(Courtesy of Department of Archaeology, The Hermitage Museum [370/746])*

are scattered. Certainly, an archaeologist would conclude that the population of a community such as New York City was substantially larger—by several orders of magnitude—than the population of a rural town in Nebraska or Iowa, at least in part by calculating the area covered by each community's structural remains and by the scatter of the artifacts found there. On this basis, Upper Paleolithic and Late Stone Age sites are not universally larger than those that date to the Middle Paleolithic or Middle Stone Age. However, archaeologists do find some sites in the Upper Paleolithic and Late Stone Age that are substantially larger than sites dating to earlier periods. Mal'ta, for example, covers an area of some 600 square meters (about 7,500 square feet; Chard 1974:20), with the remains of numerous dwellings similar to those described earlier. Randall White (1982) interprets these as places of aggregation, sites that people repeatedly visited at times of the year when resources in the area may have been particularly abundant.

6. Movement of raw materials across long distances, implying greater social integration of distant and diverse groups. In south-central Europe, tools made of flint have been found more than 100 kilometers (65 miles) from their source (Oliva 1993:52). Apparently highly valued material such as obsidian (volcanic glass) from Hungary is found in Paleolithic sites up to 500 kilometers (325 miles) away (Oliva 1993:52). Similar instances of trade across great distances are found in Late Stone Age Africa as well. Obsidian originating in East Africa has been found in sites many kilometers from its source (Phillipson 1993). Even in cases where quite serviceable stone was locally available, people nevertheless often used material obtainable only at great distances. The discovery of raw materials many miles from their sources may indicate the existence of an extensive network of trade in the Upper Paleolithic. The ability to trade across great distances implies geographically broad social connections.

7. Elaborate burials including personal items to accompany the deceased. We saw in Chapter 9 that the Neandertals were the first hominids to bury their dead and include grave goods. As Frank Harrold's analysis shows (1980), Neandertal burials were rather simple when compared to those of anatomically modern humans in the Upper Paleolithic. Compare Neandertal burials—with their handful of stone tools or animal bones—with the extreme case of the Upper Paleolithic burials at the site of Sungir', located about 150 kilometers (100 miles) northeast of Moscow (White 1993). Dating to at least 30,000 to 25,000 ya, the site contains five burials (an older male, an adult female, a young girl, a teenage boy, and an individual whose sex has not been determined). These Sungir' graves are filled with objects, primarily items of adornment (see Figure 7.25). Nearly 3,000 finely worked ivory beads, some apparently part of a beaded cap, were found with the body of the old man. On his arms were twenty-five finely carved bracelets made from woolly mammoth ivory. The young boy's body was surrounded by more than 4,900 ivory beads, and he wore a belt decorated with 250 polar fox teeth; there was an ivory pin at his throat, an ivory lance and carved ivory disk at his side, and an ivory sculpture of a woolly mammoth under his shoulder (all data on the Sungir' graves taken from White 1993:287–96). The Sungir' burial goods obviously represent an enormous investment in time and energy. They also seem poignantly to reflect the care and love provided to the dead by their living comrades. In this respect, perhaps especially, the humanity of these people is clearly recognizable.

8. Production of the first recognizable works of art in the form of paintings and sculpture.   Beginning as early as 43,000 ya and continuing until about 10,000 ya, human groups in Europe, Africa, and Australia produced some of the world's first art. In this 33,000-year period, which, as Margaret Conkey (1983) points out, constitutes the first two-thirds of human art history, Upper Paleolithic people produced a remarkable variety of artwork in numerous media and styles. They carved stone, bone, antler, and ivory; produced bas-reliefs; made ceramic figurines; engraved objects with both naturalistic figures and abstract designs; and painted fantastic friezes on cave walls.

The earliest African art yet found has been dated to about 28,000 ya (Phillipson 1993). Stone slabs with painted and engraved images of animals have been excavated from deposits dating to this time at the Apollo 11 Cave site in southern Namibia (Wendt 1976). The animals are natural renderings of the fauna of southern Africa at the time. The oldest known art in the New World dates to between 11,200 and 10,000 ya in the Caverna da Pedra Pintada in Brazil (Roosevelt et al. 1996). Red-pigment images in that cave and others in the region include concentric circles, human handprints, and spirit beings (see the discussion of the site later in this chapter).

Ancient Australia also has a rich history of painted and etched designs. (We will discuss the initial settlement of Australia later in this chapter.) Some of the oldest Australian rock art consists of channels etched by human fingers into the soft surfaces of Koonalda Cave on the Nullarbor Plain, judged to be at least 20,000 and as much as 30,000 years old. A stencil-like design found at the Laura South site in the Cape York Peninsula may be as much as 25,000 years old. Ancient Australians depicted their natural and spirit worlds in the many images they created. Graceful depictions of kangaroos, emus, fish, turtles, human beings, spirit beasts, and more adorn rock faces and cave walls of ancient Australia. According to Mulvaney and Kamminga (1999), native Australians appear to have been the most prolific of the world's early artists, producing many thousands of images across the entire extent of their continent in a number of different styles.

FIGURE 11.9 Geographical distribution of Upper Paleolithic European cave paintings. Most of the sites are clustered in the area of Franco-Cantabria in south-west France and northern Spain. *(After Jochim 1983)*

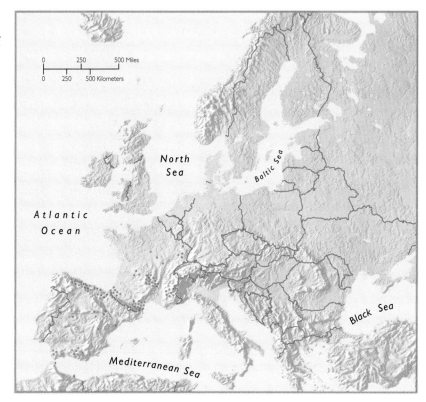

Art in the European Upper Paleolithic

The European Upper Paleolithic cave paintings and engravings capture the imagination; a few hundred caves with paintings are known, most of them clustered in southwest France and northern Spain, the region called Franco-Cantabria (Figure 11.9). In often naturalistic works, the ancient artists painted bison, oxen, horses, deer, mammoths, ibex, rhinoceros, lions, and bears. Though there is a great deal of variation, many of the animals are by no means simplistically or childishly rendered but are sophisticated, fluid, and natural. These images were painted on the cave walls from as much as 36,500 to 10,000 ya (Bahn and Vertut 1988).

Cave Paintings

How remarkable are the Upper Paleolithic cave paintings? Consider this: in 1879, when the first cave paintings were discovered at Altamira, in Spain, they were roundly denounced as a hoax. Many perceived them as being far too impressive to have been produced by ancient humans. One researcher went so far as to accuse Spanish priests of having been the hoaxsters, perpetrating a fraud in an attempt to fool and then humiliate evolutionists (Saura Ramos 1998). As more and more of the painted caves were discovered in the late nineteenth and early twentieth centuries, however, it became clear that these images were not the product of a modern trickster but were, instead, part of an artistic tradition that lasted tens of thousands of years.

The artwork is striking indeed, moving even artists and scientists to speak in superlatives. One of the greatest artists of the twentieth century, Pablo Picasso, was referring to these paintings when he said, "Not one of us could paint like that" (in Saura Ramos 1998:8). Anthropologist Pat Shipman, after viewing a set of paintings for the first time, commented, "I had looked at photographs of Lascaux [one of the best known caves], of course, so I knew that the paintings were beautiful; but what I did not know was that they would reach across 17,000 years to grab my soul" (1990:62).

Natural pigments were produced by grinding into powder ochre for orange, yellow, and red; iron oxides for brown; and manganese dioxide for black. The powder was then mixed with a binding agent such as grease, marrow, or blood. Using fingers, wooden spatulas, and brushes made of twigs or even animal hair, the artists applied the paint to their prehistoric canvases—the cave walls of Lascaux, Roc de Sers, Trois Fréres, Niaux, and Chauvet in France; Altamira and Casares in Spain; and many others.

The painted figures of these caves are not static or two-dimensional. They seem to move across the cave walls with rippling muscles and straining sinews (Figure 11.10). A herd of woolly mammoths, extinct for more than 10,000 years, lives again as they march single file across the cave wall at Rouffignac. A spectacular grouping of bison, perhaps poised to flee, is frozen in time in the "Great Panel" on the ceiling of Altamira. A group of stiff-maned horses, calm but alert, stare out at us from a flat rock surface at Cosquer Cave in southern France, looking just as fresh as when they were painted 19,000 ya (Clottes and Courtin 1996). In the oldest yet known of the painted caves, Chauvet in the Ardèche region of south-central France, a cluster of rhinoceros stand guard today on the wall, just as they have for nearly 32,000 years (Figure 11.11). Such paintings offer us a rare glimpse into an ancient world. They are a wonderful legacy left by the ancient peoples of Europe.

Why were animals a major focus of the cave painters? One explanation might be that these early artists were performing sympathetic magic based on the belief that if you can "capture" an animal by painting it, you ensure its literal capture in the hunt (Breuil 1952). This might explain the apparent avoidance of realistic depictions of people—perhaps painting a person was thought to capture his or her spirit, soul, or essence. Another, related hypothesis is that of "trophyism," which explains the paintings as records of successful individual hunts (Eaton 1978a, 1978b, as cited in

FIGURE 11.10 The so-called Chinese horse *(above),* depicted in mid-gallop on the cave wall of Lascaux, France. The Great Black Aurochs *(opposite page)*— a species of wild cattle—also from Lascaux. Painted more than 17,000 ya, the images at Lascaux exemplify the truly artistic character of Upper Paleolithic cave paintings. *(Both photos: © Art Resource, NY)*

Conkey 1983:217). In this view, the paintings are trophies much in the way a modern hunter mounts an animal head on a wall.

Certainly, the animal species represented in the cave paintings were not randomly selected. Many of these species were the focus of the painters' subsistence quest. The cave painters depicted many of the same species whose bones are found in the hearths and trash pits of their habitation sites. There is even regional variation in the animals depicted, reflecting the geographic distribution of these food sources. For example, most of the inland painted caves are dominated by paintings of large, inland-dwelling mammals, but at Cosquer, near the French Mediterranean coast, more than one in ten of the paintings are of marine animals including seals, fish, auk (a large, extinct flightless bird, much like a penguin), and even jellyfish and octopus (Clottes and Courtin 1996).

In a detailed study, anthropologist Patricia Rice and sociologist Ann Paterson detected a pattern to how often individual animal species turned up in the paintings in a series of caves located in west-central France (1985) and northern Spain (1986). These researchers found that the Paleolithic artists depicted smaller animals such as red deer and reindeer in direct proportion to the abundance of their bones in local archaeological sites of the same period. Larger animals that would individually have pro-

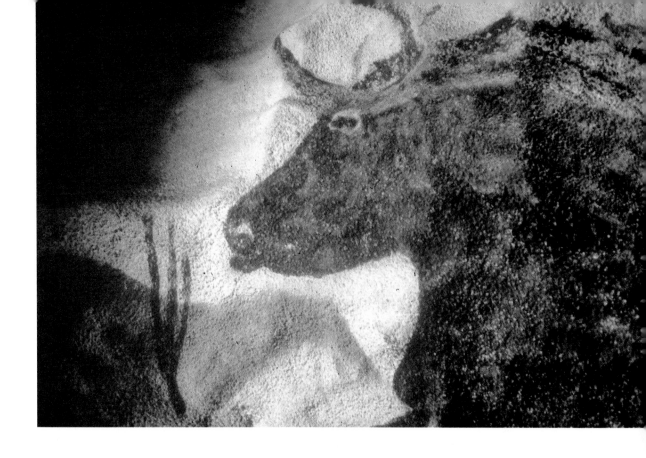

vided a lot of meat, especially horses and bison, were depicted more frequently in the caves than might have been expected from a simple count of their bones at the same sites. Rice and Paterson concluded that species frequency in the cave art largely was a function of the economic significance of the animal. The artists' favorite subjects were small animals hunted with great regularity and large animals that provided a large amount of meat even though hunted less frequently. Animals only rarely or never seen in faunal assemblages, but impressive, dangerous, and productive of large quantities of meat when they were successfully procured were also commonly selected for inclusion in the artwork. Overall, Rice and Paterson conclude that the cave art can be explained as "fertility magic, hunting magic, hunting education, and story-telling about hunting" (1985:98).

At the same time, animals of no consequence in subsistence, but impressive and dangerous, were depicted by the artists as well. For example, some paintings depict the wooly rhinoceros, a large, probably aggressive animal common in Upper Paleolithic Europe but not known to have been hunted. Chauvet Cave has depictions of about fifty wooly rhinoceros; that's more than three times the total number of these animals depicted in all of the other Upper Paleolithic painted caves combined (see Figure 11.11;

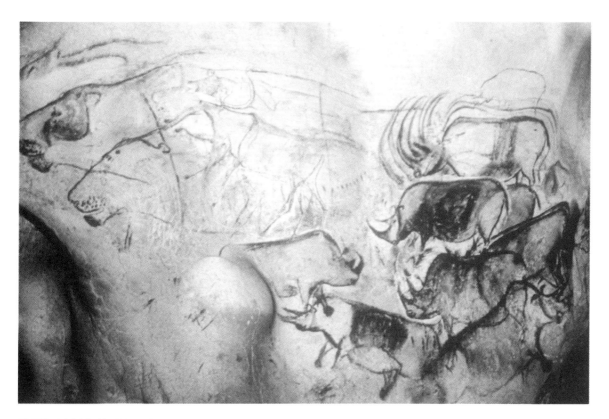

FIGURE 11.11 The Upper Paleolithic paintings at Chauvet Cave in France are among the most spectacular ever found. In caves found previously, the extinct rhinoceros species that inhabited late Pleistocene Europe was rarely depicted. At Chauvet, however, the artists portrayed about fifty of them. (© *AP/Wide World Photos*)

Chauvet 1996; Clottes 1995). Since the animals were not hunted, paintings of them could not have been "trophies." Their precise meaning is unclear, however. Perhaps the cave painters simply were in awe of these magnificent and powerful beasts and wished somehow to capture that on their stone canvases.

The placement of individual animals in the cave paintings also is not random. André Leroi-Gourhan (1982) has identified a pattern in the appearance of animals in the caves. Major sources of food including bison, oxen, and horses generally were accorded a central position within the caves themselves, as well as within individual groups of paintings. Deer, ibex, and mammoths tend to be peripheral. Dangerous creatures not part of the Upper Paleolithic diets such as rhinoceros, bears, and lions are usually far away, often deep in the recesses of caves, as much as a kilometer down narrow, winding, rock-strewn passageways.

Some researchers have interpreted what Meg Conkey (1978:74) calls the "explosion of symbolic behavior" in the Upper Paleolithic as more than simply sympathetic magic; instead, they see it as an attempt to record information in symbolic ways (Conkey 1980; Gamble 1982, 1983, 1986; Hammond 1974; Jochim 1983). These researchers propose that as human ecological circumstances changed during the Late Pleistocene, social systems changed as well. Art, these writers suggest, served the purpose of transmitting socially important information within cultural systems stressed by environmental changes.

Geometric Signs

Among the most difficult elements of ancient artwork to interpret are the simple geometric patterns. How are we to understand Upper Paleolithic paintings of wavy lines, zigzags, spirals, parallel lines, perpendicular crossing lines, and so on? Were these meaningless scrawlings—the equivalent of our doodling? Were these designs part of an ancient code that we may never decipher?

A fascinating explanation of these designs has been offered by researchers J. D. Lewis-Williams and T. A. Dowson (1988). They argue that these images derive from visual artifacts of the artists' nervous systems brought on during altered states of consciousness. The authors refer to visions that result from stimulation of the optic system during these altered states as **entoptic phenomena.** These images are not culturally controlled but result from the structure of the optic system itself and are therefore universal. When people are placed into an altered state of consciousness under experimental conditions, they report seeing six basic geometric forms—dots, wavy lines, zigzags, crosshatching or grids, concentric circles or U-shaped lines, and parallel lines (Bower 1996). These same forms are found in ancient rock art found all over the world. Perhaps through sleep deprivation, hyperventilation, staring at a flickering fire, or even ingesting psychoactive compounds (for example, plants that can induce hallucinations), shamans or priests induced these images in their own optic systems, interpreted what they saw as a vision of another world—a spirit world, perhaps—and then translated these images to cave walls as part of their religious rituals. Jean Clottes and David Lewis-Williams (1998) see suggestions of this theory in the spectacular works of art not just in the European Paleolithic but wherever ancient people have painted on rock surfaces. Some modern hunter-gatherers probably induced such visions, as well; there are about a half dozen verified accounts of the Ju/'hoansi people of southern Africa producing rock paintings or engravings in this way as late as the nineteenth century (Deacon 1999).

Human Depictions

Though there are hundreds of animal paintings on cave walls, the cave painters seemed far less interested in self-portraits. In fact, Upper Paleolithic paintings of people are rare. One of the oldest of these human portraits was found in 2000 at Cussac Cave, located in the Dordogne Valley in France (Balter 2001b). There, in addition to more than a hundred images

entoptic phenomena Visual images that result from stimulation of the optic system during altered states of consciousness.

FIGURE 11.12 Though they were accomplished artists and rendered animals with great accuracy, Upper Paleolithic artists infrequently depicted human beings, and these portrayals are often vague and schematic. An example can be seen in the engraved outline of a human female in Cussac Cave in France. Compare this image to the finely rendered cave paintings shown in Figures 11.10 and 11.11. (© *CNP/Min. Culture/Corbis Sygma*)

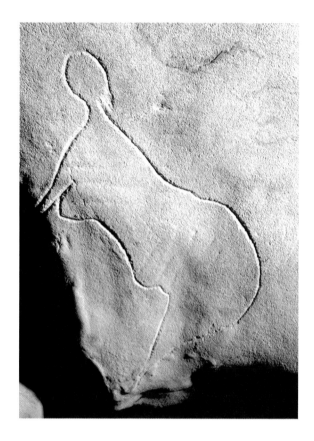

of animals (including mammoths, rhinoceros, deer, horses, and bison—incised, rather than painted, onto the wall of the cave) is the outline of what appears to be a human female (Figure 11.12). Radiocarbon dating of the human bones found in the cave date to more than 25,000 ya, and it is assumed that this date also applies to the images in the cave.

A mysterious painted image was found on a rock slab in Fumane Cave, located near Verona, Italy (Balter 2000). The stratigraphic level at which the slab was recovered has been dated to more than 32,000 ya and as much as 36,500 ya, making this image the oldest artwork yet found in Europe. Just as important as the figure's age is its appearance; it seems to be a hybrid, a bizarre combination of human and animal, with a humanlike, two-legged posture, but with an animal head with horns or antlers. The Fumane Cave researchers called the figure a "sorcerer," suggesting that the painting is of a human being wearing an animal mask or headdress, participating, perhaps, in a ceremony of some kind.

Rice and Paterson (1988) analyzed some thirty-two caves in western Europe with a total of 116 human images. Of those images where gender could be identified, 78 percent were male and only 22 percent female.

FIGURE 11.13 A 20,000-year-old "signature" left by a Paleolithic artist. This negative handprint was produced by placing a hand flat on a cave wall and then blowing paint through a hollow reed all around the hand. From the cave of Peche-Merle in France. (© *Musée de l'Homme. Photo by B. et G. Delluc*)

Males tended to be portrayed conducting some specific activity; all running, walking, or dancing figures were males. There were even three paintings of people who appear to have been speared—all males as well. Females were always represented as simply standing or lying down, usually in groups with other females. They were never portrayed in an active mode. Although we cannot be certain of the precise meaning of these paintings and patterns, certainly they reflect aspects of the differences between the lives of males and females in the Upper Paleolithic.

Though actual depictions of human beings are rare, another type of human image is more common: handprints. Sometimes these are positive images, with the painters' hands having been dipped in pigment and then pressed against the cave wall, transferring the image onto its surface. At Chauvet Cave, a single panel has forty-eight tightly clustered palm prints made in this way. Based on the size of the palms, the researchers concluded that they were the hands of a small woman or a child (Balter 1999). Another panel at Chauvet consists of ninety-two palm print impressions, likely made by a tall, adult male (Balter 1999).

Other handprint signatures are negative impressions (Figure 11.13). In these cases, a human hand was placed on the cave wall and paint was probably blown through a hollow reed all around it. Then the hand was

FIGURE 11.14 This delicately carved image of a waterfowl, found in Hohle Fels Cave, Germany, is one of several beautifully rendered depictions of animals found there. *(© AP/Wide World Photos)*

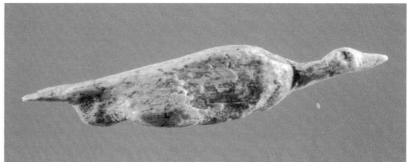

FIGURE 11.15 Called *Der Löwenmensch* ("the lion man"), this artifact was found in Hohlenstein-Stadel cave in Germany and depicts what appears to be a strange chimera, a combination of a lion and a human being. We cannot determine precisely what the sculptor intended in creating this fanciful creature, but certainly it is a reflection of a "modern" human intellectual capacity. *(Photo by Thomas Stephan, © Ulmer Museum)*

taken away from the wall surface, leaving the original color where the hand was and pigment all around it, defining the hand's outline.

It is, of course, impossible to know precisely what these artists intended to convey with their handprints. On the other hand, it seems a safe bet that in leaving impressions of their hands—their "signatures"—on these cave walls, the artists were making a statement we can understand and recognize: "We were here!"

Carvings and Engravings

Upper Palolithic artists did not restrict their work to two-dimensional paintings. They also produced carvings and engravings. Some, like the cave paintings, were naturalistic depictions of the animals they encountered in their daily lives. Two of the oldest of these have been found in excavations in Hohle Fels Cave in southwestern Germany. Dating to between 33,000 and 30,000 ya, the figurines depict a graceful waterfowl in flight (Figure 11.14) and the head of what appears to be a wild horse (Conrad 2003). Another series of Upper Paleolithic animal carvings has been found in Germany that includes depictions of bears, lions, and mammoths (Sinclair 2003).

Again, as with the cave paintings, Upper Paleolithic artists did not restrict themselves to realistic portrayals of animal life. They also produced remarkable carvings of hybrid creatures, part animal and part human. Along with the water bird and horse in the 33,000- to 30,000-year level at Hohle Fels Cave, archaeologists found the carving of a two-legged creature that appears to be a human being from the neck down but a lion from the neck up. *Der Löwenmensch* ("the lion man") from Hohlenstein-Stadel Cave in Germany, may be a bit younger but even more clearly shows a human, standing on two legs, with what appears to be a lion's head (Figure 11.15).

The meaning of carvings like these is not immediately apparent, but they may reflect aspects of the spiritual world of Upper Paleolithic people,

FIGURE 11.16 A 32,000-year-old engraved antler plaque from Abri Blanchard, France, which Alexander Marshack interprets as a calendar based on the phases of the moon. (© 2006 President and Fellows of Harvard College, Peabody Museum, Alexander Marshack)

a world inhabited by animals whose courage and ferocity they hoped to emulate and creatures who combined the essences of those animals and human beings.

The people who produced these spectacular works of art may also have been making simple, though remarkable, advances in science. A 32,000-year-old fragment of antler found in a French cave bears a succession of some sixty-nine incised marks. After examining it under a microscope, science writer Alexander Marshack (1972a, 1972b) noted that the marks were made with a number of different tools and that they resembled the succession of lunar phases, the correct order and number for more than two months (Figure 11.16). Marshack believes that this and other artifacts indicate that these people not only produced the first true art but also made the first calendars.

Venus Figurines

Other examples of three-dimensional works produced by Upper Paleolithic artists are the so-called **Venus figurines**, generally faceless women carved in limestone or ivory or made of baked clay. Created between 32,000 and 10,000 ya, the figurines have long been thought to represent a mother goddess or to reflect an Upper Paleolithic ceremonialism regarding fertility. The stereotypical Venus figurines possess exaggerated secondary sexual characteristics (large breasts and buttocks) and swollen bellies (Figure 11.17) that make them look like pregnant women. It has been suggested that the Venus figurines may be seen as self-portraits by Upper

Venus figurines Sculptures of women, sometimes with exaggerated secondary sexual characteristics, dating to as much as 32,000 ya.

FIGURE 11.17 The famous "Venus of Willendorf." The precise meaning of the so-called Venus figurines is unknown. Only some possess the stereotypical exaggerated secondary sexual features and pregnant appearance. (© *Naturhistorisches Museum Wien, Neg. #9057F*)

Paleolithic women (McDermott 1996). It is interesting to point out in this regard that a photograph taken by a pregnant woman of herself, with the lens of the camera pointed down from her face to her bare breasts and abdomen, shows a striking resemblance to those Venus figurines that appear to depict pregnancy.

The pregnant-looking figurines, however, represent only a small fraction of the sculptures. Patricia Rice (1981) has examined in detail a group of 188 Venus figurines and found their shape, size, and form to be quite varied (Figure 11.18). There were thin and fat women, women with large breasts and women with small breasts, pregnant and not pregnant women, and women who were, by Rice's careful estimation, old, middle-aged and young. Rice (1981:408) suggests that the apparent age spread of the women depicted in her sample of figurines is similar to the actual age distribution in historical hunter-gatherer populations. Rice deduces that the Venus figurines are renderings of women of all ages and states of fertility. In her view, the figurines can't be used to support a hypothesis of a fertility cult.

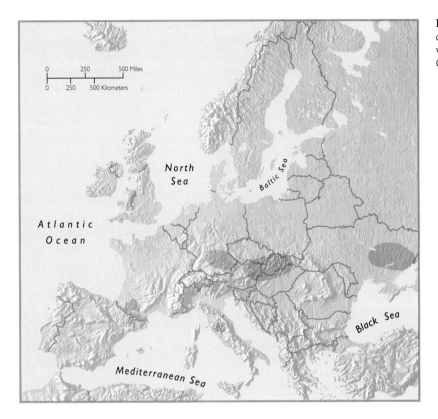

FIGURE 11.18 Geographical distribution of Venus figurines, which cluster outside Franco-Cantabria. *(After Gamble 1983)*

The Implications of Upper Paleolithic Artwork

Did people in the Upper Paleolithic practice sympathetic magic, worship a fertility goddess, mark their ritual sites with paintings, make calendars based on their observation of lunar phases, and paint visions seen during altered states of consciousness? We cannot be certain. John Halverson (1987) goes so far as to suggest that the art may have had no meaning at all, in the sense that no special and now indecipherable code was ever attached to it. The title of his article maintains that Upper Paleolithic art was simply "art for art's sake" and that the paintings and sculptures were produced simply out of a sense of "delight in appearance" (Halverson 1987:68).

Of course, it is reasonable to suggest that Upper Paleolithic artists and those who viewed the art were "delighted" by it. However, it is also reasonable to point out that art has a deeper meaning to the artist and his or her audience than simply the fact that it looks pretty. Who produces art, what images are considered appropriate to depict, where it is displayed, and who gets to view it reflect the social, political, economic, and ideological contexts of the times when the art was produced. Ancient art provides a window into the world of our ancestors, and it makes sense for us to peer through that window in our attempt to better understand their world.

The tradition of painting images on the walls of caves has continued into the modern era. The historically recorded meanings of these modern works may provide us with insights into the artwork of the Paleolithic (Clottes and Lewis-Williams 1998).

Some of the best known rock art produced in modern times is that of the Ju/'hoansi people of southern Africa (Phillipson 1993). People who lived during the lifetimes of some of the artists of the more recent African rock art were interviewed by European missionaries who entered their territory in the late nineteenth century (Lewis-Williams and Dowson 1998). Interestingly, at least some of this artwork includes exquisitely detailed and naturalistic depictions of animal life that are similar to and artistically the equal of those of the Upper Paleolithic. Also, though there are no deep caverns in the region where the African paintings are located, smaller, shallow rockshelters were available and used as repositories of the paintings.

Though we cannot use recent Ju/'hoansi art as a perfect model for the art of the Upper Paleolithic of Europe—or, for that matter, the ancient rock art of southern Africa—ethnographic information about the African art summarized by Jean Clottes and David Lewis-Williams (1998), as mentioned earlier, can provide us with an interesting perspective on the significance and meaning of such paintings to the hunting and gathering people that produced them.

The Ju/'hoansi artwork was spiritual in intent and meaning. Animals that lived in the area the Ju/'hoansi people inhabited, especially the eland, a large antelope that furnished an important portion of the diet of the Ju/'hoansi, were viewed by them as imbued with power and, as Clottes and Lewis-Williams (1998) characterize it, "potency." Clottes and Lewis-Williams maintain that paintings of eland and other animals served as "reservoirs" of this potency or power (p. 33). Even some eland blood might have been mixed into the paint to provide a further spiritual connection between the actual animal and its painted depiction.

Painting the animal in special places—in caves, for instance, which were viewed by the Ju/'hoansi as portals to an underworld of spirits—was not simply an artistic or historical act but a way of mediating the connection between this world and the spirit world. Ju/'hoansi shamans or spiritual leaders would visit these sacred places and, in a trance, bridge the gap between our ordinary world and a world inhabited by spirits. The powerful images of potent animals facilitated the connection to that world and allowed shamans to pass into it. The images painted on cave walls by ancient people might have served a similar function.

It is impossible at present to fully explain the art of the Upper Paleolithic, although the work of Jochim, Conkey, Gamble, Rice and Paterson, and Clottes and Lewis-Williams has provided great insight into its possible meaning. What is clear is that in viewing the world around them and in translating that reality through a prism of human understanding and belief into engravings, sculptures, carvings, and paintings, the people of the European Upper Paleolithic were exhibiting the depth of their intelligence and the degree of their humanity. Whichever hypothesis provides the best explanation for the art of the Upper Paleolithic (and they need not all be mutually exclusive), one thing is clear: in painting cave walls, carving figurines, and engraving bone, ivory, and antler, the people of the Upper Paleolithic in Europe left us an impressive artistic legacy.

Brave New Worlds

Not surprisingly, anatomically modern humans were able to survive in all the environments their predecessors had inhabited before them. But modern humans could also thrive under conditions that had previously proved insurmountable and to migrate into areas that were previously unreachable.

Australia

Prehistoric migration into Australia poses an interesting problem. Australia has been separate from the Asian landmass for over 30 million years. During periods when the extent of glaciation was at a peak, Java, Sumatra, Bali, and Borneo were connected to each other in a single landmass called **Sunda,** while Australia, New Guinea, and Tasmania were joined into a single landmass called **Sahul,** or **Greater Australia** (Figure 11.19). The **Wallace Trench,** which divided Sunda from Sahul, was so deep (nearly 7,500 meters, or 4.66 *miles*) that ocean waters separated these landmasses even when the worldwide sea level was at its lowest.

Coming to Australia   As a result, any population movement into Greater Australia necessarily involved the use of watercraft. Today this would entail a sea voyage of 1,500 kilometers (932 miles), with a few possible stops in between. At the time of presumed initial migration, however, the sea level was lower and more of the continental shelves of Asia and Australia were exposed, making the voyage substantially shorter. Anthropologist Joseph Birdsell (1977) has suggested a series of possible routes from Sunda to Sahul during these periods of lowered sea level (see Figure 11.19). One route starts on the eastern shore of what is today Borneo, continues east through the island of Sulawesi, and includes several island hops to northwest New Guinea. The longest gap between islands would have been about 70 kilometers (43 miles); the mean length of the eight gaps in this route is only about 28 kilometers (17 miles; Birdsell 1977:127). Another possible route begins in Java, crosses the Indonesian archipelago, and then continues south to Timor and on to Australia. This route also contains eight ocean crossings with a maximum of 87 kilometers (54 miles) and a

Sunda The combined landmass of the modern islands of Java, Sumatra, Bali, and Borneo. These islands became a single, continuous landmass during periods of glaciation and attendant lowered sea level during the Pleistocene.

Sahul The landmass of "Greater Australia" including Australia proper, New Guinea, and Tasmania, formed during periods of glacial maxima in the Pleistocene.

Greater Australia Another name for Sahul.

Wallace Trench A sea chasm more than 7,500 meters (more than 4.5 miles) deep, separating Java and Borneo from Greater Australia (Australia, New Guinea, and Tasmania).

FIGURE 11.19 When sea level was lowered during the Pleistocene, the islands of Southeast Asia were joined to the continent in a landmass called Sunda. At the same time, New Guinea, Australia, and Tasmania were joined into a single landmass called Sahul, or Greater Australia. Even during glacial maxima, Sunda and Sahul were separated by water so migrants from the former to the latter must have come by boat, probably island-hopping along one or more of the routes depicted.

mean of a little more than 19 kilometers (12 miles) between landfalls (Birdsell 1977:127).

The Archaeology of the First Australians   As might be expected for a large island landmass with a hot, dry desert interior, the oldest archaeological sites in Greater Australia are located around the perimeter of the continent. As archaeologist Sandra Bowdler (1977, 1990) points out, in all likelihood, people entered Australia from the north and then spread along the coast, inhabiting areas with tropical coastal environments similar to the places from which they migrated. They moved inland along major rivers, shifting their subsistence focus from marine to riverine resources.

The timing of the first human settlement of Australia continues to be a point of contention. At question is the accuracy of the dates derived from some of the older sites (Mulvaney and Kamminga 1999). To be sure, archaeologists agree that Australia has an extensive history of settlement, but the argument about timing, for the most part, concerns whether that extensive history can be traced back to only 40,000 ya or to as much as 60,000 ya. Archaeologists J. F. O'Connell and J. Allen (1998) reviewed the interpretations of a number of ancient Australian sites and concluded that, ultimately, while there is strong evidence for the human settlement of that continent for 40,000 years, the evidence for an older date for the first human migration is not very strong.

Among the Australian sites proposed as dating to more than 50,000 ya are Malakunanja II (Roberts et al. 1990) and Nauwalabila, both in Arnhem Land in the north of the country. A number of researchers are very skeptical, however, of the very old dates derived from these sites because of problems with stratigraphy and because the technique used to date the sites, optically stimulated luminescence, may be inaccurate (Mulvaney and Kamminga 1999; O'Connell and Allen 1998).

The Lake Mungo 3 skeleton, the remains of an anatomically modern human, is one of the oldest human remains found in Australia. Lake Mungo is one of a number of dry lake beds located in the Willandra Lakes region of southeastern Australia. Though some have argued that the skeleton lends support to the older, 60,000-year date (Thorne et al. 1999), the geological deposit in which the burial was encountered has been dated to no more than about 43,000 ya (Brown 2000). If the date of the geological deposit is correct, this would represent an absolute maximum age for the skeleton, whose grave, rather obviously, could only be placed in a deposit sometime after that deposit was laid down (Bowler and Magee 2000). Radiocarbon dating of the oldest Australian sites confirms an antiquity of more than 40,000 years, generally in the range of 42,000 to 48,000 years, but does not support a claim of greater antiquity (Gillespie 2002).

Modern native Australians have very robust skeletal features including rather massive (by modern human standards) brow ridges. Lake Mungo 3, however, is very lightly constructed; technically it is gracile, which raises questions about the relationship between the person represented by this skeleton and the present aboriginal people of Australia. In one scenario, Australia was populated at least twice by two very different-looking groups of people; first by a light-boned people who may have died out and later by a more robustly boned group who are the ancestors of modern aborigines (Jones 1992). Fragments of a skeleton (W.L. 50) were recovered just north of Lake Mungo. Dating to between 30,000 and 20,000 ya, W.L. 50 exhibits a very robust morphology with thick cranial bones and quite large brow ridges. One interpretation is that people looking like W.L. 50 represent the second wave of immigrants to Australia who were ancestors of modern aboriginal Australians.

In a competing view, the original gracile migrants to Australia evolved the more robust features of modern Australian natives over time. In this scenario, W.L. 50 does not represent a member of a population separate from that of Lake Mungo 3 but rather a descendant of that earlier gracile group. There simply is insufficient evidence at this time to determine which of these hypotheses better reflects what actually occurred—or if some other alternative better explains the data.

The oldest human sites in Greater Australia are located along the coast or in interior areas once drained by rivers or dotted with lakes (Figure 11.20). The earliest known settlement of New Guinea is located at Bobongara Hill, on the north coast on an ancient, exposed coral reef. The site has been dated to 40,000 B.P. by thermoluminescence (Groube et al. 1986).

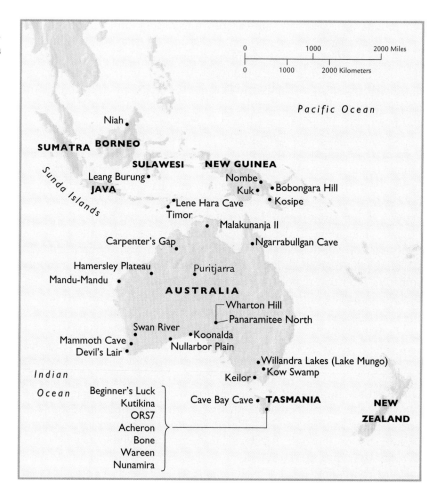

Among the oldest Australian sites whose dating is universally accepted is Swan River (the Upper Swan Bridge site) in southwestern Australia. About 200 artifacts—including stone chips, worked flakes, and flakes with edges exhibiting wear—have been found there. The site has been dated to between 40,000 and 35,000 ya (Jones 1992). Also in southwest Australia is the cave site of Devil's Lair. Radiocarbon dates derived from a series of hearths that contained the remains of kangaroos killed, butchered, and eaten by the cave's human inhabitants place occupation of the cave at 38,000 to 32,000 ya (Jones 1992). At Mammoth Cave, burned bones, possible stone artifacts, and charcoal have been dated to between 37,000 and 31,000 ya (White and O'Connell 1982). A small early occupation of Ngarrabullgan Cave in north Queensland has been dated by optically stimulated luminescence to 37,000 ya, and the Carpenter's Gap Rockshelter in central Kimberly has been radiocarbon-dated to close to 40,000 ya (Mulvaney and Kamminga 1999).

The Willandra Lakes region of western New South Wales has been a treasure trove of archaeological data related to the early human settlement of Australia. The so-called lakes are dry, the remnants of ancient, Pleistocene water bodies. Lake Mungo itself, already mentioned in reference to the Lake Mungo 3 skeleton, has produced additional, unequivocal evidence of occupation dating back to at least as early as 32,750 ya (Barbetti and Allen 1972). Fireplaces, some stone cores and flakes, steep-edged scraping tools, an earth oven, and the burned eggs of emu (a large, flightless bird indigenous to Australia) have been found. Charcoal from the fireplaces produced radiocarbon dates ranging from 24,020 to 32,750 years old (Barbetti and Allen 1972:48).

The remains of a cremated human female (Lake Mungo 1) were found at another Lake Mungo site. Like the Lake Mungo 3 find, she was anatomically modern and rather gracile in her physiology, lacking the large brow ridges or heavy buttressing bone typical of modern Australian natives. She has been dated to 24,700 ya (Mulvaney and Kamminga 1999).

Australia's Dry Interior   Between 25,000 and 20,000 ya, human groups moved into the dry interior of central Australia. The Puritjarra rockshelter in the Cleveland Hills of central Australia was occupied by 22,000 ya (M. A. Smith 1987). Other interior rockshelter sites on the Hamersley Plateau in western Australia date to 21,000 and 26,000 B.P. (Jones 1987).

Conditions in the interior were entirely different from those at the humid coast. The ability of the first Australians to migrate into a formerly unknown territory, to expand across thousands of miles, and to adapt to entirely new and alien environments is a testament to their resourcefulness. Such resourcefulness and inventiveness is what makes us human.

The Americas

Just as with Australia, there is no broad consensus concerning the timing of the earliest settlement of the New World by human beings. For several decades, the dominant perspective was that the Americas were settled by small groups of people traveling from northeast Asia into northwest North America, between 13,000 and 12,000 ya. They may have come in one, two, or three waves, and all modern Native American people are descended from these Late Pleistocene Asian migrants.

Many archaeologists, however, are now calling this **paradigm** into question. New sites, new techniques for interpreting archaeological data, and the reassessment of sites found previously have convinced some that the Americas may have been settled far earlier than the tail end of the Pleistocene—perhaps 20,000, 30,000, 40,000, or even 50,000 ya—and that northeast Asia may not have been the sole geographic source for ancient

paradigm Overarching perspective, approach, or view.

FIGURE 11.21 When the sea level dropped during the Pleistocene, the Bering Land Bridge was exposed. This 1,500-km-wide platform connected northeast Asia and northwest North America, allowing Asian populations to migrate into and populate the New World.

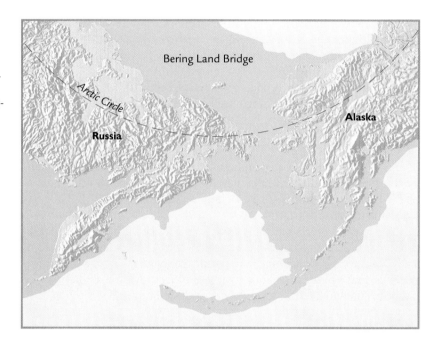

migrants to the New World. As a result, there is an active and vigorous debate among archaeologists, linguists, and biological anthropologists about the precise ethnic and geographic source of the New World's native peoples and the timing of their arrival in the Americas. Though much of the data supports the current paradigm, not all of it does, at least not clearly.

There seems to be a growing consensus that until more research is conducted, there will continue to be disagreement on this question. What we will present here only represents a summary of what is now known, but we can provide no absolute answers to the questions when or how. As we stated, it is an exciting, if confusing, time in American prehistory.

Walking or Boating to the New World   Unlike the situation in Australia, the trip to the Americas could have been made entirely by land. Several times during the Pleistocene, when a substantial amount of the earth's water was locked up in glaciers, sea level was reduced by 125 meters (more than 400 feet) or more, exposing a wide platform of land some 1,500 kilometers (more than 900 miles) across that connected northeast Asia—Siberia—with northwest North America (Figure 11.21). What is now the Bering Sea and Bering Strait, separating eastern Russia from Alaska by only 150 kilometers (just over 90 miles), was then the Bering Land Bridge, now called **Beringia,** across which animals and people moved. The precise chronology of the exposure and flooding of the land bridge is unknown, but we are fairly certain that it was intermittently avail-

Beringia A broad expanse of land more than 1,500 kilometers (1,000 miles) across, connecting northeast Asia with northwest North America during periods of sea level depression in the Pleistocene. People living in Asia walked east across the land bridge or traveled along its coast into the lands of the Western Hemisphere, likely at least 15,000 ya and possibly more.

able for human movement between 75,000 and 35,000 ya (Hopkins 1982). Further, we know it was exposed continuously from about 35,000 to 11,000 ya (Elias et al. 1996). Recent analysis of sediments off the Australian coast points to a late glacial maximum of three hundred years duration between 22,000 and 19,000 ya (Yokoyama et al. 2000). Worldwide sea level was at a low point during this time span, and Beringia would have been at its most extensive. This same evidence indicates a general warming accompanied by a rise in sea level immediately following 19,000 ya. It should also be pointed out that in recent historical times, long after the land bridge had disappeared, the Bering Strait froze over, allowing people and animals to pass from one hemisphere to another across what amounts to an "ice bridge." There would have been nothing to prevent such movement during cold spells of past interstadials or interglacials even when the land bridge would not have been available.

Though a land bridge would have provided a convenient avenue from northeast Asia into northwest North America, we have already seen in the example of Australia, and in even earlier instances in the movement of *Homo erectus* onto the Indonesian island of Flores (see Chapter 9) that human beings and even ancestral forms of hominids were capable of traversing narrow stretches of ocean such as the Bering Strait. There is no reason to believe that maritime people could not have accomplished the same thing and entered into the New World during periods when there was not a land connection between Asia and America.

Archaeological findings clearly bear this out. For example, recent work on Prince of Wales Island in Alaska indicates the presence of human beings with a maritime economy at the end of the Pleistocene (Dixon 1999). Paleontologist Timothy Heaton found human remains in On Your Knees Cave that have been dated to about 10,500 ya. Isotope analysis of the bones indicated that the individual's diet consisted almost entirely of marine foods (Dixon 1999:118). This individual may have been an Asian migrant or, more likely, the descendant of Asian migrants who moved along the coast as they explored southward.

From Siberia to Alaska   The movement of people into and across Beringia need not have been intentional. Groups of migratory hunter-gatherers living in northeast Asia may have followed the movement of large game animals onto the land bridge and eventually into the Americas, either through the interior of Beringia or along its coast. This journey thrust these people, unintentionally, into the role of pioneers with a new world to explore and settle. The question is, when might this have happened?

Siberia deserves its reputation for having a miserable climate, making the conduct of archaeology there difficult—one reason that Siberia is poorly known archaeologically. Based on the limited work that has been done there, it appears that there was not a substantial human occupation much before 30,000 B.P. (Meltzer 1993a:161). The oldest clear evidence of

FIGURE 11.22 Locations of some of the oldest archaeological sites known in the New World and sites in Siberia representing possible source populations for these first settlers of the Americas.

human occupation yet found in eastern Siberia is the Yana RHS site (Pitulko et al. 2004). Radiocarbon dating shows that people were living along the banks of the Yana River 27,000 ya. Their economy was based on hunting large game animals such as reindeer, bison, woolly mammoth, and musk ox. It is likely, therefore, that if ancient Siberians entered into the New World via Beringia, it must have been after they first settled Siberia, in other words, sometime after 30,000 ya (Meltzer 1989, 1993a, 1993b; Owen 1984).

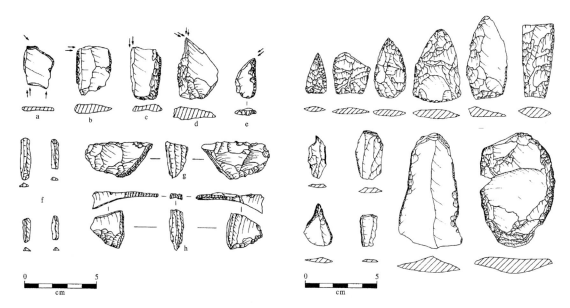

FIGURE 11.23 Stone tools from the Nenana *(right)* and Denali *(left)* cultures of Alaska. Dating to as much as 11,800 ya, the Nenana stone tool assemblage, with bifacially flaked blades, is similar to that seen in some sites in eastern Russia and also similar to later industries in America south of Alaska. Dating to about 10,000 ya, Denali tools also resemble artifacts found in Siberia, possibly evidence of a second, later wave of Asian migrants to the New World in the Late Pleistocene. *(Nenana and Denali tools courtesy William Powers)*

A number of Siberian sites dating between 18,000 and 14,000 B.P. represent the most likely population sources for the American migrants (Figure 11.22). For example, Dyuktai Cave, located on the Aldan River in central Siberia, dates to about 18,000 B.P. (Yi and Clark 1985). Dyuktai, in particular, is significant for the form of stone tools found there. There are some striking similarities between the small **wedge-shaped cores** and microblades made at Dyuktai (and a number of sites in central Siberia of similar age) and tools found in Alaska several thousand years later, which are part of the **Denali Complex** (Figure 11.23). Denali Complex sites date to after 10,700 B.P. In one view (Powers and Hoffecker 1989), people with wedge-shaped core technology constitute a second, somewhat later migration from Siberia to Alaska (see Figure 11.23). Sites become more numerous in Siberia in the period after 13,000 ya. For example, finely made, symmetrical, bifacially flaked spear points have been found along the shore of Ushki Lake in the central Kamchatka peninsula. The oldest Ushki occupation has now been dated to about 11,300 B.P. (Goebel et al. 2003). Interestingly, the stone tools found at Ushki resemble those found in Alaska in what is called the **Nenana Complex** (see Figure 11.23). The Nenana

wedge-shaped cores Cores shaped like wedges from which blades are struck.

Denali Complex A stone tool technology seen in the American Arctic consisting of wedge-shaped cores, microblades, bifacial knives, and burins. Dates to after 10,700 B.P.

Nenana Complex Stone tool complex in Alaska, dating from 11,800 to 11,000 B.P. Nenana includes bifacially flaked spear points similar to tools made in eastern Russia about 14,000 ya.

Complex also includes bifacially flaked spear points, and Alaskan sites exhibiting the Nenana Complex assemblage also date to the period between 11,800 and 11,000 ya (Powers and Hoffecker 1989). As we will see, bifacially flaked spear points also are a major component of the toolkit of at least some of the early settlers of the New World south of Alaska. So the Ushki makers of bifacial spear points represent at least one potential source for New World people and culture.

How Old Are the Oldest New World Sites?   As noted, there is controversy over the timing of the earliest settlement of the Americas. People tend to get very worked up over this, but to provide some perspective, it should be pointed out that all archaeologists agree that human antiquity in the New World can be traced back more than 10,000 years; the argument concerns how much more than 10,000 years. Some scholars think that archaeological evidence in the Americas supports their belief that people have inhabited the Western Hemisphere for 20,000, 30,000, 40,000, or even more than 50,000 years. Others maintain that strong evidence exists for settlement by about 13,000 ya but not much before this. Much of the argument revolves around the legitimacy of the artifacts being analyzed (Were the oldest of these really made by people or just fortuitously shaped natural sherds of stone or bone?) and the accuracy of the dates derived from or applied to the artifacts. A handful of the sites dating to more than 13,000 ya—or dating to around that period but located far from Beringia, implying a much older date for entry into the New World—deserve our attention.

A New World site near Beringia that may represent the habitation of some of the first settlers of the New World is Bluefish Caves (Cinque-Mars 1978). The site has a wide variety of animal bones, including those of woolly mammoth, horse, caribou, bison, and sheep. Many of the bones show evidence of butchering with stone tools, which have also been recovered at the site. The tools found there include sharp-cutting flakes, burins for engraving bone, and stone hammers for making the stone tools. The chert from which the tools were made is not native to the limestone ridge in which the caves are situated, indicating either that the raw material for making the tools or the completed tools themselves must have been brought in by humans (Morlan 1983). Radiocarbon dates derived from bones recovered in the caves have yielded dates of 15,500 and 12,900 B.P.

It would be helpful for archaeologists researching the movement of people from northeast Asia into the New World if there were a large number of sites of this age in Alaska or the Canadian Yukon, representing a first wave of migration. Unfortunately, there aren't. Perhaps such sites exist but simply have not been found—a reasonable possibility in an enormous region where climate and geography make it very difficult to conduct archaeological research. Of course, another possibility for the general absence of sites is simply that they aren't there because the standard and long-accepted

FIGURE 11.24 Proposed boundaries of the Cordilleran and Laurentide ice sheets of North America. Though the two may have coalesced in some localized areas during glacial maxima, for long periods an ice-free corridor may have existed by which people south of Alaska could have migrated into North America south of the ice sheets. *(Courtesy of David Meltzer).*

route from interior Siberia, through Beringia, and into the interior of the American Arctic was not commonly used by settlers of the New World.

Migrants who followed this interior route faced another challenge—a layer of glacial ice, more than a kilometer thick, to the south. Two primary ice fields covered North America during glacial stages of the Pleistocene: the Cordilleran ice sheet, centered in the Rocky Mountains, and the Laurentide sheet that originated in northeastern Canada (Figure 11.24). These two ice sheets spread in all directions and coalesced during glacial maxima, creating at least a temporary, impenetrable barrier to the southward movement of animals or humans. The overall timing and extent of this barrier is still uncertain, but even when there was an ice-free corridor between the two fields, it may have been inhospitable for large game animals and therefore of little interest to human hunters. Pollen studies indicate that when an ice-free corridor was available for travel before 14,000 ya, vegetation was too poor to support large populations of animals (Mandryk 1990)—and without animals to hunt, there would have been no reason for humans to be there. No direct archaeological evidence indicates a human presence in the corridor before 11,000 ya (Burns 1990).

Nevertheless, people must have traveled south through the corridor before this time because there are sites south of the ice sheets that predate

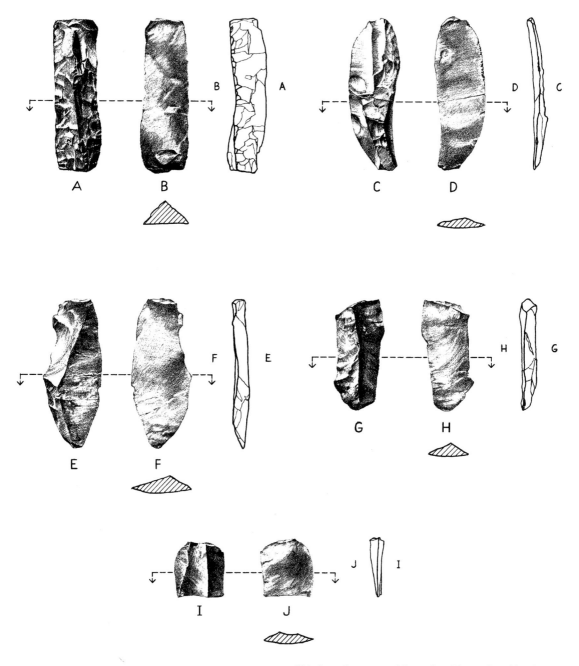

FIGURE 11.25 A series of blade tools recovered from the oldest cultural level at Meadowcroft Rockshelter in western Pennsylvania. These blades and a handful of bifacial knives and one spear point have been dated to approximately 12,800 ya. *(Courtesy J. M. Adovasio, Mercyhurst College)*

FIGURE 11.26 The so-called Miller Lanceolate projectile point *(far left)* found in the earliest indisputable cultural level at Meadowcroft Rockshelter in western Pennsylvania. The layer in which the point was found dates to 12,800 ya. The four other projectile points here—similar in appearance to the Meadowcroft specimen—were found at other sites in Pennsylvania. *(Courtesy of James Advasio, Mercyhurst Archaeological Institute)*

11,000 B.P. One of the best examples is the Meadowcroft Rockshelter near Pittsburgh, Pennsylvania (Advasio et al. 1990). Over thousands of years of occupation, humans made tools, cooked food, and threw away trash, taking advantage of the natural protection afforded by the small cave. In a meticulous excavation, part of an ambitious, multidisciplinary research project, a deeply stratified deposit with cultural material was excavated. These researchers have found material that may have the oldest radiocarbon dates associated with human activity in the New World. Sealed beneath a rock fall at the base of the sequence were more than 400 stone tools, including blades (Figure 11.25), knives with retouched edges, and an unfluted, bifacial projectile point, all dated to at least 12,000 B.P. (Figure 11.26). Six dates older than 12,800 B.P. have been associated with these tools. Meadowcroft is a long way from Beringia, which implies that entry into the New World occurred earlier than 12,800 B.P.

Recent research in the American southeast has revealed a number of archaeological sites potentially even older than Meadowcroft, including Topper in South Carolina and Cactus Hill in Virginia. At Topper (Figure 11.27), sharp stone flakes that appear to have been intentionally struck from stone cores were found by a team led by archaeologist Albert Goodyear (1999) in a stratigraphic layer below so-called **Clovis** artifacts, which have long been presumed to be the oldest kinds of tools found in the New World (see the discussion of Clovis that appears later in this chapter). Radiocarbon dates at Topper sites have been equivocal, but noncultural material from a layer immediately beneath the stone flakes dated to about 20,000 ya, so the tools may be close to that old.

In the 2004 summer field season, in another part of the site, Goodyear and his students found a deep stratum sprinkled with chipped stone flakes

Clovis A long, bifacially flaked, stone spear point characterized by channels or flutes on both faces.

FIGURE 11.27 Artifacts from two sites in eastern North America, Topper in South Carolina and Cactus Hill in Virginia. The Topper artifacts (*top*)—chipped-stone cutting tools—were found in a stratigraphic layer below one containing Clovis artifacts and dated to 11,000 ya and above a culturally sterile layer dated to 20,000 ya. The Cactus Hill artifacts (*bottom*)—including a stone scraping tool, stone blades, and a stone core—were found in an undisturbed layer 15 centimeters (6 inches) below one in which Clovis artifacts were found. (Top: *SCIAA-USC, Daryl P. Miller;* bottom: *© Kenneth Garrett/National Geographic Society Image Collection*)

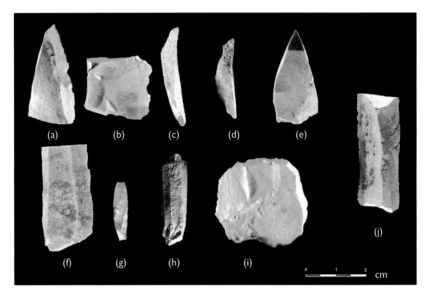

(Wilford 2004). Some of these pieces of stone may be tools, others may be fragments discarded in the toolmaking process. One of Goodyear's students also recovered flecks of charcoal in the same soil level. The archaeological community was stunned in late 2004, when Goodyear announced the results of radiocarbon dating of this charcoal: 50,000 years. The date is singular and, as a result, many are skeptical. Archaeologists eagerly await the details of the site and of this extraordinary date.

FIGURE 11.28 These stone tools from Monte Verde, in Chile, date to as early as 12,500 B.P. *(Courtesy of Tom Dillehay)*

At Cactus Hill (see Figure 11.27), stone projectile points were found 15 centimeters below a layer in which typical Clovis tools were found. The pre-Clovis layer was radiocarbon dated to 18,000 ya (Stokstad 2000), though some question whether the date was derived from older charcoal that had mixed with a younger archaeological deposit. Interestingly, the Cactus Hill tools are similar to some of the artifacts found at Meadowcroft, so it is possible that these sites together represent the remains of a small, thinly distributed human population in North America that dates to sometime between 13,000 and 20,000 ya.

Also of great importance, because of its age, location, and the incredible degree of preservation of organic remains, is Monte Verde, located on Chinchihuapa Creek in central Chile near the coast (Dillehay 1989, 1997a, 1997b). Hundreds of stone artifacts have been recovered at Monte Verde, including long, slender spear points and cutting and scraping tools (Figure 11.28). Led by archaeologist Tom Dillehay, excavators also found well-preserved wooden lances and stakes that may have been used to hold down the bases of hide-covered tents. The site is situated in a deposit of wet peat, and this depositional environment resulted in a high degree of preservation. Researchers have recovered the bones of animals killed and butchered at the site, pieces of mastodon meat and skin tissue, and fragments of almost seventy different plant species. They have also identified wooden hut foundations (Figure 11.29). Nine of the ^{14}C dates for the main occupation range from about 13,500 to 11,800 B.P. It must be pointed out that an extremely acrimonious debate has arisen concerning the interpretation of Monte Verde. Archaeologist Stuart Fiedel (1999) has raised a number of questions about the excavation and analysis of the site, asserting that much of the site is, in fact, a natural deposit and that the cultural material is far younger than the excavators claim. The principal investigator of the site, Tom Dillehay (Dillehay et al. 1999), has responded, but the issue remains controversial.

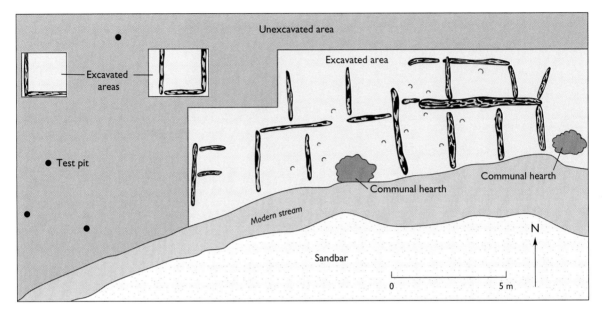

FIGURE 11.29 The remarkable level of preservation apparent at Monte Verde, in Chile, belies the great antiquity of the site's occupation. Dating to about 13,000 ya, Monte Verde, though more than 16,000 kilometers from the Bering Land Bridge, is nevertheless one of the oldest sites known in the Americas.

Monte Verde is even further from Beringia than Meadowcroft, raising the question of how Asian migrants reached the area so early. Excavator Tom Dillehay (1999) suggests that the inhabitants of Monte Verde and a number of less firmly dated sites in South America (especially Taima Taima in Venezuela and several rockshelter sites in Brazil) represent the descendants of a founding migration of northeast Asians who entered the New World through Beringia but not its interior. Using watercraft, these people would have traveled east along the Beringian coast and then south along the Pacific coast of the New World. There is little evidence of their migration because most of the sites, located along the coast, would have been inundated by rising seawater as the glaciers melted at the end of the Pleistocene.

Recent underwater research conducted by scientists Daryl W. Fedje and Heiner Josenhans has resulted in a chart showing a part of the western coast of northwestern North America as it would have looked more than 10,000 ya, before the ice sheets melted and the sea level rose (Fedje and Josenhans 2000). Evidence collected from this ancient and now submerged coastline suggests a hospitable environment with river valleys, floodplains, and lakes. Fedje and Josenhans even found a stone artifact at a level dated to about 10,000 ya, now situated 53 meters below modern sea level. This research indicates that the coastal route may have been a viable alternative to an interior one by 10,000 ya and possibly substantially earlier.

Dillehay (1999) suggests that coastally adapted migrants entered South America sometime between 14,000 and 12,000 ya, previous to the invention of Clovis stone tool technology. Archaeologist David Meltzer, going even further back in time, suggests that the age of the Monte Verde site implies a time of entry into the New World before 20,000 ya (1997:755). A couple of coastal sites in Peru dating to around 11,000 ya— Quebrada Jaguay (Sandweiss et al. 1998) and Quebrada Tacahuay (Keefer et al. 1998)—are too late to be ancestral to Monte Verde but reflect a very early coastal adaptation (most of the food found at the sites came from the ocean or shoreline) that may be similar to that of the first coastal migrants.

What Do Their Skeletons Tell Us about the First Americans?   Our sample of skeletons of the first Americans is a small one. Altogether, there are the bones of fewer than thirty individuals in the Americas that can be dated to before 8,500 ya (Steele 2000). Among the oldest are the female skeleton from Midland, Texas (originally called "Midland Man" but now known to have been a female), dated by uranium series to 11,600 ya (Hoppe 1992) and "Tepexpan Man" in Mexico (probably another female) with a date of 11,000 B.P. A small group of other human remains have been dated to between 11,500 and 10,500 ya: the Pelican Rapids find (known as "Minnesota Man," another misidentified female), the Marmes skull from Washington State, "Arlington Man" from Santa Rosa Island off of California (Owen 1984), and remains at the Wilsall site (also called Anzick) in Montana and Mostin site in northern California (Taylor 1991). Cerro Sota 2 from Chile is about 11,000 years old. Several individuals from Lagoa Santa in Brazil are probably 10,000 years old. Two nearly complete skeletons from Nevada—Spirit Lake and Wizard's Beach—have both been dated to more than 9,000 ya. The Kennewick skeleton in Washington State is a little more than 9,000 years old.

The anatomical features of these early skeletons pose an interesting problem. Most archaeologists believe that the source of both ancient and modern Native Americans was ancient northeast Asians who crossed into the New World through interior or coastal Beringia. There are many similarities between skeletons of modern Native Americans and modern northeast Asian natives. However, these oldest American skeletons do not closely resemble either modern Native Americans or modern native peoples of northeast Asia. For example, the skulls of the most ancient Americans tend to have longer and narrower faces than either modern Native Americans or northeast Asians. Also, when viewed from the top, the ancient American skulls are not as round; their braincases are longer and narrower than either modern Native Americans or northeast Asians.

There is a considerable amount of acrimony, misunderstanding, and controversy concerning the appropriateness of the excavation, analysis, and storage of the skeletons of Native Americans by scientists who are, by and large, not Native Americans. After all, what some scientists might consider to be fascinating specimens are considered by other people to be grandmother and grandfather! The record of scientists and the American government has been less than exemplary on this issue, in some cases condoning the collection of the remains of very recently deceased Indians, even battlefield casualties, for museums and research institutes (Thomas 2000). Some Native Americans consider archaeology to be little more than grave robbing, and given the injustices of the past, it is not surprising so many feel this way. As a result, when Native American skeletons are found, the possibility of resistance, mistrust, even legal action, is unfortunately high.

One such case involves "Kennewick Man," or "The Ancient One," whose bones were found in 1996 in Columbia, Washington. The case created emotional and intellectual divisions because of a fundamental difference in how those most directly involved viewed the remains. On the one hand, local Indians saw the remains as belonging to an individual they considered to be an ancestor and whose bones should have immediately been reburied. On the other hand, scientists viewed the skeleton as a spectacular archaeological remain, so complete and ancient that it could tell us much about life in America at a time we know so little about; for them, reburial would have resulted in a tragic loss of valuable information about the past.

Because of the controversy concerning who the bones should go to—scientists who wished to study them or local Indian groups that hoped to rebury them—the federal government became involved. Lawsuits were filed by Indians who wanted The Ancient One returned and by scientists who wanted to study Kennewick Man. The government required enough analysis to determine if the skeleton is, indeed, that of a Native American and, therefore, subject to the Native American Graves Protection and Repatriation Act, the law that governs the disposition of Indian remains. A detailed analysis of Kennewick prepared by biological anthropologists Joseph Powell and Jerome C. Rose (published online at *www.cr.nps.gov/aad/kennewick/*) indicates that the Kennewick skeleton is not all that similar to modern Native Americans or northeast Asians. Instead, it more closely resembles the skeletons of the Ainu of Japan, the inhabitants of southern Asia, and even some Polynesians.

Does this mean that skeletal analysis disproves the Beringian paradigm? No. There is no reason to insist that modern Native Americans should look precisely like their ancestors of more than 10,000 ya. Remember our discussion of evolution in Chapter 3. The appearance of modern Native Americans is the result of thousands of years of evolutionary processes, gene flow, and natural selection. As Powell and Rose (1999) note, the skeletons of ancient ancestors in other parts of the world are not always a good match for the modern peoples of the same region.

The most recent court decision in July 2005 at last allows for a thorough scientific examination of the Kennewick remains. The nine-year (!) battle produced hard feelings on both sides and made adversaries of people who should have been able to work together. Time, energy, and resources were wasted. Resolution took so long that Rob Bonnichsen, one of the scientists who hoped to examine the remains, passed away during the litigation. The Kennewick incident is a model for how not to solve issues revolving around the examination of human remains.

The recent analysis of the 10,300-year-old human remains found in On Your Knees Cave in Alaska is a much better model for how such research can be conducted. Local Native Americans were involved from the beginning and viewed the scientific examination of the human remains found in the cave as enabling them to learn not just about but also *from* their ancestors: "We viewed the remains as offering us knowledge. We wanted the knowledge for current and future generations" is how a Tlingit tribal member, Rosita Worl—who happens also to be a cultural anthropologist—put it (Dalton 2005:162).

And what has the ancient ancestor shared with us all? So far quite a bit, especially because scientists have been able to extract mitochondrial DNA (mtDNA) from the teeth. The mtDNA of Native Americans comprise five distinctly different DNA clusters called **haplogroups** (Derenko et al. 2001; Gibbons 1993, 1996b; Stone and Stoneking 1993). All Native American groups exhibit at least one of the haplogroups. All five haplogroups are also found among northeast Asians, suggesting a rather close genetic relationship between modern Asians and modern Native Americans. A European team of geneticists has concluded that the amount of genetic difference between Native Americans and northeast Asians suggests that the two groups separated about 25,000 to 20,000 ya (Gibbons 1996b). In a recent study of 2,198 men, geneticist Mike Hammer found the greatest degree of genetic similarity between Native Americans and Asians from the region of Lake Baikal in southern Siberia (cited in Culotta 1999b).

The mtDNA extracted from teeth found in On Your Knees Cave place the individual firmly among Native Americans, specifically mtDNA group D (of A, B, C, D, and X). In the New World, mitochondrial haplogroup D is found in modern Native Americans in California, Illinois, Mexico, and Chile. Interestingly, Group D is also found in eastern China, suggesting a possible link, however indirect, between, specifically, the Han ethnic group there and Native Americans (Dalton 2005).

Paleo-Indians: If Not the First, the First Successful   Though much disagreement exists about these possible older sites, there is little disagreement about the human population explosion that occurred in the New World after 12,000 ya. We call these peoples the **Paleo-Indians.** Whether they were new arrivals or people descended from earlier migrants, they had a hunting-gathering economy with a seasonal emphasis on the big game that flourished in North America at the tail end of the Pleistocene. Using large-bladed Clovis points, with their characteristically chipped channels or flutes on the faces to facilitate attachment to a shaft, Paleo-Indians

haplogroup A biological lineage defined by a cluster of specific, co-occurring genetic markers. Five major haplogroups characterize Native Americans, and all also occur in East Asia. An additional haplogroup found in some Native Americans is also found in Europe, West Asia, and Southwest Asia, but has not yet been found in East Asia.

Paleo-Indian A New World culture, based on big-game hunting and characterized by fluted points, present from about 12,000 to 10,000 ya.

FIGURE 11.30 Fluted points of the Paleo-Indian settlers of North America: the earlier Clovis point, dated to 11,700–11,000 B.P. from the Richey Clovis Cache (*left*), and the later Folsom, a variant on the fluted point technique, dated to after 11,000 B.P. With such weapons, these first inhabitants of the Americas hunted the large game animals that flourished at the end of the Pleistocene. *(Both photos courtesy of R. M. Gramly, Great Lakes Artifact Repository; right, artifact courtesy of Dr. Douglas Sirkin)*

hunted woolly mammoths, now-extinct bison, horses, caribou, and other large game animals (Figure 11.30). At sites such as Olsen-Chubbuck, Colorado (Wheat 1972), and Casper, Wyoming (Frison 1974), there is evidence for bison drives where hundreds of animals were driven over cliffs or into sandy traps in communal hunts. Doubtless these peoples also collected roots, seeds, nuts, and berries when in season.

These people were enormously successful and quickly spread throughout the entire New World (see Figure 11.22). After their initial appearance perhaps 14,000 or 13,000 ya in Alaska, we find sites throughout the American Midwest by 11,500 ya. By 11,000 ya, they had reached as far east as Maine, and by 9,500 ya, we find traces of their presence at the southern tip of South America.

Paleo-Indians were not just plains-dwelling hunters of Pleistocene big game. They lived in many diverse habitats, including tropical rainforest to the south and tundra in the north. An early South American site displaying the great range of Paleo-Indian adaptation has been excavated recently by a team of researchers led by archaeologist Anna C. Roosevelt (Roosevelt et al. 1996). The Caverna da Pedra Pintada site is located in the Amazon basin in Brazil. There, researchers recovered more than 30,000 stone flakes and 24 formal tools including triangular, stemmed, bifacial points from a layer in the cave that has been radiocarbon dated to between 11,200 and 10,000 ya. Preserved remains of plants and animals used by the Paleo-Indian inhabitants show quite clearly that when the site was occupied, the area was, as it is today, a tropical rainforest. Abundant remnants of tree fruits, fish, mollusks, birds, and small and large game attest to the broad food base of the cave's occupants.

Also found in the same layer as the Paleo-Indian artifacts of this site were hundreds of lumps and drops of red pigment and two chunks of painted cave wall. The chemistry of the drops of red pigment match that of painted images found on the wall, implying a similar age for the paintings. The Pedra Pintada paintings, therefore, may be the oldest known examples of cave art in the New World.

The Paleo-Indians may have been too successful. It has been suggested that their population grew so quickly and their skill as hunters was so remarkable that they contributed to the extinction of many large animals already strained by the change in climate at the end of the Pleistocene (Martin 1982). The horse, woolly mammoth, mastodon, bison, and ground sloth—all probably hunted extensively by the Paleo-Indians—became extinct sometime after these people arrived on the scene. Others believe that environmental change at the end of the Pleistocene played a more important role in the extinctions of many species of large game animals. Biologist R. Dale Guthrie (1990) suggests that the Pleistocene-Holocene boundary was unlike previous periods of warming, producing far more drastic consequences for large herbivores hunted by humans and also for small rodents and other species that were not part of the Paleo-Indians' diet.

The Arctic

The final "brave new world" we will briefly touch upon is not a previously uninhabited continent but a region not previously exploited by human beings: the Arctic. Archaic *Homo sapiens*, especially the Neandertals, had evolved a highly successful adaptation for life on the tundra. As just shown, modern human beings also occupied some very cold, harsh territory as they expanded into the Asian tundra and eventually across the Bering Land Bridge into the North American tundra. But even the cold-adapted Neandertals did not penetrate into the ice-covered region of the Arctic, and anatomically modern humans did not enter this region until fairly late in prehistory. The oldest archaeological evidence for occupation of the Arctic dates to only about 4,500 ya.

Life is difficult for humans in the Arctic. Even fresh water, the most basic necessity of life, is largely unavailable in liquid form for most of the year and must be processed by heating ice. The Arctic is severely cold much of the year, yet wood is not widely available as a fuel because trees cannot grow under these conditions. Human settlement of the Arctic, therefore, required an extremely sophisticated material culture with tailored clothing and well-insulated shelters to protect people from the cold, and a highly specialized toolkit to exploit the resources available in such an environment. As anthropologist Moreau Maxwell (1993:209) points out, when the Arctic was finally settled by human beings, it was the last of the "habitable lands" to be mastered by our species.

In the New World, the spread of people throughout the Arctic is signaled by the appearance of a series of stone artifacts of the **Arctic Small Tool Tradition.** This tradition includes small blades barely 2.5 centimeters long used in cutting and carving, equally small burins for engraving bone and antler in the production of harpoons and sewing needles, small blades inset into bone and antler arrow and spear points, and even smaller microblades about 1 centimeter long set into handles and used for such tasks as butchering and skinning animals and manufacturing watertight clothing from their skins (Maxwell 1993).

In the American Arctic, these small tools spread remarkably quickly across the north, appearing first in Alaska about 4,500 ya and turning up all the way in Greenland about 4,000 ya. The modern descendants of the people bearing this culture are the Inuit (commonly known as Eskimo), whose lifeway is emblematic of our species' remarkable ability to adapt to even the most extreme of environmental circumstances.

Arctic Small Tool Tradition
A stone tool tradition dating to about 4,500 B.P. in the Arctic, that involved the production of small blades used in cutting and carving, small burins, and even smaller microblades.

Summary

Though there are glimmers apparent in the archaeological record by 100,000 ya, it isn't until after about 50,000 ya that a remarkable transformation occurred, resulting in cultures all over the world with a decidedly modern cast. The cultures of the period are characterized by the production of blade tools; a broadening of the subsistence base; an increase in the size of some sites, implying the practice of temporary population aggregation; the use of bone, antler, ivory, and shell in toolmaking;

the manufacture of nonutilitarian items, some of which served as items of personal adornment; the extensive use of nonlocal, exotic raw materials; the regular placement of elaborate grave goods, including items of personal adornment, in burials; and the first appearance of artwork in the form of naturalistic paintings, fanciful sculptures, and engraved bone and antler.

In the Late Pleistocene, human populations migrated into three previously uninhabited continents: Australia and North and South America. Greater Australia (Australia, New Guinea, and Tasmania) was populated by coastally adapted Southeast Asians who arrived by boat more than 40,000 ya. The New World was settled by northeast Asians who walked across or sailed along the southern coast of a vast land bridge connecting the Old and New Worlds during glacial maxima. This occurred by at least 13,000 ya and perhaps closer to 20,000 ya. Some of these early settlers moved south along the Pacific coast, occasionally turning inland toward the east, and settled new and previously unexplored territories. Others likely moved south through an ice-free corridor in the interior of North America, into the American west, where they invented a new projectile-point technology. Their fluted points allowed them to expand across two continents. These Clovis people may not have been the first arrivals; some sites in both North and South America may be older. But Clovis certainly represents the first broadly successful occupation of the New World.

Study Questions

1. In what ways does the culture of the Upper Paleolithic represent a great behavioral leap beyond that of the Middle Paleolithic? Why are the behaviors recognized for the Upper Paleolithic considered to be essentially modern?

2. How can the sophisticated artwork of the Upper Paleolithic be explained? Why did people of the Upper Paleolithic paint on cave walls, carve figurines, and scratch geometric designs on bone, antler, and ivory?

3. When and how were Australia and New Guinea peopled? What technology must these first settlers have possessed to accomplish this?

4. When and how was the New World peopled? How is the migration of these people related to glacial advance and retreat?

5. Who is "Kennewick Man," and why is he an important source of information about the peopling of the New World?

6. Were the Clovis people the first human settlers of the New World? Consider the evidence for a pre-Clovis migration to the New World.

Key Terms

Upper Paleolithic	entopic phenomena	Denali Complex
Late Stone Age	Venus figurines	Nenana Complex
Middle Paleolithic	Sunda	Clovis
Middle Stone Age	Sahul	haplogroup
Gravettian	Greater Australia	Paleo-Indian
Solutrean	Wallace Trench	Arctic Small Tool
projectile point	paradigm	Tradition
Magdelanian	Beringia	
microblades	wedge-shaped cores	

For More Information

For technical information concerning the Middle to Upper Paleolithic cultural transition, see the articles contributed to *The Emergence of Modern Humans: An Archaeological Perspective,* by Paul Mellars. For wonderful photographs of the paintings in the cave of Lascaux, see Mario Ruspoli's *The Cave of Lascaux: The Final Photographs.* Other books focus on other caves and present excellent discussions and beautiful photographs of the art. See especially: *Images of the Ice Age,* by Paul Bahn and Jean Vertut; *Dawn of Art: Chauvet Cave,* by Jean-Marie Chauvet; *The Cave Beneath the Sea: Paleolithic Images at Cosquer,* by Jean Clottes and Jean Courtin; *The Cave of Altamira,* by Pedro A. Saura Ramos. For a more technical book-length treatment, see the thought-provoking *The Dawn of Belief: Religion in the Upper Paleolithic of Southwestern Europe,* by Bruce Dickson. *The Shamans of Prehistory,* by Jean Clottes and David Lewis-Williams, is the best book-length treatment of the hypothesis that the cave paintings represent images that ancient shamans induced through trance.

J. Peter White and James F. O'Connell's *A Prehistory of Australia, New Guinea, and Sahul* is still an excellent synthesis of the archaeology of Greater Australia. The most recently published summary of ancient Australia is John Mulvaney and Johan Kamminga's broad and detailed *Prehistory of Australia.* For a helpful discussion of the controversy over the earliest settlement of the Americas, read David Meltzer's article "Pleistocene Peopling of the Americas" in the journal *Evolutionary Anthropology.* A popular book by the same author, *Search for the First Americans,* provides an insightful discussion of the earliest settlement of the New World. A very interesting, popular treatment of the controversy surrounding the timing of the peopling of the Americas—with personal anecdotes of the author's experiences researching the topic—can be found in E. James Dixon's *Quest for the Origins of the First Americans.* Dixon's more recent book, *Bones, Boats, and Bison,* is another excellent summary of the evidence for the earliest human settlement of the Americas, with an especially good section on data from the far north. *The Settlement of the Americas: A New Prehistory,* by Tom Dillehay, the archaeologist who excavated the Monte Verde site in Chile, synthesizes the argument for the settlement of the Americas long before Clovis. For detailed information about the Paleo-Indian adaptation to the Americas, see the numerous articles in *Clovis: Origins and Adaptations,* edited by Rob Bonnichsen and K. L. Turnmire.

Beginning after 12,000 ya, much of humanity experienced a fundamental revolution in subsistence: they began planting crops (like the rice shown here) and domesticating animals. Why did this revolution take place? How did this revolution set the stage for the development of the modern world? *(©Yann Layma/Tony Stone Images)*

THE ORIGINS OF AGRICULTURE

CHAPTER CONTENTS

Life at the End of the Pleistocene

The Food-Producing Revolution

Why Food Production?

Domestication: How Can You Tell?

Hearths of Domestication

The Nutritional Impact of Agriculture

Can Agriculture Be Explained?

CONTEMPORARY ISSUE: Our Worst Mistake?

Summary

Study Questions

Key Terms

For More Information

So far in this book, we have recounted the story of human antiquity as it is now understood. The human ancestors we have discussed, whether they belonged to a species different from our own or were entirely modern, were all hunter-gatherers, relying on nature's bounty for their survival. In fact, for more than 99 percent of hominid history, our ancestors fed themselves by **foraging**—gathering wild plant foods and hunting and scavenging wild animals. It is difficult to imagine that **agriculture**, the subsistence mode that feeds virtually all people on this planet today and which we so take for granted, developed only in the very recent days of our evolutionary history. This chapter focuses on this revolutionary change in how our ancestors fed themselves, the subsistence shift from food gathering to food producing.

Life at the End of the Pleistocene

The end of the Pleistocene and the beginning of the Holocene—the modern epoch that began 10,000 ya—brought a recession of the glaciers and a general warming of the world's climate. Sites throughout the world show people adapting to these changing conditions. The cultural developments that characterize the human response to the changing climate of the end of the Pleistocene include the following:

1. People changed their subsistence focus as the animals and plants on which they had previously relied became either altogether extinct or locally unavailable.
2. Different human groups responded differently to the new environmental conditions, resulting in a far higher level of cultural diversity, even within relatively small regions, than had been seen across broad areas during the Pleistocene.
3. In many areas, this subsistence shift included exploiting a broader range of resources such as small game, fish, shellfish, and birds. Some added plant foods unavailable during glacial periods.
4. In other regions, people narrowed their subsistence focus, intensifying their use of some uniquely productive elements in the food quest.
5. Finally, in some places, the focus on certain abundant resources encouraged a shift from a nomadic existence to a more sedentary one. In some particularly rich regions, intensification of the food quest and the shift to a sedentary way of life set the stage for a revolutionary change in the relationship between people and food, a shift from food collecting to food production, the focus of this chapter.

Mesolithic and Archaic Cultures of the Early Holocene

As archaeologist T. Douglas Price (1991) points out, the key characteristic of the environment of Holocene Europe is its vast array of plants and animals suitable for exploitation by humans. This explosion in the diversity of resources allowed for a diversity of cultural adaptations by **Mesolithic** people, the name given to the cultures of Europe immediately following the end of the Pleistocene.

For example, the Mesolithic inhabitants at Star Carr in England hunted aurochs (wild cattle), red and roe deer, elk, ox, pig, fox, badger, beaver, and hare (Clark 1971). They also ate birds; as we know from the bones of ducks, mergansers, grebes, and cranes that have been recovered. At Mesolithic sites in southern France, a wide array of plant food remains have been recovered, including vetch, lentils, and chick peas (Price 1987). In coastal contexts, fishing played a major role in subsistence; the remains of pike, cod, ling, perch, bream, eel, and haddock have been found at

foraging A subsistence strategy based on any combination of wild food resources, including collecting wild plants, hunting wild animals, fishing, and shellfish collecting.

agriculture A subsistence strategy based on domesticated plant foods.

Mesolithic The name given to cultures in Europe at the end of the Pleistocene and before the Agricultural Revolution.

Mesolithic sites (Clark 1980). Marine mammals including ringed, harp, and grey seal were hunted, and whales and porpoises that had apparently been beached were utilized.

The Siebenlinden Mesolithic sites in southern Germany indicate that the inhabitants of the region exploited a wide range of animal and plant species (Kind 2001). These Mesolithic people can be characterized as **opportunistic foragers,** exploiting diverse plants and animals whenever the opportunity presented itself. Many of the species seen at Star Carr have also been found in the Mesolithic sites of southern Germany; the bones of large mammals such as aurochs, red deer, roe deer, elk, and wild boar are abundant in site hearths. Also, among the remains of animals recovered are those that were probably not as important for food as they were for the fur they provided, including beaver, red fox, marten, and wild cat. Plant foods also contributed to the food quest; the Mesolithic staple, hazelnut, was found at the sites, along with raspberry, wild apple, and weedy, seed-bearing plants, including knotweed and common lamb's quarters.

In North America, the waning stages of the Pleistocene saw the extinction of many tundra-adapted large-game species and their replacement with more modern fauna. The **Archaic** period (9,000 to 3,000 ya) cultures in North America represent the beginning of regionalization, as cultures settled into different post-Pleistocene environments. Strategies for survival in the northeastern woodlands, southwestern desert, northwestern coast, and elsewhere were established. For example, piñon nuts became a major component of the diet throughout much of the desert west. In the east, cultures evolved with specific adaptations to the coast, to the area around the Great Lakes, and to the forested interior. Groups pursued different combinations of hunting, fishing, collecting shellfish, and exploiting seed and nut plants, each group specialized to adapt to the resources available locally.

In South Carolina, Georgia, Tennessee, Kentucky, West Virginia, and Florida, sites dating to the Archaic period are characterized by substantial accumulations of the remains of freshwater shellfish, particularly mussels. The enormous mounds of shells that mark these sites and give them their designation—the **Shell Mound Archaic**—have been interpreted as the accumulations of food remains of dense and sedentary groups of people. Their population density and degree of sedentism were made possible by the rich and abundant food resource of freshwater shellfish.

The Koster site in Illinois provides a wealth of information on Archaic lifeways (Struever and Holton 2000). Beginning about 7,000 ya, the residents of the site hunted deer, small mammals, and migratory ducks and geese. The carbonized seeds of smartweed, sunflower, goosefoot, pigweed, and marsh elder—plants that later were part of an indigenous agricultural revolution—were major components of their diet. Fish and freshwater shellfish were collected in the river, and hickory nuts, hazelnuts, and acorns

opportunistic foragers Hunter-gatherers whose highly flexible subsistence system allows them to exploit whatever resources become available in their area whenever they become available.

Archaic Time period in the New World that follows the Paleo-Indian period.

Shell Mound Archaic A post-Pleistocene adaptation in the American southeast marked by the development of large and dense human populations that exploited shellfish and constructed great ceremonial mounds primarily out of shells.

were harvested from the forests in the fall. Other plant foods such as groundnuts, wild duck-potatoes, cattail shoots, pecans, pawpaws, persimmons, and sassafras root rounded out the broad subsistence base at Koster.

In East Asia, we see a similar process of post-Pleistocene subsistence shifts and regionalization. For example, in Thailand, Spirit Cave was occupied more than 7,500 ya. The Khong stream at the base of the cave's cliff face provided the human inhabitants with fish and freshwater crab. Otter, bamboo rat, badger, porcupine, sambar (a large Asian deer), and pig deer were caught and eaten by cave inhabitants (Gorman 1972). The cave has also yielded the remains of twenty-two genera of plants, including bamboo, butternut, and tropical fruits (Higham 1989).

In the early Holocene of Africa and the Middle East, we see a number of sites where the subsistence emphasis seems to have shifted to plant resources sometime after 18,000 ya. Along the Nile, gazelle, hippopotamus, wild cattle, wart hog, and buffalo were still hunted, but fishing had also become important. At some Nile sites, microliths—small stone flakes set in groups into bone, wood, and antler handles—exhibit a wear pattern that indicates their use in sickles for harvesting plant food (Butzer 1982). The abundance of grinding stones used for processing seeds also points to a focus on plants for food. Finally, the presence of carbonized grains of wild barley, wheat, rye, and oats bears direct witness to the growing importance of plant foods in the diet. This shift in subsistence at the end of the Pleistocene and beginning of the modern, or Holocene, period led in some places to a radical change in the relationship between people and their environment. The rest of this chapter chronicles this revolution.

The Food-Producing Revolution

The focus of this chapter is the **Food-Producing Revolution,** or **Agricultural Revolution.** Although the impact of this change on human life certainly was revolutionary—that is, momentous—there was no abrupt change in how people fed themselves. The shift to food production was a process that transpired over several millennia in a number of different areas and then spread out from these initial hearths (Figures 12.1 and 12.2; B. Smith 1995).

Archaeologists have another name for the period when agriculture first became the dominant subsistence mode for some human groups—the **Neolithic.** Neolithic simply means "new stone" and specifically refers to the production, during this period, of a new tool type made of polished or ground stone, unlike the chipped tools of the "old stone age," or Paleolithic. Although this shift in tool type is no longer viewed as the defining element of the period, the name has stuck.

The social consequences of this shift to food producing were enormous. Ultimately, the ability to ensure a constant, reliable, and expanded

Food-Producing Revolution The shift from foraging to food production through domestication, beginning after 12,000 ya.

Agricultural Revolution Another name for the Food-Producing Revolution.

Neolithic Literally "New Stone Age." Now refers to period of the beginning of agriculture.

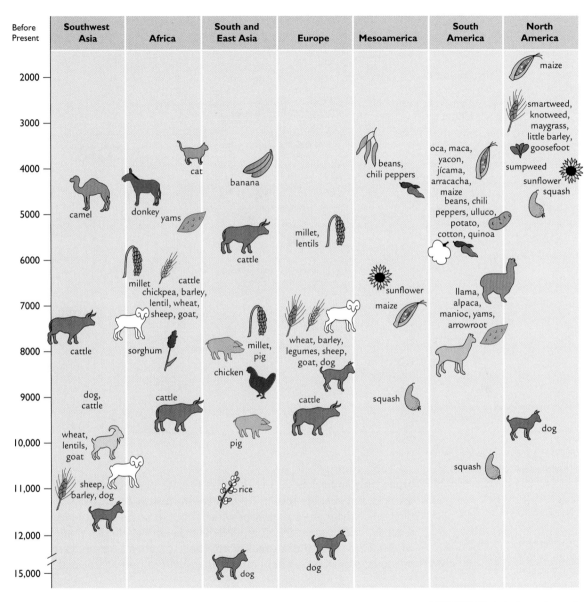

FIGURE 12.1 A chronology of domestication.

food supply allowed for an increase in sedentism and population growth, along with the development of new social structures needed to maintain order in these larger settlements. The kinds of social hierarchies made possible by—and sometimes made necessary by—the consequences of food production led to the developments that are the focus of Chapter 13.

It is not an exaggeration to say that the kind of life most of the world's people now lead was made possible by this change in subsistence, which

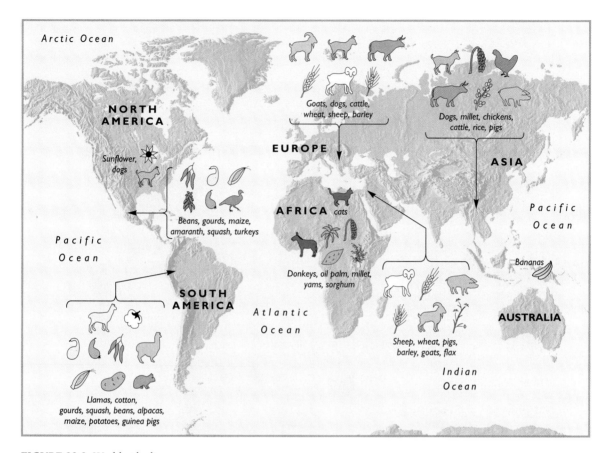

FIGURE 12.2 Worldwide distribution of apparent hearths of domesticated plants and animals.

domesticate To change, through artificial selection, the wild form of a plant or animal to a form more useful to humans; the term used for the end product of this process.

artificial selection The process where humans choose the plant or animal that will live and reproduce, based on its useful characteristics.

began only some 12,000 ya. The shift to food production marks a major break in how people related to their environment. Before, they could exploit only what nature already provided; now, they could take at least some control over the production of food. The Neolithic marks a point in time when people began to **domesticate** those plants and animals they had previously relied on for food only in their wild or undomesticated state.

The Domestication of Plants and Animals

Domestication uses **artificial selection** to change the character of a plant or animal species according to a people's own needs or purposes. Artificial selection is analogous to natural selection as Charles Darwin defined it (see Chapter 2). Darwin's hobby as a pigeon breeder, in fact, provided him with crucial insights into how natural selection might work.

In natural selection, the plants or animals that survive and reproduce are those with the characteristics best adapted for survival in a specific environment. In artificial selection, individual plants or animals are cared for and allowed to survive because they possess certain characteristics desired by humans. Those of the same species with other, less desirable traits are killed off—perhaps when very young—and not allowed to reproduce. In essence then, artificial selection is managed evolution, and the managers are people. In comparing artificial selection to natural selection, Charles Darwin (1898:47) said, "One of the most remarkable features in our domesticated races is that we see in them adaptations, not indeed to the animal's or plant's own good, but to man's use or fancy."

From Wolf to Dog

Although generally not a food species, the dog provides a good example of the process of domestication. Many of us have dogs, and we are all at least passingly familiar with some modern breeds. Although the characteristics selected for in dogs were quite different from those selected for in food species, the process of artificial selection is essentially the same.

All domesticated dogs are members of the species *Canis familiaris*. Beagles and spaniels, German shepherds and chihuahuas, St. Bernards and retrievers, toy poodles and dobermans all belong to the same species. And all are ultimately descended from a single wild species, *Canis lupus*—the wolf (Figure 12.3). Now, as we all know, wolves are intelligent, powerful, and, at times, aggressive, fierce creatures, and it is not obvious how a wolf can be bred into a Pekingese. It is, however, just a matter of artificial selection, genetic accidents, and time.

We know that the wolf was one of the first species domesticated by people—though probably not as a source of food. In a scenario suggested by **osteologist** Stanley Olsen (1985), orphaned wolf pups may have been picked up by local people and brought back to their village as a curiosity. If orphaned early enough in life, they would bond with the people raising them, who would tolerate the pups because they were little trouble and very entertaining. As the pups grew, however, most would become dangerous. Because they perceived the people around them as part of their pack, these wolves would attempt to assert themselves just as they would in the wild. People would be bitten, children might be seriously hurt, and the wolves would more than likely be killed.

There is, however, inherent variation in a wolf population. Although some wolves grow to be quite large, with enormous teeth and aggressive dispositions, others are smaller and more timid. In the wild, those wolves may be killed by larger wolves or, more likely, simply have a lower status in wolf society, where their characteristics put them at a distinct disadvantage: they eat only after the more dominant wolves get their fill; if they are males, they may not have much opportunity to mate. Within a human society, however, smaller, timid wolves might be at a tremendous advantage. Although their larger, aggressive siblings might be killed, the smaller, more

osteologist A scientist whose specialty is the study of bones, either human or animal.

FIGURE 12.3 The many breeds of dogs are all members of the species *Canis familiaris* and are all descended from the wolf, *Canis lupus*—including *(upper left)* the wolflike German shepherd, *(upper right)* the Labrador retriever, *(lower left)* the Irish wolfhound, and *(lower right)* the decidedly nonwolflike West Highland white terrier. *(German shepherd: J. M. Beatty; Labrador retriever and Irish wolfhound: M. A.. Park; West Highland white terrier: K. L. Feder)*

compliant wolves might be allowed to live. This would be especially true if they performed valuable services for the humans. Because wolves are social animals that cooperate in nature, it is likely they would do the same when raised by people, perceiving their human masters as dominant members of the pack. They might help in hunting and then, being less aggressive and assertive, contentedly wait to eat what they were given by their human masters. They might also help in protecting the village from animals and even other people; think of your dog, no matter how small and unthreatening, barking at every stranger who approaches your door.

By killing off larger wolves with dangerous characteristics and by allowing only those wolves with attractive (from a human standpoint) characteristics to survive, humans selected which animals lived to reproduce. (It is interesting to point out that, on average, when comparing a wolf and a dog of the same body mass, the dog's head—and therefore its jaws—is 20 percent smaller.) The qualities of small size and nonaggressiveness within the group would tend to be passed down to the next generation, and the selection process would continue, refining the animals to human standards. Eventually, populations of wild wolves, raised and selected for by people, became so changed according to a human blueprint that they were no longer the same species.

As genetic accidents—mutations—occurred, people discovered even more variation from which to select various desired characteristics, such as attractive fur color or extremely small size. See the stunning variation among even just the handful of dog breeds shown in Figure 12.3. Dwarfism occurs in wolves, providing the animals that led eventually to the tiny modern breeds. Gigantism—a genetic accident that leads to enormous size—also occurs in wolves, which led eventually to the enormous, larger-than-wolf breeds found today.

The same general process of selection is applicable to a plant or animal food species. For example, those individuals of a wild plant species that by genetic accident possessed characteristics desired by humans—having seeds that were bigger or hardier and easier to harvest—would be allowed to survive, reproduce, and pass down those characteristics. Those with undesirable features would be eliminated. Thus, without knowing anything about genetics, humans have genetically sculpted animal and plant species in the process of domestication via artificial selection, using the raw material provided by the inherent variation in wild species.

Why Food Production?

Agriculture began just a little after 12,000 ya. By 2,000 ya most of the world's people relied on food production for their subsistence. As anthropologist Mark Cohen (1977) has pointed out, 10,000 years is a very brief time span in the 6-million-year evolutionary history of our lineage. That in this short period several different cultures independently developed an agricultural way of life, and that many of those that didn't quickly borrowed the idea from their neighbors, shows how powerful the forces were that led to this revolution. The goal of the prehistorian is to identify and describe these forces. Doing so explains the Agricultural Revolution.

Hypotheses

> The ancient people ate meat of animals and birds. At the time of Shen Nung, there were so many people that the animals and birds became inadequate for people's wants, and therefore Shen Nung taught the people to cultivate.
> —from an early Chinese legend about a culture hero, Shen Nung (Chang 1968:79)

It might seem self-evident to us that an agricultural way of life is superior to hunting and gathering, but this is not necessarily the case. Studies have shown that hunting and gathering can be a very productive way of life, providing a great deal of security and plenty of free time (Lee 1979). Under most circumstances, agriculture is, in fact, much harder, requiring a good

TABLE 12.1	Summary of Hypotheses Proposed to Explain the Origins of Agriculture	
Hypothesis	**Proponent**	**Summary**
Oasis	V. Gordon Childe	Post-Pleistocene drying of the environment led to the concentration of people, animals, and plants at permanent water sources, or oases. There, people in close proximity to wild plants and animals studied them, tended them, and eventually domesticated them.
Sedentary	Carl Sauer	People living in areas with naturally abundant food would experiment with methods of increasing the abundance of nonfood plants. Eventually, they would apply what they learned through this experimentation to plant foods.
Readiness	Robert Braidwood	People had, by the end of the Pleistocene, accumulated knowledge about wild plants and animals in their regions. When people were intellectually ready, they domesticated those plants and animals that were amenable to domestication.
Dump heap	Edgar Anderson	Human beings disturb the habitat around their settlements as a matter of course. Certain wild plant species grow abundantly in these disturbed habitats. People soon realized that by intentionally disturbing areas, they could encourage the growth of such plants, which they then began to tend and eventually domesticate.
Coevolution	David Rindos	Domestication was not achieved intentionally or in response to a challenge or a need. Humans and the plants and animals on which they subsisted developed a symbiotic relationship in which the evolutionary fitness of all three was enhanced. Humans selected the best individuals (from their standpoint) within species and tended and encouraged them, to the exclusion of others. Human groups

deal more work and quite a bit more risk. If the hunting is bad locally, after all, it is relatively easy for a nomad to pack up and move to where it is better. Agriculture, however, represents a tremendous investment in time and energy devoted to a specific location: many hours of labor are required to clear fields; prepare the soil for planting; plant, weed, and protect the crops from animals; and harvest the crops. If, after all that work, the harvest fails, the consequences can be dire. Also, although agriculture has the potential to produce enormous quantities of food, reliance on one or a few crops can actually result in nutrition levels lower than those of hunter-gatherers (see the discussion later in this chapter). Why, then, did different groups of prehistoric people, during a relatively short time span, independently begin the process of domestication and move away from hunting and gathering?

Two ideas originally offered for this phenomenon are now rejected. Some cultures, it was suggested, domesticated plants and animals simply because their people were inherently smarter. This is nonsense because all

Hypothesis	Proponent	Summary
		evolved a dependence on certain species as these same species evolved a reliance on human encouragement. Domestication and an agricultural economy was the natural result.
Demographic	Ester Boserup	People had long recognized their ability to manipulate plants and animals through artificial selection. Because of the greatly increased amount of work this entails, however, they did not apply their knowledge of the processes of domestication until population increase and the need to produce more food necessitated it.
Marginal habitat	Lewis Binford Kent Flannery David Harris	As population grew at the end of the Pleistocene, human groups expanded into less than optimal habitats. They brought with them wild plants and animals from their source areas. These plants and animals could survive in the new areas only through the care and attention of people. People began to select only those individuals among the displaced plants and animals that thrived in the new habitat, thus leading to domestication.
Sedentism and population growth	Donald O. Henry	Some groups of nomadic foragers became more sedentary at the end of the Pleistocene, focusing on particularly productive, locally abundant wild foods. A sedentary existence encouraged population growth as infant mortality declined, life span increased, and female fertility increased. The response in some areas was to artificially raise the resource ceiling by encouraging certain plants and animals. This led to artificial selection of those plants and animals with the most beneficial characteristics, mutual dependence, and, ultimately, domestication.

human groups have a demonstrably equal capacity for intelligence. Besides, agriculture is not inherently and always "smarter" than foraging. It was also once common to explain the beginnings of agricultural life as the result of **diffusion.** According to this school of thought, cultures became agricultural when domestication was introduced to them by other groups—in other words, the process "diffused." This is, in reality, a nonexplanation. Of course, ideas and techniques do move from area to area, but this doesn't explain how they got started in the first place or why some groups might have accepted them when others did not.

We will focus briefly on a number of the more reasonable hypotheses for the origin of agriculture. Then we will present data on the major sequences of prehistoric domestication that archaeologists have developed. Finally, we will assess the hypothesis or hypotheses that best explain the data now at hand. Because each of the hypotheses was introduced and championed by individual scholars, we will present them by researcher. (These hypotheses are summarized in Table 12.1.)

diffusion The geographic movement and sharing of cultural traits or ideas.

FIGURE 12.4 Childe's Oasis hypothesis argues that the prehistoric inhabitants of Southwest Asia congregated in oases like this one in Jericho as a result of a drying trend at the end of the Pleistocene, thus setting the stage for the Agricultural Revolution. *(M. H. Feder)*

The Oasis Hypothesis

> Food-production—the deliberate cultivation of food-plants, especially cereals, and the taming, breeding, and selection of animals—was an economic revolution—the greatest in human history after the mastery of fire. (Childe 1953:23)

Prehistorian V. Gordon Childe (1942, 1951, 1953) proposed the oasis hypothesis in the 1920s. Believing that there must have been some reason why agriculture began when and where it did, Childe suggested that certain areas of the world became drier at the end of the Pleistocene. As the European glaciers melted off, weather patterns and attendant storm tracks shifted, and much less rain fell in Southwest Asia. Plant life became concentrated in areas watered by underground springs—oases (Figure 12.4). As plant life concentrated in these limited areas, animals were drawn to them, both for the water they contained and the lush stands of plants they supported. Finally, people congregated in such areas to take advantage of the water and food concentrated there.

A previously nomadic people would now have no reason to migrate and, in fact, good reason to stay put—to become **sedentary.** Their concentration in oases resulted in attempts to expand food resources by sowing seeds, weeding, and irrigating. These efforts resulted in the artificial selection of seed plants and led to domestication. Animals previously

sedentary A settlement pattern in which people mostly stay in one place.

hunted tended to live near the humans who hunted them, because the stubble from the fields of planted crops attracted them to human settlements. Such close proximity caused humans to become familiar with these animals and perhaps even to tend and eventually domesticate them through artificial selection. Thus, the shift to food production had an environmental cause in the oasis hypothesis.

The Sedentary Hypothesis

> It took man so very long to get around to the invention of agriculture that we may well doubt that the idea came easily or that it came from hunger, as is often supposed. (Sauer 1969:19)

Carl Sauer (1969), a well-known geographer, did not believe that people who were chronically short of food had the time or inclination to experiment with domestication. Too much effort devoted to an experiment with an uncertain outcome could result in starvation.

Sauer believed instead that the first agriculturalists were well-fed, sedentary people. Nomadic people would not suddenly give up established practices of migration; a migratory people, moreover, are not in one place long enough to make domestication successful. Therefore, domestication began in relatively rich areas where failed experiments in food production would have resulted in nothing more than wasted time and where people could stay in one place long enough to see a crop through from planting to harvesting. Such rich areas, in Sauer's view, also offered these prehistoric experimenters lots of raw material to experiment with. Plant and animal diversity were high, with many different species and abundant variation within those species.

Sauer also believed that the earliest agriculturalists would not be found along rivers because of water-control problems, primarily flooding. He believed that woodlands, perhaps in hilly areas, were most amenable to early cultivation, even suggesting that the first domesticates might not be food but rather poisons—used in hunting and fishing—and fibers. The area of the world that best met his criteria for early domestication was Southeast Asia.

The Readiness Hypothesis

> In my opinion there is no need to complicate the story with extraneous "causes." The food producing revolution seems to have occurred as the culmination of the ever increasing cultural differentiation and specialization of human communities. (Braidwood 1960:94)

Robert Braidwood (1960, 1975) was a well-known American prehistorian who researched the issue of domestication. He did not believe that specific environmental conditions caused domestication to take place. Braidwood ascribed the beginnings of agriculture to purely cultural or historical factors.

According to Braidwood, people began to domesticate plants when and where they did as a result of accumulating knowledge of the plants and animals that lived in their territories. In other words, familiarity breeds, well, breeding. As various groups began specializing in this process, they became expert in the characteristics of particular plant or animal species, a familiarity that resulted first in domestication and then agriculture. In Braidwood's view, agriculture began where it did because these were areas where the wild ancestors of plants and animals amenable to artificial selection were found.

The Dump Heap Hypothesis

> It is now becoming increasingly clear that the domestication of weeds and cultivated plants is usually a process rather than an event. (Anderson 1956:766)

Edgar Anderson (1952, 1956) was an eminent plant biologist interested in the beginnings of cultivation. In his dump heap hypothesis, Anderson suggested that certain plant species he called "camp followers" established themselves in the kind of disturbed habitat that humans produced in and around their villages. Such plants flourished where people dug up the ground, set fires, discarded their organic refuse, and so on. As people noticed the concentrations of these plants around their villages, they began to exploit them. They realized rather quickly that they could further encourage the growth of these plants by purposely creating the disturbances that had previously and accidentally attracted the plants. Because these plants were tended, unconscious artificial selection would have eventually resulted in domestication. Here domestication is viewed as an inevitable by-product of how people alter the landscape.

The Coevolution Hypothesis

> Man selects, but his selection is similar to nature's—he selects the best, the most useful, the most desirable, the most vigorous, the most successful (in other words, the most "fit") plant present in the immediate environment at a given time. (Rindos 1984:4)

Anthropologist David Rindos questioned all hypotheses proposed to explain agriculture that are based on intentionality. He did not believe that humans consciously or deliberately became agricultural. He viewed agriculture as merely a point along a continuum of human-plant relationships.

In this view, we cannot speak of agriculture as an invention developed to respond to a problem or even as an accidental discovery that then became important in human subsistence. Instead, in Rindos's view, humans and the plants and animals on which they subsisted became mutually dependent. In Rindos's terminology, humans and these species "coevolved." During such coevolution, selection took place not through conscious experimentation to "improve" a plant or animal species but simply as a by-product of how people collected and used those plants and animals. Artificial selection simply occurred as economically sensible decisions were made concerning which individuals within a plant or animal species to eliminate, harvest, hunt, tend, or encourage. In turn, human groups evolved a dependence for their subsistence on certain plant and animal species, and cultural practices (scheduled seasonal movement, dispersing seeds, tending wild plants, differential hunting) evolved to maximize food output.

In Rindos's view, we can no more say that people intentionally selected certain plants to domesticate than we can say that certain plants or animals selected humans to tend them. Instead, plants and animals and people and their cultures evolved together in what amounts to a symbiotic relationship. Human groups increased their evolutionary fitness by ensuring and expanding their food base, and the evolutionary fitness of certain species of plants and animals was increased as humans protected, watered, weeded, fenced in, and, in general, tended to them. Rindos maintained that domestication was a natural result of this mutual dependence. Agriculture was the ultimate result.

The Demographic Hypothesis

> It is more sensible to regard the process of agricultural change in primitive communities as an adaptation to gradually increasing population densities, brought about by changes in the rates of natural population growth or by immigration. (Boserup 1965:117–18)

Ester Boserup (1965) was an agricultural economist. Technically, her hypothesis concerns the evolution of complex agricultural systems, not the origins of domestication. Her explanation, however, can certainly be extrapolated to cover the Agricultural Revolution as well, and it has been used by prehistorians in this way.

Agriculture demands a tremendous investment of time and labor. People would not make such an investment, Boserup contended, unless they had to—that is, unless it was necessary for their survival. Boserup believed that population increases forced people to adopt more intensive subsistence strategies in order to feed a greater number of mouths. New techniques of agriculture are not so difficult to develop, but ordinarily they are not used because they require more work than older, less-intensive techniques. Thus, the Agricultural Revolution was triggered by demographics.

The Marginal Habitat Hypothesis

> Change in the demographic structure of a region which brings about the impingement of one group on the territory of another would also upset an established equilibrium system and might serve to increase the population density of a region beyond the carrying capacity of the natural environment.

Under these conditions, manipulation of the natural environment in order to increase its productivity would be highly advantageous. (Binford 1968:328)

Lewis Binford (1968), an American archaeologist whose work we have previously discussed, also argued that the beginnings of domestication were driven by population growth. In Binford's view, as in Boserup's, agriculture is not so difficult to invent, but it is not terribly attractive because it requires so much work. Because most societies have strategies for maintaining their population below the **carrying capacity** of the natural environment, they remain in equilibrium. In other words, most societies keep their population below the maximum that can be fed in a given environment, and everything goes smoothly.

When climate changed at the end of the Pleistocene, however, certain areas became extremely rich in food resources, leading to increased sedentism and, perhaps, marked population growth. Eventually, in Binford's view, some cultures overshot the carrying capacity of their local environment and were forced to expand into less attractive or marginal areas that had lower carrying capacities. Competition with people already living in these areas led to pressure to apply more intensive strategies of subsistence. This led to tending plants and animals, artificial selection, and, ultimately, domestication.

Kent Flannery (1965, 1967, 1968, 1973), another American archaeologist, added to Binford's scenario. He suggested that when groups expanded into neighboring, less productive areas as a result of population growth, they might have brought along with them some of the plant or animal species that were native to their richer home areas in a conscious attempt to increase the productivity of their new homes. Because these species were not naturally adapted to these marginal habitats, however, the only way they would survive was with human assistance. Animals might be sheltered and tended and plants planted, weeded, watered, and protected. New selectional pressures, both natural and artificial, would result, and domestication would follow. Flannery (1968) viewed this as a process of **deviation amplification.** Once a small change occurs in the relationship of people to their food resources, greater changes result. The need to expand the food base by investing increasing amounts of time in tending wild resources can only be satisfied by a greater degree of sedentism. This sedentism produces a greater reliance on tended species—there is no longer as much time to hunt and gather wild foods. Population may increase as a result of greater sedentism through, for example, lower infant mortality. This in turn requires the production of even more food to feed more mouths, which is made possible by an increased investment of time, and so on.

Also following Binford, David Harris (1977) suggested that a hunter-gatherer society in equilibrium with its environment could be shifted to-

carrying capacity The number of organisms a given habitat can support.

deviation amplification The process by which a small change in one part of a cultural system results in larger changes in the rest of the culture, which, in turn, amplify the original change.

ward food production as a result of a reduction in the availability of a staple food resource. Such a reduction, he suggested, could lead to an intensification and specialization of the food quest; other food resources, in other words, would be more intensively exploited. Where these alternative food resources were available at fixed points, Harris contended, group mobility would be reduced, and local population would increase. This would lead to a need to further intensify the food quest to feed more mouths, which might result in tending and artificial selection to increase productivity.

The Sedentism and Population Growth Hypothesis   Archaeologist Donald O. Henry (1989) proposed another explanation for the origins of food production, at least as this relates to the Levant. His hypothesis includes several elements of the explanations described above, including an environmental shift, an attendant shift in subsistence, and population increase. Henry suggested that at the end of the Pleistocene, as a result of a changing environment, some groups abandoned foraging for an extensive number of wild foods and adopted a strategy of sedentism and a focus on a smaller number of particularly productive, locally abundant wild foods. This produced an inherently unstable subsistence system: when nomadic broad-based foragers were faced with a food shortage, they could simply move to where food was more abundant or shift their subsistence focus to other wild plant foods. On the other hand, sedentary peoples might not have wished to displace their entire society and adopt a new **settlement pattern**. Instead, under the right circumstances and with the right kinds of plants and animals, they could have artificially raised the "resource ceiling" (Henry 1989:4) of their territory by tending and encouraging economically important wild crops—by planting seed beds, fencing in plots, or corralling animals.

In Flannery's sense, this may have further disturbed the equilibrium of the system. Henry suggested that in some regions, sedentism and human encouragement of certain crops or animals led to a dramatic increase in human populations for a number of reasons. A sedentary existence would have resulted in a decrease in infant mortality and increased longevity among the aged, both of whom could have survived more easily than in a nomadic existence, with its greater potential risk for mishaps. Beyond this, in some regions (Henry pointed to Southwest Asia; see the discussion later in this chapter), the shift to a more sedentary existence would have contributed to higher fertility levels overall. A diet higher in cereal foods produces proportionally more body fat, leading to higher fertility among women. Also, cereals are easily digested foods that would have supplemented and then replaced mother's milk as a primary food for older infants. Since lactation inhibits fertility, earlier weaning would have resulted in the closer spacing of births and the potential for a greater number of live births for each woman.

settlement pattern The distribution of archaeological sites and the analysis of their functions in relation to each other and to features of the environment.

FIGURE 12.5 Larger seeds produce faster-germinating and quicker-growing plants; these plants have an advantage under the culturally controlled environment of the seed bed. Smaller, slower-germinating seeds are selected against. Through this artificial selection, people produce crops that produce larger seeds that, in turn, produce more food. Compare these wild marsh elder, sunflower, and squash seeds *(top to bottom, left)* with domesticated examples *(top to bottom, right)*. *(© Chip Clark 1995)*

testa A seed coat; the protective wrapping around the part of the seed that sprouts.

Domestication: How Can You Tell?

Before we test these hypotheses by reference to site data, we need to explain how the early stages of domestication can be recognized archaeologically. Certainly, full-scale agricultural villages look very different from hunter-gatherer villages, and we can recognize this difference in the ground. But what about the transition, when settlement patterns really hadn't yet changed much? We must look at the remains of the plants and animals being exploited to see if human selection has caused any alteration from the wild state. Even this identification is not terribly easy during early stages of domestication. The changes can be extremely subtle; the vagaries of preservation being what they are. Moreover, it is virtually impossible to distinguish absolutely between ancient wild plants and animals and early domesticated species. But a number of features can be used to begin to distinguish domesticated from wild plants or animals.

Recognizing Domesticated Plants

For plant species, domestication alters at least four reasonably recognizable characteristics.

Seed Size   When seeds or fruits are the part of the plant eaten, people artificially select for those individuals of a species that produce larger seeds or fruits, perhaps in an attempt to extract a greater amount of food from each plant. It also may come about as an accident of what archaeologist Bruce Smith (1992a) calls "seed bed selection." In this view, ancient people intentionally planted the seeds of wild plants to increase the number of economically valuable wild crops growing. Like all gardeners, they planted more seeds than can be accommodated in the seed bed. Because plants that germinate slowly or later than others are likely to get weeded out and because larger seeds germinate more quickly, plants that began as large seeds were selected for in this human-controlled environment. Remember, in this scenario, at least initially, people were not intentionally selecting plants for survival because they produced large seeds; it is simply that the plants that began their existence as large seeds were more likely to survive human selection in the seed bed. After several generations of plantings, the mean seed size of plants became bigger and also more homogeneous as large seeds were regularly selected for (Figure 12.5).

Seed Coat Thickness   In temperate zones, seed-coat thickness is a crucial variable in determining whether the plant that grows from that seed will survive. The seed coat, or **testa.** is the protective wrapping around the part of the seed that actually sprouts. A thicker seed coat may forestall germination until the last killing frost of early spring. Also, some wild plant species rely on animals for seed propagation. Birds, for example, eat seeds and then fly off. Seeds with thinner seed coats are more readily digested, but those with thicker coats pass through the birds' digestive systems intact, whereupon they are excreted. These undigested seeds then fall to the ground and may germinate and grow, thus spreading the plant species into a new area.

A thick seed coat, therefore, is advantageous in nature and is selected for; seeds with thick coats are more likely to survive cold snaps and a bird's digestive tract and produce next year's wild crop. In a human-controlled seed bed, however, a thicker seed coat delays germination and confers a significant *disadvantage* because early sprouting and vigorous growth is desired and is, therefore, selected for. Also because seeds with a thicker seed coat sprout later than thin-coated seeds, they will be smaller compared to quick-germinating seeds with thin coats; as a result, they are more likely to be culled when the seed bed is thinned out. In this way, thinner seed coats, sometimes disadvantageous in nature, are selected for by people. A comparison of the seed coats of archaeological specimens and their modern wild counterparts can sometimes aid in distinguishing early domesticates from wild plants; the domesticates have thinner seed coats (B. Smith 1992a).

Seed-Dispersal Mechanisms and Terminal Clusters   In nature, plants evolve mechanisms for dispersing seeds to produce the next generation of their species. Seeds tend to be distributed throughout the plant; that way, if any part of the plant becomes damaged, seeds from the undamaged parts can still survive. Beyond this, when ripe, some seeds are blown to the ground by the wind, are knocked off by passing animals, or attach themselves to the fur of animals. Others may be eaten by animals or birds but remain undigested, to be excreted and, in a sense, planted elsewhere. For any of these mechanisms to work, the seeds have to become readily detachable from the plant at the appropriate time.

Easily detached seeds, however, pose a problem in human exploitation. If most of the seeds fall to the ground and then have to be picked up and cleaned of soil, harvesting becomes inefficient and time-consuming. In the process of domestication, humans select for those individual plants that are at a disadvantage in nature because their seeds tend not to fall off when handled roughly. As Bruce Smith (1995) points out, seeds that are located in tight clusters at the end of plant stalks rather than dispersed throughout the plant are also more conveniently harvested by humans. As a result, seeds with this characteristic are more likely to be selected by humans. Evidence for plant domestication, then, includes an alteration in the attachment of seeds or fruits to the plant. In domestication, attachment areas lose their naturally brittle character and allow for greater adhesion of the seed to the plant, and seeds tend to be more clustered at the ends of stalks (Figure 12.6).

FIGURE 12.6 In the wild, many seed-producing plants have seeds in numerous, small clusters throughout the plant, rendering harvest difficult. Humans tend to select for those individual plants that produce large numbers of seeds in compact clusters. Compare wild lamb's quarter on the right with its domesticated variety on the left. *(Left, reprinted by permission from "The Emergence of Agriculture," by Bruce D. Smith, copyright 1995, The New York Botanical Garden; right, courtesy Bruce D. Smith)*

Geographic Distribution   As Flannery (1965) proposes, when humans expand their territory, perhaps as a result of population growth and resulting dispersion, they often take food resources with them. In this way, wild plants may be introduced into areas where they do not grow naturally. Another early sign of domestication, then, is the appearance of a plant species in an area where its wild ancestors are not found.

Recognizing Domesticated Animals

Several characteristics of early animal domestication can be seen in the archaeological record as well.

Size Selection   As with seed plants, humans may select animals on the basis of size. With the domestication of the wolf, for example, smaller individuals were preferred and selected for. This preference shows up very nicely in the archaeological record of the earliest domesticated dogs, which had smaller jaws but large, wolflike teeth (Olsen 1985). In the process of domesticating cattle, smaller size also was selected for, again probably for the reason of safety. Wild horses, on the other hand, were selected for larger size because their function was to carry loads, pull carts, and transport people. Any sort of ordered change in the size of a species over time, either larger or smaller, may indicate the beginning of domestication.

Geographic Distribution   As with plants, one indication of the domestication of animals is their appearance in habitats where they are not found naturally. As people moved into new territories, they may have brought formerly wild animals with them. Different selection pressures, both natural and artificial, on the species in the new habitat may have resulted in their further alteration.

Population Characteristics   Hunting wild animals involves a great deal of chance. Animals killed may be male or female, very young, very old, or in the prime of life. Certainly, hunting is not entirely random, and hunters may focus their attention on particular animals, but they may not be able to exercise much control over which animal they finally kill. On the other hand, humans have a far greater degree of control over which domesticated animals they kill. Most people who keep animals avoid killing females for the obvious reason that they produce more animals; very few males are necessary to maintain a herd, so herders often kill and eat young males and let females survive to an old age. In addition, in some species—cows, goats, and sheep, for example—females produce milk that humans can either ingest as is or make into cheese, so it makes sense to keep females alive as long as they can produce this valuable resource. In the case of tended and domesticated animals, the population statistics of the animals killed should show a recognizable difference from the statistics for hunted animals.

Osteological Changes   Changes occur in the bones of animals when they are penned and prevented from engaging in their normal activity. Such changes are not genetic; they result from the difference in lifestyle. The bones of wild animals tend to be denser and stronger to allow the animals to withstand the rigors of life in the wild. In contrast, penned animals not allowed to roam freely and not forced to escape predators do not develop this denser microscopic architecture. Such osteological changes do not necessarily indicate domestication; they may occur even in wild zoo animals. Such alterations, however, do imply a change in the relationship between people and the animals on which they subsist, probably indicating at the very least the initial stages of animal domestication.

Some osteological changes may reflect the ways in which animals are being used by people, which may imply tending or domestication. For example, horse teeth dating to about 6,000 ya found at archaeological sites in the Ukraine exhibit a particular kind of wear not seen in any older horse remains (Barber 1999). This wear—just like that seen in modern, domesticated horses—is caused by a bit, the part of the harness placed in the horse's mouth. It is likely, then, that these ancient Ukrainians had tamed horses to the point where they could harness them for riding. Such a level of control suggests that domestication of the horse was well under way.

Hearths of Domestication

We are now in a position to discuss in some detail archaeological data relevant to the question of the invention of agriculture. We will focus on those areas of the world where domestication seems to have occurred, at least in part, independently. These areas are Southwest Asia, Africa, East Asia, southern Europe, Mesoamerica, western South America, and North America (see Figure 12.2).

Southwest Asia

Long before there is any evidence for the kind of artificial selection described above, it is clear that people of Southwest Asia living in an area called the **Levant**—a stretch of uplands across modern-day Israel, Lebanon, and Syria—had already developed subsistence systems reliant on the wild versions of plants that would eventually become the basis of an agricultural way of life. For example, evidence recovered at the Ohalo II site in Israel (Piperno et al. 2004) shows that by 20,000 ya, people were eating the seeds of wild grasses that would become—and that continue to be—staples in agricultural systems in the Middle East and, ultimately, all over the world, namely, barley and wheat. A reliance on the wild ancestors of crops that would form the basis of agriculture in Southwest Asia is clearly seen in the period from 13,000 to 9800 B.P. in what is called the **Natufian** culture (Figure 12.7)

The Natufian   Natufian sites are mostly in caves, although some open-air camps have been located. These sites are all nonagricultural; there is no evidence that domestication of any plant or animal species had yet taken place. The Natufians relied for subsistence on wild **cereal** crops that grew abundantly in the Levant and which later became the world's first domesticates (Bar-Yosef 1998; Figure 12.8). For example, kernels and stalks of wild wheat and barley have been found at many Natufian sites. At Mureybet and Abu Hureyra, in Syria, a wild wheat and vetch (a **legume**—plants that produce pods with seeds) have been found in roasting pits dated to more than 11,000 ya. Carbonized kernels of wild barley as well as lentils, chick peas, and field peas have been recovered at Wadi Hama 27 in Jordan, dated to 12,000 B.P.

Levant The area along the eastern shore of the Mediterranean, including Greece, Turkey, Syria, Lebanon, Israel, and Egypt.

Natufian Late Paleolithic–Early Neolithic culture of Southwest Asia, dated from 13,000 to 9800 B.P.

cereal Any plant, especially grasses, that produces starchy grains.

legume A family of flowering plants that produce pods containing seeds.

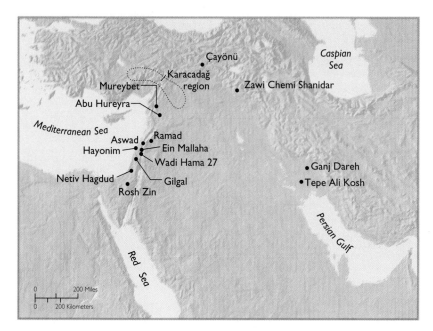

FIGURE 12.7 Locations of Southwest Asian archaeological sites mentioned in the text where evidence of domestication has been recovered.

Artifacts from these sites, as well as archaeological features reflecting food storage and preparation, also indicate Natufian reliance on wild cereal grains. Researchers have found grinding stones (or mortars), food storage pits, pits for roasting plant foods, and flint microblades. The stone mortars certainly could have been used for grinding plant material, but the evidence from the microliths is even more compelling. These tiny, very sharp stone blades inset into bone, wood, and antler handles were used much like modern sickles to harvest wild grains—most probably wheat, barley, and oats. The stone blades exhibit a sheen, or polish, that has been shown through replicative experiments to be the result of cutting the stalks of cereal plants such as wheat and barley (Unger-Hamilton 1989).

Archaeologist Ramona Unger-Hamilton (1989) has conducted an experiment focusing on the tools that may have been used to harvest the wild and early domesticated cereal crops of the Levant. After making 295 stone blades and then using them to harvest a number of locally available wild and domesticated plant species, she compared the wear patterns (see Chapter 7) on these experimental tools with those she found on 761 prehistoric blades from sites in Israel dating from 12,000 to 8,000 ya. She found that one-quarter of the blades from Natufian sites and three-quarters of the more recent tools had striations, or scratches, that were just like those she experimentally produced when harvesting cereal crops from tilled soil. In her experiment, when harvesting grains from tilled soil, the sickle handle in which the blades were inset invariably would scrape the ground, giving the blades these characteristic scratch marks. Unger-Hamilton

FIGURE 12.8 Domesticated early in the Neolithic of Southwest Asia, wheat remains one of the world's most important food crops. *(© FWP/FAD; Food and Agricultural Organization, United Nations; F. Mattioli)*

interpreted this evidence to indicate that tilling the soil and harvesting the cereals that grew there began with the Natufian culture.

Harvesting and storing abundant, dependable, and nutritious wild cereals, legumes, and nut foods supported a more sedentary way of life for the Natufian people. Natufian sites reflect this developing sedentism in a sophisticated architectural pattern of permanent villages. At Ein Mallaha, Hayonim Cave, and Rosh Zin in Israel, archaeologists have excavated house remains with stone foundations ranging from 2 to 9 meters (about 6 to 28 feet) in diameter (Henry 1989). The work invested in the construction of these homes clearly indicates that they were intended for long-term use.

Karim Shahir   Our focus now shifts to the Zagros Mountains of northeastern Iraq, where sites of the Karim Shahir culture have been excavated. One of the most important of these sites is Zawi Chemi Shanidar (see Figure 12.7), which dates to 10,600 B.P. (Wright 1971). The site is characterized by round hut floors within a cave. Artifacts include some microliths, grinding and milling stones, beads, rings, pendants, and axes. Most important, though, are the faunal remains—almost exclusively the bones of sheep. The bones themselves were not so different from the bones of ordinary wild mountain sheep, but the population distribution of the animals is striking. Almost all the bones from Zawi Chemi Shanidar are from young animals. As discussed, that kind of consistency almost certainly implies that the people were in control of the population of animals they were feeding on. Such control implies tending, if not incipient domestication.

The First Food Producers   Sometime around 11,000 ya, Natufians and Karim Shahirians appear to have produced the first domesticated plants

(Henry 1989; Maisels 1990; Miller 1992). Archaeologist Ofer Bar-Yosef (1998) suggests that colder and drier conditions that prevailed in the Levant after 11,000 ya led to a decline in the abundance of the wild cereals that were of such great importance to Natufian subsistence. Bar-Yosef continues by proposing that the Natufians, recognizing the lower yields of wild cereals that they so depended on, responded by attempting to artificially increase yields. By tending natural stands of wild cereals—perhaps by protecting them from animals and watering plants during dry spells—or by planting wild seeds in seed beds, the Natufians may have produced an artificial environment (an environment provided by people rather than by nature) for the plants and shifted the most significant selection process from natural to artificial.

The results of such activity are easier to gauge archaeologically than the process itself. For example, at Netiv Hagdud and Gilgal in Israel and at Ganj Dareh in Iran, recovered barley kernels have been identified as an early domesticated version of that cereal. The size and form of the kernels are distinct from those of wild barley, showing features present in the domesticated grain. At Aswad in Syria and Çayönü in Turkey, domesticated wheats known as **emmer** and **einkorn** have been dated to more than 10,000 B.P. At both of these sites, lentils may also have been cultivated; at Aswad, 55 percent of the seeds of food plants recovered were from cultivated peas and lentils (Miller 1992:48).

As mentioned earlier in this chapter, the population characteristics of wild and domesticated animal species differ. In most species, males are larger, more aggressive, and more dangerous than females. Add this to the fact that males are largely—but not entirely—superfluous. An individual male can sire a nearly unlimited number of offspring in a given year, so a lot of males aren't needed to maintain a herd. Each female, on the other hand, may be able to produce only a single offspring in a given year, so to increase the size of a herd it makes sense to keep females alive as long as possible, to get the maximum output of calves, lambs, or whatever. As a result, when humans control a population of animals, it makes sense for them to keep females alive and to kill off and eat right away most of the young males—before they get big and dangerous—sparing only a sufficient number of them to ensure the survival of the captive population. This pattern of control is evidenced in the archaeological record by a disproportionate number of bones of young males in the **faunal assemblage.**

Just such a pattern was recognized in the excavation of Ganj Dareh in Iran. Dating to 10,000 ya, the bones of goats recovered at the site are morphologically no different from those of wild members of the species. In fact, the goats at Ganj Dareh appear to be wild animals; artificial selection had not been applied long enough to result in any difference, at least any difference recognizable on their bones. The population profile of the bone assemblage, however, indicates a level of population control over the goats that is unlikely to occur among wild, free-roaming, hunted animals. Researchers Melinda Zeder and Brian Hesse (2000) found that a disproportionate

emmer A variety of wheat, *Tripsicum turgidum*. The source of cultivated wheat in the modern world.

einkorn A variety of wheat, *Tripsicum monococcum*. Not a significant agricultural crop today.

faunal assemblage The animal bones recovered at an archaeological site. Identifying species, sex, and age at death of the animals represented by these bones is helpful in distinguishing wild from domesticated animal species associated with a site.

number of the goat remains are, in fact, those of subadult males. At 10,000 ya, the residents of Ganj Dareh seem to have had a level of control over the goats that represents an early stage in their domestication.

Ali Kosh   In the early to mid-1960s, a multidisciplinary project was undertaken in the Deh Luran Plain of southwestern Iran. The project was directed by archaeologists Frank Hole, Kent Flannery, and James Neely (1969). Their objective was to investigate the nature of early domestication and the development of settled village life in Southwest Asia. Among the sites located in their research were two, Tepe Ali Kosh and Tepe Sabz, that provided useful data.

At Ali Kosh, from 9450 to 8700 B.P., the investigators defined the *Bus Mordeh phase* of occupation (Figure 12.9). The site was relatively small, as were the individual structures, made from local red clay. The Bus Mordeh people depended for their subsistence, at least in part, on hunting wild gazelle, wild ox, boar, and ass. They also fished, as evidenced by the remains of carp and catfish in their trash pits. The Bus Mordeh people were also pretty clearly at an early stage in the domestication of goats. As at Ganj Dareh 500 to 1,000 years earlier, the population distribution of the animals can best be interpreted as indicating tending. Most of the animals killed at Ali Kosh during the Bus Mordeh phase were young males, thus protecting females for breeding (Hole et al. 1969:344). Interestingly, Ali Kosh is outside the natural habitat of wild goats in Southwest Asia, suggesting the intentional movement of the animals by people, another indicator of the management of the animals. Finally, the goats during this phase at Ali Kosh were, on average, smaller than the tended wild goats at Ganj Dareh, and their horns are somewhat differently shaped. Both facts may indicate that the wild but managed animals of 1,000 years earlier were now becoming modified through artificial selection (Zeder and Hesse 2000).

The Bus Mordeh phase also provides evidence for domestication of plants, but as in Tehuacán in Mexico (see later in the chapter), domesticates seem to have played a minor dietary role as yet. Thousands of seeds were recovered in the Bus Mordeh levels at Ali Kosh. Most represented wild alfalfa, vetch, goosefoot, and other wild grasses and legumes. The domesticated versions of emmer wheat and two-row barley were also found at this level, but they represent less than 10 percent of the seeds recovered, indicating a very small contribution to the diet (Hole et al. 1969:343).

The period of 8700 to 7950 B.P. at Tepe Ali Kosh is called the *Ali Kosh phase*. It is unknown whether the site grew larger, but certainly individual structures were larger and more substantial. Here we can see again the rather slow development of a reliance on food production. By this time, Ali Kosh was an agricultural and herding village, but much of the diet still consisted of wild animals and plants, as well as fish. In this phase, the osteological evidence shows quite clearly that the goats were domesticated. In addition, about 40 percent of the seeds recovered in these levels were

FIGURE 12.9 Excavation of the Bus Mordeh occupation of Tepe Ali Kosh. *(Frank Hole)*

from domesticated versions of emmer wheat and two-row barley (Hole et al. 1969:347). Not surprisingly, many small flint blades (for harvesting) and grinding stones (for processing) were recovered.

From 7950 to 7550 B.P., the *Mohammad Jaffar phase,* the people at Ali Kosh were building larger and more substantial houses. They still hunted gazelle and other animals and collected wild plants for part of their subsistence. They also planted wheat and barley and herded both goats and increasing numbers of domesticated sheep.

At the Tepe Sabz site, in the period 7450 to 6950 B.P., two significant shifts in food-production strategies occurred. First, there was a change of emphasis from goats to sheep. Second, at least beginning in this phase, these people started to use irrigation to expand the area available to them for agriculture. After this period, the population of the Deh Luran Plain exploded. There were more villages, which grew larger and more stable.

In summary, at first domesticates were a minor part of the diet on the Deh Luran Plain. Population was still low, but increased effort in food production resulted in large increases in the amount of food produced, which allowed for increased population, which in turn led to a demand for more agriculture. Eventually, this effect led to the necessity of artificially increasing the amount of cultivatable land through irrigation. Irrigation resulted in an even higher output of food, which then allowed for increased population.

Domesticating Wheat   The emmer and einkorn wheat that grew wild in the hills of Southwest Asia at the end of the Pleistocene was used by local hunter-gatherers. Modern experiments have shown that large amounts of these wild grains can be harvested (Harlan et al. 1966). These wild wheat kernels are also higher in protein than modern domesticated wheat.

The plants pose a number of problems, however. The **rachis** of wild wheat—the point of attachment of the seeds to the plant—becomes quite brittle when the kernels are ripe. In fact, wild emmer wheat and barley growing near some of the older archaeological sites in the region can be harvested only during a very short period because they ripen quickly, their rachises become quite brittle, and the strong winds common to the region can blow the individual grains off the plant and onto the ground (Bower 1989b). As mentioned previously, this characteristic makes sense under natural conditions—plants that produce seeds that can be easily dislodged when ripe and that fall to the ground to produce next year's crop are at an adaptive advantage. But as mentioned before, this characteristic renders harvesting wild wheat problematic for human beings—the seeds fall off the plant too readily and at inopportune times. This provides a rationale for human selection of only those plants with nonbrittle rachises. Also, each kernel of wild wheat is encased in a tough rind, or **glume.** The wheat still needs a good deal of processing to remove the edible kernels from the inedible glumes.

But wild wheat stands have mutants that possess tough, nonbrittle rachises and naked glumes. Only a very few genes are involved in determining these characteristics. Under natural conditions, neither tough rachises nor naked glumes are advantageous. It appears, however, that people who were collecting wild wheat in Southwest Asia at the end of the Pleistocene were artificially selecting for those very characteristics (Figure 12.10).

This selection need not have been intentional, especially at the beginning of the process. It may simply have been the case that a greater proportion of the seeds of plants with nonbrittle attachments made it back to the village; a greater fraction of the seeds attached by a brittle rachis fell off during harvest and transport. As a result, seeds that fell to the ground in and around the village and germinated there tended to be those that produced plants with nonbrittle attachments. Plants with the nonbrittle characteristic, therefore, became concentrated around human habitations. In this way, plants with an advantageous feature from the perspective of human harvesters were being selected for without the humans necessarily being aware of the process.

A variety of molecular archaeology may pinpoint precisely where this process occurred. The DNA of 261 lineages of modern wild wheat

rachis The area of attachment between seeds and other seeds or between seeds and other parts of a plant.

glume Seed case in which an individual cereal grain is enclosed on the plant.

EINKORN   **EMMER**

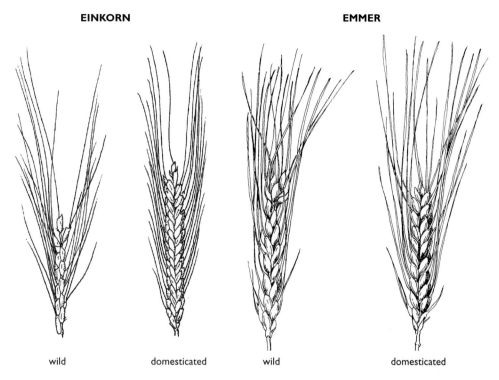

wild   domesticated   wild   domesticated

FIGURE 12.10 A comparison of the seed head of wild and domesticated wheat. The brittle rachis (where the seeds are attached) of wild wheat allows for the dispersion of seeds; the nonbrittle rachis selected for in domestication allows for ease in human harvesting.

(einkorn) including 11 that grow abundantly in the Karacadağ Mountain region of southeast Turkey has been examined (Heun et al. 1997). Researchers compared the DNA of the wild wheat strands to that of 68 lines of modern, domesticated einkorn wheat. Their results were informative; of all the wild varieties sampled, the 11 lines of Karacadağ wheat were the most genetically similar to the modern domesticated varieties examined. The presence of archaeological sites in the same region with evidence of the very early domestication of einkorn (for example, Abu Hureyra) further supports the hypothesis that strands of wild wheat today growing in the Karacadağ Mountain region are descended from the same wild wheat that served as the ancestor of the einkorn domesticated more than 10,000 ya in Southwest Asia.

Additional evidence of early steps in domestication in Southwest Asia comes from the 8,600-year-old site of Mureybet in northern Syria, where researchers have found the remains of wild wheat and barley. These crops were not native to the region and probably came from a source some 160 kilometers to the north in the Zagros Mountains of Turkey. This is good evidence for human intervention. Probably people from the Zagros Mountains brought these crops with them as they expanded their territory into northern Syria, where they planted and tended them.

FIGURE 12.11 Locations of African archaeological sites mentioned in the text where evidence of domestication has been recovered.

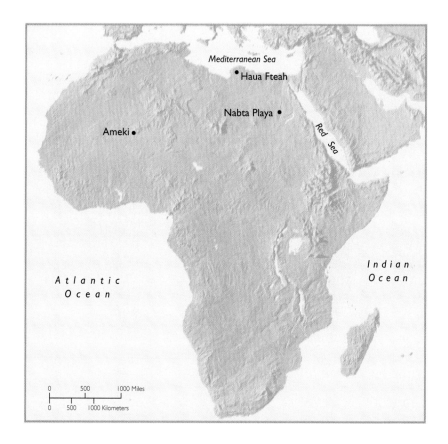

There is also evidence for the very early domestication of a plant important not so much as a source of food but for the fiber it provided. The flax plant was the principal source of fiber for textiles in much of the Old World in antiquity, and remains of domesticated flax have been found in archaeological contexts in Southwest Asia dating to more than 8,000 ya (Zohary and Hopf 1994). Mureybet in Syria, Çayönü in Turkey, Ali Kosh in Iran, and Ramad in Syria have all produced evidence of flax domestication at this time; at all of these sites, recovered flax seeds dating to before 8000 B.P. are significantly larger than seeds from wild flax plants.

Africa

Just as we saw in Southwest Asia, there is a long history in Africa of the use of the wild progenitors of plants and animals whose domesticated versions became important elements of an indigenous agriculture (Figure 12.11). For instance, at Nabta Playa in northeastern Africa, excavators have found more than one hundred cooking features and recovered thousands of seeds representing some forty different species of wild plants. The most common

FIGURE 12.12 Domesticated in the African Neolithic, sorghum is a primary source of protein in some modern African agricultural systems. *(Food and Agriculture Organization, United Nations; J. van Acker)*

seeds found at Nabta Playa were sorghum and a number of varieties of millet. Both are grass crops that produce edible seeds. Though not well known outside the semiarid tropics, millet and sorghum are the primary sources of protein in some modern African agricultural systems (Figure 12.12).

The sorghum seeds found at Nabta Playa look like those of the wild plant. There is no evidence of selection for larger or thinner-coated seeds than in wild varieties. On the other hand, the chemistry of the fats contained in the preserved Nabta Playa seeds is more similar to that of the modern domesticate. Though the seeds are not believed to represent a domesticated variety of sorghum just on the basis of their chemistry, as the researchers point out, it is a "short step" from the intensive use of wild plants to their domestication (Wendorf et al. 1992:724).

Additional evidence for domestication in Africa comes from Egypt, where domesticated wheat, barley, sheep, goats, and cattle are present in

437

sites along the Nile dating to more than 7,000 ya. Haua Fteah Cave in Libya shows evidence of domesticated sheep and goats in a level dated to before 6800 B.P. (Clark 1976).

Domesticated cattle have long played an important role in African agriculture. To figure out the source of those cattle and whether the breeds were local or imported, researchers examined the genetic background of fifty existing breeds with long histories on the African continent (Bradley et al. 1998; Hanotte et al. 2002). One of those modern breeds, the zebu (*Bos indicus*), exhibits a diagnostic hump directly behind the neck. The oldest African rock ark depicting cattle in Africa, however, shows animals without that hump; so it would seem that the zebu is not the first domesticated cattle species in Africa but was introduced later. In fact, genetic evidence traces the source of this breed back about 6,000 years in the Indus Valley in what is today Pakistan. It likely was introduced into eastern Africa sometime thereafter through trade and migration. Cattle breeds without the hump (*Bos taurus*) are also common in modern Africa, particularly north of the Sahara Desert. Genetic evidence traces these humpless varieties to the Middle East, where they were domesticated by about 8,000 ya. Archaeological evidence indicates that humpless cattle were introduced into Africa by 6,500 ya through trade and migration across a wide swath at the north of the continent.

Hanotte et al.'s (2002) genetic analysis indicates that among Africa's modern domesticates, there is a third, genetically distinctive group of cattle. This third group, today most commonly found in southern Africa, represents a group of cattle breeds that can be traced genetically to the indigenous African species *Bos primigenius*. This species was almost certainly domesticated by Africans in their own independent episode of animal domestication that may have occurred as much as 10,000 ya.

Another domesticated animal with a long history in Africa, though not for food but rather as a beast of burden, was the donkey. Archaeological and genetic evidence indicates that donkey domestication occurred in Africa by about 5,000 ya. Researchers compared the mtDNA of modern donkeys living in 52 countries in Asia, Africa, and Europe to that of wild asses in Africa and Asia (Beja-Pereira et al. 2004). No matter their current geographic location, the domesticated donkeys fell into just two mitochondrial groups, each of which was genetically similar to one of the two varieties of African wild asses. Both of the modern mitochondrial donkey groups were genetically dissimilar to Asian wild asses. The authors of the study propose that there were two, independent domestications of donkeys from wild asses and that both of these domestications were accomplished in Africa. In their view, donkeys spread only later into Asia and Europe.

Food Producers in Africa South of the Sahara   The data are very sparse for southern Africa, but domestication appears to have taken place independently south of the Sahara. Domesticated pearl millet has been found dating to as much as 6,500 ya at the Ameki site in Mali (Harlan 1992). At around 5000 B.P., we find evidence of sorghum and at least two other varieties of domesticated millet (finger and foxtail); these were not Asian or European plants, so they were probably the result of local domestication. Each sorghum plant produces a number of stems with clusters of seeds that, in the wild, mature at different times. In the process of domestication, the plants selected for produced seeds maturing all at the same time for ease of harvest (Harlan et al. 1976). A host of other plants unknown in the rest of the Neolithic world were domesticated in sub-Saharan Africa as well, including *tef* and *fonio* (cereals), groundnuts (similar to peanuts), *enset* (a relative of the banana), and *noog* (which produces an edible oil).

Also in western Africa, a non-Asian variety of rice was domesticated. Yams were another important crop, but tubers are notoriously difficult to study archaeologically because they do not produce hard parts that might be preserved. Sheep, goats, pigs, and cattle came into the area from the north and quickly became significant components in the subsistence of many sub-Saharan African agriculturalists. Recent palynological evidence suggests that the oil palm, an important domesticated tree that produces oil used in cooking, wood for construction, leaves for thatching, and fibers for cordage, was probably domesticated at about 2800 B.P. (Sowunmi 1985). It is at about this time that pollen analysis in Western Africa shows a decrease in the percentages of several wild tree species and a dramatic increase in the oil palm.

East Asia

Excellent preservation has allowed researchers to reconstruct much of the diet of the people who lived at Spirit Cave in northwestern Thailand (Figure 12.13; Gorman 1969; Solheim 1972). As early as 12,000 ya, we can see the utilization of water chestnuts, beans, soybeans, almonds, and cucumbers. These plants were probably not yet domesticated at this time. As in Southwest Asia and Africa, however, the data show an early post-Pleistocene focus on the wild antecedents of those species that were to be domesticated shortly afterward and were to become mainstays of local diet right up to the present. The data are sparse for the period after this, but we do know that by 6000 B.P., fully agricultural villages had evolved. The site of Non Nok Tha in northeast Thailand, with domesticated rice, cattle, and pigs, is an example (Figure 12.14).

Rice (Figure 12.15) is emblematic of East Asian agriculture today, and it appears to have been one of the first crops domesticated there. Grains, husks, and other plant remains of domesticated rice dating to as much as 11,500 ya have been found by researcher Syuichi Toyama at sites located along the middle section of the Chang Jiang (Yangtze) River in central China (Normille 1997). Additional sites where early rice has been found

FIGURE 12.13 Locations of East Asian archaeological sites mentioned in the text where evidence of domestication has been recovered.

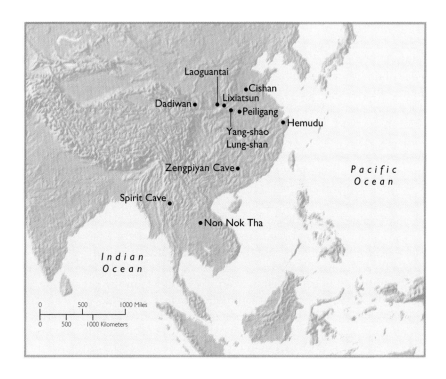

FIGURE 12.14 The Non Nok Tha site in Thailand is an early agricultural site in Southeast Asia. *(Courtesy W. G. Solheim II)*

both upstream and downstream of the middle Chang Jiang are younger than this, suggesting that the middle Chang Jiang was the source of east Asian rice domestication and that domesticated rice spread along the river in both directions.

FIGURE 12.15 Today, rice is emblematic of East Asian agricultural systems. The earliest domesticated rice in China has been identified at the Hemudu site on the Chang Jiang River just south of Shanghai with a radiocarbon date of about 11,500 B.P. (© *Yann Layma/Tony Stone Images*)

The earliest evidence of possible animal domestication in China dates to about 10,000 ya at Zengpiyan Cave in Guilan in southeast China. A large proportion (85 percent) of the animal bones are those of pigs younger than two years of age (Chang 1986:102–3). This age distribution implies that the animals were not being hunted but were kept and tended, with some animals held for breeding purposes and surplus piglets killed for food. Also, the canine teeth in the Zengpiyan pigs are smaller than in a wild pig population, which may show the artificial selection of animals with smaller, less dangerous teeth.

In the deciduous forest of northern China, the earliest food-producing culture yet encountered is called **Peiligang** and is seen at sites such as

Peiligang The earliest Neolithic culture in north China with well-established farming villages dated to 8,500 to 7,000 ya.

441

FIGURE 12.16 Locations of southern European archaeological sites mentioned in the text where evidence of domestication has been recovered.

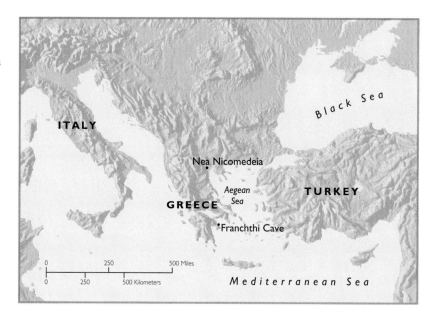

Cishan, Peiligang, Laoguantai, Dadiwan, and Lixiatsun (Chang 1986). Dating to between 8,500 and 7,000 ya, Peiligang sites were well-established farming villages, though hunting, fishing, and gathering wild plants continued to be important. Domesticated crops include foxtail millet, broomcorn millet, and Chinese cabbage. Domesticated animals include pig, dog, and chicken.

Yang-shao   Preagricultural people in central China practiced a nomadic way of life, fishing and hunting deer, elephant, and bear. Sometime after 8,000 ya, sedentary villages of what is called the **Yang-shao** culture developed in the Huang He River valley, in which the domesticated versions of foxtail millet, pigs, and dogs were eaten (Chang 1986). Domesticated rice has been recovered at the Hemudu site on the Chang Jiang River just south of Shanghai; this site has a radiocarbon date of about 7000 B.P. (Crawford 1992:25). Only later did these people begin to raise chickens, sheep, horses, and cattle.

Here again, though the data are not nearly as detailed as for Southwest Asia, we see the slow acceptance of domesticates, for wild plant foods remained important to the Yang-shao people long after they began using cultivated ones. Full-scale agricultural villages did not appear until the appearance of the **Lung-shan** culture a few thousand years later. Unfortunately, the time period that interests us most in terms of the actual development of domestication is still very poorly known for East Asia.

Yang-shao The early Neolithic culture of China dated to about 8,000 ya.

Lung-shan The first fully agricultural people in China, dated to about 6,000 ya.

FIGURE 12.17 Franchthi Cave, in Greece, was occupied during the Late Pleistocene and early post-Pleistocene. Wild species of crops that would later be domesticated, such as oats, barley, peas, and lentils, were eaten by the inhabitants more than 11,000 ya. *(Thomas W. Jacobsen)*

Europe

In southern Europe at the end of the Pleistocene (Figure 12.16), we see a pattern of big-game hunting with an emphasis on wild cattle, deer, ass, bison, and mountain goat (Milisauskas 1978; Whittle 1985). A typical site is Franchthi Cave in Greece, where these animals were hunted about 11,000 ya (Figure 12.17). By 9500 B.P., we see a decrease in the size of the animal species being hunted and a marked increase in the presence of fish bones and other aquatic resources. This seems to indicate a shift to coastal resources, as the coasts were beginning to stabilize after the sea-level rise that accompanied glacial melt-off. Although the data are unclear, the emphasis on coastal resources may indicate an increase in sedentism; commonly, coastal areas are rich enough to allow hunter-gatherers to abandon nomadism. Such a shift, however, may have resulted in a population increase or at least increased local population densities sufficient to force some groups to try to intensify the subsistence quest. Such an intensification may have resulted in the shift from food gathering to food production. At Franchthi Cave, we also see the exploitation of wild oats, barley, peas, and lentils between 13,000 and 11,000 B.P. (Hansen 1991), showing the use of wild crops that were soon to become important domesticates.

Europe's First Food Producers   After 8000 B.P. in southern Europe, sites become larger and more permanent, and evidence of domestication is clear. These early European sites, however, are not full-scale farming villages. Domesticated plants and animals appear to have been grafted onto an in-place hunting-gathering economy that continued even after domestication began. Domesticated plants and animals did not replace wild varieties; they supplemented them.

In the examples presented so far in this chapter, the Agricultural Revolution was not so much revolutionary but evolutionary, with the slow development of food-producing strategies occurring over an extended period of time. The situation in southern Europe is a bit different. Joao Zilhao (2001) points out that unlike the case in Southwest Asia, East Asia, and Africa, food production seems not so much to be an indigenous development but a process introduced from the outside, appearing comparatively rapidly and fully formed. The domesticated plants that first turn up in Europe at about 8000 B.P. are traceable to Southwest Asia, where they had been domesticated at least 1,000 years earlier.

It is rather easy to imagine contact between early agriculturalists living in the Levant and southern Europeans living along the Mediterranean coast. Almost certainly Southwest Asian domesticated plants and animals were introduced into Europe through this contact. Along with their proximity, the similarity in climate also enabled the movement of Southwest Asian domesticates into southern Europe. These crops thrived under the environmental conditions in parts of southern Europe, and the established schedule of planting and harvesting could be maintained. For example, at Franchthi Cave, domesticated emmer wheat appears without antecedents at about 8000 B.P. Two-rowed barley, another Southwest Asian domesticate, was important in the diet of the cave's inhabitants; they also relied on domesticated sheep and goats whose source, again, was probably Southwest Asia. At around the same time or soon after, early farming villages appear along the Mediterranean coasts of Italy and France, where the Southwest Asian domesticates of wheat, barley, lentils, sheep, and goats contributed to the diet. It is important to point out that at the sites mentioned, wild plants continued to play an important role in subsistence. Many of the same species that contributed to subsistence before the introduction of domesticates—deer, wild pig, fish, and sea mammals—continued to do so.

Just as we have seen in southern Asia and Africa, domesticated cattle were a significant part of the subsistence base of the European Neolithic. However, unlike the situation we have discussed for the Middle East, the Indus Valley, and Africa, it does not seem that cattle were independently domesticated in Europe. Genetic analysis of nearly 400 living animals from the Middle East, Africa, and Europe, along with data derived from the bones of a now-extinct wild European cattle species, traces the domestic cattle of Europe ultimately to the domesticated cattle of Southwest Asia, specifically the species *Bos taurus* (Troy et al. 2001). This conclusion is supported by the fact that the DNA of modern European cattle is genetically more similar to that of Middle Eastern cattle than to the wild European samples. Cattle, then, represent another example of a species initially domesticated elsewhere and then brought into Europe as part of the shift from foraging to food production.

An Agricultural Europe   Beginning about 7,500 ya, we see the first nearly completely agricultural economies in Europe, still based on a suite of Southwest Asian domesticates. For example, at Nea Nicomedeia on the Aegean coast of Greece, the hunting of wild deer, wild pig, and hare had become a minor part, along with fishing, of the subsistence quest; only about 10 percent of the animal bones found at the site were of wild species. Seventy percent of those bones were from domesticated sheep and goat, and pig and cattle made up the rest (Rodden 1965; B. Smith 1995). Wheat, barley, and legumes were the primary agricultural crops. After about 7,200 ya, fully agricultural economies based on the growing of wheat, barley, and lentils and the raising of sheep, goat, cattle, and pig are seen throughout Greece and Italy.

The essentially Southwest Asian agricultural economy that had successfully transplanted to southern Europe could not penetrate north into the more temperate conditions of central Europe, however. As Bruce Smith (1995:102) points out, it took a shift in the scheduling of planting and harvesting to allow for an agricultural economy there; in a calendar more familiar to North Americans, crops were planted in the spring and harvested in the fall, the opposite of the situation to the south. Emphasizing wheat, legumes, barley, and cattle, agriculture spread rapidly throughout central Europe after 6,700 ya.

Mesoamerica

What rice is to East Asia and wheat is to Southwest Asia, maize (corn) is to the New World. Among the many important agricultural contributions native inhabitants of the New World made to the diet of people throughout the world, maize is certainly the most significant. Current archaeological evidence indicates that maize was not, however, the first wild plant domesticated in the New World (Figure 12.18). That distinction belongs to the common squash (*Cucurbita*) plant. Archaeological evidence gathered from Guilá Naquitz Cave in Oaxaca, Mexico, indicates that the squash being eaten by the inhabitants between 10,000 and 8,000 ya produced seeds that were larger than those produced by wild squash and possessed thicker rinds and larger stems—to accommodate larger fruits—than wild

FIGURE 12.18 Locations of Mesoamerican archaeological sites mentioned in the text where evidence of domestication has been recovered.

FIGURE 12.19 Teosinte may be the wild ancestor of maize. Pictured here is a modern variety (*Zea mays parviglumis*) from the Rio Balsas in Mexico that may be the form from which domesticated maize is descended. *(Courtesy of Dolores Piperno, Smithsonian Tropical Research Institute)*

squash (B. Smith 1997). Archaeologist Bruce Smith indicates that these changes resulted from people planting and tending initially wild crops as they thinned out later-germinating, slower-growing individual sprouts.

Though the common squash may have bragging rights as the first crop domesticated in the New World, certainly maize has been the most significant contribution by Native Americans to our modern diet. In the most recent data published by the Food and Agricultural Organization of the United Nations (Kasnakoglu 2004), worldwide maize production exceeds that of wheat, potatoes, soybeans, and barley and is behind only sugarcane and rice in terms of raw tonnage harvested by the world's farmers. Suggestive evidence for a preliminary step in the domestication of maize has been found at the San Andrés site in Mexico's tropical province of Tabasco, in wetlands along the Gulf of Mexico (Pope et al. 2001). Here, pollen grains of the wild ancestor of maize, the highland grass **teosinte,** have been found in levels dating to 7,100 ya. Called "God's corn" by the Aztecs, the teosinte plant looks rather like the maize plant. Instead of cobs with kernels, however, it produces a seed spike with rows a few inches long with five to ten seeds each (Figure 12.19). A single plant can produce thousands of seeds that fall to the ground when the spike becomes brittle and is shattered by any movement or disturbance.

We know that teosinte was used as a prehistoric food source, but quite a bit of work is involved in harvesting and preparing the seeds for eating: the brittleness of the spike leads to the loss of seeds, the individual seeds are very small, and the seed cases are extremely tough and difficult to di-

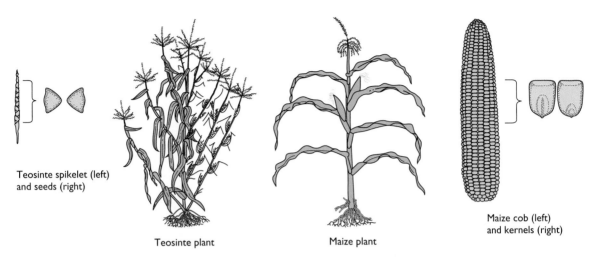

Teosinte spikelet (left)
and seeds (right)

Teosinte plant

Maize plant

Maize cob (left)
and kernels (right)

gest—tough enough, in fact, to survive in the digestive tracts of birds that may eat them, as discussed earlier in this chapter. However, a mutation in a single gene changes the extremely tough and stony fruitcase that encapsulates each teosinte kernel into a far more easily processed and much more readily digestible naked kernel (Wang et al. 2005). Thus, a single mutation transforms a nutritious but difficult plant into a nutritious and far more convenient plant food (Figure 12.20).

Though teosinte is a wild crop, its occurrence at the San Andrés site likely was the result of human intervention. Earlier in this chapter, we pointed out that one of the clues of the early stages of domestication is the occurrence of a species outside of its normal geographic range. When people expanded into a new territory where only unfamiliar plant foods grew, they may have brought along with them seeds or roots of the wild plants on which they subsisted back home and then planted and encouraged their growth in the new, alien territory. Teosinte is a highland plant; as Pope and his coworkers point out, teosinte is not native to the coastal wetlands of Tabasco where San Andrés is located (Pope et al. 2001:1373). The presence of teosinte at a site located outside of its natual range likely was facilitated by the inhabitants of San Andrés. Archaeological evidence suggests that the inhabitants were clearing off parts of the forest by burning in an attempt to artificially produce a habitat conducive to teosinte's survival.

Soon thereafter, about 7,000 ya, at San Andrés, some of the recovered pollen is recognizable as that of domesticated maize. Some of the oldest maize cobs have been found dating to 6,250 ya at Guilá Naquitz Cave. These cobs don't resemble what we buy today at the local farm stand or supermarket (Figure 12.21). These early maize specimens are, essentially, minicobs that produced tiny kernels of domesticated corn.

Clearly, archaeologists at San Andrés and Guilá Naquitz have revealed some of the early steps in maize domestication. However, equally clearly,

FIGURE 12.20 With its brittle rachis and tough glumes, teosinte (*left*), a wild Mexican grass called "God's corn" by the Aztecs, is the most likely candidate for wild maize. It is here compared to maize (*right*). The fruitcase of teosinte can be converted to the cob and naked kernels of maize by changes in a single gene or, at most, very few genes. (*From Beadle in Reed 1977*)

teosinte The wild ancestor of maize.

FIGURE 12.21 Series of maize cobs from Tehuacán, dated to after 5,000 ya. The cob on the right is of the modern variety. (*© Robert S. Peabody Museum of Archaeology*)

researchers have not yet reached far enough back in time nor far enough back in the sequence to reveal the first steps taken by the native people of the New World in their conversion of a wild crop into one of the domesticated pillars that support modern subsistence the world over. Thus, their work continues. Based on an analysis of mutation rates for maize, it has been estimated that teosinte was first genetically modified about 9,000 ya (Matsuoka et al. 2002:6083). Just as we have seen for the other plants and animals domesticated in the ancient world, domestication of maize was not an event but a process that transpired over thousands of years.

The Tehuacán Valley Project   In the late 1950s and early 1960s, American archaeologist Richard MacNeish (1964, 1967) began conducting archaeological surveys in highland Mexico. MacNeish was looking for early evidence of maize (Figure 12.22). He focused on dry caves in the highlands because these regions would have better preservation of ancient organic material and because botanist Paul Mangelsdorf (1958), an expert on maize, had declared that it had originally been a highland grass species. Searching through several highland valleys with freshwater sources, MacNeish came upon the Tehuacán Valley (Figure 12.23). After scrambling through some thirty-eight caves where organic preservation would have been best, he was finally successful. A few test pits dug in Coxcatlan Cave produced six of the most primitive-looking maize cobs anyone had ever seen.

FIGURE 12.22 Maize was domesticated approximately 7,000 years ago by the native people of Mesoamerica. It continues to be one of the world's most important food crops, the most significant of the many contributions Native Americans have made to the subsistence base of the modern world. *(Food and Agriculture Organization, United Nations; I. Velez)*

FIGURE 12.23 The Tehuacán Valley, looking past El Riego Cave on the left. Here Richard MacNeish discovered evidence for a sequence of New World agricultural development. *(© Robert S. Peabody Museum of Archaeology. Photo by R. S. MacNeish and Paul Manglesdorf)*

This initial find inspired the Tehuacán Valley Project, one of the largest and most ambitious archaeological expeditions ever undertaken. From 1961 to 1964, fifty experts in various fields converged on the valley. Major excavations were conducted on twelve sites, and hundreds of others were tested. What resulted was a nearly continuous stratigraphic sequence of human occupation of the valley from 12,000 B.P. to A.D. 1500. By follow-ing this sequence and by applying accelerator-mass-spectrometry to date some of the maize cobs, we can construct a picture of human cultural evo-lution in the valley—an evolution that included the development of a food-producing economy.

Highland cultures in Tehuacán and probably other upland valleys at the end of the Pleistocene depended to a great degree on hunting (Flannery 1967). Of greatest importance at the lowest levels of Coxcatlan Cave were pronghorn antelope and jackrabbit, animals that can be most easily hunted by groups. Pronghorn travel in herds, and jackrabbits live above ground and can be run into nets in large numbers. As climate changed at the end of the Pleistocene, both these animal species became extinct in the Mexican uplands. They were replaced by whitetail deer and cottontail rabbit, ani-mals best hunted by solitary hunters or small groups. Deer are solitary ani-mals; cottontail rabbits live in burrows and cannot be netted in large numbers. It is likely, therefore, that people living in the valley at the end of the Pleistocene found it necessary to broaden their subsistence quest and to spread their numbers out over more territory to exploit these more widely scattered animal resources. As a result of this change in settlement pattern, the people possibly also intensified their exploitation of plant species.

At many of the caves excavated in the project, human paleofeces had been preserved, producing a total of 116 fecal deposits. The analysis of these deposits allowed an extremely detailed reconstruction of the inhabi-tants' diet. For example, in the paleofeces from El Riego Cave, MacNeish's coprologist, E. O. Callen (1967), recovered undigested remains of wild beans, amaranth (a grain), chili peppers, and avocados. Also in the paleo-feces were the remains of domesticated squash. The squash found here was *not* a primitive version of a domesticate; it was entirely different from its wild antecedent.

Using the paleofeces and other data, MacNeish (1967) has attempted to reconstruct the settlement pattern in the valley. During the initial pe-riod, winter occupations were small hunting camps. In the spring, popu-lations coalesced into larger camps along the rivers. During the spring and summer, various wild seeds and cactus pods were important elements of the diet. Wild fruits were exploited when they ripened in the fall. Domes-ticates would have been incorporated into a still rather nomadic way of life, serving only as a minor element in the diet in the spring and summer.

A New World Agricultural Revolution   At another site in the valley, Abe-jas, we can see increasing reliance on domesticates. By the time this cave was occupied, the domesticates included maize, squash, and beans, the triumvirate that was to become the basis of subsistence for most of the agricultural peoples of the pre-Columbian New World.

The sites that date to this period in the valley after 4,700 ya exhibit a size and degree of sedentism previously unknown in the area. MacNeish

(1967) has suggested that what had been temporary spring and summer camps along streams were now becoming permanent base camps at which at least some members of the population stayed year-round. We are probably seeing the process of deviation amplification suggested by Flannery (1968), where a small, initial change or deviation in a traditional cultural practice related to subsistence has an enormous ripple effect across the culture, resulting in a fundamental lifestyle change.

For agriculture to make a significant contribution to the diet, people need to become more sedentary. The more sedentary they become, however, the greater the need to produce food because they can no longer roam around as much in the food quest. At the same time, the very old and the very young can make significant contributions to the subsistence quest; they can weed, sort seeds, and perform other light work. In the period we are examining, this very labor in fact may have extended people's life spans and thus increased overall population, which, in turn, would have put pressure on the subsistence system to produce more food. Thus, the original deviation from the traditional subsistence practice became amplified, further necessitating a shift toward food production.

A cave site, Ajalpa, picks up the story and again exhibits what appears to be a still very slow evolution toward an agricultural way of life. Domesticates now made up a part of the diet, the rest still supplied by hunting wild animals and gathering wild plants. Finally, the Santa Maria site exhibits an acceleration in the shift to food production.

Isotope analysis of human bones found in the Tehuacán Valley shows a clear jump in the reliance on maize and related tropical grasses early and then little change thereafter (Farnsworth et al. 1985). Based on the isotope analysis, the overall diet of these people did not change much for several millennia.

Combining MacNeish's reconstruction with the isotope data, it appears that the inhabitants of the valley went through a long period of increasing sedentism before adopting a fully agricultural way of life. This lengthy period of dietary reliance on tropical grasses—including, perhaps, the wild progenitor of maize—is similar to the situation seen in Southwest Asia.

South America

One difficulty posed in assessing the history of agriculture in the tropics, including much of the New World south of Mexico, derives from the fact that at least some of the most important crops domesticated there are root crops that leave little in the way of durable archaeological evidence, for example, no seeds, cobs, or shells. However, durable residues in the form of **starch grains** (small fragments of starch) and **phytoliths** (microscopic, inorganic particles; see Chapter 7) are sometimes found in the crevices of stone tools used to process plants, including their roots. Starch grains and phytoliths are morphologically species-specific, and their identification on

starch grains Small fragments of starch produced by plants. Because starch grain shapes are unique to individual plant species, when they are preserved on tools used to process plants, they can be recovered and used to identify plant species.

phytoliths Microscopic fragments of silica produced in plant cells. Phytolith form is species-specific, enabling researchers to identify plants that grew in an area and those that may have been used by ancient humans or human ancestors.

FIGURE 12.24 Locations of South American archaeological sites mentioned in the text where evidence of domestication has been recovered.

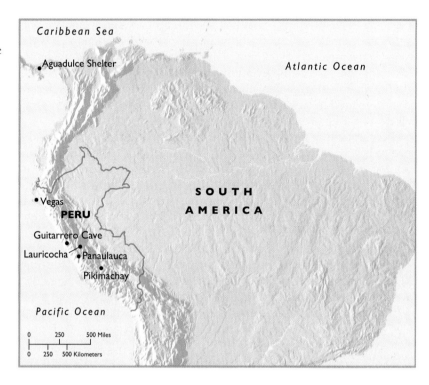

tools allows researchers to pinpoint what foods were being processed by ancient people. For example, by examining starch grains on stone grinding tools at the Aguadulce Shelter site in Panama, Dolores Piperno and colleagues (2000) have identified such domesticated root crops as manioc, yams, and arrowroot, dating to nearly 7,000 ya. Starch grains from domesticated maize also were recovered from those same grinding stones dating close to 7,000 ya, about the time of maize's earliest appearance in Mexico (Piperno et al. 2000).

In South America proper (Figure 12.24), the remains of domesticated lima beans, common beans, and chili peppers have been found in Guitarrero Cave dating to 5,000 ya (Kaplan et al. 1973; Lynch et al. 1985). Also, maize phytoliths have been found adhering to the surfaces of pottery sherds recovered at sites dating to 4,200 ya in coastal Ecuador (Brown 2001). To the east, in Uruguay, phytoliths and starch grains from domesticated varieties of squash (4190 B.P.) and beans (3050 B.P.) have been recovered from grinding stones found in the La Plata Basin (Iriarte et al. 2004).

Some of the earliest evidence for the domestication of quinoa—an extremely important crop in the agriculture of South America (Figure 12.25)—has been found at Panaulauca Cave in Peru. Quinoa plants produce nutritious seeds with a healthy mix of amino acids superior to the better-

FIGURE 12.25 Quinoa plants produce nutritious seeds with a healthy mix of amino acids superior to the better-known grains. Quinoa seeds with thinner seed coats than wild specimens have been dated to South American sites between 5000 and 4000 B.P. and continue to be an important source of protein on that continent. *(Courtesy John F. McCamant)*

known grains. Quinoa seeds with thinner seed coats than wild specimens have been dated there to between 5000 and 4000 B.P. (B. Smith 1995:173).

South American Root Crops   Several different varieties of domesticated potatoes were developed by ancient South Americans by at least 4,000 ya and possibly earlier. The potato was unknown in ancient Europe, though it became an important crop there in the sixteenth century A.D. after it was introduced by people who had traveled to the New World. This South American crop became a dietary mainstay in parts of northern Europe. A terrible famine occurred in Europe—most severely in Ireland—when much of the potato crop was killed by a blight in the 1840s.

Other high-altitude roots were domesticated and relied on as sources of food in the South American uplands. For example, *oca*, second in importance only to the potato, produced nutritious tubers at altitudes up to 13,500 feet. Also, the root crops *yacon, ulluco, mashua,* and *arracacha* and the legume *jícama* were important contributors to the diet (Figure 12.26). The turniplike *maca* was cultivated at elevations of 14,000 feet. The Inca civilization in western South America (see Chapter 13) relied more heavily on root crops than any of the world's ancient civilizations.

FIGURE 12.26 Root crops were an important food source for the high-altitude civilizations of South America. Along with the potato, other high-altitude crops such as *oca, ulluco,* and *mashua* contributed to the diet. (*Dr. Steven R. King*)

Cotton Domestication and Animal Husbandry   In South America, domestication included at least one significant nonfood crop: cotton. Evidence of its domestication can be traced back to about 5000 B.P.

South America also provides data for the most significant animal domestication in the New World (Kent 1987; Wing 1977). There are four types of **camelids** in South America: the wild guanaco and vicuña and the domesticated llama and alpaca. The precise relationships among these four types are still unknown—all four are interfertile. Some researchers suggest that the guanaco was domesticated to produce both the llama and the alpaca (Figure 12.27). In any event, the llama was primarily a beast of burden and the alpaca a source of wool; both were used for food. The llama and alpaca show signs of domestication before 5000 B.P., according to finds in Pikimachay Cave and Lauricocha Cave in Peru (Wing 1977).

North America

For a long time, it was thought that the shift from foraging to agriculture among the native people of North America was entirely the result of diffu-

camelid The family of large ruminant animals that includes Bactrian camels and dromedaries in the Old World and llamas, alpacas, vicuñas, and guanacos in the New World.

FIGURE 12.27 Llamas, probably the most important animal domesticated in the New World, were used as beasts of burden and as food. Here, a packtrain of llamas carries firewood in southern Peru. (© *Loren McIntyre*)

sion. It was believed that the maize, beans, and squash agriculture that developed in Mesoamerica diffused north and that the native North Americans, who were foragers, "borrowed" the idea wherever the environment made that shift feasible.

Maize is a tropical crop, not native to North America, and domesticated maize turns up earlier in the archaeological record in Mesoamerica than in North America; it is quite clear, therefore, that maize agriculture did, indeed, diffuse from Mexico into what is now the United States. However, it is now also clear that some of the native people of North America were already experiencing their own agricultural revolution prior to the appearance of maize in their territory.

North American Squash   Archaeological evidence indicates that soon after 5,000 ya, a local variety of squash was domesticated independently by North American natives as part of an indigenous and separate agricultural revolution that preceded the introduction of Mesoamerican maize and beans (B. Smith 1989, 1992a, 1992b, 1995). Squash seeds recovered at the Phillips Spring site in Missouri (Figure 12.28), dated to 4500 to 4300 B.P., are early domesticates with seeds significantly larger than their modern wild counterparts (B. Smith 1995).

North American Seed Crops   Other native crops known to have been domesticated by the Indians of the eastern woodlands were sunflower

FIGURE 12.28 Locations of North American archaeological sites mentioned in the text where evidence of domestication has been recovered.

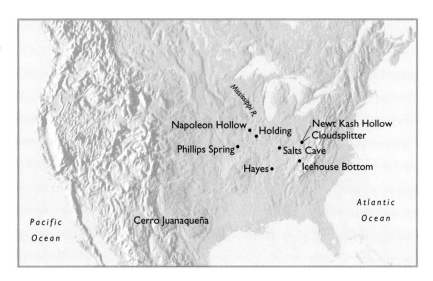

(Figure 12.29), sumpweed (also known as marsh elder), pigweed (also called lamb's quarter), and goosefoot—all producers of starchy or oil-rich seeds. Sumpweed seeds recovered from a 4,000-year-old deposit at Napoleon Hollow in Illinois, for example, are uniformly larger (by almost a third) than the seeds of wild sumpweed (Ford 1985). Domesticated sunflower with seeds substantially bigger than those of wild varieties has been dated to 4265 B.P. at the Hayes site in central Tennessee (B. Smith 1995). Dating to about 3400 B.P., goosefoot seeds from the Newt Kash Hollow and Cloudsplitter rockshelters in Kentucky have significantly thinner seed coats than those of wild plants, indicating selection for faster-growing sprouts. At Salts Cave in Kentucky, 119 preserved fecal deposits associated with a radiocarbon date of 3450 B.P. (Yarnell 1977:864) contain an abundance of sunflower and sumpweed seeds, whose large size is indicative of domestication.

The Adoption of Maize   The earliest evidence for the use of maize in North America postdates the appearance of the domesticated local foods by about 2,000 years. The oldest archaeological evidence for the use of maize in North America has been found at the Icehouse Bottom site in eastern Tennessee with a radiocarbon date of 1775 B.P. (Chapman and Crites 1987). The Holding site east of St. Louis, which has also produced maize, may be slightly older (B. Smith 1995:191).

As important as it was to become in the diets of many North American natives, for nearly 1,000 years maize was only a minor supplement to

FIGURE 12.29 The sunflower was one of a number of crops domesticated by Native Americans living north of Mexico. The many-headed sunflower shown here is similar to some wild varieties. *(K. L. Feder)*

their subsistence. Analysis of the carbon isotope chemistry of prehistoric human bones in North America (see Chapter 7) indicates that a shift away from local domesticates to a heavy reliance on maize did not occur until sometime between A.D. 900 and 1000. All of the wild and indigenously domesticated crops of eastern North America follow a different photosynthetic pathway than maize and possess a different concentration of ^{13}C than does maize. Human bones in North America show a big jump in ^{13}C concentration and, by inference, in maize consumption at about this time (B. Smith 1995:200).

The Nutritional Impact of Agriculture

Although a shift to agriculture almost always results in increased amounts of food, the diet of agriculturalists is not always nutritionally superior to that of hunter-gatherers. In fact, analysis of the skeletons of some prehistoric agriculturalists shows a marked increase in the incidence of diseases related to dietary deficiencies.

A good example of this comes from the work of physical anthropologist George Armelagos and his students (Goodman and Armelagos 1985), who analyzed hundreds of skeletons from the Dickson Mound site in Illinois. The skeletons date to the period A.D. 950 to 1200—before maize agriculture made its appearance, during the transition period, and after its acceptance. The skeletons of the site's inhabitants show the effects of dietary emphasis on a single crop, in this case, maize, which, while providing large quantities of food, led to an unvaried diet lacking in some important nutrients. Twice as many of the skeletons after the adoption of agriculture show evidence of anemia and three times as many exhibit the osteological effects of bacterial infections when compared to the skeletons of the earlier hunter-gatherers. Beyond this, the bones of the children of the agriculturalists are narrower and shorter, showing a delayed growth rate in their early years. Among agriculturalists who relied on single crops or very few crops, there was higher infant mortality and a shortened average life span. So, it may be, at least in some cases, that the varied diet of hunter-gatherers was more nutritionally complete than that of many agriculturalists. The health of people often suffered, therefore, in their attempt to produce a greater quantity of food when this resulted in a less varied diet. So, we may infer, there must have been a significant motivation to produce more food.

In another study, researchers found that the relationship between longevity and subsistence base is a bit more complicated. Archaeologists in Israel found that among 217 Natufian (preagricultural subsistence) and 262 Neolithic (agricultural subsistence) skeletons, there was an *increase* of more than five years (from 32.2 to 37.6) in mean adult male age at death among the agriculturalists and a decrease of more than five years (from 35.5 to 30.1) among females (Eshed et al. 2004). The authors of this study conclude that the abundant and reliable subsistence base provided by agriculture may have resulted in increased and even prolonged female fertility. This, they propose, may have increased not only the number of pregnancies most women endured, but also the likelihood of encountering the many serious complications of childbirth, leading, the researchers contend, to their higher mortality rate. In this case, at least, it appears that the adoption of an agricultural way of life was disadvantageous primarily to women, and it was their longevity that decreased as a result of the Food-Producing Revolution.

Can Agriculture Be Explained?

Earlier in this chapter, we presented some hypotheses for explaining the Food-Producing Revolution (see Table 12.1). We then examined data on the actual sequences of the evolution of food production in Mesoamerica, Southwest Asia, East Asia, Europe, South and North America, and Africa (see Figure 12.1 for a summary time chart). We are now left to ask which hypothesis or hypotheses are borne out by the data. In truth, the data are too limited even for the most well-known sequences to provide a definitive answer, but we can isolate the useful aspects of each of the proposed explanations and—to use an appropriate metaphor—winnow out those that do not bear up under scrutiny.

Childe's oasis hypothesis is probably not correct in positing a significant drying of the environment as a factor. Evidence now shows that this particular long-term climate change did not occur. Beyond this, the key elements of his hypothesis are not borne out. The idea that only an oasis situation would allow people to become knowledgeable about plants and animals makes no sense. Hunter-gatherers the world over possess detailed knowledge about the plants and animals on which they subsist.

Sauer was correct at least in terms of proposing that a certain degree of sedentary life was a significant factor in the development of agriculture. But other aspects of his hypothesis are not supported. Aside from the dog, early domesticates were, for the most part, food sources. Also, although the data are meager, Southeast Asia was certainly no earlier and perhaps a bit later in developing an agricultural way of life than was Southwest Asia.

Braidwood may have been correct in assuming that people would not begin the process of domestication without having significant knowledge about the species they were domesticating, but this does not explain the timing of the Agricultural Revolution or the fact that it was so widespread.

Anderson is certainly correct that domestication may have been accidentally encouraged by many of the practices of hunter-gatherers. But again, his hypothesis really does not approach the question of why they would have gone through the extra bother of an agricultural way of life.

Rindos's hypothesis of coevolution is intriguing. It is particularly valuable as a way of looking at the process of domestication, providing an evolutionary framework for how it may have come about. Rindos's hypothesis does not necessarily contradict hypotheses based on population growth. Rather, it is a valuable model for how the relationship between people and the plants and animals on which they depended might, in some cases, inevitably have led to a more productive subsistence system that would have allowed for a greater yield to feed an expanding population base.

The hypotheses of Boserup, Binford, Flannery, Harris, and Henry, which are really complementary and not competing, are perhaps the most attractive. Together, they take into account environmental, demographic, and cultural factors. The problem is that one key element of all their explanations—population growth impinging on the carrying capacity of local environments—cannot, at present, be shown to have occurred immediately prior to the beginning of domestication.

Nevertheless, following Binford's model, we can propose a tentative scenario: at the end of the Pleistocene, some cultures adjusted their adaptations in response to climatic changes wrought by the melting of the ice sheets. Some groups shifted their subsistence focus to habitats that allowed for a more sedentary existence—coasts, river banks, and so on. Such sedentism may have produced larger, or at least denser, populations. The rich food resources were localized, and group mobility decreased. The old and the lame could make significant contributions to the food quest. Where previously children had been a burden—only representing more mouths to feed—now they too could become active in the food quest when that quest focused on collecting foods such as shellfish, bird eggs, or seeds. The birth rate may have increased as fertility increased, and the proportion of surviving babies may have increased as well. An increase in population, however, may have upset the previously evolved equilibrium between human populations and their environments, causing groups to overshoot the carrying capacity of their territories. This may have resulted in expansion into marginal or less attractive habitats and subsequent intensification and specialization of the food quest. Historical hunter-gatherers are known to have broadcast the seeds of their wild food plants, so it is not difficult to believe that people at the end of the Pleistocene did the same out of necessity. We need only assume that in attempting to expand their wild food plants (or animals) into new habitats or to intensify their productivity within the same area, they would, as a matter of course, have selected for more productive, more easily harvested, more easily processed, or more tractable individuals of a species. These folks were not stupid. They depended on wild species for their survival. They knew how plants and animals propagated. It would have been a short step for them to assist in propagation and to make the end products more amenable to human use through artificial selection.

The domestication of plants and animals was not an inevitable outcome of climate change or population expansion at the end of the Pleistocene or beginning of the Holocene, nor was it the only economic basis for the development of complex societies such as those we'll discuss in Chapter 13. For example, it has been suggested (Moseley 1975) that the extremely rich ecosystems of the Pacific coast of South America provided natural resources in sufficient abundance, density, and reliability that societies exhibiting great social and political complexity developed there before the shift to agriculture. In more recent times, Native Americans living along the northwest coast of North America found an environment so abundant, with resources so concentrated, that again greatly complex societies with powerful rulers or chiefs emerged without the domestication

CONTEMPORARY ISSUE
Our Worst Mistake?

The fabric of modern life depends absolutely on the subsistence mode called agriculture. Without a steady, reliable, predictable—not to mention enormous—food supply, modern life with its cities, universities, and, yes, anthropologists simply would not be possible. One might think it obvious, therefore, that agriculture—the invention that more than anything else has made modern life possible—was a good thing. But not everyone agrees. UCLA medical school scientist and writer Jared Diamond (1987) has provocatively characterized the Food-Producing Revolution as "the worst mistake in the history of the human race."

It is an interesting assertion. Diamond points out that hunter-gatherers, in many instances, led relatively easy lives. In response to the stereotype many of us hold of the short, hard lives and hand-to-mouth existence of hunter-gatherers, they often have it better than those who rely on agriculture. Their diets frequently are healthier, providing more protein and more variety than those of agriculturalists. And, even in those few, relatively poor areas where the last hunter-gatherers were pushed by expanding agriculturalists, they didn't need to work very long for the necessities of existence. Agriculture, with its clearing of land, tilling of soil, planting, weeding, watering, and harvesting, is exceedingly hard work, and farmers typically work far more hours than hunter-gatherers.

While most hunter-gatherers practice a broad-spectrum subsistence strategy that includes regularly collecting dozens of different kinds of foods, agriculturalists often devote all of their energies to a very small number of crops—generally rice, corn, or wheat. These high-carbohydrate crops are extremely productive and can feed many more people than hunting or gathering, but, because they are lacking in some essential amino acids, they can lead to a rather poor diet. Also, if a pestilence befalls a major crop, people will starve because they have little else to fall back on.

Beyond this, Diamond points out, it was the enormous output that agriculture could achieve that led to class societies. Where there is the potential for surplus food production, there is the potential for groups of haves who control the extra and have-nots who need that food in times of trouble. Eventually, Diamond asserts, agriculture led to class societies where most were poor and worked their lives away for those few wealthy individuals who controlled the food surplus.

Thus, in Diamond's accounting, people at the end of the Pleistocene had two primary choices: They could maintain their hunting and gathering way of life and invent new ways of keeping population down to ensure enough food for their small populations, or they could allow population to grow and intensify the food quest through plant and animal domestication. The irony, in Diamond's view, was that those who made the smart decision—the hunter-gatherers who opted to keep population down and maintain their traditional subsistence mode—were quickly overrun by those who allowed their populations to grow.

What are we to make of this? Diamond does have a point. Certainly, without agriculture there can be no wealth or classes or wars to dispute who should have that wealth. Equally certainly, however, there could be no anthropologists or UCLA medical school professors. Indeed, agriculture brings with it good and bad. And ultimately, as with nearly all other cultural inventions, the results are up to us.

of plants and animals and the attendant development of agriculture. There was no need to artificially raise the resource ceiling here simply because that ceiling was so high naturally.

Nevertheless, as great as nature's bounty may be in some places, it seems no match for what is possible through the process of artificial selection and the application of agricultural technology. The human ability to produce a reliable and concentrated wealth of food and other resources through agriculture and animal husbandry is unmatched by natural ecosystems. That ability forever altered human cultural evolution and led to the far-reaching developments to be discussed in the next chapter of this book—and, indeed, to our current chapter in human history.

Summary

Beginning sometime after 12,000 ya, human groups in Southwest Asia, sub-Saharan Africa, Southeast Asia, southern Europe, Mesoamerica, coastal South America, and central North America began to domesticate the plants and animals on which they depended for their subsistence. That is, they began to produce their own food rather than simply gather what nature provided. Many hypotheses have been proposed for this fundamental change in how people fed themselves. It seems that the best explanation involves the necessity to feed more mouths as human populations grew in the above-mentioned regions at the end of the Pleistocene. In Southwest Asia, wheat, barley, sheep, and goats were the primary domesticates, whereas in Africa, they were yam, sorghum, millet, and oil palm; in Southeast Asia, rice, millet, cattle, and pigs; in southern Europe, sheep, goats, cattle, wheat, and barley; in Mesoamerica, maize, beans, and squash; in South America, quinoa, root crops (including potatoes, *oca, jícama, maca,* and *ulluco*) maize, beans, llamas, alpacas, and cotton; and in North America, squash and seed crops such as sunflower and marsh elder.

In a relatively short time—something less than 10,000 years—the vast majority of the world's people had adopted an agricultural mode of subsistence. Agriculture allowed for larger, denser populations and necessitated new social structures for controlling and organizing the dense, sedentary settlements that resulted. Ultimately, in some regions, the shift to an agricultural way of life led to the development of cities, civilization, and eventually modern life.

Study Questions

1. What are the key characteristics of human adaptation to the post-Pleistocene world? What is the meaning of the diversity of archaeological remains dated to the Mesolithic in the Old World and the Archaic in the New World?
2. Describe artificial selection and compare it to natural selection. Explain what domestication is and how artificial selection leads to the domestication of plants and animals.
3. How have various scientists attempted to explain the Food-Producing Revolution?

4. What characteristics did people select for in wild plants and animals? Considering this, how can the archaeological remains of domesticated species be distinguished from those of wild ancestors?
5. How has "molecular archaeology" contributed to the search for the sources of domesticated wheat and maize?
6. When and where did people first domesticate plants and animals? What species were domesticated in these world areas?

Key Terms

foraging	osteologist	emmer
agriculture	diffusion	einkorn
Mesolithic	sedentary	faunal assemblage
opportunistic foragers	carrying capacity	rachis
Archaic	deviation	glume
Shell Mound Archaic	amplification	Peiligang
Food-Producing	settlement pattern	Yang-shao
Revolution	testa	Lung-shan
Agricultural	Levant	teosinte
Revolution	Natufian	starch grains
Neolithic	cereal	phytoliths
domesticate	legume	camelid
artificial selection		

For More Information

If you are interested in the details of specific hypotheses on the origins of agriculture or if you would like to know more about the development of agriculture in a specific region, any of the works cited in this chapter would be a good place to start. A volume edited by C. Wesley Cowan and Patty Jo Watson titled *The Origins of Agriculture* has many excellent articles on the shift to food production in a number of world areas. Daniel Zohary and Maria Hopf have provided a virtual encyclopedia of Old World domesticated plants in *Domestication of Plants in the Old World*. Perhaps the best discussion of our current understanding of the Food-Producing Revolution throughout the Old and New Worlds can be found in Bruce Smith's splendid book, *The Emergence of Agriculture*. Finally, a monograph by Mark Cohen, *The Food Crisis in Prehistory*, gives a detailed argument for demographically driven hypotheses of the origin of prehistoric agriculture.

Monumental construction works, such as the colossal statues at Abu Simbel in Egypt, are the unique products of state societies. How did civilization evolve from a Neolithic base of egalitarian farming communities? Are civilizations destined to collapse? *(M. H. Feder)*

THE EVOLUTION OF CIVILIZATION

CHAPTER CONTENTS

The Meaning of Civilization

Explaining the Evolution of Civilization

Hearths of Civilization

Why Did It Happen?

CONTEMPORARY ISSUE: The Collapse of
    Civilization

Summary

Study Questions

Key Terms

For More Information

The images are evocative indeed: the sun sets behind the great pyramid of the pharaoh Khufu (better known by his Greek name, Cheops) at Giza in Egypt; the dark, humid jungle frames the majestic Temple of the Jaguars at the ancient Mesoamerican city of Tikal; the "skeleton" of urban sprawl that is the ancient Indus Valley city of Mohenjo-daro crawls up-slope toward the citadel that marks the political heart of the settlement. Although each is unique, these and other images reflect the culmination of what appears to have resulted from common, unifying processes of cultural evolution. For want of a better term, we characterize these great tombs, pyramids, and cities as evidence of civilization. They symbolize and de-marcate a way of life far different from any that had preceded it in the ancient world.

FIGURE 13.1 Locations of the world's earliest civilizations.

The Food-Producing Revolution set the stage for developments that were to characterize a number of world areas after about 6,000 ya. Beginning close to that time, perhaps as a consequence of the shift to agriculture, with its potential for producing enormous surpluses of food—and the attendant potential for the accumulation of wealth and power—the Neolithic pattern of small, largely autonomous farming villages became radically altered in some world areas (Figure 13.1). Social and political systems were transformed beyond recognition. The kind of life people led was entirely different from what it had been. This new way of life is the focus of this chapter.

The Meaning of Civilization

civilization Cultures with a food surplus, social stratification, labor specialization, rule by power, monumental construction projects, and a system of recordkeeping.

What is **civilization?** Common usage usually implies a level of social sophistication or gentility. The dictionary definition ordinarily includes reference to a society at "an advanced state of intellectual, cultural, and technological development" marked by "advances in the arts and sciences" and the invention of writing. Confusion over the precise meaning has led some to abandon its use as a scientific term. We will use it here for lack of a better, inclusive expression.

To be categorized as civilizations, cultures must possess the following common features (Childe 1951; Haas 1982; Tainter 1988):

1. Food and labor surplus controlled by an elite
2. Social stratification
3. A formal government
4. Specialization of labor
5. Monumental public works
6. Densely populated settlements
7. A system of recordkeeping

As we will see, each of the early civilizations you are probably already familiar with possessed many, though not necessarily all, of these qualities.

Food and Labor Surplus

Food surplus is a requirement for the development of a civilization. In most societies in the beginning of the Neolithic, the great majority of people probably contributed to the food quest. Because food output was still relatively low, it was necessary for a large proportion of the population to be directly involved in food production. A very few individuals may have specialized in religious activities or leadership, but they were the exceptions. With the development of higher-yield strains of crops, more efficient methods of agriculture, and, in some areas, the use of animal power to till the land, however, the percentage of a given population required to work in the fields certainly dropped.

We can see such a process taking place even today. According to census statistics, in 1920 more than 30 percent of the U.S. population lived on farms. By 1950, that figure had dropped to just a little more than 15 percent, and by 2000 less than 1.5 percent lived on farms (Figure 13.2). Looked at another way, before 1920 each American farmer, on the average, supplied food products for about seven people (Figure 13.3). By the 1940s each American farmer produced enough food to feed almost eleven people. By 1970 that figure jumped to fifty people, and by 1980 the American farmer produced enough food to feed almost eighty people (Kranzberg 1984). These figures have continued to grow; according to the agribusiness Archer Daniel Midlands (in one of their television commercials), in the 1990s, on average, each American farmer produced enough food to feed 130 people, the vast majority of whom are free, therefore, to engage in other pursuits.

Social Stratification

In egalitarian societies like those of most hunter-gatherers, people within the same age and sex categories are essentially equal; they have the same rights and privileges, similar responsibilities, and about equal wealth. Most

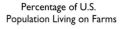
Percentage of U.S. Population Living on Farms

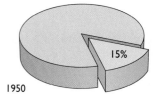
1920   30%

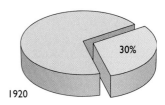
1950   15%

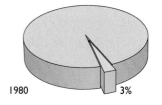
1980   3%

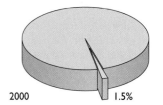
2000   1.5%

Farm
Nonfarm

FIGURE 13.2 Drop in the percentage of U.S. population living on farms, 1920–2000.

Average Number of
People Fed by a Single Farmer

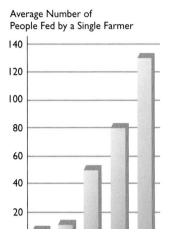

FIGURE 13.3 Approximate mean number of people fed by each American farmer in 1920, 1940, 1970, 1980, and 1990.

social stratification The presence of acknowledged differences in social status, political influence, and wealth.

state Class societies, often rigidly stratified into social levels, with a ruling class controlling the populace not by consensus but by coercion and force.

tribe A grouping of people organized largely by kinship. There is no central ruler, but individuals may obtain prestige and a degree of authority through their achievements.

chiefdom A level of socio-political integration more complex than the tribe but less so than the state.

Paleolithic and many early Neolithic societies were probably egalitarian or pretty close to it. On the other hand, societies with **social stratification** have fixed layers of power, leadership, social status, and wealth. People are born into social strata and remain there for their entire lives. Ordinarily there is a hierarchy with a ruler such as a chief, king, pharaoh, or emperor on top, followed by his or her family and religious rulers or military leaders, special workers such as craftspeople, and perhaps everyone else—farmers and soldiers, for example—below them. In other words, building a pyramid is made possible by a social system shaped like a pyramid (Figure 13.4).

Formal Government

All civilizations, as we are using the term here, are **state** societies. Along with social stratification, the defining characteristic of a state is a formal government, defined by archaeologist Joseph Tainter (1988:26) as a "specialized decision-making organization with a monopoly of force, and with the power to draft for work, levy and collect taxes, and decree and enforce laws." The leaders of this government belong to the upper social classes.

Nonstate or prestate societies certainly have leaders, people who make important decisions and whose instructions ordinarily are heeded. But leaders in nonstate societies rule through consensus and by their abilities to persuade others to follow their commands and to marshall the opinion of the group. For example, in societies identified by anthropologists as having a tribal level of political organization, leaders, called *headmen,* don't have absolute power. **Tribes** have no laws, police force, or army to force others to obey them. They do, however, have authority—they are good at organizing labor, keeping people happy, and conducting projects that people recognize are for the good of the group. Their leadership usually results from their accomplishments and abilities. It is this earned respect that convinces people to listen and follow. If people no longer wish to listen to a headman, they don't.

Some societies possess a level of political organization more complex than that of tribes but not as complex as state societies. Anthropologists call these groups **chiefdoms.** Chiefs rule by more than simple authority; they have the ability to enforce certain types of decisions. Further, the power of a chief is legitimized on the basis of religious ideology and is supported and symbolized by having greater access to wealth. However, a chief's power is neither absolute nor exclusive. There is no formal political apparatus, no government, that legitimizes the chief's rule or backs up the chief's authority. A chief does not possess a monopoly on the use of force, and as such, power in a chiefdom may be widely distributed among sub-chiefs.

The kings, pharaohs, or emperors of state societies have much more than authority, and they rule by more than the consensus of the populace. They have coercive power—the ability to make decisions, give commands,

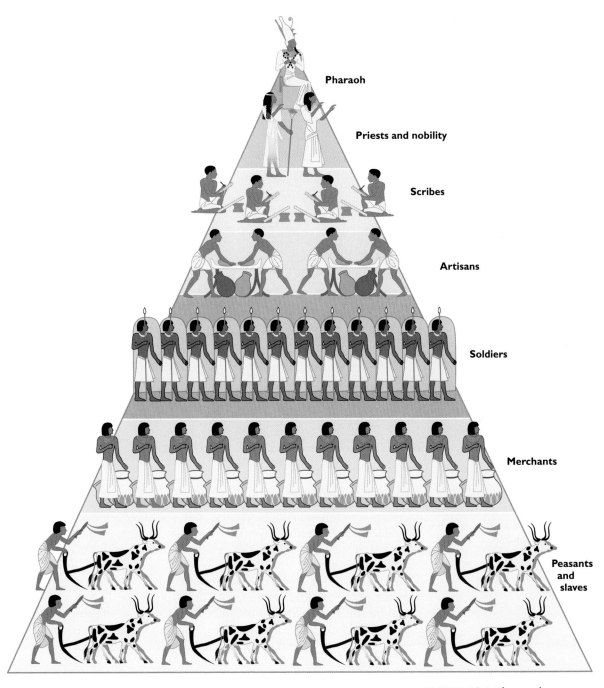

Pharaoh

Priests and nobility

Scribes

Artisans

Soldiers

Merchants

Peasants and slaves

and then make sure that those commands are carried out. Jail, enforced labor, banishment, and even execution await those who fail to heed the dictates of the ruler of a state society. And, unlike chiefs, the rulers of state societies sit atop a formal government that further concentrates, magnifies, and formalizes their power, and they have fixed laws and possess the ability to enforce those laws.

FIGURE 13.4 The social systems of state societies are pyramidal. The very few who rule, supported by a small class of nobles and specialists, sit atop the social pyramid.

FIGURE 13.5 Great works of art, like these reconstructed murals at the Maya site of Cacaxtla, require the existence of full-time artists or craftspeople who specialize in their particular fields. Full-time specialists are provided for and required by state societies. (© *Charles and Josette Lenars/Corbis*)

Labor Specialization

For great monuments to be constructed, spectacular works of art to be produced, or extensive networks of canals to be built, people who are not needed in subsistence activities must specialize. It is unlikely that part-time artists could have painted the Maya murals at Cacaxtla (Figure 13.5); it stretches the imagination to believe that part-time sculptors could have produced the carvings at Abu Simbel in Egypt (Figure 13.6).

The ability of civilizations to produce great art, architecture, engineering, crafts, and science depends on specialization, and specialization can occur only when the farmers produce enough food to feed the people who are engaged in other pursuits.

The reason you can be a student for an extended period—and can go on to become a physician, engineer, computer programmer, social worker, or even an anthropologist—rests on the fact that you are not needed on the farm. Modern farmers produce far more food than they need to feed their families, and their "surplus" can be distributed to the overwhelming majority of people who do not live on farms or produce their own food and who, therefore, can do things other than raise or gather food. For

FIGURE 13.6 Monumental architectural or engineering works, such as Abu Simbel in Egypt, are products of specialized classes of workers. Specialization of labor is possible only in civilized state societies. (M. H. Feder)

complex civilizations to develop, this same process must have been true. All of the trappings of civilization—pyramids, temples, great art, science, canals, roads—are possible only when large numbers of people are freed from producing food and available to spend their time quarrying stone, building roads, serving in the army, and being priests, artisans, builders, merchants, scribes, and so on.

Monumental Works

If the trappings of civilization require the development of specialization and social stratification, we are left wondering why such works as monumental architecture, great art, and even scientific achievements are always associated with civilization and the development of the state. We can make some rather reasonable guesses. In the next section, we will approach hypotheses about why the civilized state developed in the first place. As for why it developed the way it did, however, we can suggest the following.

Civilization involves a tradeoff. In return for the protection and security such societies offer, most people end up working harder, and much of

FIGURE 13.7 The ability to organize a large labor force to construct monumental structures is one of the hallmarks of state societies, implying the existence of a food surplus to feed a large body of nonfarm workers, a socially stratified system to conscript and organize their labor, and a specialist class to design and engineer the project. Egyptian pyramids (*top*) and their Mesoamerican counterparts (*bottom*) are examples of remarkable monuments of complex state societies. (*M. H. Feder; K. L. Feder*)

that work directly benefits not themselves but other people—their rulers or leaders. To live in a state society, most people give up some of their freedom and independence. They give up living in an egalitarian society for a stratified system, and most people in a stratified society make up the bottom of the social pyramid; they work harder and have less control over their own destinies. Why would anyone consent to this? Great pyramids, burial chambers, spectacular works of art, great engineering projects, and mysterious astronomical knowledge are all symbols of the power held by the leaders of a given civilization (Figure 13.7). Archaeologist David Webster (2002:223) calls these works "grandiose public statements." These "statements," along with whatever practical needs they fulfill, represent one way in which rulers advertise in a very visible fashion what they are capable of achieving by the application of their power. In other words, by producing spectacular monuments, breathtaking art, and remarkable engineering projects, rulers of state societies are warning all who encounter these creations, "Look at what I can accomplish; don't mess with me."

As archaeologist Joseph Tainter points out, rulers in such societies need constantly to reinforce the legitimacy of their leadership. They need, in essence, to continually convince the great mass of people that their position above the masses is reasonable and justifiable. As Tainter points out, along with an army and police force, which enable rulers to impose their will on people through physical coercion, "sacred legitimization provides a binding framework" (1988:28). Monumental works such as pyramids, great tombs, and palaces serve as this "sacred legitimization."

Sacred legitimization becomes even more pervasive and powerful when the secular leader in an ancient—or modern—state is a religious leader as well. This reaches its most extreme when the king or queen is not just a priest or priestess but a divine being. In this eventuality, the dictates of the ruling elite are not passed down simply from a chief, king, emperor, or imperial majesty. Here the order to produce more food, join the workforce to build the temple, engage in war, or provide a son or daughter for service to the state originates not from just a powerful man or woman but from a god or goddess. Failure to comply with those orders endangers one's position not only in this life; it jeopardizes one's future in the next life as well.

The blending of secular and religious power is an effective way to control a large population of people, and ancient states commonly followed this pattern. The strategy proceeds along the following lines: Pharaoh is the offspring of the gods, and therefore deserves our loyalty. Pharaoh decrees that 10,000 of us shall help construct a great pyramid to be his burial chamber. We obey because we believe him to be all-powerful. After a time, the pyramid is complete, and it is spectacular. Only someone with godlike powers could have accomplished such a feat. Any doubts that we might secretly have harbored are eliminated or, at least, greatly diminished. The pharaoh's exalted position has been legitimized by his ability to produce a spectacular monument to himself.

In this light, the great achievements of civilization in the arts and sciences are made possible by the nature of civilization. At the same time, they contribute to the creation and further consolidation of such a society. In other words, such cultural achievements are both causes and effects of civilization. A pyramid, the accurate prediction of a solar eclipse, a great wall around a city are all real achievements as well as symbols of the abilities and power of a leader. Such achievements are not usually possible in egalitarian societies.

Dense Population

With the evolution of civilization usually, but not inevitably, comes the development of the city. Although no absolute line can be drawn between a large village and a small city, we mean the term *city* to indicate a settlement with a large, dense population.

Cities are usually features of civilized life. Dense populations can be more easily ruled than dispersed groups, and large groups of people are needed to support the running of the state.

A System of Recordkeeping

Finally, we come to the necessity of recordkeeping. We must be careful in this discussion not to equate recordkeeping with writing, because not all records need to be written down.

Recordkeeping is necessary for a number of reasons. Think of our own civilization. Our government can pay the bills for defense, social programs, and construction only by taxing its citizens. At one time, the United States sustained its military force through a draft, another sort of taxation—and eighteen-year-old males in the United States still need to register with the Selective Service, so though there is no draft currently, the government still keeps a record of each eighteen-year-old male. Imagine how well our government would function if it had no way of keeping track in some kind of permanent form of how much wealth each citizen produces, how much tax was paid last year and this year, the age of its citizens, military service, and the like. Without records, it would be virtually impossible to perform these functions.

The same was certainly true for early civilizations. Early civilized societies depended on a great mass of people providing at least some of their wealth in the form of labor, food, and children to support the existence of the elite and the specialists. There had to be some way of tracking each citizen's contribution. There had to be records to make sure that each farmer provided a certain percentage of grain to feed those not involved in agriculture. There had to be some way of keeping track of the labor of the citizens as soldiers or monument builders. In the late sixteenth century, the English scholar Francis Bacon penned the words "knowledge is power," and this certainly applies to the concentration of power in the hands of an elite class in ancient civilizations. The ability of an elite to codify and record information in a more or less permanent form—especially in a form that only the elites and their scribes understood—increased their ability to control that information (Figure 13.8). By controlling information through permanent recordkeeping, the elite, essentially, monopolized knowledge and, therefore, the power created by that knowledge. Without this level of control, the state could not have existed.

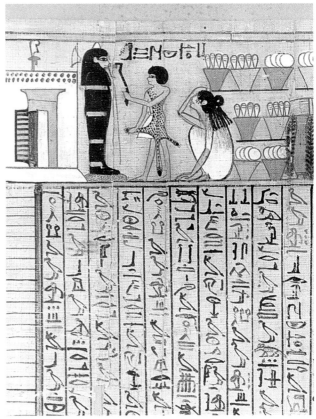

FIGURE 13.8 Examples of early systems of recordkeeping: (*top left*) cuneiform writing from Mesopotamia; (*top right*) Maya hieroglyphic writing; (*bottom left*) quipu, a nonwritten system of recordkeeping based on a series of knotted strings used by the Inca civilization of South America; and (*bottom right*) hieroglyphic writing from Egypt. A system of recordkeeping—written or not—was crucial in the development of early civilizations. (*All photos: © The Granger Collection, New York*)

475

Explaining the Evolution of Civilization

We must now address this basic question: Why did civilized states develop at all? Interestingly, we see a situation similar to the beginning of domestication. The world's first civilizations appeared in several different areas at about the same time. Where they arose is no coincidence. Such cultures could have evolved only where there was a food surplus, and such a surplus is possible ordinarily only under conditions of intensive agriculture. Because the Food-Producing Revolution occurred in a number of locations, it is not surprising that civilization later developed in many of these same areas. That it did indicates that under certain conditions, civilization may have been almost an inevitable outcome of the Food-Producing Revolution, as Jared Diamond asserted (see the "Contemporary Issue" in Chapter 12). It also implies that there were identifiable reasons for these developments.

As we did for the Agricultural Revolution, we will now present some of the hypotheses proposed by various thinkers to explain the emergence of civilization (Table 13.1).

The Explanation of Race

Some hypotheses suggested for the development of civilization in specific locations are racist. In the mid-nineteenth century, Gustav Klemm in Germany and Count J. A. de Gobineau in France both argued that race was the key factor in the development of civilization and that each civilization was unique because of biological factors (Harris 1968). Those people who had not attained a level of civilized existence were biologically unequipped to.

Very often such racist constructs could not admit that dark-skinned people had attained civilized status—despite physical evidence to the contrary. So Native American cultures such as the Maya, who clearly created a remarkable civilization, were either explained as the result of cultural borrowing or were denied the status of civilization. The impressive ruins of Great Zimbabwe, located in southern Africa, were ascribed by some to interlopers from Southwest Asia, so great was the desire to deny a connection between its massive and impressive monuments and sub-Saharan Africans (Ndoro 1997). Human history and cultural evolution were reduced to an argument based on biology. These racist explanations are not supported by any data and can be rejected.

Environmental Determinism

environmental determinism
The notion that the nature of the environment directly determines the technological level of a culture.

> Man can apparently live in any region where he can obtain food, but his physical and mental energy and his moral character reach their highest development only in a few strictly limited areas. (Huntington 1924)

Ellsworth Huntington was an early twentieth-century geographer who championed the notion of **environmental determinism**, an approach that

TABLE 13.1 Summary of Hypotheses Explaining the Evolution of Civilization

Hypothesis	Proponent	Type	Summary
Race	Various	Pseudoscience	A racist explanation that assumed that certain racial or ethnic groups were inherently superior and so evolved civilized societies.
Environmental determinism	Ellsworth Huntington	Deterministic	Human groups became more intelligent and progressed further where the environment was more challenging.
Unilinear evolution	Lewis Henry Morgan	Deterministic	Culture, in essence, drives itself forward as specific inventions are made: fire, bow and arrow, pottery, domestication, iron, writing. Without coming upon these successive inventions, cultures became stuck and did not progress.
Marxism	Karl Marx Friedrich Engels	Internal conflict	The trappings of civilization developed after the invention of private property. Some individuals became wealthy and needed to protect their wealth. Social classes and specialization followed.
Hydraulic	Karl Wittfogel	Managerial Integrative	The need to control water for irrigation purposes led to the development of organizations to build and maintain waterworks. To accomplish this, there had to be leaders and followers, and institutions originated for this purpose evolved into the bureaucracy of the state.
Circumscription	Robert Carneiro	External conflict	Societies that had effectively filled up their territory waged war against their neighbors to obtain their land. The losers in such battles became the lower class in an emerging stratified society that led to the civilized state.
Social integration	Jonathan Haas	Synthetic Conflict/ integrative	In different combinations, trade, warfare, and irrigation led to the formation of complex social and political structures. This led to social stratification with those at the top of society given differential access to resources. This, in turn, led to their accumulation of wealth and power and the need to symbolically reinforce the legitimacy of their wealth and power through the construction of monumental works.

actually had first found favor with the ancient Greeks. In attempting to explain cultural differences and the development of civilized life, Hippocrates had suggested that human behavior was the result of the interaction of four bodily "humours," or liquids: yellow bile, black bile, phlegm, and blood. Hippocrates suggested that climate was responsible for the balance of these liquids within the human body. Their relative proportions were in turn responsible for the development of the human intellect, health, and personality traits. Thus, climate was a determinant of cultural development. Even into the nineteenth century, some scholars seriously considered phlegm, bile, and blood as being responsible for culture.

Huntington, however, developed a more complex and reasoned approach to environmental determinism. He felt that climate has a direct impact on human intelligence. In this view, environments that were too easy or too naturally productive hampered cultural development—if people did not need to invent things to survive, if they were not challenged by their environment, they would not be obliged to advance and civilization would not develop. On the other hand, if the climate were too rigorous, people would be too caught up in the necessities of survival to progress beyond mere subsistence. Only those climates lying in between the too generous and the too rigorous would lead to the development of civilized life. Not coincidentally, Western European writers who supported this hypothesis viewed the climate of Europe, particularly Western Europe, as just right for such developments.

Environmental determinism began to fade in importance as a theory because it didn't work. If the European environment was so right for such developments, why did the earliest civilizations evolve elsewhere? Also, the environments in Mesopotamia, Egypt, India, China, lowland Mesoamerica, highland Mesoamerica, and South America were quite different from one another, yet each had early civilizations. Beyond this, even though the climates in these same regions had not changed since the evolution of their civilizations, the cultures had. Clearly environmental determinism is an explanatory dead end, and we can reject it as an explanation for the development of civilization.

Unilinear Evolution

> It is both a natural and proper desire to learn, if possible, how all these ages upon ages of past time have been expended by mankind; how savages, advancing by slow, almost imperceptible steps, attained the higher condition of barbarians; how barbarians, by similar progressive advancement, finally attained to civilization. (Morgan 1877:5)

Another approach to the question of why civilization developed avoided seeking causes in biology or climate or any factor outside culture itself. This approach sought to explain cultural evolution through cultural explanations. The work of Lewis Henry Morgan (1877), a nineteenth-century lawyer and early anthropologist, is of great importance here. Morgan, whom we mentioned briefly in Chapter 2, believed that all cultures developed or evolved through similar phases: "The experience of mankind has run in nearly uniform channels" (1877:15), he wrote. These general phases Morgan labeled savagery, barbarism, and civilization. Savagery and barbarism could each be broken down into early, middle, and upper stages (Figure 13.9).

Morgan's view of the development of civilization as a product of cultural evolution was essentially materialistic: Culture evolved as successive levels of material achievement were attained. His view was also economically based; Morgan considered advances in subsistence technology to be the most significant aspect of cultural evolution driving people toward civilization. Development was contingent on certain specific inventions and followed a natural sequence. As Morgan put it, "The most advanced portions of the human race were halted, so to express it, at certain stages of progress, until some great invention or discovery, such as the domestication of animals or the smelting of iron ore, gave a new and powerful impulse forward" (1877:40).

Culture, in essence, drove itself forward toward civilized life. But notice that Morgan was circular in his argument while begging the question. Civilization, he said, develops because it does. If great inventions such as iron smelting, domestication, and the alphabet were necessary to establish civilization, what caused them? Morgan had no answer to this question. He believed that inventions occurred through ingenuity and spread out from wherever they were invented. Such an approach simply cannot explain why civilization developed where it did and when it did. And these are precisely the questions we are asking.

FIGURE 13.9 The cultural evolutionary model of Lewis Henry Morgan, who believed that all cultures passed through these stages of development, although some became "stuck" in a stage.

Marxism

> Civilization is . . . the stage of development in society at which the division of labor, the exchange between individuals arising from it, and the commodity production which combines them both come to their full growth and revolutionizes the whole of previous society. (Engels 1942:233)

Karl Marx and his benefactor and collaborator Friedrich Engels developed a variation on Morgan's cultural evolutionary scheme. In a scenario laid out by Engels (1942), the domestication of animals led to specialization in animal herding. Animal domestication also allowed humans to produce far more food than was needed for subsistence. Thus, wealth—meat, milk, hides, and wool—became concentrated in the hands of those who possessed animals. There arose a need for regular exchange between the haves and the have-nots, and the excess wealth accumulated by the producers had to be defended from those who might want to take it for themselves.

As groups became larger and as exchange intensified, a class of specialists arose to conduct this new business. These were the first full-time merchants. For the first time, people not involved in subsistence or production were in charge of economic life, and they became rich and powerful at the expense of producers. In the view of Marx and Engels, the key invention of civilization was the formal governmental structure that defines state societies. With a government in place that justifies, legitimizes, and protects the power of the emerging elite, the propertied class could better maintain its wealth and benefits. In this view, struggle between emerging classes results in the development of a formal government as a political structure that on the one hand mediates and dampens such conflict and on the other allows members of the upper class to validate their position over the lower classes and to justify their exploitation of them as peasants, soldiers, workers, and even slaves. A class society with rulers, workers, and slaves results. The trappings of civilization followed, Marx and Engels proposed, as the result of the need to formalize and solidify the unequal structure of society. Thus, civilization developed from a sort of economic determinism.

The Hydraulic Hypothesis

> A large quantity of water can be channeled and kept within bounds only by the use of mass labor; and this mass labor must be coordinated, disciplined, and led. Thus a number of farmers eager to conquer arid lowlands and plains are forced to invoke organizational devices which—on the basis of premachine technology—offer the one chance of success; they must work in cooperation with their fellows and subordinate themselves to a directing authority. (Wittfogel 1957:18)

Karl Wittfogel (1957), a German historian, proposed the hydraulic hypothesis for the development of ancient civilization. He sees civilization as a logical, though not inevitable, consequence of the need to control water. To feed an expanding population, people need to bring more land under cultivation. In some regions, they do so through the construction of waterworks, canals, and aqueducts, which requires people working together and "subordinat[ing] themselves to a directing authority" (Wittfogel 1957:18). To organize and coordinate a large number of people, a centralized government may develop. There need to be canal designers, supervisors, and workers—thus, labor specialization occurs. Mathematics and a recording system may become necessary for planning and designing such projects.

The same social, economic, and political apparatus set in motion by constructing canals, Wittfogel suggests, can be used to build defensive works. Such works become necessary because territory in which so much labor has been expended becomes a tempting target for those who might wish to reap the benefits without investing the labor.

The people directly in charge of designing, constructing, and maintaining these waterworks gain importance to the society, which provides them higher economic and social status. Real power and control, and thus wealth, now rest in their hands because they can deny access to water to those who do not follow their lead or heed their commands. The organization of labor developed to produce canals can also be used to construct temples, great palaces, and impressive tombs for those important people who are in charge. The other trappings of civilization all follow from this concentration of power and serve to reinforce it. Thus, according to Wittfogel, the development of civilization is sparked by a need to increase agricultural production via development and control of water resources.

The Circumscription Hypothesis

> A close examination of history indicates that only a coercive theory can account for the rise of the state. Force, and not enlightened self-interest, is the mechanism by which political evolution has led, step by step, from autonomous villages to the state. (Carneiro 1970:734)

In the scenario of Robert Carneiro (1970), an American anthropologist, civilization developed through coercion in areas where resources, especially agricultural lands, were circumscribed—in other words, limited and bounded. Where land is not limited and bounded, people can migrate into new territories when population grows. Where it is circumscribed, however, they cannot. Mountains, deserts, seas, or other geographic features confine some peoples to a limited area. Within such a bounded area, only a small number of responses are possible if population grows: (1) restrict population growth through sexual abstinence, contraception, abortion, or infanticide; (2) intensify agriculture through irrigation or other means; or (3) seize land through warfare against neighboring groups.

In this final option, the territory of the defeated becomes incorporated into the political unit of the victor. In some cases, the members of the defeated group are also integrated into the victorious group, usually as subordinates. Warfare between increasingly larger groups, Carneiro believes, led to larger and larger political entities with progressively larger territories. In his opinion, most of the world's early civilizations evolved under conditions of geographic circumscription and developed as a reaction to them.

Hearths of Civilization

As we have said, the world's first civilizations evolved where agriculture had evolved. We will now examine the sequences in a number of these cases to assess the usefulness of the above hypotheses for explaining the evolution of civilized life. In each instance, our primary question concerns how small, sedentary, largely self-sufficient Neolithic farming villages were transformed into dense, socially stratified, urban civilizations. We will briefly discuss the prestate societies of Southwest Asia and then move on to the ancient civilizations of Mesopotamia, Egypt, India and Pakistan, China, Mesoamerica, South America, southern Europe, Africa, North America, and Southeast Asia (see Figure 13.1). Each section begins with a brief description of the civilization at its peak and then assesses the origins and development of that culture, beginning with its roots in the Neolithic.

Civilization's Roots: Chiefdoms in Southwest Asia

Jericho   The modern city of Jericho in Israel is the same town as that mentioned in the Old Testament, but the roots of Jericho go back beyond even biblical times. Excavated by archaeologist Kathleen Kenyon in the 1950s (Kenyon 1954), Jericho is now known to have been occupied more than 9,000 ya. At this very early date, Jericho may have been inhabited by more than 3,000 people in an area of about 10 acres. The entire area was encompassed by what may have been the first example of a large-scale construction project anywhere in the world—an enormous wall (Figure 13.10). This wall ranged from more than 3.5 meters (11 feet) to 7 meters (22 feet) in height with ramparts more than 9 meters (30 feet) high. Built entirely of dry-laid stone (mortar was not used), it was 2 meters thick at its base.

Trade was important to Jericho's economy. Raw materials from distant sources—including obsidian from Turkey, turquoise from the Sinai Peninsula, and cowrie shells from the Red Sea—are found at early levels of the site.

The presence of these exotic materials in burials implies the beginning of social stratification here. Most of the graves in the earliest levels at Jericho were situated in one area, and all were pretty much the same. A cluster of burials, however, was different. Clay was molded over the faces of the deceased, with cowrie shells positioned over their eyes. The significance of this practice is unknown but suggests differences in social status. Without much more than this to differentiate social groups, Jericho cannot be labeled a state society. On the other hand, with the beginning of social differentiation and the construction of a monumental wall, we can reasonably suggest that Jericho was a chiefdom-level society.

Çatalhöyük   Çatalhöyük is located in central Turkey, near the town of Çumra (Balter 1998, 2005; Hodder 2005; Mellaart 1965; Todd 1976). The oldest of the twelve occupation levels at the site dates to about 9,000 ya, and the settlement persisted for 1,000 years. The site itself is about three times the size of Jericho, covering approximately 12 hectares (30 acres), and consists of what has been estimated to be a warren of about 1,000 densely compacted, interconnected rooms (Figure 13.11). There were no broad boulevards or even narrow streets or alleyways demarcating the boundaries of separate structures or neighborhoods at Çatalhöyük. In fact, most of the houses in the community had no ground-level entrances.

FIGURE 13.10 The wall at the ancient city of Jericho, dating back 9,000 years, is the oldest known monumental construction. *(© 1990 Fred Mayer/Magnum)*

Çatalhöyük's residents moved around in their community across the rooftops and could access their own dwellings and those of their neighbors through openings in the roof. The site is the largest of its time period, and researchers estimate that as many as 10,000 lived there at its peak of occupation.

FIGURE 13.11 This artist's conception of a portion of Çatalhöyük shows the architectural complexity of this 9,000-year-old site. *(© Times Books 1988. Reproduced with permission)*

We might expect that a large, densely occupied village such as Çatal-höyük could exist only through the establishment of a vigorous agricultural economy, but archaeological evidence indicates that these people were not reliant exclusively on agriculture for their subsistence. Though the people of Çatalhöyük planted and harvested domesticated varieties of wheat and barley, and while they raised, primarily, domesticated sheep and, to a lesser extent, cattle, much of their subsistence was based on foraging for wild crops including grasses, tubers, lentils, hackberries, acorns, and pistachios (Balter 1998).

Though densely populated, Çatalhöyük did not have the characteristics of a city. There is no evidence of public architecture such as municipal buildings, palaces, temples, or governmental buildings. The great size of the settlement implies the existence of a social and political structure capable of maintaining order; however, there is little evidence for the kind of social stratification that characterizes a complex state society. The archaeological record exhibits little evidence of economic or political differentiation among the inhabitants' families. Individual domiciles all seem more or less the same, and none reflect great wealth, prestige, or power invested in any particular family. Neither do burials reflect enormous wealth or power. Families merely buried their dead under the floors of the rooms of their homes; excavators discovered the remains of seventy individuals under the floor of one such room. Though there were no elaborate tombs or rich arrays of grave goods, one group was buried consistently with proportionally more stone- and bone-bead bracelets, anklets, and necklaces; these people were not wealthy men or women but rather babies and infants (Hodder and Cessford 2004).

One of the most interesting elements appears in the otherwise unremarkable rooms in which ordinary activities such as stone and bone toolmaking, food preparation, and consumption were carried out (Hodder and Cessford 2004). The walls of these rooms were decorated with paintings, often of men in leopard-skin pelts hunting animals, usually wild bulls and stags; other images depict leopards and vultures. Further, some of the walls were decorated with sculptures of rams and bulls. Various animal bones, especially those of wild bulls, are found in concentrations at Çatalhöyük, out of proportion to their likely overall contribution to the diet, and perhaps representing ritual feasts (Hodder 2005:40).

Çatalhöyük is located near the Konya Mountains, an important source of obsidian to ancient stone toolmakers. Hodder and his crew have found obsidian castoffs and waste flakes evenly distributed throughout the site in what they interpret as the family compounds (Balter 1998). This suggests that there were stone toolmakers in most families at Çatalhöyük, not just a handful of specialists. Also, the bricks used to build the site were not the result of labor specialization. Wendy Matthews has shown that the mud bricks that make up the primary construction material of the community, as well as the plaster used to coat the bricks, are highly variable (as cited in Balter 1998:1443). In all likelihood, family groups made these materials on their own; there were no specialized brick or plaster makers following standard recipes.

Though not a state, Çatalhöyük clearly was different from other sites of the same age. The size and complexity of its architecture imply a high degree of social and political complexity. On the other hand, as large and integrated as it was, Çatalhöyük appears to have been decentralized as a community. Only further research will help us better understand how Çatalhöyük was organized and why so many people chose to congregate at the foot of the Konya Mountains 9,000 ya.

Mesopotamia

The destruction of archaeological sites and the looting of museums are merely two of the tragedies nestled within the greater tragedy of the current situation in Iraq. At the outset of the war, the U.S. military published and distributed fliers to the Iraqi populace. One, in particular, caught our

FIGURE 13.12 Copies of this broadside were among those dropped from U.S. aircraft flying over Iraq at the inception of the Iraq War. It shows two images of an icon of Mesopotamian history, the great monument known as the ziggurat at Ur. The publication's message to the Iraqi public was that the U.S.-led coalition forces did not intend to damage the ancient landmarks of Iraq. (© *AP/Wide World Photos*)

The Coalition will destroy any viable military targets.

The Coalition does not wish to destroy your landmarks.

attention. It bore two images of an archaeological icon of early civilization, the great **ziggurat** located in Ur, one of the world's first truly urban communities (Figure 13.12). On the left side of the flier two U.S. fighter jets are seen streaking over the ziggurat, firing missiles at two fleeing Iraqi vehicles. Above this image is the caption: "The Coalition will destroy any viable military targets." The right side of the flier shows a much more tranquil scene; the image of the ziggurat is identical to that on the left, but there are no jets and no military vehicles. Here the caption reads: "The Coalition does not wish to destroy your landmarks." The ultimate impact of the war on archaeological sites and on the historical treasures housed in Iraqi museums is yet to be tallied (Lawler 2003), but it is surely ironic that a region home to one of the greatest and earliest civilizations of the ancient world has suffered first through the reign of a brutal dictator and now through a period of chaos and death following his removal by U.S.-led forces.

The city of Ur was located in the region called Mesopotamia (literally, "the land between the two rivers"—the Tigris and the Euphrates). Made more than 4,000 ya, the ziggurat at Ur is a massive structure of mud brick with an exterior surface of fired brick (Figure 13.13). It stood 22 meters (72 feet) high and measured over 60 meters (200 feet) long by nearly 46 meters (150 feet) wide at its base. Steps led up to each successive platform; at the top was a small temple or shrine where priests conducted worship services (Lloyd 1978).

The cemetery at Ur contains more than 2,000 graves, 16 of which were the interments of members of the elite class. These royal tombs were as much as 9 meters (30 feet) deep and 9 meters across. The burials were placed in stone chambers with vaulted roofs—one even possessed a dome. One of the tombs, that of a queen called Pu-abi (her name appears in writing), is typical of the royal internments at Ur. In death, Pu-abi wore a headdress of gold and semiprecious stones. Around her were gold and silver

ziggurat An enormous mud-brick structure built in the form of a rectangular platform with stairs leading to the top. A monumental structure of the early Mesopotamians.

FIGURE 13.13 The ziggurat at Ur, built in stages over a lengthy period, is more than 4,000 years old. It stands 22 meters high, with a temple originally on the top platform. (© George Gerster/ Photo Researchers, Inc.)

FIGURE 13.14 This beautiful gold cup was just one of the many impressive artifacts found in the tomb of the Mesopotamian queen Pu-abi. The concentration of such wealth in the hands of an elite class of people is diagnostic of the stratified societies of even the world's oldest civilizations. (© Boltin Picture Library/Bridgeman Art Library)

containers, an intricately designed harp, a gaming table, and another 250 or so objects (Figure 13.14). Pu-abi did not have to pass on to the afterlife alone. As with the other royalty at Ur, she was accompanied by humans and animals sacrificed as part of the royal burial ceremony. In her burial chamber were two female attendants. Just outside were ten more women

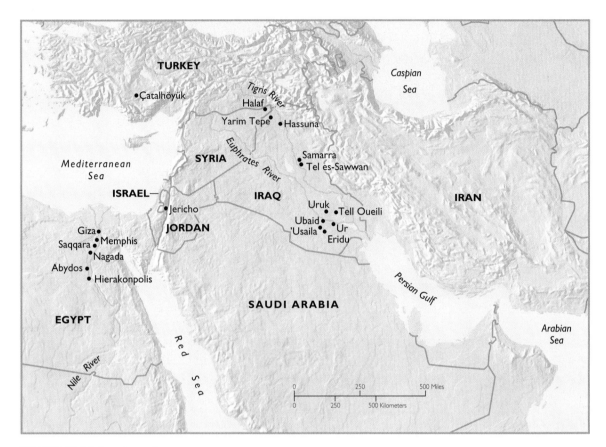

FIGURE 13.15 Locations of Southwest Asian and Egyptian sites related to the development of civilization and mentioned in the text. Modern national boundaries are shown for reference.

(one with a harp to provide musical accompaniment for the journey), five soldiers, and two oxen. Beneath Queen Pu-abi's chamber was a man's tomb—possibly her husband's. He was accompanied by six soldiers, nineteen females wearing gold headpieces, six oxen, two chariots, a lyre, a gaming table, and an exquisite silver model of a boat.

Such were the death settings of Ur nobility. Their lives were lived in even greater splendor. But how did the Neolithic farming villages described in Chapter 12 give rise to the grandeur of Ur? How did the surplus and social stratification develop that made such monuments as the ziggurat and royal tombs of Ur possible? To answer these questions, we must look back into the Neolithic of Southwest Asia.

Mesopotamian Roots   From 8000 to 6500 B.P., we see the beginning of population movement away from the foothills of the Zagros Mountains, mentioned in our discussion of the Neolithic, onto the floodplain between the two rivers (Figure 13.15). The sites of Hassuna, Samarra, and Halaf, each exhibiting distinctive pottery and architecture, have provided names to three distinctive Mesopotamian cultures with substantial temporal overlap: **Hassunan, Samarran,** and **Halafian.**

Dating from 8000 to 7200 B.P., Hassunan sites are small, typically about 100 to 200 meters (about 330 to 660 feet) in diameter, with populations estimated only in the hundreds (Lamberg-Karlovsky and Sabloff 1995:96). Despite low populations, some Hassunan sites, such as Hassuna and Yarim Tepe, do provide evidence for large-scale construction. For example, the latter has multiroomed houses with interior and exterior courtyards.

Samarran sites also show evidence of increasing architectural complexity and size, as well as increasing evidence of social differentiation. For example, the village of Tell es-Sawwan was surrounded by a monumental wall and a ditch. Samarra itself has a large fortification wall with buttresses. While most burials at Tell es-Sawwan are rather plain, others are filled with alabaster, turquoise, copper, greenstone, obsidian, carnelian (a lustrous, reddish-brown stone), and shell-bead necklaces and bracelets, implying an increasing gulf among members of the society (Lamberg-Karlovsky and Sabloff 1995). Turquoise, obsidian, and carnelian are not locally available and must have been obtained through trade.

After about 7400 B.P., a new architectural feature is seen at Samarran sites: T-shaped buildings used to house the community's grain. This communal storage suggests a pooling of labor in both farming and in the construction of the storage building.

Halaf, on the Syrian-Turkish border, shows what appear to be the earliest shrines in Mesopotamia. These circular, beehive-shaped rooms range from 5 to 10 meters (15 to 30 feet) in diameter at their base. The round buildings at some sites also contain human burials accompanied by ceremonial objects, leading some to suggest that they served as the burial places for important people.

As archaeologists C. C. Lamberg-Karlovsky and Jeremy Sabloff (1995) suggest, after 8,000 ya, economic, social, and political structures that would set the stage for later developments were beginning to form at Hassunan, Samarran, and Halafian sites.

Ubaid It is not until after about 6300 B.P., in the broad floodplain to the south, that a great leap forward was taken by the early Mesopotamians. The culture of southern Mesopotamia during this period, called Ubaid, is reflected in Tell al-'Ubaid, Tell Oueili, Eridu, 'Usaila, and Ur. These sites are larger and show evidence of specialization in pottery and metallurgy. The population at Eridu, for example, is estimated to have exceeded 5,000 (Lamberg-Karlovsky and Sabloff 1995:108) even at this early stage. The Ubaid sites show development of large temple structures that may indicate that these villages functioned as ceremonial centers as they were evolving into urban centers (Figure 13.16; Wheatly 1971). Temples probably served as granaries, administrative centers, and redistribution points for food.

Hassunan Neolithic culture in Mesopotamia dated from 8000 to 7200 B.P.; characterized by small farming villages and some reliance on hunting.

Samarran Neolithic culture of southern Mesopotamia; sites are located on the floodplain of the Tigris and Euphrates Rivers and date to after 7,500 years ago.

Halafian Neolithic culture in Mesopotamia dating from 7500 to 6700 B.P. Halafian sites generally are small farming villages.

FIGURE 13.16 An artist's impression of the temple at the early Mesopotamian city of Eridu, dated to around 5000 B.P. *(From* Art of the Ancient Near East *by Seaton Lloyd, copyright © 1961, Thames and Hudson, page 259, Praeger Publishers, an imprint of Greenwood Publishing Group, Inc., Westport, CT. Reprinted with permission)*

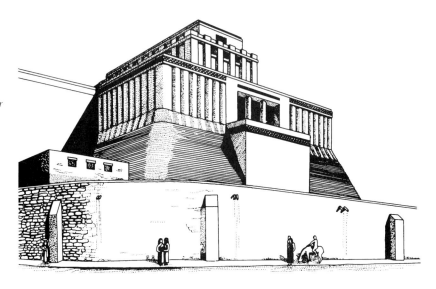

The First Cities   By about 6000 B.P., Ubaid sites had spread throughout Mesopotamia. And, finally, by 5800 B.P. or so, one of these villages, Uruk, had grown to such a size and density that it can confidently be proclaimed as the world's first true city. Unlike Çatalhöyük, described earlier, the construction of Uruk seems to have been more centralized, with construction elements more standardized. In other words, there appears to have been a controlling authority determining the community's growth and development. The existence of such an authority is characteristic of state societies.

Uruk was not isolated; it appears to have been interconnected in a settlement hierarchy that included, in descending size, smaller towns, villages, and hamlets (Crawford 1991). This pattern—large urban centers surrounded by three orders or levels of smaller settlements that owed their political, social, and economic allegiance to the city—was to be the rule for Mesopotamian **city-states.**

What Led to the Development of Civilization in Mesopotamia?   The push toward urbanization in Mesopotamia was probably encouraged by several factors. First came the need to intensify agriculture through the construction of irrigation networks as a result of population increase. By 5800 B.P., there were 17 villages, 3 large towns, and 1 city in Mesopotamia; by 4900 B.P., there were 124 villages, 20 towns, and 20 cities (Adams and Nissen 1972:18). To expand agricultural production, irrigation was necessary, and canals up to 40 kilometers (almost 25 miles) long were eventually built (Lamberg-Karlovsky and Sabloff 1995). The requirement of organizing labor to build these canals would have fostered social differen-

city-state A large politically complex society with villages surrounding a dense central population.

tiation, and differential access to irrigation water would have further segmented and stratified the society. Note how well this fits Wittfogel's hydraulic hypothesis discussed earlier.

As archaeologist Harriet Crawford (1991) suggests, the need to trade was another important impetus to urbanization. Southern Mesopotamia lacked most resources beyond fertile soil and water. Ores for the production of metals, wood for building and fuel, and stone for building had to be traded for, and such trade had to be organized. The need to organize people to engage in trading networks may have contributed toward differentiating classes as well. Unequal access to trade goods would have served to further distinguish groups of people.

Another likely factor was the presence of nonagricultural, nomadic animal herders on the peripheries of Mesopotamia. From later documentary accounts, we know that settled villagers in Mesopotamia had hostile relations with neighboring nomads. As Lamberg-Karlovsky and Sabloff (1995) point out, however, such nomads probably provided urban dwellers with livestock and, as a result of their greater mobility, may also have assisted in trade and communication. As wealth became concentrated in such dense settlements, however—effectively making it easier to steal—the need grew for protection from these nomads and from competing city-states. This may have led to the development of monumental works—not pyramids or tombs, but enormous defensive walls. Such projects require a social system unlike that of an egalitarian society.

The Role of the Temple   Early Neolithic cultures in Mesopotamia were either egalitarian, or **rank societies.** They likely had no existing social structure—no government or army—to fill the leadership roles demanded by large-scale construction or trade. There was, however, one institution where extraordinary powers resided even before social complexity increased: the temple. We have seen that shrines or temples date back to the time before the Ubaid period. Early prototypes for Mesopotamian temples are seen in Samarran sites, and the Halafian round storage buildings may have been a functional prototype. These early temples were not only places of religious worship, they also served as communal granaries.

In the view of archaeologists C. C. Lamberg-Karlovsky and Jeremy Sabloff (1995), when population grew and moved out onto the floodplain, irrigation works became a necessity. Such works required a social and political institution that could organize the labor necessary to build and maintain them. In their view, an already powerful religious elite also became the dominant political and social force in Mesopotamian society. In other words, priests first became chiefs and later kings. Control of the irrigation networks led to power, and with power came the ability to control the enormous food surplus that the evolving system produced. Together, these forces helped transform the village farming culture of Mesopotamia into what is recognized as the world's first civilization.

rank society A nonegalitarian society with a few sociopolitical levels filled by a relatively small number of people.

FIGURE 13.17 The three great pyramids at Giza. Enormous monuments such as these testify to the power wielded by the rulers of the early Egyptian state. *(M. H. Feder)*

Egypt

The name Egypt alone is enough to conjure up potent images. Great pyramids, the Sphinx, the boy-king Tutankhamun, and all-powerful pharaohs are elements of Egyptian civilization that have fascinated people for centuries.

Just consider some of the remarkable accomplishments of the culture of ancient Egypt. For example, at Giza, north of the ancient capital city of Memphis and near modern Cairo, three pyramids rise out of the desert (Figure 13.17). Each one was constructed as memorial for a different pharaoh; each is a spectacular achievement unto itself. Together they are one of the true wonders of the ancient world. The two smaller pyramids were actually built for the pharaoh Khafre and his son, Menkaure, who was pharaoh after him. It was the first and largest, however, built for the pharaoh Khufu (Khafre's father, often called by his Greek name, Cheops), that represents one of the largest and most impressive structures ever built by human beings—before or since. The Great Pyramid at Giza measures over 230 meters (750 feet) on each of the four sides of its base. Rising like an artificial mountain more than 145 meters (almost 500 feet) in height, it was constructed from nearly 2.5 million quarried stone blocks averaging 2,270 kilograms (5,000 pounds) each. Some of the larger blocks weigh more than 13,000 kilograms (30,000 pounds).

The pyramid itself was built at a level of accuracy rarely achieved even in modern construction. The smooth blocks making up the surface of the pyramid have joints a mere 0.5 millimeter ($\frac{1}{50}$ inch) in width. The pyramid is aligned to the cardinal compass directions; that this was intentional is clear from the writings of the ancient Egyptians. That alignment is almost perfect; the degree of error on the north-south sides of the pyramid is 0.09 percent, on the east-west sides 0.03 percent.

But the pyramid of Khufu is not just an enormous, accurately laid pile of limestone and granite blocks. Within the pyramid is a maze of passageways, several connected chambers, arched vaults and narrow, enigmatic shafts leading from those vaults out to the surface of the pyramid. It is, indeed, a spectacular achievement. Though the largest, the Great Pyramid is but one of almost 100 large pyramids built by the ancient Egyptians (Lehner 1997). And pyramids were just one aspect of Egyptian culture.

We are all awed by these spectacular achievements of ancient Egyptian civilization. But we want to go beyond fascination to understanding. How was the magnificence that was ancient Egypt achieved? Where did this civilization come from? How did it develop? To answer these questions, we need to go back to a time before pharaohs and pyramids. We need to examine the Egyptian Neolithic.

The Evolution of Egyptian Civilization   The Greek historian Herodotus called Egypt the "gift of the Nile." The Nile River is a narrow ribbon of life winding through a dry, lifeless desert (Figure 13.18). In Egypt a great civilization could have developed only along the banks of the Nile, so our attention must focus there.

Some Egyptologists believe that as a result of increasing competition for agricultural land, some towns became what geographers call **central places**—places viewed by the local populace as locations of great spiritual and social power. These central places were also important as a result of their strategic locations, providing them with easy access to trade routes across the desert, as well as to mineral resources found only in desert areas. After 5,500 ya, the three most important of these communities were Abydos, Hierakonpolis, and Nagada. Each dominated its own territory along the Nile in Upper Egypt, and each competed against the other for land, resources, and power. Each vied for control of all of the people in their competitors' communities, as well as for control over everyone else living up and down the Nile (Wilkinson 2003). Abydos, Nagada, and Hierakonpolis were, effectively, small city-states, similar to those in Mesopotamia, and their leaders aspired to be not just the ruler of their own community but the king of a unified Egypt with all of the additional power and wealth that would accrue to anyone in that position.

The leaders of these city-states became rich and powerful; this is clearly seen in their treatment at death. For example, the king's tomb called U-j, built at Abydos about 5,200 ya, had eight chambers, providing the deceased with a small-scale model of the royal palace in which he had lived (Wilkinson 2003). Beyond this, the king's tomb contained finely

central place The geographic focus of a political entity.

FIGURE 13.18 This photograph of the Nile, taken by astronauts aboard the Space Shuttle, shows how the river literally demarcates the boundaries of life for the inhabitants of Egypt. *(Courtesy NASA)*

made objects crafted from raw materials that would have been expensive to obtain because their sources lay far to the north in the Nile Delta. The name of the leader interred in Tomb U-j is not known, but some of the pots that were placed in his tomb bear the inscription of a scorpion. Some have, as a result, called him "King Scorpion."

Hierakonpolis   A series of excavations led by American archaeologist Michael Hoffman (1979, 1983) in the 1970s and 1980s at one of these city-states, Hierakonpolis, provides us with a glimpse into how each city-state of ancient Egypt developed. Located on a bay adjacent to the Nile, Hierakonpolis comprised about 100 inhabited acres some 5,800 ya. Habitation areas consisting of houses made of mud brick as well as wattle and daub (intertwined sticks covered with mud or clay) were surrounded by farmland, and at least 2,500 and perhaps as many as 10,000 people lived there. The town seems to have prospered during the Neolithic on the basis of a booming pottery industry. Enormous kilns and millions of fragments of broken pots have been found here, and pottery manufactured at Hiera-konpolis was probably traded to other towns along the Nile for inclusion in their fancy burials.

At Hierakonpolis during this period, the first evidence of impressive tombs appears. Although by no means comparable to the pyramids, these tombs may be the first step toward their development. The tombs were sometimes lined with mud brick; some were cut into bedrock. In a prac-tice that was to characterize later Egyptian civilization, they were filled with items to accompany the dead: finely made pottery, baskets, leather-work, woodwork, and flintwork. The tombs were covered by structures—not yet pyramids, but earth mounds and wood-and-reed buildings.

The largest and most sumptuous of the burials at Hierakonpolis and other sites dating to this period along the Nile were limited to a developing elite class. With increased population density along the Nile came the need to coordinate activity, to enforce rules and law. Although rule by simple au-thority—where there is consensus, not coercion—was possible in earlier, smaller towns, in a settlement of several thousand, rule through power was probably emerging. At Hierakonpolis, a group of leaders may have evolved simply to maintain order. This elite was in charge of producing the pottery and probably controlling trade, and excess wealth began to be concentrated in their hands. With wealth came even more power. The production of fancy pottery and the interment of people in impressive tombs may have served as symbols reinforcing the legitimacy of that leadership.

Social and political change began to accelerate by 5,500 ya in what is known as the Gerzean period. The local climate seems to have become drier, possibly because of deforestation that resulted from collecting fire-wood to feed the pottery kilns. This challenge was met at Hierakonpolis and probably elsewhere by the construction of irrigation canals, which al-lowed for intensification of agriculture even while the local climate was becoming less agreeable for it. As archaeologist Hoffman (1979, 1983) has pointed out, the power that was already concentrated in the hands of the pottery barons probably allowed them to control the construction of irri-gation canals. Once the local farmers began to rely on the canals for food production, the former pottery barons became even more powerful—they now controlled the water necessary for farming.

For a few hundred years, such developments continued at Hierakonpo-lis and elsewhere. By 5,200 ya, however, local development and expansion began to impinge on neighboring groups. Warfare among neighbors seems to have been the result. Elites in different towns began to compete among themselves for territory and for the loyalties of the people in these areas.

The Unification of Egypt   Remember that the images of scorpions were found on pots buried in the U-j tomb at Abydos. A scorpion associated with an important ruler has also been found at Hierakonpolis. There, on a

FIGURE 13.19 Found at the predynastic city-state of Hierakonpolis, the Narmer Macehead shows an oversized king carrying out what appears to be an irrigation rite. Directly in front of the king's face is a scorpion. This has been interpreted as representing the name of the king—King Scorpion— who ruled Hierakonpolis. *(© Werner Forman/Art Resource, NY)*

ceremonial macehead, the leader is shown opening an irrigation canal, and in front of the great ruler's face is the clear image of a scorpion (Figure 13.19). Some suggest that this depiction indicates that the Abydos leader buried in Tomb U-j was also considered by the people of Hierakonpolis to be their leader as well. This may be the earliest evidence of a ruler recognized not by just one community or city-state but by many. In this interpretation, King Scorpion may represent a very early attempt to unify at least some of the city-states under a single, powerful ruler.

It was not until about 5100 B.P. that a ruler of Hierakonpolis, Narmer (also known as Menes), was able to unite all villages up and down the Nile. Narmer was, indeed, the first ruler of Egypt, if not the first actual pharaoh. On a carved piece of stone found by archaeologists in Hierakonpolis in 1898, Narmer is depicted as uniting the northern and southern halves of Egypt, becoming the ruler of all who dwelled along the Nile (Figure 13.20).

With the growth of villages and then cities along the Nile, the emergence of a powerful elite class, the production of sufficient food surplus to feed this class, and the emergence of specialists such as pottery makers, we have all the prerequisites for the evolution of civilization. By 4,700 ya,

FIGURE 13.20 Dating to 5100 B.P., the Narmer Palette was found in the Egyptian site of Hierakonpolis. The ruler Narmer is shown on the left, brandishing a weapon over a defeated enemy. On the right, Narmer (the tallest character on the left in the top panel) is shown wearing the combined crowns of Upper and Lower Egypt. As the ruler of a unified Egypt, Narmer is generally thought to be the first pharaoh. *(Left: © Werner Forman/ Art Resource, NY; right: © Giraudon/ Art Resource, NY)*

a successor to Narmer, King Djoser, exploited the power that had been concentrated in his hands and caused the construction of the first Egyptian pyramid at a place called Saqqara (Figure 13.21). As kings became pharaohs and as pharaohs became all-powerful, pyramids became larger, construction projects became more ambitious, and the army increased in size. Egyptian civilization flourished.

The Indus Valley

That a spectacular early civilization developed in ancient India and Pakistan comes as a surprise to most Americans. Yet a magnificent civilization with two of the ancient world's largest early cities did indeed develop and flourish on the Indian subcontinent some 4,500 ya (Allchin and Allchin 1982; Fairservis 1975).

Mohenjo-daro was one of those cities. During its peak period—from approximately 4,500 to 4,000 ya—the religious and political life of the

FIGURE 13.21 The stepped pyramid of King Djoser at Saqqara represented an important point in the evolution of the pyramid memorial that was to characterize the tombs of later Egyptian pharaohs. *(M. H. Feder)*

city's nearly 40,000 inhabitants was centered in its citadel. There, on an enormous mud-brick mound some 450 meters (almost 1,500 feet) long, 90 meters (almost 300 feet) wide, and 12 meters (40 feet) high, were built a temple, a granary, and a bathhouse (Figure 13.22). Within the great bathhouse was a bathing pool nearly 12 meters (40 feet) long, 6 meters (20 feet) wide, and 2.5 meters (8 feet) deep. The entire citadel was surrounded by a brick wall reaching 13 meters (over 40 feet) in height in some sections and marked by square towers and bastions.

To the east of the citadel lay the lower city. Here, spread across 100 hectares (247 acres), lived the vast majority of the residents of Mohenjo-daro. Their streets were laid out according to a master plan that must have been engineered from the inception of construction (Kenoyer 1998). Major roads were aligned precisely along the cardinal directions. Wide boulevards paralleled each other in a north-south orientation. Smaller, secondary streets ran parallel to the boulevards. Still other streets were neatly perpendicular (Figure 13.23).

Other Indus civilization cities—including Mohenjo-daro's virtual twin, Harappa—followed a nearly identical plan, with streets laid out in a grid, imposing citadels constructed on artificial mounds on their western margins, large public buildings including bathhouses and granaries surrounding their citadels, and monumental walls enclosing these sacred precincts. Hundreds of small farming villages were aligned with each of these two cities, which together controlled more than 300,000 square miles of territory (Possehl 1980:2).

Mohenjo-daro and Harappa were spectacular achievements of this little-known civilization. But where did this Indus Valley culture come from? How did it develop?

FIGURE 13.22 The citadel of Mohenjo-daro, one of the Indus civilization's two great cities, which held a temple, a granary, and a bathhouse. The city had a brick-covered sewer trench with connections to separate apartments, a testament to city planning some 4,500 ya. (© *Dilip Mehta/Woodfin Camp and Associates, Inc.*)

The Evolution of the Indus Valley Civilization We can trace the roots of this civilization back to a series of Neolithic sites in an area of western Pakistan called Baluchistan (Figure 13.24). Mehrgarh is located at the foothills of the Baluchistan Mountains. Dated to 7100 B.P., this site is an extensive settlement of mud-brick structures, including a number of

FIGURE 13.23 This map of a section of the planned city Mohenjo-daro shows its major avenues, parallel and perpendicular streets, and regularly sized buildings and rooms. *(From M. Wheeler. 1968.* The Indus Civilization. *New York: Cambridge University Press. Reprinted with permission of the publisher)*

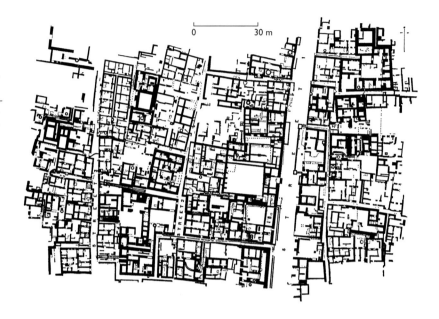

domestic units—probably the homes of individual families—containing six and sometimes nine rooms. Some separate structures appear to have been public granaries. Subsistence was provided by domesticated wheat, barley, and dates, along with cattle and water buffalo. The inhabitants of Mehrgarh also participated in a wide-ranging trade network. Conch shell from some 500 kilometers (about 310 miles) away as well as lapis lazuli and turquoise from similar distances were found at the site.

Another typical site, Kili Ghul Mohammed, was a small agricultural settlement also located in the foothills of the Baluchistan Mountains. Dated to 6000 B.P., it has evidence of domesticated wheat, goats, sheep, and cattle.

Mehrgarh and Kili Ghul Mohammed grew larger over time, indicating a general population increase. By 5,000 ya, settlement was spreading out of the foothills southward along the streams that drained the mountaintops and fed the large Indus River to the southeast.

Where previous Neolithic sites in Baluchistan each exhibited its own artifact styles in pottery and items of adornment, a certain degree of uniformity appears as people began moving out onto the floodplain of the Indus, implying greater cultural—and perhaps political—unification (Allchin and Allchin 1982). For example, a common image of a horned buffalo head appears on pottery throughout the area at many sites. Terracotta statues of women showing a standardized style also appear at many sites from this period (Figure 13.25); some have dubbed these "mother goddesses," implying a degree of religious unification as well (Allchin and Allchin 1982:163).

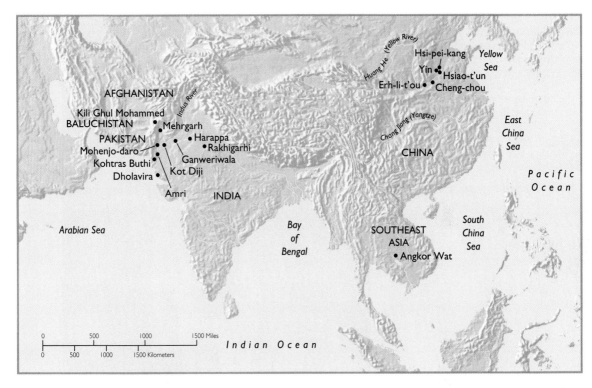

FIGURE 13.24 Locations of South Asian and East Asian sites related to the development of civilization and mentioned in the text. Modern place names are included for reference.

Sites dating to after 5000 B.P. are included in what is called the Nal culture. Kohtras Buthi is a fairly typical Nal site. Much larger than Kili Ghul Mohammed, it covers some 15 acres. Significantly, at this site we see some of the earliest evidence in the area for water-control construction. The inhabitants built a wall surrounding one end of the village, apparently to protect themselves from the intense flooding that characterizes this area in the spring. At other Nal culture sites, we see dams built across small streams for the accumulation of alluvial soils behind the dams and other dams built to impound water for irrigating fields that lie away from the rivers.

Settlement along the Indus   Apparently, population kept growing and flood-control technology kept improving. By 4500 B.P., settlement expanded onto the floodplain of the Indus River itself. The Indus is a large, unpredictable river given to violent flooding. It is unlikely that an agricultural people could have survived on its banks without sophisticated flood-control construction. Two sites that typify this period are Kot Diji and Amri. The latter contains a large number of connected mud-brick structures, and there is evidence of canal building.

FIGURE 13.25 This sculpture shows a standardized image of a mother goddess, an important deity in the Indus Valley civilization. A common, shared religion and religious iconography reflected in a shared artistic style often underly state societies, serving to unite the people within the single political entity of the state. (© *Angelo Hornak/ Corbis*)

It is at Kot Diji, however, that we see the earliest evidence for large-scale flood-control construction (Figure 13.26). This site is surrounded by a wall measuring up to 8 meters (26 feet) high and 1.5 meters (about 5 feet) thick. The base of the wall is constructed of cut limestone, and the top is made of mud brick. Such construction implies a coordinated effort by the population and may indicate the beginning of social differentiation.

Florescence of the Indus Valley Civilization   By about 4500 B.P., five large urban communities (including Mohenjo-daro and Harrappa), all

FIGURE 13.26 The excavation at Kot Diji exposed a large village site that predated Mohenjo-daro and Harappa. *(Department of Archaeology and Museums, Karachi)*

built on a similar plan, dominated social, political, and economic life in the Indus Valley. The towns of Ganweriwala and Rakhigarhi each grew to cover more than 80 hectares (about 200 acres). Another Indus community Dholavira, grew larger still, reaching an area of 100 hectares (247 acres). At its peak, Harappa spread out over more than 150 hectares (about 370 acres). The largest, Mohenjo-daro, grew to truly stupendous size, at its peak covering more than 250 hectares (617 acres; all size data were taken from Kenoyer 1998:49).

As impressive as these figures are for the areal extent of each of the Indus Valley cities 4,500 ya, they are, in fact, deceptive. The quoted sizes reflect only the extent of their urban cores, the areas across which there is archaeological evidence in the form of house remains, temple ruins, streets, industrial zones, etc. Each of the cities listed, however, also controlled expansive hinterlands, inhabited by the farmers whose produce supported the cities. In fact, an estimated 1,500 farming communities were located throughout the Indus Valley in this period, and most were intimately tied into life in one of the five cities (Kenoyer 2005:27). Most of these agricultural villages covered areas of between 1 and 10 hectares (between 2.5 and 25 acres). There also were a few larger villages between 10 and 50 hectares (between 25 and 124 acres) in expanse. Kenoyer (1998:50) calculated that each of the five Indus urban centers separately controlled a hinterland of at least 100,000 square kilometers (38,000 square miles, or a little smaller than the state of Kentucky); the largest, Mohenjo-daro, likely controlled an area of as much as 170,000 square kilometers (66,000 square miles, or about the size of Washington State).

Individual dwellings in each of the Indus cities reflected the wide range in economic, social, and political status of the inhabitants. Almost all houses had private bathrooms connected by chutes to a citywide network of drains—probably the world's first engineered sewer system. There were single-room apartments, houses with many rooms and courtyards, and great houses with dozens of rooms and private wells. Based on the kinds of tools found in different sections of these Indus cities, it is clear that certain neighborhoods were dedicated to the production of particular crafts. There were districts of metalworkers, cloth makers, potters, bakers, stoneworkers, and bead makers; the tools of these various trades have been found exclusively in their respective neighborhoods (Kenoyer 1998). It is likely that even brick making was a specialist's craft. The mud bricks used to construct most of the Indus city buildings are so uniform, they must have been made according to a standardized form, much in the same way modern brick makers adhere to established size and form standards (Kenoyer 1998). Specialization and standardization are diagnostic of ancient civilizations.

The Indus Valley civilization possessed a system of recordkeeping that still awaits a thorough translation. About 4,000 Indus inscriptions have been unearthed, dating to as much as 5,200 ya, but the script was not in widespread use until 800 years later, about 4,400 ya. Anywhere from 400 to 450 different symbols appear to have been used in the script. These consist of, for the most part, animal pictographs and abstract patterns (Figure 13.27). Kenoyer (2005:30) feels that the co-occurrence of certain symbols suggests that, in a fashion similar to that seen in the earliest Mesopotamian cuneiform and the first of the Egyptian glyphic writing, the purpose of the Indus script was for keeping track of material, including lands and goods; in other words, the script was used for economic accounting.

China

In northern Honan province of China, on the banks of the Huan River, near the modern city of An-yang, rests the ruins of the ancient city of Yin. Here, in what was the culmination of East Asia's earliest civilization, the Shang, a succession of twelve kings ruled for 273 years beginning about 3,700 ya (Chang, 1986; Gernet 1987).

In and around An-yang is a series of settlements articulated into what was the center of Shang culture. At Hsiao-t'un were the royal palaces—large structures with stamped-earth foundations, large stone support pillars, and platform altars. Around the palaces were smaller structures used to manufacture pottery, stone tools, and bone carvings and to cast bronze works of art (Figure 13.28).

Near Hsi-pei-kang was an extensive cemetery complex containing more than 1,200 burials. Eleven large tombs were found, possibly the

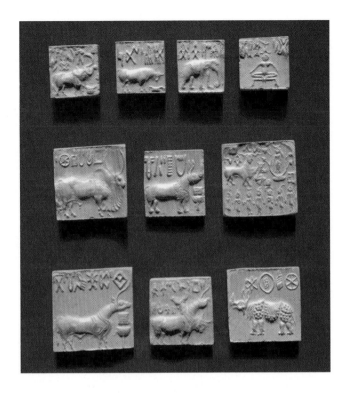

FIGURE 13.27 These inscribed ceramic tiles were found in excavations at the Indus Valley city of Mohenjo-daro and appear to reflect an early, locally developed form of writing. Though not yet deciphered, the writing appears to represent an accounting of lands, goods, and other materials. *(Charles and Josette Lenars/ Corbis)*

FIGURE 13.28 Bronze metallurgy was raised to the status of a fine art in the Shang civilization, the earliest complex state society known in China. Here, a bronze vessel called a *gui* exhibits the detailed reliefs that characterize the work of the specialist class of metallurgists in Shang society. *(© Burstein Collection/Corbis)*

FIGURE 13.29 The great rulers of the Shang civilization, China's first complex state society, were buried in splendor and accompanied on their journey to the afterlife by people sacrificed by beheading, as shown here. *(Courtesy of the Institute of History and Philology, Academia Sinica, Taiwan)*

interments of all but the last of the historically recorded Shang rulers at Yin (the twelfth supposedly died and was consumed in a fire during the destruction of the city). These royal tombs were enormous construction projects with large grave pits up to 40 meters (130 feet) long and 30 meters (nearly 100 feet) wide. Ramps as long as 50 meters (more than 160 feet) led down into the burial pits, where the kings were interred in log-lined tombs accompanied by elaborate objects manufactured of bronze, jade, antler, stone, bone, and shell. Hundreds of people were apparently sacrificed to accompany these kings into their afterlife; their decapitated remains surround the royal tombs (Figure 13.29).

The Evolution of Chinese Civilization   Although once presumed to result from outside developments, the Shang civilization is now recognized as having evolved from the Neolithic Lung-shan culture of China (see Chapter 12). The subsistence base of Shang civilization was essentially the same as that of local Neolithic cultures. Domesticated rice, millet, and wheat were the primary agricultural products. Pigs, sheep, cattle, and chickens were raised and eaten. Well into Shang times, this agricultural base was supplemented by hunting deer and bear and fishing.

Early manifestations of Shang civilization have been identified at the Erh-li-t'ou site on the Lo River in Honan province. Dated to around 3,800 ya, the site is larger than anything seen previously in East Asia, covering an area of 2.5 kilometers (1.6 miles) by 1.5 kilometers (a little less than 1 mile). Bronze and jade artifacts are common. Some of the bronzes were tools including knives, chisels, axes, adzes, arrowheads, and other weapons. Many of the bronze artifacts at the site were ceremonial or ornamental, including disks, fancy drinking vessels, and musical instruments.

Evidence of social stratification is shown in differential burial patterns. Some human remains were rather casually interred in storage or refuse pits with no accompanying grave goods. Other burials were much more elaborate, with the deceased buried in lacquered coffins. Grave goods include jade carvings, turquoise and shell jewelry, finely made ceramics, and bronzes. Finally, the presence of some headless human burials bears witness to human sacrifice.

A unique feature at Erh-li-t'ou are the remains of two palaces, far larger than any of the residences located at the site. One palace was about 100 meters (325 feet) on a side; the second was somewhat smaller. The walls of both consisted of thick berms of stamped earth.

A later site was excavated near the modern city of Cheng-chou. These remains are clearly urban in character, with residential areas, industrial zones, elite areas, and a cemetery. Surrounding the central part of the site—where large, upper-class houses and elite burials were found—was a monumental wall more than 7,000 meters (more than 22,000 feet) in circumference. It encompassed an area of more than 3 square kilometers (almost 2 square miles), stood close to 10 meters (32 feet) high, and was more than 35 meters (almost 115 feet) wide at its base. Archaeologist K.C. Chang quotes estimates that 10,000 workers must have toiled for almost two decades to construct the wall alone (1968:205). Outside the wall were residential and industrial sectors of the city, with bronze foundries, pottery factories, and bone workshops.

Although monumental works in the form of pyramids or ziggurats do not appear at Shang sites, Shang is certainly an early civilization. Large populations were concentrated in urban centers. Differential burials and variations in house size and construction clearly show social stratification. There was specialization in various crafts, including bronze metallurgy, ceramics, bone carving, and stone sculpture. Finally, there was writing. More than 100,000 inscribed bones and tortoise shells have been recovered, mostly at Yin. The writing included some 5,000 different characters, of which about 1,500 have been interpreted (Gernet 1987:47). Translations indicate that most of the writing involved divination and predictions concerning social, political, military, and economic affairs.

Mesoamerica

The ancient Mexican city of Teotihuacán stands as mute testimony to the wondrous achievements of the prehistoric civilizations of Mesoamerica. From 1,700 to 1,300 ya, Teotihuacán was the most powerful political entity in the Western Hemisphere (Adams, 1991; Lamberg-Karlovsky and Sabloff 1995; Millon et al. 1973; Sabloff 1989; Sanders and Price 1968; Weaver 1972). At its peak, Teotihuacán was a teeming city covering 23 square kilometers (9 square miles). Its population is estimated to have reached a maximum of 200,000 people. In other words, even 1,500 ya, Teotihuacán had a population that places it securely in the 100 largest modern American urban centers. As many as 1 million people may have been part of what might be considered the nation of which Teotihuacán was the capital.

The center of the city was dominated by two large pyramids connected by a broad boulevard today called the Avenue of the Dead. The smaller Pyramid of the Moon (Figure 13.30) sits at one end of the boulevard, overlooking a large plaza surrounded by several smaller pyramids and temple complexes. The avenue is lined with temples and palaces. On one side rests the spectacular Pyramid of the Sun, 210 meters (682 feet) along one side of its base and rising 64 meters (208 feet) high. Steps lead to its summit, where a small temple once stood. Near the Pyramid of the Sun are compounds, temples, and palaces. Sculpted reliefs of skulls, snakes, birds, jaguars, and mythological creatures adorn walls and ceilings everywhere. When the city was inhabited, the architecture was awash in bright color, with walls and ceilings painted blue, brown, red, green, yellow, white, and black.

Though Teotihuacán was a ruin when the Spanish arrived in the sixteenth century, the Aztecs, the powerful native people who dominated the Valley of Mexico at the time, knew of the site and revered it. The Aztecs, apparently, left offerings at Teotihuacán, and historical records even indicate that Motecuhzoma (Montezuma), the final Aztec ruler, regularly visited the ruins of the city to conduct various rituals. Even the name by which we know the city comes from the Aztec language: *Teotihuacán* means "the place of the gods" (Pasztory 1997).

Early in the third millennium B.P., Teotihuacán was just one of many small farming villages in the Valley of Mexico. Its location, however, offered its inhabitants several advantages over those of most of the other villages. Teotihuacán was located near an important source of obsidian, was adjacent to a major trade route, and was well suited to irrigation-aided agriculture. When population growth in the area challenged the ability of simple agriculture to feed the increasing number of people living there, Teotihuacán flourished.

By 2100 B.P., there were a number of developing population centers in central Mexico, yet Teotihuacán outstripped them all in growth. The key

FIGURE 13.30 The Pyramid of the Moon at the ancient city of Teotihuacán in central Mexico. Fifteen hundred years ago, Teotihuacán was a metropolis of 200,000 people. *(M. H. Feder)*

to Teotihuacán's success was not only the advantages noted above but also a volcanic eruption that decimated its rivals. To take advantage of its obsidian resource, miners of the stone, makers of tools, and full-time traders were needed. A greater emphasis on irrigation allowed for the production of more food, which in turn allowed a greater proportion of the population to engage in specialties related to the obsidian trade. Great power and wealth rested in the hands of the elite who controlled both trade and irrigation.

At its peak, Teotihuacán's urban core is marked by 2,000 enormous, multifamily apartment house compounds built on a consistent and fixed grid. The consistency in the arrangement of these compounds reflects an ancient Mesoamerican version of urban planning, implying a high level of control of city development by a ruling authority.

Some of the compounds consist of large, finely made rooms, many of which exhibit beautifully rendered, colorful murals (Figure 13.31). Some of these same apartments open up onto very private interior patios. Almost certainly, these were the homes of important families: rich and politically connected administrators, soldiers of high military rank, and,

FIGURE 13.31 Detailed and colorful wall art decorated the homes of the Teotihuacán elite. *(Richard A. Crooke/Corbis)*

perhaps, priests (Pasztory 1997). Two-thirds of the residential compounds are much smaller, not as finely made, and lack interior patios. These likely were inhabited by the urban working class; most of them probably were farmers or craft workers (Millon 1992). There is little evidence of abject poverty or urban blight at Teotihuacán; even the smallest, simplest compounds appear to have been rather livable, and like the apartments of some of their wealthy neighbors, some had artfully rendered murals.

Teotihuacán was a hub of politics and commerce in ancient Mesoamerica. Houses and tombs that reflect the styles and practices of other ancient Mesoamerican state societies are found in clusters at Teotihuacán. These may have been the homes and graves of foreign merchants or dignitaries who represented the political and economic interests of their home territories in the center of the most powerful political entity of their time.

Teotihuacán's power declined after A.D. 600, and its collapse began to accelerate after A.D. 700. It is not at all clear, but the death throes of Teotihuacán may have been the result of internal dissension. While there is no evidence of an invasion by an outside force, there does appear to have been substantial burning in ceremonial areas and, especially, in the Ciudadela, that part of the city where Teotihuacán's rulers resided. After the

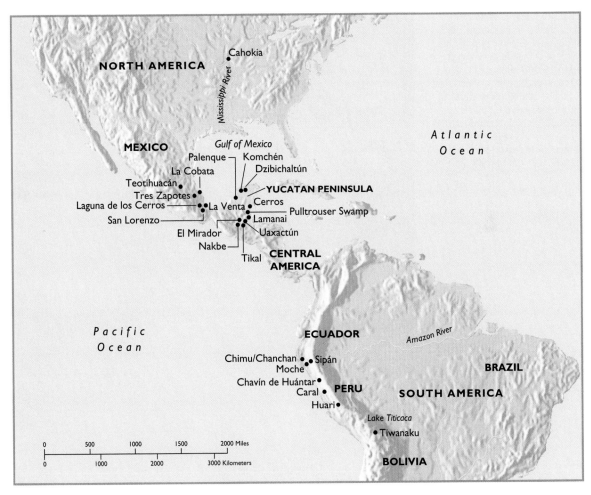

FIGURE 13.32 Locations of New World sites related to the development of civilization and mentioned in the text. Modern place names are included for reference.

burning of the Ciudadela, people seem to have abandoned the city, ending Teotihuacán's reign as Mesoamerica's great city-state.

The Evolution of Mesoamerican Civilization   Teotihuacán, of course, did not appear without antecedents (Figure 13.32). Beginning about 3200 B.P., the trajectory of cultural evolution in Mesoamerica changed significantly although there is no major change in subsistence technology or urbanization. In the uplands and lowlands, people relied on maize, beans, and squash as their food base. In the lowlands, they practiced a form of agriculture called *slash-and-burn*. Typical in subtropical and tropical forest lowlands, slash-and-burn involves cutting trees, burning them to release their nutrients quickly into the soil, planting and harvesting, and then moving on to other areas, allowing the harvested area to return to forest.

FIGURE 13.33 An enormous head carved from a single block of basalt, a volcanic rock. Some of these Olmec heads weighed up to 18,000 kilograms (about 20 tons) each. The raw materials for these monolithic sculptures were transported to Olmec ceremonial centers located up to 130 kilometers (80 miles) from their source in the Tuxtla Mountains. (© Robert & Linda Mitchell)

Olmec The artistic and iconographic style in Mesoamerica, starting about 3200 B.P.

After 3200 B.P., a cultural convergence similar to that seen in the Indus Valley about 4500 B.P., appears. In this case, a unique style of art permeates most of Mesoamerica. The style, called **Olmec**, appears to represent not just a single set of art motifs but a unified ideology with a shared iconography and common forms of artistic expression, including depictions of a half-human, half-jaguar god; the use of jade; the production of iron-ore mirrors; the construction of large earthen platforms; the construction of earthen pyramids; and the carving of huge basalt boulders into the form of human heads. Altogether, seventeen such monumental, sculpted portraits have been found: ten at San Lorenzo, four at La Venta, two at Tres Zapotes, and one at La Cobata. The largest is 3.3 meters (nearly 11 feet) tall and weighs nearly 18,000 kilograms (40,000 pounds; Figure 13.33).

Along with this converging style and the belief system inferred from it appears a different kind of settlement concentrated in the lowlands of the modern Mexican states of Veracruz and Tabasco. Three major sites have been discovered—La Venta, San Lorenzo, and Laguna de los Cerros—that appear not to be villages or cities but rather ceremonial centers.

Archaeologist Richard Diehl (2004) calls them "regal-ritual centers," places where priests and economic elites lived, carried out rituals, and controlled the populations who owed their allegiance to the center. Each of these regal-ritual centers seems to have been located to exploit a particular set of natural resources and to furnish those resources to the rest of Olmec society (Grove 1996). For example, Laguna de los Cerros is near the Tuxtla Mountains, rich in the volcanic rock used in sculpture and construction. San Lorenzo was in an area possessed of extremely fertile soil. In addition, the nearby Coatzacoalcos River provided an avenue along which raw materials and finished goods were traded across the Olmec realm. La Venta was close to sources of rubber, salt, and cacao—the source for chocolate (Grove 1996).

The Olmec moved monumental amounts of earth to construct platforms and pyramids and to modify the landscape of their ceremonial centers. For example, San Lorenzo is situated on a natural topographic eminence that had been added to and flattened by its inhabitants. It is estimated that the top 9 meters (10 feet) of the plateau on which the community is located was artificially built up. The earthen platform built at La Venta is more than 32 meters (105 feet) high and contains more than 2 million cubic meters (75 million cubic feet) of earth.

Archaeologists Linda Schele and David Freidel characterize the Olmec in this way: "They were the people who forged the template of world view and governance" that marked Mesoamerican civilization for more than two millennia (1990:38). Monumental undertakings such as earthen pyramids and huge sculptures reflect the Olmec's ability to command and organize the labor of a large number of people, typical of chiefdom and state societies.

As seen previously in the case of the evolution of complex societies in Mesopotamia, the growing authority of leaders in Olmec society is reflected in the archaeological record of their burials. At La Venta, for example, one ruler or chief was buried in a sandstone sarcophagus carved into an elaborate depiction of a caiman (a Central and South American crocodile). Like this elite burial, most Olmec rulers were interred with many beautifully rendered artworks including jewelry, sculptures, and celts (axe-like implements), many of them carved of highly polished jade or greenstone (Figure 13.34).

FIGURE 13.34 An Olmec ceremonial jade carving with a humanlike face. Jade was widely used in Olmec art and is believed to have been of great religious significance. (*Courtesy Department of Library Services. American Museum of Natural History. Neg. #K9850*)

In addition to these three ceremonial centers there were a number of smaller centers, including the very impressive site of Tres Zapotes in Veracruz and a few others where material evidence of the ability to harness a large pool of labor and to expend surplus wealth has been found. None of these communities were urban, but they hardly were sparsely inhabited. There are over two hundred individual house mounds at San Lorenzo and population estimates for the largest Olmec sites are generally about 1,000 people. This includes the small elite class that inhabited residences placed on top of the raised earthen platforms and the larger population of individuals who served the needs of each center's elite, including artisans and farmers. These centers likely relied on the labor of tens of thousands of people living in the many small farming villages and regional centers in the surrounding area (Adams 1991:59).

Why Did Olmec Develop?   Population growth may be part of the reason that the Olmec pattern developed. In the tropical lowlands of the Mexican Gulf Coast, the richest agricultural lands are located on natural levees produced by the rivers that flow through it. These rich regions seem to have attracted a large portion of the growing population.

Archaeologist Michael Coe (1968) has proposed that families that used the productive lands along the Gulf Coast probably produced agricultural surpluses, enabling them to amass wealth. Their wealth gave them the power to mobilize regional populations to produce monumental works such as the pyramids and other earthworks. As Tainter (1988) has pointed out, such works would have served ritually to legitimize the elevated social and economic status of this developing elite (also see Lowe 1989).

Small farming villages located in close proximity to valuable resources like rich agricultural land became regionally significant as the residences of a developing elite class—hence the rise of the ceremonial centers.

Certainly, we can see in Olmec the beginning of the process of state formation in Mesoamerica, but the question remains why? Beyond the fact that the Olmec appears to be a unifying art style, we do not know what else it signified to the ancient people of Mesoamerica. William Sanders and Barbara Price (1968) suggest that "microgeographical zoning" led to competition among groups in areas with different sets of resources. Population grew with the advent of slash-and-burn agriculture in the natural richness of the lowland environment. A single ideology reflected in a pan-regional art style may have unified disparate groups who needed to trade with each other.

The Maya   Various regional civilizations followed the Olmec in Mesoamerica. The Maya, located in the lowlands of Mexico, Honduras, Belize, and Guatemala, are one of the best known (Sabloff 1994).

The origins of the Maya can be traced back to 2,650 ya. The earliest evidence of monumental public architecture is seen by about 2300 B.P., at

FIGURE 13.35 This large stone platform topped by a temple is located at Dzibichaltún in the northern Yucatán. Dated to about 2300 B.P., Dzibichaltún and a handful of sites from the same period exhibit evidence of some of the earliest public architecture in the Maya realm. *(K. L. Feder)*

places such as Nakbe, El Mirador, Lamanai, Cerros, and Tikal in the south and Komchén and Dzibichaltún in the north (Figure 13.35). Such structures were related to Maya religion, and these early ceremonial centers probably housed members of a religious elite and their attendants. Some settlements, such as Cerros, located on a bay by the mouth of a river, became trading centers (Freidel 1979). Here, raw materials such as obsidian and jade, finely crafted goods from these raw materials, agricultural products such as cotton and cacao, and perhaps fine ceramics were distributed, contributing to the wealth and power of the developing religious elite (Sabloff 1994:115).

A highly productive agricultural system focusing on maize (see Chapter 12) provided subsistence for the Maya. Food surpluses allowed for population growth. As a result of this growth as well as the movement of people from the countryside to the population centers, some Maya villages developed into true cities with large, dense populations. These cities first appeared less than 2,300 ya.

The energy and resources needed to support large, competing population centers and the expanding elite class grew. This probably led to increased competition for resources—and even for people, on whose labor the economic, political, and social systems relied. There is evidence of defensive earth embankments at some Maya cities at this time, and there are numerous depictions in Maya art of military conflicts as cities fought against one another.

The Maya relied on a broad range of agricultural techniques to feed their growing population. One of their primary subsistence practices, slash-and-burn agriculture, requires quite a bit of land (perhaps 20 acres for each family) and quickly depletes the soil of its nutrients, requiring a long fallow period for the soil to regain its productivity. Shortening the fallow time to obtain a greater yield from a plot of land in the short term can deplete the soil of its nutrients in the long term, resulting in lower productivity. As a result, the Maya added other, more intensive agricultural techniques including terracing hills, planting kitchen gardens, tree-cropping, and building raised fields in swamps (McKillop 1994). By mounding up fields in wetlands, as they did at the Pulltrouser Swamp site in Belize, the Maya were able to use areas previously too wet to farm and to farm the same plots every year (Turner and Harrison 1983).

By about 1,900 ya, the essential characteristics of the ancient Maya civilization had become fully developed: a royal family headed by a powerful king; a socially stratified society with an elite class; impressive temples, palaces, and stone altars; an art style characterized by images of death and human sacrifice; a hieroglyphic language; screenfold books made of long strips of bark paper folded into a series of connected pages with narratives in that written language; stelae—upright stone slabs with carved messages in that same hieroglyphic language; a written number system; a dual calendar of 365 and 260 days; a ritual ball game; a veneration of jade and related green and blue-green semiprecious stones; and the use of chocolate in a ceremonial beverage. After these features had developed, about 1,750 ya (A.D. 250 in the modern calendar), the Maya civilization reached its ascendance, called the Classic period of Maya history.

The number of Classic period urban centers—Webster (2002:151) calls them "regal-ritual cities"—grew to about 40 or 50. These centers were largely politically independent of one another, city-states serving as the capitals of separate Maya polities. Each city-state was ruled by its own royal dynasties, and each dynasty decreed the construction of pyramids and temples that were a direct reflection of its power.

By 1,350 ya Tikal, in Guatemala, had a resident population of at least 40,000 people and perhaps thousands more in the surrounding countryside (Figure 13.36). Tikal also shows evidence of neighborhoods where particular craftspeople lived, producing stone tools, ceramics, and wooden implements.

Like most ancient city-states, each Maya city required the labor of a large population living in the expansive areas around the urban center, primarily farmers whose agricultural surplus provided the economic basis for the existence of the elites, the construction of their monuments, and trade for their exotic raw materials. Because the Maya homeland is not enormously agriculturally productive, David Webster (2002:140) estimates that 90 percent of the Maya were farmers whose labor was used to construct the great temples and pyramids.

Through the remarkable and persistent work of many scholars, the Maya are beginning to speak to us in their own voice across the centuries (see Schele and Freidel's splendid book, *A Forest of Kings: The Untold Story of the Ancient Maya* for a discussion of the translation of Maya writing). Their writing tells of a fascinating culture of more than fifty independent city-states spread across some 100,000 square kilometers (almost 40,000 square

FIGURE 13.36 The Temple of the Giant Jaguar at the classic Maya site of Tikal in Guatemala. At its peak, Tikal had a resident population of more than 40,000. (*M. A. Park*)

miles) of Mesoamerica. The story of the Maya is one of great achievements in science and engineering, bloody and protracted wars, and an intriguing belief in the cyclicity of time and history. Deciphering the Maya written language has made enormous strides in recent years. Continued success will allow for more complete understanding of the Maya civilization.

South America

The Romans of the New World, the Inca held their far-flung empire together by military might. First fully consolidated in A.D. 1476, and at its peak immediately before the Spanish conquest in A.D. 1534, the Inca empire controlled 2,000 miles and millions of people along the South American coast from northern Ecuador to southern Chile (Cobo 1653; Patterson 1973).

The Inca called their empire Tawantinsuyu, meaning "the four parts together." The amalgamation of tens of thousands of people in the "four parts"—north, south, east, and west—is an accurate description of the Inca empire. The Inca accomplished the joining of the four parts largely through military conquest. By using a professional standing army of more than 80,000 soldiers and by constructing 48,000 kilometers (30,000 miles) of roadways, they were able to conquer and control a vast territory (Figure 13.37).

As you might expect, the enormous army of the Inca inspired fear in the hearts of its neighbors, some of whom joined the empire not out of any love for the Inca but as a result of their pragmatic desire to avoid a war they almost certainly would lose. For example, given a choice between war with the Inca and "voluntarily" becoming a part of Tawantinsuyu, the small and far less powerful state called Chincha, located on Peru's southern coast, put into practical use the philosophy, "if you can't beat 'em, join 'em." The rulers of Chincha, like many others, recognized the inevitability of Inca hegemony, and by joining the empire they spared their society a pointless war.

It has been estimated that at the height of the Inca empire, only 1 percent of its population consisted of ethnic Inca (D'Altroy 2003:231). As a result, there always was a high degree of tension between the Inca and the non-Inca people over whom they ruled. The Inca understood that the resentment felt by those who joined Tawantinsuyu as a result of military defeat—or fear of such a defeat—could undermine the unity of their empire. To control their subjects, the Inca built administrative centers in the capitals of the states they defeated in battle and in the states that elected to join them. The Inca then installed an ethnic Inca in each of these administrative centers to act as governor. At the same time, representatives of the non-Inca people were moved to Cuzco, the Inca capital, effectively serving, as Morris and von Hagen (1993) characterize it, as hostages.

At the same time, the Inca did not depose local deities as they deposed local autonomous rulers. Instead, local gods were incorporated into the Inca pantheon. All people living under the Inca state, however, had to learn the language of the Inca, Quechua. Today, this language is still the primary tongue of the central Andes region.

Metallurgists in copper, bronze, silver, and gold, the Inca were also fine stonemasons, and their architecture is a major legacy of this culture. Using neither mortar nor cement, they constructed enormous walls of in-

FIGURE 13.37 The royal estate of Machu Picchu is located high in the Andes Mountains. Enormous, complex construction projects like this are diagnostic of cultures labeled "civilizations." (P. Nute)

tricately carved blocks made of volcanic stone. The precision with which individual blocks were fitted together is impressive. Gold and silver adorned the walls and temples of Cuzco.

The Roots of Civilization in South America   The 4,500-year-old site of Caral is located in the Supe River Valley, 23 kilometers (14 miles) from the Pacific coast and 200 kilometers (about 124 miles) north of Lima, the

FIGURE 13.38 This aerial view of Caral in Peru shows the monumental scale of pyramid construction undertaken by the inhabitants. The site's age of more than 4,500 years places it at the beginning in the New World of monumental architecture and the complex society necessary for its construction. (© *AP/Wide World Photos*)

modern capital of Peru (Solis et al. 2001). The site covers about 65 hectares (160 acres) and includes evidence of what may be the oldest monumental construction project yet found in the ancient New World, the huge earth and stone "truncated," or flat-topped, Piramide Mayor. The monument stands more than 18 meters (60 feet) tall, covers an area of about 24,000 square meters (6 acres), and contains 200,000 cubic meters (7 million cubic feet) of river cobbles and cut stone fill, all moved and mounded up by human effort one basketful at a time (Solis et al. 2001:723). Piramide Mayor is the largest of six pyramids at the site, demarcating a rectangular plaza that likely was the social and spiritual center of the community (Figure 13.38).

Caral probably had a large population, and there is clear evidence of a socioeconomic hierarchy at the site. Each of the six pyramids at Caral is associated with its own clusters of rooms with well-made, plaster-covered walls. Other residential areas at the site exhibit the remains of less elaborate and less substantial structures of wooden poles, cane, and mud. The more substantial buildings were likely the homes of Caral's elite; the wood and mud structures were the homes of the community's commoners (Pringle 2001).

Archaeological evidence suggests a subsistence base at Caral consisting of an array of domesticated plant foods including squash, beans, guava, *lucuma* (a round, green fruit), *pacay* (a sweet and smooth-textured legume), and *camote* (sweet potato). Caral's inhabitants also consumed large quantities of shellfish, notably mussels and clams, from the coast. That the coast is 200 kilometers away indicates that trade played an important role in Caral's development.

The Supe River Valley is not inherently conducive to agriculture. There is no substantial floodplain along the Supe River, and the overall dryness of the area makes an agriculturally based subsistence strategy problematic. Excavators propose that the inhabitants of Caral could have produced enough food for the large resident population only if they had expanded the agricultural fields by building irrigation canals. When not building great pyramids, Caral's labor force would have been able to dig and maintain these canals. The need to build canals to increase the amount of arable land in order to feed a growing population might explain why people would have worked cooperatively in the first place. And once a group of people followed the command of whoever was in charge of canal building, the social distinctions and economic inequality apparent at Caral may have become permanent.

Jonathan Haas, Winifred Creamer, and Alvaro Ruiz (2004) have continued to investigate the river valleys north of Lima, finding 20 major sites in the Supe, Pativilca, and Fortaleza valleys. Dating to as much as 5,200 ya, these sites reflect a consistent pattern including substantial populations; the construction of stone structures and terraced, flat-topped pyramids so large that they would have required the combined and coordinated labor of much of the community; and sunken circular plazas as large as 40 meters (131 feet) across.

By about 4,000 ya along South American's Pacific coast, we begin to see the development of a number of complex societies, each ensconced within its own river valley and each exhibiting some of the features that will later define civilization in South America.

The Evolution of South American Civilization   These river valleys are cut by streams draining the Andes, running parallel to each other and westward onto Peru's coastal plain. Resources are similar from valley to valley but differ depending on one's location within an individual valley. Archaeologist Thomas Patterson (1973) maintains that these valleys, each providing a complete mix of resources, appear to have been self-contained cultural units in early South American prehistory. Seasonal movements occurred within the confines of individual valleys, and there was little intervalley contact. By 4,000 ya, this general isolation among the inhabitants of different valleys led to cultural differentiation.

At the same time, population was increasing within valleys as agriculture replaced hunting and gathering. As elsewhere, agriculture led to a more sedentary settlement pattern. The patchy nature of resource availability led to differentiation within valleys. Where people could previously get whatever they needed simply by moving within a single valley, they now needed to trade to obtain resources available in other parts of the valley. Some villages, situated where resources were more abundant, became richer at the expense of others. Perhaps as validation of this differentiation, ceremonial centers begin to grow at this time.

As populations increased and approached the carrying capacities of the valleys, the need to trade and cooperate with people in neighboring

FIGURE 13.39 The religious art style—the iconography—of Chavín, like the Olmec in Mesoamerica, served to unify a geographically broad group of people, setting the stage for their political unification in a series of powerful, complex state societies. (© *Boltin Picture Library/Bridgeman Art Library*)

Chavín The artistic and iconographic style of Peru starting 3,000 ya.

repoussé A method of decorating thin metal where the pattern is hammered up from the underside.

valleys arose. Then, beginning about 3,000 ya, there occurred what archaeologist Richard Burger calls "a decisive change in Central Andean prehistory" that resulted in a "radical restructuring of earlier Andean cultures" (1988:99). A common artistic and iconographic style called **Chavín** quickly spread along natural routes of communication and trade within and across the valleys. The style consisted of relief and full sculptures of jaguars, caimans, snakes, and eagles, as well as humans with jaguarlike features (Figure 13.39). Along with these images came the spread of technological innovations in textiles and metallurgy, including new methods of manufacturing textiles, the widespread use of gold, methods of alloying gold and silver, soldering, sweat-welding, and the **repoussé** method of decorating gold objects (Burger 1992).

The style seems to have been centered at Chavín de Huántar in north-central Peru. Here, at about 3000 B.P., a pyramid and temple complex 13 meters (more than 40 feet) high and over 200 meters (650 feet) along one side was built. Within this complex are many relief sculptures in typical Chavín style and a 4-meter (13-foot) tall carved column of granite representing a standing man with jaguar fangs and snakes for hair.

Chavín may have served a function similar to that of the Olmec culture in Mesoamerica—a facilitator of trade, communication, and cooperation among previously alien people. Sharing the same art style and, probably more significantly, the same religious belief system with the same gods would have made interaction that much easier. Burger suggests that the spread of this common style and ideology may have resulted from

FIGURE 13.40 The Moche culture Pyramid of the Sun stood 41 meters (over 130 feet) in height. Begun about 1,900 ya, it consists of more than 143 million adobe bricks. (© Tony Morrison/South American Pictures)

some sort of broad crisis among the people living in their separate Andean river valleys. Chavín, in this interpretation, may have started as a local cult that seemed to many to offer a mystical solution to the crisis.

Whatever the reason, Chavín did, for the first time, join the various valley cultures in a set of common cultural practices related to religion. It therefore set the stage for later political amalgamation of the various valley polities into larger, inclusive empires.

At about 1,900 ya on the north coast of Peru, we see the Moche site, with its 41-meter-high (more than 130 feet) stepped Pyramid of the Sun made up of 130 million sun-dried bricks (Figure 13.40); the spread of a unique pottery style far beyond the confines of its own valley (Conklin and Moseley 1988); and the presence of spectacular burials of a class of warrior-priests. The Moche were accomplished potters. They commonly painted naturalistic scenes on their pots, depicting everyday life, rituals, plants, and animals. Some of the pots were shaped into extremely realistic depictions of human faces and people engaged in various activities (Figure 13.41). These images represent a wonderful artistic legacy and also provide us with a detailed glimpse into Moche life and culture.

The royal cemetery of the Moche elite has been found about 150 kilometers (95 miles) north of the Pyramid of the Sun, in the village of Sipán

FIGURE 13.41 This ceramic vessel in the shape of a blind beggar playing the flute is typical of the splendid work in clay produced by the ancient Moche culture of western South America. (© *Gianni Dagli/Corbis*)

(Alva and Donnan 1993, 1994). One tomb in the cemetery, dating to about 1,660 ya, contained the remains of a man in his late thirties or early forties (Figure 13.42; Alva and Donnan 1994:29). The tomb was filled with turquoise, copper, silver, and gold jewelry. To his right lay a gold and silver scepter; on his left was a staff of cast silver. On his head was a feathered headdress; in death, he also wore nose ornaments and a beaded chest covering. Also accompanying this lord of the Moche were hundreds of pottery vessels, some quite elaborate and displaying human shapes; a number were in the form of warriors vanquishing their enemies. Two other men appear to have been sacrificed as part of the burial ceremony.

FIGURE 13.42 Warrior priests in pre-Inca western South America were buried in fabulous tombs surrounded by great amounts of wealth. This tomb in Sipán, Peru, was discovered by grave robbers and then excavated by archaeologists. *(Nathan Benn)*

The Moche lord was also accompanied by llamas, a dog, three women, and a child.

The clothing, ornamentation, and headdresses of those buried at Sipán match artistic depictions of warriors from other Moche sites. In those depictions, victorious warriors are presented with the hands and feet of their enemies as trophies. Alva and Donnan discovered the remains of human hands and feet associated with the major burials at Sipán. On this basis, the Sipán burials are characterized as those of warrior-priests.

By 1,400 to 1,200 ya, two separate civilized states, Tiwanaku and Huari, came into existence. Again, the respective capitals of these states are marked by monumental architecture, far-flung trading networks, differentiated burials, and a level of artistic skill implying specialization. Art and architectural styles, religious motifs, and burial patterns of the Tiwanaku and Huari civilizations spread over hundreds of square miles through expansion, friendly incorporation, and conquest. As archaeologists William Conklin and Michael Moseley (1988) point out, Tiwanaku and Huari represent the development of a kind of large-scale "national" Andean unity.

FIGURE 13.43 Major sites of the Minoan civilization on Crete. Knossos, with its large palace, is the largest and most complex of these sites.

By about 1,000 ya, another large state, the Chimu, evolved, with its 15-square-kilometer (6-square-mile) capital, Chanchan. The Chimu built an expansionist, militaristic empire. They followed the practice of split inheritance, in which the son of the king inherited only his title while others in a king's family inherited his wealth, property, and land—along with the right to collect the taxes, the proceeds of which they were obliged to use to maintain the king's burial. This fueled the military expansionism of the new king, who wanted to acquire new lands and subjects to support the state and his kingship. The Chimu were the precursors of the Inca, who also practiced this policy of split inheritance. The Inca ascended to supremacy when they defeated the Chimu in war.

Southern Europe

The city of Knossos was the center of what certainly was Europe's first literate civilization (Cherry 1987; Warren 1987). Built on the island of Crete close to 4,000 ya, it was the nucleus of the **Minoan** civilization, the influence of which was felt throughout the central Mediterranean (Warren 1975; Figure 13.43). The social and political hub of Knossos was the Labyrinth, a palace built in 3,880 B.P. that covered an enormous area of some 20,000 square meters (215,000 square feet) and may have contained 1,000 separate rooms or chambers (Castleden 1990:8; Figure 13.44). It is a remarkable structure made of mud brick, marked with numerous columns tapered from top to bottom, and painted in browns and reds. Its interior walls were covered with paintings showing details of Minoan life and belief 3,800 ya: priestesses gaze at visitors across the millennia; an athlete-acrobat performs a handstand on the back of an enormous bull in a palace fresco; the images of two animals that appear to be a mythical

Minoan The earliest European civilization, centered on Crete and beginning about 4,000 ya.

FIGURE 13.44 Looking down into one of the rooms of the palace at Knossos on Crete. The columns have been reconstructed and repainted, conveying only an impression of how beautiful the palace had once been. *(M. H. Feder)*

mixture of dogs and birds flank what seems to be a throne; and beautifully rendered dolphins frolic among a school of fish.

The palace at Knossos was the hub of a civilization that stood at the hub of a vast network of trade encompassing the Aegean region of the Mediterranean. This trade—focused on olives, particularly valuable for their oil—may have been a key contributor to the importance of the island, leading to the evolution of a complex political and economic entity.

The power of Knossos began to fade after about 3,400 ya while the importance of the **Mycenaeans** on the Greek mainland grew at its expense. The Mycenaeans were accomplished traders, too, although their focus was not on olives but copper and tin. These two metals, when alloyed, produce bronze, a material far more durable and useful than either of the metals from which it was made. Perhaps resulting from a need to keep records of trade, the Mycenaeans expanded on the writing system first developed by the Minoans.

The Mycenaeans flourished until a bit after 3,200 ya when invasions from the north sapped their strength, leading to the destruction of their

Mycenaean The civilization of Greece that followed the Minoans and preceded the Greek city-states.

FIGURE 13.45 Locations of sites related to the development of African civilization south of Egypt and mentioned in the text.

civilization. The fall of the Mycenaeans paved the way for the ascendance of the Greek city-states that produced the architecture, science, and philosophy that contributed so greatly to the development of Western society.

Africa, South of Egypt

The evolution of civilization in Africa presents us with a long, complex, richly detailed story. Once thought to reflect only a late reaction to developments in other regions, the cities, the states, and civilizations in sub-Saharan Africa are now known to have been ancient and in some cases to have developed independently from other areas (Connah 1987; Figure 13.45).

Perhaps the oldest African civilization south of Egypt—in what the Egyptians called Kush and today we call Nubia—is the 3,500-year-old civilization of Kerma (Connah 1987). Kerma, located on the east bank of the Nile in modern Sudan, covers 60,000 to 100,000 square meters (15 to 25 acres) and is surrounded by a monumental wall some 10 meters (33 feet) high. The wall includes huge mud-brick towers nearly 20 meters (66 feet) high.

FIGURE 13.46 The pyramids of the rulers of Meroë, an African civilization located to the south of pharaonic Egypt and dated to between 2500 and 2200 B.P. (© *Jonathan Blair/Corbis*)

East of Kerma is a large cemetery where members of Kerma's upper classes were buried. Individuals were placed on finely made wooden beds, some encased in gold. Well-crafted items were entombed with them: bronze swords, bronze razors, fine clothing of leather, fans made of ostrich feathers, and large quantities of pottery. The most impressive grave in the cemetery, that of Tumulus X, represents the final resting place of an obviously important ruler, surrounded by the sacrificed remains of close to 400 retainers (O'Connor 1993).

The best known of the ancient Nubian civilizations is that of Meroë, dated from about 2,250 to 1,650 ya. The city of Meroë covered an area of about 750,000 square meters (185 acres). The center of the settlement consisted of a maze of monumental structures made of mud brick and faced with fired brick. These buildings appear to have been palaces, meeting halls, temples, and residences for both nobility and their workers. The central area of Meroë was surrounded by a monumental wall of mud brick. Excavations east of the city have revealed a commoners' graveyard where about 600 simple interments were found. In comparison, beautifully constructed small, stone pyramids capped the graves of Meroë's nobility who were buried in the North Cemetery. (Figure 13.46).

Southeast of Nubia is the city of Axum, in modern Ethiopia. Here the inhabitants built a four-towered "castle" some 2,000 ya. In Axum and its surrounding towns, researchers have found enormous, narrow towers,

FIGURE 13.47 Ruins of the 600-year-old stone enclosure at Great Zimbabwe in southern Africa. Great Zimbabwe was the central place of an indigenous southern African civilization. *(© Jason Laure/Woodfin Camp)*

each carved from single blocks of stone. The tower at Axum, for instance, is carved from a block of granite and stands 21 meters (69 feet) tall. False windows and doors have been carved into its four sides, making it look similar to a modern skyscraper.

Another ancient African civilization south of the Sahara is that of Jenne-jeno in Mali (McIntosh and McIntosh 1982). Jenne-jeno was a true city more than 1,000 ya, with a population of between 10,000 and 20,000 people. It shows evidence of public works, particularly in the form of its 2-kilometer (1.2-mile) surrounding wall. Jenne-jeno probably developed before any substantial contact with Arabs living north of the Sahara, so it was truly an indigenous, independent prehistoric Sub-Saharan kingdom. The city may have served as a trading center, bartering its rich agricultural products for salt, iron, and copper—the last obtained from sources 1,000 kilometers (over 620 miles) away (McIntosh and McIntosh 1982:414).

Dating to the fourteenth and fifteenth centuries A.D., the ruins of Great Zimbabwe, in southern Africa, consist of two main groups a little more than half a kilometer apart: the Hill Complex and the Great Enclosure. The modern African nation of Zimbabwe, in which the ruins of Great Zimbabwe are located, takes its name from the ancient site. The Great Enclosure may have housed Zimbabwe's economic and political elite (Ndoro 1997; Figure 13.47). The Hill Complex is a large, dry-laid stone ruin surrounded by a huge wall more than 11 meters (36 feet) high enclosing an area of more than an acre. It may have served as a residential area. Located above the surrounding terrain, it also was well-positioned to serve as a lookout to alert Great Zimbabwe's inhabitants of approaching danger. Be-

FIGURE 13.48 Monk's Mound contains about 50 million cubic meters (60 million cubic yards) of earth, covers an area of about 57,000 square meters (or about 14 acres), and rises to about 30 meters (100 feet) at its summit It is the central earthwork in a Native American settlement containing more than 120 smaller mounds. At its peak at around A.D. 1200, Cahokia's population probably exceeded 5,000. *(K. L. Feder)*

tween the Great Enclosure and the Hill Complex is an unbroken series of stone walls, enclosures, and foundations—in essence, the heart of an ancient city with a population of at least 2,000 adults (Ndoro 1997) and estimated by some to be as high as 18,000 (Connah 1987:184). The splendid and precise masonry with herringbone and chevron designs incorporated into the towers, platforms, and bastions of the large Zimbabwe structures reflects the great technological, architectural, and engineering sophistication of the people who built them.

When the site was stripped of its artifacts in the late nineteenth century by collectors interested in selling whatever might be found, many items of gold and iron were recovered. Unfortunately, Great Zimbabwe was not investigated by archaeologists until the early twentieth century, by which time much of the site had been damaged by looters.

The area around Great Zimbabwe contains more than 300 additional sites that appear to have been inhabited by people bearing the same culture. It seems clear that Great Zimbabwe was the capital of a far-reaching political entity (Ndoro 1997).

North America

Cahokia was not a full-fledged city, but the argument can be made that it was on its way to becoming one. Some 200 earthen mounds, platforms, and pyramids were spread across its 18 square kilometers (7 square miles; Figure 13.48). In the core of the settlement was Monk's Mound, the largest pyramid, covering more than 57,000 square meters (14 acres), containing over 50 million cubic meters (60 million cubic yards) of earth, and rising more than 30 meters (100 feet) over the river floodplain. In volume, Monk's Mound rivals the size of the pyramids of Mesoamerica and of many of those built in Egypt. From its summit, one can still gaze out on a large open plaza encompassed by large mounds: flat-topped pyramids, conical mounds, and low-lying earthworks.

Surrounding 200 acres of the main part of the settlement with its eighteen major mounds (including Monk's Mound), was a log wall or palisade with bastions and watchtowers. That wall was constructed from an estimated 20,000 logs, and it was rebuilt three times. The wall was as monumental a feat as Monk's Mound itself, enclosing the central part of the settlement and protecting the homes of Cahokia's elite. At its peak, Cahokia was a settlement of 5,000 or more inhabitants (some estimates range up to 20,000), including priests, artisans, merchants, farmers, and kings. Its rulers were buried in sumptuous splendor in log-lined tombs with precious artifacts of stone, shell, and copper. One ruler was laid out on a cape made of over 20,000 drilled and sewn shell beads. Also in his tomb were more than 1,000 beautifully made arrow points, a copper tube, sheets of mica, and numerous shaped stones (called *chunky stones*). Around his grave were the remains of more than sixty other people, all killed to accompany the chief to the afterlife.

With its food surplus, specialists, stratification, and dense settlement and as the economic and political center of a geographically broad entity, Cahokia has the appearance of an early stage of a civilization (Pauketat 1994). But Cahokia is not in the Indus or Nile valleys. It is not in northern China or Mesoamerica. Cahokia is found on the Illinois side of the Mississippi River, just east of St. Louis. For more than 500 ya, Cahokia was the center of a Native American chiefdom.

Southeast Asia

In Kampuchea (Cambodia) in Southeast Asia lie the ruins of the spectacular Khmer civilization. There, between A.D. 800 and 1300, seventy-two temples and monuments were constructed of sandstone, laterite (a hard red soil), and brick. Each complex of temples represented the capital of the Khmer state during the reign of successive kings. Angkor Wat, built after A.D. 1100, is the largest and most impressive (P. T. White 1982; Figure 13.49). The temple at Angkor Wat is surrounded by a rectangular outer gallery over 800 meters (0.5 mile) long. The walls of the gallery are covered with bas-relief sculptures depicting important events and personages in Hindu mythology. There are eight huge panels of reliefs, each close to 2 meters (6 feet) high and from 50 to 100 meters (160 to 300 feet) long. One panel depicts the Hindu creation myth; another contains 1,700 relief sculptures of spirit women. There is also an interior gallery with hallways connecting it to the outer gallery. At the center is the temple of

FIGURE 13.49 The Khmer civilization constructed a series of magnificent temples from A.D. 800 to 1300. Angkor Wat, the largest, was built after A.D. 1100. (© *Joson/zefa/Corbis*)

Angkor Wat itself, a hauntingly beautiful building with five intricately carved domes.

Water control seems to have been the key to Khmer civilization. Through a series of enormous reservoirs called *barrays* and miles of canals, the Khmer were able to produce two and sometimes three yearly rice harvests. The western barray is, in its way, as monumental and impressive as the temple complex. Constructed at ground level with dikes, this reservoir is 8 kilometers (5 miles) long and 2.25 kilometers (1.25 miles) wide.

Khmer civilization fell as a result of warfare with neighboring groups that had previously been under the sway of Khmer rule. Warfare today threatens the remains of this once great civilization.

Why Did It Happen?

The evolution of civilization is difficult to chronicle (Figure 13.50)—and even more difficult to explain. There are numerous gaps in the archaeological record, which become gaps in our thinking.

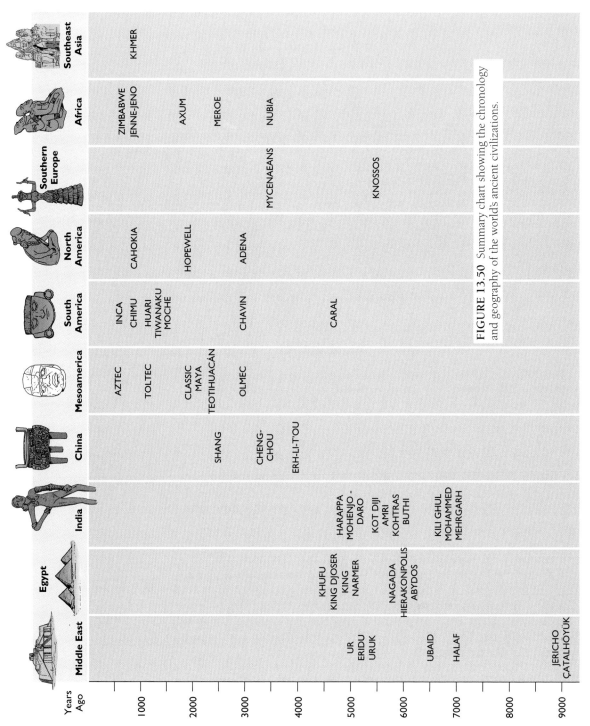

FIGURE 13.50 Summary chart showing the chronology and geography of the world's ancient civilizations.

As you read the brief descriptions in the preceding pages, you may have recognized some of the factors mentioned earlier in the hypotheses about the emergence of civilization (see Table 13.1). As Lamberg-Karlovsky and Sabloff have pointed out, each civilization had its own unique character, but "some strikingly similar developmental patterns characterized the beginnings of agriculture and the later rise of civilizations in both the Old and New World localities" (1995:214). Irrigation certainly played an important role in almost all the societies discussed, but it cannot be shown to have occurred first and therefore cannot have been in all places a prime cause. It is certainly the case that circumscription of resources served as a catalyst in the emergence of the civilized state, but a catalyst is not necessarily a cause. Managing trade of highly desirable localized resources seems to have been an important factor in all the examples discussed. You see the problem: it becomes a chicken-and-egg argument. We cannot determine which, if any, of those characteristics used to define civilization were causes, which were effects, and which were both.

Archaeologist Joseph Tainter (1988:32) has provided a valuable taxonomy of the hypotheses proposed for the origin of civilization. He categorizes the scientifically based hypotheses we have discussed—and myriad others—as follows:

1. *Managerial.* Managerial hypotheses maintain that civilization developed in response to a need for more complex forms of political integration. In other words, the need arose in some societies to accomplish specific complex tasks such as the construction of irrigation canals or the management of trade for valuable items not locally available. Managerial hierarchies developed to oversee these new, complex tasks, which led to social stratification and the other trappings of civilization. Clearly, the hydraulic hypothesis of Wittfogel fits into this category, as do explanations specifically pointing to trade as the cause of the development of civilization in Mesopotamia or Mesoamerica.
2. *Internal conflict.* In this perspective, class conflict is the prime mover behind the rise of civilization. The institutions of the state evolved to protect the wealth and power of the privileged few who, by luck and greed, had managed to accumulate more than their neighbors. Marxist theories fit into this category.
3. *External conflict.* In this view, civilization evolved in response to an external threat and to administer those groups defeated in warfare. The circumscription hypothesis of Carneiro belongs here.
4. *Synthetic.* Any explanations that combine several interrelated processes belong in this category.

Though we can offer no definitive answer to the question "What caused civilization to develop?" we can say that post-Pleistocene agricultural societies were living in various states of equilibrium with their

CONTEMPORARY ISSUE

The Collapse of Civilization

In his insightful and popular book *Collapse: How Societies Choose to Fail or Succeed,* scientist and writer Jared Diamond (2005) proposes five contributing factors to the collapse of complex societies, what we have labeled "civilizations" in this book: (1) environmental degradation caused by the practices of a society; (2) natural cycles of climate change that diminish the ability of the food producers in a society to grow enough food to feed the citizens of the state; (3) warfare, especially against other state societies; (4) the inability to obtain vital resources except from geographic regions beyond the borders or control of the state; and (5) a society's response to the first four items listed.

Diamond's first cause sees collapse as resulting directly from the practices of the society. The expansion of agricultural land by clearing vast swaths of tropical woodlands, the construction of irrigation canals, the reclamation of wetlands, the use of petrochemical fertilizers are, in many cases, temporary and inherently unstable fixes. They allow the production of more food in the short run, but they can also lead to population increase and the exponential growth in the economic cost of maintaining the viability of these new agricultural lands. It's a recipe for disaster that may lead to collapse.

Diamond's second explanation lies outside of human control or fault. As you have seen in this book, over the past 1.8 million years, cycles of human evolution and cultural development have been superceded by the natural rhythms of the Pleistocene. America's strength rests, at least in part, on our ability to feed ourselves, but what would (or, more likely, what *will*) happen when the next period of glaciation descends on North America and the so-called breadbasket of our nation becomes covered by a mile-thick layer of ice?

Diamond's third cause of collapse is war. Great and powerful societies compete with their great and powerful contemporaries for land, resources, and people, and this competition too often leads to the battlefield. The leaders of these great and powerful societies, of course, recognize this and invest an enormous portion of their nations' treasures in preparing for that eventuality. War and the preparation for war can become so burdensome that collapse is the inevitable outcome, even for the winners of those wars.

Diamond's fourth cause of collapse is based on the fact that natural resources can be distributed in ways that are patchy and unpredictable. A nation blessed with an abundance of agricultural lands may lack other vital resources, for instance, metal or wood. The development of powerful civilizations in the ancient—as well as the modern—world depended absolutely on their ability to obtain natural resources

environments. Some of these states of equilibrium, however, were unstable. Archaeologist David Clarke identifies a state of unstable equilibrium as one in which a "small displacement from the equilibrium state gives rise to a cumulatively greater displacement from that specific state" (1978:48). Relatively minor perturbations from without or within—such as population growth, climate change, technological advance, or outside threat—may have upset that delicately balanced equilibrium and changed the equation for survival. Decisions were made, challenges met, and strategies revised to respond to these changes. Canals may have been built, population density increased, agriculture intensified, or trading networks that were not necessarily available within their own borders. To ensure a steady flow of such resources, civilizations have relied on trade and alliance, as well as military conquest. It is hardly necessary to point out how much of modern politics is based on the fundamental need of industrial nations to obtain oil from those limited parts of the world where oil is still abundant and relatively easy and, therefore, inexpensive to procure. The oil embargo of the 1970s, when oil-producing nations withheld oil from the West, caused massive economic disruption, and there is always the potential in such disruptions for the dissolution of nations for whom oil is the lifeblood of their economies.

Diamond's fifth explanation places the burden on the societies themselves. How do we respond to the havoc we wreak on the environment including global warming, air and water pollution, and the erosion of topsoil?

Beyond this, how do we react to short-term environmental catastrophes? This question is particularly relevant as we write this; cleanup has just begun in the devastated American Gulf Coast in the wake of Hurricane Katrina. Do we learn from this tragedy and invest in a levy system that may protect communities against a Category 5 hurricane? Do we build away from the coast and allow for a natural buffer against the sea? Or do we blithely go back to business as usual, replicating pre-Katrina New Orleans, a marvelous city but one situated in an inherently precarious location? It has been estimated that reconstruction of New Orleans, Gulfport, Biloxi, and dozens of other communities will cost more than 200 billion dollars. How many more such bills can our nation pay before we are bankrupted?

Some suggest that the arms race essentially bankrupted the Soviet Union and led to its collapse. Will the billions the United States is now spending on its war against terrorism—a war against an enemy without borders or armies but one that hijacks airliners and flies them into buildings—protect or impoverish us? With gasoline at more than $3.00 a gallon, will we substantially change our energy habits by investing in alternative ways to fuel our industries, heat and cool our homes, and power our transportation?

It is one thing to consider the collapse of ancient civilizations and quite another to contemplate the collapse of your own. Let us hope that the subtitle of Diamond's book—*How Societies Choose to Fail or Succeed*—is correct and that our fates rest not in an inevitable and unavoidable downward spiral intrinsic to civilization, but in our ability to respond to the challenges of change.

established. Under conditions of unstable equilibrium, these new approaches, though perhaps solving initial challenges, sometimes produced a ripple effect that greatly transformed other aspects of culture. Patterns of social integration had to change to make such activities possible. Power was invested in emerging elites to build canals or walls, completely altering established social systems. Wars of conquest were initiated, changing the political nature of a region. Certain groups of people obtained differential access to resources by controlling trade. Such changes in turn may have triggered a spiral of change as a new equilibrium was sought but not attained. Changes in subsistence or trade may have required more coordination of individuals, triggering changes in social structure. The maintenance of this new order may have required symbols in order to perpetuate and justify itself. Use of these symbols, in turn, put more power in the hands of the leaders of the new social order. This power would have enabled even greater accomplishments in architecture and science.

Thus, myriad factors impinging on agricultural groups in the Indus and Nile valleys, Mesopotamia, highland and lowland Mesoamerica, China, South America, North America, southern Africa, southern Europe, and Southeast Asia may have set in motion forces whose ultimate impact on these societies was enormous. In the broadest sense, we are all living with the consequences of those changes.

Summary

Beginning sometime after 6,000 ya in several world areas, fundamental changes occurred in the social and political lives of human groups. The food surplus made possible by the Food-Producing Revolution allowed for a dramatic increase in cultural complexity that resulted in the development of what we call civilization.

Characterized by densely populated settlements, specialization of labor, social stratification, monumental public works, a system of recordkeeping, and the production of a food surplus, the world's earliest civilizations developed in Mesopotamia, in the Nile Valley of Egypt, the Indus Valley of Pakistan, northern China, the highlands and lowlands of Mesoamerica, and the mountain valleys of the Andes in South America. Other complex states and chiefdoms developed in southern Europe, sub-Saharan Africa, Kampuchea in Southeast Asia, and the North American Midwest.

The reasons postulated for the development of these societies have been varied: race, environment, invention, class struggle, the need for groups to subordinate themselves to authority, and warfare. There seems to be no point in suggesting a single cause for the development of civilizations in general, or even in individual cases. Civilizations are complex entities with complex explanations. Viable propositions include aspects of both conflict-based and integrative mechanisms. Thus, it is likely that in some world areas, as population grew, complex bureaucratic structures developed to facilitate group projects such as the construction of city walls or irrigation networks; specialist classes originated to coordinate trade for materials unavailable locally; and competition may have led to warfare, with defeated groups becoming subordinate classes. As social distinctions developed, monumental projects became common as members of the newly emerged elite classes felt compelled to legitimate in some concrete ways the stratified social system. In this way, civilization, with all of its concomitants, evolved in these many areas around the world.

Study Questions

1. What are the key characteristics of the world's first civilizations, or state societies?
2. How are such monumental works as pyramids, great palaces, and temples part of a feedback system in the increasing investment of power in the hands of an elite; in other words, how are monumental works both an effect and a cause of the development of the state?
3. How have various thinkers attempted to explain the rise of civilization? What appear to be essential commonalities wherever early civilization developed?
4. When and where did people first develop civilization? Was it rare or common? Did it occur independently in many areas, or was there a single source from which it spread into other regions?
5. How do conflict and integration models explain the evolution of early state societies?
6. Do state societies inevitably collapse? Is such collapse necessarily tragic for the people living in them?

Key Terms

civilization	ziggurat	Olmec
social stratification	Hassunan	Chavín
state	Samarran	repoussé
tribe	Halafian	Minoan
chiefdom	city-state	Mycenaean
environmental	rank society	
determinism	central place	

For More Information

C. C. Lamberg-Karlovsky's and Jeremy A. Sabloff's (1995) *Ancient Civilizations: The Near East and Mesoamerica* provides excellent summaries of the various hypotheses explaining the development of state society. The book also discusses in-depth the development of civilization in Mesopotamia, Egypt, the Indus Valley, and Mesoamerica. Though the time period discussed is a bit later than that focused on here, John Romer's *Ancient Lives: Daily Life in Egypt of the Pharaohs* provides remarkable insight into life in ancient Egypt. Graham Connah's *African Civilizations* provides the best recent discussion on the development of civilization on that continent. Jonathan Kenoyer's book *Ancient Cities of the Indus Valley Civilization* provides a detailed and up-to-date perspective on the society that produced Mohenjo-Daro and Harappa. For a comprehensive discussion of the

Olmec, see Richard Diehl's *The Olmecs: America's First Civilization.* David Webster's *The Fall of the Ancient Maya* is a terrific book, providing a very readable account of the story of the Maya. One of the best sources on the ancient Maya continues to be Linda Schele and David Freidel's *A Forest of Kings: The Untold Story of the Ancient Maya.* Esther Pasztory provides a very thoughtful analysis of Teotihuacán in *Teotihuacán: An Experiment in Living.*

K. C. Chang's *The Archaeology of Ancient China* is a good source of information on the Shang civilization. Thomas Patterson's *America's Past: A New World Archaeology* examines the development of the state in South America. *National Geographic* has published fine articles on the cultures of Cahokia (George Stuart's "Who Were the 'Mound Builders'?") and Angkor Wat (P. T. White's "The Temples of Angkor: Ancient Glory in Stone"). *Angkor Wat: Time, Space, and Kingship,* by Eleanor Mannikka, is a wonderful source for information about the Khmer civilization. Jonathan Haas's *The Evolution of the Prehistoric State* and Joseph Tainter's *The Collapse of Complex Societies* are especially useful treatments of the birth and death of civilizations. For a wonderfully written examination of the collapse of civilizations, both ancient and modern, see Jared Diamond's *Collapse: How Societies Choose to Fail or Succeed.*

EPILOGUE
What Don't We Know?

Science magazine is, essentially, the publication of record for science in the United States. The equivalent publication in Great Britain is *Nature*. Both are venerable, weekly periodicals in which scientists from many fields often choose to announce their latest, most important discoveries. Detailed descriptions of scientific discoveries or breakthroughs may take months or even years to see print in highly specialized journals, but those first announcements, usually just a few pages long, often appear first in *Science* or *Nature*. You may have noted that many of the articles we cite in this textbook, usually relating to new and important discoveries in paleoanthropology or archaeology—announcements of newly discovered fossil hominids, important breakthroughs in artifact analysis, or the revelation of significant archaeological sites—originate in one of these two publications.

One issue of *Science,* in particular, caught our attention because it broke from tradition. Rather than the usual compendium of articles from a wide variety of fields announcing recent discoveries—brief announcements concerning what we newly know about the world—the July 1, 2005 issue had a theme: what we *don't* know about the world around us. In fact, the issue itself was titled "125 Questions: What We Don't Know." It enumerated in a detailed way what the featured authors felt were today's most important and exciting questions in astronomy, physics, biology, paleoanthropology, archaeology, and more. Some might wonder why such an esteemed periodical would devote an entire issue to what scientists don't know—to what is, essentially, an admission of ignorance—but their puzzlement would reflect a misunderstanding of science and the scientific method. Science doesn't shy away from mysteries or merely "admit" to not being able to solve them. The fact that there are so many unanswered questions and mysteries—about the universe, our planet, life, and ourselves—provides science with a purpose; unanswered questions are precisely what make science so exciting in the first place.

With this thought-provoking issue in mind, we have decided to end this edition of *Human Antiquity* by briefly discussing what we don't yet know about our subject, questions for which we do not yet have adequate answers but for which, we hope, our understanding will be much more complete in the future.

What Are the Intellectual Capabilities of Our Closest Relatives, and What Does This Imply about How We Should Treat Them?

We've known for some time that chimpanzees make tools (see Chapter 5). We know now that bonobos do as well, and that gorillas and orangutans at least use tools. We also know that our closest relatives lead complex social lives, so much so that it's not anthropomorphizing to use human terms to describe the behaviors of chimps and bonobos. Thus, for example, chimpanzees have "friends"; they regularly spend time together and embrace one another upon reuniting after an absence. Chimpanzees also have "enemies" whom they shun. Moreover, studies have shown there to be group differences among chimpanzees in toolmaking and social behaviors, what some have termed "traditions" or even "cultures."

In artificial situations, we have taught chimps, bonobos, and gorillas the rudiments of human language. This is a communication system they don't use in the wild but which, obviously, their brains are capable of once we teach them to use a nonspeaking vehicle such as sign language or a symbolic keyboard.

However, because we can't fully communicate with our evolutionary relatives, it is difficult to fully assess their intellectual abilities, at least in human terms. Yet anecdotal evidence keeps coming in and seems to increasingly indicate that the apes have a surprising degree of analytic, creative, and flexible behavior.

All this speaks to the similarity of our species, and, indeed, our separation of seven million years at most argues that our bodies and behaviors are homologous—variations of the same evolutionary adaptive themes. But, even so, we can ask whether the obvious differences in our behaviors are differences of degree or kind? That is, are we so different that, despite our recent common ancestry with the apes, we humans are a qualitatively different sort of creature? Perhaps we are an example of an emergent property in which existing attributes, in this case the mental capacities common to the hominoids, came together in us in an interactive combination that is nonadditive, that is, where the whole is greater than the sum of its parts. The jury is still out on this.

In another, related area of interest, we freely acknowledge our evolutionary closeness when we use nonhuman primates for medical and psychological experiments. The premise of such experiments is that these species are homologous to humans, at least for the physiological and behavioral factors being tested, and can therefore be used to further medical advances on behalf of *humans*.

But this, then, begs the question of the morality of giving apes human diseases or of subjecting them to psychological distresses in the name of medical or psychological research. If they respond in ways similar to us—if they are essentially like us—have we any right to, in short, use and abuse them? This is an ongoing and complex philosophical question for which even the relevance of scientific data is an issue.

Who Were the First Members of the Human Lineage, and What Triggered Our Divergence from the Evolutionary Lineage That Led to the Modern Apes?

We are interested not only in who we are now but also when we began our evolution and how that happened. There are now about a half dozen proposed candidates for the first member of our lineage (see Chapter 8), and even more specific schemes than that when authorities attempt to "connect the dots" by drawing evolutionary lines among fossils to construct a family tree.

Since the exposure of Piltdown as a fraud, we have replaced the focus on big brains with a focus on bipedalism as the adaptation that set into motion and defined our evolutionary line. Indeed, we proceed with the assumption that if a fossil shows evidence of bipedalism, it is a hominid. We describe some of the early hominids as "bipedal apes," to show the primacy of that adaptation.

But is that a safe or even a reasonable assumption? As Stephen Jay Gould pointed out, while the overall tree of life might have the shape of an inverted triangle—diversity of life in general increasing over time—individual portions of the tree take the shape of a stereotyped Christmas tree, with more diversity early in a broad taxon's history that is then pared down by natural selection to fewer lines as time and adaptive competition go on.

Thus, is it not possible that some of the fossils suggested as early hominids—in some cases, *the* earliest hominid—might be something else: members of an extinct lineage? Perhaps, in fact, bipedalism evolved in primates more than once, and so some of those fossils are, literally, bipedal apes. And so, carrying the question further, perhaps the only fossils we can be sure are members of our specific lineage are those that show an increase in brain size over the chimpanzee-sized brains of all the supposed hominid fossils before about 2.5 mya. Thus, in a more modern, sophisticated sense, we are back to the assumption that prompted the Piltdown fraud. And as a further implication of this question, if we don't know who the earliest hominids were, how old they were, nor what they looked like, we can't say for sure what the circumstances were that produced the speciation event separating our line from that of our closest relatives. Our origins remain, really, as enigmatic as ever.

How Are Premodern Groups of Humans Related, and How and When Did *Homo sapiens* Evolve?

There is an ongoing debate over these questions (see Chapter 10), and it can get heated at times. Why? At issue is more than the search for scientific truth. At issue also is the philosophical question of, evolutionarily speaking, just *who* we are. Are all living and recent *Homo sapiens* a new and recent species, different at that level from the Neandertals and other so-called archaic humans? Or are we the current manifestation of a much older, temporally and spatially variable species and, thus, literal biological siblings with those other human types?

How much variation do we acknowledge and accept within our species? Some who see us as a new, separate species insist that the Neandertals, for example, as similar as they are to us, are *not* us; in other words, there are some profound differences between us. Others accept that, especially in the past, our evolving species displayed more geographic variation and, certainly, variation over time, so they welcome the Neandertals and others into our species.

Such philosophical matters are, of course, irresolvable, as all philosophical matters are. But so too, at the moment, are the empirical aspects of the question. Lacking the ultimate proof of species identity—the ability to interbreed—we may never know if we are a separate species from those other groups. Extensive DNA data could eventually solve the problem, but so far we have only short sequences of genetic material from fossils, and those are not particularly old. The chances of recovering sufficient DNA from each fossil group is slim.

So the question of our ancestry is one question that we may never answer and, thus, a puzzle we will have to live with.

What Did—and What Does—the Art of the Upper Paleolithic and Late Stone Age Mean?

Some people refer to it as "the artistic impulse," that seemingly universal human practice of producing two- and three-dimensional images that serve no apparent goal other than delighting the maker in the making and/or the observer in the observing. Beautiful or ugly, crude or sophisticated, simple or complex, realistic or abstract, these drawings, etchings, paintings, sculptures, and the like all fit under the broad heading *art*. They are all uniquely a product of the human mind.

In this book, we have traced evidence of this behavior among our ancestors dating back to more than 30,000 ya. Glimmers of this artistic impulse may go back even more deeply in time (see Chapter11).

Art surrounds us: finger-painted masterpieces are hung by magnets on refrigerators, crude sexual images are inked onto college classroom desks, paintings of soaring beauty and layered meaning are found in museums all over the world, Harry Potter fan art is scattered across the Internet in literally thousands of Web sites, the human body serves as the canvas for elaborate tattoos. We express our feelings about the world around us, we convey messages about our devotion, we protest, we complain, we pray, we attack, we tell our story, we convey our joy, and we simply create beauty by employing the symbolic expression that underlies all art.

Certainly, we recognize our ties to those human ancestors who, more than thirty millennia ago, created art by painting images on cave walls, by sculpting representations of pregnant women, and by making items of personal adornment to suspend from chains worn around their necks or to pin to their cloaks. The humanity of our ancient ancestors may represent the ultimate impetus for their production of art; they were humans, and human beings express themselves through art. Art is part of the package that defines the modern human mind.

But what was the proximate cause for the ancient art? What were the immediate, self-conscious reasons for making art during the Upper Paleolithic and Late Stone Age? If we were able to travel back through time and ask a cave painter of the Upper Paleolithic why he or she was depicting a horse on a rock canvas deep in the warren of tunnels in a dark cave, what would the answer be? If we asked our ancient ancestors why they were sculpting the image of woman, wearing a necklace, pecking the representation of a giraffe on a boulder, dragging their fingers in swirls across a soft clay surface, what would they answer? What reason would they give for making what we recognize and label as artwork? We simply don't have the answer to this question.

What Triggered the Food-Producing Revolution?

Most of us take it for granted that the Agricultural Revolution of more than 10,000 ya was a good thing and that the adoption of and reliance on an agricultural way of life just makes sense. So the domestication of plants and animals and the shift to food production as discussed in Chapter 12 seems like an obvious development.

Our ancient ancestors adopted an agricultural way of life because it was a smart thing to do, resulting in a food base that was more abundant, more reliable, safer, and just plain better than the hunting and gathering practices of our even more ancient ancestors.

But not so fast. You likely noticed that though we discussed in Chapter 12 a number of hypotheses to explain the Agricultural Revolution, we didn't conclude that any one of them actually explains things, at least not entirely. It turns out, often to the surprise of twenty-first-century people who take for granted the superiority of an agriculturally based subsistence, that in many circumstances a hunting and gathering economy proved highly effective, producing an abundant, diverse, and fairly reliable food base and taking a lot less work than an agriculturally based economy. In many environments, foragers rarely wanted for food and could hunt and gather more than enough for themselves, their families, and their communities in fewer weekly work hours than many horticulturalists and agriculturalists. Also, unlike many early agriculturalists who concentrated on a small number of highly productive crops, hunter-gatherers often practiced a broad-spectrum approach to subsistence. In many circumstances, the diets of foragers were more complete than those of agriculturalists. Furthermore, disease, drought, or an early frost could destroy the subsistence base of an agricultural group reliant on a single or very few primary crops; the same conditions would have had less of an impact on the widely varied diet of a hunting-gathering group. Some of their favorite foods might be wiped out, but because they were already primed to exploit a broad array of wild foods in their territories, foragers could respond to adverse environmental conditions simply by shifting their subsistence emphasis as needed.

This clears up one issue but leaves another, equally important one. Because of the obvious trade-offs that accompany the adoption of a food-producing way of life—longer work hours, and inherent risks of focusing on a small number of crops in exchange for a potentially plentiful food base—agriculture was not developed and adopted "just because." There must have been ample reason for accepting the longer work hours and the attendant risks. But what those reasons are, we just don't know.

How Do We Explain the Shift to Social, Political, and Economic Complexity That Led, in the Short Term, to the World's First Civilizations and, in the Long Term, to Our Own Modern Way of Life?

Certainly, there are benefits to living in a complex society. The development of a formal government with a consistently applied set of laws and the accompanying establishment of a police force may result in a level of order that benefits many people in a society. A highly trained and well-organized military force of a kind that often developed even in the most ancient complex societies can provide a significant level of protection to its citizens from the depredations of nasty neighbors. The growth of a large coterie of specialists may result in access to finely crafted and often useful goods to an increasingly large segment of a society's population. The organization of trade and commerce under a controlling authority may ensure the free flow of goods and services and result in the standardization of costs, weights, and measures, which increases the likelihood that the average person will actually get what he or she pays for in economic transactions.

At the same time, however, each of these benefits reflects a trade-off, and within each resides the certainty of the loss of individual freedom and personal control. For example, with a policing force comes the potential for the abuse of those who don't understand or agree with the rules and regulations of the society, many of which provide a drastically different level of benefit to different classes of people. A baker might appreciate the laws that deter the theft of his inventory, but Jean Valjean in *Les Miserables* would feel quite differently, being imprisoned for twenty years for the crime of stealing a loaf of bread to feed his starving family. The clear benefits of defense provided by a standing army are mitigated by the dangers of a force that has the power to circumvent the laws established by the civic authority. Beyond this, consider the personal cost when an individual's protection from external threats requires the conscription and ultimate loss of a teenage child called to military service. Moreover, all of the benefits of a complex society come with a monetary cost. Every complex society has its version of the IRS, and people's lands, homes, and the materials they grow and produce are inevitably taxed to pay for the functions carried out by that society.

Human antiquity is characterized, in several places and at several times, by the development of complex state societies (see Chapter 13). In each of these places and at each of these times, human beings, on some level, must have recognized and assessed the trade-offs inherent in the movement toward social, economic, and political complexity and, either as a result of fear or rationality—and likely some combination of the two—acquiesced in that shift. The key question that remains is, Why did this happen, in ancient Mesopotamia, Egypt, the Indus Valley, Mexico, Peru, and other places? What factor or factors served as the tipping point in the development of the ancient state, making the adoption of a complex society a reasonable decision? We simply do not know.

How Can Only 30,000 Genes in Our Genome Make Us Human Beings, and Which of Those Genes Make Us Uniquely Human?

If you were surprised by our statement in Chapter 4 that so few genes could initiate and guide the development of an organism as complex as a human, you weren't alone. Only a few years ago, scientists were guessing that at least 100,000 genes must be responsible for producing us. Now we know that we have only about twice the number of genes as a fruit fly! How could that be? We are, objectively speaking, so much more complex an organism than a fly, and we certainly like to think of ourselves as *the* most complex of nature's products.

We have some tantalizing hints as to the answer in the so-called Hox genes, which code for basic body parts—legs, eyes, and so on—and are the same in many organisms across the taxonomic spectrum. A basic gene that initiates the shaping of beaks in birds, for example, is the same one that humans possess for shaping faces. Moreover, the new and exciting field of evolutionary development (called "evo-devo") is showing that major changes in evolution may involve mutations of a relatively few genes that regulate developmental rate and direction in individual organisms.

But we are still a long way from understanding just how genes—which are, in a sense, nothing more than templates and some instructions for building proteins—can make a creature that, for example, can write and read these paragraphs. No other organism on earth can do that, not even our closest relatives. So, while it's not surprising that one possible genetic difference between humans and chimps relates to brain development (see Chapter 5), that still doesn't come close to answering the question as to what makes us *us,* especially when considering how our brains generate our minds. At the moment, the answer to that query is: We really don't have a clue.

GLOSSARY OF HUMAN AND NONHUMAN PRIMATES

Adapidae (ah-da'-pih-day) A group of early primates from the then-connected landmass of North America and Europe dated to more than 50 mya and thought to be ancestral to prosimians such as lemurs and lorises.

Aegyptopithecus (ee-gyp'-tow-pith'-ah-cuss) An extinct monkey with several apelike traits. Discovered in Egypt and dating to 34 mya, it may represent a form of primate ancestral to Old World monkeys and apes.

Ankarapithecus (ahn-kah-rah-pith'-ah-cuss) Fossil ape genus from Turkey, dated at 9.8 mya, that shows similarities to *Sivapithecus.*

Anthropoidea (an-throw-poi'-dee-ah) One of the two suborders of order **Primates** (the other is **Prosimii**). Means "humanlike" and includes monkeys, apes, and hominids.

Ardipithecus kadabba (ar-di-pith'-ah-cuss kah-dah'-bah) An earlier species of *Ardipithecus* from Ethiopia and dated at 5.8 to 5.2 mya; interpreted by some as bipedal. The subspecies name means "base family ancestor" in the Afar language.

Ardipithecus ramidus (ar-di-pith'-ah-cuss rah'-mi-dus) A hominid species from Ethiopia and dated at about 4.4 mya, based on skeletal fragments and teeth. Not yet fully documented or accepted, it is thought by its discoverers to represent one of the earliest species in the hominid line; thus the species name, which means "root" in the local language.

Australopithecus afarensis (os-tral-oh-pith'-ah-cuss ah-far-en'-sis) A fossil species from East Africa, a well-established species in the hominid line. Dated from 3.7 to 3 mya, *afarensis* had a small, chimp-sized brain but walked fully upright.

Australopithecus africanus (os-tral-oh-pith'-ah-cuss ah-frih-can'-us) A fossil hominid species from South Africa dated from about 3 mya to 2.3 mya. Similar to **A. afarensis,** it may well be a direct evolutionary descendant of that species. It retains the chimp-sized brain and is fully bipedal.

Australopithecus anamensis (os-tral-oh-pith'-ah-cuss ana-men'-sis) Found in Kenya and dating from 4.2 to 3.8 mya, it is the earliest well-documented fully bipedal hominid.

Australopithecus bahrelghazalia (os-tral-oh-pith'-ah-cuss bar-el-gah-zahl'-ya) A new species of this genus, based on a jaw and several teeth found in Chad and dated at 3.5 to 3 mya. The species name is based on an Arab name for a nearby riverbed. It is noteworthy as the only early hominid found outside of East Africa or southern Africa.

Australopithecus garhi (os-tral-oh-pith'-ah-cuss gar'-hee) Recently discovered fossils from Ethiopia, dated to 2.5 mya, that display resemblances to both **Australopithecus afarensis** and early *Homo,* leading some authorities to consider them a new species and a direct ancestor of *Homo.*

Catarrhini (cat-ah-rine'-eye) One of two infraorders of suborder **Anthropoidea** (the other is infraorder **Platyrrhini,** the New World monkeys). Catarrhini is the infraorder of the Old World monkeys, apes, and hominids. Along with the geographical distinction, catarrhines can be distinguished from platyrrhines by their narrow nose, fewer premolar teeth, and lack of a prehensile tail.

Cercopithecidae (sir-co-pith-ah-sigh'-day) The taxonomic family of all monkeys of Europe, Africa, and Asia.

Cercopithecoidea (sir-co-pith-ah-coy'-dee-ah) The superfamily of all monkeys of Europe, Africa, and Asia.

Eoanthropus   (ee-oh-an′-throw-puss)   Meaning "dawn man," the taxonomic name given the Piltdown fossil announced in 1912. *Eoanthropus* had a very humanlike cranium but an apelike jaw, fulfilling the expectations of the time concerning the appearance of the earliest humans. It was later proven to be a fraud, and the name is no longer valid.

Eosimiidae   (ee-oh-sim-ee′-ih-day)   A group of early primates from Asia, dated at around 45 mya, that may represent direct ancestors of monkeys, apes, and hominids.

Equatorius   (ee-kwa-tor′-ee-us)   A fossil genus from East Africa dated at 15 mya and showing similarities in arm and ankle structure to the modern chimpanzee. Lumped by some authorities into **Kenyapithecus.**

Gigantopithecus   (ji-gan-tow-pith′-ah-cuss)   A fossil ape genus from 7 mya to perhaps 300,000 ya in China, India, and Vietnam. The largest primate known, it may have reached a height of 12 feet when standing erect and weighed up to 1,200 pounds.

Gorilla gorilla   (go-ril′-a go-ril′-a)   The gorilla (well, duh), one of the three great ape species from Africa and the largest living primate.

Hominidae   (ho-mih′-nih-day)   The family of modern and extinct human species, defined as the primates that are habitually bipedal. Members of this group are called hominids.

Hominoidea   (ho-min-oy′-dee-ah)   The superfamily that includes the large, tailless primates: apes and hominids, living and extinct.

Homo antecessor   (ho′-mow an-tee-sess′-or)   A newly proposed species from Spain and dated at 780,000 ya or more. The fossils show a mix of primitive and modern features and are interpreted by their discoverers as possibly ancestral to **Homo heidelbergensis** and **H. neanderthalensis.** This species is not widely recognized at present.

Homo erectus   (ho′-mow ee-reck′-tuss)   A fossil hominid species dated from at least 1.8 mya to perhaps as late as 27,000 ya. First appearing in Africa, *H. erectus* was the first hominid species to expand beyond that continent. Fossils are found throughout Africa and Asia. There is abundant archaeological evidence and a few fossils indicating presence in Europe after 1 mya. Members of this species had an average brain size about two-thirds that of modern humans, made advances in stone tool technology, and late in their existence were able to control fire.

Homo ergaster   (ho′-mow er-gas′-ter)   A proposed new species that includes the earliest **H. erectus** fossils from East Africa. These specimens are said by some experts to be different enough that they represent a separate species ancestral to both *H. erectus* and, later, **Homo sapiens,** but the idea is not universally accepted.

Homo floresiensis   (ho′-mow floor-ee-zee-en′-sis)   A proposed new species from the Indonesian island of Flores, dated to as recently as 13,000 ya and characterized by a diminutive body size (3 feet 5 inches) and small brain (380 ml). *H. floresiensis* is, however, associated with stone tools, hunting, and fire.

Homo habilis   (ho′-mow hah′-bill-us)   A fossil hominid species dated from about 2.3 to 1.6 mya and found in East Africa. Fully bipedal and with an average brain size of 680 ml, *H. habilis* was the first confirmed hominid stone toolmaker. Because this was the first hominid with a brain larger than that of a chimpanzee and because of the association with stone tools, it is thought to be the earliest member of our genus, *Homo.*

Homo heidelbergensis   (ho′-mow high-del-berg-en′-sis)   A proposed species from Africa, Asia, and Europe, dated at between 475,000 and 200,000 ya. *H. heidelbergensis* had a modern human brain size but retained primitive features such as brow ridges, prognathism, and postorbital constriction.

Homo neanderthalensis   (ho′-mow nee-an-dir-tall-en′-sis)   The name once applied to the Neandertals, indicating that they were a different species from **Homo sapiens.** In the past, this interpretation was based on an exaggeration of some of the differences between them and modern humans. At present, there is a debate as to whether Neandertals represent a separate species or are simply the European and Southwest Asian populations of premodern *Homo sapiens.* If they are indeed part of a distinct species, the name might be reinstituted.

Homo rudolfensis   (ho′-mow rue-dolf-en′-sis)   Species name given by some authorities to certain specimens of **Homo habilis,** including the well-known skull ER 1470.

Homo sapiens   (ho′-mow say′-pee-ens)   The taxonomic name for modern and some premodern (archaic) humans. There is some debate as to whether or not this name covers certain fossil forms.

Hylobatidae   (high-low-bat′-ah-day)   The family that includes the gibbons and siamangs, the arboreal, so-called lesser apes of Southeast Asia. They are highly efficient brachiators.

Kenyanthropus platyops (ken-yan'-throw-puss plat'-ee-ops) A new fossil genus from Kenya, dated at 3.5 mya and suggested by some authorities, because of its flat face and other features, to represent a better human ancestor than any species of *Australopithecus*. Thus far, it is based on only two specimens.

Kenyapithecus (ken-ya-pith'-ah-cuss) Fossil genus from East Africa dated at 15 mya. A possible candidate for the first hominoid. According to some authorities, includes fossils classified as ***Equatorius.***

Macaca (mah-cah'-cah) A highly successful genus within family **Cercopithecidae** with representative species from North Africa to Japan.

Morotopithecus (mow-row-tow-pith'-ah-cuss) Fossil genus from Uganda dated at 20 mya. A possible candidate for the first hominoid it may have been capable of occasional upright walking.

Omomyidae (oh-mow-me'-ah-day) A group of early primates that lived in the then-connected landmass of North America and Europe. Dated to 60 mya, they are thought to be ancestral to tarsiers and perhaps **Anthropoidea** as well.

Orrorin tugenensis (or-or'-in too-gen-en'-sis) A new fossil genus from Kenya, based on thirteen specimens and dated at 6.2 to 5.6 mya. Its purported bipedal features have led some to suggest it represents the ancestor of all later hominids. The identity and features of this form are still a matter of much debate.

Ouranopithecus (oo-ran'-oh-pith'-ah-cuss) An ape form from Greece dated at 10 to 9 mya. With some hominidlike features, it is thought by some to be a member of the ape line that led to the hominids.

Pan A genus within family **Pongidae** that includes the two chimpanzee species from Africa: ***Pan troglodytes,*** the common chimpanzee, and ***Pan paniscus,*** the bonobo or pygmy chimpanzee.

Pan paniscus (pan pan-iss'-cuss) The bonobo, sometimes called the pygmy chimpanzee, one of the three living great ape species from Africa.

Pan troglodytes (pan trog-low-dye'-tees) The chimpanzee, one of the three living great ape species from Africa.

Papio (pah'-pee-oh) A genus within superfamily **Cercopithecoidea** (the Old World monkeys), which comprises several species of baboons, large monkeys living in social groups on the African savannas.

Paranthropus aethiopicus (par-an'-throw-puss ee-thee-o'-pih-cuss) A hominid species from East Africa dated from 2.8 to 2.2 mya, the first of the so-called robust hominids, having large, rugged features associated with chewing. Its other features, including brain size, are so similar to members of genus *Australopithecus* that many authorities still include it in that genus. It is thought that the species was adapted to a diet of tough, gritty, hard vegetable foods. The most famous, and first, specimen is the "Black Skull."

Paranthropus boisei (par-an'-throw-puss boys'-ee-eye) A robust hominid of East Africa dated from 2.2 to 1 mya. It had large facial features associated with chewing, although less pronounced than in ***P. aethiopicus.*** The first specimen was "Zinjanthropus." Sometimes included in genus *Australopithecus.*

Paranthropus robustus (par-an'-throw-puss row-bus'-tuss) A robust hominid of southern Africa dated from 2.2 to 1.5 mya. It is marked by robust chewing features, although less so than in either ***P. aethiopicus*** or ***P. boisei.*** The postcranial skeleton and the brain size remain similar to those of *Australopithecus.* It is sometimes included in that genus.

Platyrrhini (plat-ee-rine'-eye) One of two infraorders of suborder **Anthropoidea** (the other is suborder **Catarrhini,** the Old World monkeys, apes, and hominids). Platyrrhines include the New World monkeys. Members of this group can be differentiated from the catarrhines by their broad nose, greater number of premolar teeth, and, at least in several species, prehensile tail.

Plesiadapiformes (pleez-ee-ah-dah'-pih-form-ees) A branch of archaic primates from sites in present-day North America that became extinct about 55 mya.

Pongidae (pon'-jih-day) The family of the so-called great apes, the orangutans of Southeast Asia and the gorillas, chimpanzees, and bonobos of Africa.

Pongo pygmaeus (pon-go pig-may'-us) The orangutan, the only great ape from Southeast Asia.

Primates (pry-mate'-ees) An order within class Mammalia consisting of large-brained, arboreal mammals with stereoscopic color vision and grasping hands (and sometimes feet). Includes prosimians, monkeys, apes, and hominids.

Prosimii (pro-sim′-ee-eye)   One of two suborders of order **Primates** (the other suborder is **Anthropoidea**). Prosimians are the more primitive of the two suborders; they retain features of some of the oldest primate fossils. Many lack color vision, are nocturnal, and have limited opposability of the thumb.

Sahelanthropus tchadensis   (sah-hale-an′-throw-puss chad-en′-sis)   A possible fossil hominid from Chad, dated at 7 to 6 mya. Despite some apelike features, it has other cranial features that some claim make it the earliest hominid.

Sivapithecus   (she′-vah-pith′-ah-cuss)   A fossil ape from India and Pakistan, dated from 15 to 12 mya, and thought to be ancestral to the orangutan.

GLOSSARY OF TERMS

Terms in boldface type are defined elsewhere in the Glossary.

absolute dating Any dating technique in which a specific age, year, or range of years can be assigned to an object or site. Also called **chronometric dating**. Compare with **relative chronological sequence.**

accelerator mass spectrometry (AMS) A technique in **radiocarbon dating** in which the actual number of ^{14}C atoms (or a proportion of them) is counted.

Acheulian A toolmaking tradition of *Homo erectus* in Europe and Africa. Includes **hand axes**, cleavers, and **flake tools.**

adaptation The adjustment of an organism to a particular set of environmental conditions.

adapted See **adaptation.**

Agricultural Revolution See **Food-Producing Revolution.**

agriculture A subsistence strategy based on domesticated plant foods.

allele A variant of a gene. Most genes possess more than one allele, the different alleles conveying different instructions for the development of a certain **phenotype** (for example, blue eyes versus brown eyes and type O, A, or B blood).

allele frequency The percentage of times a certain **allele** appears in a population relative to the other possible alleles of the same gene.

amino acid The chief component of **proteins**; the building block of all life.

analogy In evolution, a trait that is similar in function in two or more species but that is unrelated evolutionarily. See **homology.**

anthropological linguistics The anthropological study of language.

anthropology The **holistic** and integrative study of the human species. Anthropology includes the study of human biology, human physical evolution, human cultural evolution, and human **adaptation.**

arboreal Adapted to life in the trees.

archaeology A branch of **anthropology** that focuses on cultural evolution through the study of the material remains of past societies.

Archaic The time period in the New World that follows the **Paleo-Indian** period. The Archaic begins at the end of the Pleistocene and represents a period of cultural **adaptation** to the new postglacial environment.

Arctic Small Tool Tradition A stone tool tradition dating to about 4500 B.P. in the Arctic, characterized by small blades, barely 2.5 centimeters long, used for cutting and carving, small burins for engraving bone and antler in the production of harpoons and sewing needles, small blades inset into bone and antler arrow and spear points, and even smaller **microblades** about 1 centimeter long set into handles and used for various tasks such as butchering and skinning animals and manufacturing watertight clothing from their skins.

argon/argon (Ar/Ar) dating A recent refinement of **potassium/argon dating**. Measures the decay of one isotope of the gas argon (^{40}Ar) into another (^{39}Ar).

artifact Any object usually found at an archaeological site that was made by humans. Also, a natural object consciously modified for a specific use.

artificial selection The process by which human beings choose those members of a plant or animal species that will live and reproduce and those that will not. The animals or plants selected are those that possess characteristics desirable to humans.

association   Objects found together in the same archaeological or geological stratum in proximity to one another are said to be in association.

Aurignacian   The stone tool technology associated with anatomically modern *Homo sapiens* in Europe beginning about 34,000 ya. Includes long, narrow blade tools.

base pair   The bonded pairs of bases (A with T and G with C) in the DNA molecule.

Beringia   A broad expanse of land more than 1,500 kilometers (1,000 miles) across, connecting northeast Asia with northwest North America during periods of sea level depression in the **Pleistocene.** People living in Asia walked east across the land bridge or traveled along its coast into the lands of the Western Hemisphere at least 15,000 ya and possibly more.

bifacial   A stone tool that has been worked on both sides.

biological anthropology   See **physical anthropology.**

biostratigraphy   The patterned appearance of plant and animal fossils in **strata.** The fossils of more ancient organisms are found in older, deeper strata, while those of more recent organisms are found in younger, generally higher layers.

bipedal   Having the ability to walk on two feet.

brachiate   The ability to swing through trees using arms and hands.

breeding population   A population within a species with some degree of genetic isolation from other populations of that species. See **deme.**

Bronze Age   The period in European prehistory when people began making bronze tools.

calibration curve   The curve derived for the correlation of tree-ring and radiocarbon dates.

camelid   The family of large ruminant animals that includes Bactrian camels and dromedaries in the Old World and llamas, alpacas, vicuñas, and guanacos in the New World.

carbon isotope analysis   Analysis of the proportion of ^{12}C and ^{13}C in a sample.

carrying capacity   The number of organisms a given habitat or region can support.

catastrophist   An adherent to the hypothesis of catastrophism—that the world was produced through a series of catastrophic events, usually including Noah's flood. Compare to **uniformitarianism.**

central place   The geographic focal point of a political entity. A large city or ceremonial center with religious structures is often the central place of an ancient state or a chiefdom. Elites lived in central places.

cereal   Any plant, especially grasses, that produces starchy grains.

Châtelperronian   A stone tool industry associated with late Neandertals in Europe. It appears to reflect an amalgam of the older Neanderthal **Mousterian** industry and the **Aurignacian** of anatomically modern humans.

Chavín   The artistic and iconographic style that appeared about 3,000 ya and spread across groups that had been culturally separate and that lived in a series of river valleys in the western Andes in Peru. Chavín apparently set the stage for the development of larger, politically united entities in western South America.

chiefdom   A level of sociopolitical integration more complex than the **tribe** but less so than the **state.** Chiefdoms are less rigidly structured than state societies, and without the formal structure of a government behind the office, a chief's power is less than that of a king or pharaoh.

chromosome   A strand of DNA in the nucleus of a cell that carries genetic information passed down to subsequent generations.

chronometric dating   See **absolute dating.**

city-state   A large, politically complex entity, including a dense central population with surrounding villages owing allegiance to the city, characteristic of the early civilization of Mesopotamia.

civilization   Used in this book for cultures with an agricultural surplus, **social stratification,** labor specialization, a formal government, monumental construction projects, and a system of recordkeeping. Cultures evolved into early civilizations in a number of world areas from local **Neolithic** adaptations.

cladistics   A taxonomic classification based on actual order of evolutionary branching. Compare with **phenetic taxonomy.**

cline   A geographic continuum in the variation of a specific **phenotype.**

Clovis   A long, bifacially flaked stone spear point characterized by channels or flutes on both faces. Clovis points date to the period 11,500 to 11,000 ya and are found throughout North America and parts of South America.

codominant   Used to describe the situation that occurs when neither allele of a gene pair is **dominant** and both are expressed in the organism.

codon   A section of the DNA molecule that codes for a particular **amino acid.**

comparative biology   The study of the similarities and differences among plants and animals.

comparative collection   An aggregation of modern specimens used in the identification of ancient remains found at archaeological or paleontological sites; for example, a comparative collection of seeds, wood types, or animal bones. An osteological comparative collection is a "bone library," useful not only in the identification of species but also the sex, age at death, and health status of the animal.

comparative osteology   The study of bones of different animal species.

competitive exclusion   The process by which one **species** outcompetes others for resources in a particular area.

compliance archaeology   Archaeological research mandated by government regulations aimed at historic and environmental preservation.

coprolites   Fossilized feces, useful in reconstructing a paleo-diet. **Paleofeces.**

core tool   A tool made by taking **flakes** off a stone nucleus.

creationist   One who believes that a supernatural power was directly or indirectly responsible for the origin of the universe, the earth, and all living things.

creation myth   A myth that explains the origin of the world and its inhabitants.

cultural anthropology   The branch of **anthropology** that focuses on cultural behavior. **Archaeology, ethnography,** and **anthropological linguistics** are included in cultural anthropology.

cultural evolution   Changes in cultural patterns over time.

cultural technique   A dating method based on cultural comparisons and the processes of culture change. A site may be dated based on the degree of similarity between the **artifacts** found there and those from other sites where absolute dates have been derived. Cultural dating techniques also include **seriation.**

culture   A nongenetic means of **adaptation.** Those things people invent or develop and then pass down, including political, social, technological, economic, and ideological systems.

Darwinian gradualism   The same as **gradualism.**

deduction   A step in the scientific method. After developing a general explanation (a **hypothesis**) from specific observations through the process of **induction,** deduction is the step of suggesting those things that must be true (new data) if the hypothesis is valid.

deme   A genetically isolated population within a species; generally, the same as a breeding population and often physically distinguishable from other demes. See **breeding population.**

Denali Complex   A stone tool technology seen in the American Arctic consisting of **wedge-shaped cores, microblades,** bifacial knives, and burins and dated to after 10,700 B.P.. Several features of the Denali Complex are reminiscent of elements of older complexes in northeast Asia, particularly that of Dyuktai Cave.

dendrochronology   A dating technique based on the unique, nonrepeating sequence of tree-ring widths.

deoxyribonucleic acid (DNA)   The molecule that contains the genetic code.

deviation amplification   The process by which a small change in one part of a cultural system results in larger changes in the rest of the culture, which then amplify the original change. The development of agriculture and civilization reflect such processes.

diaphysis (plural *diaphyses*)   The shaft of a long bone— for example, the femur, humerus, and tibia.

differential reproduction   The process by which some individuals of a species are more successful than others at surviving, attracting mates, producing offspring, and hence passing down their characteristics. See **natural selection.**

diffusion   The geographic movement and sharing of cultural traits or ideas.

direct historical approach   One method of **ethnographic analogy.** The historically recorded behavior of descendants of a group whose archaeological remains are being studied is used as the source for models or analogies in an attempt to understand the ancient culture.

diurnal   Active during the daytime.

domesticate   To change, through **artificial selection,** the wild form of a plant or animal to a form more useful to humans. The end product species is also called a domesticate.

dominance hierarchy   A social pattern seen in animal species in which certain individuals have preferential access to food, mates, and social activities.

dominant   Of a pair of **alleles,** the one that is expressed in the **heterozygous** condition.

ecofact   An element found in an archaeological context that exhibits human activity but was not made by people and so is not, strictly speaking, an **artifact.**

egalitarian   Societies in which, within the same age-sex categories, all people are more or less equal in terms of wealth, social standing, and authority.

einkorn   A variety of wheat; *Tripsicum monococcum.* An important domesticate in the **Neolithic** but not a significant agricultural crop today. Compare with **emmer.**

electrical resistivity survey   A noninvasive procedure used in archaeological prospecting in which an electrical current is passed through the ground. Variations in resistance to the current may signal the location of archaeological **artifacts** or **features.**

electron spin resonance (ESR) dating   A dating technique that measures the buildup of electrons in crystalline materials. Can be applied to sites from more than a few thousand to more than 10 million years old.

emmer   A variety of wheat; *Tripsicum turgidum.* An early domesticate of the **Neolithic** in Southwest Asia and the source of cultivated wheat in the modern world. Compare with **einkorn.**

enamel hypoplasia   Damage in the form of pits and cracks in the enamel of the adult teeth resulting from malnutrition or disease during early childhood, long before the adult teeth emerged.

endocast   A natural or artificial cast or model of the interior of a fossil skull. In nature, loose material may fill a skull and harden, producing a model of the surface of the brain the skull housed. In the lab, latex or similar material can be poured into the skull or painted onto the interior surface, again producing a model of the surface of the brain.

endogamy   Marriages restricted to those within the same social group. Exogamy is marriage restricted to those outside the social group.

entoptic phenomena   Visual images that result from stimulation of the optic system during altered states of consciousness. Geometric designs in cave art of the **Upper Paleolithic** have been explained by some researchers as resulting from entoptic phenomena.

environmental determinism   The notion, popular in the nineteenth century, that the nature of the environment directly determines the technological level of a culture. Determinists assumed that more challenging environments produce more developed cultures.

enzyme   A **protein** in the body that causes and in part controls chemical processes.

epiphyseal union   The fusion during growth of the end of a long bone **(epiphysis)** to the shaft **(diaphysis).**

epiphysis   The end or cap of a long bone. Long bones have two epiphyses.

estrus   In many nonhuman mammals, the period during which a female is fertile; also, the signals indicating this condition to males of the species.

ethnoarchaeology   Conducting ethnographic research among a living people from the perspective of an archaeologist, focusing on the processes by which people's behavior becomes translated into the archaeological record.

ethnocentric   Judging another society's values in terms of one's own social values.

ethnographic analogy   A technique in archaeological analysis in which a written description of the lifeway of a contemporary or historically recorded group is used as a model for interpreting the archaeological record.

ethnography   A subfield within **cultural anthropology** that involves the intensive study of a human group. The ethnographer lives with a group of people, often for a number of years. Also applied to the written work produced by an ethnographer.

ethology   The study of the behavior of organisms under natural conditions.

evolution   Change over time with reference to biological species. Also, changes within cultural systems.

excavation units   Individually dug sections at an archaeological **site.**

faunal analysis   The examination of animal remains from archaeological sites. Faunal analysis is helpful in the reconstruction of diet, seasonality, and subsistence technology.

faunal assemblage   The animal bones recovered at an archaeological site. Identifying the species, sex, and age at death of the animals represented by these bones is helpful in distinguishing wild from **domesticated** animal species associated with a site.

feature   A nonportable element of a site, composed of **artifacts** or organic debris or both. Features reflect an activity or set of activities. Trash pits, fireplaces, graves, and tool-manufacturing stations are all examples of features.

field survey   The process whereby archaeological sites are discovered in the field. Surface walkovers, **test pits,** and aerial photography are important aspects of field survey.

fission   The division, or splitting up, of a **breeding population.**

flake   A stone fragment removed from a core. Flakes with sharp points or edges may be used as tools without modification or can be further shaped or sharpened.

flake tool   See **flake.**

flotation   A technique in which soil matrix and archaeological material are separated by the use of water. Some organic materials such as seeds and charcoal will float and can be skimmed off the surface of standing water.

Food-Producing Revolution   The slow shift among human groups, beginning after 12,000 ya, from **foraging** to food production through the process of domestication. Also called **Agricultural Revolution.**

forager   See **hunter-gatherer.**

foraging   A subsistence strategy based on any combination of wild food resources, including collecting wild plants, hunting wild animals, fishing, and shellfish collecting.

foramen magnum   The hole in the base of the skull through which the spinal cord emerges and around the outside of which the top vertebra articulates.

foraminifera   Microscopic marine organisms whose exoskeletons are used in the analysis of the oxygen isotope ratio in seawater. This ratio varies in proportion to the amount of the earth's water that is in land-based **glaciers.**

founder effect   Differences in an isolated population of a species caused by the characteristics of those individuals that randomly established the isolate.

gamete   The cells of sexual reproduction; for example, sperm and eggs.

gamete sampling   The form of **genetic drift** that operates when genes are passed to offspring in proportions that differ from those of the parental population.

gene   Generally, the portion of the DNA molecule that codes for a specific **protein.**

gene flow   The exchange of genes among populations of a species through interbreeding.

gene pool   All **alleles** within a population.

genetic drift   The change in **allele frequencies** caused by random fluctuations within a population over time.

genetics   The study of the mechanism of inheritance and the physical results of that mechanism.

genome   The total genetic endowment of an organism.

genotype   The **alleles** possessed by an organism. Compare with **phenotype.**

glacial   See **glacial period.**

glacial period   Phases of the **Pleistocene Epoch** during which worldwide temperature dropped and substantial, long-term glacial expansion occurred. There have been as many as eighteen separate glacial periods over the last 1.6 million years, each lasting thousands of years. Compare with **interglacial.**

glacier   A massive body of ice that, through a number of processes, can expand and move.

glume   The seed case in which an individual cereal grain is enclosed on the plant.

gradualism   The view in evolution that **speciation** is slow and steady with cumulative change. Compare with **punctuated equilibrium.**

Gravettian   A toolmaking tradition of the **Upper Paleolithic** characterized by the production of small blades and denticulate knives. Dated from 27,000 to 21,000 B.P.

Greater Australia   See **Sahul.**

grooming   The practice among social primates in which one animal cleans the fur of another. This behavior helps promote social cohesion.

ground penetrating radar (GPR)   A noninvasive technique used in archaeological prospecting in which an electromagnetic pulse is passed through the soil. Variations in the pulse as it reflects off buried objects may signal the location of archaeological remains, for example, walls or foundations.

growth arrest lines   Horizontal cracks at the ends of the long bone shafts resulting from malnutrition during childhood. Also called **Harris lines,** after the researcher who first recognized their cause.

haft   To attach a wooden handle or shaft to a stone or bone point.

Halafian   A **Neolithic** culture in Mesopotamia dating from 7500 to 6700 B.P. Halafian sites generally are small farming villages.

half-life   The amount of time it takes for half of a **radioactive isotope** to decay to a stable isotope.

hand axe   A bifacial, all-purpose stone tool, axelike in shape, which was produced by *Homo erectus.*

haplogroup   A biological lineage defined by a cluster of specific, co-occurring genetic markers. Five major haplogroups characterize Native Americans, and all also occur in East and Central Asia.

Hardy–Weinberg equilibrium   The formula that shows **genotypic** percentages within a population under hypothetical conditions of no evolutionary change.

Harris lines   See **growth arrest lines.**

Hassunan   A **Neolithic** culture in Mesopotamia dating from 8000 to 7200 B.P. Characterized by small farming villages where subsistence was based on the growing of wheat, barley, peas, and lentils. Hunting was still an important part of subsistence.

heterozygous   Possessing two different **alleles** in a gene pair. Compare with **homozygous.**

holistic   A study that views its subject as a whole made up of integrated parts.

Holocene   The modern geological epoch that began about 10,000 ya with the end of the **Pleistocene.**

hominid   Any member of the taxonomic family Hominidae. Modern humans and our ancestors; the **bipedal** primate.

homology   In **evolution,** a trait shared by two or more species through inheritance from a common ancestor. See **analogy.**

homozygous   Possessing two of the same **alleles** in a gene pair. Compare to **heterozygous.**

hunter-gatherer   A society that relies on naturally occurring sources of food. Also called **forager.**

hypothesis   In the **scientific method,** a testable explanation of a phenomenon. Compare with **theory.**

induction   A step in the **scientific method.** The process of developing a general explanation (called a **hypothesis**) from specific observations. Compare with **deduction.**

inheritance of acquired characteristics   The incorrect idea that traits acquired by adaptation during an organism's lifetime could be passed to its offspring, once proposed as a mechanism for evolution.

in situ   In place. An **artifact, ecofact,** or **feature** that remains in its exact place of discovery is said to be *in situ.*

intelligence   The relative ability of an organism to take in, store, process, and utilize information from the environment.

intelligent design   The idea that an intelligent designer played a role in some aspect of the evolution of life on earth, usually the origin of life itself. Generally, a thinly disguised version of **scientific creationism.**

interglacial   A long-term phase during the **Pleistocene** between glacial periods, when glacial ice receded and worldwide temperature increased.

interstadial   A short-term, relatively minor period of glacial retreat during longer phases of general glacial advance. Compare with **glacial periods.**

K/Ar dating (potassium/argon dating)   An **absolute dating** technique based on the decay of a **radioactive isotope** of potassium into argon. Often used to date volcanic rock that can be stratigraphically related to archaeological materials. The long **half-life** of the radioactive isotope of potassium generally renders the technique useful only for materials more than 100,000 years old. It is often applied to fossil hominid sites.

knuckle walking   Walking on the backs of the knuckles of the hand, typical of the African apes.

Late Stone Age   Term for the final phase of the Stone Age in Africa, dating to between 40,000 and 10,000 ya.

Laurasia   The former northern landmass made up of parts of present-day North America and Eurasia. Where **primates** first evolved 65 mya.

law of superposition   The stratigraphic law that the more recent geological layers are superimposed over older ones.

legume   A large family of flowering plants that produce pods that contain seeds. Garden peas, snap beans, lima beans, lentils, and chick peas are all legumes domesticated during the **Neolithic.**

Levallois   A sophisticated and efficient tool technology involving striking uniform flakes from a prepared stone core. Levallois dates to about 200,000 ya.

Levant   The area along the eastern shore of the Mediterranean, including Greece, Turkey, Syria, Lebanon, Israel, and Egypt.

Lower Paleolithic   Term used for the earliest period of hominid toolmaking in Africa, Europe, and Asia, dating to as much as 2.5 mya (in Africa) to about 250,000 ya throughout the Old World.

Lower Pleistocene   The first part of the **Pleistocene** from 1.6 mya to 780,000 ya.

Lung-shan   The first fully agricultural people in China, dated to about 6,000 ya.

Magdelanian   A late **Upper Paleolithic** toolmaking culture in Europe dating from 16,000 to 11,000 B.P. Known from sites primarily in France and Spain, the Magdelanian material culture included finely made barbed harpoons, carved decorative objects, and cave paintings.

master sequence   The general and relatively consistent pattern of tree-ring-width variation across time within a given region.

matrilocal   A type of society in which a married couple lives with the wife's family.

Mesolithic   The name given to cultures in Europe at the end of the **Pleistocene** and before the **Food-Producing Revolution.** Adaptations of the Mesolithic usually reflect a change from those of the **Paleolithic** as plant and animal communities changed with the waning of the glaciers.

messenger ribonucleic acid (mRNA)   The form of ribonucleic acid that carries the genetic code out of the cell nucleus and into the cytoplasm, where it is translated into **proteins.**

microblades   Small, usually extremely sharp, stone blades. Microblades were set into handles of bone, wood, antler, and so on.

midden   A pile of trash produced by the inhabitants of a settlement.

Middle Paleolithic   Term used for the time period in Europe after the **Lower Paleolithic** and before the **Upper Paleolithic,** dating to between 250,000 and 40,000 ya, encompassing the cultures of premodern varieties of human beings, including the Neandertals.

Middle Pleistocene   The second phase of the **Pleistocene** from 780,000 to 200,000 ya.

Middle Stone Age   Term used for the time period in Africa after the Early Stone Age and before the **Late Stone Age,** dating to between 250,000 and 40,000 ya, encompassing the cultures of premodern varieties of human beings, including those transitional between premodern and anatomically modern *Homo sapiens.*

Minoan   The earliest civilization in Europe. Centered on the island of Crete and beginning about 4,000 ya, it appears to have been a city-state with Knossos as its capital.

mitochondrial (mtDNA) DNA   Genetic material contained in the mitochondria of cells. Analysis of mitochondrial DNA (mtDNA) of modern humans has provided researchers with an estimate for the age of anatomically modern *Homo sapiens.*

monogenic   A trait coded for by a single gene.

Mostly-Out-of-Africa model   The hypothesis that *Homo sapiens* is about 2 million years old as a species but that most of the genetic variation and phenotypic features of modern humans have an African origin.

Mousterian   The Middle **Paleolithic** culture associated with the European and Southwest Asian Neandertals that included a unifacial flake tool technology.

Movius Line   A geographic break between the manufacture of **hand axes** and that of simple stone chopping tools. Hand axes appear to the west of this line—located in eastern India—but generally not east of it.

multilinear   The accepted notion that different cultures pass through any one of a number of possible sequences of change. Compare with **unilinear.**

Multiregional Evolution (MRE) model   The hypothesis that *Homo sapiens* is about 2 million years old and that modern human traits evolved in geographically diverse locations and then spread through the species. Compare with **Recent African Origin model**

mutation   Any change in an organism's genetic material.

Mycenaean   The civilization in Greece that followed that of the **Minoans** and preceded that of the Greek city-states.

myth   A story, usually invoking the supernatural, to account for some aspect of the world.

Natufian   The Late **Paleolithic**–Early **Neolithic** culture of Southwest Asia, dated from 13,000 to 9800 B.P.

natural selection   Evolution based on the relative reproductive success of individuals within a species, the degree of success determined by the individual's adaptive fitness. See **differential reproduction.**

Nenana Complex   Perhaps the oldest identified stone tool complex in Alaska, dating from 11,800 to 11,000 B.P. Predating the **Denali Complex,** Nenana includes bifacially flaked, unfluted spear points. Nenana bifaces are similar and perhaps related to tools made in eastern Russia about 12,000 ya.

neocortex   The part of the brain of complex organisms responsible for memory and thought, in other words, for **intelligence.**

Neolithic   Literally, "New Stone Age," now seen as the period characterized by domestication of plants and animals.

neutron activation analysis   A procedure that reveals the chemical signature of a raw material. Samples of a specific raw material (for example, turquoise, obsidian, or clay) from a series of different geographic sources are irradiated with neutrons. Different elemental constituents in each sample then emit radiation at levels unique to each element, producing a signature for each source. When artifacts are analyzed in the same way, they can be associated with the source from which the raw material originated.

niche   The ecological address of an organism; the actual space inhabited by the organism as well as the organism's functional place in a community of organisms—where it lives as well as what it does to make a living.

nocturnal   Active at night.

notochord   A long cartilaginous rod that supports the body and protects the dorsal nerve. The evolutionary precursor of the vertebral column.

nuclear DNA   The genetic material contained in the nucleus of a cell. See **deoxyribonucleic acid.**

nuclear family   The family unit made up of parents and their offspring.

occipital   The bone of the rear of the skull. The occiput tends to be rounded and smooth in anatomically modern human beings and angled and rough in nonmodern hominids.

Oldowan   The tool technology associated with *Homo habilis* approximately 2.5 mya. Sharp-edged flakes were produced by striking a stone core.

Olmec   Dating to after about 3200 B.P. in Mesoamerica, the Olmec people produced a number of large ceremonial centers with great earthworks, finely carved jade sculptures, and massive basalt carvings of human heads. The religious iconography of Olmec art seems to have served as a unifying element in ancient Mesoamerica.

opportunistic foragers   Hunter-gatherers whose highly flexible subsistence system allows them to exploit whatever resources become available in their area, whenever they become available.

opposability   The ability of the thumb to touch (oppose) the tips of the other digits on the same hand.

oscillating selection   Adaptive variation around a norm, rather than in one direction, in response to environmental variation in a species' habitat.

osteologist   A scientist who studies bones, either human or animal.

Out-of-Africa model   Another name for the **Recent African Origin model.**

paleoanthropologist   A **biological anthropologist** specializing in the study of human fossil remains.

paleoclimatologist   A specialist in ancient climatic conditions.

paleoethnography   The process of performing an **ethnography** of an archaeological culture; studying a people by excavating their material remains and attempting to reconstruct their lifestyle based on these remains.

paleofeces   See **coprolites.**

Paleo-Indian   New World cultures, based on big-game hunting and characterized by fluted points, present from about 12,000 to 10,000 ya.

paleopathology   The study of disease and nutritional deficiency in prehistoric populations, usually with reference to the study of their skeletons.

palynology   The identification of plants through the remains of their pollen grains.

Pangea   The supercontinent that included parts of all present-day landmasses, which began to break up about 138 mya.

paradigm   An overarching perspective, approach, or view.

parent material   The term used to indicate the source material of a particular soil. The parent material is often local bedrock that, through various processes of erosion, becomes soil.

particulate   In the study of heredity, the idea that traits are controlled separately by individual particles rather than all together by a single agent. The genetic theory of heredity.

patrilocal   A type of society in which a married couple lives with the husband's family.

pebble tool   A chipped stone tool made from a pebble or cobble. **Flakes** are struck off the pebble to produce a sharp-edged tool.

Peiligang   The earliest **Neolithic** culture in north China with well-established farming villages dated to 8,500 to

7,000 ya. Cultigens included foxtail millet, broomcorn millet, and Chinese cabbage, but not rice. Domesticated animals include pig, dog, and chicken.

petrographic analysis Examination of the morphology of a lithic source by the analysis of thin slices of rock. Can be used to determine the source of raw materials used by past people.

phenetic taxonomy A classification system based on existing phenotypic features and adaptations. Compare with **cladistics.**

phenotype Any physical or chemical trait that can be observed or measured. The expression of the genetic code. Compare with **genotype.**

physical anthropology The branch of **anthropology** that focuses on humans as a biological species.

phytolith Microscopic, inorganic particles produced by plants. Phytoliths are extremely durable and species-specific. Enormous databases have been compiled allowing researchers to identify the species from which the phytoliths originated.

plate tectonics The movement of the plates of the earth, caused by their interaction with the molten rock of the earth's interior. The cause of continental drifting.

Pleistocene The geological time period, from about 1.6 mya to 10,000 ya, characterized by a series of glacial advances and retreats.

Pliocene The geological time period dated from 5 million to 1.6 million ya, during which the first **hominids** appeared in Africa.

point mutation The **mutation** of a single letter in a **codon.**

polygenic A trait coded for by more than one gene.

polymorphism A trait showing variation within a **species** that is the result of genetic variation.

population Any reproductive unit within a species; may be the species itself.

postmarital residence pattern Where a new couple lives after they marry.

postnatal dependency The period after birth when a young animal is dependent on adults for survival, which is relatively long among humans.

postorbital constriction A narrowing of the skull behind the eyes, as viewed from above.

potassium/argon dating See **K/Ar dating.**

prehensile Grasping, with particular reference to the hands and feet of primates. The tails of a few New World monkeys are also prehensile.

primate A large-brained, **arboreal** mammal with **stereoscopic vision** and grasping hands and (often) feet.

primatologist An anthropologist who studies **primates.**

prognathism A protrusion of the lower portion of the face.

progressive The now-rejected idea that evolution is always producing organisms that are better by current cultural standards.

projectile point A pointed tool or weapon—generally a stone, bone, or antler tip hafted onto a shaft, often of wood—which is thrown or shot at a target, usually a hunted animal. Includes spear points and arrowheads.

prosimian A member of the group of **primates** with the most primitive features, that is, that most resemble the earliest primates.

protein One of a family of molecules that are the main constituent of cells and that carry out cellular functions. Compare with **amino acid.**

protein synthesis The process by which the genetic code puts together **proteins** in the cell.

proton magnetometry A noninvasive technique used in archaeological prospecting in which a proton magnetometer measures the strength of the earth's magnetic field at the surface. Variations in that magnetic field may signal the location of buried remains including walls and foundations.

provenience The precise, measured location of archaeological artifacts.

pubic symphysis Articulation between the two halves of the pelvis at the pubis.

punctuated equilibrium The evolutionary theory that species remain stable for most of their history and that new species arise fairly suddenly as the result of mutations. Compare with **gradualism.**

quadrupedal Having the ability to walk on four legs.

rachis The area of attachment between seeds and other seeds or between seeds and other parts of a plant. A brittle rachis is an adaptive advantage in nature but selected against by humans in **artificial selection.**

radioactive isotope An unstable form of an element that decays to a stable form, the rate of which can be used to date archaeological evidence.

radiocarbon dating   A **radiometric dating** technique using the decay rate of a **radioactive isotope** of carbon found in organic remains.

radiometric dating   A chronometric dating technique that uses the known rate of decay of radioactive elements found in the item to be dated.

random sample   Randomly selected points within a research area tested for the presence of archaeological material. The goal is to obtain a **representative sample** of sites in a region.

rank society   A nonegalitarian society with a few sociopolitical levels filled by a relatively small number of people.

Recent African Origin (RAO) model   The hypothesis that *Homo sapiens* recently evolved as a separate species in Africa and then spread to replace more archaic populations. Compare with **Multiregional Evolution model.**

recessive   Of an **allele** pair, the one that is not expressed when combined in the heterozygous state with a dominant allele. Compare with **dominant.**

recombination   The exchange of genetic material between pairs of chromosomes during meiosis. An important source of genetic variation.

relative chronological sequence   A sequence of sites, events, or artifacts arranged in the relationship of older to younger. See **absolute dating.**

remote sensing   Procedures in archaeological site survey in which sites are searched for and examined, once discovered, through noninvasive techniques, that is, without moving any soil.

replication   In experimental **archaeology,** facsimiles of archaeological specimens are produced and used in order to analyze how ancient people manufactured and utilized their **artifacts** and **features.** Also, in genetics, the copying of the genetic code during the process of cell division.

repoussé   A method of decorating thin metal, including gold, in which the pattern is beaten up from the underside.

representative sample   A small sample of a large population in which the characteristics of the sample (ages, sizes, activities, functions, etc.) proportionally match those found in the overall population.

sagittal crest   A ridge of bone running front to back along the top of the skull for the attachment of major chewing muscles. Typical of gorillas.

sagittal keel   A sloping of the sides of the skull toward the top, as viewed from the front.

Sahul   The landmass of **Greater Australia** including Australia proper, New Guinea, and Tasmania, formed during periods of glacial maxima in the **Pleistocene.**

Samarran   A **Neolithic** culture of southern Mesopotamia. Samarran sites are located on the floodplain of the Tigris and Euphrates Rivers and date to less than 7,500 ya. There is evidence of communal works, including irrigation canals, fortification walls, and communal grain storage structures.

savanna   A tropical grassland with trees scattered throughout. It is probably on the savanna that the **hominid** adaptation of **bipedal** locomotion first became adaptively significant.

science   The method of inquiry that attempts to explain phenomena through observation and the development and testing of hypotheses.

scientific creationism   The belief that scientific evidence exists supporting the religious claim that the universe is the product of divine creation.

scientific method   The process by which phenomena are explained through observation and the development and testing of **hypotheses.**

sedentary   A settlement pattern in which people largely stay in one place or settlement year-round, although some members of the population may still be mobile in the search for food and raw materials.

segregation   The breaking up of **allele** pairs during the production of gametes.

seriation   A process of establishing a **relative chronological sequence** based on the statistical pattern of replacement of styles of a type of artifact.

settlement pattern   The distribution of archaeological sites and the analysis of their functions in relation to one another and to features of the environment.

sexual dimorphism   The differential physical appearance of the sexes of a species.

sexual selection   The form of selection in which mating partners are actively, rather than randomly, chosen by individuals within a population based on such things as appearance, presence of a nest site, and successful competition with other potential mates.

shared, derived characteristics   A trait shared by two species or groups of species that is not found in other groups, resulting from descent from a common ancestor.

Shell Mound Archaic   A post-Pleistocene adaptation in the American Southeast in which freshwater shell fish were exploited by large and dense human populations that constructed large ceremonial mounds primarily out of shells.

site   Any place that contains evidence of a past human presence.

social stratification   The presence of acknowledged differences in social status, political influence, and wealth among the people within a society.

Solutrean   An Upper **Paleolithic** culture of France and Spain, dating from 21,000 to 16,000 ya, that included the manufacture of finely made, leaf-shaped, bifacial spear points.

sounding   A test excavation. Usually a small pit or column dug to expose stratigraphic layers and to search for archaeological material. Another name for **test pit.**

spatial context   The location and associations of an **artifact, ecofact,** or **feature.** Precisely where and with what something is found can provide information concerning how the object was made, used, or discarded.

speciation   The evolution of new **species** from existing species.

species   A group of organisms that can produce fertile offspring among themselves but not with any other group. A closed genetic population, usually physically distinguishable from other populations and with a unique **gene pool.**

stadial   A short-term period of extreme cold and rapid glacial advance during a longer-term period of general, slow glacial expansion or retreat.

starch grains   Small fragments of starch produced by plants. Because starch grain shapes are unique to individual plant species, when they are preserved on tools used to process plants, they can be recovered and used to identify plant species.

state   Class societies, often rigidly stratified into social levels, with a ruling class controlling the populace not by consensus but by coercion and force. The rulers in a state society have the power to levy and collect taxes, to establish and enforce laws, and to conscript people to do the work of the state.

stereoscopic vision   The ability to see in three dimensions; depth perception.

strata (singular, *stratum*)   Layers; here, distinct and distinguishable layers of rock and soil.

stratigraphy   The arrangement of rocks and soil in layers.

Sunda   The combined landmass of the modern islands of Java, Sumatra, Bali, and Borneo plus Southeast Asia, which joined during periods of glacial maxima and attendant lowered sea level during the **Pleistocene.**

suture   The line of contact between the bones that make up the skull, analysis of which can be used to provide an estimate for the age at death of an individual.

symbiosis   A close, prolonged relationship between two or more different organisms of different species that may be, but is not necessarily, beneficial to members of the different species.

taphonomy   The analysis of how animal and plant remains become part of the archaeological or paleontological record.

taxon   A category within a taxonomic classification; plural, *taxa.* See **taxonomy.**

taxonomy   A systematic classification based on similarities and differences among the things being classified.

teosinte   Called "God's corn" by the Aztecs, the plant that is the wild ancestor of domesticated maize.

testa   A seed coat. The protective wrapping around the part of the seed that sprouts.

test boring   A small excavation to establish the presence of an archaeological site, often a narrow column of soil extracted by the use of a hollow metal tube.

test pit   See **sounding.**

theory   A **hypothesis** that has been tested repeatedly and has been well supported by evidence and experimental testing is elevated to the status of theory.

toolkit   A group of tools often found in spatial association at an archaeological site that was used together to form a particular task.

torus   A continuous ridge of bone.

trace element analysis   A process in which the geographic source of a raw material can be determined through the analysis of small or trace amounts of impurities.

transect   A line of systematically located test pits.

transfer ribonucleic acid (tRNA)   The form of ribonucleic acid that lines up **amino acids** in their proper sequence along the **messenger RNA** to make **proteins.**

trephining   Cutting a hole in the skull of a living person, usually for medical purposes.

tribe   A grouping of people organized largely by kinship. There is no central ruler, but individuals may obtain prestige and a degree of authority through their achievements.

uniformitarianism   The concept that biological and geological processes that affected the earth in the past are still in operation today, and vice-versa. Compare with **catastrophist.**

unilinear   The now-discredited notion that all cultures pass through the same sequence of change. Compare with **multilinear.**

Upper Paleolithic   Term used for the final phase of the Paleolithic in Europe, dating to between 40,000 and 10,000 ya, associated with the first appearance of anatomically modern humans in Europe.

Upper Pleistocene   The final phase of the **Pleistocene** from 200,000 to 10,000 ya.

uranium series   Dating technique based on calibration of the decay of uranium isotopes to their various "daughter" isotopes and elements, including thorium and protactinium.

Venus figurines   Carved figures in stone, ivory, antler, and clay that depict women, often, but not always, with exaggerated secondary sexual characteristics. Among the first sculptures produced by humanity, the oldest date to 32,000 ya.

Wallace Trench   A sea chasm more than 7,500 meters (more than 4.5 miles) deep, separating Java and Borneo from **Greater Australia** (Australia, New Guinea, and Tasmania).

wear pattern   The mark left on stone tools as a result of their use. Such marks include polishing, striations, chipping, and scarring. Analysis of wear patterns can provide information concerning how and on what raw material a tool was used.

wedge-shaped cores   Cores shaped like wedges from which blades are struck, found in sites in Siberia dating to after 20,000 ya and as part of the **Denali Complex** in the American Arctic.

Yang-shao   The early **Neolithic** culture of China, dated to about 8,000 ya.

ziggurat   An enormous mud-brick structure built in the form of a rectangular platform with stairs leading to the top. Monumental structures of the early Mesopotamians.

zygote   A fertilized egg before cell division begins.

BIBLIOGRAPHY

Abbate, E. et al. 1998. One-million-year-old *Homo* cranium from the Danakil (Afar) Depression of Eritrea. *Nature* 393: 458–60.

Ackerman, J. 1998. Dinosaurs take wing. *National Geographic* 194(7): 74–99.

Adams, R. E. W. 1991. *Prehistoric Mesoamerica.* Norman: University of Oklahoma Press.

Adams, R. McC., and H. Nissen. 1972. *The Uruk Countryside.* Chicago: University of Chicago Press.

Adovasio, J., O. Soffer, and B. Kilma. 1996. Upper Paleolithic fibre technology: Interlaced woven finds from Pavlov I, Czech Republic, c. 26,000 years ago. *Antiquity* 70: 269.

Adovasio, J. M., J. Donahue, and R. Stuckenrath. 1990. The Meadowcroft rockshelter radiocarbon chronology—1975–1990. *American Antiquity* 55: 348–53.

Agnew, N., and M. Demas. 1998. Preserving the Laetoli footprints. *Scientific American* 279(3): 44–55.

Aiello, L., and C. Dean. 1990. *An Introduction to Human Evolutionary Anatomy.* New York: Academic Press.

Alexander, R. McN. 1995. Standing, walking and running. In *Gray's Anatomy,* 38th ed. New York: Churchill Livingston.

Allchin, B., and R. Allchin. 1982. *The Rise of Civilization in India and Pakistan.* Cambridge, Eng.: Cambridge University Press.

Allsworth-Jones, P. 1990. The Szeletian and the stratigraphic succession in central Europe and adjacent areas: Main trends, recent results and problems for resolution. In *The Emergence of Modern Humans: An Archaeological Perspective,* ed. P. Mellars, pp. 160–242. Ithaca, NY: Cornell University Press.

Alva, W., and C. B. Donnan. 1993. *Royal Tombs of Sipán.* Los Angeles: Fowler Museum of Culture History.

———. 1994. Tales from a Peruvian crypt. *Natural History* 103(5): 26–34.

Ambrose, S. H. 1998. Late Pleistocene human population bottlenecks, volcanic winter, and differentiation of modern humans. *Journal of Human Evolution* 34: 623–51.

Anderson, E. 1952. *Plants, Life and Man.* Boston: Little, Brown.

———. 1956. Man as a maker of new plants and new plant communities. In *Man's Role in Changing the Face of the Earth,* Vol. 2, ed. W. L. Thomas, Jr., pp. 767–77. Chicago: University of Chicago Press.

Appleman, P. (ed.). 1979. *Darwin,* 2nd ed. New York: Norton.

Ardrey, R. 1961. *African Genesis: A Personal Investigation into the Animal Origins and Nature of Man.* New York: Dell.

Arensburg, B., L. A. Schepartz, A. M. Tiller, B. Vandermeersch, and Y. Rak. 1990. A reappraisal of the anatomical basis for speech in Middle Paleolithic hominids. *American Journal of Physical Anthropology* 83: 137–46.

Arsuaga, J.-L., I. Martinez, A. Garcia, J.-M. Carretero, and E. Carbonell. 1993. Three new human skulls from the Sima de los Huesos Middle Pleistocene site in Sierra de Atapuerca, Spain. *Nature* 362: 534–37.

Asfaw, B., W. H. Gilbert, Y. Beyene, W. K. Hart, P. R. Renne, G. WoldeGabriel, E. S. Vrba, and T. D. White. 2002. Remains of *Homo erectus* from Bouri, Middle Awash, Ethiopia. *Nature* 416: 317–20.

Asfaw, B., T. White, O. Lovejoy, B. Latimer, S. Simpson, and G. Suwa. 1999. *Australopithecus garhi:* A new species of early hominid from Ethiopia. *Science* 284: 629–35.

Asimov, I. 1969. *Asimov's Guide to the Bible.* New York: Avenel Books.

Attenborough, D. 1979. *Life on Earth.* Boston: Little, Brown.

Awadalla, P., A. Eyre-Walker, and J. M. Smith. 1999. Linkage disequilibrium and recombination in hominid mitochondrial DNA. *Science* 286: 2524–25.

Bahn, P. G. 1994. *Homo erectus* in Europe. *Archaeology* 47(6): 25.

———. 1996. Treasure of the Sierra Atapuerca. *Archaeology* 49(1): 45–48.

———. 1998. Neanderthals emancipated. *Nature* 394: 719–21.

Bahn, P. G., and J. Vertut. 1988. *Images of the Ice Age.* London: Smith and Son.

Bailey, G. N. 1978. Shell middens as indicators of postglacial economies: A territorial perspective. In *The Early Postglacial Settlement of Northern Europe: An Ecological Perspective,* ed. P. Mellars, pp. 37–63. Pittsburgh: University of Pittsburgh Press.

Balter, M. 1998. Why settle down? The mystery of communities. *Science* 282: 1442–45.

———. 1999. New light on the oldest art. *Science News* 283: 920–22.

———. 2000. Paintings in Italian cave may be oldest yet. *Science* 290: 419–21.

———. 2001a. Anthropologists duel over modern human origins. *Science* 291: 1728–29.

———. 2001b. Stone age artists—or art lovers—unmasked. *Science* 294: 31.

———. 2004. Skeptics question whether Flores hominid is a new species. *Science* 306: 1116.

———. 2005. *The Goddess and the Bull: Çatalhoyuk: An Archaeological Journey to the Dawn of Civilization.* New York: Free Press.

Balter, M., and A. Gibbons. 2000. A glimpse of humans' first journey out of Africa. *Science* 288: 948–50.

———. 2002. Were "little people" the first to venture out of Africa? *Science* 297: 26–27.

Barber, E. W. 1999. *The Mummies of Ürümchi.* New York: Norton.

Barbetti, M., and H. Allen. 1972. Prehistoric man at Lake Mungo, Australia, by 32,000 years B.P. *Nature* 240: 46–48.

Barinaga, M. 1992. "African Eve" backers beat a retreat. *Science* 255: 686–87.

Bartsiokas, A., and M. H. Day. 1993. Lead poisoning and dental caries in the Broken Hill hominid. *Journal of Human Evolution* 24: 243–49.

Bartstra, G. J., S. Soegondho, and A. V. D. Wijk. 1988. Ngandong man: Age and artifacts. *Journal of Human Evolution* 17: 325–37.

Bar-Yosef, O. 1998. The Natufian culture of the Levant, threshold to the origins of agriculture. *Evolutionary Anthropology* 7: 159–77.

Bass, W. 1971. *Human Osteology: A Laboratory and Field Manual of the Human Skeleton.* Columbia: Missouri Archaeological Society.

Beadle, G. 1977. The Origin of *Zea mays.* In *Origins of Agriculture,* ed. C. A. Reed, pp. 615–36. The Hague: Mouton.

Beaumont, P., H. deVilliers, and J. C. Vogel. 1978. Modern man in sub-Saharan Africa prior to 49,000 years B.P.: A review and evaluation with particular reference to Border Cave. *South African Journal of Science* 74: 409–19.

Begley, S., and F. Gleizes. 1989. My grandad, Neandertal? *Newsweek,* October 16, pp. 70–71.

Begun, D. R. 2000. Knuckle-walking and the origin of human bipedalism. Paper delivered at the 69th annual meeting of the American Association of Physical Anthropologists. San Antonio.

———. 2003. Planet of the apes. *Scientific American* 289(2): 74–83.

Beja-Pereira, A. etal. 2004. African origins of the domestic donkey. *Science* 304: 1781.

Belfer-Cohen, A., and N. Goren-Inbar. 1994. Cognition and communication in the Levantine Lower paleolithic. *World Archaeology* 26: 144–57.

Belfer-Cohen, A., and E. Hovers. 1992. In the eye of the beholder: Mousterian and Natufian burials in the Levant. *Current Anthropology* 33: 463–71.

Benefit, B. R. 1999. *Victoriapithecus:* The key to Old World monkey and catarrhine origins. *Evolutionary Anthropology* 7(6): 155–74.

Ben-Itzhak, S., P. Smith, and R. A. Bloom. 1988. Radiographic study of the humerus in Neandertals and *Homo sapiens sapiens. American Journal of Physical Anthropology* 77: 231–42.

Berger, L. 1998. Redrawing our family tree? *National Geographic* 194(2): 90–99.

Berger, T. D., and E. Trinkaus. 1995. Patterns of trauma among the Neandertals. *Journal of Archaeological Science* 22: 841–52.

Bermúdez de Castro, J. M., J. L. Arsuaga, E. Carboneli, A. Rosas, I. Martinez, and M. Mosquera. 1997. A hominid from the Lower Pleistocene of Atapuerca, Spain: Possible ancestor to Neandertals and modern humans. *Science* 276: 1392–95.

Berreman, G. D. 1991. The incredible "Tasaday": Deconstructing the myth of a "stone-age" people. *Cultural Survival Quarterly* 51(1): 3–45.

Biegert, J. 1963. The evaluation of characteristics of the skull, hands, and feet for primate taxonomy. In *Classification and Human Evolution,* ed. S. L. Washburn, pp. 116–45. Chicago: Aldine.

Binford, L. 1968. Post-Pleistocene adaptations. In *New Perspectives in Archaeology,* eds. L Binford and S. Binford, pp. 313–41. Chicago: Aldine.

———. 1978. *Nunamiut Ethnoarchaeology.* New York: Academic Press.

———. 1981. *Bones: Ancient Men and Modern Myths.* New York: Academic Press.

———. 1985. Ancestral life ways: The faunal record. *Anthroquest* 32: 1, 15–20.

Binford, L., and S. Binford. 1966. A preliminary analysis of functional variability in the Mousterian of Levallois facies. *American Anthropologist* 68: 239–95.

Binford, L., and K. Chuan. 1985. Taphonomy at a distance: Zhoukoudian, "The Cave Home of Beijing Man." *Current Anthropology* 26: 413–43.

Binford, L., and N. M. Stone. 1986. Zhoukoudian: A closer look. *Current Anthropology* 27: 453–76.

Binford, S. 1968. Variability and change in the Near Eastern Mousterian of Levallois facies. In *New Perspectives in Archaeology,* eds. L. Binford and S. Binford, pp. 49–60. Chicago: Aldine.

Birdsell, J. H. 1977. The recalibration of a paradigm for the first peopling of Greater Australia. In *Sunda and Sahul: Prehistoric Studies in Southeast Asia, Melanesia, and Australia,* eds. J. Allen, J. Golson, and R. Jones, pp. 113–67. New York: Academic Press.

Bischoff, J. L., N. Soler, J. Maroto, and R. Julià. 1989. Abrupt Mousterian/Aurignacian boundary at c. 40 ka B.P.: Accelerator ^{14}C dates from l'Arbreda Cave (Catalunya, Spain). *Journal of Archaeological Science* 16: 563–76.

Blinderman, C. 1986. *The Piltdown Inquest.* Buffalo: Prometheus Books.

Bloch, J. I., and D. M. Boyer. 2002. Grasping primate origins. *Science* 298: 1606–9.

Blumenschine, R. J. et al. 2003. Late Pliocene *Homo* and hominid land use from Western Olduvai Gorge, Tanzania. *Science* 299: 1217–21.

Boaz, N. T., and R. L. Ciochon. 2001. The scavenging of "Peking Man." *Natural History* 110(2): 46–51.

Boëda, E., J. Connan, D. Dessort, S. Muhesen, N. Mercier, H. Valladas, and N. Tisnérat. 1996. Bitumen as a hafting material on Middle Paleolithic artefacts. *Nature* 380: 336–38.

Boëda, E., J. M. Geneste, C. Griggo, N. Mercier, S. Muhesen, J. L. Reyss, A. Taha, and H. Valladas. 1999. A Levallois point embedded in the vertebra of a wild ass *(Equus africanus):* Hafting projectiles and Mousterian hunting weapons. *Antiquity* 73: 394–402.

Boesch, C. 1999. A theory that's hard to digest. *Nature* 399: 653.

Bonnichsen, R., and K. L. Turnmire. (eds.). 1991. *Clovis: Origins and Adaptations.* Corvallis, OR: Center for the Study of the First Americans.

Bordes, F. 1972. *A Tale of Two Caves.* New York: Harper & Row.

Boserup, E. 1965. *The Conditions of Agricultural Growth: The Economics of Agrarian Change Under Population Pressure.* Chicago: Aldine.

Boucher de Perthes, J. 1847. *Celtic and Antediluvian Antiquities.* Paris.

Boule, M., and H. V. Vallois. 1923. *Fossil Men.* 1957 ed. New York: Dryden Press.

Bouyssonie, A., J. Bouyssonie, and L. Bardon. 1908. Découverte d'un squelette humain mousterien à la Bouffia de la Chapelles-aux-Saints (Correze). *L'Anthropologie* 19: 513–18.

Bowdler, S. 1977. The coastal colonisation of Australia. In *Sunda and Sahul: Prehistoric Studies in Southeast Asia, Melanesia, and Australia,* eds. J. Allen, J. Golson, and R. Jones, pp. 205–46. New York: Academic Press.

———. 1990. Peopling Australasia: The "Coastal Colonization" hypothesis re-examined. In *The Emergence of Modern Humans: An Archaeological Perspective,* ed. P. Mellars, pp. 327–43. Ithaca, NY: Cornell University Press.

Bowen, D. Q. 1979. Quarternary correlations. *Nature* 277: 171–72.

Bower, B. 1987a. Stone Age site gets pushed back in time. *Science News* 132: 199.

———. 1987b. Uncovering life by an ancient lake. *Science News* 131: 264.

———. 1989a. Ritual clues flow from prehistoric blood. *Science News* 136: 405.

———. 1989b. Stone blades yield early cultivation clues. *Science News* 135: 101.

———. 1989c. Talk of ages. *Science News* 136: 24–26.

———. 1990. Civilization and its discontents. *Science News* 137: 136–39.

———. 1995a. Fossil hints at hominids' European stall. *Science News* 147: 85.

———. 1995b. Human genetic origins go nuclear. *Science News* 148: 52.

————. 1996. Visions on the rocks. *Science News* 150: 216–17.

————. 1999a. Fossil may expose humanity's hybrid roots. *Science News* 155: 295.

————. 1999b. Neandertal hunters get to the point. *Science News* 156.

————. 1999c. Neandertals show staying power in Europe. *Science News* 156: 277.

————. 2000. Neandertals' diet put meat on their bones. *Science News* 157: 389.

Bowlby, J. 1990. *Charles Darwin: A New Life.* New York: Norton.

Bowler, J. M., and J. Magee. 2000. Redating Australia's oldest human remains: A skeptics view. *Journal of Human Evolution* 38: 719–26.

Brace, C. L. 2005. *"Race" Is a Four-Letter Word: The Genesis of the Concept.* New York: Oxford University Press.

Bradley, D. G., R. T. Loftus, P. Cunningham, and D. E. MacHugh. 1998. Genetics and domestic cattle origins. *Evolutionary Anthropology* 7: 79–86.

Bradley, R. S. 1985. *Quarternary Paleoclimatology: Methods of Paleoclimatological Reconstruction.* Boston: Allen and Unwin.

Braidwood, R. 1960. The agricultural revolution. *Scientific American* 203(3): 130–48.

————. 1975. *Prehistoric Men.* Glenview, IL: Scott, Foresman.

Bräuer, G. 1984. A craniological approach to the origin of anatomically modern *Homo sapiens.* In *The Origins of Modern Humans: A World Survey of the Fossil Evidence,* eds. F. H. Smith and F. Spencer, pp. 327–410. New York: Liss.

Bräuer, G., H. J. Deacon, and F. Zipfel. 1992. Comments on the new maxillary finds from Klasies River Mouth, South Africa. *Journal of Human Evolution* 23: 419–22.

Bräuer, G., and C. Stringer. 1997. Models, polarization, and perspectives on modern human origins. In *Conceptual Issues in Modern Human Origins Research,* ed. G. A. Clark and C. M. Willermet. New York: Aldine de Gruyter.

Bräuer, G., Y. Yokoyama, C. Falguères, and E. Mbua. 1997. Modern human origins backdated. *Nature* 386: 337.

Breuil, H. 1952. *Four Hundred Centuries of Cave Art.* Montignac, France: Centre D'études et de Documentation Prehistorique.

Brice, W. R. 1982. Bishop Ussher, John Lightfoot, and the age of creation. *Journal of Geological Education* 30: 18–24.

Bridges, P. S. 1995. Skeletal biology and behavior of ancient humans. *Evolutionary Anthropology* 4(4): 112–20.

Brown, F., J. Harris, R. Leakey, and A. Walker. 1985. Early *Homo erectus* skeleton from West Lake Turkana. *Nature* 316: 788–92.

Brown, K. 2001. New trips through the back alleys of agriculture. *Science* 292: 631–33.

Brown, P. 2000. The first Australians: The debate continues. *Australasian Science* (May): 28–31.

Brown, P. et al. 2004. A new small-bodied hominin from the Late Pleistocene of Flores, Indonesia. *Nature* 431: 1055–61.

Bruhns, K. O. 1994. *Ancient South America.* Cambridge, Eng.: Cambridge University Press.

Brunet M. 2002. Reply to Wolpoff et al. 2002. *Nature* 419: 582.

Brunet M. et al. 2002. A new hominid from the Upper Miocene of Chad, Central Africa. *Nature* 418: 145–55.

Buffon, G. 1749. *Histoire Naturelle.* Paris: De l'Imprimerie Royale.

————. 1778. *Epochs of Nature.* Paris: De l'Imprimerie Royale.

Burger, R. L. 1988. Unity and heterogeneity within the Chavin Horizon. In *Peruvian Prehistory,* ed. R. W. Keating, pp. 99–144. Cambridge, Eng.: Cambridge University Press.

————. 1992. *Chavin and the Origins of Andean Civilization.* New York: Thames and Hudson.

Burns, James A. 1990. Paleontological perspectives on the ice-free corridor. In *Megafauna and Man: Discovery of America's Heartland,* eds. L. D. Agenbroad, J. I. Mead, and L. W. Nelson, pp. 61–66. Hot Springs, SD: The Mammoth Site of Hot Springs and Northern Arizona University.

Buttrick, G. A. (ed.). 1952. *Interpreter's Bible.* New York: Abingdon Press.

Butzer, K. 1971. *Environmental Archaeology: An Ecological Approach to Prehistory.* New York: Aldine-Atherton.

————. 1982. *Archaeology as Human Ecology.* Cambridge, Eng.: Cambridge University Press.

Byrne, R. W., and J. M. Byrne. 1988. Leopard killers of Mahale. *Natural History* 97(3): 22–26.

Callen, E. O. 1967. Analysis of the Tehuacán coprolites. In *The Prehistory of the Tehuacán Valley: Vol. 1:* Environment and Subsistence, ed. D. Byers, pp. 261–89. Austin: University of Texas Press.

Cann, R. L., M. Stoneking, and A. C. Wilson. 1987. Mitochondrial DNA and human evolution. *Nature* 325: 31–36.

Carbonell, E., J. M. B. de Castro, J. L. Arsuaga, J. C. Díaz, A. Rosas, G. Cuenca-Bescós, R. Sala, M. Mosquera, and X. P. Rodriguez. 1995. Lower Pleistocene hominids and artifacts from Atapuerca-TD6 (Spain). *Science* 269: 826–30.

Carneiro, R. 1970. A theory of the origin of the state. *Science* 169: 733–38.

Carr, K. W., J. M. Adovasio, and D. R. Pedler. 1996. Paleoindian populations in trans-Appalachia: The view from Pennsylvania. Paper presented at the Integrating Appalachian Archaeology Conference. New York State Museum, Albany.

Cartmill, M. 1992. New views on primate origins. *Evolutionary Anthropology* 1(3): 105–11.

———. 1993. *A View to a Death in the Morning: Hunting and Nature Through History.* Cambridge, MA: Harvard University Press.

———. 1997. The third man. *Discover* (September): 56–62.

Castleden, R. 1990. *The Knossos Labyrinth.* London: Routledge.

Cavalli-Sforza, L. L. 1991. Genes, peoples and languages. *Scientific American* 265(5): 104–10.

Cavalli-Sforza, L. L., and F. Cavalli-Sforza. 1995. *The Great Human Diasporas: The History of Diversity and Evolution.* Reading, MA: Addison-Wesley.

Cavallo, J. A. 1990. Cat in the human cradle. *Natural History* 99(2): 53–60.

Chagnon, N. 1977. *Yąnomamö: The Fierce People,* 2nd ed. New York: Holt, Rinehart & Winston.

Chagnon, N. 1997. *Yąnomamö.* 5th ed. New York: Holt, Rinehart & Winston.

Chang, K. C. 1968. *The Archaeology of Ancient China.* New Haven, CT: Yale University Press.

———. 1986. *The Archaeology of Ancient China.* 2nd ed. New Haven, CT: Yale University Press.

Chapman, J., and G. D. Crites. 1987. Evidence for early maize (*Zea mays*) from Icehouse Bottom Site, Tennessee. *American Antiquity* 52: 318–29.

Chard, C. 1974. *Northeast Asia in Prehistory.* Madison: University of Wisconsin Press.

Chase, P., and H. Dibble. 1987. Middle Paleolithic symbolism: A review of current evidence and interpretations. *Journal of Anthropological Archaeology* 6: 263–96.

Chauvet, J.-M. 1996. *Dawn of Art: The Chauvet Cave.* New York: Abrams.

Chen T., Q. Yang, and E. Wu. 1994. Antiquity of *Homo sapiens* in China. *Nature* 368: 55–56.

Chen, T., and Z. Yinyun. 1991. Paleolithic chronology and possible coexistence of *Homo erectus* and *Homo sapiens* in China. *World Archaeology* 23(2): 147–54.

Cherry, J. F. 1987. Island origins: The early prehistoric Cyclades. In *Origins: The Roots of European Civilisation,* ed. B. Cunliffe, pp. 16–29. Chicago: Dorsey Press.

Childe, V. G. 1942. *What Happened in History.* Baltimore: Pelican Books.

———. 1951. *Man Makes Himself.* New York: Mentor Books.

———. 1953. *New Light on the Most Ancient East.* New York: Norton.

Churchill, S., and E. Trinkaus. 1990. Neandertal scapular glenoid morphology. *American Journal of Physical Anthropology* 83: 147–60.

Churchill, S. E. 1998. Cold adaptation, heterochrony, and Neandertals. *Evolutionary Anthropology* 7(2): 46–61.

Cinque-Mars, J. 1978. Bluefish Cave I: A Late Pleistocene eastern Beringian cave deposit in the northern Yukon. *Canadian Journal of Anthropology* 3: 1–32.

Ciochon, R., J. Olsen, and J. James. 1990. *Other Origins: The Search for the Giant Ape in Human Prehistory.* New York: Bantam Books.

Clark, G. 1971. *Excavation at Star Carr.* Cambridge, Eng.: Cambridge University Press.

———. 1980. *Mesolithic Prelude.* Edinburgh: University of Edinburgh Press.

Clark, J. D. 1976. Prehistoric population pressures favoring plant domestication in Africa. In *Origins of African Plant Domestication,* eds. J. R. Harlan, J. M. J. De Wet, and A. B. L. Stemler, pp. 67–106. The Hague: Mouton.

Clark, J. D. et al. 2003. Stratigraphic, chronological and behavioral contexts of Pleistocene *Homo sapiens* from Middle Awash, Ethiopia. *Nature* 423: 747–52.

Clarke, D. 1978. *Analytical Archaeology.* New York: Columbia University Press.

Clarke, R. J. 2000. What the StW 573 *Australopithecus* skeleton reveals about early hominid bipedalism. Paper delivered at the 69th annual meeting of the American Association of Physical Anthropologists. San Antonio.

Clottes, J., 1995. Rhinos and lions and bears (Oh, my!). *Natural History* 104(5): 30–35.

Clottes, J., and Courtin J. 1996. *The Cave Beneath the Sea: Paleolithic Images at Cosquer.* New York: Abrams.

Clottes, J., and D. Lewis-Williams. 1998. *The Shamans of Prehistory: Trance and Magic in the Painted Caves.* New York: Abrams.

Cobo, B. 1653. *History of the Inca Empire.* 1979 ed. Austin: University of Texas Press.

Coe, M. 1968. *America's First Civilization*. New York: Van Nostrand.

Cohen, M. 1977. *The Food Crisis in Prehistory*. New Haven, CT: Yale University Press.

Collard, M., and L. C. Aiello. 2000. From forelimbs to two legs. *Nature* 404: 339–40.

Coltorti, M., M. Cremaschi, M. C. Delitala, D. Esu, M. Fornaseri, A. McPherron, M. Nicoletti, R. van Otterloo, C. Peretto, B. Sala, V. Schmidt, and J. Sevink. 1982. Reversed magnetic polarity in an early Lower Paleolithic site in central Italy. *Nature* 300: 173–76.

Conkey, M. 1978. Style and information in cultural evolution: Toward a predictive model for the Paleolithic. In *Social Archaeology: Beyond Subsistence and Dating*, eds. C. Redman, M. J. Berman, E. V. Curtin, W. T. Langhorne, N. M. Versaggi, and J. C. Wanser, pp. 61–85. New York: Academic Press.

———. 1980. The identification of prehistoric hunter-gatherer aggregation sites: The case of Altamira. *Current Anthropology* 21: 609–39.

———. 1981. A century of Paleolithic cave art. *Archaeology* 34(4): 20–28.

———. 1983. On the origins of Paleolithic art: A review and some critical thoughts. In *Mousterian Legacy*, ed. E. Trinkaus, pp. 201–27. Oxford, Eng.: British Archaeological Reports, International Series, 164.

Conklin, W. J., and M. E. Moseley. 1988. The patterns of art and power in the Early Intermediate period. In *Peruvian Prehistory*, ed. R. W. Keatinge, pp. 145–63. Cambridge, Eng.: Cambridge University Press.

Connah, G. 1987. *African Civilizations*. Cambridge, Eng.: Cambridge University Press.

Conrad, N. J. 2003. Palaeolithic ivory sculptures from southwestern Germany and the origins of figurative art. *Nature* 426: 830–32.

Conroy, G. C. 1997. *Reconstructing Human Origins: A Modern Synthesis*. New York: Norton.

Constable, G., and the Editors of Time-Life. 1973. *The Neanderthals*. New York: Time-Life Books.

Conyers, L. B. 2004. *Ground Penetrating Radar for Archaeology*. Walnut Creek, CA: AltaMira Press.

Cook, J., C. B. Stringer, A. P. Current, H. P. Schwarcz, and A. G. Wintle. 1982. A review of the chronology of the European Middle Pleistocene hominid record. *Yearbook of Physical Anthropology* 25: 19–65.

Coon, C. S. 1962. *The Origin of Races*. New York: Knopf.

Coppens, Y. 1994. East side story: The origin of humankind. *Scientific American* 270: 88–95.

Cowan, C. W., and P. J. Watson. (eds.). 1992. *The Origins of Agriculture: An International Perspective*. Washington, DC: Smithsonian Institution Press.

Cowen, R. 1995. *History of Life*. 2nd ed. Boston: Blackwell.

Crawford, G. W. 1992. Prehistoric plant domestication in East Asia. In *The Origins of Agriculture: An International Perspective*, eds. C. W. Cowan and P. J. Watson, pp. 7–38. Washington, DC: Smithsonian Institution Press.

Crawford, H. 1991. *Sumer and the Sumerians*. Cambridge, Eng.: Cambridge University Press.

Crompton, R. H., L. Y. W. Weijie, M. Günther, and R. Savage. 1998. The mechanical effectiveness of erect and "bent-hip, bent-knee" bipedal walking in *Australopithecus africanus*. *Journal of Human Evolution* 35(1): 55–74.

Crelin, E. S. 1987. *The Human Vocal Tract: Anatomy, Function, Development, and Evolution*. New York: Vantage Press.

Cronin, J. E., N. T. Boaz, C. B. Stringer, and Y. Rak. 1981. Tempo and mode in hominid evolution. *Nature* 292: 113–22.

Culotta, E. 1995. Human origins: Asian hominids grow older. *Science* 270: 1116–17.

———. 1999a. Anthropologists probe bones, stones, and molecules. *Science* 284: 1109–11.

———. 1999b. A new human ancestor? *Science* 284: 572–73.

Dahlberg, F. 1981. *Woman the Gatherer*. New Haven, CT: Yale University Press.

Dalton, R. 2005. Caveman DNA hints at map of migration. *Nature* 436: 162.

D'Altroy, T. N. 2003. *The Incas*. Oxford: Blackwell.

Darwin, C. R. 1898. *On the Origin of Species by Means of Natural Selection*. 6th ed., 1872. New York: Appleton.

Davis, R. S., and V. A. Ranov. 1999. Recent work on the Paleolithic of central Asia. *Evolutionary Anthropology* 8: 186–93.

Day, M. H. 1971. Postcranial remains of *Homo erectus* from bed IV Olduvai Gorge, Tanzania. *Nature* 232: 283–87.

———. 1986. *Guide to Fossil Man*. 4th ed. Chicago: University of Chicago Press.

Deacon, H. J., and R. Shuurman. 1992. The origins of modern people: The evidence from Klasies River. In *Continuity or Replacement: Controversies in* Homo sapiens *Evolution*, eds. G. Bräuer and F. Smith, pp. 121–30. Rotterdam: Balkema.

Deacon, J. 1999. South African rock art. *Evolutionary Anthropology* 8(2): 48–63.

Dean, M. C., C. B. Stringer, and T. G. Bromage. 1986. Age at death of the Neandertal child from Devil's Tower,

Gibraltar and the implications for students of general growth and development in Neandertals. *American Journal of Physical Anthropology* 70: 301–9.

De Bonis, L., and G. D. Koufos. 1994. Our ancestor's ancestor: *Ouranopithecus* is a Greek link in human ancestry. *Evolutionary Anthropology* 3(3): 75–83.

Deetz, J. 1965. *The Dynamics of Stylistic Change in Arikara Ceramics.* Urbana: University of Illinois Series in Anthropology, No. 4.

Defleur, A., T. White, P. Valensi, L. Slimak, and É. Crégut-Bonnoure. 1999. Neanderthal cannibalism at Moula-Guercy, Ardèche, France. *Science* 286: 128–31.

de Heinzelin, J., J. D. Clark, T. White, W. Hart, P. Renne, G. WoldeGabriel, Y. Beyene, and E. Vrba. 1999. Environment and behavior of 2.5-million-year-old Bouri hominids. *Science* 284: 625–29.

Deino, A., P. R. Renne, and C. C. Swisher III. 1998. ^{40}Ar/^{39}Ar dating in paleoanthropology and archaeology. *Evolutionary Anthropology* 6(2): 63–75.

de Lumley, H. 1969. A Paleolithic camp at Nice. *Scientific American* 220(5): 42–50.

———. 1975. Cultural evolution in France in its Paleolithic setting during the Middle Pleistocene. In *After the Australopithecines: Stratigraphy, Ecology and Culture Change in the Middle Pleistocene,* eds. K. Butzer and G. Issac, pp. 745–807. The Hague: Mouton.

Dennell, R. 1986. Needles and spear-throwers. *Natural History* 95(10): 70–78.

Derenko, M. V., T. Grzybowski, B. A. Malyarchuk, J. Czarny, D. Miscicka-Sliwka, and I. A. Zakharov. 2001. The presence of mitochondrial haplogroup X in Altaians from south Siberia. *American Journal of Human Genetics* 69: 237–41.

Dethlefsen, E., and J. Deetz. 1966. Death's heads, cherubs, and willow trees: Experimental archaeology in colonial cemeteries. *American Antiquity* 31: 502–10.

Dettwyler, K. A. 1991. Can paleopathology provide evidence for "compassion"? *American Journal of Physical Anthropology* 84: 375–84.

de Waal, F., and F. Lanting (photographer). 1997. *Bonobo: The Forgotten Ape.* Berkeley: University of California Press.

Diamond, J. 1987. The worst mistake in the history of the human race. *Discover* 8(5): 64–66.

———. 1989. The great leap forward. *Discover* 10(5): 50–60.

———. 2005. *Collapse: How Societies Choose to Fail or Succeed.* New York: Penguin.

Dibble, H. 1987. The interpretation of Middle Paleolithic scraper morphology. *American Antiquity* 52: 108–18.

Dickson, D. B. 1990. *The Dawn of Belief: Religion in the Upper Paleolithic of Southwestern Europe.* Tucson: University of Arizona Press.

Diehl, R. A. 2004. *The Olmecs: America's First Civilization.* London: Thames and Hudson.

Dikov, N. N. 1978. Ancestors of Paleoindians and proto-Eskimo-Aleuts in the Paleolithic of Kamchatka. In *Early Man in America from a Circum-Pacific Perspective,* ed. A. L. Bryan, pp. 68–69. Edmonton, Canada: Archaeological Researches International.

Dillehay, T. D. 1989. *Monte Verde: A Late Pleistocene Settlement in Chile, Vol. 1: Paleoenvironment and Site Context.* Washington, DC: Smithsonian Institution Press.

———. 1997a. The battle of Monte Verde. *The Sciences* (January/February): 28–33.

———. 1997b. *Monte Verde: A Late Pleistocene Settlement, Vol. 2: The Archaeological Context and Interpretation.* Washington, DC: Smithsonian Institution Press.

———. 1999. The Late Pleistocene cultures of South America. *Evolutionary Anthropology* 7(6): 206–16.

———. 2000. *The Settlement of the Americas: A New Prehistory.* New York: Basic Books.

Dillehay, T. D., M. Pino, J. Rosen, C. Ocampo, P. Riva, D. Pollack, and G. Henderson. 1999. Reply to Fiedel, Part 1. *Discovering Archaeology* 1(6): 12–14.

Dixon, E. J. 1993. *Quest for the Origins of the First Americans.* Albuquerque: University of New Mexico Press.

———. 1999. *Bones, Boats, and Bison: Archaeology and the First Colonization of Western North America.* Albuquerque: University of New Mexico Press.

Dolhinow, P., and A. Fuentes (eds.). 1999. *The Nonhuman Primates.* Mountain View, CA: Mayfield.

Donnelly, P., S. Tavaré, D. J. Balding, and R. C. Griffiths. 1996. Technical comments: Estimating the age of the common ancestor of men from the ZFY intron. *Science* 272: 1357–58.

Doyle, A. C. 1981. *The Celebrated Cases of Sherlock Holmes.* London: Octopus Books.

Duarte, C., J. Mauricio, P. B. Pettiee, P. Souto, E. Trinkaus, H. Van der Plicht, and J. Zilhão. 1999. The early Upper Paleolithic human skeleton from the Abrigo od Lagar Velho (Portugal) and modern emergence in Iberia. *Proceedings of the National Academy of Sciences* 96: 7604–9.

Dunham, I., N. Shimizu, B. A. Roe, S. Chissoe, et al. 1999. The DNA sequence of human chromosome 22. *Nature* 402(December 2): 489–95.

Eldredge, N., and S. J. Gould. 1972. Punctuated equilibria: An alternative to phyletic gradualism. In *Models in Paleobiology,* ed. T. S. Schopf, pp. 82–115. San Francisco: Freeman, Cooper.

Elias, S., S. K. Short, C. H. Nelson, and H. H. Birks. 1996. Life and times of the Bering Land Bridge. *Nature* 382: 60–63.

Engels, F. 1942. *The Origin of the Family, Private Property and the State.* 1972 ed. Chicago: Kerr.

Eshed, V., A. Gopher, T. B. Gage, and I. Hershkovitz. 2004. Has the transition to agriculture reshaped the demographic structure of prehistoric populations? New evidence from the Levant. *American Journal of Physical Anthropology* 124: 315–29.

Fagan, B. 2000. *In the Beginning: An Introduction to Archaeology.* Upper Saddle River, NJ: Prentice Hall.

Fairservis, W. A. 1975. *The Roots of India.* Chicago: University of Chicago Press.

Falk, D. et al. 2005. The brain of LB1, *Homo floresiensis. Science* 308: 242–45.

Farnsworth, P., J. Brady, M. DeNiro, and R. S. MacNeish. 1985. A re-evaluation of the isotopic and archaeological reconstructions of diet in the Tehuacán Valley. *American Antiquity* 50: 102–16.

Feder, K. L. 1997. Site Survey. In *Field Methods in Archaeology,* 7th ed., eds. T. R. Hester, H. J. Shafer, and K. L. Feder, pp. 41–68. Mountain View, CA: Mayfield.

———. 2006. *Frauds, Myths, and Mysteries: Science and Pseudoscience in Archaeology.* 5th ed. Mountain View, CA: Mayfield.

Fedigan, L. M., and L. Fedigan. 1988. Gender and the study of primates. *Curricular Module for the Project on Gender and Curriculum.* Washington, DC: American Anthropological Association.

Fedje, D. W., and H. Josenhans. 2000. Drowned forests and archaeology on the continental shelf of British Columbia, Canada. *Geology* 28: 99–102.

Feibel, C. S., F. H. Brown, and I. McDougal. 1989. Stratigraphic context of fossil hominids from the Omo Group deposits: Northern Turkana basin, Kenya and Ethiopia. *American Journal of Physical Anthropology* 78: 595–622.

Ferris, T. 1988. *Coming of Age in the Milky Way.* New York: William Morrow.

Fiedel, S. J. 1999. Artifact provenience at Monte Verde: Confusion and contradictions. *Discovering Archaeology* 1(6): 1–12.

Flannery, K. 1965. The ecology of early food production in Mesopotamia. *Science* 147: 1247–56.

———. 1967. Vertebrate fauna and hunting patterns. In *The Prehistory of the Tehuacán Valley: Vol. 1: Environment and Subsistence,* ed. D. Byers, pp. 132–77. Austin: University of Texas Press.

———. 1968. Archaeological systems theory in early Mesoamerica. In *Anthropological Archaeology in the Americas,* ed. B. J. Meggers. Washington, DC: Anthropological Society of Washington.

———. 1973. The origins of agriculture. *Annual Review of Anthropology* 2: 271–310.

Fleagle, J. G. 1988. *Primate Adaptation and Evolution.* San Diego: Academic Press.

Flint, R. F. 1971. *Glacial and Quarternary Geology.* New York: Wiley.

Flood, J. 1990. *Archaeology of the Dreamtime: The Story of Prehistoric Australia and Its People.* New Haven, CT: Yale University Press.

Folger, T., and S. Menon. 1997. Or much like us? *Discover* (January): 33.

Ford, R. 1985. Patterns of prehistoric food production in North America. In *Prehistoric Food Production in North America,* ed. R. Ford, pp. 341–64. Anthropological Papers, Vol. 75. Ann Arbor: Museum of Anthropology, University of Michigan.

Fossey, D. 1983. *Gorillas in the Mist.* Boston: Houghton Mifflin.

Franciscus, R. G., and E. Trinkaus. 1988. Nasal morphology and the emergence of *Homo erectus. American Journal of Physical Anthropology* 75: 517–27.

Frayer, D. W., M. H. Wolpoff, A. G. Thorne, F. H. Smith, and G. G. Pope. 1993. Theories of modern human origins: The paleontological test. *American Anthropologist* 95: 14–50.

———. 1994. Getting it straight. *American Anthropologist* 96: 424–38.

Freeman, L. G. 1973. The significance of mammalian faunas from Paleolithic occupations in Cantabrian Spain. *American Antiquity* 38: 3–44.

Freidel, D. 1979. Culture areas and interaction spheres: Contrasting approaches to the emergence of civilization in the Maya lowlands. *American Antiquity* 44: 6–54.

Frere, J. 1800. Account of flint weapons discovered in Hoxne in Suffolk. *Archaeologia* 13: 204–5.

Frison, G. B. (ed.). 1974. *The Casper Site.* New York: Academic Press.

Fritz, G. 1994. Are the first American farmers getting younger? *Current Anthropology* 35(3): 305–9.

Fu, Y-X, and W-H Li. 1996. Estimating the age of the common ancestor of men from the ZFY intron. *Science* 272: 1356–57.

Gabunia, L., A. Vekua, D. Lordkipanidze, C. C. Swisher III, R. Ferring, A. Justus, M. Nioradze, M. Tvalchrelidze, S. C. Antón, G. Bosinski, O. Jöris, M. A. de Lumley, G. Majsuradze, and A. Mouskhelishvili. 2000. Earliest Pleistocene cranial remains from Dmanisi, Republic of Georgia: Taxonomy, geological setting, and age. *Science* 288: 1019–25.

Gaffney, E. S., L. Dingus, and M. K. Smith. 1995. Why cladistics? *Natural History* 104(6): 33–35.

Galdikas, B. 1995, *Reflections of Eden: My Years with the Orangutans of Borneo*. Boston: Little, Brown.

Gamble, C. 1982. Interaction and alliance in Paleolithic society. *Man* 17: 92–107.

———. 1983. Culture and society in the Upper Paleolithic of Europe. In *Hunter–Gatherer Economy in Prehistory: A European Perspective,* ed. G. Bailey, pp. 210–11. Cambridge, Eng.: Cambridge University Press.

———. 1986. *The Paleolithic Settlement of Europe.* Cambridge, Eng.: Cambridge University Press.

Gargett, R. H. 1989. Grave shortcomings: Evidence for Neandertal burial. *Current Anthropology* 30: 157–90.

Gebo, D. L., M. Dagosto, K. C. Beard, T. Qi, and J. Wang. 2000. The oldest known anthropoid postcranial fossil and the early evolution of the higher primates. *Nature* 404: 276–78.

Gebo, D. L., L. MacLatchy, R. Kityo, A. Deino, J. Kingston, and D. Pilbeam. 1997. A hominoid genus from the early miocene of Uganda. *Science* 276: 401–4.

Gee, H. 2001. Return to the planet of the apes. *Nature* 412: 131–32.

Gernet, J. 1987. *A History of Chinese Civilization.* Cambridge, Eng.: Cambridge University Press.

Gibbons, A. 1993. Geneticists trace the DNA trail of the first Americans. *Science* 259: 312–13.

———. 1996a. Did Neandertals lose an evolutionary "arms" race? *Science* 272: 1586–87.

———. 1996b. The peopling of the Americas. *Science* 274: 31–33.

———. 1997a. Tracing the identity of the first toolmakers. *Science* 276: 32.

———. 1997b. Y chromosome shows Adam was an African. *Science* 278: 804–5.

———. 1998a. Genes put mammals in age of dinosaurs. *Science* 289: 675–76.

———. 1998b. Which of our genes make us human? *Science* 281: 1432–34.

Gillespie, R. 2002. Dating the first Australians. *Radiocarbon* 44: 455–72.

Gish, D. T. 1979. *Evolution: The Fossils Say No!* San Diego: Creation Life Publishers.

Godfrey, L. R., and M. R. Sutherland. 1996. Paradox of peramorphic paedomorphosis: Heterchrony and human evolution. *American Journal of Physical Anthropology* 99: 17–42.

Goebel, T., M. R. Waters, and M. Dikova. 2003. The archaeology of Ushki Lake, Kamchatka, and the Pleistocene peopling of America. *Science* 301: 501–6.

Goodall, J. 1971. *In the Shadow of Man.* Boston: Houghton Mifflin.

———. 1986. *The Chimpanzees of Gombe: Patterns of Behavior.* Cambridge, MA: Belknap Press.

———. 1990. *Through a Window: My Thirty Years with the Chimpanzees of Gombe.* Boston: Houghton Mifflin.

———. 1995. A message from Jane Goodall. *National Geographic* 187(6): 129.

Goodman, A. H., and G. Armelagos. 1985. Disease and death at Dr. Dickson's mound. *Natural History* 94(9): 12–18.

Goodyear, Albert C. 1999. Results of the 1999 Allendale Paleoindian expedition. *Legacy* 4(1–3): 8–13.

Gore, R. 1996. The dawn of humans: Neandertals. *National Geographic* 189(1): 2–35.

———. 1997. The first steps. *National Geographic* 191(2): 72–97.

Gorman, C. 1969. Hoabinhian: A pebble-tool complex with early plant associations in Southeast Asia. *Science* 163: 671–73.

———. 1972. Excavations at Spirit Cave, North Thailand: Some interim impressions. *Asian Perspectives* 13: 79–107.

Gould, S. J. 1977. *Ever Since Darwin.* New York: Norton.

———. 1980. *The Panda's Thumb.* New York: Norton.

———. 1983. Part 4: Teilhard and Piltdown. In *Hen's Teeth and Horse's Toes.* New York: Norton.

———. 1985. *The Flamingo's Smile.* New York: Norton.

———. 1987a. Bushes all the way down. *Natural History* 96(6): 12–19.

———. 1987b. Empire of the apes. *Natural History* 96(5): 20–25.

———. 1987c. Life's little joke. *Natural History* 96(4): 16–25.

———. 1988. A novel notion of Neanderthal. *Natural History* 97(6): 16–21.

———. 1991. *Bully for Brontosaurus.* New York: Norton.

———. 1993a. *The Book of Life.* New York: Norton.

———. 1993b. *Eight Little Piggies.* New York: Norton.

———. 1993c. Fall in the house of Ussher. In *Eight Little Piggies: Reflections in Natural History.* New York: Norton.

————. 1994. The evolution of life on earth. *Scientific American* 271(4): 84–91.

————. 1995. *Dinosaur in a Haystack.* New York: Harmony Books.

————. 1996. *The Mismeasure of Man.* 2nd ed. New York: Norton.

Gove, Harry E. 1996. *Relic, Icon or Hoax? Carbon Dating the Turin Shroud.* Philadelphia: Institute of Physics Publishing.

Grant, P., and R. Grant. 2000. Non-random fitness variation in two populations of Darwin's finches. *Proceedings of the Royal Society of London* 267(1439): 131–38.

Grant, P. R., and B. R. Grant. 2002. Unpredictable evolution in a 30-year study of Darwin's finches. *Science* 296: 707–11.

Grauer, A. L. (ed.). 1995. *Bodies of Evidence: Reconstructing History Through Skeletal Analysis.* New York: Wiley-Liss.

Grayson, D. K. 1983. *The Establishment of Human Antiquity.* New York: Academic Press.

Greene, J. C. 1959. *The Death of Adam: Evolution and Its Impact on Western Thought.* Ames: Iowa State University Press.

Grine, F. E., and D. S. Strait. 2000. The phylogenetic relationships of recently described early hominid species.

Groube, L., J. Chappell, J. Muke, and D. Price. 1986. A 40,000 year-old human occupation site at Huon Peninsula, Papua New Guinea. *Nature* 324: 453–55.

Grove, D. 1996. The Olmec. *Arqueologia Mexicana* 2(12).

Groves, C. P. 1989. A regional approach to the problem of the origin of modern humans in Australasia. In *The Human Revolution: Behavioural and Biological Perspectives in the Origins of Modern Humans,* eds. P. Mellars and C. Stringer, pp. 274–85. Princeton, NJ: Princeton University Press.

Grün, R. 1993. Electron spin resonance dating in paleoanthropology. *Evolutionary Anthropology* 2(5): 172–81.

Grün, R., P. B. Beaumont, and C. B. Stringer. 1990. ESR dating evidence for early modern humans at Border Cave in South Africa. *Nature* 344: 537–39.

Grün, R., et al. 1996. Direct dating of Florisbad hominid. *Nature* 382: 500–501.

Grün, R., and C. B. Stringer. 1991. Electron spin resonance dating and the evolution of modern humans. *Archaeometry* 33: 153–99.

Guth, A. H. 2000. Genesis: The sequel. *Natural History* 109(February): 77–79.

Guthrie, R. D. 1990. Late Pleistocene faunal revolution— New perspective on the extinction debate. In *Megafauna and Man: Discovery of America's Heartland,* eds. L. D. Agenbroad, J. I. Mead, and L. W. Nelson, pp. 42–53. Hot Springs, SD: The Mammoth Site of Hot Springs and Northern Arizona University.

Gutin, J. 1995. Do Kenya tools root birth of modern thought in Africa? *Science* 270: 1118–19.

Haas, J. 1982. *The Evolution of the Prehistoric State.* New York: New York University Press.

Haas, J., W. Creamer, and A. Ruiz. 2004. Dating the Late Archaic occupation of the Norte Chico region of Peru. *Nature* 432: 1020–24.

Habgood, P. J. 1992. The origin of anatomically modern humans in east Asia. In *Continuity or Replacement: Controversies in* Homo sapiens *Evolution,* eds. G. Bräuer and F. Smith, pp. 273–87. Rotterdam: Balkema.

Haile-Selassie, Y. 2001. Late Miocene hominids from the Middle Awash, Ethiopia. *Nature* 412: 178–81.

Haile-Selassie, Y., G. Suwa and T. D. White. 2004. Late Miocene teeth from middle Awash, Ethiopia, and early hominid dental evolution. *Science* 303: 1503–5.

Halverson, J. 1987. Art for art's sake in the Paleolithic. *Current Anthropology* 28: 63–71.

Hammer, M. F., and S. L. Zegura. 1996. The role of the Y chromosome in human evolutionary studies. *Evolutionary Anthropology* 5(4): 116–34.

Hammond, N. 1974. Paleolithic mammalian faunas and parietal art in Cantabria: A comment on Freeman. *American Antiquity* 39: 618–19.

Hanotte, O., D. G. Bradley, J. W. Ochieng, Y. Verjee, E. W. Hill, and J. E. O. Rege. 2002. African pastoralism: Genetic imprints of origins and migrations. *Science* 296: 336–39.

Hansen, J. M. 1991. *The Paleoethnobotany of Franch-thi Cave, Greece.* Bloomington: Indiana University Press.

Harlan, J. 1992. Indigenous African agriculture. In *The Origins of Agriculture: An International Perspective,* eds. C. W. Cowan and P. J. Watson, pp. 59–70. Washington, DC: Smithsonian Institution Press.

Harlan, J. R., J. M. J. De Wet, and A. Stemler (eds.). 1976. Plant domestication and indigenous African agriculture. In *Origins of African Plant Domestication,* pp. 3–22. The Hague: Mouton.

Harlan, J. R., J. M. J. De Wet, A. Stemler, and D. Zohary. 1966. Distribution of wild wheats and barley. *Science* 153: 1074–80.

Harmon, R., J. Glaze, and K. Nowak. 1980. ^{230}Th/^{234}U dating of travertines from the Bilzingsleben archaeological site. *Nature* 284: 132–35.

Harris, C. L. (ed.) 1981. *Evolution: Genesis and Revelations.* Albany: State University of New York Press.

Harris, D. 1977. Alternative strategies toward agriculture. In *Origins of Agriculture,* ed. C. A. Reed, pp. 179–243. The Hague: Mouton.

Harris, M. 1968. *The Rise of Anthropological Theory.* New York: Cromwell.

Harrold, F. B. 1980. A comparative analysis of Eurasian Paleolithic burials. *World Archaeology* 12: 195–211.

———. 1989. Mousterian, Châtelperronian and early Aurignacian in Western Europe: Continuity or discontinuity. In *The Human Revolution: Behavioural and Biological Perspectives in the Origin of Modern Humans,* eds. P. Mellars and C. Stringer, pp. 677–713. Princeton, NJ: Princeton University Press.

Hattori, M. et al. 2000. The DNA sequence of human chromosome 21. *Nature* 405: 311–19.

Hayden, B. 1993. The cultural capacities of Neandertals: A review and re-evaluation. *Journal of Human Evolution* 24: 113–46.

Hedges, S. B., S. Kumar, K. Tamura, and M. Stoneking. 1992. Technical comments. *Science* 255: 737–39.

Heim, J. L. 1968. Les restes Neandertaliens de La Ferassie 1: Nouvelles données sur la stratigraphie et inventure de squelettes. *Computes Reneud de l'Academie del Sciences, Series D* 266: 576–78.

Henning, G. J., W. Herr, E. Weber, and N. I. Xirotiris. 1981. ESR-dating of the fossil hominid cranium from Petralona Cave, Greece. *Nature* 292: 533–36.

Henry, D. O. 1989. *From Foraging to Agriculture: The Levant at the End of the Ice Age.* Philadelphia: University of Pennsylvania Press.

Henshilwood, C., F. d'Errico, M. Vanhaeren, K. V. Niekerk, and Z. Jacobs. 2004. Middle Stone Age shell beads from South Africa. *Science* 304: 404.

Henshilwood, C. S., F. d'Errico, R. Yates, Z. Jacobs, C. Tribolo, G. A. T. Duller, N. Mercier, J. C. Sealy, H. Valladas, I. Watts, and A. G. Wintle. 2002. Emergence of modern human behavior: Middle Stone Age engravings from South Africa. *Science* 295: 1278–80.

Hester, T. R., H. J. Shafer, and K. L. Feder, eds. 1997. *Field Methods in Archaeology.* 7th ed. Mountain View, CA: Mayfield.

Heun, M., R. Schäfer-Pregl, D. Klawan, R. Castagna, M. Accerbi, B. Borghi, and F. Salamini. 1997. Site of einkorn wheat domestication identified by genetic fingerprinting. *Science* 278: 1312–13.

Higham, C. 1989. *The Archaeology of Mainland Southeast Asia.* Cambridge, Eng.: Cambridge University Press.

Hodder, I. 2005. Women and men at Çatalhoyuk. *Scientific American: Special Edition* 15(1): 35–41.

Hodder, I., and C. Cessford. 2004. Daily practice and social memory at Çatalhoyuk. *American Antiquity* 69: 17–40.

Hoffman, M. 1979. *Egypt Before the Pharaohs.* New York: Knopf.

———. 1983. Where nations began. *Science* 83 4(8): 42–51.

Hole, F., K. Flannery, and J. A. Neely. 1969. *Prehistory and Human Ecology of the Deh Luran Plain: An Early Village Sequence from Khuzistan, Iran.* Ann Arbor: University of Michigan Press.

Holden, C. 1998. No last word on language origins. *Science* 282: 1455–58.

———. 1999. Patrimony debate gets ugly. *Science* 285: 195.

———. 2001a. Dinner in a mound. *Science* 291: 587.

———. 2001b. Oldest human DNA reveals Aussie oddity. *Science* 291: 230–31.

Holliday, T. W. 1997. Postcranial evidence of cold adaptation in European Neandertals. *American Journal of Physical Anthropology* 104: 245–58.

Holloway, R. 1980. Indonesian "Solo" (Ngandong) endocranial reconstructions: Preliminary observations and comparisons with Neandertal and *Homo erectus* groups. *American Journal of Physical Anthropology* 53: 285–95.

———. 1981. The Indonesian *Homo erectus* brain endocasts revisited. *American Journal of Physical Anthropology* 55: 503–21.

Hopkins, D. 1982. Aspects of the paleogeography of Beringia during the late Pleistocene. In *The Paleoecology of Beringia,* eds. D. M. Hopkins, J. V. Matthews Jr., C. E. Schweger, and S. B. Young, pp. 3–28. New York: Academic Press.

Hoppe, K. 1992. Antiquity of oldest American confirmed. *Science News* 142: 334.

Hovers, E., S. Ilani, O. Bar-Yosef, and B. Vandermeersch. 2003. An early case of color symbolism: Ochre use by early modern humans in Qafzeh Cave. *Current Anthropology* 44: 491–522.

Hovers, E., Y. Rak, and W. Kimbell. 1996. Neandertals of the Levant. *Archaeology* 49(1): 49–50.

Howard, R. W. 1975. *The Dawn Seekers: The First History of American Paleontology.* New York: Harcourt Brace Jovanovich.

Howell, F. C. 1960. European and northwest African Middle Pleistocene hominids. *Current Anthropology* 1: 195–232.

———. 1966. Observations on the earlier phases of the European Lower Paleolithic. Special publication of *American Anthropologist* 68: 88–201.

Hublin, J.-J. 1996. The first Europeans. *Archaeology* 49(1): 36–44.

Hublin, J.-J., F. Spoor, M. Braun, F. Zonneveld, and S. Condemi. 1996. A late Neanderthal associated with Upper Paleolithic artefacts. *Nature* 381: 224–26.

Huddleston, L. E. 1967. *Origins of the American Indians: European Concepts 1492–1729.* Austin: University of Texas Press.

Huntington, E. 1924. *Civilization and Climate.* New Haven, CT: Yale University Press.

Hutton, James. 1959. *Theory of the Earth: With Proofs and Illustrations,* 1795 ed., 2 vols. Weinheim, Germany: H. R. Engelmann and Wheldon & Wesley.

Ikeya, M. 1982. Petralona Cave dating controversy: Response to Henning et al. *Nature* 299: 281.

Ingmanson, E. 1996. Tool-using behavior in the wild *Pan paniscus:* Social and ecological considerations. In *Reaching into Thought: The Minds of the Great Apes,* eds. A. Russon, K. Bark, and S. Taylor. Cambridge, Eng.: Cambridge University Press.

Ingmanson, E., and H. Ihobe. 1992. *Predation and meat eating by* Pan paniscus. Paper presented at the 61st annual meeting of the American Association of Physical Anthropology. Las Vegas.

Ingmanson, E., and T. Kano. 1993. Waging peace. *International Wildlife* (November/December): 30–37.

International HapMap Consortium. 2003. The international HapMap project. *Nature* 426: 789–96.

International SNP Map Working Group. 2001. A map of human genome sequence variation contains 1.42 million single nucleotide polymorphisms. *Nature* 409: 928–33.

Iriarte, J., I. Holst, O. Marozzi, C. Listopad, E. Alonso, A. Rinderknecht, and J. Montana. 2004. Evidence for cultivar adoption and emerging complexity during the mid-Holocene in the La Plata basin. *Nature* 432: 614–17.

Issac, G. 1977. *Olorgasailie: Archaeological Studies of a Middle Pleistocene Lake Basin in Kenya.* Chicago: University of Chicago Press.

Jablonski, N. G., and G. Chaplin. 2000. Do theories of bipedalization stand up to anatomical scrutiny? Paper presented at the 61st annual meeting of the American Association of Physical Anthropologists. Las Vegas.

Jaeger, J.-J. et al. 1999. A new primate from the Middle Eocene of Myanmar and the Asian early origin of anthropoids. *Science* 286: 528–30.

James, S. 1989. Hominid use of fire in the Lower and Middle Pleistocene. *Current Anthropology* 30: 1–11.

Jia, L., and W. Huang. 1990. *The Story of Peking Man.* New York: Oxford University Press.

Jochim, M. 1983. Paleolithic cave art in ecological perspective. In *Hunter–Gatherer Economy in Prehistory: A European Perspective,* ed. G. Bailey, pp. 212–19. Cambridge, Eng.: Cambridge University Press.

Jochim, M. A. 1998. *A Hunter-Gatherer Landscape: Southwest Germany in the Late Paleolithic and Mesolithic.* New York: Plenum.

Johanson, D., and M. Edey. 1981. *Lucy: The Beginnings of Humankind.* New York: Simon & Schuster.

Johanson, D., and J. Shreeve. 1989. *Lucy's Child: The Discovery of a Human Ancestor.* New York: Morrow.

Jones, R. 1987. Pleistocene life in the dead heart of Australia. *Nature* 328: 666.

———. 1989. East of Wallace's Line: Issues and problems in the colonization of the Australian continent. In *The Human Revolution: Behavioural and Biological Perspectives in the Origins of Modern Humans,* eds. P. Mellars and C. Stringer, pp. 743–82. Princeton, NJ: Princeton University Press.

———. 1992. The human colonisation of the Australian continent. In *Continuity or Replacement: Controversies in* Homo sapiens *Evolution,* eds. G. Bräuer and F. Smith, pp. 289–301. Rotterdam: Balkema.

Kaessmann, H., V. Wiebe, and S. Pääbo. 1999. Extensive nuclear DNA sequence diversity among chimpanzees. *Science* 286: 1159–61.

Kaiser, J. 1995. Blood from a stone: Tests for prehistoric blood cast doubt on earlier results. *Science News* 147: 376–77.

———. 1996. Were cattle domesticated in Africa? *Science* 272: 1105.

Kano, T. 1990. The bonobos' peaceable kingdom. *Natural History* 99(11): 62–71.

Kaplan, L., T. F. Lynch, and C. E. S. Smith, Jr. 1973. Early cultivated beans (*Phaseolus vulgaris*) from an intermontaine Peruvian valley. *Science* 179: 76–77.

Kasnakoglu, H. 2004. *FAO Yearbook: Production 2003.* Rome: Food and Agriculture Organization of the United Nations.

Kay, R. F., C. Ross, and B. A. Williams. 1997. Anthropoid origins. *Science* 275: 797–804.

Ke, Y. et al. 2001. African origin of modern humans in East Asia: A tale of 12,000 Y chromosomes. *Science* 292: 1151–53.

Keefer, D. K., S. D. de France, M. E. Moseley, J. B. Richardson III, D. R. Satterlee, and A. Day-Lewis. 1998. Early maritime economy and El Niño events at Quebrada Tacahuay, Peru. *Science* 281: 1833–35.

Keeley, L. H. 1980. *Experimental Determination of Stone Tool Use: A Microwear Analysis.* Chicago: University of Chicago Press.

Keith, A. 1927. *Concerning Man's Origin.* London: Watts.

Kennedy, K. A. R. 1975. *Neanderthal Man.* Minneapolis: Burgess Press.

———. 1976. *Human Variation in Space and Time.* Dubuque, IA: Brown.

———. 1999. Paleoanthropology. *Evolutionary Anthropology* 8: 165–85.

Kennedy, K. A. R., A. Sonakia, J. Chimet, and K. K. Verma. 1991. Is the Narmada hominid an Indian *Homo erectus? American Journal of Physical Anthropology* 86: 475–96.

Kenoyer, J. M. 1998. *Ancient Cities of the Indus Valley Civilization.* Oxford, Eng.: Oxford University Press.

———. 2005. Uncovering the keys to the lost Indus cities. *Scientific American: Special Edition* 15(1): 24–33.

Kent, J. 1987. The most ancient south: A review of the domestication of the Andean camelids. In *Studies in the Neolithic and Urban Revolutions,* ed. L. Manzanilla, pp. 169–84. Oxford, Eng.: British Archaeological Review.

Kenyon, K. 1954. Ancient Jericho. *Scientific American* 190(4): 76–82.

Kerr, R. A. 2001. Evolutionary pulse found, but complexity as well. *Science* 293: 2377.

Keyser, A. W. 2000. New finds in South Africa. *National Geographic* 197(5): 76–83.

Kind, C. J. 2001. The Mesolithic Sites of Siebenlinden: Baden-Württenberg. www.landesdenkmalamt-bw.de/english/archaeol/siebenlinden/index.php

Kingston, J. D., B. D. Marino, and A. Hill. 1994. Isotopic evidence for Neocene hominid paleoenvironments in the Kenya rift valley. *Science* 264: 955–59.

Klein, R. G. 1989. *The Human Career: Human Biological and Cultural Origins.* Chicago: University of Chicago Press.

———. 1993. Hunter-gatherers and farmers in Africa: The transformation of a continent. In *People of the Stone Age: Hunter-gatherers and Early Farmers,* ed. G. Burenhult. San Francisco: HarperSanFrancisco.

———. 1994. The problem of modern human origins. In *Origins of Anatomically Modern Humans,* eds. M. Nitecki and D. Nitecki, pp. 3–17. New York: Plenum.

———. 1999. *The Human Career: Human Biological and Cultural Origins.* Chicago: University of Chicago Press.

Knecht, H., A. Pike-Tay, and R. White. 1993. Introduction. In *Before Lascaux: The Complex Record of the Early Upper Paleolithic,* eds. H. Knecht, A. Pike-Tay, and R. White, pp. 1–4. Boca Raton, FL: CRC Press.

Kramer, A. 1991. Modern human origins in Australasia: Replacement or evolution. *American Journal of Physical Anthropology* 86: 455–73.

———. 1993. Human taxonomic diversity in the Pleistocene: Does *Homo erectus* represent multiple hominid species? *American Journal of Physical Anthropology* 91: 161–71.

Kranzberg, M. 1984. Technological revolutions. *National Forum: The Phi Kappa Phi Journal* 64(3): 6–10.

Krings, M., H. Geisert, R. W. Schmitz, H. Krainitzki, M. Stoneking, and S. Pääbo. 1999. DNA sequence of the mitochondrial hypervariable region II from the Neanderthal type specimen. *Proceedings of the National Academy of Sciences* 96(10): 5581–85.

Krings, M., A. Stone, R. W. Schmitz, H. Krainitzki, M. Stoneking, and S. Pääbo. 1997. Neandertal DNA sequences and the origin of modern humans. *Cell* 90(1): 19–30.

Kuban, G. 1989a. Elongate dinosaur tracks. In *Dinosaur Tracks and Traces,* eds. D. D. Gillette and M. G. Lockley, pp. 57–72. New York: Cambridge University Press.

———. 1989b. Retracing those incredible mantracks. *National Center for Science Education Reports* 94(4): 13–16.

Kunzig, R. 1997. The face of an ancestral child. *Discover* 18(12): 88–101.

Kurtén, B. 1968. *The Pleistocene Mammals of Europe.* London: Weiderfield and Nicholson.

Lahr, M. M., and R. Foley. 2004. Human evolution writ small. *Nature* 431: 1043–44.

Laitman, J., and R. C. Heimbach. 1984. The basicranium and upper respiratory system of African *Homo erectus* and early *Homo sapiens. American Journal of Physical Anthropology* 63: 180.

Lamberg-Karlovsky, C. C., and J. A. Sabloff. 1995. *Ancient Civilizations: The Near East and Mesoamerica.* Prospect Heights, IL: Waveland Press.

Landau, M. 1991. *Narratives of Human Evolution.* New Haven, CT: Yale University Press.

Langdon, J. H. 2005. *The Human Strategy: An Evolutionary Perspective on Human Anatomy.* New York: Oxford.

Larick, R., and R. Ciochon. 1996. The first Asians. *Archaeology* 49(1): 51–53.

Larsen, C. S., and R. M. Matter. 1985. *Human Origins: The Fossil Record.* Prospect Heights, IL: Waveland Press.

Lawler, A. 2003. Mayhem in Mesopotamia. *Science* 301: 582–89.

Leakey , M. G., C. S. Feibel, I. McDougall, and A. Walker. 1995. New four-million-year-old hominid species from Kanapoi and Allia Bay, Kenya. *Nature* 393: 62–65.

Leakey, M. G., C. S. Feibel, I. McDougall, C. Ward, and A. Walker. 1998. New specimen and confirmation of an early age for *Australopithecus anamensis*. *Nature* 393: 62–66.

Leakey, M. G., F. Spoor, F. H. Brown, P. N. Gathogo, and L. N. Leakey. 2003. A new hominin calvaria from Ileret (Kenya). Paper delivered at the 72nd Annual Meeting of the American Association of Physical Anthropologists, Tempe, Arizona.

Leakey, M. G., F. Spoor, F. H. Brown, P. N. Gathogo, C. Kiarie, L. N. Leakey, and I. McDougall. 2001. New hominid genus from eastern Africa shows diverse Middle Pliocene lineages. *Nature* 410: 433–40.

Leakey, R., and R. Lewin. 1992. *Origins Reconsidered: In Search of What Makes Us Human*. New York: Doubleday.

———. 1995. *The Sixth Extinction: Patterns of Life and the Future of Humankind*. New York: Doubleday.

Leakey, R. E. F., and A. Walker. 1985a. A fossil skeleton 1,600,000 years old: *Homo erectus* unearthed. *National Geographic* 168(5): 624–29.

———. 1985b. Further hominids from the Plio-Pleistocene of Koobi Fora, Kenya. *American Journal of Physical Anthropology* 67: 135–63.

Lee, R. 1979. *The !Kung San: Men, Women, and Work in a Foraging Society*. Cambridge, Eng.: Cambridge University Press.

Lee, R. B., and I. DeVore (eds.). 1968. *Man the Hunter*. Chicago: Aldine.

Lehner, M. 1997. *The Complete Pyramids*. New York: Thames and Hudson.

Leiberman, P. 1984. *The Biology and Evolution of Language*. Cambridge, MA: Harvard University Press.

Leigh, S. 1992. Cranial capacity evolution in *Homo erectus* and early *Homo sapiens*. *American Journal of Physical Anthropology* 87: 1–13.

Leroi-Gourhan, A. 1982. *The Dawn of European Art: An Introduction to Paleolithic Cave Painting*. Cambridge, Eng.: Cambridge University Press.

Lévêque, F. 1993. The Castelperronian industry of Saint-Césaire: The Upper Level. In *Context of a Late Neandertal, Vol. 16*. eds. F. Lévêque, A. M. Backer, and M. Guilbaud. Madison, WI: Prehistory Press.

Lévêque, F., A. M. Backer, and M. Guilbaud (eds.). 1993. *Context of a Late Neandertal*. Monographs in World Archaeology. Vol. 16. Madison, WI.: Prehistory Press.

Lewin, R. 1982. *Thread of Life: The Smithsonian Looks at Evolution*. Washington, DC: Smithsonian Books.

———. 1984. Unexpected anatomy of *Homo erectus*. *Science* 226: 529.

———. 1987. *Bones of Contention: Controversies in the Search for Human Origins*. New York: Simon & Schuster.

Lewis-Williams, J. D., and T. A. Dowson. 1988. The signs of all times. *Current Anthropology* 29(2): 201–17.

Lewontin, R. 1982. *Human Diversity*. New York: Scientific American Library.

Lieberman, D. E. 1999. Homology and hominid phylogeny: Problems and potential solutions. *Evolutionary Anthropology* 7(4): 142–51.

Little, P. 1999. The book of genes. *Nature* 402: 467–68.

Lloyd, S. 1978. *The Archaeology of Mesopotamia*. London: Thames and Hudson.

Long, A., B. Benz, J. Donahue, A. Jull, and L. Toolin. 1989. First direct AMS dates on early maize from Tehuacán, Mexico. *Radiocarbon* 31: 1035–40.

Lopez, B. 1986. *Arctic Dreams: Imagination and Desire in a Northern Landscape*. New York: Bantam.

Lovejoy, C. O., and E. Trinkaus. 1980. Strength and robusticity of the Neandertal tibia. *American Journal of Physical Anthropology* 53: 465–70.

Lowe, G. W. 1989. The heartland Olmec: Evolution of material culture. In *Regional Perspectives on the Olmec*, eds. R. J. Sharer and D. C. Grove, pp. 33–67. New York: Cambridge University Press.

Lu, Zun'e. 1987. Cracking the evolutionary puzzle: Jinniushan Man. *China Pictorial* 4: 34–45.

Lyell, C. 1873. *The Geological Evidences of the Antiquity of Man*. London: Murray.

Lynch, T. F., R. Gillespie, J. A. J. Gowlett, and R. E. M. Hedges. 1985. Chronology of Guitarrero Cave, Peru. *Science* 229: 864–67.

MacNeish, R. S. 1964. Ancient Mesoamerican civilization. *Science* 143: 531–37.

———. 1967. An interdisciplinary approach to an archaeological problem. In *The Prehistory of the Tehuacán Valley: Vol. 1: Environment and Subsistence*, ed. D. Byers, pp. 14–23. Austin: University of Texas Press.

Maisels, C. K. 1990. *The Emergence of Civilization: From Hunting and Gathering to Agriculture, Cities, and the State in the Near East*. New York: Routledge.

Mandryk, Carole A. 1990. Could humans survive the ice-free corridor?: Late-glacial vegetation and climate in west central Alberta. In *Megafauna and Man: Discovery of America's Heartland*, eds. L. D. Agenbroad, J. I. Mead, and L. W. Nelson, pp. 67–79. Hot Springs, SD: The Mammoth Site of Hot Springs and Northern Arizona University.

Manglesdorf, P. 1958. Reconstructing the ancestor of corn. *Proceedings of the American Philosophical Society* 102: 454–63.

Mannikka, E. 1996. *Angkor Wat: Time, Space, and Kingship.* Honolulu: University of Hawai'i Press.

Marean, C., and Z. Assefa. 1999. Zooarcheological evidence for the faunal exploitation behavior of Neandertals and early modern humans. *Evolutionary Anthropology* 8(1): 22–37.

Marean, C. W., and S. Y. Kim. 1998. Mousterian large-mammal remains from Kobeh Cave: Behavioral implications for Neanderthals and modern humans. *Current Anthropology* 39(Supplement): S79–S92.

Marks, A. E. 1990. The Middle and Upper Paleolithic of the Near East and the Nile Valley: The problem of cultural transformations. In *The Emergence of Modern Humans: An Archaeological Perspective,* ed. P. Mellars, pp. 56–80. Ithaca: Cornell University Press.

———. 1993. The early Upper Paleolithic: The view from the Levant. In *Before Lascaux: The Complex Record of the Early Upper Paleolithic,* eds. H. Knecht, A. Pike-Tay, and R. White, pp. 5–21. Boca Raton, FL: CRC Press.

Marks, J. 1995. *Human Biodiversity: Genes, Race, and History.* New York: Aldine.

———.2002. *What It Means To Be 98% Chimpanzee: Apes, People, and Their Genes.* Berkeley: University of California Press.

Marshak, A. 1972a. Cognitive aspects of Upper Paleolithic engraving. *Current Anthropology* 13: 445–77.

———. 1972b. *The Roots of Civilization.* New York: McGraw-Hill.

Martin, P. S. 1982. The pattern of meaning of Holarctic mammoth extinction. In *Paleocology of Beringia,* eds. D. Hopkins, J. Matthews, C. Schweger, and S. Young, pp. 399–408. New York: Academic Press.

Martin, R. D. 1990. *Primate Origins and Evolution: A Phylogenetic Reconstruction.* Princeton, NJ: Princeton University Press.

———. 1993. Primate origins: Plugging the gaps. *Nature* (May 20): 223–24.

Mason, S. L. R., J. G. Hather, and G. C. Hillman. 1994. Preliminary investigation of the plant macro-remains from Dolni Vestonice II, and its implications for the role of plant foods in Paleolithic and Mesolithic Europe. *Antiquity* 68: 48–57.

Matsuoka, Y., Y. Vigouroux, M. Goodman, J. Sanchez G., E. Buckler, and J. Doebley. 2002. A single domestication for maize shown by multilocus microsattelite genotyping. *Proceedings of the National Academy of Science* 99: 6080–84.

Maxwell, M. 1993. Pioneers of the Arctic: The last of the habitable lands. In *The First Humans: Human Origins and History to 10,000 B.P.,* ed. G. Hurnehult, pp. 209–25. San Francisco: Harper San Francisco.

Mayor, A. 2000. *The First Fossil Hunters: Paleontology in Greek and Roman Times.* Princeton: Princeton University Press.

———. 2005. *Fossil Legends of the First Americans.* Princeton, NJ: Princeton University Press.

McCollum, M. A. 1999. The robust australopithecine face: A morphogenic perspective. *Science* 284: 301–4.

McConnell, J. B. 1988. Whence we've come, where we're going, how we're going to get there. In *Biotechnology and the Human Genome,* eds. A. D. Woodhead and B. J. Barnhart, pp. 1–4. New York: Plenum.

McCrone, J. 1991. *The Ape That Spoke: Language and the Evolution of the Mind.* New York: Avon Books.

McCrossin, M. L. 1997. New postcranial remains of *Kenyapithecus* and their implications for understanding the origins of hominoid terrestriality. Paper delivered to the 66th annual meeting of the American Association of Physical Anthropologists. St. Louis.

McDermott, F., R. Grün, C. B. Stringer, and C. J. Hawkesworth. 1993. Mass-spectrometric U-series dates for Israeli Neanderthal/early modern hominid sites. *Nature* 363: 252–55.

McDermott, L. 1996. Self-representation in Upper Paleolithic female figurines. *Current Anthropology* 37: 227–76.

McDougall, I., F. H. Brown, and J. G. Fleagle. 2005. Stratigraphic placement and age of modern humans from Kibish, Ethiopia. *Nature* 433: 733–36.

McGrew, W. C. 1998. Culture in nonhuman primates? *Annual Review of Anthropology* 27: 301–28.

McIntosh, S., and R. McIntosh. 1982. Finding West Africa's oldest city. *National Geographic* 162(3): 396–418.

McKillop, H. 1994. Ancient Maya tree-cropping. *Ancient Mesoamerica* 5: 129–40.

Mellaart, J. 1965. *Earliest Civilizations of the Near East.* London: Thames and Hudson.

Mellars, P. (ed.). 1990. *The Emergence of Modern Humans: An Archaeological Perspective.* Ithaca, NY: Cornell University Press.

Meltzer, D. J. 1989. Why don't we know when the first people came to North America? *American Antiquity* 54: 471–90.

———. 1993a. Pleistocene peopling of the Americas. *Evolutionary Anthropology,* pp. 157–69.

———. 1993b. *Search for the First Americans.* Washington, DC: Smithsonian Books.

———. 1997. Monte Verde and the Pleistocene peopling of America. *Science* 276: 754–55.

Menon, S. 1997. Neanderthal noses. *Discover* (March): 30.

Mercier, N., H. Valladas, J.-L. Joron, J.-L. Reyss, F. Lévêque, and B. Vandermeersch. 1991. Thermoluminescence dating of the late Neanderthal remains from Saint-Césaire. *Nature* 351: 737–39.

Milisauskas, S. 1978. *European Prehistory.* New York: Academic Press.

Millar, R. 1972. *The Piltdown Men.* New York: Ballantine Books.

Miller, N. 1992. The origins of plant cultivation in the Near East. In *The Origins of Agriculture: An International Perspective,* eds. C. W. Cowan and P. J. Watson, pp. 39–58. Washington, DC: Smithsonian Institution Press.

Millon, R., B. Drewit, and G. Cowgill. 1973. *The Teotihuacan Map: Urbanization at Teotihuacan,* Vol. 1. Austin: University of Texas Press.

Minugh-Purvis, N. 1995. The modern human origins controversy. *Evolutionary Anthropology* 4(4): 140–47.

Molnar, S. 1998. *Human Variation: Races, Types, and Ethnic Groups.* 4th ed. Englewood Cliffs, NJ: Prentice-Hall.

Monastersky, R. 1991. Tales from ice time: Two holes through Greenland offer a glimpse of climates past and future. *Science News* 140: 161–76.

———. 1992. New date resets geologic clocks. *Science News* 141: 14.

Montagu, A. (ed.). 1964. *The Concept of Race.* New York: Collier.

Morgan, L. H. 1877. *Ancient Society.* 1964 ed. Cambridge, MA: Belknap Press.

Morlan, R. E. 1983. Pre-Clovis occupation north of the ice sheets. In *Early Man in the New World,* ed. R. Shutler, Jr., pp. 47–63. Beverly Hills: Sage.

Morris, C., and A. V. Hagen. 1993. *The Inka Empire and Its Andean Origins.* New York: American Museum of Natural History.

Morris, J. 1980. *Tracking Those Incredible Dinosaurs and the People Who Knew Them.* San Diego: Creation Life Publishers.

Morse, D. 1969. *Ancient Disease in the Midwest.* Springfield: Illinois State Museum.

Morse, D., J. Duncan, and J. Stoutamire (eds.). 1983. *Handbook of Forensic Archaeology and Anthropology.* Tallahassee, FL: Published by the editors, distributed by Bill's Bookstore.

Morwood, M. J., P. B. O'Sullivan, F. Aziz, and A. Raza. 1998. Fission-track ages of stone tools and fossils on the east Indonesian island of Flores. *Nature* 392: 173–76.

Moseley, M. E. 1975. *The Maritime Foundations of Andean Civilization.* Menlo Park, CA: Cummings Publishing.

Movius, H. 1953. The Mousterian cave of Teshik-Tash, south-central Uzbekistan, Central Asia. *Bulletin of the American School of Prehistorical Research* 17: 11–71.

Mowat, F. 1987. *Woman in the Mists.* New York: Warner Books.

Muchmore, E. A., S. Diaz, and A. Varki. 1998. A structural difference between the cell surfaces of humans and great apes. *American Journal of Physical Anthropology* 107: 187–98.

Mulvaney, J., and J. Kamminga. 1999. *Prehistory of Australia.* Washington, DC: Smithsonian Institution Press.

Napier, J. R., and P. H. Napier. 1985. *The Natural History of the Primates.* London: British Museum (Natural History).

Natural History. 1991–1992. Rediscovering the Maya. *Natural History.*

Ndoro, W. 1997. Great Zimbabwe. *Scientific American* 277(5): 94–99.

Newcomer, M. 1971. Some quantitative experiments in handaxe manufacture. *World Archaeology* 3: 85–94.

Nichols, M., J. Goodall, G. B. Schaller, and M. G. Smith. 1993. *The Great Apes: Between Two Worlds.* Washington, DC: National Geographic Society.

Nilsson, G. E. 1999/2000. The cost of a brain. *Natural History* 108(5): 94–99.

Normille, D. 1997. Yangtze seen as earliest rice site. *Science* 275: 309.

———. 2001. Gene expression differs in human and chimp brains. *Science* 292: 44–45.

Nova. 1993. *This Old Pyramid.* Boston: WGBH-TV.

O'Brien, E. M. 1984. What was the Acheulean hand ax? *Natural History* 93(7): 20–23.

O'Brien, S. J., and R. Stanyon. 1999. Ancestral primate revealed. *Nature* 402: 356–66.

O'Connell, J. F., and J. Allen. 1998. When did humans first arrive in Greater Australia and why is it important to know? *Evolutionary Anthropology* 6(4): 132–46.

O'Connor, D. 1993. *Ancient Nubia: Egypt's Rival in Africa.* Philadelphia: University Museum, University of Pennsylvania.

Oliva, M. 1993. The Aurignacian in Moravia. In *Before Lascaux: The Complex Record of the Early Upper Paleolithic,* eds. H. Knecht, A. Pike-Tay, and R. White, pp. 37–55. Boca Raton, FL: CRC Press.

Olsen, S. J. 1985. *Origins of the Domestic Dog.* Tucson: University of Arizona Press.

Ovchinnikov, I., A. Götherström, G. Romanova, V. Kharitonov, K. Lidén, and W. Goodwin. 2000. Molecular analysis of Neanderthal DNA from the northern Caucasus. *Nature* 404: 490–92.

Ovey, C. (ed.). 1964. *The Swanscombe Skull: A Survey of Research on a Pleistocene Site.* Royal Anthropological Institute of Great Britain and Ireland, Occasional Paper 20.

Owen, R. 1984. The Americas: The case against an Ice-Age human population. In *The Origins of Modern Humans: A World Survey of the Fossil Evidence,* eds. F. H. Smith and F. Spencer, pp. 517–64. New York: Liss.

Pääbo, S. 1985. Molecular cloning of ancient Egyptian mummy DNA. *Nature* 314: 644–45.

Pääbo, S., J. A. Gifford, and Allan C. Wilson. 1988. Mitochondrial sequences from a 7,000 year old brain. *Nucleic Acids Res.* 16: 9775–87.

Page, C., and J. Cort. 1997. *Secrets of Lost Empires: Stonehenge.* Boston: WGBH.

Parés, J. M., and A. Pérez-González. 1995. Paleomagnetic age for hominid fossils at Atapuerca archaeological site, Spain. *Science* 269: 830–32.

Park, M. A. 1979. *Dermatoglyphics as a Tool for Population Studies: An Example.* Unpublished doctoral dissertation. Bloomington: Indiana University Department of Anthropology.

———. 2005. *Biological Anthropology.* 4th ed. Mountain View, CA: Mayfield.

Partridge, T. C., D. E. Granger, M. W. Caffee, and R. J. Clarke. 2003. Lower Pliocene hominid remains from Sterkfontein. *Science* 300: 607–12.

Passingham, R. E. 1982. *The Human Primate.* Oxford, Eng.: Freeman.

Pasztory, E. 1997. *Teotihuacan: An Experiment in Living.* Norman: University of Oklahoma Press.

Patterson, T. 1973. *America's Past: A New World Archaeology.* Glenview, IL: Scott, Foresman.

Pauketat, T. R. 1994. *The Ascent of Chiefs: Cahokia and Mississippian Politics in Native America.* Tuscaloosa: University of Alabama Press.

Pearsall, D. 1989. *Paleoethnobotany: A Handbook of Procedures.* New York: Academic Press.

Pearson, O. M. 2000. Postcranial remains and the origin of modern humans. *Evolutionary Anthropology* 9(6): 229–47.

Pfeiffer, J. E. 1969. *The Emergence of Man.* New York: Harper & Row.

Phillipson, D. W. 1993. *African Archaeology.* Cambridge, Eng.: Cambridge University Press.

Pilbeam, D. 1984. The descent of the hominoids and hominids. *Scientific American* 250(3): 84–96.

———. 1986. Human origins. *David Skomp Distinguished Lecture in Anthropology.* Bloomington: Indiana University.

Piperno, D. R., A. J. Ranere, I. Holst, and P. Hansell. 2000. Starch grains reveal early root crop horticulture in the Panamanian tropical forest. *Nature* 407: 894–97.

Piperno, D. R., E. Weiss, I. Holst, and D. Nadel. 2004. Processing of wild cereal grains in the Upper Paleolithic revealed by starch grain analysis. *Nature* 430: 670–73.

Pitulko, V. V., P. A. Nikolsky, E. Y. Girya, A. E. Basilyan, V. E. Tumskoy, S. A. Koulakov, S. N. Astakhov, E. Y. Pavlova, and M. A. Anismov. 2004. The Yana RHS site: Humans in the Arctic before the last glacial maximum. *Science* 303: 52–56.

Pope, G. 1988. Recent Advances in Far Eastern Paleoanthropology. *Annual Reviews in Anthropology* 17: 43–77.

———. 1989. Bamboo and human evolution. *Natural History* 50–54.

———. 1992. Craniofacial evidence for the origin of modern humans in China. *Yearbook of Physical Anthropology* 35: 243–98.

Pope, K. O., M. E. D. Pohl, J. G. Jones, D. L. Lentz, V. V. Nagy, F. J. Vega, and R. Potts. 1984. Home bases and early hominids. *American Scientist* 73: 338–47.

Possehl, G. L. 1980. *Indus Civilization in Saurashtra.* Delhi, India: B. R. Publishing.

Post, P. W., Jr., F. Daniels and R. T. Binford. 1975. Cold injury and the evolution of "white" skin. *Human Biology* 47: 65–80.

Potts, R. 1996. Evolution and climate variability. *Science* 273: 922–23.

———. 1998. Variability selection in hominid evolution. *Evolutionary Anthropology* 7: 81–96.

Poulianos, A. N. 1971. Petralona: A Middle Pleistocene cave in Greece. *Archaeology* 24(1): 6–11.

Powell, E. 2005. The turquoise trail. *Archaeology* 58(1): 24–29.

Powell, J., and J. C. Rose. 1999. Report on the osteological assessment of the "Kennewick Man" skeleton. www.cr.nps.gov/aad/kennewick.

Power, M. 1991. *The Egalitarians—Human and Chimpanzee: An Anthropological View of Social Organization.* Cambridge, Eng.: Cambridge University Press.

Powers, W. R., and J. F. Hoffecker. 1989. Late Pleistocene settlement in the Nenana Valley, central Alaska. *American Antiquity* 54: 263–87.

Price, T. D. 1987. The Mesolithic of western Europe. *Journal of World Prehistory* 1: 225–305.

———. 1991. The view from Europe: Concepts and questions about terminal Pleistocene societies. In *The First Americans: Search and Research,* eds. T. D. Dillehay and D. J. Meltzer, pp. 185–208. Boca Raton, FL: CRC Press.

Pringle, H. 1997. Ice Age communities may be earliest known net hunters. *Science* 277: 1203–4.

———. 1998. New women of the Ice Age. *Discover* (April): 62–69.

———. 2001. The first urban center in the Americas. *Science* 292: 621–22.

Prum, R. O., and A. H. Brush. 2003. Which came first, the feather or the bird? *Scientific American* 288(3): 84–93.

Quitmyer, I. R. 2001. Origin and environmental setting of ancient agriculture in the lowlands of Mesoamerica. *Science* 292: 1370–73.

Radner, D., and M. Radner. 1982. *Science and Unreason.* Belmont, CA: Wadsworth.

Ragir, S. 2000. Diet and food preparation: Rethinking early hominid behavior. *Evolutionary Anthropology* 9(4): 153–55.

Rak, Y. 1990. On the differences between two pelvises of Mousterian context from the Qafzeh and Kebara Caves, Israel. *American Journal of Physical Anthropology* 81: 323–32.

Rak, Y., and B. Arensberg. 1987. Kebara 2 Neandertal pelvis: First look at a complete inlet. *American Journal of Physical Anthropology* 73: 227–31.

Ray, J. 1974. *The Wisdom of God Manifested in the Works of the Creation.* New York: Georg Olms Verlag.

Read-Martin, C. E., and D. W. Read. 1975. *Australopithecus* scavenging and human evolution: Approach from fauna analysis. *Current Anthropology* 16: 359–68.

Reeves, R. H. 2000. Recounting a genetic story. *Nature* 405: 283–84.

Relethford, J. H. 1997. *The Human Species: An Introduction to Biological Anthropology.* 3rd ed. Mountain View, CA: Mayfield.

———. 2001. *Genetics and the Search for Modern Human Origins.* New York: Wiley-Liss.

———. 2003. *Reflections of Our Past: How Human History Is Revealed in Our Genes.* Boulder, CO: Westview.

Relethford, J. H., and H. C. Hardpending. 1995. Ancient differences in population size can mimic a recent African origin of modern Humans. *Current Anthropology* 36: 667–74.

Rice, P., 1981. Prehistoric Venuses: Symbols of motherhood or womanhood. *Journal of Anthropological Research* 37: 402–14.

Rice, P., and Paterson, A. 1985. Cave art and bones: Exploring the interrelationships. *American Anthropologist* 87: 94–100.

———. 1986. Validating the cave art-archaeofaunal relationship in Cantabrian Spain. *American Anthropologist* 88: 658–67.

———. 1988. Anthropomorphs in cave art: An empirical assessment. *American Anthropologist* 90: 664–74.

Richard, A. F. 1985. *Primates in Nature.* New York: Freeman.

Richards, M. P., P. B. Pettitt, E. Trinkaus, F. H. Smith, M. Paunovic, and I. Karacanic. 2000. Neanderthal diet at Vindija and Neanderthal predation: The evidence from stable isotopes. *Proceedings of the National Academy of Sciences* 97: 7663–66.

Richmond, B. G., and D. S. Strait. 2000. Evidence that humans evolved from a knuckle-walking ancestor. *Nature* 404: 382–85.

Ridley, M. 1996. *Evolution.* Boston: Blackwell.

Rightmire, G. P. 1979a. Cranial remains of *Homo erectus* from Beds II and IV, Olduvai Gorge, Tanzania. *American Journal of Physical Anthropology* 51: 99–116.

———. 1979b. Implications of Border Cave skeletal remains for later Pleistocene evolution. *Current Anthropology* 20: 23–35.

———. 1984. *Homo sapiens* in sub-Saharan Africa. In *The Origins of Modern Humans: A World Survey of the Fossil Evidence,* eds. F. H. Smith and F. Spencer, pp. 295–326. New York: Liss.

———. 1985. The tempo of change in the evolution of Mid-Pleistocene *Homo.* In *Ancestors: The Hard Evidence,* ed. E. Delson, pp. 255–64. New York: Liss.

———. 1990. *The Evolution of* Homo erectus: *Comparative Anatomical Studies of an Extinct Human Species.* New York: Cambridge University Press.

———. 1998. Human evolution in the Middle Pleistocene: The role of *Homo heidelbergensis. Evolutionary Anthropology* 6(6): 218–27.

Rightmire, G. P., and H. Deacon. 1991. Comparative studies of Late Pleistocene human remains from Klasies

River Mouth, South Africa. *Journal of Human Evolution* 20: 131–56.

Rindos, D. 1984. *The Origins of Agriculture: An Evolutionary Perspective.* Orlando, FL: Academic Press.

Roberts, R. G., R. Jones, and M. A. Smith. 1990. Thermoluminescence dating of a 50,000-year-old human occupation site in northern Australia. *Nature* 345: 153–56.

Robins, A. H. 1991. *Biological Perspectives on Human Pigmentation.* Cambridge: Cambridge University Press.

Roche, H., A. Delagnes, J.-P. Brugal, C. Feibel, M. Kibunjia, V. Mourre, and P.-J. Texier. 1999. Early hominid stone tool production and technical skill 2.34 my ago in West Turkana, Kenya. *Nature* 399: 57–60.

Rodden, R. J. 1965. The early Neolithic village in Greece. *Scientific American* 212(4): 83–91.

Rogan, P. K., and J. J. Salvo. 1990. Molecular genetics of pre-Columbian South American mummies. *UCLA Symposium in Molecular Evolution* 122: 223–34.

Rogers, J., P. B. Samollow, and A. G. Comuzzie. 1996. Estimating the age of the common ancestor of men from the ZFY intron. *Science* 272: 1360–61.

Romer, J. 1984. *Ancient Lives: Daily Life in Egypt of the Pharaohs.* New York: Holt, Rinehart and Winston.

———. 1988. *Testament: The Bible and History.* New York: Holt.

Roosevelt, A. C. et al. 1996. Paleoindian cave dwellers in the Amazon: The peopling of the Americas. *Science* 272: 373–84.

Rose, M. 1995. The last Neandertals. *Archaeology* 48(5): 12–13.

Roush, W. 1996. Corn: A lot of change from a little DNA. *Science* 272: 1873.

Rowe, N. 1996. *The Pictorial Guide to the Living Primates.* East Hampton, NY: Pogonius Press.

Rowlett, R. M., M. G. Davis, and R. B. Graber. 1999. Friendly fire. *Discovering Archaeology* 1(5): 82–89.

Ruff, C. B. 1993. Climatic adaptation and hominid evolution: The thermoregulatory imperative. *Evolutionary Anthropology* 2(2): 53–60.

Ruspoli, M. 1986. *The Cave of Lascaux: The Final Photographs.* New York: Abrams.

Sabloff, J. 1989. *The Cities of Ancient Mexico: Reconstructing a Lost World.* New York: Thames and Hudson.

———. 1994. *The New Archaeology and the Ancient Maya.* New York: Scientific American Library.

Sagan, C. 1977. *The Dragons of Eden: Speculations on the Evolution of Human Intelligence.* New York: Random House.

———. 1980. *Cosmos.* New York: Random House.

Sanders, W., and B. Price. 1968. *Mesoamerica: The Evolution of a Civilization.* New York: Random House.

Sandweiss, D. H., H. McInnis, R. L. Burger, A. Cano, B. Ojeda, R. Paredes, M. Sandweiss, and M. D. Glasscock. 1998. Quebrada Jaguay: Early South American maritime adaptations. *Science* 281: 1830–32.

Sargis, E. J. 2002. Primate origins nailed. *Science* 298: 1564–65.

Sarich, V. 1971. A molecular approach to the question of human origins. In *Background for Man,* eds. P. Dolhinhow and V. M. Sarich, pp. 60–81. Boston: Little, Brown.

Sauer, C. 1969. *Seeds, Spades, Hearths, and Herds: The Domestication of Animals and Foodstuffs.* Cambridge, MA: MIT Press.

Saura Ramos, P. A. 1998. *The Cave of Altamira.* New York: Abrams.

Savage-Rumbaugh, S., and R. Lewin. 1994. *Kanzi—The Ape at the Brink of the Human Mind.* New York: John Wiley.

Savage-Rumbaugh, S., and R. Lewin. 1994. Ape at the brink. *Discover* 15(9): 91–98.

Savage-Rumbaugh, S., S. Shanker, and T. J. Taylor. 1998. *Apes, Language, and the Human Mind.* New York: Oxford University Press.

Savaria. 1965. *The Popol Vuh.* Guatemala: Publicaciones Turisticas.

Schele, L., and D. Freidel. 1990. *A Forest of Kings: The Untold Story of the Ancient Maya.* New York: Morrow.

Schick, K. D., and N. Toth. 1993. *Making Silent Stones Speak: Human Evolution and the Dawn of Technology.* New York: Simon and Schuster.

Schiffer, M. B. 1978. *Behavioral Archaeology.* Orlando: Academic Press.

Schmid, P. 2000. Functional interpretation of the Laetoli footprints. Paper delivered at the 69th annual meeting of the American Association of Physical Anthropologists. San Antonio.

Scholz, M., L. Bachmann, G. J. Nicholson, J. Bachmann, I. Giddings, B. Rüschoff-Thale, A. Czarnetzki, and C. M. Pusch. 2000. Genomic differentiation of Neanderthals and anatomically modern man allows a fossil DNA-based classification of morphologically indistinguishable hominid bones. *American Journal of Human Genetics* 66: 1927–32.

Schwartz, J. H. 1995. *Skeleton Keys: An Introduction to Human Skeletal Morphology, Development, and Analysis.* New York: Oxford.

Semaw, S., P. Renne, J. W. K. Harris, C. S. Feibel, R. L. Bernor, N. Fesseha, and K. Mowbray. 1997. 2.5-million-year-old stone tools from Gona, Ethiopia. *Nature* (January 23): 333–36.

Shackleton, N., J. Backman, H. Zimmerman, D. V. Dent, M. A. Hall, D. G. Roberts, D. Schnitker, J. G. Baldauf, A. Despraires, R. Homrighausen, P. Huddleston, J. B. Keene, A. J. Kaltenback, K. A. O. Krumsiek, A. C. Morton, J. W. Murray, and J. Westberg-Smith. 1984. Oxygen isotope calibration of the onset of ice-rafting and history of glaciation in the North Atlantic region. *Nature* 307: 620–23.

Shackleton, N. J., and N. D. Opdyke. 1973. Oxygen isotope and paleomagnetic stratigraphy of equatorial Pacific core V28-238: Oxygen isotope temperatures and ice volumes on a 10^5 and 10^6 year scale. *Quaternary Research* 3: 39–55.

———. 1976. Oxygen-isotope and paleomagnetic stratigraphy of Pacific core V28-239 Late Pliocene and latest Pleistocene. In *Investigation of Late Quaternary Paleoceanography and Paleoclimatology,* eds. R. M. Cline and J. Hays, pp. 449–64, Vol. 145: Geological Society of America.

Shapiro, H. L. 1974. *Peking Man.* New York: Simon & Schuster.

Sharer, R., and W. Ashmore. 1993. *Archaeology: Discovering Our Past.* 2nd ed. Mountain View, CA: Mayfield.

Shea, B. T. 1989. Heterochrony in human evolution: The case for neoteny reconsidered. *Yearbook of Physical Anthropology* 32: 69–101.

Shea, J. 1989. A functional study of the lithic industries associated with hominid fossils in Kebara and Qafzeh Caves, Israel. In *The Human Revolution: Behavioural and Biological Perspectives in the Origins of Modern Humans,* eds. P. Mellars and C. Stringer, pp. 611–25. Princeton, NJ: Princeton University Press.

———. 1998. Neandertal and early modern human behavioral variability: A regional scale approach to lithic evidence for hunting in the Levantine Mousterian. *Current Anthropology* 39(Supplement): S45–S61.

Sherwood, R. J. 2000. The status of early *Homo.* Paper delivered at the 69th annual meeting of the American Association of Physical Anthropologists. San Antonio.

Shipman, P. 1984. Scavenger hunt. *Natural History* 93(4): 20–27.

———. 1986. Scavenging or hunting in early hominids: Theoretical frameworks and tests. *American Anthropologist* 88: 27–43.

———. 1990. Old masters. *Discover* 11(7): 60–65.

Shipman, P., and J. Rose. 1983. Evidence of butchery and hominid activities at Torralba and Ambrona: An evaluation using microscopic techniques. *Journal of Archaeological Science* 10: 465–74.

Shreeve, J. 1994. *Erectus* rising. *Discover* (September): 80–89.

———. 1995. *The Neandertal Enigma: Solving the Mystery of Modern Human Origins.* New York: William Morrow.

———. 1996a. New skeleton gives path from trees to ground an odd turn. *Science* 272: 654.

———. 1996b. Sunset on the savanna. *Discover* 17(7): 116–25.

———. 1999. Secrets of the gene. *National Geographic* 196(4): 42–75.

———. 2006. The greatest journey. *National Geographic* 209(3): 73.

Sillen, A., and C. K. Brain. 1990. Old flame: Burned bones provide evidence of an early use of fire. *Natural History* 99(4): 6–10.

Simek, Jan F. 1992. Neanderthal cognition and the Middle to Upper Paleolithic transition. In *Continuity or Replacement: Controversies in* Homo sapiens *Evolution,* eds. G. Braüer and F. Smith, pp. 231–46. Rotterdam: Balkema.

Simerly, C. et al. 2003. Molecular correlates of primate nuclear transfer failures. *Science* 300: 297.

Simons, E. 1964. The early relatives of man. *Scientific American* 211(1): 50–62.

Simons, E. L., and T. Rasmussen. 1994. A whole new world of ancestors: Eocene anthropoideans from Africa. *Evolutionary Anthropology* 3(4): 128–39.

Simons, M. 1996. New species of early human reported found in Africa. *The New York Times.* May 23, p. A8.

Sinclair, A. 2003. Art of the ancients. *Nature* 426: 774–75.

Singer, R., and J. Wymer. 1982. *The Middle Stone Age at Klasies River Mouth in South Africa.* Chicago: University of Chicago Press.

Sloan, C. P. 1999. Feathers for *T. rex? National Geographic* 196(November): 99–107.

Smith, B. 1989. Origins of agriculture in Eastern North America. *Science* 246: 1566–70.

———. 1992a. Prehistoric plant husbandry in eastern North America. In *The Origins of Agriculture: An International Perspective,* eds. C. W. Cowan and P. J. Watson, pp. 101–19. Washington, DC: Smithsonian Institution Press.

———. (ed.). 1992b. *Rivers of Change: Essays on Early Agriculture in Eastern North America.* Washington, DC: Smithsonian Institution Press.

———. 1995. *The Emergence of Agriculture.* New York: Scientific American Library.

———. 1997. The initial domestication of *Cucurbita pepo* in the Americas 10,000 years ago. *Science* 276: 932–34.

Smith, B. H. 1993. The physiological age of KNM-WT 15000. In *The Nariokotome* Homo erectus *skeleton*, eds. A. Walker and R. Leakey, pp. 195–220. Cambridge, MA: Harvard University Press.

Smith, F., E. Trinkaus, P. B. Pettitt, I. Karavanic, and M. Paunovi. 1999. Direct radiocarbon dates for Vindija G1 and Velika PeCina Late Pleistocene hominid remains. *Proceedings of the National Academy of Sciences* 96: 1281–86.

Smith, F. H. 1984. Fossil hominid from the Upper Pleistocene of central Europe and the origins of modern Europeans. In *The Origins of Modern Humans: A World Survey of the Fossil Evidence*, eds. F. H. Smith and F. Spencer, pp. 137–210. New York: Liss.

———. 1991. The Neandertals: Evolutionary dead ends or ancestors of modern people. *Journal of Anthropological Research* 47(2): 219–38.

———. 1994. Samples, species, and speculations in the study of modern human origins. In *Origins of Anatomically Modern Humans*, eds. M. Nitecki and D. Nitecki, pp. 227–52. New York: Plenum.

Smith, F. H., A. B. Falsetti, and S. M. Donnelly. 1989. Modern human origins. *Yearbook of Physical Anthropology* 32: 35–68.

Smith, F. H., and F. Spencer (eds.). 1984. *The Origins of Modern Humans: A World Survey of the Fossil Evidence*. New York: Liss.

Smith, J. M. 1984. Science and myth. *Natural History* 93(11): 10–24.

Smith, M. A. 1987. Pleistocene occupation in arid Central Australia. *Nature* 328: 710–11.

Smuts, B. 1985. *Sex and Friendship in Baboons*. Hawthorne, NY: Aldine.

———. 1995. Apes of wrath. *Discover* (August): 35–57.

Soffer, O. 1993. Upper-Paleolithic adaptations in central and eastern Europe and man-mammoth interactions. In *From Kostenki to Clovis: Upper Paleolithic-Paleoindian Adaptations*, eds. O. Soffer and N. Preslov, pp. 31–50. New York: Plenum.

Solecki, R. S. 1971. *Shanidar: The First Flower People*. New York: Knopf.

Solheim, W. 1972. An earlier agricultural revolution. *Scientific American* 226(4): 34–41.

Solis, R. S., J. Haas, and W. Creamer. 2001. Dating Caral, a preceramic site in the Supe Valley on the central coast of Peru. *Science* 292: 723–26.

Sowunmi, M. A. 1985. The beginnings of agriculture in West Africa: Botanical evidence. *Current Anthropology* 26: 127–29.

Spencer, F. 1990. *Piltdown: A Scientific Forgery*. New York: Oxford University Press.

Sponheimer, M., and J. A. Lee-Thorp. 1999. Isotopic evidence for the diet of an early hominid, *Australopithecus africanus*. *Science* 283: 368–69.

Stanford, C. 1999. *The Hunting Apes: Meat Eating and the Origins of Human Behavior*. Princeton: Princeton University Press.

Stanford, C. B. 1995. To catch a colobus. *Natural History* 104(1): 48–55.

———. 1999. Gorilla warfare. *The Sciences* 39(4): 18–23.

Stedman, H. H., B. W. Kozyak, A. Nelson, D. M. Thesier, L. T. Su, D. W. Low, C. R. Bridges, J. B. Shrager, N. Minugh-Purvis, and M. A. Mitchell. 2004. Myosin gene mutation correlates with anatomical changes in the human lineage. *Nature* 428: 415–18.

Steele, D. G. 2000. The skeleton's tale. *Discovering Archaeology* 2(1): 61–62.

Stern, J. T., Jr. 2000. Climbing to the top: A personal memoir of *Australopithecus afarensis*. *Evolutionary Anthropology* 9(3): 113–33.

Steudel, K. 1996. Limb morphology, bipedal gait, and the energetics of hominid locomotion. *American Journal of Physical Anthropology* 99(2): 345–56.

Stiebing, W. H., Jr. 1993. *Uncovering the Past: A History of Archaeology*. New York: Oxford University Press.

Stipp, J. J., J. H. A. Chapell, and I. McDougall. 1967. K/Ar age estimate of the Pliocene-Pleistocene boundary in New Zealand. *American Journal of Science* 265: 462–74.

Stokstad, E. 2000. "Pre-Clovis" site fights for recognition. *Science* 288: 247.

Stone, A. C., and M. Stoneking. 1993. Ancient DNA from a pre-Columbian Amerindian population. *American Journal of Physical Anthropology* 92: 463–71.

Stoneking, M. 2001. From the evolutionary past . . . *Nature* 409: 821–22.

Strait, D. S., and F. E. Grine. 1999. Cladistics and early hominid phylogeny. *Science* 285: 1210.

Strait, D. S., F. E. Grine, and M. A. Moniz. 1997. A reappraisal of early hominid phylogeny. *Journal of Human Evolution*. 32(1): 17–82.

Straus, L. G. 1989. Age of the modern Europeans. *Nature* 342: 476–77.

Straus, W. L., and A. J. E. Cave. 1957. Pathology and the posture of Neandertal Man. *Quarterly Review of Biology* 32: 348–63.

Stringer, C. 2003. Out of Ethiopia. *Nature* 423: 692–95.

Stringer, C., and R. McKie. 1996. *African Exodus: The Origins of Modern Humanity.* New York: Holt.

Stringer, C. B. 1974. A multivariate study of the Petralona skull. *Journal of Human Evolution* 3: 397–404.

———. 1988. The dates of Eden. *Nature* 331: 565–66.

———. 1989. The origin of early modern humans: A comparison of the European and non-European evidence. In *The Human Revolution: Behavioural and Biological Perspectives in the Origins of Modern Humans,* eds. P. Mellars and C. Stringer, pp. 232–44. Princeton, NJ: Princeton University Press.

———. 1990. The emergence of modern humans. *Scientific American* 263(6): 98–104.

———. 1992a. Reconstructing recent human evolution. *Philosophical Transactions of the Royal Society of London (B)* 337: 217–24.

———. 1992b. Replacement, continuity, and the origin of *Homo sapiens.* In *Continuity or Replacement: Controversies in* Homo Sapiens *Evolution,* eds. G. Bräuer and F. Smith, pp. 9–24. Rotterdam: Balkema.

———. 1993. Secrets of the pit of the bones. *Nature* 362: 501–2.

———. 1994. Out of Africa: A personal history. In *Origins of Anatomically Modern Humans,* eds. M. Nitecki and D. Nitecki, pp. 149–74. New York: Plenum.

Stringer, C. B., and P. Andrews. 1988. Genetic and fossil evidence for the origin of modern humans. *Science* 239: 1263–68.

Stringer, C. B., and C. Gamble. 1993. *In Search of the Neanderthals.* New York: Thames and Hudson.

Stringer, C. B., and R. Grün. 1991. Time for the last Neandertals. *Nature* 351: 701–2.

Stringer, C. B., R. Grün, H. P. Schwarcz, and P. Goldberg. 1989. ESR dates for the hominid burial site of Es Skhul in Israel. *Nature* 338: 756–58.

Stringer, C. B., J. J. Hublin, and B. Vandermeersch. 1984. The origin of anatomically modern humans in western Europe. In *The Origins of Modern Humans: A World Survey of the Fossil Evidence,* eds. F. H. Smith and F. Spencer, pp. 51–136. New York: Liss.

Struever, S., and F. A. Holton. 2000. *Koster: Americans in Search of Their Prehistoric Past.* Garden City, NY: Anchor Press/Doubleday.

Strum, S. 1987. *Almost Human.* New York: Random House.

Stuart, G. E. 1972. Who were the "mound builders"? *National Geographic* 142(6): 783–801.

Susman, R. L. 1994. Fossil evidence for early hominid tool use. *Science* 265: 1570–73.

Sussman, R. W. 1997. Exploring our basic human nature: Are humans inherently violent? *AnthroNotes* 19(3): 1–6, 17–19.

Suwa, G. et al. 1997. The first skull of *Australopithecus boisei.* *Nature* 389: 489–92.

Svoboda, J. 1993. The complex origin of the Upper Paleolithic in the Czech and Slovak Republics. In *Before Lascaux: The Complex Record of the Early Upper Paleolithic,* eds. H. Knecht, A. Pike-Tay, and R. White, pp. 23–36. Boca Raton, FL: CRC Press.

Swisher, C. C., G. H. Curtis, T. Jacob, A. G. Getty, A. Suprijo, and Widiasmoro. 1994. Age of the earliest known hominids in Java, Indonesia. *Science* 263: 1118–21.

Swisher III, C. C., W. J. Rink, S. C. Antón, H. P. Schwarcz, G. H. Curtis, A Suprijo, and Widiasmoro. 1996. Latest *Homo erectus* of Java: Potential contemporaneity with *Homo sapiens* in Southeast Asia. *Science* 274: 1870–74.

Szabo, B., and D. Collins. 1975. Ages of fossil bones from British interglacial sites. *Nature* 254: 680–82.

Tainter, J. A. 1988. *The Collapse of Complex Societies.* Cambridge, Eng.: Cambridge University Press.

Takai, M., F. Anaya, N. Shigehara, and T. Setoguchi. 2000. New fossil materials of the earliest New World monkey, *Branisella boliviana,* and the problem of platyrrhine origins. *American Journal of Physical Anthropology* 111: 263–81.

Tattersall, I. 1992. The many faces of *Homo habilis. Evolutionary Anthropology* 1(1): 33–37.

———. 1993. *The Human Odyssey: Four Million Years of Human Evolution.* New York: Prentice Hall.

———. 1995. *The Fossil Trail: How We Know What We Think We Know About Human Evolution.* New York: Oxford University Press.

———. 2000. Once we were not alone. *Scientific American* 282(1): 56–62.

———. 2001. How we came to be human. *Scientific American* 285(6): 56–63.

———. 2003. Stand and deliver: Why did early hominids begin to walk on two feet? *Natural History* (November): 61–64.

Tattersall, I., and J. Schwarz. 2000. *Extinct humans.* Boulder, CO: Westview.

Taveré, S., C. R. Marshall, O. Will, C. Soligo, and R. D. Martin. 2002. Using the fossil record to estimate the age of the last common ancestor of extant primates. *Nature* 416: 726–29.

Taylor, R. E. 1991. Frameworks for dating the Late Pleistocene peopling of the Americas. In *The First Americans: Search and Research,* eds. T. D. Dillehay and D. J. Meltzer, pp. 77–111. Boca Raton, FL: CRC Press.

Templeton, A. R. 1993. The "Eve" hypothesis: A genetic critique and reanalysis. *American Anthropologist* 95: 51–72.

———. 1996. Gene lineages and human evolution. *Science* 272: 1363.

———. 1997. Testing the out of Africa replacement hypothesis with mitochondrial DNA data. In *Conceptual Issues in Modern Human Origins Research,* eds. G. A. Clark and C. M. Willermet, pp. 329–60. New York: Aldine de Gruyter.

Templeton, A. R. 2002. Out of Africa again and again. *Nature* 416: 45–51.

Thieme, H. 1997. Lower Paleolithic hunting spears from Germany. *Nature* 385: 807–10.

Thomas, D. H. 1989. *Archaeology.* 2nd ed. New York: Holt, Rinehart & Winston.

———. 2000. *Skull Wars: Kennewick Man, Archaeology, and the Battle for Native American Identity.* New York: Basic Books.

Thorne, A., R. Grün, G. Mortimer, N. A. Spooner, J. J. Simpson, M. McCulloch, L. Taylor, and D. Curnoe. 1999. Australia's oldest human remains: Age of the Lake Mungo skeleton. *Journal of Human Evolution* 36(6): 591–612.

Thorne, A. G., and M. H. Wolpoff. 1992. The multiregional evolution of humans. *Scientific American* 266(4): 76–83.

Tishkoff, S. A., E. Dietzsch, W. Speed, A. J. Pakstis, J. R. Kidd, K. Cheung, B. Bonné-Tamir, A. S. Santachiara-Benerecetti, P. Moral, M. Krings, S. Pääbo, E. Watson, N. Risch, T. Jenkins, and K. K. Kidd. 1996. Global patterns of linkage disequilibrium at the CD4 locus and modern human origins. *Science* 271: 1380–87.

Tobias, P. V. 1987. The brain of *Homo habilis:* A new level of organization in cerebral evolution. *Journal of Human Evolution* 16: 741–61.

Todd, I. A. 1976. *Catal Hüyük in Perspective.* Menlo Park, CA: Benjamin/Cummings.

Toth, N. 1985. The Oldowan reassessed: A close look at early stone artifacts. *Journal of Archaeological Science* 2: 101–20.

Trinkaus, E. (ed.). 1983a. Neanderthal postcrania and the adaptive shift to modern humans. In *The Mousterian Legacy,* pp. 165–200. Oxford: British Archaeological Reports, International Series, 164.

———. 1983b. *The Shanidar Neandertals.* New York: Academic Press.

———. 1984. Western Asia. In *The Origins of Modern Humans: A World Survey of the Fossil Evidence,* eds. F. H. Smith and F. Spencer, pp. 251–94. New York: Liss.

———. 1986. The Neandertals and modern human origins. *Annual Review of Anthropology* 15: 193–218.

Trinkaus, E., and P. Shipman. 1993. *The Neandertals: Changing Images of Mankind.* New York: Knopf.

Trinkaus, E., and D. D. Thompson. 1987. Femoral diaphyseal histophometric age determinators for the Shanidar 3, 4, 5 and 6 Neandertals and Neandertal longevity. *American Journal of Physical Anthropology* 72: 123–29.

Trinkhaus, E., and I. Villemeur. 1991. Mechanical advantages of the Neandertal thumb in flexion: A test of an hypothesis. *American Journal of Physical Anthropology* 84: 249–60.

Troy, C. C., D. E. MacHugh, J. F. Bailey, D. A. Magee, R. T. Loftus, P. Cunningham, A. T. Chamberlain, B. C. Sykes, and D. G. Bradley. 2001. Genetic evidence for Near-Eastern origins of European cattle. *Nature* 410: 1088–91.

Turner, B. L., and P. Harrison (eds.). 1983. *Pulltrouser Swamp: Ancient Maya Habitat, Agriculture, and Settlement in Northern Belize.* Austin: University of Texas Press.

Tuross, N., and T. D. Dillehay. 1995. The mechanism of organic preservation at Monte Verde, Chile and the use of biomolecules in archaeological interpretation. *Journal of Field Archaeology* 22: 97–101.

Tylor, E. B. 1871. *Primitive Culture: Part I—The Origins of Culture.* 1958 ed. New York: Harper and Brothers.

Unger-Hamilton, R. 1989. The epi-Paleolithic southern Levant and the origins of cultivation. *Current Anthropology* 30: 88–103.

Valdes, V. C., and J. L. Bischoff. 1989. Accelerator ^{14}C dates for Early Upper Paleolithic (Basal Aurignacian) at El Castillo Cave (Spain). *Journal of Archaeological Science* 16: 577–84.

Valladas, H., J. L. Reyss, J. L. Joron, G. Valladas, O. Bar-Yosef, and B. Vandermeersch. 1988. Thermoluminescence dating of Mousterian "Proto-Cro-Magnon" remains from Israel and the origin of modern man. *Nature* 331: 614–16.

Van Peer, P. 1992. *The Levallois Reduction Strategy.* Monographs in World Archaeology. Vol. 13. Madison, WI: Prehistory Press.

Van Peer, P., and P. M. Vermeersch. 1990. Middle to Upper Paleolithic transition: The evidence for the Nile Valley.

In *The Emergence of Modern Humans: An Archaeological Perspective,* ed. P. Mellars, pp. 139–59. Ithaca, NY: Cornell University Press.

Van Riper, A. B. 1993. *Men Among the Mammoths: Victorian Science and the Discovery of Human Prehistory.* Chicago: University of Chicago Press.

Van Tilburg, J. A. 1995. Moving the moai: Transporting the megaliths of Easter Island: How did they do it? *Archaeology* 48(1): 34–43.

Vekua, A. et al. 2002. A new skull of early *Homo* from Dmanisi, Georgia. *Science* 297: 85–89.

Videan, E. N., and W. C. McGrew. 2000. Bipedality in chimpanzees and bonobos: Testing hypothesized selection pressures. Paper delivered at the 69th annual meeting of the American Association of Physical Anthropologists. San Antonio.

Vietmeyer, N. 1992. Forgotten roots of the Incas. In *Chilies to Chocolate: Food the Americas Gave the World,* eds. N. Foster and L. S. Cordell, pp. 95–104. Tucson: University of Arizona Press.

Vignaud, P. et al. 2002. Geology and palaeontology of the Upper Miocene Toros-Menalla hominid locality, Chad. *Nature* 418: 152–55.

Villa, P. 1982. Conjoinable pieces and site formation processes. *American Antiquity* 47: 276–90.

Wade, N. 1998. Human or chimp? 50 genes are the key. *New York Times* (October 20): F1,4.

Walker, A. 1993. Perspectives on the Nariokotome discovery. In *The Nariokotome* Homo erectus *Skeleton,* eds. A. Walker and R. Leakey, pp. 411–30. Cambridge, MA: Harvard University Press.

Walker, A., and R. Leakey (eds.). 1993. *The Nariokotome* Homo erectus *Skeleton.* Cambridge, MA: Harvard University Press.

Walker, A., and C. B. Ruff. 1993. The reconstruction of the pelvis. In *The Nariokotome* Homo erectus *Skeleton,* eds. A. Walker and R. Leakey, pp. 221–33. Cambridge, MA: Harvard University Press.

Walker, A., and P. Shipman. 1996. *The Wisdom of the Bones.* New York: Vintage Books.

Walsh, J. E. 1996. *Unraveling Piltdown: The Science Fraud of the Century and its Solution.* New York: Random House.

Walsh, P. D. et al. 2003. Catastrophic ape decline in western equatorial Africa. *Nature* 422: 611–14.

Wang, H., T. Nussbaum-Wagler, B. Li, Q. Zhao, Y. Vigouroux, M. Faller, K. Bomblies, L. Lukens, and J. F. Doebley. 2005. The origin of the naked grains of maize. *Nature* 436: 714–19.

Wang, R.-L., A. Stec, J. Hey, L. Lukens, and J. Doebley. 1999. The limits of selection during maize domestication. *Nature* 398: 236–39.

Ward, C., M. Leakey, and A. Walker. 1999. The new hominid species *Australopithecus anamensis. Evolutionary Anthropology* 7(6): 197–205.

Ward, S., B. Brown, A. Hill, J. Kelley, and W. Downs. 1999. *Equatorius:* A new hominoid genus from the Middle Miocene of Kenya. *Science* 285: 1382–86.

Warren, P. 1975. *The Aegean Civilizations.* Oxford, Eng.: Elsevier Phaidon.

———. 1987. Crete: The Minoans and their gods. In *Origins: The Roots of European Civilisation,* ed. B. Cunliffe, pp. 30–41. Chicago: Dorsey Press.

Watson, J. D. 1968. *The Double Helix.* New York: Athenaeum.

Weaver, K. 1985. The search for our ancestors. *National Geographic* 168(5): 560–623.

Weaver, M. P. 1972. *The Aztecs, the Maya, and Their Predecessors: Archaeology of Mesoamerica.* New York: Seminar Press.

Webster, D. 2002. *The Fall of the Ancient Maya: Solving the Mystery of the Maya Collapse.* London: Thames and Hudson.

Weiner, J. 1994. *The Beak of the Finch: A Story of Evolution in Our Time.* New York: Knopf.

Weiner, J. S. 1955. *The Piltdown Forgery.* London: Oxford Press.

Weiner, J. S., and B. G. Campbell. 1964. The taxonomic status of the Swanscombe skull. In *The Swanscombe Skull: A Survey of Research on a Pleistocene Site,* ed. C. Ovey, pp. 175–209. Royal Institute of Great Britain and Ireland, Occasional Paper 20.

Weiner, S., Q. Xu, P. Goldberg, J. Liu, and O. Bar-Yosef. 1998. Evidence for the use of fire at Zhoukoudian, China. *Science* 281: 251–53.

Weiss, G., and A. von Haeseler. 1996. Technical comments: Estimating the age of the common ancestor of men from the ZFY intron. *Science* 272: 1359–60.

Wendorf, F., A. E. Close, R. Schild, K. Wasylikowa, R. A. Housley, J. R. Harlan, and H. Królik. 1992. Saharan exploitation of plants 8,000 years B.P. *Nature* 359: 721–24.

Wendt, W. E. 1976. Art mobilier from the Apollo 11 Cave, South West Africa: Africa's oldest dated works of art. *South African Archaeological Bulletin* 31: 5–11.

Wheat, J. B. 1972. *The Olsen–Chubbuck Site: A Paleo-Indian Bison Kill.* Salt Lake City: Memoirs of the Society for American Archaeology, No. 26.

Wheatly, P. 1971. *The Pivot of the Four Quarters.* Chicago: Aldine.

White, F. J. 1996. *Pan paniscus* 1973 to 1996: Twenty-three years of field research. *Evolutionary Anthropology* 5(1) 11–17.

White, J. P., and J. F. O'Connell. 1982. *A Prehistory of Australia, New Guinea, and Sahul.* New York: Academic Press.

White, P. T. 1982. The temples of Angkor: Ancient glory in stone. *National Geographic* 161(5): 552–89.

White, R. 1982. Rethinking the Middle-Upper Paleolithic transition. *Current Anthropology* 23(2): 169–92.

———. 1993. Technological and social dimensions of "Aurignacian-age" body ornaments across Europe. In *Before Lascaux: The Complex Record of the Early Upper Paleolithic,* eds. H. Knecht, A. Pike-Tay, and R. White, pp. 277–99. Boca Raton, FL: CRC Press.

White, T. 1986. Cut marks on the Bodo cranium: A case of prehistoric defleshing. *American Journal of Physical Anthropology* 69: 503–9.

White, T. D. 2001. Once we were cannibals. *Scientific American* 285(2): 58–65.

———. 2003. Early hominids—diversity or distortion? *Science* 299: 1994–97.

White, T. D., B. Asfaw, D. DeGusta, H. Gilbert, G. D. Richards, G. Suwa, and F. C. Howell. 2003. Pleistocene *Homo sapiens* from Middle Awash, Ethiopia. *Nature* 423: 742–47.

White, T. D., and P. A. Folkens. 1991. *Human Osteology.* San Diego: Academic Press.

White, T. D., G. Suwa, and B. Asfaw. 1994. *Australopithecus ramidus,* a new species of early hominid from Aramis, Ethiopia. *Nature* 371: 306–12.

———. 1995. Corrigendum. *Nature* 375: 88.

White, T. D., G. Suwa, S. Simpson, and B. Asfaw. 2000. Jaws and teeth of *Australopithecus afarensis* from Maka, Middle Awash, Ethiopia. *American Journal of Physical Anthropology* 111: 45–68.

Whiten, A., and C. Boesch. 2001. The cultures of chimpanzees. *Scientific American* (January): 60–67.

Whiten, A., J. Goodall, W. C. McGrew, T. Nishida, V. Reynolds, Y. Sugiyama, C. E. G. Tutin, R. W. Wrangham, and C. Boesch. 1999. Cultures in chimpanzees. *Nature* 399: 682–85.

Whittle, A. 1985. *Neolithic Europe: A Survey.* Cambridge, Eng.: Cambridge University Press.

Wilford, J. N. 2004. The oldest Americans may prove even older. *New York Times.* June 29, p. F1.

Wilkinson, T. 2003. Who were the first kings of Egypt? In *The Seventy Great Mysteries of Ancient Egypt,* ed. B. Manley, 28–32. London: Thames and Hudson.

Williams, S. 1991. *Fantastic Archaeology: The Wild Side of North American Prehistory.* Philadelphia: University of Pennsylvania Press.

Wilmsen, E. 1974. *Lindenmeier: A Pleistocene Hunting Society.* New York: Harper & Row.

Wilmut, I. 1998. Cloning for medicine. *Scientific American* 279(6): 58–63.

Wilson, A. C., and R. L. Cann. 1992. The recent African genesis of humans. *Scientific American* 266(4): 68–73.

Wing, E. 1977. Animal domestication in the Andes. In *Origins of Agriculture,* ed. C. A. Reed, pp. 837–60. The Hague: Mouton.

Wittfogel, K. 1957. *Oriental Despotism: A Comparative Study of Total Power.* New Haven, CT: Yale University Press.

Wolpoff, M. 1980a. Cultural remains of Middle Pleistocene hominids. *Journal of Human Evolution* 9: 339–58.

———. 1980b. *Paleoanthropology.* New York: Knopf.

———. 1984. Evolution in *Homo erectus:* The question of stasis. *Paleobiology* 10: 389–406.

———. 1988. The place of the Neandertals in human evolution. In *The Emergence of Modern Humans: Biocultural Adaptations in the Later Pleistocene,* ed. E. Trinkaus, pp. 97–141. New York: Cambridge University Press.

———. 1989. Multiregional evolution: The fossil alternative to Eden. *The Human Revolution: Behavioural and Biological Perspectives in the Origins of Modern Humans,* eds. P. Mellars and C. Stringer, pp. 62–108. Princeton, NJ: Princeton University Press.

———. 1998a. Concocting a divisive theory. *Evolutionary Anthropology* 7(1): 1–3.

———. 1998b. Neandertals: Not so fast. *Science* 282: 1991.

Wolpoff, M., and R. Caspari. 1997. *Race and Human Evolution: A Fatal Attraction.* New York: Simon & Schuster.

Wolpoff, M., X. Z. Wu, and A. G. Thorpe. 1984. Modern *Homo sapiens* origins: A general theory of hominid evolution involving the fossil evidence from East Asia. In *The Origins of Modern Humans: A World Survey of the Fossil Evidence,* eds. F. H. Smith and F. Spencer, pp. 411–84. New York: Liss.

Wolpoff, M. H., J. Hawks, and R. Caspari. 2000. Multiregional, not multiple origins. *American Journal of Physical Anthropology* 112: 129–36.

Wolpoff, M H., J. Hawks, D. W. Frayer, and K. Hunley. 2001. Modern human ancestry at the peripheries: A test of the replacement theory. *Science* 291: 293–97.

Wolpoff, M. H., B. Senut, M. Pickford, and J. Hawks. 2002. Brief communication. *Nature* 419: 581–82.

Wolpoff, M. H., A. G. Thorne, F. H. Smith, D. W. Frayer, and G. G. Pope. 1994. Multiregional evolution: A worldwide source for modern human populations. In *Origins of Anatomically Modern Humans,* eds. M. Nitecki and D. Nitecki, pp. 175–99. New York: Plenum.

Wong, K. 1998. Ancestral quandary. *Scientific American* 278(1): 30–32.

———. 2003. An ancestor to call our own. *Scientific American* 288(1): 54–63.

———. 2005. The littlest human. *Scientific American* 292(2): 56–65.

Wood, B. 2002. Hominid revelations from Chad. *Nature* 418: 133–35.

Wood, B., and M. Collard. 1999. The human genus. *Science* 284: 65–71.

Wood, B. A. 1984. The origin of *Homo erectus. Courier Forschungsinstitut Seckenberg* 69: 99–111.

———. 1992. Early hominid species and speciation. *Journal of Human Evolution.* 22:351–65.

Woodhead, A. D., and B. J. Barnhart. 1988. *Biotechnology and the Human Genome.* New York: Plenum.

Wrangham, R. W. 2000. A view on the science: Physical anthropology at the millennium. *American Journal of Physical Anthropology* 111: 445–49.

Wright, G. 1971. Origins of food production in Southwestern Asia: A survey of ideas. *Current Anthropology* 12: 447–77.

Wu, R. (Woo Ju-kang). 1985. New Chinese *Homo erectus* and recent work at Zhoukoudian. In *Ancestors: The Hard Evidence,* ed. E. Delson, pp. 245–48. New York: Liss.

Wu, R. (Woo Ju-kang) and S. Lin. 1983. Peking Man. *Scientific American* 248(6): 86–94.

Yamei, H., R. Potts, Y. Baoyin, G. Zhengtang, A. Deino, W. Wei, J. Clark, X. Guangmao, and H. Weiwen. 2000. Mid-Pleistocene Acheulean-like stone technology of the Bose Basin, South China. *Science* 287: 1622–26.

Yarnell, R. 1977. Native plant husbandry north of Mexico. In *Origins of Agriculture,* ed. C. A. Reed, pp. 861–78. The Hague: Mouton.

Yellen, J. E., A. S. Brooks, E. Cornelissen, M. J. Mehlman, and K. Stewart. 1995. A Middle Stone Age worked bone industry from Katanda, Upper Semliki Valley, Zaire. *Science* 268: 553–56.

Yi, S., and G. Clark. 1985. The "Dyuktai Culture" and New World origins. *Current Anthropology* 26: 1–13.

Yokoyama, Y., K. Lambeck, P. De Deckker, P. Johnsston, and L. K. Fifield. 2000. Timing of the Last Glacial Maximum from observed sea-level minima. *Nature* 406: 713–16.

Yoon, C. K. 1998. Iguanas sail from Guadeloupe to Anguilla and into history. *New York Times* (October 8).

Zeder, M., and B. Hesse. 2000. The initial domestication of goats (*Capra hircus*) in the Zagros Mountains 10,000 years ago. *Science* 287: 2254–57.

Zhu, R. X. et al. 2001. Earliest presence of humans in northeast Asia. *Nature* 413: 413–17.

Zilhao, J. 2001. Radiocarbon evidence for maritime pioneer colonization at the origins of farming in west Mediterranean Europe. *Proceedings of the National Academy of Sciences,* 98: 14180–14185.

Zimmer, C. 1994. Cows were in the air. *Discover* 15(9): 29.

Zohary, D., and M. Hopf. 1994. *Domestication of Plants in the Old World.* Oxford: Clarendon Press.

INDEX

Page numbers in italic type refer to figures or tables.

absolute dating, 179
Abu Simbel, *464, 470, 471*
Abydos site (Egypt), 495
accelerator mass spectrometry (AMS), 181
Acheulian toolmaking, 280–284, *281, 282*
Adam and Eve, *5*
Adapidae, 135
adaptation, 28, 144–147
 Pleistocene epoch, 408
 sickle cell anemia, 87–88
Adovasio, James, 363
Aegyptopithecus, 136, *136*
Africa. *See also* Egypt
 agriculture, 410, 436–439, *437*
 civilizations, *528,* 528–531, *535*
 climate/vegetation zones, 241, *241*
 domestication, 436–439, *437*
 Holocene, 410
 Homo erectus in, 272
 Homo habilis, 263–264
 Homo sapiens, modern, 323–324, 330–335
 Homo sapiens, premodern, *310,* 321
 models of human evolution, 320–323, 325, 331, 334–339, 351
 monumental works, *529*
 site locations, 171, *171, 224,* 235, *237,* 238, 245, 246, 262, 263, 271, 285, *328,* 358, *436, 437,* 439, 494–495, *495,* 530
African Exodus: The Origins of Modern Humanity (McKie/Stringer), 351

agriculture, *406,* 407–462. *See also* domestication
 Africa, 410, 436–439, *437*
 definition, 407
 diet and, 457
 by diffusion, 417
 Europe, 408–410, *442,* 443–445
 food and labor surplus, 467
 food production, 415–423
 hypotheses for, 415–423, *416–417,* 459–462
 irrigation, 535
 maize (corn), 445–448, *446, 447, 448, 449,* 450, 455–457
 Mesoamerica, 445–451
 North America, 454–457
 nutritional impact, 458
 "resource ceiling," 423
 slash-and-burn, 511
 South America, 451–454
 Southeast Asia, 410, 439–442
 Southwest Asia, 428–436, *430,* 445
 Tehuacán Valley, 448–451
 Teotihuacán, 508–509
 wheat, 431, 434–436, *435*
Aguadulce Shelter site (Panama), 452
Ali Kosh site (Iran), 432–434, *433*
allele frequency, 82
alleles, 75, 78
 codominant, 81
 dominant, 78
 frequency of, 82
 heterozygous, 78
 homozygous, 78
 mutations and, 78
 recessive, 78
Allen, J., 382
Altamira cave (Spain), 369

Ambrona site (Spain), 286
Ameki site (Mali), 439
American Sign Language, primate use of, 127
Americas, 385–391, 393, 396–402. *See also* Mesoamerica; North America; South America
 Archaic period, 408–410
 Arctic, 401–402
 first settlements, 390–391
 glacial periods, 391, *391*
 land migration, *386,* 386–390
 Paleo-Indians, 399–401
 site locations, *26, 164, 178,* 364–365, 367, *388,* 393, *395, 395, 396, 396,* 397, 401, 409, 445, 450, 452, 454, 455, 456, *456,* 458
 skeletal remains, 397–399
 tools, *389, 392, 394, 395*
 underwater research, 396–397
amino acids, 54, 74
amphioxus, *109*
AMS. *See* accelerator mass spectrometry
analogies, 144–146, *145*
 ethnographic, 158–161
Ancient Society (Morgan), 38
"The Ancient One," 398
Anderson, Edgar, 420
Angkor Wat, 532, *533*
Ankarapithecus, 137
anthropod primates, 120–123, 126–127
anthropological linguistics, 12
Anthropology, 11–14. *See also* cultural anthropology; physical (biological) anthropology
apes, *125,* 126. *See also* primates
 extinction of, in Africa, 140
appearance, reconstruction of, 215–217

Archaeopteryx, 70, 98
Archaic period, 408–410
archeology, 166–176
    Australia, 382–385
    compliance, 172
    data collection, *173,* 173–177, *174*
    dating sites, 177–187
    definition, 12–13
    dietary reconstruction, 194–198
    environment reconstruction,
        191–194, *193, 194*
    ethnoarcheology, 188
    ideology reconstruction, 202–203
    reconstructing pathways, 187–203
    sexual identification, 208–210
    site discovery process, 167–172
    social system reconstructing,
        199–200
    technology restructuring, 189–191,
        192
    trade reconstruction from, 200–202
Arches National Monument (Utah), *22*
Arctic, 401–402
Arctic Small Tool Tradition, 402
Ardipithecus kadabba, 238, 245, 253
Ardipithecus ramidus, 230, 232, 232, 236,
    245
argon/argon dating, 183–184
"Arlington Man," 397
Armelagos, George, 458
art
    in Africa, 367
    Australia, 367
    Chavin style, *522,* 522–523
    civilization, *470,* 470–471
    Olmec style, *512, 513,* 513–514
    personal adornment, 364–365, *365*
    rock art, 380
    South America, 367, *524*
    Upper Paleolithic, 358, 364–365,
        367–381, 544
artifacts, 126, 167
    Egyptian, *496, 497*
    Indus Valley, *502, 505*
    Mesopotamia, *487*
    Shang civilization, *505*
artificial selection, 412–413
As You Like It (Shakespeare), 18
Asia
    fossil sites, *203,* 265, 277, 278, *278,*
        364, 366, 389
    site locations, 410
associations, 174
Attenborough, David, 150

Aurignacian toolmaking, 329–330, *361*
Australia
    archeology, 382–385
    art, 367
    early settlements, 381–385
    Greater, 381, *382*
    site locations, 383–385, *384*
    Upper Paleolithic migration, 381–385
australopithecines
    definition of, 64
    endocasts, *288*
    evolution of, 227, 247–249
    fossils, 65
Australopithecus afarensis, 230, 233–234,
    234, 235
    characteristics of, 234–235
    habitat, 245
    knuckle-walking, 240
    "Lucy," 233, *234*
    phylogenetic relationships, 248
Australopithecus africanus, 227, *230, 247*
Australopithecus anamensis, 230, 233,
    233, 234
    habitat, 245
    knuckle-walking, 240
Australopithecus bahrelghazalia, 235,
    245
Australopithecus garhi, 249
Axum civilization, 529–530

baboons, 147–148, *148. See also* primates
    estrus, 148, *149*
Babylonian creation myths, 8
Bacon, Francis, 474
Bar-Yosef, Ofer, 431
behavior patterns
    bonobos, 154–158, *157*
    chimpanzees, 150–153
    gorillas, 149
    Homo erectus, 277–288
    in humans, 128–129
    primates, 116–117
    reconstruction of, 217, *218,* 219
Bellantoni, Nick, *14*
Beringia, 386, 386–387
Bible, 8, 18
bifacial tools, 280–281, *282, 328*
Big Bang theory, 50–53, *51, 67*
Binford, Lewis, 264, 285, 422
biology, etymology, 26–27
biostratigraphy, 45
bipedalism
    as adaptive response, 64, *64*
    benefits of, 239–242

    evolutionary evidence from bones,
        240
    in hominid evolution, 112, 227–228,
        232–236
    models for emergence, 242–244
    in primates, 112
Birdsell, Joseph, 381
Black Skull, 249–250, *250*
Blombos Cave (South Africa), 358, *359*
blood cells, *80*
blood types, 343–345
    worldwide distribution, *344*
Bobongara Hill site (Australia), 383
body build, 345–346
Boker Tachtit site (Israel), 361
bones. *See also* fossils; skulls, fossil
    age at death from, 210–211
    in Americas, 397–399
    appearance reconstruction from,
        215–217
    australopithecines, *288*
    behavior pattern reconstruction from,
        217, *218,* 219
    behavior reconstruction from,
        128–129
    cut marks, 287, *287*
    diet reconstruction from, 194–198,
        195
    dinosaurs, *26*
    excavation unit ethics, 175–176
    Gran Dolina cave, *293*
    health reconstruction from, 211–212,
        214
    human skeleton, *203*
    Neandertals, 298, *302*
    occipital, in hominid skulls, 266
    Olduvai Gorge, *263*
    sexual dimorphism, 208, *209*
    species definition and identification
        from, 205–208
    "Turkana Boy," *271*
Bonnischen, Rob, 399
bonobos, *125, 142, 155. See also*
    primates
    behavior patterns, 154–158, *157*
    dominance hierarchy among, 156
    intelligence, 542
    taxonomy, *118*
Bos primigenius, 438
Bos Taurus, 445
Boserup, Ester, 421
Boucher de Perthes, Jacques, 36
Bowdler, Sandra, 382
The Boys from Brazil (Levin), 100

brachiation, 114–115
Braidwood, Robert, 419
brains
    early *Homo,* 264
    size increase during human
        evolution, 65, 290–296
Bräuer, G., 336
breeding populations, 82
Bronze Age, 191
Bryan, William Jennings, 43, *43*
Bryce Canyon (Utah), *16*
Burger, Richard, 522
burials
    Neandertal ceremonialism, 304–306,
        305, 366
    North America, *203*
    Olmec, 513
    Shang civilization, *506*
    South America, *525*
    Upper Paleolithic, 366–367
Burnet, Reverend Thomas, 19
Bus Mordeh people, 432–433, *433*

Cactus Hill, 393, *394,* 395
Cahokia civilization, *531,* 531–532
calibration curves, 185, *186*
Callen, E.O., 450
camelids, 454
cannibalism, among Neandertals,
    307–308
Caral site (Peru), 519–520, *520*
carbon dating. *See* radiocarbon dating
carbon isotope analysis, 197, 451
Carneiro, Robert, 481
carrying capacity, 422
Cartmill, Matt, 134, 351
carvings/engravings
    Upper Paleolithic, *376,* 376–378, *377*
Caspari, Rachel, 321
Çatalhöyük (Turkey), 482, *484,*
    484–485
Catarrhini, 118, 120
catastrophists, 19
cattle, domestication of, 427, 438, 444
Cavalli-Sforza, L.L., 352
cave bears, 306–307
cave paintings, 369–376, *372*
    animal symbolism, 370–373
    "Chinese horse," *370*
    Europe, *374*
    geometric signs, 373
    "Great Black Aurochs," *371*
    handprints, 375, *375*
    human depictions, 373–376, *374, 375*

radiocarbon dating, 374
    Upper Paleolithic, *356, 368,* 369–376
Caverna de Pedra Pintada (Brazil), 367,
    401
cells
    blood, *80*
    division, *79*
    donor, for genetic cloning, 100
    structure, *73*
central places, 493
Cercopithecidae, *118,* 120
Cercopithecoidea, *118,* 120
cereal crops, 429
Chalmers, Reverend Thomas, 22
Chang, K.C., 507
Châtelperronian toolmaking, 330
Chauvet Cave (France), *372*
Chavin style, *522,* 522–523
Chen-chou site (China), 507
chiefdoms, 468
Childe, V. Gordon, 418
chimpanzees, *125,* 126–127, *127,*
    149–154, *152, 154. See also*
        bonobos; primates
    behavior patterns, 150–153
    dominance hierarchy among, 152
    genetic similarities to humans, *131,*
        331
    Goodall on, 149–150
    gorillas v., 150
    intelligence, 542
    taxonomy, *118*
    tool use, *127*
    vocal apparatus, *289*
China, 504, 506–507
    civilizations, 506–507, *535*
    cultures, 506–507
    social stratification, 507
"Chinese horse," *370*
chromosomes, 74, 90–91
chronometric dating, 179–186
Chuan, Kun Ho, 285
circumscription hypothesis, 481
city-states, 490
civilization, 465–538, 545–546
    Africa, *528,* 528–531
    art, *470,* 470–471
    chiefdoms, 468
    China, 504, 506–507
    chronology, *535,* 535–536
    collapse of, 536–537
    definition, 466–467
    earliest locations, *466*
    Egypt, 492–497

Europe, 526–528
    evolution hypotheses, 476, *477,*
        478–481, *479,* 535
    formal government development,
        468–469
    Indus Valley, 497–504
    labor specialization, 470–471
    Mesoamerica, 508–517
    Mesopotamia, *475,* 485–491
    monumental works, 471–473
    North America, *531,* 531–532
    population growth, 474
    racist explanations, 476
    role of temples in, 491
    social stratification, 467–468
    South America, 518–526
    Southeast Asia, 532–533
    in Southwest Asia, 428–436,
        483–497, *488*
    as state societies, 468
    trade and, 491
    tribes, 468
cladistic classification, 110–113, *112*
    evolution under, *111*
Clarke, David, 536
clines, 348
Clottes, Jean, 373, 380
Clovis artifacts, 393, 397
codominance, 81
codons, 74
Coe, Michael, 514
coevolution hypothesis, 420–421, 459
collagen, 73
*Collapse: How Societies Choose to Fail or
    Succeed* (Diamond), 536–537
Columbus, Christopher, 34, *35*
comparative biology, 24
comparative collection, 194
comparative osteology, 205
competitive exclusion, 255
compliance archeology, 172
Conkey, Margaret, 367, 372
Conklin, William, 525
coprolites, 198
Cordilleran ice sheet, 391, *392*
core tools, 260
cradleboards, 217
    effects of, *218*
Crawford, Harriet, 491
Creamer, Winifred, 521
creation myths, 3–8
    ancient Hebrews, *5, 6,* 17–18
    Babylonian, 8
    evolution and, 9, 11

creation myths (continued)
    Maya, 6–7, 6, 7
    Yąnomamö, 2–4, 2–4, 3, 7, 12
creationalists, 24
Cucurbita, 445
cultural anthropology, 12–13
cultural evolution, 32–38
    biblical creation myths, 32, 34
    multilinear, 38
    unilinear, 38, 478–479, 479
cultural techniques
    dating by, 186–187
culture, 12–13
cuneiform writing, 475
Cussac Cave (France), 374

Darrow, Clarence, 43, 43
Dart, Raymond, 65, 227
Darwin, Charles, 29, 33, 39, 72, 100,
    412–413
Darwinian gradualism, 94, 95
Darwin's finches, 85–86, 86, 96–99, 97
dating, 189
    argon/argon, 183–184
    calibration curves, 185, 186
    chronometric techniques, 179–186
    cultural techniques, 186–187
    dendrochronology, 184–185, 185
    potassium/argon, 182–183
    radiocarbon dating, 180–182
    seriation, 187
    stratigraphy, 177, 177–178, 183
Davis, Michael, 285
Dawson, Charles, 225
deduction, 9
Deetz, James, 199–200
del Bene, Terry, 190
demes, 82
demographic hypothesis, 421
Demosthenes, 106
Denali Complex, 389, 389
dendrochronology, 184–185, 185, 191
deoxyribonucleic acid (DNA), 74–75,
    75, 76
    base pairs, 331
    codons, 74
    genomes, 77–78
    haplogroups, 399
    human v. chimpanzee, 131, 331
    mutation rates, 332
    recovery from ancient remains,
        207
    replication of, 74
    SNPs, 349–350

Der Lowenmensch ("the lion man"), 376,
    376
deviation amplification, 422
Devil's Lair site (Australia), 384
Dholvira site (Pakistan), 503
Diamond, Jared, 461, 476
diaphysis, 210
Dickson Mound site (Illinois), 458
Diehl, Richard, 513
diet
    agriculture and, 457
    Archaic period, 408–410
    archeological reconstruction,
        194–198, 195
    carbon isotope analysis, 197
differential reproduction, 84
diffusion, 417
Dillehay, Tom, 198, 395, 396
Dinosaur National Monument
    (Utah/Colorado), 26
dinosaurs, 60
    bones, 26
    extinction of, 60
Djoser (King of Egypt), 497
Dmanisi site (Russia), 277, 278
DNA. See deoxyribonucleic acid
DNA analysis
    computer-generated tree, 333
    mitochondrial DNA, 331
    for modern humans, 207–208
    nuclear, 331
    types, 331–332
    Y-chromosomes, 331, 334
dogs, 414
    domestication of, 413–415
Dolni Vestonice I site (Czech Republic),
    362
domestication
    Africa, 436–439, 437
    animals, 454, 455
    artificial selection, 412–413
    cattle, 427, 438, 444
    chronology, 411, 411–412
    definition, 412
    dogs, 413–415, 414, 426–427
    Europe, 443–444
    Mesoamerica, 445–451
    North America, 454–457
    osteological changes, 427–428
    plants, 424–428
    rice, 439–440, 441
    South America, 451–454
    Southeast Asia, 439–441, 441
    Southwest Asia, 428–436

wheat, 431
    worldwide distribution, 412
dominance hierarchy, 116
    among bonobos, 156
    among chimpanzees, 152
dominant alleles, 78
donor cells, for genetic cloning, 100
Dowson, T.A., 373
The Dragons of Eden (Sagan), 54
Dubois, Eugene, 265
Dumpheap Hypothesis, 420
dwarfism, 415
Dyuktai Cave (Siberia), 389

Earth, 18–23, 53
    early cellular evolution, 57
    landmass movements, 57
ecofacts, 179
egalitarianism, 160–161
Egypt
    artifacts, 496, 497
    central places, 493
    civilizations, 493–495, 535
    monumental works, 464, 471, 472,
        492, 492–493, 498
    unification of, 495–497
Ein Mallaha site (Israel), 430
einkorn (Tripsicum monocuccum), 431
El Riego Cave (Mexico), 450
Eldredge, Niles, 97
electrical resistivity surveys, 168
electron spin resonance (ESR), 184
emmer (Tripsicum turgidum), 431, 444
enamel hypoplasia, 214
endocasts, skull fossils, 279–280, 288
endogamy, 343, 350
Engels, Friedrich, 479
entoptic phenomena, 373
Enuma Elish, 8
environment, reconstruction of,
    191–194, 193, 194
environmental determinism, 476, 478
enzymes, 73
Eoanthropus, 226, 255
Eosimiidae, 135
epiphyseal union, 210, 212
epiphysis, 210
Epochs of Nature (Buffon), 21
Equatorius, 137
Erh-li-t'ou site (China), 507
ESR. See electron spin resonance
estrus, 148, 149
ethnoarcheology, 188
ethnocentrism, 158

ethnographic analogies, 158–161, 190
ethnography, 189–190
    direct historical approach, 190
ethology, 147
Europe
    agriculture, 408–410, *442,* 443–445
    cave paintings, 369–376
    civilizations, 526–528, *535*
    domestication, 443–444
    early settlements, 444
    Mesolithic, 408–410
    Neandertals, 329–330
    site locations, 24–25, 278, 285, 286,
        290–293, *293,* 296, 327, *329,* 362,
        408
evolution. *See also* hominid evolution;
        Homo sapiens, modern; human
        evolution; natural selection
    of australopithecines, 227, 247–249
    of civilization, 476, 477, 478–481,
        479
    under cladistic classification, *111*
    creation myths and, 9, 11
    cultural, 32–38
    definition, 9
    fossils as evidence of, 19
    inheritance of acquired statistics,
        28–29, 78–81, 86
    intellectual history timelines, *40–41*
    Lamarck's model, *29*
    mutation as process of, 90–91
    under phenetic classification, 110,
        110
    of primates, *132,* 132–139
    processes of, *90*
    progressive, 29–30
    punctuated equilibrium model, 97,
        99
    unilinear, 38, 478–479, *479*
excavation units, 175–176
extinction
    of dinosaurs, 60
    of great apes, 140
    natural selection and, 31
    during Pleistocene, 409

"fairy stones," 36
Farmington River Archeological Project,
    14
farms, United States populations, *467,*
    468
faunal analysis, 194–196
faunal assemblage, 431
features, site, 167

Feder, Ken, *14*
Fedje, Daryl W., 397
Fiedel, Stuart, 395
field surveys, 168
fire, control of, 284–286
fission, 92, *93*
flake tools, 260–261, *261, 282*
Flannery, Kent, 422, 432
flax plant, 436
flotation, 194
Food and Agricultural Organization,
    446
Food-Producing Revolution, 410–415,
    461, 544–545. *See also* agriculture;
    domestication
    United States farm populations, *467,*
        468
foragers, 158
    opportunistic, 409
foraging, 407
foramen magnum, 227, *229*
foraminifera, 193
Fossey, Dian, 149
fossils. *See also* skulls, fossil
    ancient Greeks and Romans, 24–25
    australopithecines, 65
    dinosaur bones, 26
    discovery of, 19, *20*
    early hominid sites, *231*
    modern *Homo sapiens, 309,* 325
    primates, 135–137
founder effect, 92
Franchthi Cave (Greece), *443,* 443–444
Francois's langurs, *117*
Freeman, Leslie, 362
Frere, John, 36
Friedel, David, 513
Fumane Cave, 374

Galdikas, Biruté, 149
gametes, 78
    sampling, 92
Ganj Dareh site (Israel), 431
gelada baboons, *124*
gene pools, 92
genes, 72, 74
    alleles, 75
    monogenic, 81
    polygenic, 81
genetic cloning, 100–101
    for reproduction, 100
    therapeutic, 101
genetic code, 72–78. *See also*
        deoxyribonucleic acid

chromosomes, 74
    deoxyribonucleic acid, 74–75, *75*
    Messenger ribonucleic acid, 74
    for sickle cell anemia, 79–80
genetic drift, 91–93, 346
    fission, 92, *93*
    founder effect in, 92
    gamete sampling, 92
genetic flow, 91–92, 346, 350
genetics
    definition, 72
    genes, 72, 74
    genetic code, 72–78
    modern *Homo sapiens* evidence,
        323–324, 330–335
    of populations, 82–84
    primate relationships, 129–132
genomes, human, 77–78, 546–547
genotypes, 77
Geography (Ptolemy), *33*
*The Geological Evidences of the Antiquity
    of Man* (Lyell), 37
geometric signs, 373
gibbons. *See also* primates
    taxonomy, *118*
    white-handed gibbon, *124*
gigantism, 415
Gigantopithecus, 137
glacial periods, 273
    in Americas, 391, *391*
glaciers, 273
Glazier Blade Cache, *176*
glume, 434
Gobineau, J.A. de, 476
Goodall, Jane, 149–150
Goodyear, Albert, 393
gorillas, *125, 150. See also* primates
    behavior patterns, 149
    chimpanzees v., 150
    Diane Fossey and, 149
    taxonomy, *118*
Gould, Stephen Jay, 97, 99
governments, formal
    city-states, 490
    definition, 468
    development, 468–469
    Marxism, 479–480
    recordkeeping, 474–475
    sacred legitimization, 472–473
GPR. *See* ground penetrating radar
Graber, Robert, 285
gradualism, *94, 95*
Gran Dolina cave (Spain), 290–293
    bone fossils, *293, 293*

Grant, Peter, 85
Grant, Rosemary, 85
Gravettian toolmaking, 361
"Great Black Aurochs," *371*
Great Enclosure site (Zimbabwe),
    530–531
Great Rift Valley (East Africa), *224, 245,
    246*
Great Zimbabwe, *530,* 530–531
Greeks, discovery of fossils, 24–25
grooming, 117, *117*
ground penetrating radar (GPR), 169,
    170
growth arrest lines, 214, *215*
Guila Naquitz Cave (Mexico), 445
Guthrie, R.D., 401

Haas, Jonathan, 521
hafts, 304, 305
Halafian culture, 489
half-life, 180
Halverson, John, 379
Hames, Raymond, *13*
Hammer, Mike, 399
hand axes, 280–281, *281, 282, 283*
    Movius Line, *283,* 283–284
Hansell, Patricia, 197
haplogroups, 399
Harappa site, 498
Harbottle, Garman, 201
Hardy-Weinberg equilibrium, 83–84
Harris, David, 422
Harris lines, 214, *215*
Harrold, Frank, 330, 366
Hassunan culture, 489
Haua Fteah Cave (Israel), 361
health, reconstruction of, 211–212, 214
Heaton, Timothy, 387
Hebrew creation myths, *5, 6, 7,* 17–18
hemoglobin, 79–80
Henry, Donald O., 423
Herodotus, 493
Hesse, Brian, 431
heterozygotes, 78
Hierakonpolis, 494–495
hieroglyphics, *475*
Hill Complex site (Zimbabwe),
    530–531
Hippocrates, 478
Hoffman, Michael, 494
Hohle Fels Cave (Germany), 376
Hohlenstein-Stadel Cave (Germany),
    376
Holding site, 456

Hole, Frank, 432
holistic, definition, 11–12
Holloway, Ralph, 279, 288
Holocene epoch, 273
    Africa, 410
Holst, Irene, 197
hominid evolution
    bipedalism in primates, 112,
        227–228, 232–236
    classification, 236–239, 253–254
    Homo comparisons, 262–264
    overview of fossil record, *230*
    summary of species, *252*
Hominidae, *118,* 126
hominids. *See also* australopithecines
    definition, 65
    early fossil sites, *231*
    occipital bones, 266
    teeth, *248*
Hominoidea, *118,* 121
Homo
    brain size, 264
    classification, 263–264
    culture, 264
    early hominid comparisons, 262–264
    toolmaking, 260–262
Homo antecessor, 290–291, *291, 292,*
    313,
Homo erectus, 265–268, 270, 272, 313,
    322
    in Africa, 272
    behaviors of, 277–288
    cranial characteristics, *279,* 279–280,
        294
    evolution of, 277–288
    features, 266–268, 278
    fire, 284–286
    fossil location sites, 265–268,
        266–267, 267, 268
    hunting and scavenging, 286–288
    intelligence, 280
    language, 288–290
    Mostly-Out-of-Africa hypothesis, 338
    skulls, *269, 270, 278*
    stone tools, 280–284
Homo ergaster, 265–268, *266,* 313, 322
    cranial characteristics, *294*
    fossil location sites, 265–267, *266,
        267, 268*
    skulls, *269, 270*
Homo floresiensis, 314, 314–315
Homo habilis, 263–264
Homo heidelbergensis, 290–291, *291,
    292,* 294–296, 313, 322

cranial characteristics, *242*
    Neandertals v., 298
    skull fossils, *295*
Homo neanderthalensis, 291–292, 313,
    322. *See also* Neandertals
Homo rudolfensis, 263–264
Homo sapiens
    characteristics of, 106
    evolution of, 66, 542–543
    models of origins, 321, *322*
    Neandertals v., 298, 325
Homo sapiens, modern, 308–313
    biological diversity, *319,* 341–352,
        342
    cultural evidence, 327–330
    evolution of, 335–337, 543–544
    genetic evidence, 323–324, 330–335
    models of evolution, 320–323, 325,
        331, 334–339, 351
    natural selection among, 343–348
    physical features, 321–322, 326
    premodern v., 320, 322–323
    races, 348–352
    toolmaking, 327, *328, 329*
Homo sapiens, premodern
    in Africa, *310,* 321
    fossils, *309*
    modern v., 320, 322–323
    skulls, *311, 312*
    toolmaking, 327
homologies, 144–146, *145*
homozygotes, 78
Hooke, Robert, 19, *20,* 25
house sparrows, *349*
Hovenweep National Monument, *170*
Hsi-pei-kang site, 505
human evolution. *See also* hominid
    evolution; *Homo sapiens,* modern
    brain size increase, 65, 290–296
    cultural evidence, 327–330
    genetic evidence, 323–324, 330–335
    genetic flow, 346, 350
    Homo sapiens, 66
    language groups, 352, *353*
    models of evolution, 320–323, 325,
        331, 334–339, 351
    Multiregional Evolution hypothesis,
        320–323, *324,* 331, 335
    natural selection, 343–348
    polymorphisms, 343–344
    races, 348–352
humans. *See also* primates
    behavior patterns, 128–129
    blood types, 343–345

brain size increase during evolution, 65
genetic similarities to chimpanzees, *131*, 331
genomes, 77–78, 546–547
intelligence, 128
Linnaean taxonomy of, *108, 118*
locomotion, 128
as primates, 9, 127–129
pygmy, 315
reproduction, 128
senses, 127–128
skeleton, *206*
Hungtington, Ellsworth, 476
hunter-gatherers, 158, 305
hunting
 Homo erectus, 286–288
 Neandertals, 305
 Upper Paleolithic, 362–363
Hutton, James, 22, 39, 67
Huxley, Thomas Henry, 319
hydraulic hypothesis, 480–481
Hylobatidae, *118*, 122–123
hypotheses, 9
 agriculture, 415–423, *416–417*, 459–462
 circumscription hypothesis, 481
 coevolution hypothesis, 420–421, 459
 hydraulic hypothesis, 480–481
 marginal habit hypothesis, 421–423
 Mostly-Out-of-Africa hypothesis, 337–339, *338, 338*
 Multiregional Evolution hypothesis, 320–323, *324,* 331, 335, 351
 null hypothesis, 83
 oasis hypothesis, *418,* 418–419, 459
 Out-of-Africa hypothesis, 320
 readiness hypothesis, 419–420
 Recent African Origin hypothesis, 320–321, *322,* 335–337, 351
 sedentary hypothesis, 419, 460
 sedentism and population growth hypothesis, 423

Ice Ages, 273–275. *See also* glacial periods
"Ice Man," *204,* 205
Icehouse Bottom site (Kentucky), 456
ideology, reconstruction of, 202–203
in situ, definition, 176
Inca civilization, 519–520
 Machu Picchu, *519*
induction, 9

Indus Valley, 497–504
 artifacts, *502, 505*
 civilizations, 499–501, *535*
 cultures in, 501
 early settlements, 501–502
 fluorescence, 502–504
inheritance of acquired statistics, 28–29, 78–81, 86
 as particulate, 72
Iniut people, 159, *347*
intelligence
 bonobos, 542
 chimpanzees, 542
 Homo erectus, 280
 human, 128
 in primates, 116
Intelligent Design, 42–46
interglacials, 273–274
The International Union for Conservation of Nature and Natural Resources, 140
interstadials, 273
irrigation, 535

"Java Man," 265, *269*
Jenne-jenno civilization, 530
Jericho (Israel), 482, *483*
Johanson, Donald, 233
John Paul II (Pope), 42
Josenhans, Heiner, 397
"Juanita" (human fossil), *204*
Ju/'hoansi people, 159, *160,* 380
Just so Stories (Kipling), 9

Kanzai (bonobo), 156
K/ar dating, 182
Karim Shahir site, 430
Katanda site (Democratic Republic of Congo), 327, *329,* 358
Kebara Cave site (Israel), 303
Keely, Lawrence, 190, *191*
Keith, Sir Arthur, 255
"Kennewick Man," 398
Kenyan, Kathleen, 482
Kenyanthropus platytops, 238, 253
Kenyapithecus, 137
Kerma civilization, 528
Khmer civilization, 533
Khoisan people, 334
Kili Ghul Mohammed site, 500
Kiowa tribe, 25
Klasies River Mouth site (Africa), 327, *328,* 358
Klein, Richard G., 363

Klemm, Gustav, 476
Knecht, Heidi, 359
Knosses, 526–527, *527*
knuckle-walking, 240
Kohtras Buthi site (Pakistan), 501
Koobi Fora site (Kenya), 285
Koster site (Illinois), 409
Kot Diji site (Pakistan), 502–503, *503*
Ksar Akil site (Lebanon), 361

La Cobata site (Mexico), 513
La Venta site (Mexico), 513
Laetoli footprints, *237*
Laetoli site (Tanzania), 235, *237*
Laguna de los Cerros, 513
Lake Baringo site (Kenya), *328,* 358
Lake Mungo sites (Australia), 383, 385
Lake Turkana sites (Kenya)
 skeleton fossils, *271*
 skull fossils, *262*
Lamarck, Jean-Baptiste de, 26
 evolution model, *29*
 Philosophie Zoologique, 28
Lamberg-Karlovsky, C.C., 491
language
 anthropological linguistics, 12
 groups, human evolution of, 352, *353*
 Homo erectus, 288–290
 vocal apparatus, *289*
Late Stone Age, 359
Laurasia, 58, 134
Laurentide ice sheet, 391, *392*
Lauricocha Cave (Peru), 454
law of superposition, 177
Leakey, Louis, 149, 237, 252
Leakey, Maeve, 237, 277
Leakey, Mary, 235, 236, 252
legumes, 429
Leroi-Gourhan, André, 372
L'Escale cave (France), 285
Levallois toolmaking, 296, *297*
Levant, 423, 428–429
Lewis-Williams, David, 373, 380
Lewontin, Richard, 350
Lindenmeier site (Colorado), 199
linguistics. See anthropological linguistics
Linnaean taxonomy, 106–110, *107*
 of humans, *108*
Linné, Carl von. *See* Linneaus, Carolus
Linneaus, Carolus, 24, 106
locomotion
 for humans, 128
 in primates, 114–115

London Society of Antiquaries, 36
Lord of the Rings (Tolkein), 315
Lower Paloelithic, 260
Lower Pleistocene, 276, *276*
Loy, Tom, 198
"Lucy" (*A. afarensis*), 233, *234*, 235
Lung-shan people, 442
Lycaenops, 95
Lyell, Charles, 22, *23*, 39, 67

Macaca, 122
Machu Picchu, *519*
MacNeish, Richard, 448
Magdelanian toolmaking, 361
maize (corn), 445–448, *446, 447, 448,*
    449, 450, 455–457
  Maya civilization, 515
Malakunanja II site (Australia), 383
malaria, 87, 89
  worldwide frequency of, *89*
Mal'ta site (Russia), *364,* 366
Mammoth Cave (Australia), 384
Mangelsdorf, Paul, 448
marginal habit hypothesis, 421–423
Marks, Anthony, 359
Marshack, Alexander, 377
Marx, Karl, 479
Marxism, 479–480
Masai people, *347*
Mason, Sarah, 363
matrilocal societies, 199
Matthews, Wendy, 485
Maxwell, Moreau, 402
Maya civilization
  characteristics, 516–517
  creation myths, 6–7, *6, 7*
  maize (corn), 515
  monumental works, 470
  origins of, 514–515
  temples, *515*
Mayor, Adrienne, 24
McBearty, Sally, 327
McGrew, W.C., 153
Meadowcroft Rockshelter
    (Pennsylvania), *392,* 393
Mehgarh site (Pakistan), 500
meiosis, *79*
Mendel, Gregor, 72
Meroë people, 529
Mesoamerica
  agriculture, 445–451
  civilizations, *535*
  cultures in, 489
  domestication, 445–451

evolution of civilization, 508–517
  Inca civilization, 519–520
  maize (corn), 445–448, *446, 447, 448*
  Maya civilization, 514–518
  monumental works, 465, *472, 515,*
    517
  Olmec civilization, *512,* 512–514,
    513
  pyramids, *472,* 508, *509*
  sculpture, *201*
  site locations, 445, *446,* 450, 452,
    511, 513, 516
  Teotihuacán, 508–511
  Ubaid, 489–490
Mesolithic culture, 408–410
Mesopotamia, 485–491
  artifacts, *487*
  city-states, 490
  development of, 488–489
  monumental works, *486*
  recordkeeping, *475*
  temples, *490, 491*
  ziggurats, *486, 487*
messenger ribonucleic acid (mRNA), 74
metallurgy, 519
Meteor Crater (Arizona), *61*
microblades, 361
middens, 194
Middle East
  civilizations, *535*
  site locations, 303, 358, 361, 430,
    431, 432–434, *433,* 497–498, *498,*
    499, 500, 501
Middle Paleolithic, 359
  Upper Paleolithic comparisons,
    359–368
Middle Pleistocene, 276, *276*
Middle Stone Age, 359
migration
  to Americas, *386,* 386–390
  to Australia, 381–385
"Minnesota Man," 397
Minoan civilization, *526,* 526–527
Mississippi Delta, 22, *23*
mitochondrial deoxyribonucleic acid
    (mtDNA), 331, 334
mitosis, *79*
Moche Culture Pyramid, *523*
Moche site (Peru), 523–525
Mohammad Jaffar phase, 433
Mohenjo-daro site (Pakistan), 497–498,
    499, 500
monkeys. *See also* primates
  snow monkeys, *123*

spider monkeys, *122*
  taxonomy, *118*
Monks Mound, *531,* 531–532
monogenic genes, 81
Monte Verde (Chile), 395, *395,* 396,
    396
monumental works, *517*
  Africa, *529*
  civilization and, 471–473
  Egyptian pyramids, *464, 471, 472*
  Maya, 470, *515, 517*
  Mesoamerica, 465, *472, 509, 515, 517*
  Mesoamerican carved heads, 512,
    512
  Mesopotamia, *486*
  North America, *531,* 531–532
  sacred legitimization of, 472–473
  South America, 520, *523*
  Southeast Asia, *533*
  temples, *490, 491*
  ziggurats, *486, 487*
Moreno Glacier (Argentina), *258, 274*
Morgan, Lewis Henry, 478
  Ancient Society, 38
Moropithecus, 137
Morris, Desmond, 106
Moseley, Michael, 525
Mostly-Out-of-Africa hypothesis,
    337–339, *338*
  Homo erectus, 338
"mother goddesses," 500, *502*
Mousterian toolmaking, 303, *304*
Movius line, *283,* 283–284
Mpongwe people of Gabon, 9
MRE. *See* Multiregional Evolution
    hypothesis
mRNA. *See* Messenger ribonucleic acid
M16 nebula, *48, 52*
mtDNA. *See* mitochondrial
    deoxyribonucleic acid
multilinear evolution theory, 38
Multiregional Evolution hypothesis
    (MRE), 320–323, *324,* 331, 335,
    351
  requirements, 323
mutations, 78
  deoxyribonucleic acid, 332
  in evolutionary process, 90–91
  gene flow and, 91
  genetic drift and, 91
  point, 80
Mycenaean civilization, 527–528
myths. *See also* creation myths
  definition, 2

Nabta Playa site (Northeast Africa), 437
Nal culture, 501
Narmer Macehead, *496*
Native American Graves Protection and Reparation Act, 398
Native Americans, European explanation of, 34
Natufian cultures, 429–430, 458
natural selection, 23–26, 84–91, *87*
  definition, 31
  differential reproduction, 85
  extinction and, 31
  in modern *Homo sapiens,* 343–348
  oscillating selection, 96
  sexual selection, 85
  speciation, 96
  variation in, *30*
A Natural History (Buffon), 20–21
Nauwalabila site (Australia), 383
Neandertals
  altruism, 307
  appearance, 215, 298–301, *301, 306*
  burial ceremonialism, 304–306, *305,* 366
  cannibalism, 307–308
  cave bears and, 306–307
  cranial characteristics of, 298, *302*
  cultural practices, *306*
  discovery, 296–297
  in Europe, 329–330
  fossil sites, *300*
  Homo heidelbergensis v., 298
  Homo sapiens v., 298, 325
  hunting, 305
  locations, 296, 298, *299*
  skeletal features, *303*
  skull fossils, *298*
  in Southwest Asia, 329
  toolmaking, 303
  vocal tracts of, 308
Necrolemur, 135
Neely, James, 432
Nefertiti (Queen), 217
Nelson Bay Cave (Canada), 364–365
Nenanai Complex, 389, *389*
neocortex, 128, *129*
Neolithic period, 410, 458
Netiv Hagdud site (Israel), 431
neutron activation analysis, 201, *201*
Newcomer, Mark, 281
Ngangdong site (Java), 278
Ngarrabullgan Cave (Australia), 384

niches, 84
Nile River, 493, *494*
  site locations, 494–495
Non Nok site (Thailand), 439
North America
  agriculture, 454–457
  burial artifacts in, *203*
  civilizations, *531,* 531 532, *535*
  monumental works, *531,* 531–532
  site locations, *26, 164, 178,* 364–365, 445, 450, 455, 456, *456,* 458, *511,* 516
notochord, 108, *109*
Nubia civilization, 528
nuclear deoxyribonucleic acid (DNA), 331
nuclear family, 159
null hypothesis, 83
nutrition. *See* diet

oasis hypothesis, *418,* 418–419, 459
occipital bones, 266
O'Connell, J.F., 382
Old Brooks Site (Connecticut), *178*
"Old Man," 307, *307*
Oldowan toolmaking, *260,* 260–262, *261,* 264
Olduvai Gorge site (Tanzania), 171, *171, 263*
Olmec civilization, 512–514
  burial ceremonialism, 513
  development of, 514
Olmec style, *512, 513,* 513–514
Olorgesailie site (Spain), 286
Olson, Stanley, 413
Omomyidae, 135
On the Origin of Species (Darwin), 31, 72, 298
On Your Knees Cave (Alaska), 387, 399
Opdyke, Neil, 275
opportunistic foragers, 409
opposability, 115
orangutans, 126. *See also* primates
  Galdikas and, 149
  Southeast Asian, *104*
  taxonomy, *118*
The Origin of Races (Koon), 351
Orrorin tugenensis, 238, 245, 253
oscillating selection, 96
osteologists, 413
Ouranopithecus, 137
Out-of-Africa hypothesis, 320
oxygen isotope curve, 275

paleoanthropologists, 14
paleoclimatologists, 273
paleoethnography, 189
paleofeces, 198, 450
Paleo-Indians, 399–401. *See also* Native Americans
  toolmaking, *400*
Paleolithic periods. *See* Lower Paleolithic
paleopathology, 211. *See also* health, reconstruction of
palynology, 193
Pan paniscus. See bonobos
Pan troglodytes. See chimpanzees
Pangea (landmass), 58
Papio, 122, 147
paradigm, 385
Paranthropus, 231, 236
Paranthropus aethiopicus, 249
Paranthropus boisei, 230, 250, *251,* 252
Paranthropus robustus, 230, 250, *251*
parent materials, 177
Park, Michael, *14*
particulate, 72
Paterson, Ann, 370
patrilocal societies, 199
Patterson, Thomas, 521
Pawnee tribe, 25
Pearson, O.M., 336
pebble tools, 260
Peiligang culture, 441–442
"Peking Man," 265, *269*
  fossil locations, 265
Periboriwä, 3
personal adornment, 364–365, *365*
petrographic analysis, 200
Peyrère, Isaac de, 36
Pfeiffer, John, 284
phenetic classification, evolution under, 110, *110*
phenotypes, 78
Phillips Spring site (Missouri), 455
Philosophie Zoologique (Lamarck), 28
photoevaporation, *52*
physical (biological) anthropology, 12–13, 166
phytoliths, 197, *198,* 285, 451
Picasso, Pablo, 369
Pike-Tay, Anne, 359
Pikimacahy Cave (Peru), 454
Piltdown fraud, 226, *226,* 255, 543
Piperno, Dolores, 197, 452
Piramide Mayor, 520

Pithecanthropus erectus, 265
plants. *See* agriculture
plate tectonics, 57, *57*
Platyrrhini, 118, 120
Pleistocene epoch, 259, 273–276, *275*
    adaptation, 408
    extinction during, 409
    glacial chronology, *276*
Pliocene epoch, 273
point mutations, 80
polygenic genes, 81
polymorphisms, 343–344
    body build, 345–346, *347*
    skin color, 345, *346*
Pongidae, *118,* 123, 126
Pongo pygmaeus. See orangutans
Pope, Geoffrey, 284
Popol Vuh, 6, 6–7, 7
populations
    breeding, 82
    civilization and, 474
    demographic hypothesis, 421
    fission, 92, *93*
    genetics of, 82–84
    sedentism and population growth
        hypothesis, 423
    on United States farms, *467, 468*
postmarital residence patterns, 199
postnatal dependency, 116
postorbital constriction, 294
potassium/argon dating, 182–183
Potts, Richard, 245, 254
Powell, Joseph, 398
prehensile hands and feet, 114, *115*
Price, T. Douglas, 408
primates. *See also* anthropod primates;
      prosimian primates
    American Sign Language use by,
       127
    arboreal, 62, 113
    behavior patterns, 116–117
    bipedalism among, 112
    definition, 58
    early, 58, *59*
    evolution of, *132,* 132–139
    fossils, 135–137
    genetic and relationships, 129–132
    glossary of, 548–551
    human similarities in, 9
    intelligence, 116
    locomotion, 114–115
    quadrupedalism among, 112
    reproduction, 114–115
    senses, 113–114

    taxonomy, *110, 111, 112,* 117–123,
       118, 126–127
    worldwide distribution, *119*
primatologists, 14
Primitive Culture (Taylor), 38
prognathism, 235, *327*
progressive evolution, 29–30
projectile points, 361
prosimian primates, 62, *62,* 62–63,
    117–120
    diurnal, 118
    nocturnal, 118
    taxonomy, *118*
proteases, 132
protein synthesis, 74, *76*
proteins, 72–73
    collagen as, 73
    enzymes, 73
proton magnetometry, 168, *169*
provenience, 174
Ptolemy, *33*
Pu-abi, 486–488
pubic symphysis, 210–211
Pulltrouser Swamp site (Belize), 516
punctuated equilibrium, 97, *99*
Punnett squares, *93*
pygmy chimpanzees. *See* bonobos
pygmy humans, 315
Pyramid of the Moon (Mexico), 508, *509*
Pyramid of the Sun (Mexico), 508
pyramids
    Africa, *529*
    Egyptian, *464, 465, 492,* 492–493,
      498
    Mesoamerica, *472,* 508, *509*
    South America, 520, *523*

Qafzeh cave (Israel), 358
quadrupedalism, among primates, 112
Quebrada Jaguay site (Peru), 397
Quebrada Tacahuay site (Peru), 397
quinoa, 452–453, *453*
quipu, *475*

Race and Human Evolution: A Fatal
    Attraction (Caspari/Wolpoff), 351
races, human, 348–352
    civilization and, 476
    clines, 348
rachis, 434
radioactive isotopes, 179
radiocarbon dating, 180–182. *See also*
    dating
    cave paintings, 374

radiometric dating, 179
random samples, 172
Ranere, Anthony, 197
rank societies, 491
RAO. *See* Recent African Origin
    hypothesis
readiness hypothesis, 419–420
Recent African Origin (RAO)
    hypothesis, 320–321, *322,*
    335–337, 351
    requirements, 323
recessive alleles, 78
recordkeeping, 474–475, *475*
"regal-ritual centers," 513, 516
relative chronological sequence, 177
Relethford, John, 337
remote sensing, 168–169, *169*
replication, 74
repoussé method, 522
representative samples, 172
reproduction
    in humans, 128
    among primates, 114–115
"resource ceiling," 423
rice, domestication of, 439–440, *441*
Rice, Patricia, 370, 378
Rindos, David, 420
ring-tailed lemurs, 62
rock art, 380
Romans, discovery of fossils, 24–25
Roosevelt, Anna C., 401
root crops, 453, *454,* 455
Rose, Jennie, 287
Rose, Jerome, 398
Rowlett, Ralph, 285
Ruiz, Alvaro, 521

Sabloff, Jeremy, 491
sacred legitimization, 472–473
Sagan, Carl, 53
    The Dragons of Eden, 54
sagittal crest, 235
sagittal keel, 266
Sahelanthropus tchadensis, 239, 245, 253
Sahul (landmass), 381, *382*
Samarran culture, 489
San Lorenzo site (mexico), 513
Sarich, Vincent, 130
Sauer, Carl, 419
savannas, 63, *63*
Schele, Linda, 513
science, 2
Scientific Creationism, 42–46
scientific method, 9

Scopes, John T., 43
sedentary, definition, 418
sedentary hypothesis, 419, 460
sedentism and population growth
    hypothesis, 423
"seed bed selection," 424
seed coat thickness, 424–425
seed dispersal mechanisms, 425, 426
seed size, in domestication, 424, 424
seed-dispersal mechanisms, 425
segregation, 78
senses
    in humans, 127–128
    in primates, 113–114
seriation, 187, 188
settlement patterns, 423
settlements, Upper Paleolithic, 365–366
sex, archeological identification of,
    208–210
sexual dimorphism, 208
    in skull and pelvis, 209
sexual selection, 85
Shackleton, Nicholas, 275
Shakespeare, William, As You Like It, 18
Shang civilization, 504, 506
    artifacts, 505
    burial ceremonialism, 506
shared derived characteristics, 111
Shea, John, 303
Shell Mound Archaic, 409
Shipman, Pat, 264, 287, 369
Shreeve, James, 277
sickle cell anemia, 79–81
    adaptive fitness of, 87–88
    allele frequency for, 81
    genetics of, 79–80
    worldwide frequency of, 88
Sima de los Huesos site (Spain), 296
sites (archeological). See also specific
        sites
    definition, 167
    preservation of, 221, 221
Sivapithecus, 137, 138
skeletons. See also bones
    human, 206
    syphilis effects on, 213
skin color, 345
    worldwide distribution, 346
skulls, fossil
    casting, 216
    endocasts, 279–280, 288
    Homo erectus, 269, 270, 279
    Homo ergaster, 269, 270
    Homo heidelbergensis, 295

Lake Turkana sites, 262
    modern Homo sapiens, 311, 312
    Neandertals, 298
    sexual dimorphism, 208, 209
slash-and-burn, 511
slender loris, 120
Smilodectes, 134
Smith, Bruce, 424–425, 446
Smith, John Maynard, 42
snow monkeys, 123
social stratification, 507
    civilization, 467–468
social systems, 469. See also civilization
    methods of reconstructing, 199–200
Soleilhac site (France), 278
Solutrean toolmaking, 361, 362
sorghum, 437, 437
soundings, 172
South America
    agriculture, 451–454
    art, 367, 524
    burial ceremonialism, 525
    Chavin style, 522, 522–523
    civilizations, 518–526, 519–520, 535
    monumental works, 519, 520, 523
    site locations, 367, 395, 395, 396,
        396, 397, 401, 452, 454, 511,
        519–520, 523–525
Southeast Asia
    agriculture, 410, 439–442
    animal domestication, 441
    civilizations, 532–533, 535
    monumental works, 533
    orangutans, 104
    rice, 439–440, 441
    site locations, 410, 439, 440, 441,
        501, 505, 507
Southeast Asian orangutan, 104
Southwest Asia. See also Middle East
    agriculture in, 428–436, 430, 445
    civilizations, 428–436, 483–497
    Levant, 428
    Neandertals, 329
    site locations, 429, 501
spatial contexts, 174
speciation, 96, 100, 337
species
    definition, 11–12, 205
    identification through bones,
        205–208
    origin of, 94–99
spider monkeys, 122
Spirit Cave (Thailand), 410, 439
Square Tower House (Colorado), 164

stadials, 273
starch grains, 451
Starr Carr site (England), 408
state societies, 468
stereoscopic vision, 114, 114
Stone Age, 37–38. See also Middle
        Paleolithic; Upper Paleolithic
Stone, Nancy, 285
strata (stratum), 25–26
    geological, 27
stratigraphy, 26, 178
    dating of sites, 177, 177–178, 183
Stringer, Christopher, 320, 335
Stromatolites, 56
Sunda (landmass), 381, 382
sunflowers, 457
Sungir' site (Russia), 203
supernovas, 53
sutures, 210, 211
Swan River site (Australia), 384
syphilis, skeletal effects of, 213

Tainter, Joseph, 468, 473, 535
taphonomy, 196. See also diet
tarsiers, 120, 121
Tasaday people, 158–159
Tatersall, Ian, 320
"Taung baby," 227, 228
Tawantisuyu. See Inca civilization
taxon, 110
taxonomy, 24, 106–113
    cladistics, 110–113, 112
    Linnaean, 106–110
    primates, 117–123, 118, 126–127
technology, prehistoric, 189–191, 190,
        192
teeth, eruption aging, 210
Tehuacán Valley Project, 448–451, 449
Temple of the Giant Jaguar, 517
temples, 491
    Khmer, 533
    Maya, 515
    Mayan, 515, 517
    Mesopotamia, 490, 491
    as monumental works, 490, 491
    role in civilizations, 491
Templeton, Alan, 337
teosinte, 446, 446–447
Teotihuacán, 508–511
    agriculture, 508–509
    wall art, 510
"Tepexpan Man," 397
"termite fishing sticks," 126
Terra Amata (France), 278

test borings, 172
test pits, 172
theory, definition, 10–11
Theory of the Earth (Hutton), 21
therapeutic cloning, 101
Thomsen, Christian Jurgen, 38
Thorne, Alan, 329
"thunder stones," 36
timelines, intellectual history, *40–41*
"Tollund Man," *204*
toolkits, 329
toolmaking. *See also* core tools; flake
    tools; pebble tools
  Acheulian, 280–284, *281, 282*
  in Americas, *389*
  Arctic, 402
  Aurignacian, 329–330, *361*
  bifacial tools, 280–281, *281, 328*
  from bone/ivory/antler, 364
  Châtelperronian, 330
  chimpanzees, *127*
  early hominids, 262–263
  Gravettian, 361
  hafts, 305
  Homo erectus, 280–284
  Homo evolution, 260–262
  Levallois, 296
  Magdelanian, 361
  modern *Homo sapiens,* 327
  Mousterian, 303, *304*
  Oldowan, *260,* 260–262, *261,* 264
  Paleo-Indians, *400*
  premodern *Homo sapiens,* 327
  Solutrean, 361, *362*
  Upper Paleolithic, *360,* 360–362, *361,*
    362
  wear patterns, 190, *191*
Topper site (South Carolina), 393, *394*
Toros-Menalla site (Chad), 238
Torralba site (Spain), 286
torus, 266
Toyama, Syuichi, 439
trace element analysis, 200
trade, 200–202
  civilization and, 491

transects, 172, *173*
transfer RNA (tRNA), 74
trephining, 212, *214*
Tres Zapotes site (Mexico), 513
tribes, 468
tRNA. *See* transfer RNA
"trophyism," 369
Tubalcain, 36
Tulmeadow North site, *175*
"Turkana Boy," 268, *271*
Tuross, Noreen, 198

Ubaid cultures, 489–490
Unger-Hamilton, Ramona, 429
Uniformitarianism, 19–23
unilinear evolution theory, 38,
    478–479, *479*
United States. *See also* North America
    farm populations, *467, 468*
universe
    Big Bang theory for, 50–53, *51, 67*
    conceptual history of, as calendar
    year, *54–55*
Upper Paleolithic
    art from, 358, 364–365, 367–381,
    544
    Australian migration, 381–385
    bone/ivory/antler tools, 364
    burial ceremonialism, 366–367
    carvings/engravings, *376,* 376–378,
    377
    cave paintings, *356, 368,* 369–376
    geometric signs, 373
    hunting, 362–363
    material mobility, 366
    Middle Paleolithic comparisons,
    359–368
    personal adornment, 364–365, *365*
    settlement size increase, 365–366
    stone tool technologies, *360,*
    360–362, *361, 362*
    Venus figurines, 377–378, *378*
Upper Pleistocene, *276, 276*
uranium series, 184
Ussher, Archbishop James, 18

"variability selection," 245
Venus figurines, 377–378, *378*
"Venus of Willendorf," *378*

Walker, Alan, 280
Wallace, Alfred Russell, 29, 39, 72
Wallace Trench, 381
water control, 533
wear patterns, 190, *191*
Webster, David, 473, 516
wedge-shaped cores, 389, *389*
wheat
    domestication of, 431, 434–436, *435*
    einkorn, 431
    emmer, 431, 444
    glume, 434
    rachis, 434
White, Randall, 359, 365, 366
white-handed gibbon, *124*
Willandra Lakes (Australia), 385
Wilmsen, Edwin, 199
Wilson, Allan, 130
*The Wisdom of God Manifested in the
    Works of Creation* (Ray), 18
Wittfogel, Karl, 481
Wolpoff, Milford, *301,* 321, 329
Wood, Bernard, 254
Worl, Rosita, 399

Yang-shao culture, 442
Yąnomamö (tribe), 2–4, *13*
    creation myths for, 2–5, *3,* 7, 12
Y-chromosomes, 331, 334
Y-5 cusp patterns, *137*

Zallinger, Rudolph, *60, 306*
Zawi Chemi Shanidar site, 430
Zeder, Melinda, 431
Zengpiyan Cave (China), 441
Zhoukoudian cave site (China), 265
ziggurats, 486, *487*
Zilhao, Joao, 444
Zinjanthropus, 252, 260–261
zygomatic arch, *251*
zygotes, 78